COLLECTIVE SECURITY

COLLECTIVE SECURITY

ALEXANDER ORAKHELASHVILI

OXFORD
UNIVERSITY PRESS

OXFORD
UNIVERSITY PRESS

Great Clarendon Street, Oxford OX2 6DP

Oxford University Press is a department of the University of Oxford.
It furthers the University's objective of excellence in research, scholarship,
and education by publishing worldwide in

Oxford New York

Auckland Cape Town Dar es Salaam Hong Kong Karachi
Kuala Lumpur Madrid Melbourne Mexico City Nairobi
New Delhi Shanghai Taipei Toronto

With offices in

Argentina Austria Brazil Chile Czech Republic France Greece
Guatemala Hungary Italy Japan Poland Portugal Singapore
South Korea Switzerland Thailand Turkey Ukraine Vietnam

Oxford is a registered trade mark of Oxford University Press
in the UK and in certain other countries

Published in the United States
by Oxford University Press Inc., New York

© Alexander Orakhelashvili 2011

The moral rights of the author have been asserted

Crown copyright material is reproduced under Class Licence
Number C01P0000148 with the permission of OPSI
and the Queen's Printer for Scotland
Database right Oxford University Press (maker)

First published 2011

British Library Cataloguing in Publication Data

Data available

Library of Congress Control Number: 2011922689

Typeset by SPI Publisher Services, Pondicherry, India
Printed in Great Britain
on acid-free paper by
CPI Antony Rowe, Chippenham, Wiltshire

ISBN 978–0–19–957984–6 (Hbk)

1 3 5 7 9 10 8 6 4 2

Acknowledgements

The work on this study has taken nearly three years of my academic life, covering my affiliation to three academic institutions: Oxford University, the British Institute of International and Comparative Law, and finally, Birmingham University. I am grateful to all these institutions for their continuous support and for their invaluable resources. The three confidential referees who read my initial proposal encouraged me to pursue the proposed path of research. Luke Price, research assistant here at the Law School, was very helpful for reading and correcting the proofs. As usual, the tremendously supportive role performed by the commissioning and production editors at Oxford University Press has been instrumental throughout the process that culminated in this book. In this respect, I am grateful to John Louth, Alex Flach, Merel Alstein, and Ela Kotkowska for their helpful and productive approach to this project, from the original proposal right up to publication.

AO
Birmingham, 21 December 2010

Table of Contents

Table of Cases

EUROPEAN COURT OF HUMAN RIGHTS

EU COURTS

INTERNATIONAL ADMINISTRATIVE TRIBUNALS

INTERNATIONAL COURT OF JUSTICE

INTERNATIONAL CRIMINAL TRIBUNAL FOR THE FORMER YUGOSLAVIA

SPECIAL COURT FOR SIERRA LEONE

NATIONAL COURTS

Table of Treaties and Resolutions

INTERNATIONAL TREATIES

UN GENERAL ASSEMBLY RESOLUTIONS

List of Abbreviations

ADF	Arab Defence Force
AFSOUTH	(NATO) Allied Forces Southern Europe
AMIB	African Union Mission in Burundi
AMIS	African Union Mission in Sudan
AMISOM	African Union Mission in Somalia
ARF	ASEAN Regional Forum
ASEAN	Association of Southeast Asian Nations
ASF	African Standby Force
AU	African Union
CAR	Central African Republic
CARICOM	Caribbean Community
CEWARN	(IGAD) Conflict Early Warning and Response Mechanism
CEWS	(AU) Continental Early Warning System
CFSP	(EU) Common Foreign and Security Policy
CINCSOUTH	(NATO) Commander-in-Chief South
CIS	Commonwealth of Independent States
CJTF	(NATO) Combined Joint Task Force
CSTO	(CIS) Collective Security Treaty Organization
DPKO	*see* UNDPKO
DRC	Democratic Republic of the Congo
ECCAS	Economic Community of Central African States
ECHR	European Convention on Human Rights
ECOMOG	Military Observer Group of ECOWAS
ECOWAS	Economic Community of West African States
ESDP	European Security and Defence Policy
EU(3D)	[Avoiding] Duplication of NATO efforts, Decoupling European defence from NATO, and Discrimination against non-NATO states
EUFOR RD Congo	EU Force in the Democratic Republic of the Congo
EUMC	EU Military Committee
EUMS	EU Military Staff
EWR	Early Warning Report
FOMAC	Multinational Peace Force in Central Africa
FRY	Former Republic of Yugoslavia
IAEA	International Atomic Energy Agency
ICC	International Criminal Court
ICCPR	International Covenant on Civil and Political Rights
ICTY	International Criminal Tribunal for the Former Yugoslavia
IFOR	(NATO) Implementation Force

IGAD	(East African) Inter-Governmental Authority on Development
IGASOM	IGAD Peace Support Mission in Somalia
IIA	Iraqi Interim Administration
ILC	UN International Law Commission
ILO	International Labour Organization
ILOAT	ILO Administrative Tribunal
ISAF	(Afghanistan) International Security Assistance Force
ISDSC	SADC Organ on Politics, Defence, and Security Co-operation, Inter-State Defence and Security Committee
KFOR	NATO-led Kosovo Force
LAS	League of Arab States
MARAC	(ECCAS) Early Warning, Observation, and Monitoring System
MICIVIH	OAS/UN Civilian Mission in Haiti
MINUSTAH	United Nations Stabilization Mission in Haiti
MISAB	Inter-African Mission to Monitor the Implementation of the Bangui Agreements
MNB	Multinational Brigades
MNF	Multi-National Force in Iraq
MONUC	United Nations Mission in DR Congo
MSC	ECOWAS Mediation and Security Council
NAC	North Atlantic Council
NAM	Non-Aligned Movement
NATO SHAPE	NATO Supreme Headquarters Allied Powers Europe
NPFL	National Patriotic Front of Liberia
NPT	Nuclear Non-proliferation Treaty 1968
NRF	NATO Response Force
OAS	Organization of American States
OAU	Organization of African Unity (now African Union)
OECS	Organization of Eastern Caribbean States
OIC	Organization of the Islamic Conference
ONUB	UN Operation in Burundi
ONUC	UN Operation in the Congo
OSCE	Organization for Security and Co-operation in Europe
PCIJ	Permanent Court of International Justice
PMAD	Protocol relating to Mutual Assistance on Defence
PSC	(AU) Peace and Security Council; (EU) Political and Security Committee
PSO	Peace Support Operations
ROE	Rules of Engagement
RRF	Rapid Reaction Force
RUF	(Sierra Leone) Revolutionary United Front

SACEUR	(NATO) Supreme Allied Commander Europe
SADC	Southern African Development Community
SCR	UN Special Committee Resolution
SCSL	Special Court for Sierra Leone
SFOR	(NATO) Stabilization Force
SG/HR	Secretary-General of the Council of the European Union/High Representative Common Foreign and Security Policy
SHAPE	(NATO) Supreme Headquarters Allied Powers, Europe
SNA	Somali National Alliance
SRSG	(UN) Special Representative of the Secretary-General
TCN	Troop-contributing Nation
TEU	Treaty on European Union (Maastricht Treaty)
TFG	Transitional Federal Government
UfP	Uniting for Peace
UNAMID	United Nations–African Union Mission in Darfur
UNAMIR	UN Assistance Mission for Rwanda
UNAMSIL	UN Mission in Sierra Leone
UNCLOS	UN Convention on the Law of the Sea 1982
UNDPKO	UN Department of Peacekeeping Operations
UNEF	UN Emergency Force
UNFICYP	UN Peacekeeping Force in Cyprus
UNGA	UN General Assembly
UNIFIL	UN Interim Force in Lebanon
UNITA	National Union for the Total Independence of Angola
UNITAF	Unified Task Force in Somalia
UNMIBH	United Nations Mission in Bosnia and Herzegovina
UNMIH	UN Mission in Haiti
UNMIK	UN Mission in Kosovo
UNMIS	UN Mission in Sudan
UNMISET	UN Mission in East Timor
UNMOVIC	UN Monitoring, Verification, and Inspection Commission
UNOCI	UN Operation in Côte d'Ivoire
UNOGIL	UN Observation Group in Lebanon
UNOMIL	UN Observer Mission in Liberia
UNOSOM	United Nations Operation in Somalia
UNPROFOR	UN Protection Force (in Yugoslavia)
UNSC	UN Security Council
UNSCOM	UN Special Commission
UNTAC	UN Transitional Authority in Cambodia
UNTAES	UN Transitional Authority in Eastern Slavonia
UNTAET	UN Transitional Administration in East Timor

Introduction

The quest for the prevention of war and the preservation of peace has pervaded political and legal thinking for several centuries past. Many ideas and projects notwithstanding, the first genuine collective security institution was the League of Nations, established in 1919 in recognition of the fact that the international system at that time, based on an equilibrium between and concert of European great powers, had broken down. A distinctively new multilateral arrangement was needed that would deal with problems of war and peace in a formalized context—it would be based on a written international agreement and operate through regularly scheduled sessions, public discussion, and officially adopted documents. The procedure specified in the League Covenant would define the cause of action and standing to raise it, as well as the measures to be implemented in response to an outstanding threat to peace and security. The simple but cardinal difference these arrangements made to existing patterns of informal concerts and secret diplomacy was that the problem of international peace and security became a matter of law.

Ever since, legal arrangements have come to be viewed as the principal tool for enhancing and upgrading the effectiveness of collective security arrangements. The breakdown of the League system in the 1930s was followed by lengthy negotiations in 1944 and 1945 at the Dumbarton Oaks and San Francisco conferences to establish collective security arrangements suitable for the post-Second World War environment, culminating in the adoption of the United Nations Charter.

However, ever since its establishment, the UN has been viewed as insufficient, given that its action is contingent on the unanimity of five permanent members in the Security Council. Hence, multiple regional arrangements have been established to compensate for the insufficiency of the UN by providing a regional capability to deal with regional crises. This process of multiplying institutions has raised the question how and in what manner these institutions are supposed to cohabit within the same international legal system.

Despite the abundance of writings on these matters, so far there has been no comprehensive study of collective security that covers all the pertinent institutions and arrangements. Collective security is a complex and multifaceted process and can be approached in a variety of ways. To illustrate, in the Cold War period, the issues attracting heaviest attention in doctrine and practice were the scope of domestic jurisdiction under Article 2(7) of the UN Charter, and the competence of the UN General Assembly to authorize the use of force under the 'Uniting for Peace' resolution. The period since the Cold War has witnessed an increasing attention to proposals for reform of the UN Security Council, and a growing emphasis on human security and the 'responsibility to protect'. Obviously a study that examines collective security in a comprehensive manner has to be premised on such delimitation of its scope as will ensure the proper focus on its principal underlying themes.

Two principal themes underlie this monograph. In the first place, collective security is a product of law: the powers of collective security organs exist because, and to the extent that, they are delegated to these organs by states party to their constituent instruments. Therefore the ultimate measure of collective security decisions and operations lies with a consensual imperative as the structural principle of the international legal system. Collective security action has to fit within the consensual limits of delegation. It is the consensual positivist approach that holds the key to identifying the extent of the potential of jurisdictional and operational capabilities vested in institutions. This is usefully, and inevitably, complemented by the process of interpreting constituent instruments and decisions adopted pursuant to them, to identify the content of particular decisions, the intention behind them, and their impact on the ground.

The second principal theme of this monograph refers to the process by which collective security institutions multiply. The primacy of the United Nations, as provided for in its Charter (notably Article 103), obviously requires collective security to be viewed as a single comprehensive system covering the United Nations together with regional and sub-regional organizations. Chapter VIII of the UN Charter is the constitutional basis for this comprehensive system, and defines the criteria for the valid existence and activities of regional arrangements in various contexts. However, as regional institutions develop, increasingly they assert their own policies regarding the collective security process, and at times contradict policy choices made by UN organs, above all the Security Council. Sometimes this affects the outcomes on the ground, thus constraining the real impact that Security Council decisions can have.

The entire system of collective security is multilevel and multidimensional, and has to be examined from a bottom-up perspective that is free of any blanket preconception that a particular level of collective security should inherently enjoy primacy over others. The answer to this problem is rather more nuanced, and focuses on the legal frameworks of specific collective security institutions, and policies adopted by those institutions. Given that this process develops within the context of a consensual legal system, the only permissible solutions can be those that enjoy a sufficient degree of international consensus.

This inevitably requires identifying underlying principles by which competence is allocated, based on which institutions can arrange for a sustainable division of labour between one another, and claim legitimacy for their actions and policies. The principles widely recognized and practised include 'complementarity' and 'subsidiarity'; those that are repeatedly articulated in various contexts but remain contested, falling short of commanding a general acceptance, include 'primacy', 'non-subordination', and 'autonomy'. The focus on these principles is at the core of this study. The principal focus on competence allocation is concentrated in Chapter 3, although subsidiarity and complementarity are considered in other chapters to the extent necessary to examine particular aspects of collective security.

1

Essence and Definition of Collective Security

1. State Security and Collective Security

Collective security refers to collective action in response to a collectively identified threat. From the League of Nations period onwards, attempts were undertaken to formulate a definition of collective security, bearing in mind its historical, political, and ethical aspects.[1] The 2004 UN High-Level Panel Report denoted as a central challenge the fashioning of a new and broader meaning of collective security—its responsibilities, strategies, and institutions—if this system is to be effective and equitable.[2] The Report provides no definition of collective security, whether as a matter of an inadvertent omission or as an implied position that no definition is necessary since collective security institutions exist anyway. Still, defining collective security is required, not to prove that it exists but to explain what it is.

States are at the roots of the international system. No collective security is feasible unless it draws on fundamental security needs of states. As the High-Level Panel Report specifies, the founders of the UN were preoccupied with state security, in terms of collective reaction against aggression.[3] Security of each state is a value in itself: it covers the preservation by states of their territory, values, development, and the quality of life of their population.[4] What a state's national security comprises, overall, is determined by national opinion. International security concerns have to be identified in the international context where there is neither a government nor a homogeneous socio-political opinion. The only possible way of 'securitizing' particular matters is an agreement between states. Normal ways to do that are multilateral treaties, summit declarations, and institutional declarations adopted by the UN General Assembly or Security Council. The 1975 Helsinki Final Act, for instance, expresses the consensus of European and North American states on aspects of national and international security.

---

[1] M Borquin, General Report on the Preparatory Memoranda Submitted to the General Study Conference, in M Borquin (ed.), *Collective Security, A Record of the Seventh and Eighth International Studies Conferences*, Paris 1934–London 1935 (Paris: International Institute of Intellectual Cooperation, 1936), 3 at 6.

[2] *A More Secure World: Our Shared Responsibility, Report of the Secretary-General's High-Level Panel on Threats, Challenges and Change*, A/59/565, December 2004, 11, 22.

[3] Ibid, 15.

[4] Cf. A Collins (ed.), *Contemporary Security Studies* (New York: Oxford University Press, 2007), 3; P Morgan, 'Security in International Politics: Traditional Approaches', in ibid, 14.

The principle of national safety stated in Article 8 of the League of Nations Covenant makes it clear that international peace and security is premised on the ability of states to protect their own security. The Organization of American States (OAS) Declaration on Security in the Americas specifies that 'each state has the sovereign right to identify its own national security priorities and to define strategies, plans, and actions for addressing threats to its security, in accordance with its legal system and with full respect for international law'.[5] According to Article 4 Treaty on European Union (TEU), 'national security remains the sole responsibility of each Member State'. The African Union (AU) Declaration on the Common African Defence and Security Policy affirms that national and international securities are mutually interlinked, by proclaiming that

the security of one African country is inseparably linked to the security of other African countries, and the African continent as a whole. Accordingly, any threat or aggression on one African country is deemed to be a threat or aggression on the others, and the continent as a whole.[6]

Hence, protecting basic rights and interests of states is at the heart of every viable collective security arrangement.

Security can be regarded either as an absolute and objective, or as a subjective matter of psychological perception. In a world consisting of nation states guided by their own national security interests, which interests are often in mutual conflict, it is not easy to identify the aspects of the absolute, objective, or universal security of a 'collective'. It is absurd to expect that security interests of one state or group of states will be seen as forming part of universal law and obligation. It is quite likely that the security of one state could mean insecurity for another state.[7] This is even more so in a world riddled with ideological divisions.

Individual state security can merge with collective security only if the latter reflects the former. In order for this to happen, a lowest common denominator of the security of individual states has to be identified. As Nincic explains,

each member of a system of collective security should therefore construe security as consisting of only those elements which are genuinely essential to the life and growth of the nation concerned. The notion of security cannot, therefore, be left to the individual and necessarily subjective appreciation of each individual State, as was the case in the yet unorganised and more or less anarchic international community, but should be objectively defined by the norms of the international legal order. Security should, moreover, be equal for all. Such equality and the framing of the concept of security in objective and normative terms, constitute the essential prerequisites for the construction of a system of collective security.[8]

---

[5] *Declaration on Security in the Americas*, 28 October 2003, para. 4(a).
[6] Adopted at Sirte (Libya), 28 February 2004, para 12(i).
[7] Cf. F Coppola, 'The Idea of Collective Security', in Borquin (n 1 above.), 145–6; see also Morgan, n 4 above, 18.
[8] D Nincic, *The Problem of Sovereignty in the Charter and in the Practice of the United Nations* (Leiden: Nijhof, 1970), 81–2; quoting Ehrlich that security relates to the protection of interests protected by the existing legal order, ibid., 82.

Collective security thus understood imposes universal concepts on national policies;[9] it is, then, about an international compromise on permissible limits to how states perceive security, and means by which they can maximize their security. In order to achieve its aims, collective security has to be premised on a sound understanding of legitimate, fundamental, security interests of states as expressed in agreed norms and principles. The ability of states to preserve their security is necessarily premised on their ability to enjoy territorial supremacy, sovereignty, and to be protected against external intervention, as is reflected in fundamental principles of international law.

A distinctive feature of collective security is its formal character. States attempt to obtain security through domination, balance of powers, or alliances. The balance of power system attempts to achieve security by balancing competing alliances. Collective security is premised on general interests shared by all states and aims to protect those interests by concentrating force.[10] It is a public process involving the identification of a threat and the selection of a response by relying on normative standards and transparent procedures, as opposed to mere political consensus within a selected group of states. Collective security is above all a matter of interpreting and applying a legal framework consisting of constituent treaties, summit communiqués and declarations, and institutional decisions of binding or recommendatory character.

2. Validity and Feasibility of the Idea of Collective Security

Ever since its inception in 1919, collective security has been expected to operate above and beyond traditional patterns of international politics, to operationalize 'universal moral obligations' through the concert of great powers.[11] This approach presupposes, to some extent, a selfless commitment by states. Claude points out that states should be prepared to entrust their destiny to collective security institutions, fight for friends and foes alike whenever they are victims of aggression, and not engage in alliances, because this would mean discriminating between friends and foes which is alien to a 'basic proposition of collective security'.[12] The Chatham House Report prepared in the inter-war period stressed that the viability of collective security depends on the readiness of states to act beyond their self-interest. It was observed that

the danger of a break-down of the system thus arises if it appears that the nations are not sufficiently interested in the preservation of peace, apart from all other interests, to act up to

---

[9] HC Johnson and G Niemeyer, 'Collective Security: The Validity of an Ideal', 8 *International Organization* (1954), 19 at 20, 35.

[10] A Plant, 'Report on Collective Security', in Borquin (n 1 above), 132.

[11] EB Haas, 'Types of Collective Security: An Examination of Operational Concepts', 49 *American Political Science Review* (1955), 40 at 40, 42; KW Thompson, 'Collective Security Re-examined', 47 *American Political Science Review* (1953), 761, also speaks of 'a minimum of political solidarity and moral community' among great powers as a precondition for collective security.

[12] I Claude, *Swords Into Plowshares*, 3rd edn. (New York: Random House, 1964), 233.

their obligations when it comes to the point. Every failure to enforce the law or to make it wholly effective weakens the strength of the law and helps to render it effectively futile.[13]

Still, collective security operates against the background that 'governments lack a strong sense that they are a part of a larger (political, economic, social, cultural) entity in international politics with overarching interests, goals, perspectives and values they all share'.[14] Furthermore, 'although States might engage in the occasional act of security cooperation, anarchy ultimately and decisively causes them to seek advantage over their neighbours, and to act in a self-interested and self-help manner.'[15] States are shy of agreeing to international commitments in the area of security because they are not certain whether those will prove adequate if their security should be endangered.[16] When proceeding from the realist premise, the idea of collective security could seem unnatural, because 'a system of independently conceived national security policies implies the expectation of war as the dominant factor'.[17] According to Kolb, 'collective security seems a too rational and abstract construct to fit political realities'. In reality state interests and positions do not suit collective security requirements conceptually.[18] If states are guided by their national interest and if that interest makes it natural to fight wars or pursue expansion, it is indeed unnatural and anti-historical to expect them to engage in wars for collective good. Such an arrangement expects states to make wars against the nature, and effectively oppose the development of, history, which has been driven by their national self-interest.[19] It has been aptly pointed out that 'if we are to expect nations to act in [a] disinterested and international way, we must expect them to cease to be nations'. Nevertheless, 'in those exceptional cases in history when an overly powerful State developed an insatiable appetite for conquest, a form of "collective security" always came into existence.'[20] After all, it was states that realized after the First World War that a collective forum such as the League of Nations was necessary to avoid greater dangers to their security. The League of Nations and the United Nations have introduced 'vague but strongly felt notions of sin and righteousness' and called for a world of unselfish foreign policies. 'While never fully realised, this concept has to a considerable degree influenced international reality.'[21]

[13] *International Sanctions*, A Report by a Group of Members of the Royal Institute of International Affairs, 1935 (Oxford: Oxford University Press, 1938), 211.

[14] Morgan, n 4 above, 17.

[15] Cf E Adler and M Barnett, 'Security Communities in Theoretical Perspective', in Adler and Barnett (ed.), *Security Communities* (Cambridge: Cambridge University Press, 1998), 3.

[16] Morgan, n 4 above, 19.

[17] Johnson and Niemeyer, n 9 above, 19.

[18] R Kolb, 'The Eternal Problem of Collective Security: From the League of Nations to the United Nations', 26 *Refugee Studies Quarterly* (2007), 221.

[19] Cf Borquin, n 1 above, at 7.

[20] R Stromberg, 'The Idea of Collective Security', 17 *Journal of the History of Ideas* (1956), 250 at 259–60.

[21] Johnson and Niemeyer, n 9 above, 21, 27.

Thus, collective security cannot be written off in realist terms. Although the establishment of the UN collective security mechanism was criticized as inimical to the world political order, soon after it started operating Hans Morgenthau, the founder of the American wing of political realism, demonstrated that, instead of establishing a new idealist pattern of international politics, the UN became yet another platform for the interaction and confrontation of states in terms of their national interest and power positions. Morgenthau has criticized statements by American and British statesmen that the establishment of the UN would bring the end of power politics.[22] In addition, a sound realist approach acknowledges the complexity of power positions in the international system, and that an unpunished aggression can set a precedent for further aggression. Collective security is premised on the realist recognition of the need for collectively authorized action within transparent limits, and for the use of national power to that end against the recalcitrant power. The aim is to manage and institutionalize the use of power to achieve collective security aims.

The League of Nations Covenant was adopted against the background of President Wilson's proposal that violation of Covenant engagements would place the wrongdoer state under an automatic boycott, entailing its isolation from the rest of the world.[23] Thus, Article 16 of the Covenant stipulated that League members would

undertake immediately to subject it to the severance of all trade or financial relations, the prohibition of all intercourse between their nationals and the nationals of the covenant-breaking State, and the prevention of all financial, commercial or personal intercourse between the nationals of the covenant-breaking State and the nationals of any other State, whether a Member of the League or not.

Collective security under the UN Charter involves little automation and decisions are largely discretionary.[24] Immediate automatic action is not provided for, still less any obligation on individual members to assist the state which has been attacked, even under treaties of allegiance such as the North Atlantic Treaty. Such lack of automaticity obviously diminishes the overall efficiency of these institutions.

A radical criticism of the UN Charter was voiced by Borchard, who did not believe that peace can be enforced by peace-loving nations against aggressors in a world of sovereign states subject to no higher authority. The Charter had to be amended to remove a war-making function from it and turn the UN into an assembly for the consideration of international problems, notably in the economic sphere.[25] According to Stromberg, the formula of UN collective security proved useless and redundant, because it was premised on the utopia of idyllic unity among great powers in tackling threats, and instead has caused traditional alliances to

---

[22] H Morgenthau, 'Diplomacy', 55 *Yale Law Journal* (1945–6), 1067 at 1070.
[23] Cf Chatham House, n 13 above, 2.
[24] M Koskenniemi, 'The Place of Law in Collective Security', 17 *Michigan Journal of International Law* (1995–6), 455 at 457.
[25] E Borchard, 'The Impracticability of "Enforcing" Peace', 55 *Yale Law Journal* (1945–6), 966 at 966–8, 972.

reappear.[26] Arguably prevention of wars is thus possible, not through establishing collective security, but through equilibrium of power between states. If states were to fight wars where their national interest is not affected, this effort to repress war would transform local wars into world wars.[27]

Against this background, Haas proposed a theory of collective security which 'should not be based on the assumption of selfless motives'. This helps to explain the limited success of collective security and meets 'the tests of conceptual acceptability within the world conditions defined for them'. Ad hoc concerts of power depend on accidental confluences of power and are unstable. Permissive enforcement is a concept based on the willingness of great powers to act. Balancing remains the concept most relevant in formulating a theory of collective security, and its main virtue is that it does not assume selfless behaviour at the root of collective security. The UN should be a forum where contending regional systems negotiate and compromise, thus making the UN a balancer.[28]

'Permissive enforcement' is based on UN-authorized action but without the organization being directly involved. This enables major powers to undertake economic and military measures in the service of national policy but under global symbols.[29] This can be performed in practice in the way mandated by the UN Charter under Chapter VII, or through improvised but controversial approaches such as the Uniting for Peace resolution of the UN General Assembly. As Haas has pointed out, delegation to a single great power of authority to use military force is a vital concomitant of 'permissive enforcement'. The action in Korea in the 1950s would have been organized the same way if the UN force had been a purely US force. 'Universal collective security principles and procedures, by implication, are to be applied only to authorise and justify the regional or bilateral steps to be taken.'[30] This approach substantially limits the distinctive significance of collective security, though premised on its monopoly of the legitimizing role in the area of enforcement. Even if several instances of collective security action (such as the US-led war in the Persian Gulf in 1991, or 1994's French involvement in Rwanda on the basis of Security Council Resolution 929), are seen as collective and multilateral in formal terms but self-serving and interest-driven in essence, still they are collectively authorized interventions in pursuance of global aims and within carefully drafted limits.

Over centuries the idea of establishing institutional security frameworks for transforming the anarchic nature of the international system into a more peaceful and ordered international community has been part of political and academic thinking.[31] Such thinking has been manifested, as Hans Morgenthau illustrated, by Wilsonian idealism at the time when the League of Nations was established and

---

[26] Stromberg, n 20 above, 254.
[27] Coppola, n 7 above, 147–8.
[28] Haas, n 11 above, 60–2.
[29] Ibid, 48.
[30] Ibid, 50.
[31] For an illustration see EH Carr, 'The League of Peace and Freedom—An Episode in the Quest for Collective Security', *International Affairs* (1935), 836. This is a 'transformational' approach, which

by enthusiasm about the UN's potential to bring into operation new policies and procedures and displace the patterns of 'old' diplomacy.[32] Questions whether collective security is a valid notion, or even feasible, were being asked long after the League of Nations had been established,[33] given that the idea of collective security related to the idea of transforming the chaos of international relations into a peaceful order similar to national societies safeguarded by police, where law prevails and violence is not an ordinary expectation.[34] According to Claude,

collective security has generally been regarded as a halfway house between the terminal points of international anarchy and world government. Given the assumption that the former has become intolerable and the latter remains, at least for the foreseeable future, unattainable, collective security is conceived as an alternative, far enough from anarchy to be useful and far enough from world government to be feasible.[35]

On this view collective security might appear to be a shortcut to evade the natural givens of international society that are indisputable from any doctrinal point of view. As Thompson observes,

a legal arrangement imposed upon political and social conditions incompatible with its fulfillment makes successful political action difficult. Therefore it is essential in considering the reality of collective security that we understand fully its assumptions and requirements.[36]

Viewing collective security as an ideology-driven framework misunderstands the basis from which collective security derives its legitimacy. The powers, functions, and tasks of collective security institutions are determined through inter-state agreements. The rationale behind setting up collective security institutions is not to give effect to a particular ideology, nor to set one part of the world against another in a crusade-style confrontation, but to preserve the consensually identified causes of peace that are recognized by all major elements of international society. As Sir Alfred Zimmern has pointed out,

the League of Nations was never intended to be, nor is it, a revolutionary organization. It accepts the world as it finds it and merely seeks to provide a more satisfactory means for carrying on some of the business which these States transact between one another. It is not even revolutionary in the more limited sense of revolutionising the methods for carrying on international business. It does not supersede the older methods. It merely supplements them.[37]

This straightforward and down-to-earth explanation, although uttered in relation to the League specifically, can be generalized as an accurate description of the entire

---

sees collective security as an idea, political project, or ideology, as opposed to the product of state agreement and part of an overall political and legal context.

[32] Morgenthau, n 22 above, 1067.

[33] Plant, n 10 above, 132–3.

[34] Johnson and Niemeyer, n 9 above, 20; Thompson, n 11 above, 753 at 755; Stromberg, n 20 above, 255.

[35] Claude, n 12 above, 224; Stromberg, ibid, 252, 254–5.

[36] Thompson, n 11 above, 758.

[37] Sir Alfred Zimmern, *The League of Nations and the Rule of Law* (London: Macmillan, 1936), 4.

system of collective security. The League of Nations Covenant envisaged this organization as complementing the regular means of dispute settlement on the basis of subsidiarity. Articles 12 and 13 of the Covenant provided that disputes between League members should be submitted to arbitration or judicial organs. More specifically,

[d]isputes as to the interpretation of a treaty, as to any question of international law, as to the existence of any fact which if established would constitute a breach of any international obligation, or as to the extent and nature of the reparation to be made for any such breach, [were] declared to be among those which are generally suitable for submission to arbitration or judicial settlement.

However, if disputes 'likely to lead to a rupture' were not submitted for arbitral or judicial settlement, they were covered by the League Council's jurisdiction under Article 15 of the Covenant. These arrangements are largely replicated in Articles 33, 36, and 37 of the United Nations Charter.[38]

As a product of international law, collective security cannot transform (through the back door) the legal and political system of which it is a product. Collective security of the whole serves as a superstructure to ordinary patterns of conflict resolution. As explained above, the end of the First World War led states to recognize that

the old system of individual security by each state had broken down. The impossibility, perhaps even undesirability, of a world federal state was recognized. Hence, an attempt was made to arrive at a new system of collective security by international organization on a quasi-universal scale; that is, by norms of particular international law, by a basic treaty which would adopt some of the features of an advanced municipal legal order, and yet remain within the framework of international law. The end envisaged was a loose confederation of sovereign states which would accept by treaty certain restrictions of their sovereignty. The term 'collective security' was coined for this system.[39]

Collective security is thus a legal arrangement operating in the existing legal environment. It develops through the ordinary process of international law. It is there, not to advance ideas, nor to fit itself to particular patterns of governance, but to perform tasks that have been consensually delegated to it.

3. Categories and Definitions

Collective security refers to the collective, that is the group of states which unites around a set of common values and principles and includes, on a permanent basis, the institutional capacity to determine, case by case, whether the values and principles in question have been encroached upon and take the action to safeguard them and preserve or restore the state of things that they require. Defining collective security also demonstrates the degree of legitimacy the idea commands. The term 'collective security' first appeared in France in the early 1930s, to describe

---

[38] See Chapter 2 below.
[39] J Kunz, 'The Idea of "Collective Security" in Pan-American Developments', 6 *Western Political Quarterly* (1953), 658 at 659.

a far older idea, which history has understood in terms of collective or concerted action to maintain the existing international status quo or general tranquillity. This idea contemplates such action as could be taken against states which are not part of the particular security arrangement involved.[40] In one view, collective security is normally 'introverted', in contrast to the 'extroverted' collective self-defence treaties meant to counter an external aggressor. But both are designed to counter acts of aggression.[41] Kolb specifies that collective security includes two essential elements: a triggering event and collective, binding decision making.[42]

As widely recognized, the distinct, and indispensable, condition for collective security is an appropriate international machinery, binding obligations clearly set forth in legal instruments,[43] 'a written Constitution, statutory meetings at regular intervals, and a material centre',[44] 'a multilateral treaty, whereby Contracting Parties create an international agency vested with the power to employ force against aggressors (and perhaps other law-breakers)'.[45] Kelsen emphasized that 'we speak of collective security when the protection of the rights of the States, the reaction against the violation of the law, assumes the character of a collective enforcement action'.[46]

Collective security assumes a status quo, or situation of peace, and seeks to secure this prevailing status quo through prohibiting acts of aggression.[47] Collective security envisages 'a state of affairs in which attempts to change the status quo by violence are unlawful and doomed to frustration through opposition in overwhelming force'.[48] Without solving the problem of war, and coordinating responses to it, collective security will solve no other problem.[49] Accordingly, Johnson and Niemeyer define collective security 'as a system based on the universal obligation of all nations to join forces against an aggressor State as soon as the fact of aggression is determined by established procedure'.[50] As Borquin specified, collective security 'carries with it necessarily—by definition, it may be said—a more or less far-reaching renunciation by States of the use of armed violence to secure justice for themselves and, to put it more generally, to make their will prevail'. In the League

---

[40] D Nincic, n 8 above, 80.

[41] Y Dinstein, *War, Aggression and Self-Defence* (Cambridge: Cambridge University Press, 2005), 278.

[42] Kolb, n 18 above, 220.

[43] Thompson, n 11 above, 758.

[44] FP Walters, Introduction, in Mowat *et al*, *Problems of Peace*, 10th Series (London: George Allen & Unwin Ltd, 1936), 1 at 2.

[45] Dinstein, n 41 above, 278.

[46] H Kelsen, 'Collective Security and Collective Self-Defence under the Charter of the United Nations', 41 AJIL (1948), 783 at 783–4.

[47] Thompson, n 11 above, 758; J Morris and H McCoubrey, 'Regional Peacekeeping in the Post-Cold War Era', 6 *International Peacekeeping* (1999), 129 at 130; Nincic, n 8 above, 80–1,

[48] Cf Kunz, n 39 above, 658 at 659.

[49] P Noel-Baker, 'The Future of the Collective System', in Mowat *et al*, n 44 above, 178 at 179; RL Butterworth, 'Organizing Collective Security: The UN Charter's Chapter VIII in Practice', 28 *World Politics* (1976), 197 at 197–8.

[50] Johnson and Niemeyer, n 9 above, 19 at 20, 35.

of Nations context this included obligations under both the Covenant and the 1928 Paris Pact.[51]

The UN system is likewise based on a comprehensive prohibition of the use of force in Article 2(4) of the UN Charter. Only two exceptions are admitted to this prohibition: use of force in self-defence against an armed attack, or as authorized by the Security Council under Article 42 of the Charter. In practice, states have claimed other bases for using force, such as anticipatory self-defence, pre-emptive action, or humanitarian intervention, but all such claims have been repudiated by a great many states as incompatible with the Charter and general international law. Consequently, the use of force going beyond exceptions admitted in the Charter constitutes an act of aggression as defined in General Assembly Resolution 3314(1974), and consequently a legitimate cause of action for collective security institutions.

Diverse notions are advanced doctrinally and politically, such as conflict prevention, conflict management, and conflict resolution. It is interesting to consider what might be the relationship of those 'other' concepts with the (overarching) concept of collective security. Conflict prevention is understood as a set of actions to avoid situations escalating into a conflict or crisis. Conflict management arguably refers to actions confronting a conflict that has already broken out and consists of peace-making and peace-enforcement measures. Conflict resolution is vaguely described as a set of post-conflict reconstructive efforts to address the causes that led to the conflict, to impose a (partial) settlement on a crisis, and to consolidate the cessation of violence.[52] Conflict prevention can be operational—short-term operational efforts using political or military means to prevent a conflict or forestall escalating violence—or long-term structural—aiming at risk reduction and consisting of developmental or economic efforts to address the root causes of conflicts.[53] Within the EU framework, conflict prevention focuses 'on preventing the outbreak and spreading of violent conflicts through early action, and on preventing the recurrence of violent conflict'. This way, the EU commits itself to help African organizations and governments in dealing with root causes of conflicts.[54]

Crisis management is a set of arrangements and procedures to control a crisis and shape its future course,[55] while its resolution is being sought.[56] Crisis management

---

[51] Borquin, n 1 above, 10.

[52] V Kronenberger and J Wouters, 'Introduction', in Kronenberger and Wouters (ed.), *The European Union and Conflict Prevention—Policy and Legal Aspects* (The Hague: TMC Asser Press, 2004), XXIII; S Blockmans and R Wessel, 'The European Union and Crisis Management: Will the Lisbon Treaty Make the EU More Effective?', 14 *Journal of Conflict and Security Law* (2009), 265 at 269.

[53] H Wulf and T Debiel, 'Conflict Early Warning and Response Mechanisms: Tools for Enhancing the Effectiveness of Regional Organisations? A Comparative Study of the AU, ECOWAS, IGAD, ASEAN/ARF and PIF', Crisis States Research Centre Working Paper Series No, 2, Working Paper No. 49, May 2009, 3; Kronenberger and Wouters, ibid, XXIV; J Nino Perez, 'Conflict Indicators Developed by the Commission—The Check-List for Root Causes of Conflict/Early Warning Indicators', in Kronenberger and Wouters, ibid, 5.

[54] The Council Common Position 2004/85/CFSP of 26 January 2004 concerning conflict prevention, management and resolution in Africa and repealing Common Position 2001/374/CFSP, Articles 2 and 4.

[55] J Kriendler, 'NATO Crisis Management', in Kronenberger and Wouters, n 52 above, 415 at 417.

[56] Blockmans and Wessel, n 52 above, 269.

encompasses all measures intended to prevent or defuse a humanitarian crisis or a conflict, mitigate its effects on human populations once it has broken out, stabilize the region after a ceasefire has been reached, and prevent the recurrence of conflict in the long term. It ranges from good offices or economic and diplomatic pressure to a full-fledged military campaign. It also includes humanitarian aid, rescue operations, peace-keeping, and peace-enforcement.[57] Thus understood, crisis management can include a broad spectrum of measures that differ in their type, duration, and effect. Overall, crisis management places greater emphasis on involvement than on solution.

Crisis management as part of the European Security and Defence Policy (ESDP) involves both the element of 'proper' collective security with the military arm engaged in peace operations, and civilian crisis management dealing with law enforcement and local situation-monitoring in potential crisis areas. The activities in question include 'police missions, rule of law missions, civilian administration missions, civil protection missions, peace monitoring missions, support missions to EU Special Representatives, border assistance missions and security sector reform missions'.[58] How civilian crisis management differs from more general activities relating to technical cooperation and development assistance is relative.[59] The 1999 NATO Strategic Concept defines the tasks of crisis management as 'to contribute to preventing crises and, should they arise, defusing them at an early stage'. Crisis management thus understood is not conceptually different from conflict prevention.[60] As is generally recognized, the difference between these terms is blurred in practice.[61] For instance, action adopted in the wake of a crisis, intended to prevent the resurgence of armed violence in the short, medium and longer term, could fall within the realm of both peace building and (future) conflict prevention. The same holds true for the 'fuzzy concept of crisis management', which 'serves as a catch-all phrase for both military and civilian ESDP operations, whether they are deployed to prevent conflict from bursting into crisis, assist in enforcing the peace, keep the peace or build the peace'.[62]

Early warning can include any initiative that focuses on systematic data collection, analysis and formulation of recommendations (including risk assessment), and alerts a recognized authority (such as the UN Security Council) to a new (or renewed) threat to peace at a sufficiently early stage. This task includes anticipating the escalation of conflicts, estimating the magnitude and timing of

---

[57] M Reichard, *The EU–NATO Relationship* (Aldershot: Ashgate,2006), 241–2.

[58] Blockmans and Wessel, n 52 above, 269.

[59] The Secretary-General has proposed that 'the root causes of conflicts at the early stages of prevention' can be addressed by development and humanitarian agencies of the UN: *Report of the Secretary-General on the Prevention of Armed Conflict*, S/2001/754 – A/55/985, 7 June 2001, para 13.

[60] Strategic Concept, para. 32.

[61] This is illustrated by J Wouters and F Naert, 'The EU and Conflict Prevention', in Kronenberger and Wouters, n 52 above, 542–3, who give examples of definitions of peacemaking and crisis management.

[62] Blockmans and Wessel, n 52 above, 269.

emerging threats, describing plausible scenarios, and presenting decision makers with options.[63]

The essence of collective security is described in Article 1 of the UN Charter as follows: 'to maintain peace and security by the prevention and removal of threats to the peace'; thus conflict prevention is essentially an element of collective security. The 1992 summit statement of Security Council members reaffirms 'their commitment to the collective security system of the Charter to deal with threats to peace and to reverse acts of aggression'.[64]

Thus, it can be seen that the concept of collective security is overarching and broad, and can include in itself a variety of tasks such as conflict prevention, crisis management, peace-keeping, or peace-enforcement, as required to enable the relevant institution to deal with threats as their gravity and magnitude require. The Agenda for Peace sets the conflict prevention issues as one of the priorities:

It is the essence of the concept of collective security as contained in the Charter that if peaceful means fail, the measures provided in Chapter VII should be used, on the decision of the Security Council, to maintain or restore international peace and security in the face of a 'threat to the peace, breach of the peace, or act of aggression'.[65]

Without such preliminary preventive procedures under Chapter VI it would be impossible to ascertain whether a coercive collective security action was warranted. A valid concept of collective security thus includes mediation, conciliation, investigation, and fact finding as aspects of conflict prevention.

Article 2 of the African Union Peace and Security Council (PSC) Protocol defines PSC as 'a collective security and early-warning arrangement to facilitate timely and efficient response to conflict and crisis situations in Africa'. Its role is broad and includes conflict management and intervention. Article 1 of the 1999 Economic Community Of West African States (ECOWAS) Mechanism Protocol on Conflict Prevention Mechanism establishes within ECOWAS 'a mechanism for collective security and peace to be known as "Mechanism for Conflict Prevention, Management, Resolution, Peace-keeping and Security"'.

Chapter VI of the OAS Charter is titled 'Collective security'. Article 28 specifies that an act of aggression against one member of OAS constitutes aggression against all member States; Article 29 provides a comprehensive view of collective security including collective self-defence, specifying that

if the inviolability or the integrity of the territory or the sovereignty or political independence of any American State should be affected by an armed attack or by an act of aggression that is not an armed attack, or by an extracontinental conflict, or by a conflict between two or more American States, or by any other fact or situation that might

---

[63] Cf Wulf and Debiel, n 53 above, 3; Nino Perez, n 53 above, 3 at 7–8.

[64] Statement by the Security Council Presidency on behalf of the Council's membership, S/23500, 31 January 1992, at 2.

[65] *An Agenda for Peace—Preventive diplomacy, peacemaking and peace-keeping*, Report of the Secretary-General pursuant to the statement adopted by the Summit Meeting of the Security Council on 31 January 1992, A/47/277–S/24111, 17 June 1992, para. 42.

endanger the peace of America, the American States, in furtherance of the principles of continental solidarity or collective self-defense, shall apply the measures and procedures established in the special treaties on the subject.

These provisions refer to threats and consequent measures, and demonstrate that the idea of collective self-defence is related to that of collective security.

Conflict prevention, crisis management, conflict resolution, and peace-building are tasks subsumed by the framework of collective security. Collective security is an older and widely accepted concept dealing with the sum of universal and regional efforts to address threats to international peace. It enjoys a more general acceptance, greater consistency, and better validity than other related concepts. In addition, organizations which have developed the idea of crisis management, such as NATO and the EU, have committed themselves to act within the broader framework of the UN's collective security.[66]

4. Collective Security and Legal Constraints

It is not rational to defend collective security for its own sake and unless it establishes a durable system of sustained peace. As Stromberg pointed out,

collective security has hardly received the critical analysis it requires. . . . A certain aura of sanctity has surrounded it, because it has seemed to carry the honorific cause of internationalism against nationalism, idealism against cynicism, peace against war. But we need no longer respect the pretensions to holiness of an idea which seems to issue in so much unholiness.[67]

More precisely, as Claude has specified, collective security focuses on the instigation of sanctions, without offering a theoretical guide to determining the limits of community coercion, and establishing a settlement after the successful squelching of aggression.[68] The instigation of sanctions is at the core of the collective security idea, but limits on the harmful consequences thereof and the ultimate objective of collective security efforts can be inflated in this process. As Kelsen observed, the UN Charter does not exclude the possibility of unsettled disputes. In certain cases decisions on enforcement or on obligations of states (such as the withdrawal of troops from the relevant territory) cannot be achieved.[69] In addition, as Brierly pointed out, 'there is nothing in the Charter to preclude the Security Council from deciding that a threat to the peace would most conveniently be met by another Hoare–Laval or Munich solution at the expense of a weak power'.[70] Due to voting arrangements under the Charter, no action can be taken unless it is supported by all permanent members of the Security Council.

---

[66] See Chapter 3 below.
[67] Stromberg, n 20 above, 263.
[68] Claude, n 12 above, 255.
[69] Kelsen, n 46 above, 789–90.
[70] JL Brierly, 'The Covenant and The Charter', 23 *British Yearbook of International Law* (1946), 83 at 87.

Arguably, the Charter thus falls short of achieving its purposes, as it allows political considerations to prevail over legal considerations.[71]

If this approach is right, the more collective security expands, the greater is the possibility that it can be turned into a national policy tool with far-reaching implications, and thus the more likely it is to defeat its original purpose. This factor makes it vital to clarify how far collective security action can expand, which can only be done by focusing on legal aspects, above all interpretation of legal instruments that specify the scope of delegated powers.

Historically, 'collective security began with a theory based on an analogy with law and the criminal.' The Wilsonian concept of collective security relied on the right cause being taken up against those who engage in aggressive and criminal conduct. However, even in the early period of the UN difficulties were revealed in assigning the adjectives 'right' and 'wrong' to different parties.[72] The mandate of the League of Nations had been inspired by the need to safeguard international law, as is clear from the Preamble of its Covenant. The Preamble refers to 'the acceptance of obligations not to resort to war', to understanding of international law 'as the actual rule of conduct among Governments', and to 'the maintenance of justice and a scrupulous respect for all treaty obligations in the dealings of organised peoples with one another'. Article 10 stipulated a fundamental obligation on every member State to respect the territorial integrity and political independence of other Members.

Ludwick Ehrlich, one of the leading legal minds in the inter-war period, conceived collective security as part of a 'well-organised system of defence of legal rights' that reduces to a minimum the likelihood of successful violations of state rights. The concept of security had to be understood in relation to interests guaranteed by international law. 'National safety' under Article 8 of the League of Nations Covenant meant the protection of interests safeguarded by international law, further reinforced by Article 10. Ehrlich concluded that 'security, in the legal sense of the term, means the actual protection of the interests which are safeguarded by the existing legal system.'[73] Similarly, Noel-Baker observed that not only must the law of collective security proscribe war, but law must be upheld in every case where it is infringed.[74] Without this legal element collective security has no

---

[71] Ibid, 88–91; Nincic, n 8 above, 87; on a related but different note, Goodrich considers it improbable that the Security Council would achieve better results in Abyssinian and Manchukuo affairs than the League did, because of great powers being able to block the enforcement action: 'within the area of possible operation, the actual effectiveness of the United Nations system will depend upon political conditions which, if they had existed, would have also assured the success of the League of Nations.' LM Goodrich, 'From League of Nations to United Nations', 1 *International Organization* (1947), 3 at 18.

[72] Stromberg, n 20 above, 255.

[73] L Ehrlich, 'The Development of International Law and the Problem of Collective Security', in Borquin, n 1 above, 152 at 153–5; the function of collective security to uphold and safeguard international law contrasted with the hitherto dominant pattern of thinking and activity in international relations that emphasized only national interest and force: ibid., 227.

[74] Noel-Baker, n 49 above, 192–3.

distinctive value and becomes just another tool for wielding power, without a distinct legitimacy.

Arguably the UN Charter provisions on enforcement 'depart from the earlier, more juridical, conception of collective security'. The Security Council is not required to enforce international law but only to maintain peace and security, and is a political organ.[75] The Council is certainly not required to act to enforce the entire body of international law. The principal motivation for its enforcement action should be the existence of a threat to or breach of the peace as specified under Chapter VII of the Charter. But in almost every instance, the Council's use of its enforcement powers results in the enforcement of international law. As further pointed out, 'the behaviour of a State cannot easily be challenged solely on grounds of "policy".' It is preferable to demonstrate a deviation from legal rules if one wishes to gain the support of those not directly involved.[76]

According to Kelsen, the UN collective security mechanism is meant to enforce peace not law, and can compromise law for the sake of peace. It may even require one conflicting state to cede territory to another in the interest of peace. In such cases the UN enforcement machinery can create new law.[77] Eagleton claims that the UN Security Council is not restricted to legal principles; the Charter puts security above justice and order above law.[78] Further, according to Franck the Charter establishes the primacy of peace over justice.[79]

In conceptual and policy terms, a dichotomy between law and peace could mean that the legal consequences of illegal acts should be replaced by some other consequences designed under the Council's discretion. However, addressing peace and security through policy considerations only produces conceptually insoluble dilemmas, since none of the conflicting policy considerations is better than any other. The key to the outcome lies in a systemic understanding of peace and security, the way the community of states views this concept, as opposed to what it might be if viewed from a particular policy perspective. This is reflected in Article 1 of the UN Charter, according to which the principal purpose of the United Nations is

[t]o maintain international peace and security, and to that end: to take effective collective measures for the prevention and removal of threats to the peace, and for the suppression of acts of aggression or other breaches of the peace, and to bring about by peaceful means, and in conformity with the principles of justice and international law, adjustment or settlement of international disputes or situations which might lead to a breach of the peace.

---

[75] O Schachter, *International Law: Theory and Practice* (Leiden: Nijhoff, 1991), 389–90.

[76] O Schachter, 'The Quasi-Judicial Role of the Security Council and the General Assembly', 58 AJIL (1964), 960 at 962; R Higgins, 'The Place of International Law in the Settlement of Disputes by the Security Council', 64 AJIL (1970), 17.

[77] Kelsen, n 46 above, 788–9; see also statements of some governments in the early years of the Security Council that references to law were unhelpful because the Council's function was to maintain peace, in Higgins, ibid, 9–10.

[78] C Eagleton, 'The Jurisdiction of the Security Council Over Disputes', 40 AJIL (1946), 513.

[79] T Franck, 'The United Nations as Guarantor of International Peace and Security' in C Tomuschat (ed.), *The United Nations at the Age of Fifty* (The Hague: Kluwer, 1995), 25 at 26.

According to Kelsen, conformity with the principles of justice and international law is required only for the settlement of disputes, not for enforcement measures. Kelsen also argues that justice is not the same as international law, and that

the question arises whether the one or the other shall be maintained in case of conflict. Since the Charter gives no answer to this question and no definition of the concept of justice, the organ of the United Nations which has to apply the provision of the Charter has the choice between justice, or what this organ considers to be justice in the case at hand, and positive international law. In essence this means that the Charter does not strengthen but rather weakens respect for the obligations of international law.[80]

However, as Higgins observed, there is no evidence 'that the framers of the Charter saw any great distinction between law and justice; the terms were used synonymously, even if somewhat redundant'. Governments plead that a dispute should be sorted in accordance with justice as opposed to law when they know their legal case to be weak; or when they want the existing legal status quo to be revised.[81]

In addition, the concept of peace and security under the UN Charter has no meaning that is essentially different from, still less inimical, to international law. The UN General Assembly set down the early position of the UN on this matter in its Resolution 290(IV) of 1 December 1949 on Essentials of Peace. According to this resolution, the UN Charter 'lays down basic principles necessary for an enduring peace; that disregard of these principles is primarily responsible for the continuance of international tension' (paragraph 1). The resolution then specifies that states must refrain from threatening or using force contrary to the Charter, 'from any threats or acts, direct or indirect, aimed at impairing the freedom, independence or integrity of any State, or at fomenting civil strife and subverting the will of the people in any State', to 'carry out in good faith its international agreements', to observe human rights and to settle international disputes by peaceful means (paragraphs 2, 4, 6, and 11).

This demonstrates the position of the organization that the concept of peace is firmly premised on the observance of fundamental principles of international law, and that compliance with international law is a condition for peace. This requires viewing peace against the structural background of international law: there will be peace when states can exercise their rights unharassed. Action for peace cannot be validly motivated by contempt for the legal rights of states. If the fundamental rights of a state are essential to peace, then their exercise cannot as such be understood as a threat to or breach of the peace. Therefore, from the outset early doctrinal views on the primacy of peace over justice have been articulated inconsistently and constituted a fallacy.

It would therefore be unsound to see collective security aimed at political resolution of pertinent crises as opposed to their resolution based on legal merit.

---

[80] H Kelsen, 'The Preamble of the Charter—A Critical Analysis', 2 *Journal of Politics* (1946) 134 at 155–7.
[81] Higgins, n 76 above, 9–11.

If the 'political' aim conflicts with legal imperatives, then international society has conflicting policies as to what outcome conduces to the maintenance or restoration of peace and security in the relevant case. This is well illustrated by the reaction to the Security Council's handling of the conflict in Cyprus. As illustrated, with the cease-fire in Cyprus and deployment of the UN Peacekeeping Force in Cyprus (UNFICYP),

> there was a sense in which the effectiveness of the United Nations in helping to conclude and secure respect for ceasefires actually worked against the achievement of the broader objective of preventing aggression, since it placed a premium on a State achieving a rapid military success which a ceasefire then enabled it to consolidate in the knowledge that the United Nations would not compel it to give up the territory it had occupied.[82]

In a number of its resolutions the UN Security Council has consistently taken the view that it does not view its peace and security mandate as isolated from, still less opposed to, enforcement of international law. In the preamble to Resolution 514 (1982) regarding the war between Iran and Iraq, the Council recalled provisions of Article 2 of the Charter and that the reestablishment of peace and security in the region required the strict adherence to these provisions. According to the preamble of Resolution 836(1993) on Bosnia,

> the lasting solution to the conflict in the Republic of Bosnia and Herzegovina must be based on the following principles: immediate and complete cessation of hostilities; withdrawal from territories seized by the use of force and 'ethnic cleansing'; reversal of the consequences of 'ethnic cleansing' and recognition of the right of all refugees to return to their homes; and respect for sovereignty, territorial integrity and political independence of the Republic of Bosnia and Herzegovina.

In the preamble to Resolution 1556(2004) on Darfur, the Council urges 'all the parties to take the necessary steps to prevent and put an end to violations of human rights and international humanitarian law and underlin[es] that there will be no impunity for violators', welcoming 'the commitment by the Government of Sudan to investigate the atrocities and prosecute those responsible'. Further, in operative paragraph 6 the Council demands

> that the Government of Sudan fulfil its commitments to disarm the Janjaweed militias and apprehend and bring to justice Janjaweed leaders and their associates who have incited and carried out human rights and international humanitarian law violations and other atrocities,... and expresses its intention to consider further actions, including measures as provided for in Article 41 of the Charter of the United Nations on the Government of Sudan, in the event of non-compliance.

Thus, the Council directly links the applicability of Chapter VII economic sanctions to the implementation of international legal standards on the prosecution of serious international crimes.

---

[82] C Greenwood, 'The United Nations as Guarantor of International Peace and Security: Past, Present and Future—A United Kingdom View', in Tomuschat (ed.), n 79 above, 58 at 64.

In the preambles to Resolution 1564(2004) and 1591(2005), the Council noted that the ultimate resolution of the crisis in Darfur must include the safe and voluntary return of internally displaced persons and refugees to their original homes, which is a critical factor for the consolidation of the peace process. Paragraph 3 of the same resolution specifies a number of Article 41 measures against the perpetrators' violations of human rights and humanitarian law, namely the denial to such individuals of entry to and transit through the territories of all states (paragraph 3(d)), and freezing the financial assets of such individuals and any entities owned or controlled by them (paragraph 3(e)).[83]

The *Responsibility to Protect* Report stresses that the UN is a 'law-enforcing collective security organization' and that the Security Council is at the heart of the international law-enforcement system, possessing the unique authority to validate peace-enforcement operations, given that the use of force is otherwise illegal.[84] A systemic understanding of peace and security has also been upheld within other collective security institutions. The OAS manifested just such an integral vision by insisting on restoring status quo under Article 7 of the Inter-American Treaty on Reciprocal Assistance 1947 (Rio Treaty).[85] On 15 July 1969 the OAS committee invoked Article 7 and called upon Honduras and El Salvador to cease hostilities and restore *status quo ante bellum*. The El Salvador Government's position was that, if acceptance of the committee's formula resulted in violent social upheaval because of intense public feeling, consequently action would have to be taken in steps. The OAS committee disagreed, reasoning that Article 7 of the Rio Treaty was indivisible, and that a conditional reply to a resolution adopted by the Organ of Consultation was not acceptable to the OAS. Although El Salvador continued to reject this approach, on 18 July the Organ of Consultation adopted a resolution that embodied the committee's approach.[86]

---

[83] For more examples of such resolutions see Chapter 4 below.

[84] *The Responsibility to Protect*, Report of the International Commission on Intervention and State Sovereignty (December 2001), para. 6.12.

[85] Article 7 reads as follows: 'In the case of a conflict between two or more American States, without prejudice to the right of self-defense in conformity with Article 51 of the Charter of the United Nations, the High Contracting Parties, meeting in consultation shall call upon the contending States to suspend hostilities and restore matters to the *status quo ante bellum*, and shall take in addition all other necessary measures to reestablish or maintain inter-American peace and security and for the solution of the conflict by peaceful means. The rejection of the pacifying action will be considered in the determination of the aggressor and in the application of the measures which the consultative meeting may agree upon.'

[86] LTG, 'A Microcosmic View of the OAS: The Honduras–El Salvador Conflict', 57 *Virginia Law Review* (1971), 291 at 296–7.

2

Collective Security Institutions

1. The United Nations System in General

The UN collective security system operates mainly through three principal organs of the UN. The Security Council, which consists of 15 member States and decides by unanimous vote of its permanent members as specified in Article 27 of the Charter, has a monopoly over enforcement actions. The General Assembly is an organ with universal representation, but lacks enforcement powers. The International Court of Justice is the principal judicial organ of the UN and clarifications it has given in contentious or advisory cases have determined many issues of the law of collective security. The UN Secretary-General mostly performs the role of implementing the decisions adopted by the Council and the Assembly, and of interpreting their decisions on the ground.

2. The Nature and Primary Responsibility of the UN Security Council

According to Article 24 of the Charter, the Security Council has primary responsibility in the area of peace and security. In carrying out this primary responsibility the Council acts on behalf of the entire UN membership. The relevance of this provision has been objected to, since the Council decides for the UN, not for member States.[1] But a clause like this cannot be read out of the Charter as superfluous and devoid of meaning,[2] especially since a representative part of the UN membership can express an adverse view on the Council's decisions.

The two principal types of Council activities are peaceful settlement of disputes and situations under Chapter VI, and enforcement action under Chapter VII.[3] The multitude of responsibilities allocated to the Council raises the question

---

[1] F Seyersted, *Common Law of International Organisations* (Leiden: Brill, 2008), 372; H Kelsen, *The Law of the United Nations* (London: Stevens, 1950), 280; J Delbrück, 'Article 24', in B Simma (ed.), *The Charter of the United Nations—A Commentary* (New York: Oxford University Press, 2002), 404.

[2] As the representative of Ghana stated in the Security Council's discussion of the Lockerbie matter after the International Court's 1998 judgment on preliminary objections, taking views from the wider membership of the UN under Article 24 in this case called 'for an end to sanctions against Libya and the pacific settlement of the dispute over the Lockerbie affair', S/PV.3864, 20 March 1998, 56.

[3] The Council's role under Chapter VI is covered in this chapter while the matters arising under Chapter VII are mainly examined in Chapters 4 and 5.

what is the essential nature of this organ—political, administrative, quasi-judicial, fact finding, or other—but the Charter does not expressly clarify this. The International Court specified in the *Reparations* case that the UN is a 'political body, charged with a political task of an important character'.[4] Then arguably, unless the Charter otherwise specifies, component parts of the UN—its principal and subsidiary organs—also have a political character. The Council is composed of representatives who receive political instructions.[5]

Along with being influenced by political factors, the Council is established by law. Its powers, functions, and the degree to which it can take political considerations into account are also determined by law. The International Court confirmed in the *Admissions* case that the political character of an organ does not release it from a duty to observe the law, let alone place it above the law.[6] As the International Criminal Tribunal for the Former Yugoslavia specified, the Council 'is not a judicial organ and is not provided with judicial powers (though it may incidentally perform certain quasi-judicial activities such as effecting determinations or findings)'.[7] What also matters, however, is that (while not designated as a judicial organ) the Council can regard law-enforcement tasks as inherent to its principal peace and security mandate. In the *Application for Review* Advisory Opinion, the International Court pronounced on the nature of political and judicial organs, using the example of the Committee of Applications for Review of UN Administrative Tribunal Judgments. As the Court pointed out,

Certainly, being composed of member States, the Committee is a political organ. Its functions, on the other hand, are merely to make a summary examination of any objections to judgments of the Tribunal and to decide whether there is a substantial basis for the application to have the matter reviewed by the Court in an advisory opinion. These are functions which, in the Court's view, are normally discharged by a legal body. But there is no necessary incompatibility between the exercise of these functions by a political body and the requirements of the judicial process, inasmuch as these functions merely furnish a potential link between two procedures which are clearly judicial in nature.[8]

If, consequently, a political organ is statutorily entrusted with tasks that are essentially judicial, this obviously impacts on the nature of its powers, functions, and procedures. An organ in question remains a political organ, but what it can do—and any safeguards it has to observe—depend on the nature of the task as well as the statutory framework.

The essence of an organ's quasi-judicial character is that, even where it is not established as a court, it can administer justice the way courts do, that is decide on

---

[4] *Reparation for Injuries Suffered in Service of the United Nations*, ICJ Reports 1949, 179.

[5] D Ciobanu, *Preliminary Objections Related to the Jurisdiction of the United Nations Principal Organs* (Leiden: Nijhoff, 1975), 3–5.

[6] *Admission of a State to the Membership of the United Nations* (Advisory Opinion), *ICJ Reports*, 1947–8, 64; see also *Prosecutor v Tadić*, Case IT-94-1-AR72, ICTY Appeal Chamber, 2 October 1995, paras 20–8.

[7] *Prosecutor v Tadić*, Case IT-94-1-AR72, Appeal Chamber, 2 October 1995, para 37.

[8] *Application for Review of Judgment No 158 of the United Nations Administrative Tribunal*, *ICJ Reports* 1973, 166 at 173.

complex issues of attribution to establish the responsibility of the relevant entity, through a proper assessment of evidence and a fair hearing. Principal features are independence from state influences, competence to apply rules to facts, and the ability to reach final decisions within their mandate, irrespective of whether such decisions are binding.[9] The basis for all of this is the delegation of the relevant authority to an organ by states party to its constituent instrument. Unlike the quasi-judicial role of organs such as the UN Human Rights Committee under the 1966 Civil and Political Rights Covenant or the Committee against Torture under the 1984 Torture Convention—to which have been delegated the task of interpreting and applying the relevant treaties to ensure their uniform implementation—the Charter does not designate the Council as the sole organ that can interpret the Charter authoritatively or conclusively, not even if its decisions are binding under Article 25. That the Council is not properly equipped to exercise quasi-judicial tasks is reflected in Article 36, which indicates that legal disputes should normally be referred to the International Court. In addition, the fact that the Council (as well as the General Assembly) may establish subsidiary organs (such as ad hoc criminal tribunals, administrative tribunals, or the UN Compensation Commission) that may perform a judicial or quasi-judicial role, confirms that the principal organs understand their own lack of judicial or quasi-judicial powers.

Given that criminal accountability was seen as an indispensable part of restoring peace and security in the former Yugoslavia, the Council established a Criminal Tribunal to deal with this task. In other cases, however, the Council's own decisions and pronouncements are based on findings and conclusions that can sensibly be arrived at only through the criminal justice process. Targeted sanctions against individuals suspected of involvement in terrorism are premised on postulations of criminality and thus share the character of criminal sanctions. These sanctions are administered by sanctions committees established by the Council that have neither adequate composition nor the necessary qualities for making such legal findings.[10]

One of the causes of the Council's involvement with the Iranian nuclear enrichment issue was a divergence of views between Iran, the International Atomic Energy Agency (IAEA), and the UN, regarding the scope of Iran's obligations regarding the use of nuclear energy, more specifically its decision in 2007 to revert to the old Code 3.1 of its Safeguards Agreement with the IAEA.[11] The new Agreement was initially accepted by Iran in 2003, but not ratified by its parliament. The Agency's position was that Code 3.1 could not be modified unilaterally, and that '[t]he Agency's right to verify design information provided to it is a continuing right, which is not dependent on the stage of construction of, or the presence of nuclear material at, a facility'.[12] The matter then

---

[9] GJH van Hoof and K de Vey Metsdagh, 'Mechanisms of International Supervision', in P van Dijk (ed.), *Supervisory Mechanisms in International Economic Organisations* (The Hague: TMC Asser Press, 1984), 22.

[10] For detail on targeted sanctions see Chapter 5 below.

[11] Statement of the IAEA Legal Adviser to the Meeting of the Board of Governors, March 2009, para 1.

[12] *Implementation of the NPT Safeguards Agreement and Relevant Provisions of Security Council Resolutions in the Islamic Republic of Iran*, GOV/2007/22, 23 May 2007, paras 12–14.

turned on two legal questions: whether Iran was bound by the unratified agreement, and if so, whether Iran could modify it unilaterally.

Security Council Resolution 1803(2008) took a clear position on this matter. In the preamble the Council noted 'with concern that Iran has taken issue with the IAEA's right to verify design information which had been provided by Iran pursuant to the modified Code 3.1', and then reiterated the Agency's finding quoted above.[13] The Council's entire approach is framed as a legal argument, which is then used to justify further action under Chapter VII. However, while treating alleged violations of the Nuclear Non-proliferation Treaty (NPT) as a cause of action, it is not certain that the Council adopted the proper standard of proof in ascertaining the existence of a breach of that Treaty, relying on presumptive concerns instead of established facts.

In relation to Security Council Resolutions 731(1992), 748(1992) and 883 (1993), adopted after the Lockerbie aerial incident, the Libyan representative submitted to the Council that claims contained in these resolutions could only be resolved through impartial adjudication: demands to extradite Libyan terror suspects to the USA or the UK ran counter to the legal framework of extradition law, demands to compensate victims prejudiced the principle that one should be presumed innocent until proved guilty, and demands that Libya should provide proof of the guilt of those suspects ran counter to the principle that those who raise charges should prove guilt as well. All these demands 'related to legal procedures and any dispute over them is a legal one'. However, 'the countries concerned immediately transformed the question from a legal to a political one by submitting it to the Security Council.'[14] It secured the adoption of a resolution that embodied essentially judicial and prosecutorial findings. The Arab League representative disapproved of the Security Council's handling of the Libyan matter, observing that the Council acted, at the same time, as investigator, judge, jury, and sentencer.[15]

---

[13] For the Iran–IAEA Safeguards Agreement see INFCIRC/214, 13 December 1974. The scope of Iran's pertinent obligations was described in the IAEA Director General's Report:

> The Subsidiary Arrangements General Part in force with Iran from 1976 to 26 February 2003 included what was, until 1992, standard text which called for provision to the Agency of design information on a new facility no later than 180 days before the introduction of nuclear material into the facility, and the provision of information on a new LOF [location outside facility] together with the report relating to the receipt of nuclear material at the LOF. With the acceptance by Iran on 26 February 2003 of the modifications to the Subsidiary Arrangements proposed by the Agency, the Subsidiary Arrangements General Part now requires Iran to inform the Agency of new nuclear facilities and modifications to existing facilities through the provision of preliminary design information as soon as the decision to construct, to authorize construction or to modify has been taken, and to provide the Agency with further design information as it is developed. Information is to be provided early in the project definition, preliminary design, construction and commissioning phases.

Implementation of the NPT Safeguards Agreement in the Islamic Republic of Iran, GOV/2003/40, 6 June 2003, para 15.

[14] Letter dated 8 January 1992 from the Permanent Representative of the Libyan Arab Jamahiriya to the UN Secretary-General, 31 ILM (1992), 725 at 726; S/PV.3864, 20 March 1998, 4–5 (Libya).

[15] Quoted in J Quigley, 'Security Council Fact-Finding: A Prerequisite to Effective Prevention of War', 7 *Florida Journal of International Law* (1992), 191 at 242, 245: Quigley comments that the standard of evidence the Council presumably used was that of probable cause (ibid, 242). In allocating blame for a criminal offence to individuals and to a state for organizing that crime, this standard is plainly inadequate.

In general, the Council is entitled to make legal determinations within the limits of international law and as part of its peace and security mandate. According to Schachter, drafters of the Charter might have believed that empowering the Council to make legal determinations and declare states in violation of international law could impede its action to maintain and restore peace. The Council's task is not to make legal determinations but to adopt acceptable decisions that parties will implement.[16] However, the Council resorts to legal qualifications on a regular basis and often treats violations of international law as its cause of action.[17] It is moreover unlikely that, where international law is violated, the Council's decision will be acceptable to the aggrieved party unless this is based on the respect for that party's rights.

Higgins regards complaints about the law's inflexibility in relation to political decision-making as unjustified and disapproves of 'the position that legal decisions cannot resolve disputes, because they fail to accommodate the interests of one of the parties'. The Council has to comply with the law but it can also pronounce on questions in ways other than by applying law to facts. Political and legal elements in the Council's role are not mutually exclusive. The Council has a wide political discretion but its solutions and recommended adjustments have to be in accordance with international law. 'This political operation *within* the law, rather than decision according *to* the law, which is the [International] Court's function, allows the Council to address itself to problems with a very considerable number of facts.'[18] This means that the Council might not be obliged to adopt decisions strictly replicating legal consequences of the relevant situation. Its decisions can include politically chosen measures and steps, but within the scope left free by, and thus consistent with, legal requirements. Political operation of the Council within the law does not presuppose, but instead is essentially different from, the primacy of political considerations over legal ones.

3. Powers of the Security Council under Chapter VI

Chapters VI and VII of the UN Charter constitute a common framework enabling the Council to respond to a dispute or crisis in the way its gravity or magnitude requires. It will be recalled that at the San Francisco conference the US delegation described the Security Council's involvement with crises as a process of graduated stages justifying the Council's intervention to the extent necessary.[19] Therefore, Chapters VI and VII constitute one structural and systemic whole. The purpose of Chapter VI is to determine how the Council should deal with disputes and situations likely to endanger peace, but also to guide the Council in determining whether the dispute or situation has matured to justify the activation of Chapter VII.

---

[16] O Schachter, 'The Quasi-Judicial Role of the Security Council and the General Assembly', 58 AJIL (1964), 960–1.

[17] For detail see Chapter 1 above and Chapter 4 below.

[18] R Higgins, 'The Place of International Law in the Settlement of Disputes by the Security Council', 64 AJIL (1970), 1 at 14, 16 (emphasis in original).

[19] Cf, EL Kerley, 'The Powers of Investigation of the United Nations Security Council', 55 AJIL (1961), 892 at 895.

Chapters VI and VII can also be used together. Resolution 1590(2005) on Sudan, for instance, was adopted both under chapters. In the preamble the Council makes an Article 39 determination. Operative paragraphs establish the UN Mission in Sudan (UNMIS), consisting of 10,000 military personnel to support the implementation of the peace agreement. The resolution invokes Chapter VII only in paragraph 16 when it authorizes UNMIS to use force in implementing its mandate. The same applies to the establishment of UNAMID—a joint UN–African Union mission in Darfur—under Resolution 1769(2007). There are thus no inherent dividing lines between Chapters VI and VII, apart from those preserving certain kinds of decision for Chapter VII exclusively (under Articles 41 and 42). To illustrate this point further, arms control inspection organs such as UNSCOM and UNMOVIC have been established under Chapter VII Resolutions 687(1991) and 1284(1999). Yet both organs could only operate in Iraq on the basis of the latter's sovereign consent. The fact that they were established under Chapter VII was due to their being part of broader Chapter VII operations *in casu*, which does not preclude the Council from conducting similar inspection programmes under Chapter VI should its objectives in other cases so demand.

The Charter provides no definition of a dispute or situation in relation to which the Council is empowered to act. Dispute has to be understood in its generally accepted sense as a disagreement on the point of fact or law, or an opposition of one entity's views to those of another. Situation is a broader notion and can involve any context—inter-state or intra-state—that potentially endangers international peace and security, which understanding is confirmed by reference in Article 34 to situations that might lead to international friction. To the extent a situation involves elements of a dispute it has to be addressed as a matter of dispute settlement under Article 33. If these means are inherently or contextually unsuitable to adjusting that situation, the Council should consider what other means are available for addressing it under Chapters VI or VII.

The starting-point principle is provided in the first paragraph of Article 33 which specifies that

[t]he parties to any dispute, the continuance of which is likely to endanger the maintenance of international peace and security, shall, first of all, seek a solution by negotiation, enquiry, mediation, conciliation, arbitration, judicial settlement, resort to regional agencies or arrangements, or other peaceful means of their own choice.

The second paragraph provides that '[t]he Security Council shall, when it deems necessary, call upon the parties to settle their dispute by such means'. As Eagleton observes, dispute settlement obligations under the Charter begin when voluntary efforts to that effect have failed. The Charter 'devotes five out of the six articles in Chapter VI to this preliminary phase of voluntary agreement.' Articles 34 to 36 are essentially part of the concept of Article 33.[20]

---

[20] C Eagleton, 'The Pacific Settlement of Disputes under the Charter', 246 *Annals of the American Academy of Political and Social Science* (1946), 24 at 25.

There is an obligation to try the regional and bilateral means of settlement, not to persist with local agencies up to the point of obtaining solution. As Kelsen observes, under Article 33 'the formula "to seek a solution" is too vague, and the parties to the dispute are not bound, in case one of the means indicated in this paragraph fails, to try another and finally to apply the one which alone guarantees a settlement, namely, arbitration or judicial decision'.[21]

Article 36 enables the Council to interfere, 'at any stage', in a dispute or situation dealt with bilaterally or regionally. Article 37 applies to situations when other means of adjustment or settlement fail. Under Article 36 the Council can recommend procedures or methods, while under Article 37 it can recommend solutions, because it can be satisfied that the dispute or situation has not otherwise been resolved. Article 36 provides that the Council can interfere in a dispute or situation *while it is being resolved*, which means that it must have reasons for this. The most plausible reason can be that the bilateral or regional effort is insufficient, inadequate, or biased, and thus cannot constitute a genuine peace and security effort. Otherwise, there is no reason why Article 36 should empower the Council to interfere in disputes that are being resolved anyway. Thus, subsidiarity is inherent to Article 36.

In the Lockerbie matter, Libya argued before the Council that Resolution 731 (1992) had been adopted in clear violation of Article 33(1), which requires using the dispute settlement means provided under the 1971 Montreal Convention.[22] Resolution 731 was directly intended to circumvent these requirements by rebranding an essentially legal dispute as a political and security dispute, having the same object as the original legal dispute. The US and UK representatives contended that the Council was not dealing with a dispute regarding the interpretation and application of Article 14 of the Montreal Convention but with Libya's alleged participation in terrorism as a matter of peace and security,[23] it remaining the case that these states and Libya disagreed on whether Article 14 covered the situation. The dispute between them existed in the most proper sense of this term.

The same applies to allegations voiced in the Council that Libya's involvement in terrorism rendered 'normal' dispute settlement mechanisms inappropriate.[24] A mere, unsubstantiated allegation of such involvement could not render inappropriate those *fora* under the Charter which are designed precisely for this task, yet not taken advantage of *in casu*. Simple unwillingness of one disputant to resolve the issue through the means provided under Article 33 does not make that dispute inherently unsuitable for resolution through such means. The Council's proper action in such cases is to reaffirm the availability of dispute settlement means under Article 33, not prematurely to overtake them. In relation to just such disputes alleged to threaten peace, Articles 33, 34, and 36 provide procedures to clarify the

---

[21] H Kelsen, 'The Settlement of Disputes by the Security Council', 2 *International Law Quarterly* (1948), 173 at 174–5.
[22] Convention for the Suppression of Unlawful Acts Against the Safety of Civil Aviation, signed at Montreal, 23 September 1971; S/PV.3864, 20 March 1998, 5 (Libya).
[23] See statements quoted in F Beveridge, 'The Lockerbie Affair', 41 ICLQ (1992), 907 at 910.
[24] Cf ibid.

merit of the issue, and allow for the Council's interference only if it cannot be dealt with by traditional means. These provisions do not justify rebranding a dispute with a view to evading the subsidiarity of the Council's role.

Furthermore, Libya submitted that the matter was legal and had to be dealt with by the International Court,[25] presumably in line with Article 36 of the Charter. The 1995 Addis Ababa resolution of the Organization of African Unity (OAU) on the Lockerbie crisis maintained that the dispute settlement provisions of Chapter VI apply even if the Council has invoked Chapter VII. The OAU's position was accompanied by its asseessment of Security Council sanctions against Libya as illegal and disproportionate. The OAU Council of Ministers called on all parties to resolve the crisis by resorting to means provided for under Article 33, with the overall objective of trying suspects in a third country.[26] With this position, the OAU disagreed with the objectives the Council had set in Resolutions 731, 748, and 883.

Article 37(1) of the Charter states that '[s]hould the parties to a dispute of the nature referred to in Article 33 fail to settle it by the means indicated in that Article, they shall refer it to the Security Council'. As Goodhart illustrates, Article 37(1) essentially embodies a subsidiarity approach:

this article makes it compulsory on the parties to refer a dispute, which cannot be otherwise settled, to the Security Council. As a complement to this there is a duty on the Security Council either to take action under Article 36 or to recommend appropriate terms of settlement. It was therefore not contemplated by the Charter that the dispute might be left, so to speak, suspended in the air.[27]

This way the Council's subsidiary role reflects the need for effectiveness across the entire collective security framework.

The Charter does not specify conditions on which it can be determined that recourse to bilateral and regional means of settlement is no longer required. While under Article 37(1) 'the parties are obligated to refer their dispute to the Security Council when the means of their own choice have failed to achieve a settlement', the Council could assume jurisdiction even if not all parties agree whether other means of settlement have failed. Nevertheless,

no guidance or authority is provided for determining whether the 'means of their own choice' under Article 33 have actually failed, should one of the parties deny such failure and insist upon continuing negotiations. It seems reasonable to believe that, in the face of such a disagreement, the Council would itself decide whether 'means of their own choice' had actually failed, and whether, therefore, the Council could take up the dispute under Article 37.[28]

---

[25] Letter dated 18 March 1992 from the Secretary of the People's Committee for Foreign Liaison and International Cooperation of the Libyan Arab Jamahirya addressed to the Secretary-General, 31 ILM (1992), 742; see also S/PV.3864, 20 March 1998, 6 (Libya).

[26] CM/Res.1587 (LXII), 21–5 June 1995, para 8; the Arab League expressed a similar position, Resolution adopted by the Council of the League of Arab States on 16 January 1992, 1992, 31 ILM (1992), 727.

[27] A Goodhart, 'North Atlantic Treaty Organization', 79 *Recueil des Cours de l'Académie de Droit International de la Haye* (II–1951), 183 at 200.

[28] Eagleton, n 20 above, 26.

However, in doing so, the Council cannot just assert but has to properly demonstrate that other means of dispute settlement have failed, either because some parties do not accept a particular method of settlement, or because the use of that method does not lead to a feasible result.

Another aspect of subsidiarity in the Council's competence is that '[i]f the Security Council deems that the parties have not yet fulfilled the requirement of Article 33, paragraph 1, it may refuse to intervene under Article 37, paragraph 2'.[29] This point is reinforced by the use of different wordings in Articles 33 and 37 to emphasize the gradualist nature of the Council's involvement. Disputes and situations under Article 33 are 'likely' to endanger international peace; disputes which justify the Council's own action, presumably after it has been established that traditional (including regional) means are unworkable or inadequate, are the ones that, as the higher threshold requirement under Article 37(2) suggests, are 'in fact likely' to endanger international peace.

According to Kelsen, under Article 37, 'after a dispute has been referred to it,' the Council 'shall first decide whether the continuance of it is in fact likely to endanger the maintenance of international peace and security'.[30] This is essentially a preliminary issue of competence. The Council's responsibility in this context is functional, for it may issue recommendations relating only to disputes that are 'in fact likely' to endanger international peace. It may not be crucial whether this likelihood test is regarded as subjective or objective. What matters is that the Council's membership can make a collective determination of this kind under Article 37(2) if it is intelligibly demonstrated how the factual background of the dispute makes danger to international peace likely and, moreover, how this is still the case where bilateral and regional procedures are available and not resorted to. In other words, the burden lies with the Council to demonstrate that, considering all factors, the situation in question meets the test provided by Article 37(2).

Chapter VI thus seems to contain an adverse presumption against the Council's involvement in disputes and situations that are being, or can be, suitably resolved or adjusted by available means of dispute resolution, and are thus deemed not to be likely to endanger international peace. This in its turn creates an expanded presumption against the propriety of the Council's activation of Chapter VII in such situations. In general terms, subsidiarity works, not by allocating competence between different free-standing levels of collective security that can ride in their own directions and operate following independent perceptions and policies, but by doing so within a single collective security framework whose foundations are laid in Chapters VI and VIII of the Charter.

The nature of the Council's recommendations under Article 37(2) is subject to debate. Kelsen suggests that the Council is authorized to recommend a settlement involving an infringement of a party's rights if it considers this settlement 'just' or, under Article 37, 'appropriate', and contends that

---

[29] Kelsen, n 21 above, 178.
[30] Ibid, 177.

there is hardly any difference between the two terms, since it is upon the Security Council to decide what is 'just' or 'appropriate'. In case of a territorial dispute the Council might recommend as appropriate that one party shall cede a part of the disputed territory to the other party, regardless of whether the latter has any legally justifiable claim to this territory.[31]

Higgins disagrees with Kelsen's contention that the Council's recommended terms of settlement need not be in accordance with international law and may infringe upon the rights of parties. The word 'appropriate' in Article 37(2) is not used in contradistinction to law. Appropriateness refers to the discretion exercisable within and constrained by international law.[32]

A further tool operationalizing the subsidiarity principle in relation to the Council's powers is its power to investigate situations under Article 34, clarify their nature, and establish whether and to what extent the Council's interference with them is justified. As Kelsen specified, the parties' view as to whether a dispute is going to endanger peace and security does not bind the Security Council, which can itself ascertain, by way of investigation under Article 34, whether that is the case.[33] Article 34 provides that

[t]he Security Council may investigate any dispute, or any situation which might lead to international friction or give rise to a dispute, in order to determine whether the continuance of the dispute or situation is likely to endanger the maintenance of international peace and security.

Thus the initial condition triggering the Council's power is the existence of any inter-state dispute or of any situation—international or internal—that might lead to international friction. The Council has the power to investigate these to establish whether they are likely to endanger international peace and thus justify its exercise of powers under Articles 33, 36, 37, or ultimately 39. As Eagleton specified,

the Security Council is given by Article 34 a limited but important right to investigate not as to the merits of the case, but as to whether or not the dispute is one whose continuance might endanger the peace. If the Council were to determine that the dispute is one of this nature, the sole result would be to enable the Council to advise the parties to this effect and to recommend to the parties that they follow one of the procedures of Article 33.[34]

But the use of Article 34 also provides the Council with the option to determine whether it should proceed with finding a 'threat to the peace' under Article 39, once Chapter VI processes have properly been gone through or the situation in question has been demonstrated to be incapable of address through such means.

---

[31] Ibid, 182; see also H Kelsen, 'Sanctions under the Charter of the United Nations', 12 *Canadian Journal of Economics and Political Science* (1946), 429 at 434, arguing that, even if the Security Council is bound by international law and justice, it still can choose to which of the two to adhere.

[32] Higgins, n 18 above, 9.

[33] Kelsen, n 21 above, 180, 184.

[34] Eagleton, n 20 above, 25.

A crucial question is whether Article 34, apart from entitling the Council to investigate, also obliges states to permit an investigation or empowers the Council to impose an investigation contrary to the wishes of states. When a member refuses to permit an investigation, a violation of the Charter arises and a member's unwillingness to cooperate with the Council, and desire to conceal the factual situation, become clear.[35] The Council's ability to resort to Article 34 is instrumental in enabling it to use the range of its Chapter VII powers.

4. Decisions of the Security Council

(a) General Nature and Types

Attempts to identify the nature of Security Council resolutions have produced a doctrinal trend towards reasoning by analogy. Given the diversity of subject matter the Council deals with and the generality of measures contained in some of its resolutions, writers tend to view these as pieces of global legislation as opposed to decisions adopted in relation to a particular dispute or situation.[36] Domestic analogies are generally misleading because they attempt to reconceptualize the actual legal nature of resolutions, and project premises underlying domestic legal systems which simply do not obtain in the international legal system. What matters ultimately is the delegated nature of the Council's powers under the Charter and the limits on those powers.

Decisions of the Council are not formally designated as treaties, but are still agreements on which the states concerned can place reliance. Their binding force does not differ from that of treaties. They are not time-limited but apply to the pertinent situation unless and until one of the following conditions—broadly similar to those under the law of treaties—materializes: (a) the Council decides to terminate a resolution or replace it by another one; (b) the time limit on a resolution (or on a particular measure it specifies) expires; (c) material breach of a resolution deprives it of its rationale; (d) conflict arises between a resolution and any legal requirements which the Council is obliged to observe.[37]

Bailey and Daws suggest that 'decisions' of the Council under Article 27 refer to all its decisions, including those under Chapter V on organizational issues, under Chapter VI on dispute settlement, and both recommendations and decisions under Chapter VII.[38] This uniform understanding is useful to help the voting procedure under Article 27 to make sense across the board under the Charter. But it also prompts the question whether the Charter provides for a 'decision' in a generic

---

[35] Kerley, n 19 above, 893, 903.

[36] E Rosand, 'The Security Council as "Global Legislator": Ultra Vires or Ultra Innovative?' 28 *Fordham International Law Journal* (2004–5), 542.

[37] In relation to termination of treaties see Articles 53, 54, 56, 59, 60, and 64 of the 1969 Vienna Convention.

[38] SD Bailey and S Daws, *The Procedure of the UN Security Council* (New York: Oxford University Press, 1998), 263.

sense as a free-standing category of acts adopted by the Council, or merely regards 'decisions' as procedural decisions preliminary to adopting a recommendatory resolution under Chapter VI, indicating provisional measures under Article 40, adopting operational decisions under Chapter V on organizational matters, or resorting to enforcement measures under Chapter VII.

The actual enforcement is denoted in Article 41 as 'measures' meant to give effect to the Council's decisions. Hence, the Council's decisions are by default those which, being antecedent to those 'measures', prescribe a substantive line of conduct or outcome. Given that Article 41 can be used only after a threat to the peace has been identified under Article 39,[39] a 'decision' under Article 41 can be either a decision under Article 40,[40] or (given that the use of Article 40 is not mandatory) a decision the adoption of which is implied in or consequent upon the threat identification under Article 39 as a premise for resorting to measures under Articles 41 and 42, by way of specifying the objective of these 'measures'.

(b) Binding Force

Article 25 of the Charter requires member States to accept and carry out the Council's decisions in accordance with the Charter. The International Court affirmed in the *Namibia* case that Article 25 makes the Council's decisions binding, whether or not they are adopted under Chapter VII.[41] As further suggested, Article 25 confers binding force on Security Council decisions, not on its resolutions per se. Resolutions under Chapter VI, apart from those initiating investigations under Article 34, are not decisions, while most resolutions under Chapter VII are.[42] At least a *prima facie* case can thus be made that there are 'decisions' in the general sense of Article 27 and, more specifically, decisions as opposed to recommendations.[43] The question what can be denoted a 'decision', then, ultimately bears on the overall effectiveness of the Council's peace and security mandate. Bailey and Daws admit that the Charter alone is an insufficient basis for resolving differences as to what decisions of the Council are binding.[44] The Court in *Namibia* did

---

[39] Articles 39 and 41 seem to be in a circular mutual relationship, since the former gives the Council power to 'decide what measures shall be taken in accordance with Articles 41 and 42', while the latter provides for adopting enforcement measures 'to give effect to its decisions'.

[40] For instance, in Resolution 598(1986) regarding the war between Iran and Iraq, the Council specified that under Articles 39 and 40 the parties had to observe an immediate cease-fire, discontinue all military action, withdraw their forces to internationally recognized boundaries, release all prisoners of war, and cooperate with the Secretary-General's investigative and consultative efforts (paragraphs 1 to 4). Resolution 1696(2006) regarding Iranian nuclear enrichment emphasizes that the Council acted under Article 40 'to make mandatory the suspension required by the IAEA'.

[41] *Legal Consequences of the Continued Presence of South Africa in Namibia (South West Africa) notwithstanding Security Council Resolution 276* (Advisory Opinion), *ICJ Reports* 1971, 53.

[42] R Churchill, 'Conflicts between United Nations Security Council Resolutions and the 1982 United Nations Convention on the Law of the Sea, and Their Possible Resolution', 85 *US Naval War College International Law Studies Series* (2009), 143 at 145.

[43] Bailey and Daws, n 38 above, 264, point out this diverse use of the term 'decision' in official Security Council publications such as the Repertory and the annual *Resolutions and Decisions of the Security Council*.

[44] Bailey and Daws, ibid, 264.

not subscribe to viewing all Council 'decisions' (in the sense of Article 27) as binding. It specified that the language of a 'decision' should be interpreted to see if it had been intended to bind.[45] This has to be ascertained by the usual methods of interpretation.[46]

Dinstein suggests that 'it is not altogether free of doubt which decisions are covered by Article 25', though Chapter VII decisions are indisputably binding.[47] The view that the Council can take binding decisions only under Chapter VII has long been articulated both in practice and in doctrine.[48] This view aims to provide 'a rough and ready, convenient and simple guide to the drafting of resolutions, which through constant reiteration by its adherents has taken on, for them, the status of international law'. But this approach sets up a formalistic dichotomy between binding decisions under Chapter VII and acts adopted under Chapter VI.[49] It is not obvious at all that this view is supported either by the text and structure of the Charter or by major authorities eliciting its meaning. There is no requirement under the Charter to associate recommendatory decisions exclusively with Chapter VI and binding decisions exclusively with Chapter VII. As the Court specified in *Namibia*, if the Council's binding powers were restricted to Chapter VII, Article 25 would have been placed within that Chapter. Moreover, Article 25 applies across the board while provisions on recommendations (such as Articles 37, 38, and 39) apply in specifically determined circumstances.

Binding force of a resolution can entail obliging states to perform particular things as opposed to leaving them with a choice, presumably because the Council regards the relevant outcome as necessary—not optional—for maintenance or restoration of peace and security. The Council can issue clear-cut binding demands, such as those addressed to Iraq under Resolution 687(1991) regarding the admission of weapons inspectors to specified locations. There can also be operative decisions, consisting in conclusive, operational findings, or specification of a particular arrangement, which

---

[45] n 41 above, 53.

[46] B Conforti, *The Law and Practice of the United Nations* (The Hague: Kluwer, 2005), 194–5.

[47] Y Dinstein, *War, Aggression and Self-Defence* (Cambridge: Cambridge University Press, 2005), 289.

[48] For instances from practice see Kerley, n 19 above, 895. In doctrine, this view is held by A Pellet, 'The Road to Hell is Paved with Good Intentions. The United Nations as a Guarantor of International Peace and Security: A French Perspective', in C Tomuschat (ed.), *The United Nations at the Age of Fifty* (The Hague: Kluwer 1995), 113 at 124; Higgins quotes the British Government's view that only after activating Chapter VII through Article 39 can the Council adopt a binding decision under Article 39: R Higgins, 'The Advisory Opinion on Namibia: Which UN Resolutions Are Binding under Article 25 of the Charter?', 21 ICLQ (1972), 270, 277. De Wet argues with some vigour that none of Chapter VI provisions facilitated adoption of Resolution 260(1970) (dealt with in *Namibia*) and it was instead a Chapter VII decision, even though the Court went to some length to give the opposite impression: E de Wet, *Chapter VII Powers of the UN Security Council* (Oxford: Hart, 2004), 39–40. But this view is self-contradictory, because there is no provision under Chapter VII that would explain the binding force of Resolution 276, which included neither coercive measures under Articles 41 and 42, nor provisional measures under Article 40, and still less constituted a recommendation under Article 39.

[49] N White, *Keeping the Peace* (Manchester: Manchester University Press, 1997), 62; H Nasu, 'Investigation *Proprio Motu* for the Maintenance of International Peace and Security', 23 *Australian Yearbook of International Law* (2004), 105 at 127–8.

will then produce a binding obligation on states not to conduct themselves in a way that could adversely affect a particular enterprise. For instance, the Council's establishment of a peace-keeping force and specification of its mandate produces binding obligation on states to respect it.[50]

Under Chapter VI, decisions on the substantive outcome of disputes are recommendatory, while decisions calling upon states to resolve disputes potentially threatening international peace are binding. Chapter VII provides for the issue of recommendations under Article 39, orders binding states to provisional measures under Article 40, and binding decisions to apply sanctions under Article 41. Decisions to authorize the use of force under Article 42 are not strictly binding on anyone, in the sense of demanding a particular line of conduct, as they merely authorize the use force based on an offer by states to do so under the Council's mandate. These are better termed as operative decisions, and produce legal effect(s) that states are bound not to upset. On a general plane, the ICTY characterized Chapter VII powers as follows:

These powers are coercive *vis-à-vis* the culprit State or entity. But they are also mandatory *vis-à-vis* the other Member States, who are under an obligation to cooperate with the Organization (Article 2, paragraph 5, Articles 25, 48) and with one another (Article 49), in the implementation of the action or measures decided by the Security Council.[51]

None of the above categories can accommodate some decisions on material issues intended as binding. Resolutions adopted under Chapter VI or Chapter VII can restate an existing international legal position that does not depend on affirmation in the Council's resolutions.[52] An instance of this is Resolution 242(1967) adopted in the wake of Six-Day War; Resolution 276(1970) on South Africa's violation of the Mandate Agreement regarding Namibia; or Resolution 301(1971) on South African Bantustan territories. The Council's resolutions often include calls to withdraw from an occupied territory, to respect the self-determination of peoples, to withhold recognition from illegal state-like entities, to enable refugees and internally displaced persons to return to their homes, or to prosecute perpetrators of international crimes.

It has been argued that, at most, what the Council can do under Chapter VI is to advise the parties on terms or procedures of settlement, and that states are free to accept or reject that advice.[53] The US delegation at the San Francisco Conference developed a more dynamic and functional approach to identify parameters of the binding force of the Council's resolutions. Since the Council's intervention in crises

---

[50] For detail see Chapter 7 below.
[51] *Tadić*, n 7 above, para 31 (emphasis removed).
[52] On relevant fundamental principles of international law not being dependent on postulation in Security Council resolutions see, for detail, A Orakhelashvili, *Peremptory Norms in International Law* (New York: Oxford University Press, 2006), Chapter 13.
[53] A Eide, 'Peace-Keeping and Enforcement by Regional Organizations: Its place in the United Nations System', 3 *Journal of Peace Research* (1966), 125 at 131.

is graduated to meet the degree of its necessity, its decisions assume binding quality 'only as they relate to the prevention or suppression of breaches of peace'.[54] This dynamic approach requires asking a basic interpretative question: what functions of the Council require the mandatory character conveyed by Article 25 in order to enable the Council to meet its primary responsibility to maintain international peace and security? While all Chapter VII functions directly relate to this task, the same does not apply to all Chapter VI powers:

It is not essential to the maintenance of peace that parties to a dispute or situation resort to the specific method of settlement, or terms of settlement, recommended by the Security Council under Chapter VI, so long as they continue their efforts to arrive at a solution. Thus, actions by the Council under Articles 36, 37, and 38 are properly termed recommendations. It is essential, however, that the parties take measures to arrive at a solution, and should they fail to do so, the Security Council can require them to do so under Article 33(2).

This framework underlines the Council's subsidiary role under Chapter VI to oversee parties' dispute settlement efforts as opposed to imposing a settlement.

The investigative power under Article 34 enables the Council to determine its own competence to deal with a given question, which is 'essential if the Council is to operate at all'. Therefore, the Council's decision under Article 34 must be seen as being covered by Article 25.[55] This approach reflects the need to interpret the Charter as a treaty in accordance with the principle of effectiveness, to enable the Council to exercise its mandate effectively; but it also illustrates that the effective interpretation approach actually gives expression to the subsidiary role of the Council in relation to bilateral and regional modes of adjustment, as long as these remain within the requirements of the Charter, and makes the binding force of the Council's decisions conditional on its observance of the principle of subsidiarity.

It is possible for the Council to adopt decisions, binding or operative, without resorting to Chapter VII. Resolution 338(1973), adopted outside Chapter VII, '*[d]ecides* that, immediately and concurrently with the cease-fire, negotiations shall start between the parties concerned under appropriate auspices aimed at establishing a just and durable peace in the Middle East' (paragraph 3). Resolution 340 (1973) which among other things set up UNEF II, '*[d]emands* that immediate and complete cease-fire be observed and that the parties return to the positions occupied by them at 1650 hours GMT on 22 October 1973' (paragraph 1). The binding force of this resolution is emphasized in the Secretary-General's report on the establishment of UNEF II, in particular regarding the parameters of the right to self-defence to be exercised by this force. The Report emphasizes that, since the parties are bound to comply with this decision of the Council, the force will

---

[54] Cf Kerley, n 19 above, 895.
[55] Kerley, n 19 above, 896–7; Nasu, n 49 above, 107.

be entitled to exercise its right to self-defence to the extent needed to forestall attempts to prevent it from realizing its mandate.[56] Precisely the same principle was reiterated regarding the exercise of the mandate of UNIFIL established under Resolution 425(1978), to ensure that the binding requirement set in paragraph 2 of that resolution, even if employing the words 'calls upon', would be enforced.[57]

In Resolution 797(1992) on Mozambique, not adopted under Chapter VII, the Council '[d]emands that all parties and others concerned in Mozambique take all measures necessary to ensure the safety of United Nations and all other personnel deployed pursuant to this and prior resolutions' (paragraph 5). The force concerned, ONUMOZ, was deployed under Chapter VI. But even though consensual and non-coercive, the effective implementation of that mission justified the Council's implied power to adopt a binding decision as it did, for without ensuring the safety of this peace-keeping mission and thus enabling it to carry out its tasks, the rationale of its establishment, albeit consensual, would have been undermined.

What also matters is the Council's use of a particular wording. The words 'call upon' can convey a recommendation or a binding decision, depending on whether the resolution suggests that a particular step or action called upon is a necessary one. In Resolution 217(1965), the Council, under Chapter VII, '[c]all[ed] upon all States to refrain from any action which would assist and encourage the illegal régime and, in particular, to desist from providing it with arms, equipment and military material, and to do their utmost in order to break all economic relations with Southern Rhodesia, including an embargo on oil and petroleum products' (paragraph 8). The *Namibia* Opinion is premised on the binding force of Resolution 276(1970) in which the Council 'called upon' all states 'to refrain from any dealing with the Government of South Africa which are inconsistent' with the Council's finding the occupation of Namibia illegal and South African acts in relation to that territory invalid. 'Call upon' in Resolution 665(1990) is not a recommendation but authorizes maritime interdiction measures to enforce sanctions against Iraq, not initially binding but, once taken up, obligatory for third states to regard. The Council's 'request' to UNPROFOR under Resolution 781 (1992) 'to monitor compliance with the ban on military flights, including the placement of observers where necessary at airfields in the territory of the former Yugoslavia' is not a recommendation either, given (moreover) that the Council imperatively states in the preamble that 'the establishment of a ban on military flights in the airspace of Bosnia and Herzegovina constitutes an *essential element* for the safety of the delivery of humanitarian assistance and a decisive step for the cessation of hostilities in Bosnia and Herzegovina', that is, a core element of this entire Chapter VII effort. Contexts in which 'call upon' can reflect a binding obligation include paragraph 11 of Resolution 1816(2008) dealing with repression of piracy along the coasts of Somalia. The Council

---

[56] S/11052/Rev.1, 2, para 4(d).
[57] S/12611, paras 2(a) and 4(d).

[c]alls upon all States, and in particular flag, port and coastal States, States of the nationality of victims and perpetrators or piracy and armed robbery, and other States with relevant jurisdiction under international law and national legislation, to cooperate in determining jurisdiction, and in the investigation and prosecution of persons responsible for acts of piracy and armed robbery off the coast of Somalia.

Given that repression of piracy is in any case under universal jurisdiction, states are already obliged to cooperate in prosecuting persons suspected of piracy, and the Council's resolution reflects just that.

Higgins considers that 'call upon' is stronger than 'recommend'.[58] The use of the words 'call upon' and 'request' is stronger that 'invite' and 'encourage', even though leaving some uncertainty as to whether a binding decision has been intended. However, the Security Council 'called upon' states to observe sanctions imposed on Yugoslavia, Haiti, and Iraq, and this was clearly intended as binding.[59] In any case, the complexity of the framework within which the Council operates and the diversity of situations it addresses militate against assigning a fixed effect to the words 'call upon' and 'request'. Instead, whether their use gives rise to binding decisions has to be clarified by reference to all relevant factors relating to the resolution's text, context, and drafting history, along with the test under the *Namibia* case.

Some writers suggest that the imposition of a binding settlement does not fall outside the Council's competence.[60] But no specific basis for this has ever been located in the Charter, even though Article 25 gives the Council the power to adopt binding decisions. Assuming that the Council can impose binding settlement of disputes or territorial settlement is also structurally inconsistent. There is no evidence or authority that the Council's general power to adopt binding decisions—upheld in *Namibia*—extends beyond what is required for the reversal of serious violations of international law. For the rest of its peace and security mandate, the Council possesses binding powers only to the extent expressly specified in the Charter.

In relation to the substantive outcome of a dispute, the Charter specifies types of decision the Council can adopt on every pertinent issue. Chapter VI deals with recommending such terms of settlement as the Council may consider appropriate (Article 37(2)). Article 39 speaks of recommendations in relation to core Chapter VII situations. Article 40 provides for binding decisions of a provisional type, falling short of final settlement of the pertinent controversy. To assert that the Council is entitled to impose a binding settlement is to read into the Charter a qualitatively new type of power. If the Council were endowed with the power to settle disputes with final and binding force—going much further than any of its expressly stated powers—the Charter would have stated this expressly. Such power is too important

---

[58] Higgins, n 48 above, 278.
[59] Churchill, n 42 above, 146.
[60] M Koskenniemi, 'The Place of Law in Collective Security', 17 *Michigan Journal of International Law* (1995–6), 455 at 486; M Matheson, 'United Nations Governance of Postconflict Societies', 95 AJIL (2001), 76 at 85, contending that the Council can be justified 'in directing a permanent change in some aspect of the status, boundaries, political structure, or legal system of territory within a State'.

and distinct to be implied, since only that which is generically similar or inherent to what is expressly stated can be implied.[61] Consequently, the projection of a power to impose binding settlements has no realistic prospect of being viewed with approval by the membership of the United Nations.

As Halderman points out, the 'peaceful settlement' function is concerned with substantive issues relating to international disputes and situations. It was deliberately intended that the UN powers in such matters do not go beyond recommendation. Enforcement action is different, in comprising action by the organization itself, and connotes a power of decision.[62] Thus enforcement measures under Chapter VII are tools to re-establish peace (which may include the enforcement of international law already binding on states), not to enable the Council to design a substantive settlement of its own. The Council in its practice regards these enforcement measures as a tool to uphold existing agreements, to induce the parties to reach an agreement, or to enforce international law, as opposed to imposing a binding solution of its own. In one of its most robust involvements under Chapter VII the Council underlined in Resolution 770(1992) 'the imperative need for an urgent negotiated political solution to the situation in the Republic of Bosnia and Herzegovina to enable that country to live in peace and security within its borders'. If the Council insisted on anything, it was only requirements under fundamental principles of international law (such as territorial integrity, non-use of force, non-intervention, and the right of displaced persons to return home), to guide the political solution to be agreed as between the parties (Resolution 787(1992)). Similarly, the robust Chapter VII action under Resolution 816(1993) was meant to enforce the flight ban agreed by parties themselves.

(c) Interpretation of Security Council Resolutions

Security Council resolutions are agreements reached through complex negotiations between State-members of the Council, although their validity outlives the Council's composition at that moment. The competence to interpret resolutions is not expressly allocated to any organ. The Council is arguably in a favourable position to interpret its own decisions, as it does on occasions.

In the course of their activities subsidiary organs, such as sanctions committees, will interpret pertinent resolutions. On occasions the Council has adopted a committee's interpretation in a resolution of its own, adopted to clarify previous resolutions on the matter, for instance regarding sanctions against FRY. However, the Council does not expressly confer on the committees the competence to interpret. A related problem is the lack of consistency between interpretations produced by different committees, in the absence of a coordinating mechanism.[63]

---

[61] See further Section 6 below.
[62] JW Halderman, 'Regional Enforcement Measures and the United Nations', 52 *Georgetown Law Journal* (1963), 89 at 101–2.
[63] M Scharf and J Dorosin, 'Interpreting UN Sanctions: The Rulings and Role of the Yugoslavia Sanctions Committee', 19 *Brooklyn Journal of International Law* (1993), 771 at 813–5, 820–2, 826.

Furthermore, a proper—and needed—interpretation of collectively adopted resolutions can be prevented by the adverse political position of a single member of the relevant committee. If this occurs in practice, the Council might be prevented from reacting to it due to a political deadlock.

Individual states do not have a regular competence to interpret Security Council resolutions. Positions of states and state groupings can still set parameters to the general acceptability of resolutions. International courts and tribunals can interpret Security Council resolutions, but only if the matter has been properly brought before them in accordance with provisions governing their jurisdiction.[64]

The Secretary-General's views expressed in his/her reports can be reflected in the Council's subsequent resolutions. A report can provide a point of reference as to the meaning and reach of the relevant resolution. Secretary-General Hammarskjold asserted a power to interpret resolutions and to follow his own interpretative attitude should the Council fail to respond to his invitation to clarify a matter. Member States could contest these interpretations before the Council but they cannot insist on renegotiating until and unless the Council adversely pronounces on the matter.[65] If the Council's interpretation conflicts with that of the Secretary-General, the former prevails. However, the difficulty of obtaining the Council's authoritative interpretation arguably means that in practice the Secretary-General will assert an authoritative interpretation of his delegated powers without that being subject to agreement with member States.[66]

All this demonstrates that reliance merely on agencies of interpretation can in practice produce insoluble difficulties, because every agency can be either politically deadlocked, prevented from engaging with interpretation due to jurisdictional restrictions, or have no distinct legitimacy in this process. Therefore, the proper use of the principles of interpretation assumes a crucial importance.

Resolutions are consensual instruments and international law is well equipped with rules to interpret them, above all under the 1969 Vienna Convention on the Law of Treaties.[67] Although not formally applicable to resolutions, Articles 31 and 32 of the Convention constitute customary law on interpretation which, given that there is no alternative set of interpretative rules, must be deemed to apply to resolutions. It is suggested that the drafting of resolutions is a complex process, some aspects of which are known publicly and others not, and that the 'overall political background' has to be considered in interpreting resolutions. Arguably, then, 'it becomes highly artificial, and indeed to some extent simply not possible, to

---

[64] As confirmed by, among others, the International Court in the *Kosovo* Opinion: *Accordance with international law of the unilateral declaration of independence in respect of Kosovo*, General List No 141, Advisory Opinion of 22 July 2010, paras 46, 85.

[65] Cf D Sarooshi, *The United Nations and Development of Collective Security* (New York: Oxford University Press, 1999), 57–9.

[66] D Sarooshi, 'The Role of the United Nations Secretary-General in United Nations Peace-Keeping Operations', 20 *Australian Yearbook of International Law* (1999), 279 at 286–7.

[67] UNTS 1155, 331.

seek to apply all the Vienna Convention rules *mutatis mutandis* to SCRs' [Security Council resolutions].[68] But resolutions are not more political than other international transactions which also undergo a complex drafting process yet are subject to the Vienna Convention regime.

The International Court suggested in the *Kosovo* Advisory Opinion that

> [w]hile the rules on treaty interpretation embodied in Articles 31 and 32 of the Vienna Convention on the Law of Treaties may provide guidance, differences between Security Council resolutions and treaties mean that the interpretation of Security Council resolutions also requires that other factors be taken into account. Security Council resolutions are issued by a single, collective body and are drafted through a very different process than that used for the conclusion of a treaty.[69]

The Court does not specify what these 'other factors' are, nor how the drafting process of resolutions is 'very different' from that of treaties. In reality both these processes involve reaching agreement between states, enshrining that agreement in text, and enabling the relevant states to place reliance on it whenever their rights and obligations are at stake. In general, it is not uncommon in the Court's jurisprudence to pay lip service to the 'special' nature of certain 'non-treaty' acts, but ultimately interpret them in compliance with the Vienna Convention regime.[70] The nature of Council resolutions also reflects two principal structural considerations—givens of a nature impossible to bypass in any consistent interpretative exercise—namely agreement between Council members and the Council's collective will to achieve stated objectives. There is no authority justifying deviation from the sequence of interpretation methods specified under the Vienna Convention.

Principles of interpretation, and their order of priority, reflect the nature of the instrument interpreted. With regard to treaties, rules under Articles 31 and 32 are arranged to demonstrate the agreement between states in the most authentic way. A restrictive interpretation can prevent the resolution from achieving its aims; an expansive interpretation can project outcomes that exceed the consent and agreement of the Council's membership. The effective interpretation of resolutions corresponds with the Council's task to act in the face of a threat to peace and security by adopting decisions that will genuinely contribute to eliminating or reducing that threat. This said, effective interpretation requires effective construction of what has been agreed upon by the Council as a collective organ; it does not involve assessment of whether the decision, as agreed upon, offers an effective contribution to peace and security.

---

[68] M Wood, 'The Interpretation of Security Council Resolutions', 2 *Max-Planck Yearbook of UN Law* (1998), 74, 79–81, 95, although in principle accepting the law of treaties analogy as per Lord McNair: ibid, 95.

[69] *Kosovo* Opinion, n 64 above, para 94.

[70] In *Fisheries Jurisdiction* (Spain/Canada) the International Court stated that the optional clause declarations of the acceptance of the Court's jurisdiction are *sui generis* instruments. However, the actual process of interpretation in this case was conducted in the way a faithful application of the 1969 Vienna Convention would require, by reliance on the textual meaning of the Canadian declaration as the crucial factor in ascertaining its meaning: *Fisheries Jurisdiction (Spain v Canada), ICJ Reports*, 1998, 432, especially paragraphs 61–80.

The International Court in *Namibia* specified that interpretation of resolutions should focus on 'all circumstances [that] might assist in determining the legal consequences of the resolution'. This does not mean that all interpretative factors are the same. The principal method is to refer to their plain, ordinary meaning in the light of their object and purpose. The appeal decision in *Tadić* demonstrates, in relation to Article 5 of the ICTY Statute, that resolutions should be interpreted like treaties, in line with Article 31 of the Vienna Convention. On this ground the Tribunal concluded that a discriminatory animus towards crimes against humanity was not a requirement of the ICTY Statute, as part of Resolution 827(1993). The Council had not intended to create new crimes by legislating, but only to establish jurisdiction over existing crimes. The Secretary-General's Report on the basis of which the Council adopted the Statute did not have the same legal standing and binding authority as the Statute. The Report had been 'approved' by the Council, and was explanatory to the Statute which had been 'adopted'. If a manifest contradiction should arise between the Statute and the Report, the Statute must prevail. In other situations, the Report could provide an authoritative interpretation of the Statute. Consequently, even if a discrepancy between the Report and the Statute was conspicuous, the wording of Article 5 clearly and unambiguously prevents resorting to secondary sources of interpretation, such as the Report. The literal interpretation of Article 5 necessarily prevailed.[71]

Wood argues that, since resolutions often are not clear, simple, concise, or unambiguous, often negotiated by non-lawyers, in haste and under considerable political pressure, they often contain a deliberate ambiguity.[72] The notion of deliberate ambiguity could be used for political purposes to justify conduct that is not approved by the Council, and thus for reading into resolutions entitlements that are not there, which desperately need justification in the interpretative framework. Silence in a resolution, on the other hand, is not the same as ambiguity but rather means that the Council has not adopted a decision on the relevant matter. It is unsound to assume that parties to a written instrument would agree to dispose of important substantive questions in an unwritten way, by silence. Only if the matter is the one which is necessarily implied in a point expressly dealt with in the text, which is qualitatively and essentially contingent upon it, can it then be implied that the Council has decided the point accordingly.

The context of a Security Council resolution can include discussions at the adoption stage, if these reveal that a number of states upheld a particular meaning and others did not contradict it. In practical terms, it is highly unlikely that states participating in these discussions at the time when a resolution is adopted will, in any significant numbers, uphold any interpretation that is incompatible with the text.[73] A high threshold of proof will normally be needed to demonstrate that discussions within the Council have led to an agreement between members. The ICTY in the *Tadić* appeal decision had to assess statements made in the Council,

---

[71] *Tadić*, IT-94-1, Appeal Chamber, Judgment of 15 July 1999, paras 295–6.
[72] Wood, n 68 above, 82.
[73] For an exception, see China's position regarding the powers of UNAMID, in Chapter 7 below.

after adoption of the Statute, by three states (France, the USA, and Russia) on importing into Article 5 a qualification concerning discriminatory intent. The US remarks were expressly couched as an 'interpretative statement', setting out the understanding 'that other members of the Council share our view regarding the following clarifications related to the Statute'. The Appeals Chamber denied that these three statements can be considered as part of the 'context' of the Statute, pursuant to the general rule of construction under Article 31 of the Vienna Convention. Those statements did not form an 'agreement' relating to the Statute. Even if the USA had spelled out what (it claimed) was understood, 'it would seem difficult to conclude that there emerged an agreement in the Security Council designed to qualify the scope of Article 5 with respect to discriminatory intent'.[74]

In the earlier *Tadić* Appeal Decision on Jurisdiction, the Tribunal gave more weight to statements of the USA, the UK, and Hungary that reaffirmed the broad textual meaning of Article 3 of the ICTY Statute which, according to the Tribunal, lists war crimes in a manner which is merely illustrative, not exhaustive. 'Since no delegate contested these declarations, they can be regarded as providing an authoritative interpretation of Article 3.'[75] State views conforming to the literal meaning of the text are thus authoritative while those that contradict the text are irrelevant. The use of the textual method led to an effective interpretation which ensured effective prosecution of crimes under the Statute. The establishment of the ICTY was meant to put a stop to all serious violations of humanitarian law in the former Yugoslavia. Article 3 fully realized this primary purpose: not to leave unpunished any such serious violation.[76] In similar terms, effective interpretation of treaties follows from Article 31 of the Vienna Convention.[77]

The object and purpose of a Security Council resolution draws on the agreement among Council members in the case at hand. Preambles can be a useful point of reference. Even if, as has been suggested, preambles could include provisions that were not adopted as operative paragraphs,[78] they are still adopted as the Council's statement of objectives and thus guide the interpretation of a resolution. In the *Namibia* case the preamble to Resolution 276(1970) made the difference and enabled the International Court to declare the resolution to be binding. That preamble specified that the Council was '[m]indful of its responsibility to take necessary action to secure strict compliance with the obligations entered into by States Members of the United Nations under the provisions of Article 25 of the Charter'.[79]

The object of treaties can be one-off or continuous. If the object and purpose of a resolution are one-off, that resolution, or its pertinent part, will be deemed to lapse upon the attainment of that object. If a resolution contains a demand not linked to a specific period, it is active until the demand is met. But if a resolution authorizes a

---

[74] *Tadić*, n 71 above, paras 298–300.
[75] *Tadić*, n 7 above, paras 87–8.
[76] Ibid, para 89.
[77] As confirmed by the International Law Commission, II *Yearbook of the ILC* 1966, 219.
[78] Cf Wood, n 68 above, 86–7.
[79] *Namibia, ICJ Reports* 1971, 53.

specific action to deal with a specific threat, then it lapses as soon as that action is completed.

Subsequent practice and agreement are of limited importance as interpretative factors. To validly qualify as such, the practice in question has to positively demonstrate the agreement of the Council's membership to the resolution's meaning, as Article 31(1)(b) of the Vienna Convention requires, and that this has been reached through the Council's decision-making procedure under Article 27 of the Charter.

Preparatory work and circumstances surrounding the adoption of a resolution (such as records of discussion, letters by member States to the Council, or reports by the Secretary-General) can indicate the meaning of a resolution. If, for instance, a resolution is silent as to its legal basis, preparatory work can be helpful to highlight whether this was identified at the adoption stage. If, however, the relevant basis or circumstance had been referred to by some member States but contradicted by others, and did not end up as part of the text of a resolution, it can be presumed that this basis had been supported by individual members but not by the Council collectively. Conversely, if some members denied the existence of a potential legal basis for a resolution (which the text does not mention) and others have not identified it, this might be evidence that the resolution had been adopted without a proper legal basis.

In the appeal decision in *Tadić* the issue arose whether the US, UK, and Hungarian statements in the Security Council (which could not qualify as context for the ICTY Statute) formed part of the *travaux préparatoires*. Even as such, they would not be indispensable aids to interpretation. Under customary international law codified in Article 32 of the Vienna Convention, the *travaux* constitute a supplementary means of interpretation and 'may only be resorted to when the text of a treaty or any other international norm-creating instrument is *ambiguous or obscure*'. The wording of Article 5 was clear and there was no need to rely upon those statements.[80] In some cases, the materials related to adoption of a resolution are not publicly available.

One important aspect in which the interpretation of resolutions can differ from that of treaties relates to the relevance of general international law. Article 31(3)(c) of the Vienna Convention enables rules of general international law to be taken into account for interpreting undefined provisions in treaties, and also enables general international law to prevail over what might actually be required under the treaty's ordinary meaning, because treaties form *lex specialis* in relation to custom.[81] This is not inevitably the case with Security Council resolutions, which can prevail over treaties under Article 103 of the Charter, but not over general international law. Hence, resolutions generally have to be seen as not prejudicing the operation of general international law. As the ICTY specified in the *Blaškić* case, a Chapter VII resolution can prevail over the rules of general international law to a limited extent that is inherent in the designation of a particular measure as required, for instance, by specific obligations imposed on states under Article 29 in terms of cooperation

---

[80] *Tadić*, n 71 above, para 300 (emphasis in original).
[81] For detail and analysis see A Orakhelashvili, *Interpretation of Acts and Rules in Public International Law* (New York: Oxford University Press, 2008), Chapter 10.

with the Tribunal.[82] Apart from that, as the *Tadić* appeal judgment confirmed, a Security Council resolution has to be interpreted as not intended to displace any rule of general international law.[83]

(d) The Consequences of Breaches of Resolutions

There is a conceptual and normative difference between a violation of a Security Council resolution that is valid and in force, and a refusal to carry out a Council decision that exceeds its competence.[84] Unlike rules under the law of treaties, there is no codified set of rules dealing with legal consequences of breaches of resolutions. The Council's own position in relation to a breach can be of prominent importance in determining the consequences. The Council can issue additional demands or resort to coercion of the recalcitrant party under Chapter VII. To illustrate, Resolution 1295(2000) adopted under Chapter VII stressed the obligation of all member States to comply fully with the enforcement measures imposed against UNITA in the Council's previous resolutions and stated its readiness to consider appropriate action against states that violate these measures.

In institutional terms, sanctions committees are established to oversee the operation of particular sanction regimes. Resolution 724(1991) established the FRY sanctions committee 'to consider any information brought to its attention by States concerning violations of the embargo', and to recommend appropriate measures in response to that. The note issued by the President of the Security Council regarding the work of sanctions committees specifies that

Member States should provide the sanctions committees with all information available on alleged violations, and sanctions committees should seek to clarify all cases of alleged violations of sanctions regimes. The UN Secretariat should provide such information from all available sources and the committee's guidelines should include clear provisions for strict action to be taken by the committees on alleged violations of the sanctions regimes.[85]

Yet the Council could respond in part or not at all, if a political deadlock arose. It is thus questionable whether the legal consequences of the breach of a resolution can be limited to those emanating from the Council's reaction.

A particular decision in its entirety is what the Council collectively agrees to be the way to preserve or restore international peace and security in a particular situation. As part of that enterprise, a binding resolution could impose a complex legal framework consisting of rights of and obligations on multiple entities. The rights and obligations of every entity are, then, conditional upon those of other

---

[82] *Prosecutor v Blaškić*, Judgment on the Request of the Republic of Croatia for Review of the Decision of Trial Chamber II of 18 July 1997, Appeal Chamber, 29 October 1997, para 64.

[83] *Tadić*, n 71 above, para 287.

[84] On refusal to carry out illegal decisions of the Council see Chapter 8 below.

[85] Note by the President of the Security Council: Work of the Sanctions Committees, S/1999/92, 29 January 1999, paras 3–5; see also the Iraq Sanctions Committee Report, S/1996/700, paras 93ff, the Committee emphasizing that it will seek information from governments regarding the violations of sanctions and then consider further action.

entities. If one party fails to deliver its part, this could raise the question whether the situation on the ground still actually reflected the Council's stated objective to maintain or restore peace and security in that particular context. That situation on the ground, if perpetuated, could be substantially different from what the Council originally intended and mandated. The rationale of the resolution in question could thus be undermined and it might be rendered unworkable.

Once a situation along these lines becomes obvious, states concerned can validly declare that they will stop complying with the resolution. If, for instance, an arms embargo is imposed on both sides of a conflict and then states decide, for political reasons, to start arms shipments to one of the parties, the first step would naturally be to convey a protest and demand compliance. But if that yielded no result, there is no obvious reason why states should be obliged to continue observing restrictions on their freedom when the rationale of those restrictions had been rendered moot through the conduct of other states and the Council's inaction.

Needless to say, the right of states to reciprocal non-compliance only extends to rights and obligations that owe their existence to the resolution in question: not to any that exist under international law independently of that resolution, even if reflected in it. A related systemic limit on this reciprocity-driven process is the compliance with obligations under *jus cogens* that all entities are peremptorily obliged to offer, whether or not a particular resolution continues in force, or indeed has been adopted at all. There can be no reciprocal justification, for instance, for preventing displaced persons from returning to their homes, for conducting attacks on safe areas, or for perpetuating the aggressor's presence in an occupied territory.

5. The General Assembly

(a) The Nature of the Assembly's Powers

The General Assembly represents the entire UN membership and its substantive powers are defined in Articles 10 to 14 of the Charter. It is argued that the Assembly can appropriately deal with long-term 'root cause' aspects of peace and security, while the Security Council undertakes operative actions.[86] Such abstract considerations, however, cannot affect the allocation of powers to principal organs under the Charter. For the Assembly to carry out operative activities is premised on its right to go beyond discussion, recommendation, and internal organizational matters such as election and budget.

The general terms of Article 14 of the Charter allow the Assembly to exercise dispute-settlement functions allocated to the Council under Articles 33(2), 36, 37, and 38. As long as it uses non-binding instruments, the Assembly can exercise its dispute-settlement functions comprehensively and has the power of investigation to that effect.[87] Article 12 of the Charter provides that the Assembly shall refrain from

---

[86] Pellet, n 48 above, 121.
[87] Conforti, n 46 above, 218, 220.

acting when 'the Security Council is exercising in respect of any dispute or situation the functions assigned to it in the present Charter'. Once the Council has begun dealing with the matter, it is not justified to assume that it has ceased to do so, in the absence of some clear-cut indication.[88] Mere presence of the matter on the Council's agenda is not, however, sufficient to prevent the Assembly's involvement. Conforti suggests that Article 12 has to be understood restrictively: only if the Council is actually discussing the matter should the Assembly refrain from addressing it. In practice, pleas to prevent a question pending before the Council from being discussed before the Assembly have failed.[89]

The dynamics of the relationship between the Security Council and the General Assembly can be displayed in multiple ways. The Council could adopt binding decisions or resort to enforcement measures on the basis of a policy determined by the General Assembly. In *Namibia*, the Court made it clear that the Council's binding call on South Africa to withdraw from Namibia was made pursuant to the Assembly's decision to draw the Council's attention to the matter, acting under Article 11(2) of the Charter.[90] The Assembly could act when the Council is unwilling to do so, by adopting a resolution calling for a particular line of conduct, or an operative decision.

There is a considerable body of doctrinal opinion that the Security Council's primary responsibility can be overtaken by the General Assembly's residual responsibility if the Council fails to take action in relation to a crisis, for instance because it is prevented by a veto.[91] This approach was embodied in General Assembly Resolution 377(1950) adopted in response to the war in Korea. In paragraph 1, the Assembly

[r]esolves that if the Security Council, because of lack of unanimity of the permanent members, fails to exercise its primary responsibility for the maintenance of international peace and security in any case where there appears to be a threat to the peace, breach of the peace, or act of aggression, the General Assembly shall consider the matter immediately with a view to making appropriate recommendations to Members for collective measures, including in the case of a breach of the peace or act of aggression the use of armed force when necessary, to maintain or restore international peace and security.

This resolution envisaged transfer of the Security Council's primary responsibility to address threats to the peace and breaches of the peace to the General Assembly after the Council had dropped the matter from its agenda. This could be done through procedural voting and could be accomplished by seven affirmative votes against the opposition of as many as four permanent members. The Council's primary responsibility would thus become nominal.[92] The overall effect would

---

[88] F Vallat, 'The General Assembly and the Security Council of the United Nations', 29 *British Yearbook of International Law* (1952), 63 at 82.

[89] Conforti, n 46 above, 219–20.

[90] *ICJ Reports* 1971, 51.

[91] Vallat, n 88 above, 96; M McDougal and R Gardner, 'The Veto and the Charter: An Interpretation for Survival', 60 *Yale Law Journal* (1951), 258 at 289.

[92] LM Goodrich, 'The UN Security Council', 12 *International Organization* (1958), 273 at 279.

then be that major policy decisions on enforcement are taken through a procedural vote by evading the decision-making requirements under Article 27.

The Chapter VII wording 'where there appears to be a threat to the peace, breach of the peace, or act of aggression' is controversial because it implies the independent standing of the General Assembly to determine that such have occurred. But in relation to the use of armed force, the wording of Resolution 377 A (V)(1950) 'Uniting for Peace' (UfP) is limited to 'a breach of the peace or act of aggression', which Dinstein sees as a careful drafting through which the Assembly claimed the competence to act only if there was the basis for the use of force in self-defence,[93] which does not need the Council's authorization anyway. It is pointed out that the Assembly's decisions on enforcement action contradict the Charter by exceeding this organ's competence under Articles 11–14 of the Charter,[94] and by encroaching on the Council's monopoly over decisions on enforcement, as well as by moving into the area that is subject to veto.[95] According to Dinstein, the Assembly is not competent to place the use of force on a new juridical footing and thus cannot authorize the use of force as the Council can. When the Council fails to act, no other organ can serve as its surrogate. An Assembly resolution could be seen as at most an exhortation to members to engage in the action of collective self-defence.[96]

But there still are ways of accommodating the principle underlying the UfP resolution. The Security Council enjoys monopoly only in relation to enforcement measures under Chapter VII. Outside this area, the Council's powers are concurrent with those of other principal organs, to enable the most effective realization of collective security functions under the Charter. The *Certain Expenses* case clarified the pattern along which the Assembly and the Council share competence, especially in view of Article 11 of the Charter which requires that a matter on which 'action' is required shall be referred to the Council. As the Court specified,

the kind of action referred to in Article 11, paragraph 2, is coercive or enforcement action.... The word 'action' must mean such action as is solely within the province of the Security Council. It cannot refer to recommendations which the Security Council might make, as for instance under Article 38, because the General Assembly under Article 11 has a comparable power. The 'action' which is solely within the province of the Security Council is that which is indicated by the title of Chapter VII of the Charter, namely 'Action with respect to threats to the peace, breaches of the peace, and acts of aggression'. If the word 'action' in Article 11, paragraph 2, were interpreted to mean that the General Assembly could make recommendations only of a general character affecting peace and security in the abstract, and not in relation to specific cases, the paragraph would not have provided that the General Assembly may make recommendations on questions brought before it by States or by the Security Council. Accordingly, the last sentence of

---

[93] Dinstein, n 47 above, 317–18, adding that the UfP resolution could be drafted even more meticulously to exclude the authorization of force where this is not undertaken as self-defence in response to an armed attack.

[94] N Schrijver, 'The Future of the Charter of the United Nations', 10 *Max-Planck Yearbook of UN Law* (2006), 1 at 14.

[95] R Kolb, *Ius contra bellum, Le droit international relatif au maintien de la paix* (Basle/Louvain: Helbing Lichtenhahn/Bruylant, 2003), 116; Pellet, n 48 above, 117.

[96] Dinstein, n 47 above, 317.

Article 11, paragraph 2, has no application where the necessary action is not enforcement action.[97]

This explains how the Charter enables the Assembly to take an operative action going beyond discussion and recommendation, without encroaching upon the exclusive competence of the Council to undertake enforcement action against a state. The reliance in *Certain Expenses* on the non-exclusivity of the Council's powers related to the area in which the principal organs' competence is concurrent, notably to the Council's power to establish peace-keeping forces. The Opinion contains nothing to support the view that in the area of its exclusive powers the Council's primary responsibility could be displaced by another organ's secondary or residual responsibility merely because the Council had failed to act.

Therefore, the legality of action on the UfP pattern should not be judged in a pre-conceived manner, but depends on whether the action encroaches on the area of competence exclusively reserved by the Charter for the Security Council. If seen this way, the principle underlying the UfP resolution in itself is little more than a particular way to implement the capacity expressly granted to the Assembly under Articles 10 and 11(2) of the Charter, with the caveat that the Assembly has no power to authorize the use of force.[98]

(b) The Types of Assembly Decisions

Though generally non-binding, Assembly resolutions authoritatively state the policy and legal position accepted by the entire international community. As the International Court specified in *Namibia*, 'it would not be correct to assume that, because the General Assembly is in principle vested with recommendatory powers, it is debarred from adopting, in specific cases within the framework of its competence, resolutions which make determinations or have operative design',[99] producing legal consequences opposable to all states. As Higgins points out pertinently, 'it is rather too simple to dispose of the question merely by saying that a certain organ may only pass recommendations'.[100]

Given that the roles of the Security Council and the General Assembly are concurrent, as per *Certain Expenses*, the General Assembly is entitled to take operational and obligatory decisions. In the Suez crisis, the Assembly clearly took the view that it had such power. By Resolution 1000 (ES–I)(1956), the Assembly '[e]stablishe[d] a United Nations Command for an emergency international force to secure and supervise the cessation of hostilities', appointed its commander and '[i]nvite[d] the Secretary-General to take such administrative measures as may be

---

[97] *Certain Expenses of the United Nations (Article 17, paragraph 2, of the Charter)*, Advisory Opinion of 20 July 1962, *ICJ Reports* 1962, 164–5.

[98] H McCoubrey and J Morris, *Regional Peacekeeping in the Post-Cold War Era* (The Hague: Kluwer, 2000), 34; EB Haas, 'Types of Collective Security: An Examination of Operational Concepts', 49 *American Political Science Review* (1955), 40 at 48.

[99] *ICJ Reports* 1971, 50.

[100] Higgins, n 48 above, 273.

necessary for the prompt execution of the actions envisaged in the present Resolution' (paragraphs 1–2 and 4). By Resolution 1001 (ES–I)(1956), the Assembly '[a]uthorize[d] the Secretary-General to issue all regulations and instructions which may be essential to the effective functioning of the Force...and to take all other necessary administrative and executive action' (paragraph 7). These decisions were plainly meant to impact on the situation on the ground and to do so externally, that is beyond the internal administrative realm of the UN.

An example of concurrent competence based on the need to respond to changing circumstances is provided by the case of the mandate of the UN Observation Group in Lebanon (UNOGIL), which had originally been established by the Secretary-General under Security Council Resolution 128(1958) to ensure that no arms and personnel would penetrate the Lebanese border. Later the Council was unable to agree on extending UNOGIL's mandate, and consequently General Assembly Resolution ES–1237 (1958) empowered the Secretary-General to make 'such practical arrangements as would adequately help in upholding the purposes and principles of the Charter in relation to Lebanon and Jordan in the present circumstances, and thereby facilitate the early withdrawal of the foreign troops from the two countries' (Section II).

6. Powers of Principal Organs and Interpretation of the Charter

(a) General Aspects

Given that principal organs of the UN have competence delegated by states, they can act lawfully only within the limits of that delegation. Excessive use of delegated powers produces an illegal act. There is, however, a significant body of doctrinal and judicial opinion explaining a bulk of decisions of UN organs as initially in breach of the Charter but then validated pursuant to the maxim *ex injuria jus oritur*. As Morgenstern aptly comments, this position assumes a demonstrated illegality, while in reality much of this practice can be explained as possible interpretations of the law.[101] Across-the-board generalizations are hardly useful. Each pertinent decision has to be examined on its own, by reference to interpretative factors that influence conclusions as to whether the Charter has authorized its adoption in the first place. If the answer is affirmative, illegality becomes a non-issue. If the answer is negative, then issues arise of violation of the Charter and of excess of competence, which can be clarified by analysing the type of the action and decision concerned, how it/they contradict the Charter or other applicable rules, and the required threshold of validation if that constitutes a viable option in the relevant case.[102] Before these conclusions can be reached, however, two questions have to be examined that are crucial for determining the legality of relevant decisions. The first relates to the legal basis on which the powers of

---

[101] F Morgenstern, 'Legality in International Organisations', 48 *British Yearbook of International Law* (1975–6), 241 at 255.

[102] For detail on this latter question, see Chapter 8 below.

principal organs rest. The second relates to the capacity of principal organs to pronounce on the legality of each others' decisions.

(b) Legal Bases for the Powers of Principal Organs

Broad as the Security Council's powers are, they still are grounded in the Charter through which they have been delegated to it by states. It is argued that the Council 'has virtually never found it necessary to specify a "legal base" for its decisions' under specific provisions of the Charter, but instead 'situates itself within an international tradition in which the scope and allocation of powers are achieved with a broader brush'.[103] This position has to be taken with caution, since the broader UN membership is unlikely to accept the Council's decisions unless they can ultimately be defended by reference to powers delegated to it.

It is widely accepted that principal organs possess powers that are expressly conferred on them by the Charter, and others that are inherent to, or implied by, the expressly conferred powers and responsibilities. The implied powers doctrine is reinforced by the principle of effective interpretation of the Charter as a treaty. The rationale of effective interpretation is that, if the organ in question is to discharge its responsibilities under the Charter effectively, then it should be able to adopt such decisions as are necessary for and antecedent to that. This point was substantiated by the International Court in the *Namibia* case, addressing the power of the Security Council to respond to South Africa's breaches of its obligations under the Mandate Agreement regarding Namibia. The Court specified that

Article 24 of the Charter vests in the Security Council the necessary authority to take action such as that taken in the present case. The reference in paragraph 2 of this Article to specific powers of the Security Council under certain chapters of the Charter does not exclude the existence of general powers to discharge the responsibilities conferred in paragraph 1 . . . . the Members of the United Nations have conferred upon the Security Council powers commensurate with its responsibility for the maintenance of peace and security.[104]

Thus, the Council's standing to respond to a serious violation of international law protecting Namibia's right to self-determination justified implying into the Charter, on strictly functional terms, the appropriate power of decision even though this was not expressly mentioned there. Implied powers can only be those that correspond to the overall character of an organ under the constituent instrument and enable it to carry out functions conferred on it. In the *Certain Expenses* Opinion the International Court admitted the exercise of implied powers by principal organs to the extent that this serves the purposes of the UN.[105] The limit on the overall relevance of implied powers is that they should respect both the scope of each

---

[103] F Berman, 'The Authorisation Model', in D Malone (ed.), *The UN Security Council—From the Cold War to the 21st Century* (Boulder/London: Lynne Rienner Inc, 2004), 153 at 156; M Craven, 'Humanitarianism and the Quest for Smarter Sanctions', 13 *European Journal of International Law* (2002), 43 at 50.

[104] *ICJ Reports* 1971, 52.

[105] *ICJ Reports* 1962, 167.

organ's powers and the overall balance of competence between them.[106] The establishment of peace-keeping forces dealt with in *Certain Expenses* clearly fell within this category.

(c) The Interpretation of the Charter and Parallel Competences

If a principal organ adopts a decision it claims to be based on an express provision of the Charter, or to be inherent to or implied in its Charter-based responsibilities, it thereby purports at times to produce particular legal consequences for states—and for other principal organs—without being expressly empowered to do so. Thus, a principal organ cannot be sensibly considered to possess an ultimate power to determine the essence and scope of its expressly delegated or implied powers. This necessarily points to the relevance of the positions principal organs take regarding each others' actions and decisions. This is where the teleological aspect of Charter interpretation intertwines with its consensual aspect.

The same effectiveness principle of interpretation that explains the implied powers doctrine can justify a distribution of competence among principal organs that is conducive to the most efficient attainment of the purposes stated in the Charter. Subject to textual prescriptions by the Charter of exclusive jurisdiction to one or another principal organ (for instance, the adoption of enforcement measures only by the Security Council or the adoption of binding judgments settling disputes only by the International Court), or primacy of one organ over another (for instance, like that the Security Council enjoys over the General Assembly under Article 12), all institutional competence has to be viewed as concurrent and running parallel in different principal organs, so that the purposes of the Charter can be realized even if a particular organ is unwilling to act in a given case.

In one of the very few instances where this question has been properly confronted, Schachter observes that the Charter is fully subject to the principle that authentic interpretation of a treaty by all parties to it is as binding as the treaty itself. This also applies to 'cases where a virtually unanimous consensus in a matter of Charter interpretation is made known through statements and actions expressed separately by Governments either within or outside the United Nations, even though no vote is taken.' However the burden of demonstrating this is high. If the above is not the case, then

[t]he usual distinction then drawn is that between an interpretation of a treaty which is considered to be binding because it has been accepted by all of the parties and an interpretation which is rejected by some and therefore would be regarded as effective only if the treaty should be amended accordingly.[107]

---

[106] AIL Campbell, 'The Limits on the Powers of International Organisations', 32 ICLQ (1983), 523 at 528, 531; N Blokker, 'Is the Authorisation Authorised? Powers and Practice of the UN Security Council to Authorise the Use of Force', 11 *European Journal of International Law* (2000), 541 at 548–9.
[107] O Schachter, 'The Relation between Law, Politics and Action in the United Nations', 109 *Recueil des Cours de l'Academie de Droit International de la Haye* (1963), 169 at 186–7.

As for choice between conflicting interpretations, Schachter considers that it should be made according to 'shared values' that are enshrined in the Charter or through other consensual procedures.[108] This does not really entail policy choice but a referral to the overarching legal framework to find out which interpretation is correct.

Sir Francis Vallat has submitted that both the General Assembly and the Security Council act on their own interpretations.[109] If so, then each principal organ can adopt its own interpretation of the Charter, and in practice mutually exclusive interpretations could emerge, some of which will be right and others wrong, because the Charter cannot justify or require mutually exclusive outcomes. Conforti's argument is very much in point, specifying that

if the UN organs had the sovereign power to interpret the Charter provisions in a way that was binding on all the member States, this would be the same as saying that they had the possibility of violating them with impunity, since any decision could be justifiable in the light of a subjective and 'special' interpretation of the Charter.[110]

But Conforti's other point—that the General Assembly has no express power to review the exercise by the Security Council of its own powers—is more controversial.[111] Not only is the Assembly the organization's most representative organ, entitled to articulate the premises of legitimacy, but it is also expressly endowed with the power to pronounce on the Council's exercise of its powers. Article 10 specifically provides that the Assembly can discuss, and make recommendations on, the issues 'relating to the powers and functions of any organs provided for in the present Charter'.[112]

This question was viewed as very important at the San Francisco Conference, where Committee II/2 enquired 'how and by what organs of the Organization should the Charter be interpreted'. The Committee specified that in exercising their tasks each organ can interpret those parts of the Charter that apply to its activities. This was inherent to the functioning of each organ, and did not need to be expressly specified. The Committee observed that, while under national legal systems these questions are decided by the highest court, the nature of the UN does not invite such a specific arrangement. Instead, as needs to be understood, the Committee specified that the competence to interpret would be spread between the General Assembly, the Security Council, and the International Court, as already emerges from their powers and without this needing to be expressly specified in the

---

[108] Ibid, 197–8.
[109] Vallat, n 88 above, 67; Conforti, n 46 above, 15.
[110] Conforti, ibid, 15.
[111] Ibid.
[112] It is unfortunate that a leading commentary on the UN Charter regards these words as having no independent significance: Hailbronner and Klein, 'Article 10' in Simma, n 1 above, 262. This approach runs counter to the framework of treaty interpretation, especially the presumption of redundancy: see for detail, and other examples of applying this principle within the UN law, Orakhelashvili, n 81 above, Chapter 11.

Charter.[113] Thus the Committee opposed the principle that a judicial organ should have exclusive jurisdiction over questions of interpretation; it also said nothing to oppose judicial competence to interpret the Charter, which incidentally could be exercised by the International Court in the course of a regular adjudication. This approach is further reinforced by General Assembly Resolution 171(II) (1947) specifying that the Charter should be interpreted in accordance with principles of interpretation recognized in international law, and that the International Court as a principal organ is in the most suitable position to pronounce on such complex legal issues.

What is most important is that the Committee proposed a criterion which has so far received insufficient attention in doctrine,[114] namely 'if an interpretation made by any organ is not generally acceptable, it will be without binding force'.[115] General acceptability does not inevitably mean unanimity—although objections to an interpretation could possibly undermine its general acceptability[116]—but it seems, definitionally, to imply the absence of a significant split within the UN membership.

The underlying idea is that the Charter is a treaty, a consensual instrument, and that the further development and interpretation of open-ended, treaty-based powers has to reflect the consensual nature of this entire process. So, if an organ such as the Security Council adopts a binding decision based on an interpretation of the Charter that is not generally acceptable, this is without binding force owing to its incompatibility with the Charter.[117]

A 'generally acceptable' interpretation could be made by an organ with general representation such as the General Assembly, or by the International Court, whose decisions are based on international law in any case, which is by definition generally accepted by the membership. In terms of substantive principles of interpretation, the requirement for general acceptability could be met by construing relevant Charter provisions in terms of their ordinary meaning as placed in the context of Charter purposes and principles, or reinforced by evidence that the support of the membership qualifies that interpretation as part of 'subsequent practice' under Article 31(3)(b) of the 1969 Vienna Convention.

The 'general acceptability' thesis reflects the delegated nature of powers under the Charter and enables limits on discretionary elements under the Charter to be articulated; it also reinforces the principle that no principal organ is the ultimate judge of its own competence. This test is even more pertinent, since the Charter includes a number of notions (such as 'threat to the peace', necessity, or proportionality) which it does not define. In order for decisions relying on these notions to be legitimate, the interpretative outcome must be generally acceptable to the membership. This approach seems to be articulated in the ICTY Appeal Chamber

---

[113] 13 UNCIO, 709.
[114] For a fortunate exception see Ciobanu, n 5 above, 170ff.
[115] 13 UNCIO, 710.
[116] Ciobanu, n 5 above, 170–2.
[117] For options available to member States in such cases see Chapter 8 below.

Decision in *Tadic* where the Tribunal demonstrated that application of Article 39 of the Charter to internal conflicts was an option approved by the General Assembly and was thus generally acceptable.[118]

The general acceptability requirement further reinforces the principle stated in Article 24 that, while exercising its peace and security mandate, the Security Council shall act on behalf of the entire membership of the UN. What also most pertinently appears from the San Francisco Committee position is that the correctness of an interpretation does not depend on the binding force of the decision which is premised on that interpretation; instead, the binding force is conditional on the correctness of the interpretation underlying it. Otherwise, each principal organ would be able to interpret the Charter in its own way, which on occasions would lead to mutually conflicting interpretations, and contradict another significant principle enshrined in jurisprudence: 'that the right of giving an authoritative interpretation of a legal rule belongs solely to the person or body who has power to modify or suppress it'.[119] It should not be assumed that each organ's interpretation of its competence, and thus of the relevant provisions of the Charter, is authoritative and conclusive. In the absence of a centralized authority with regular jurisdiction over these matters, the only feasible—and statutorily permissible—position is that of *the parallelism of interpretative competences* as between the General Assembly, the Security Council, the International Court, and member States acting individually or in groups, including through regional organizations, as opposed to auto-interpretation of the Charter by any organ or entity.

(d) The Security Council and the International Court of Justice

The Charter admits of no hierarchy or subordination between the Council and the Court, nor prohibits one organ from dealing with situations pending before the other, the way Article 12 treats the relationship between the General Assembly and the Security Council.[120] As the International Court specified in *Tehran Hostages*,

[w]hereas Article 12 of the Charter expressly forbids the General Assembly [from] mak[ing] any recommendation with regard to a dispute or situation while the Security Council is exercising its functions in respect of that dispute or situation, no such restriction is placed on the functioning of the Court by any provision of either the Charter or the Statute of the Court. The reasons are clear. It is for the Court, the principal judicial organ of the United Nations, to resolve any legal questions that may be in issue between parties to the dispute.[121]

---

[118] See further Chapter 4.

[119] *Question of Jaworzina (Polish Czechoslovakian Frontier)*, PCIJ Series B, No 8, 37; as Judge Morelli further specified in *Certain Expenses*, 'the [General] Assembly is required to establish and appreciate correctly a body of factual circumstances. It must also verify the validity of the resolutions of the different United Nations organs concerning the activity to which the expenditure to be authorized or not relates.' Separate Opinion of Judge Morelli, *ICJ Reports* 1962, 224.

[120] *Lockerbie*, Dissenting Opinion of Judge Weeramantry, *ICJ Reports* 1992, 58.

[121] *Hostages* (Merits), *ICJ Reports* 1980, 22 (para 40); reaffirmed in *Nicaragua* (Jurisdiction and Admissibility), *ICJ Reports* 1984, 433–4 (para 93).

Furthermore, Article 36 of the Charter, together with Articles 36 and 38 of the Court's Statute (which contain no subject-matter limit on the Court's judicial function), precludes projecting limitations on the Court's power to deal with situations also dealt with by the Council and reduces any interpretation having this effect to a mere assertion. It is only natural that, as a judicial organ, the Court is ultimately responsible for interpretation of the Charter as a treaty, and presumably enjoys a functional primacy in determining legal issues on matters that are properly brought before it. Its views on treaty interpretation are better informed than those of the Council. Article 36 of the Charter mandates the Court's involvement precisely in the context where the Council acts to preserve peace and security; even in such contexts, legal disputes should be submitted to the Court.

In the *Lockerbie* affair the Council attempted to overtake the adjudication before the Court, despite the requirement contained in Article 36. This led the International Court to refrain from indicating provisional measures requested by Libya. Judge Bedjaoui observed that the Security Council's action under Resolutions 731 (1992) and 748(1992) prompted the Court to refrain from exercising its judicial function. The Court's abdication of its judicial function was incompatible with the Security Council's subjection to international law under Articles 1 and 24 of the Charter and with the Court's judicial function under Article 36 of its Statute.[122]

7. Legal Limits on Powers of United Nations Organs

While the United Nations organization as a whole, and as a treaty-based organization, has a limited, delegated mandate and is thus subject to international law in various ways, in practice the observance of those constraints by the Security Council has repeatedly raised the issue of legal constraints. Since the reference to principles of justice and international law under Article 1 of the Charter relates only to dispute settlement procedures, not to enforcement action under Chapter VII, in the *Lockerbie* case Judge Schwebel contended that 'it was deliberately so provided to ensure that the vital duty of preventing and removing threats to and breaches of the peace would not be limited by existing law'.[123] However, as the ICTY observed in *Tadić*,

[t]he Security Council is thus subjected to certain constitutional limitations, however broad its powers under the constitution may be. Those powers cannot, in any case, go beyond the limits of the jurisdiction of the Organization at large, not to mention other specific limitations or those which may derive from the internal division of power within the Organization. In any case, neither the text nor the spirit of the Charter conceives of the Security Council as *legibus solutus* (unbound by law).[124]

---

[122] Dissenting Opinion of Judge Bedjaoui, *ICJ Reports* 1992, 44.
[123] Dissenting Opinion of Judge Schwebel, *ICJ Reports* 1998, 76; see Chapter 1 above regarding the content of Article 1 of the Charter.
[124] *Tadić*, n 7 above, para 28.

Thus, the Security Council is subject to several kinds of legal limitation upon which the binding force of its decisions under Article 25 is contingent. The Council's decision making is subject to structural limits, relating to the allocation of powers to principal organs under the Charter. Under Article 33 the Council is meant to promote settlement of disputes through traditional means before it intervenes in them; under Article 36 the Council is meant, whenever possible, to defer judicial disputes to the International Court; under Article 39 and Chapter VII as a whole the Council can validly adopt enforcement decisions only if it identifies a genuinely existing threat justifying action of a particular type. The failure to observe these conditions can result in a decision that is beyond the Security Council's mandate.[125] Another—functional—limit on the Security Council's powers under the Charter relates to the purposes and principles of the Charter under its Articles 1 and 2, as Article 24 further affirms.[126] As the International Court observed in *Certain Expenses*, UN organs benefit from a substantial presumption in favour of the legality of acts that they undertake pursuant to purposes of the UN,[127] provided that these do not violate express provisions of the Charter.

The Security Council's powers are also subject to general, or customary, international law, on several grounds. In the first place, as an organ of an international organization the Council is as such bound by international law.[128] In the second place, a number of fundamental principles of international law (non-use of force, non-intervention, or respect for fundamental human rights) are embodied in purposes and principles of the Charter.[129] In the third place, the Security Council can be seen as estopped by its own statements concerning respect for the relevant rules and principles of international law, for instance its Resolution 1456(2003) which specifies that counter-terrorist measures have to be conducted in compliance with human rights law and humanitarian law. Human rights norms, in particular, bind the Security Council along with the standards embodied under the relevant treaties.[130] The UN position is that forces established or authorized by the Security Council are bound by humanitarian law.[131]

Substantive limitations on the Council's powers are also provided by peremptory norms of general international law (*jus cogens*),[132] which again reflect the treaty-based,

---

[125] On ultra vires decisions see Chapter 8 below.
[126] Cf, *Namibia, ICJ Reports*, 1971, 50–2.
[127] *Certain Expenses, ICJ Reports* 1962, 167.
[128] Cf *WHO Regional Office*, Advisory Opinion, *ICJ Reports*, 1980, 90.
[129] Cf *Tehran Hostages, ICJ Reports* 1980, 42.
[130] M Bossuyt, 'The adverse consequences of economic sanctions on the enjoyment of human rights', working paper, E/CN.4/Sub.2/2000/33, 9.
[131] UN Secretary-General's Bulletin on 'Observance by United Nations Forces of International Humanitarian Law', UN Doc ST/SGB/1999/13 (6 August 1999); see in general D Schraga, 'UN Peacekeeping Operations: Applicability of International Humanitarian Law and Responsibility for Operations-Related Damage', 94 AJIL (2000), 406; on the applicability of humanitarian law to the Security Council's enforcement activities in general, see Bossuyt, ibid.
[132] According to Articles 53 and 64 of the 1969 Vienna Convention, treaties conflicting with *jus cogens* are void.

delegated, and limited character of the Council's powers, construing which will inevitably require observing those public order limits that state-parties are bound to observe when concluding a treaty such as the UN Charter.[133]

Of direct importance in addressing the powers of the Security Council in relation to international law is Article 103 of the Charter which stipulates that

[i]n the event of a conflict between the obligations of the Members of the United Nations under the present Charter and their obligations under any other international agreement, their obligations under the present Charter shall prevail.

Article 103 takes this effect if certain conditions are met. In the first place, in order to command primacy under Article 103, a decision of the Security Council must be a valid one adopted in compliance with all structural, functional, and substantive limits on the Council's powers. As Wilfried Jenks observed, 'Article 103 cannot be invoked as giving the United Nations an overriding authority which would be inconsistent with the provisions of the Charter itself'.[134] In the second place, and according to the clear wording of Article 103, the Charter prevails over international agreements, not over general, or customary, international law. In the third place, Article 103 provides no relief to Security Council decisions that violate *jus cogens*.[135]

8. The Charter and the Extra-Charter Basis for Collective Security Action

Article 15 of the League of Nations Covenant gave the League Council power to make recommendations. However, as the Permanent Court specified,

[t]here is nothing to prevent the Parties from accepting obligations and from conferring on the Council powers wider than those resulting from the strict terms of Article 15, and in particular from substituting, by an agreement entered into in advance, for the Council's power to make a mere recommendation, the power to give a decision which, by virtue of their previous consent, compulsorily settles the dispute.[136]

Likewise, consent of the states concerned, as an additional legitimizing factor, can enable UN organs to do more than what is expressly specified in the Charter. In the *Namibia* case dealing with an operative decision adopted by the General Assembly, Judge Fitzmaurice developed a rather sophisticated reasoning as to why the Assembly's activities have to be limited to actions that are generically similar to those expressly conferred on it. The Assembly could not validly engage in 'extra-mural' functions such as peace-keeping operations even if there was an agreement

---

[133] For detail, see Orakhelashvili, n 52 above, Chapter 12.

[134] W Jenks, 'The Conflict of Law-Making Treaties', 30 *British Yearbook of International Law* (1951), 401 at 439.

[135] *Bosnian Genocide*, Separate Opinion of Judge *ad hoc* Lauterpacht, *ICJ Reports*, 1993, 440; M Shaw and K Wellens, *Final Report on Accountability of International Organisations* (2004), 19.

[136] *Frontier between Iraq and Turkey*, PCIJ Series B, No 12, 27.

between the UN and some member states to that effect: for that would alter the character of the organization through extraneous agreements, and impermissibly imitate a constitutional amendment. A system which only allows the Assembly to discuss and recommend cannot be replaced by another system which would allow it, in addition, to take executive action.[137] The issue here, however, is one of interpretation of the Charter as a treaty which alone can indicate what characteristics underlie, or limit, the Assembly's competence. The Charter contains no express restrictions on the Assembly's operative decision making. The object and purpose of the Charter provides room to imply powers for the Assembly to act effectively in the area of peace and security without encroaching on competences that have been exclusively reserved for other principal organs. Such an interpretation—coupled with state consent—enables the Assembly to establish peace-keeping forces in the way confirmed in *Certain Expenses*.[138] The addition of consent of states can complement the powers that principal organs already have under the Charter and thus help to identify the outer limits of their competence under Chapters VI and VII.

In *Supplement to an Agenda for Peace*, the Secretary-General clearly viewed it as an aspect of international peace and security that internal conflicts witness

the collapse of state institutions, especially the police and judiciary, with resulting paralysis of governance, a breakdown of law and order, and general banditry and chaos. Not only are the functions of government suspended, its assets are destroyed or looted and experienced officials are killed or flee the country. This is rarely the case in inter-state wars. It means that international intervention must extend beyond military and humanitarian tasks and must include the promotion of national reconciliation and the re-establishment of effective government.[139]

While addressing such situations, possibly with intrusive Chapter VII measures, the Secretary-General has not confirmed that the Council can assume governance functions within a state without that state's consent. Assuming such functions *while the collapse of government lasts* could presumably be located within the parameters of necessity for and proportionality of the Council's action, but as soon as a government is in place, the Council's governance functions will be difficult to justify on those grounds.

In the absence of an ad hoc conferral the scope of the powers of particular organs is governed solely by the constituent instrument. While an external agreement cannot determine the scope of powers of UN organs as such, being merely a request to the UN to take appropriate action,[140] it can still possess relevance for interpreting the scope of UN powers in the relevant situation, or even add to those powers. The combined operation of Charter-based powers and of an external agreement then constitutes, for that particular case, a single legal framework determining the legality of the action by

---

[137] Dissenting Opinion, *ICJ Reports* 1971, 284–7.
[138] For detail see Chapter 7 below.
[139] *Agenda for Peace—Supplement*, S/1995/1, 1995, paras 12–13.
[140] D Sarooshi, 'Conferrals by States of Powers on International Organisations: The Case of Agency', 74 *British Yearbook of International Law* (2003), 291 at 304, 307–8.

the UN. This factor also affects the scope of UN powers in terms of acting within what otherwise would be the domestic jurisdiction of states, either under a peace agreement or in the course of peace operations based on state consent. By premising its decisions on Kosovo, Bosnia, Afghanistan, and Iraq on state consent, the Security Council acknowledged the limits on its powers, the consistency of which position could prevent this organ from engaging in similar operations where consent is not forthcoming, unless the Council's objectives *in casu* were determined as requiring action against that government as such, for example in cases of aggressive war or genocide.[141] Otherwise, it is difficult to see how the administration of the state or territory in a way that overrides the will of its government can be conducive to attaining the Council's peace and security objectives, or be necessary and proportionate to that end. Even after the collapse of a government apparatus, the Council did not assume governance functions in Somalia—a case that has offered a greater justification for it to do so than any other. The Council's principal stated objective was the improvement of the humanitarian situation and to enable the Somali factions to resume the reconciliation process.[142] It is right to point out that general powers under Article 24(1) (as per

---

[141] Sarooshi, ibid, 304 considers the Security Council action under the Dayton Peace Agreement as related to the Council's choice between taking up an offer contained in a peace treaty to take the necessary measures and acting on its own under Chapter VII. Even where the Council refers to the parties' consent to the deployment of forces in Bosnia under Chapter VII, Sarooshi regards this as 'of no consequence'. But consensual conferrals should not be treated as an alternative to a Chapter VII action. Given the delegated and limited nature of the Security Council's powers and the increasingly sensitive implications of acting within the territory of states, it appears more justified to treat the Council's reference to the consent of relevant states as factoring in the Council's reflection of how far its powers reach in the face of state territorial supremacy, and how the requirements of necessity and proportionality work out in such situations. For detail on the relevance of state consent in the case of IFOR and the Dayton Agreement see Chapter 8 below. The same considerations apply to the argument regarding the establishment of UNTAES under Resolution 1037(1995), which was adopted under Chapter VII *and* responded to requests by parties under the relevant peace agreement: ibid, 305–6. There is no inherent dichotomy between the Chapter VII action and the acceptance of a consensual conferral. It was in reality precisely the latter that demonstrated the necessity and proportionality of the Council's action, for the propriety of that action and its success in achieving its tasks would have been doubtful had it not been premised on the consent of parties given through the peace agreement, as opposed to a centralized imposition of the relevant framework by the Council. See also Sarooshi, n 65 above, 62–3, for the argument that the SRSG's promulgation of the 1962 Criminal Code as criminal law in force in Somalia was problematic because the SRSG acted without an authorization to that effect being deducible from the relevant Security Council resolution. The inference is that, had the Security Council authorized this action, the SRSG could have exercised it validly. Essentially Sarooshi's argument, whether consciously or not, is premised on the lack of limits to Security Council powers in adopting such decisions. This argument has also been tested, and disapproved, by the Security Council's overwhelming reference to the consent of Iraq as authorizing the multinational presence under Resolution 1546(2004), and that of Afghanistan as approving expanding the military presence beyond Kabul. On detail see Chapters 5 and 7 below. Similarly, Resolution 940(1994) on authorizing a Chapter VII intervention to restore the democratically elected government of Haiti also relies on an invitation from the legitimate government, as well as the implementation of the Governor Island Agreement (preamble, paragraphs 3–4). See also S Ratner, 'The Cambodia Settlement Agreements', 87 AJIL (1993), 9, to the effect that the Council has never given serious consideration to this option, given its unwillingness to impose a settlement on factions that might oppose it. See further Chapters 5 and 8.

[142] See Chapter 5 below.

Namibia)[143] could possibly justify the Council's exercise of governance functions,[144] but this could only operate as an implied power, which by its nature cannot override the rights of states under general international law. This consideration becomes imperative if the delegated nature of the Council's powers is borne in mind.

Should the Security Council consider itself entitled to undertake peace enforcement measures by overriding the will of territorial states, it would arrogate to itself the role of a world legislature. However, the Council consistently avoids making such claims. The Council's involvement in repressing piracy off the coasts of Somalia illustrates this approach. In its pertinent resolutions from Resolution 1816(2008) onwards, the Council has been careful to emphasize that its action against a threat to the peace caused by piracy was conducted strictly within the applicable international legal framework. The preamble of Resolution 1816 specifies that the 1982 Law of the Sea Convention sets out the framework and guidance for dealing with the threat of piracy. It then refers to the consent of Somalia, expressed in a letter requesting 'urgent assistance in securing the territorial and international waters off the coast of Somalia for the safe conduct of shipping and navigation'. In operative paragraphs 7 and 9 the Council again emphasizes that it is guided strictly by the legal framework under which the Somali government's consent is the only legal basis for authorizing foreign navies to enter Somali territorial waters for the purpose of combating piracy. Thus the Council does not consider itself competent to authorize such operations without the consent of territorial states. If, then, the Council is not competent to override the freedoms enjoyed by states on the high seas or in their own territorial waters, it is even less empowered to assume governmental functions on the territory of a state without its consent. This again stresses the crucial relevance of the consent of the relevant Balkan states to the establishment of IFOR and UNTAES.

9. The Establishment and Operation of Subsidiary Organs

Article 7 of the Charter provides for the establishment of such subsidiary organs 'as may be found necessary'. Articles 22 and 29 enable principal organs to establish such subsidiary organs as may be necessary for the performance of their functions. The remit of Article 7 is broader than that of Articles 22 and 29, as it allows for the establishment of organs other than those needed for performance of functions of the Assembly and the Council. Normally a new organ is established because the powers expressly allocated to principal organs under the Charter are not feasible or sufficient for attaining the objectives that a principal organ identifies in relation to a particular matter. The subsidiary nature of the relevant organ points not so much to its subordinate status as to the accessory and specialized tasks allotted to it that cannot be properly exercised within the general context of the principal organs' activities.

Sanctions committees are established to administer each sanctions regime adopted by the Council. They receive and examine reports regarding the implementation

---

[143] *ICJ Reports,* 1971.
[144] Cf Sarooshi, n 65 above, 61–2.

of sanctions, respond to violations, consider requests under admitted exceptions, and report on all these matters to the Council. Sanctions resolutions such as 757 (1992) on FRY or 841(1993) on Haiti include catalogues of such powers. The note of the President of the Security Council specifies that chairpersons of the sanctions committees should make visits to the relevant regions to obtain first-hand accounts regarding the impact of sanctions. They

should monitor, throughout the sanctions regime, the humanitarian impact of sanctions on vulnerable groups, including children, and make required adjustments of the exemption mechanisms to facilitate the delivery of humanitarian assistance. The indicators for assessment developed by the Secretariat could be used by the committees.[145]

Sanctions committees have the same composition as the Security Council itself and meet at the deputy head of mission level. Each committee is chaired by a permanent representative of a non-permanent member who acts in a personal capacity, is elected for a year, and cannot be replaced by a deputy. If unable to carry out its functions, the chair can be replaced by one of the two permanent representatives who are designated as deputy chairpersons. Sanctions committees decide by consensus, on a no-objection basis, and every member effectively has a veto.[146]

The establishment of subsidiary organs does not really involve a delegation of functions by the Security Council to other organs. In all cases, decisions on what has to be done to restore peace and security under Articles 41 and 42 are taken by the Council itself and then embodied in the subsidiary organ's mandate. Moreover, the delegation approach does not work in relation to judicial organs, since the principal organ in question does not possess judicial powers to delegate in the first place. In a rather down-to-earth way, the ICTY commented in *Tadić* that the establishment of the ICTY did not signify that the Council had delegated to the Tribunal some of its powers, nor that the Council had usurped the powers of another organ, such as 'a judicial function which does not belong to it'. The Council established the Tribunal 'as an instrument for the exercise of its own principal function of maintenance of peace and security' in relation to Yugoslavia.[147] There was thus no delegation, but merely some of the Council's existing powers under Chapter VII being put into operation.[148] This reinforces the position that the enforcement of international law

---

[145] *Note by the President of the Security Council: Work of the Sanctions Committees*, S/1999/92, 29 January 1999, paras 2, 11.

[146] See, eg Guidelines of the Committee of the Security Council established by paragraph 6 of Security Council Resolution 1267(1999) of 15 October 1999 (the Al-Qaida and Taliban Sanctions Committee), version of 9 December 2008, paras 1(c)–(d); see also P van Walsum, 'The Iraq Sanctions Committee', in Malone, n 103 above, 181 at 182–3; Scharf and Dorosin, n 63 above, 774; M Bennouna, 'Les sanctions économiques des Nations Unies', 300 *Recueil des Cours de l'Académie de Droit International de la Haye* (2002), 54; G-L Burci, 'Interpreting the Humanitarian Exceptions through the Sanctions Committees', in Gowlland-Debbas, V (ed.), *UN Sanctions and International Law* (The Hague: Kluwer, 2001), 143.

[147] *Tadić*, n 7 above, para 38.

[148] Similarly, the General Assembly does not delegate its powers when establishing an administrative tribunal. The International Court pointed out (in *Effect of Awards*) that '[b]y establishing the Administrative Tribunal, the General Assembly was not delegating the performance of its own functions: it was exercising a power which it had under the Charter to regulate staff relations': *ICJ Reports*, 1954, 61. The Tribunal had to be established since the General Assembly itself had no appropriate powers.

is an inherent part of the Security Council's peace and security mandate, for which a specialized expertise is required in subsidiary organs.

A peculiar case of the establishment and operation of subsidiary organs is Resolution 687(1991) which established, after Iraq's invasion of and expulsion from Kuwait in 1990, subsidiary organs such as the Compensation Commission to administer the fund to compensate for 'any direct loss, damage, including environmental damage and the depletion of natural resources, or injury to foreign Governments, nationals and corporations, as a result of Iraq's unlawful invasion and occupation of Kuwait' (paragraphs 16 and 18). The resolution also created 'a Special Commission [UNSCOM], which shall carry out immediate on-site inspection of Iraq's biological, chemical and missile capabilities, based on Iraq's declarations and the designation of any additional locations by the Special Commission itself' (paragraph 9(b)(i)). This case illustrates that delegation of authority to subsidiary organs can produce a double-edged effect not foreseen at the time that the organ in question was established. Like many other Council decisions, the establishment of subsidiary organs is based on political agreements through which Council members purport to attain political objectives. Yet the legal dimension of establishing subsidiary organs can hold the ground in a way that upsets those political calculations, because legally the subsidiary organ is meant to carry out its duties without adverse interference from Council members. This preserves the collective dimension in the Council's decision making.

To illustrate, UNSCOM created its Information Assessment Unit to gather information, which drew an objection from the US representative. But it could not be stopped, because no consensus within the Council to that effect was forthcoming. In 1995 UNSCOM again interpreted its mandate and created a Concealment Unit, which now drew opposition from Russia, with a similar outcome. UNSCOM ignored claims by France and Russia that inspectors were overly aggressive in their tactics and compromised Iraqi sovereignty. Again, there was no consensus in the Council to censure UNSCOM.[149] The entire period in which UNSCOM operated was marred by these controversies, corroborated by allegations of espionage in Iraq. This organ was disbanded, and replaced by the Monitoring, Verification and Inspection Commission (UNMOVIC) under Resolution 1284(1999), by which means the Council traded the easement of sanctions against Iraq for a renewed consent to allow weapons inspectors to resume their activities.

Political arguments cannot resolve these dilemmas. Solutions can be found in legal safeguards which, apart from reporting procedures, can include time limits on mandates. Periodic reviews could enable the principal organ to review the subsidiary organ's activities, and ensure that they are exercised in accordance with the original

---

[149] MJ Tierney, 'Delegation Success and Policy Failure: Collective Delegation and the Search for Iraqi Weapons of Mass Destruction', 71 *Law and Contemporary Problems* (2008), 283 at 299–300.

mandate. The reason why this was not so arranged for UNSCOM was that members of the Council (such as the USA and the UK) did not agree to enable other Council members to prevent this organ's further operation, the cost of which was that neither could they themselves control UNSCOM's politically objectionable decisions. In some other cases, such as criminal and administrative tribunals, the control of a subsidiary organ's mandate through periodic review is inherently unsuitable as this would entail a political organ's interference with the administration of justice.

10. Regional Collective Security Institutions

(a) The African Union

Under its Articles 6 to 10, the African Union Constitutive Act, adopted in Lomé on 11 July 2000,[150] establishes the Assembly and Executive Council as its most important organs. The Assembly is composed of heads of state and government, and has a number of functions, including adoption of the Union's budget. The Executive Council is composed of ministers of foreign affairs. The Union's collective security system originates from the Protocol Establishing the AU Peace and Security Council that came into force in 2003.

The PSC was established to deal with all security issues.[151] The Protocol describes this organ 'as a standing decision-making organ for the prevention, management and resolution of conflicts' and 'a collective security and early-warning arrangement to facilitate timely and efficient response to conflict and crisis situations in Africa' (Article 2). The Council consists of fifteen members elected by the Assembly, ten of whom are elected for two years and five of whom for three years, to ensure continuity (Article 5). The principal objectives and functions of the Council include, under Articles 3 and 6, conflict prevention, peace-making efforts once conflicts have erupted, and development of a common defence policy. Specific powers under Article 7 are to

a. anticipate and prevent disputes and conflicts, as well as policies that may lead to genocide and crimes against humanity;
b. undertake peace-making and peace-building functions to resolve conflicts where they have occurred;
c. authorize the mounting and deployment of peace support missions;
d. lay down general guidelines for the conduct of such missions, including the mandate thereof, and undertake periodic reviews of these guidelines;
e. recommend to the Assembly, pursuant to Article 4(h) of the Constitutive Act, intervention, on behalf of the Union, in a Member State in respect of grave

---

[150] On the establishment of the AU and its structure in general see CAA Packer and D Rukare, 'The New African Union and Its Constitutive Act', 96 AJIL (2002), 365.
[151] J Levitt, 'The Peace and Security Council of the African Union and the United Nations Security Council: The Case of Darfur, Sudan', in N Blokker and N Schrijver (eds.), *The Security Council and the Use of Force* (Leiden: Martinus Nijhoff, 2005), 213 at 221.

circumstances, namely war crimes, genocide and crimes against humanity, as defined in relevant international conventions and instruments;

f. approve the modalities for intervention by the Union in a Member State, following a decision by the Assembly, pursuant to article 4(j) of the Constitutive Act;

g. institute sanctions whenever an unconstitutional change of Government takes place in a Member State, as provided for in the Lomé Declaration;

h. implement the common defense policy of the Union; . . .

o. examine and take such appropriate action within its mandate in situations where the national independence and sovereignty of a Member State is threatened by acts of aggression, including by mercenaries;

p. support and facilitate humanitarian action in situations of armed conflicts or major natural disasters;

q. submit, through its Chairperson, regular reports to the Assembly on its activities and the state of peace and security in Africa; and

r. decide on any other issue having implications for the maintenance of peace, security and stability on the Continent and exercise powers that may be delegated to it by the Assembly.

The Council's decisions have to be accepted and carried out by member States, which are also obliged to extend full cooperation to the Council's action and facilitate its operations (Article 7). The Council can meet at the level of permanent representatives, foreign ministers, or heads of state or government. It aims to operate by consensus, failing which procedural decisions are adopted by a simple majority and substantive decisions by a two-thirds majority (Article 8). The Chair of the Council—a position held by members of the Council in alphabetical order for one month each—is a focal point in communicating to the Council about situations that could threaten peace on the continent and about the progress of the Union's peace support missions (Article 10). The Protocol does not specify other entities or officials eligible to draw the Council's attention to situations falling within its mandate. Such right presumably accrues to each member of the Council.

Article 12 introduces a Continental Early Warning System which consists of

a. an observation and monitoring centre, to be known as 'The Situation Room', located at the Conflict Management Directorate of the Union, and responsible for data collection and analysis on the basis of an appropriate early warning indicators module; and

b. observation and monitoring units of the Regional Mechanisms to be linked directly through appropriate means of communications to the Situation Room, and which shall collect and process data at their level and transmit the same to the Situation Room.

The Council's chairperson reports to the Council on threats to the peace on the continent on the basis of information obtained through this system. The main instruments of the CEWS are reports compiled from open-source information that identifies potentially dangerous activities. These reports are the basis for PSC decisions, particularly over the possible deployment of the African Standby Forces.[152]

Under Article 13(2) of the Protocol, member States must take steps to establish an African Standby Force (ASF), to be involved in peace support missions decided on by the PSC or interventions authorized by the Assembly. The tasks for which the force can be used include observation, monitoring, peace keeping, and intervention. Article 13 also establishes the normative framework for a Military Staff Committee, which is required to advise and assist the PSC. Under Article 13(17) (a), after authorization by the PSC or the Assembly troop-contributing states shall immediately, upon request by the Commission, deploy standby contingents with the necessary equipment for the AU operations. According to Article 15(2), '[t]he African Standby Force shall be adequately equipped to undertake humanitarian activities in their mission areas under the control of the Chairperson of the Commission'.

The ASF is still in its early stages, and is intended to build up, by 2010, to five brigades with a strength of at least 3,000 troops each, ready to operate as an African Rapid Reaction Force.[153] In general, while the AU's peace-keeping potential is limited owing to resource constraints,[154] in practice it asserts a lead role in situations where it is getting involved jointly with the UN.

(b) The Economic Community of West African States (ECOWAS)

ECOWAS was originally established in 1975 as an organization to promote regional economic integration, as is clear from the preamble and Chapter II of the 1993 ECOWAS Revised Treaty. Article 7 of the Revised Treaty establishes the authority of heads of state and government as the supreme institution of the Community. The Authority's decisions are binding on member States. Article 10 establishes the Council of the Community. Article 12 determines that the Council shall act by regulations, which are binding on the institutions under the Council's authority. The Executive Secretary is appointed by the Authority (Article 18) and, according to Article 19, is 'the chief executive officer of the Community and all its institutions'. There is already a regional security dimension enshrined in the Revised Treaty, Article 58 of which provides for 'establishing and strengthening appropriate mechanisms for the timely prevention and resolution of intra-State and inter-State conflicts', more specifically to 'establish a regional peace and security observation system and peacekeeping forces', details to 'be defined in the relevant Protocols'.

---

[152] H Wulf and T Debiel, 'Conflict Early Warning and Response Mechanisms: Tools for Enhancing the Effectiveness of Regional Organisations? A Comparative Study of the AU, ECOWAS, IGAD, ASEAN/ARF and PIF', Crisis States Research Centre Working Paper Series No, 2, Working Paper No. 49, May 2009, 15; the early warning system is far from full operational: ibid, 17.

[153] Ibid, 14.

[154] Ibid, 15; it is also speculated that these factors can prevent the AU from fully realizing conflict prevention and security tasks that the OAU did not exercise: J Cilliers, 'Towards a Continental Early Warning System for Africa', ISS Paper 102 (Pretoria: Institute for Security Studies, April 2005), 3.

The Protocol on Non-Aggression, concluded at Lagos on 22 April 1978,[155] states in its preamble that ECOWAS cannot attain its objectives save in the atmosphere of peace in the region. Article 2 stipulates that 'Each Member State shall refrain, from committing, encouraging or condoning acts of subversion, hostility or aggression against the territorial integrity or political independence of the other Member States.' Disputes that cannot be settled peacefully shall be referred to the Authority or its committee (Article 5).

The Protocol on Mutual Assistance on Defence, concluded on 29 May 1981,[156] specifies in its preamble that 'economic progress cannot be achieved unless the conditions for the necessary security are ensured in all Member States of the Community'. The preamble views the continuous presence of foreign military bases on the African continent as possible support for aggression. The Protocol envisages the role of the Defence Council and the Defence Commission, alongside the Authority. The Defence Council is established by the authority of heads of state and consists of ministers of defence and foreign affairs (Article 7). A Defence Commission is established by the Authority, to consist of a Chief of Staff from each member State, and be responsible for technical aspects of defence matters.

The most important collective security instrument of ECOWAS is the Protocol relating to the Mechanism for Conflict Prevention, Management, Resolution, Peace-keeping and Security, adopted at Lomé on 10 December 1999. This Protocol establishes a conflict prevention mechanism, the objectives of which are, under Article 3, to

a. prevent, manage and resolve internal and inter-State conflicts under the conditions provided in Paragraph 46 of the Framework of the Mechanism ratified as per Decision A/DEC.11/10/98 of 31 October 1998;

b. implement the relevant provisions of Article 58 of the Revised Treaty;

c. implement the relevant provisions of the Protocols on Non-Aggression, Mutual Assistance in Defence, Free Movement of Persons, the Right of Residence and Establishment;

d. strengthen cooperation in the areas of conflict prevention, early-warning, peace-keeping operations, the control of cross-border crime, international terrorism and proliferation of small arms and anti-personnel mines; . . .

h. constitute and deploy a civilian and military force to maintain or restore peace within the sub-region, whenever the need arises.

The Protocol establishes a Mediation and Security Council, which comprises nine member States of which seven are elected by the Authority. The other two members are the current chairperson and the immediate past chairperson of the Authority (Articles 4 and 8). Although under Article 6 the Authority remains the highest decision-making body in the area of conflict management and peace keeping, Article 7 mandates the MSC, on the Assembly's behalf, to take

---

[155] UNTS 1690, No I–29136 (1992), 40.
[156] UNTS 1690, No I–29137 (1992), 52.

'appropriate decisions for the implementation of the provisions of this Mechanism'. As provided in Article 9, the MSC decides by two-thirds of its members' votes. More specifically, under Article 10 the Assembly must

a. decide on all matters relating to peace and security;
b. decide and implement all policies for conflict prevention, management and resolution, peace-keeping and security;
c. authorise all forms of intervention and decide particularly on the deployment of political and military missions;
d. approve mandates and terms of reference for such missions;
e. review the mandates and terms of reference periodically, on the basis of evolving situations;
f. on the recommendation of the Executive Secretary, appoint the Special Representative of the Executive Secretary and the Force Commander.

Article 11 provides that the Council will deliberate at the levels of heads of state and government, ministers, and ambassadors. Heads of state meet twice a year, and extraordinary meetings may be called. Meetings at ministerial level are held once every three months, or as needed 'to review the general political and security situation in the sub-region'. The ambassador-level meeting takes place once a month and reviews issues relating to sub-regional security. These procedures carry an important preventative function, enabling the Council to keep the security situation under control. A related function is vested in the Executive Secretary who, under Article 15, has 'the power to initiate actions for conflict prevention, management, resolution, peace-keeping and security in the sub-region. Such actions may include fact-finding, mediation, facilitation, negotiation and reconciliation of parties in conflict.' The Executive Secretary can convene meetings of the MSC and the Defence and Security Commission, deploy fact-finding and mediation missions, and implement the Council's decisions. Thus, the Executive Secretary can play the role of focal point in delivering information to other organs as to the security situation on which the functioning of those other organs depends.

The role of Executive Secretary, however, is not exclusive. Article 26 of the Protocol states that

[t]he Mechanism shall be put into effect by any of the following: a) Upon the decision of the Authority; b) Upon the decision of the Mediation and Security Council; c) At the request of a Member State; d) On the initiative of the Executive Secretary; e) At request of the Organization of African Unity or the United Nations.

The ECOWAS Peace and Security Observation System under Chapter IV of the 1999 Protocol consists of a sub-regional peace and security observation system known as the Early Warning System. This system consists of an Observation and Monitoring Centre located at the Secretariat and Observation and Monitoring Zones within the sub-region. Under Article 24, 'Member States shall be divided into zones on the basis of proximity, ease of communication and efficiency. Each zone shall be identified by a number and each shall have a zonal headquarters', which in their turn maintain working relations with local institutions.

Under Article 27, '[t]he Mediation and Security Council shall consider several options and decide on the most appropriate course of action to take in terms of intervention. Such options may include recourse to the Council of Elders, the dispatch of fact-finding missions, political and mediation missions, or intervention by ECOMOG.' The ECOWAS action in the Liberian crisis was presumably based on the Protocol relating to Mutual Assistance on Defence (PMAD),[157] consent by the Liberian Government arguably compensating for deficiencies in the legal basis for that operation.

ECOMOG was established at the first session of the Community Standing Committee in 1990.[158] Broad but careful definition of ECOMOG tasks is contained in Article 22 of the 1999 Protocol. Article 21 of the Protocol specifies that '[t]he ECOWAS Cease-fire Monitoring Group (ECOMOG) is a structure composed of several Stand-by multi-purpose modules (civilian and military) in their countries of origin and ready for immediate deployment'. In Article 22, ECOMOG is charged, among others, with the following missions:

a. Observation and Monitoring;
b. Peace-keeping and restoration of peace;
c. Humanitarian intervention in support of humanitarian disaster;
d. Enforcement of sanctions, including embargo;
e. Preventive deployment;
f. Peace-building, disarmament and demobilisation;
g. Policing activities, including the control of fraud and organised crime;
h. Any other operations as may be mandated by the Mediation and Security Council.

Under Article 28 of the Protocol member States agree to make available to ECOMOG enough units and adequate resources for the army, air force, navy, gendarmerie, police, and all other military, paramilitary, or civil formations necessary for the accomplishment of the mission. Each member State provides ECOMOG with a unit the size of which is determined after consultation with each member State. This may be the most significant provision, not because it establishes stand-by forces, which was also the case with PMAD, but because it places them under the direct control of the MSC.[159] It is observed that 'since June 2006, ECOWAS has had a rapid response force at its command—the Standby Brigade (ECOBRIG) consisting of up to 6,500 soldiers. Compared to other

---

[157] Protocol concluded at Freetown, 29 May 1981. A Abass, 'The New Collective Security Mechanism of ECOWAS: Innovations and Problems', 5 *Journal of Conflict and Security Law* (2000), 211 at 214, 220–1, further specifying that ECOWAS manifested its position as acting pursuant to PMAD, and that the criticisms of this operation related to PMAD lacking the power to use force against a state.

[158] At the meeting at Banjul in The Gambia on 6–7 July 1990; cf Abass, ibid, 213.

[159] Abass, ibid, 218. The term 'Allied Armed Forces' under PMAD envisaged national contingents provided to ECOWAS in the case of emergency.

African regional organisations ECOWAS has evolved into a front runner for security and political integration.'[160] Furthermore, 'ECOMOG is the core of the newly formed West African brigade, intended to be able to deploy 5,000 soldiers and civilians within 90 days as well as 1,500 within 30 days.'[161]

The adoption of the 1999 Protocol has manifested a significant expansion of the security dimension in the ECOWAS legal framework, most notably adding the collective security function to collective defence and the 'traditional' peace keeping under PMAD that only allowed for the deployment of interpository troops in conflicts between member States. As indicated, the 1999 Protocol contrasts with PMAD, which stated in its Article 18 that the Community would not intervene in a purely internal conflict.[162]

(c) Southern African Development Community (SADC)

The original Declaration and Treaty establishing the SADC was adopted on 17 August 1992, and its consolidated amended version on 14 August 2001. Under Article 9, the principal organs of SADC include the Summit of Heads of State or Government, the Organ on Politics, Defence, and Security Co-operation, and the Council of Ministers. A chairperson and deputy chairperson of the Organ on Politics, Defence, and Security Co-operation are elected, as specified in Article 10 of the Consolidated Treaty, by the Summit of Heads of State or Government. Article 10 also requires the structure, functions, powers, and procedures of the organ and other related matters to be prescribed in a separate Protocol.

The SADC Protocol on Politics, Defence, and Security Co-operation further specifies the role and functions of the Organ on Politics, Defence, and Security Co-operation.[163] The Protocol's preamble is premised on recognition under Chapter VIII of the UN Charter of the role of regional arrangements in dealing with such peace and security matters as are appropriate for regional action.

The Organ is accountable to the SADC Summit and reports to it. The Organ has the following structures: the chairperson, the Troika, a Ministerial Committee, an Inter-State Politics and Diplomacy Committee (ISPDC), an Inter-State Defence and Security Committee (ISDSC), and such other sub-structures as may be established by any of the ministerial committees, to implement policies in relevant areas (Articles 3, 6–7). The Troika consists of the chairperson of the Organ, the incoming chairperson (who becomes the deputy chairperson), and the outgoing chairperson. The Ministerial Committee, which comprises the ministers responsible for foreign affairs, defence, public security, and state security from each of the

---

[160] Wulf and Debiel, n 152 above, 17.

[161] Ibid, 16.

[162] Abass, n 157 above, 214. However, Article 18(2) provides that, if an internal conflict in a member State is maintained from outside, Community intervention can be conducted under Articles 6 and 9 PMAD (which relate to intervention in inter-state conflicts through Allied Armed Forces of the Community, and specify the arrangements, including the role of the Authority, Defence Council, Defence Commission, and Force Commander).

[163] Adopted on 14 August 2001.

State-parties, is responsible for coordinating the work of the Organ and its structures (Articles 4–5). Article 11 of the Protocol defines the Organ's tasks as managing conflicts by peaceful means (including preventative action) and early warning. Enforcement action is envisaged only with the UN Security Council's authorization under Article 53 of the Charter, and external military threats would be addressed through the separate Mutual Defence Pact.

(d) The Inter-Governmental Authority on Development (IGAD)

The IGAD superseded the Intergovernmental Authority on Drought and Development (IGADD) established in 1986 by six Eastern African countries then afflicted by drought: Djibouti, Ethiopia, Kenya, Somalia, Sudan, and Uganda. Although IGADD was originally intended to coordinate the efforts of member States to combat drought and desertification, it became increasingly apparent that it provided a regular forum where leaders of Eastern African countries could tackle other political and socio-economic issues. This was the principal impetus behind the adoption of the Agreement establishing IGAD.[164]

The IGAD Agreement Article 6 mentions among its principles '[n]on-interference in the internal affairs of Member States; The peaceful settlement of inter- and intra-State conflicts through dialogue; Maintenance of regional peace, stability and security'. Under Article 7, purposes include '[p]romote peace and stability in the sub-region and create mechanisms within the sub-region for the prevention, management and resolution of inter and intra-State conflicts through dialogue'.

IGAD has no special organ responsible for peace and security.[165] Under Article 9 (1), '[t]he Assembly of Heads of State and Government is the supreme organ of the Authority'. It is the main policy-making organ and adopts its decisions by consensus. Under Article 9(2)(c), the Assembly issues guidelines and monitors political issues regarding conflict prevention, management, and resolution. Under Article 10 (1), the Council of Ministers 'shall be composed of the Ministers of Foreign Affairs and one other focal Minister who shall be designated by each Member State'; its functions include making appropriate recommendations to the Assembly, including in relation to conflict prevention and resolution. Article 18 provides that

Member States shall act collectively to preserve peace, security and stability which are essential prerequisites for economic development and social progress. Accordingly Member States shall: a) take effective collective measures to eliminate threats to regional co-operation peace and stability; b) establish an effective mechanism of consultation and cooperation for the pacific settlement of differences and disputes; c) accept to deal with disputes between Member States within this sub-regional mechanism before they are referred to other regional or international organisations.

---

[164] Adopted in Nairobi, 21 March 1996, IGAD/SUM–96/AGRE–Doc; see also Cilliers, n 154 above, 12.
[165] Wulf and Debiel, n 152 above, 18.

IGAD's Conflict Early Warning and Response Mechanism (CEWARN) was established in 2000 to respond to multiple crises in the East African region. In 2002, at the summit in Khartoum, this decision was implemented through the adoption of the Protocol on the Establishment of a Conflict Early Warning and Response Mechanism for IGAD Member States, which made CEWARN an integrated structure of IGAD (Article 2). Article 1 of the Annex to the Protocol specifies the CEWARN mandate as mainly consisting in 'receive and share information concerning potentially violent conflicts as well as their outbreak and escalation in the IGAD region'. Upon receipt of that information 'the Executive Secretary shall immediately bring that information to the attention of the Committee of Permanent Secretaries'.

The Mechanism's tasks include conflict prevention by reporting on all violent conflicts in a broadly defined human security area and not just on national or state security. Operationally, CEWARN established a network of field monitors, country coordinators, national research institutes, and conflict–Early Warning Report (EWR) units at the national level, and began its work in two pilot areas on pastoral conflicts in the cross-border areas of Ethiopia, Kenya, Uganda, Sudan, Ethiopia, and Somalia. CEWARN uses a set of 52 socio-political indicators for two types of report: violent incident reports with indicators on armed clashes, raids, protest demonstrations, and other incidents; and indicators for reports on the presence and status of communal relations, civil society activities, economic activities, governance and media, natural disasters, safety and security, and social services. This arguably makes CEWARN the most developed early-warning mechanism in Africa.[166]

(e) The Economic Community of Central African States (ECCAS)

ECCAS was established in 1981 with the aim of promoting economic cooperation and integration. In 1999 it acknowledged that economic development was contingent on the peace and security status in the region, and decided to establish the Peace and Security Council for Central Africa (COPAX). In June 1999, heads of state and government agreed to adopt the Protocol on COPAX and formally integrated this organ into the ECCAS structure. The Protocol provides for the establishment of a Commission for Defence and Security, a Multinational Peace Force in Central Africa (FOMAC), and an Early Warning, Observation, and Monitoring System (MARAC).[167] MARAC's tasks include the collection and analysis of data with the primary purpose of assisting ECCAS in conflict prevention, management, and resolution activities. It has an observation and analysis centre and zonal observation and analysis centres (Article 22 of the COPAX Protocol).

---

[166] Wulf and Debiel, n 152 above, 19.
[167] In October 2002 ECCAS established the Central African multinational force—FOMAC—to be stationed in the Central African Republic at the request of the President of CAR, and to contribute to security and national reconciliation. See M Zwarenburg, 'Regional Organisations and the Maintenance of International Peace and Security: Three Recent Regional African Peace Operations', 11 *Journal of Conflict and Security Law* (2006), 483 at 499–500.

The decision adopted by ECCAS Heads and Governments on 17 June 2002 contains Standing Orders for MARAC. Article 1 of this decision specifies that MARAC 'shall be responsible for data collection and analysis in order to prevent crises and conflicts'. Article 10 specifies multiple sources from which MARAC is supposed to obtain its information, including governments, international organizations, non-governmental organizations, and research institutions, thus precluding grounds for pleading ignorance.

(f) The League of Arab States

In September 1944, a session of the Preparatory Committee of the General Arab Congress was held in Alexandria, attended by Egypt, Syria, Lebanon, Iraq, Saudi Arabia, and Transjordan, while Yemen was represented as an observer.[168] The Alexandria Protocol of 7 October 1944 specified that '[a] League will be formed of the independent Arab States which consent to join the League', with the 'Council of the League of Arab States' representing Arab states on an equal footing. In 1945, the Preparatory Committee was reconvened to consider the draft Pact of the Arab League, which was approved by the General Arab Congress on 22 March 1945. According to Article 1 of the Pact, the League is open to independent Arab states. Article 3 establishes a League Council, which is considered the supreme political organ of the League, with central responsibilities for dispute settlement and collective security.[169] Jurisdiction of the Council is specified under Article 5 which deals with dispute settlement, and Article 6 which deals with responses to aggression. According to Article 7, '[t]he decisions of the Council taken by a unanimous vote shall be binding on all the member States of the League; those that are reached by a majority vote shall bind only those that accept them'. The Secretary-General is appointed by a two-thirds majority (Article 12).

It has been traditional to hold summit conferences of the League, representing members at the highest level. The preponderant view has been that Summit Conferences should be regarded as sessions of the Council.[170] A Political Committee was established by the Council in November 1946 and has become a major policy organ of League decision making. Its work overlaps with that of the Council.[171] It seems that essentially in practice there is one single organ as between the Council, the Summit Conference, and the Political Committee.

In 1950, the Joint Defence and Economic Cooperation Treaty was concluded to strengthen the security dimension of the League. It has established a Joint Defence Council, the responsibility of which is to implement provisions of Articles 2 to 5 of the Treaty. The Council consists of the foreign ministers and the defence ministers

---

[168] I Pogany, 'The League of Arab States: An Overview', 21 *Bihar Law Journal* (1989), 41 at 43–4; M Khadduri, 'The Arab League as a Regional Arrangement', 40 AJIL (1946), 756 at 763; on the founding of the Arab League see also HN Howard, 'Middle Eastern Regional Organization: Problems and Prospects', 24(4) *Proceedings of the Academy of Political Science* (1952), 101.

[169] Pogany, ibid, 51.

[170] Ibid, 53–4.

[171] Ibid, 56.

of the contracting States or their representatives. Decisions taken by a two-thirds majority are binding on all contracting States (Article 6). The Annex to the Treaty specifies the tasks of a Permanent Military Commission, which consist in preparations and practical arrangements to carry out Treaty commitments to respond to security threats. According to Article 3 of the Treaty,

[a]t the invitation of any one of the signatories of this Treaty the Contracting States shall hold consultations whenever there are reasonable grounds for the belief that the territorial integrity, independence, or security of any one of the parties is threatened. In the event of the threat of war or the existence of an international emergency, the Contracting States shall immediately proceed to unify their plans and defensive measures, as the situation may demand.

As pointed out, the nature and type of sanctions is not defined.[172] The conclusion is that the Arab League treaties have not established an effective system of collective security.[173] However the League framework has been influential in articulating common positions of Arab states on the collective security process.

(g) The Organization of Islamic Conference (OIC)

The OIC originated in Islamic Summit Conferences held in 1969 and 1972. Its Charter was adopted in 1972, and a revised version replaced it, on adoption by the OIC Council of Foreign Ministers on 14 March 2008. The preamble and Article I list OIC objectives, which mainly relate to enhancing solidarity among Islamic states. Article 2 proclaims subjection to the principles of the UN Charter, and Article 3 specifies that any state having a Muslim majority can become a member. The organs of the OIC are, for pertinent purposes, the Islamic Summit (which is composed of heads of state and government and takes policy decisions—Articles 6 and 7), the Council of Foreign Ministers (which considers means of implementing these policies—Article 10), and a number of standing committees (Article 11).

OIC has no free-standing security structure and has not purported to conduct collective security activities. The organization is constrained to respect the domestic jurisdictions of its members (Article 2(6)). However, there is no injunction in the OIC Charter to develop a security element, either by amending the Charter, adopting an additional protocol, or through organizational practice. The principal relevance of the OIC in the collective security process has so far been its influence, as an organization consisting of 57 states covering several regions of the world, over collective security decisions of other organizations such as the UN, illustrated by the OIC role in shaping the Security Council's reaction to the crisis in Lebanon in 2006; or its pronouncements on the legality of Security Council measures such as the sanctions imposed on Libya in 1992.

---

[172] Khadduri, n 168 above, 768.
[173] Pogany, n 168 above, 63.

(h) The Organization of American States (OAS)

The Organization of American States assumes a comprehensive security competence in relation to the American hemisphere. From the 1930s, the Inter-American Conference was the supreme organ, but amendments to the OAS Charter replaced it with the OAS General Assembly, which under Article 54 of the Charter is designated as the supreme organ of OAS, deciding on the organization's policies. Article 84 of the OAS Charter provides that '[t]he Permanent Council shall keep vigilance over the maintenance of friendly relations among the Member States, and for that purpose shall effectively assist them in the peaceful settlement of their disputes'. Under Article 87 the Council may, 'by such means as it deems advisable, investigate the facts in the dispute, and may do so in the territory of any of the parties, with the consent of the Government concerned'.

The Meeting of Consultation of Foreign Ministers is an organ of consultation, which exercises functions comparable to the UN Security Council.[174] Inter-American security consultation at the foreign minister level originated in the inter-war period.[175] The Meeting is supposed to meet to deal with any situation under Articles 3 and 6 of the Rio Treaty, so is thus a

decisional body established by the Rio Treaty to deal with threats to the peace.... it can utilize the enforcement powers granted by the Rio Treaty. In either role, the Meeting of Consultation is not held at regular intervals, but is convened only at a member's request, directed to the Council of the OAS.[176]

As Article 61 of he OAS Charter specifies, '[t]he Meeting of Consultation of Ministers of Foreign Affairs shall be held in order to consider problems of an urgent nature and of common interest to the American States, and to serve as the Organ of Consultation'. As pointed out,

the Council cannot go on to act as a provisional Organ of Consultation until it has first determined that the situation warrants the calling of a Meeting of Consultation. The discussion by the Council of the character of a situation presented to it cannot, therefore, be made the occasion for the determination of the measures to be taken to meet the situation or the sanctions to be applied. That is a second step entirely distinct from the first.[177]

Traditionally the Council has respected its subordination to the titular organ of consultation by restricting itself to handling cases which appeared amenable to resolution by negotiation, persuasion, and peaceful procedures.[178] However,

---

[174] J Kunz, 'The Bogota Charter of the OAS', 42 AJIL (1948), 568 at 577.

[175] R Barliant, 'The OAS Peace and Security System', 21 *Stanford Law Review* (1969) 1156 at 1158.

[176] Ibid, 1165; see also Article 62 of the OAS Charter.

[177] CG Fenwick, 'The Competence of the Council of the Organization of American States', 43 AJIL (1949), 772 at 774.

[178] J Dreier, 'The Council of the OAS: Performance and Potential', 5 *Journal of Inter-American Studies* (1963), 297 at 306.

decisions of the Sixth Meeting of Foreign Ministers marked a substantial expansion of the Council's powers. In the matter of Venezuelan allegations against the Dominican Republic, the Meeting of Foreign Ministers assigned to the Council the highly important political task of deciding upon the adoption of additional economic sanctions against the aggressor government, and of determining when the sanctions adopted or authorized by the Meeting of Foreign Ministers should be terminated. The implication is that 'the juridical formula that the Council could exercise powers of the Inter-American Treaty on Reciprocal Assistance 1947 (Rio Treaty) only provisionally and *before* a meeting of Foreign Ministers was discarded'. The relaxation of the strict juridical limitations on the Council's powers 'opens other doors to the further development of the role which the Council may in the future play', particularly by using the doctrine of implied powers, as this might bear upon the Council's decision whether or not to convoke a Meeting of Consultation.[179] Thus there are prospects of institutional powers evolving through practice.

The causes of action for the OAS collective security mechanism are provided in Articles 3 and 6 of the Rio Treaty. Article 3 specifies the consequences of any armed attack against a member State, whether by an American or an extra-hemispheric state.[180] However, Article 6 (which covers threats other than armed attack) has been more important than Article 3 in the development of the security system in the Americas.[181]

Article 17 of the Rio Treaty specifies that decisions are adopted by a two-thirds majority. According to Article 20 '[d]ecisions which require the application of the measures specified in Article 8 shall be binding upon all the Signatory States which have ratified this Treaty, with the sole exception that no State shall be required to use armed force without its consent'. Thus, the OAS can impose binding enforcement measures. As specified, however, 'the members have never taken steps to enforce this obligation when one of them has failed to fulfill it'.[182]

In 1940, the Meeting of Foreign Ministers in Havana adopted a resolution on 'Peaceful Solution of Conflicts', recommending the institution of a committee of five members which should keep 'constant vigilance to [e]nsure that States between which any dispute exists or may arise, of any nature whatsoever, may solve it as quickly as possible'. The committee was authorized to suggest the measures and steps conducive to that end. Originally it was known as the Inter-American Committee on Methods for the Peaceful Solution of Conflicts. Its first involvement came in the dispute between the Dominican Republic and Cuba, in which the Committee ensured that negotiations were renewed; when, later, the Council thought it unadvisable to convoke the Meeting of Foreign Ministers because the situation between Haiti and the Dominican Republic was not sufficiently grave, the Committee intervened and secured adoption by the parties of a joint declaration in which they undertook not to tolerate in their territories the activities of individuals

[179] Ibid, 306–10 (emphasis in original).
[180] See further Chapter 6.
[181] Barliant, n 175 above, 1158–9; see further Chapter 4.
[182] Ibid, 1159.

and groups aiming to disturb the domestic peace in another country. The Committee then adopted the name 'Inter-American Peace Committee', and got involved in multiple controversies subsequently. The most important feature of the Committee is that it fills the gap between bilateral procedures and the Consultation Mechanism under the Rio Treaty.[183] It could thus be said that the Committee's role overlaps with that of the UN Security Council under Chapter VI.

The interaction between OAS organs manifests the absence of *litis pendens* between them. By a Resolution of 9 June 2009, the OAS General Assembly repealed the decision of the Eighth Meeting of Consultation of Ministers of Foreign Affairs, which excluded the government of Cuba from participation in the Inter-American system.[184] Effectively, one organ reversed the decision adopted by another.

(i) The Association of Southeast Asian Nations (ASEAN)

The ASEAN conflict prevention mechanism operates mainly through intergovernmental meetings at head of state or foreign minister level. An attempt was made to establish a formal conflict management mechanism through the 1976 Treaty of Amity and Cooperation, which set in place a code of conduct based on fundamental rules of international law such as sovereign equality, non-interference, and territorial integrity. Articles 14 and 15 provide for a High Council competent to recommend the settlement of disputes through means including mediation and conciliation.

The Council has not so far been constituted and no state has ever relied on the dispute-resolution provisions of the Treaty. Despite a long-standing, traditional preference for preventative diplomacy through unstructured, informal, and consensus-based arrangements, the 1990s brought about a shift in regional security thinking. The establishment of the ASEAN Regional Forum (ARF) was a major indicator of this change. However it is doubted whether ASEAN could confront a major military crisis in its region, and function as an effective collective security institution in the short or medium term.[185]

In 1999 the ASEAN Troika was established, comprising past, current, and incoming chairpeople of the organization. It is meant to be guided by the principles of consensus and non-interference. Not much progress has been reported in the work of the Troika. ASEAN's record has been described as not having resolved any conflict; all it has done is to prevent conflicts. It has facilitated discussions on sensitive issues related to Myanmar, Korea, and the South China Sea. Its 'soft' approach has helped it to defuse potential conflicts.[186] In general, consensus,

---

[183] CG Fenwick, 'Inter-American Regional Procedures for the Settlement of Disputes', 10 *International Organization* (1956), 12 at 19.

[184] Resolution on Cuba, AG/RES. 2438 (XXXIX–O/09), 9 June 2009, para 1.

[185] J Morris and H McCoubrey, 'Regional Peacekeeping in the Post-Cold War Era', 6 *International Peacekeeping* (1999), 129 at 144–5.

[186] M Caballero-Anthony, 'The Regionalisation of Peace in Asia', in M Pugh and WPS Sidhu (ed.), *The United Nations and Regional Security—Europe and Beyond* (Boulder: Lynne Rienner Inc, 2003), 195 at 198–9, 201–2; C Samli and WPS Sidhu, 'Strengthening Regional Approaches to Peace Operations', in ibid, 255 at 261.

non-confrontation, and non-interference form the basic principles of the ASEAN security and conflict resolution approach.

Given that, it is questionable whether ASEAN can fit within any acceptable definition of collective security, and it therefore could offer little in terms of collective security efforts, particularly peace-enforcement activities. However, consensual peace keeping could still be arranged under the aegis of ASEAN. ASEAN could potentially be a Chapter VI 'task manager' under Article 52 of the UN Charter; but is unsuitable for Article 53 authorization because it has no appropriate assets; still, the option of the 'able and willing' taking an enforcement action cannot be discounted. The implied powers doctrine could enable ASEAN to take matters further; that it has not yet done so is the Association's political choice, not due to lack of legal capacity.

Importantly, the 1995 ARF Concept Paper specifies the security dimension ASEAN could engage with, in terms of a comprehensive approach to peace and security and its inter-relatedness to economic growth (similar to ECOWAS). ASEAN states 'should acknowledge that periods of rapid economic growth are often accompanied by significant shifts in power relations. This can lead to conflict. The ARF will have to carefully manage these transitions to preserve the peace.'[187] The Concept Paper goes on to elaborate upon the ways to promote security and peace within the ASEAN zone, such as confidence- and security-building measures, preventative diplomacy, and conflict resolution.

ARF has not been given an independent role in conflict management, to some extent because China has resisted that idea. In none of the major acute crises in its region—Aceh, East Timor, Burma, Tibet—did ASEAN play an important role, and it has no early warning mechanism.[188] Furthermore, ASEAN's limited vision of its security mandate goes hand-in-hand with the 1992 Singapore Declaration, in which ASEAN Heads of State and Government emphasized ASEAN's commitment to the centrality of the UN role in the maintenance of international peace and security.[189]

(j) The Pacific Island Forum

The Pacific Island Forum has no security organ and merely constitutes a dialogue forum on security issues; nor does it have an early warning mechanism,[190] and its security mandate remains in an embryonic state. Yet its positions can be legitimate regional attitudes and thus count in the complementarity and subsidiarity equations. The 2002 Biketawa Declaration emphasizes the principle of non-interference in domestic affairs. The Declaration 'has been invoked twice since its promulgation

---

[187] ARF Concept Paper (1995), para 5.
[188] Wulf and Debiel, n 152 above, 21–2.
[189] Singapore Declaration 1992, para 3, 31 ILM (1992), 499.
[190] Wulf and Debiel, n 152 above, 23–4.

in 2000, with the Regional Assistance Mission to the Solomon Islands and the Pacific Regional Assistance for Nauru.'[191]

(k) The North Atlantic Treaty Organization (NATO)

NATO was established by the North Atlantic Treaty concluded at Washington in 1949, framing the Organization as a defensive alliance. Article 3 of the Treaty stipulates the duty of continuous preparedness of the allies to defend themselves, and each other, against armed attack. According to Article 4, '[t]he Parties will consult together whenever, in the opinion of any of them, the territorial integrity, political independence or security of any of the Parties is threatened'. Alliance decisions are the product of a consultation process which is meant as more than a mere exchange of views that happen to be unalterable final intentions.[192] Arguably this concept of consultation has commanded the status of a special custom of the Alliance.[193] Article 4 not only obliges consultations to occur when a threat is perceived, but also requires that no member State should act unilaterally before consultations are held.[194] This approach relies on purposive interpretation of Article 4. However, as Schwarzenberger observed, NATO members have no obligation under Article 4 beyond being committed to consultation.[195] There have been a number of instances of serious crises involving NATO members which took decisions before consulting the NATO Council, such as the arms embargo imposed by the USA on Turkey after its invasion of Cyprus and the Turkish retaliatory closure of American bases on its territory. Nor did Britain and France consult NATO regarding their action in Suez; nor the USA before invading the Bay of Pigs and the Dominican Republic in the 1960s.[196] However, these actions did not require consultation as they were simply outside Article 4 and were thus not the ones on which the Alliance is supposed to make decisions.

The Treaty does not provide any procedure for adopting the Council's acts, nor define its legal form and force. NATO has made no provision regarding the effect of its acts. As suggested,

one must analyse and interpret each Council act in its context in order to determine its normative impact. To the extent a resolution purported to impose an obligation,

---

[191] Ibid, 23; in the case of the Solomon Islands, the PIF approved a wide package of measures to strengthen the security and economic sector of the Islands, at the latter's request: Zwarenburg, n 167 above, 505.

[192] As affirmed in the report of the 'Three Wise Men' appointed to improve consultation within NATO: *Report of the Committee of Three on Non-Military Cooperation in NATO*, 23 October 1956, CT–WP/7 (Final), 16 (para 13).

[193] F Kirgis, 'NATO Consultations as a Component of National Decision-making', 73 AJIL (1979), 372 at 373.

[194] Ibid, 374–5.

[195] G Schwarzenberger, 'The North Atlantic Pact', 2 *Western Political Quarterly* (1949), 309 at 312.

[196] Kirgis, n 193 above, 386–7, 398–9.

member States in principle have acted as if they were bound by reason of their concurrence.[197]

In general, NATO acts are said to be of four types: internal decisions relating to administration; decisions prescribing rules of conduct for member States, such as those related to command and control structures, and to establishment of subsidiary organs; guidelines regarding common policies; and agreements reached within the Council or between the Council and a member.[198]

The Council has normally followed the unanimity approach as this suited the purpose of securing united action. If a member does not wish to participate in a decision nor oppose its implementation, the adopted decision will be effective for all members except the non-participant.[199] The Alliance's organs can never adopt mandatory decisions to impose military coercive measures upon member states.[200]

Even if NATO Council documents are political declarations, some unanimously accepted declarations could still constitute international agreements laying obligations on members. Considering the extensive expenditures and investments made in reliance of certain NATO arrangements, arguably member States can be estopped from denying such obligations to the serious detriment of the Organization and the other members.[201]

The Article 5 commitment to collective defence remains the principal *raison d'être* of NATO,[202] through geographic parameters imposed by Article 6 in relation to that commitment. Article 6 is thus seen as an impediment to NATO redefining its role, in which it has been engaged from the 1990s onwards.[203] The 1999 Strategic Concept emphasizes that the Alliance 'not only ensures the defence of its members but contributes to peace and stability in this region'.[204] The Strategic Concept further specifies that, while 'any armed attack on the territory of the Allies, from whatever direction, would be covered by Articles 5 and 6 of the Washington Treaty', alliance security interests can be affected by other risks of a wider nature, including acts of terrorism, sabotage, and organized crime, and by the disruption of the flow of vital resources, or the uncontrolled movement of large numbers of people, particularly as a consequence of armed conflicts. The existing NATO arrangements under Article 4 should cover new activities.[205]

It seems that these new fields of competence relate, not to NATO's implied powers (which can only exist on the basis of enabling the Alliance to effectively carry out its defensive function), but as a consensually agreed expansion to cover

---

[197] E Stein and D Carreau, 'Law and Peaceful Change in a Subsystem: "Withdrawal" of France from the North Atlantic Treaty Organization', 62 AJIL (1968), 577 at 608.
[198] Ibid, 608–10.
[199] Ibid, 606–8.
[200] T Gazzini, 'NATO's Role in the Collective Security System', 8 *Journal of Conflict and Security Law* (2003), 243.
[201] Stein and Carreau, n 197 above, 613.
[202] For detail see Chapter 6 below.
[203] Morris and McCoubrey, n 185 above, 138.
[204] Para 6.
[205] Ibid, para 24.

tasks qualitatively different from those set out in Article 5. The 1994 NATO Summit Declaration reaffirmed the readiness to perform these tasks under the authority of the UN Security Council.[206] To perform these non-Article 5 tasks, NATO has developed the required capabilities. The 1994 Brussels Ministerial Meeting endorsed the concept of Combined Joint Task Forces (CJTF) to enable more flexible and mobile deployment of NATO forces, including the establishment of new missions.[207]

The creation of a NATO Response Force (NRF) was proposed by Defence Secretary Rumsfeld at the NATO defence ministers' meeting on 25 September 2002, as a 21,000-strong force, of all three services. The 2002 Prague Summit likewise specified the intention to create a NATO response force. The initial operating capability was attained by 2003 and war games have been conducted since then.[208] The full operational capability of NRF was announced at the 2006 NATO summit in Riga.[209]

(l) The Western European Union (WEU)

The WEU was originally established under the 1954 Modified Brussels Treaty as a defence alliance obliging member States to provide assistance if one of the contracting parties should suffer armed attack (Article V). But the treaty framework does not limit the WEU to self-defence: it also provides for collective security arrangements. Article VIII(3) of the Modified Brussels Treaty provides that '[a]t the request of any of the High Contracting Parties the [WEU] Council shall be immediately convened in order to permit Them to consult with regard to any situation which may constitute a threat to peace'.

The WEU has allotted itself an operational role outside the core task of common defence, by adopting the Petersberg Declaration of 19 June 1992, stating its readiness to undertake humanitarian and rescue tasks, peace-keeping tasks, and sending combat forces in crisis management, including peace-making, to support (on a case-by-case basis) implementation of conflict prevention and crisis management measures mandated by the Organization for Security and Co-operation in Europe (OSCE) or UN Security Council.[210] In addition, the Petersberg Declaration has defined further tasks which the WEU may undertake outside Europe. But the Declaration is ultra vires the functions of the Council of Ministers because, even though the WEU Treaty does not explicitly provide for such an evolution of the organization's activities, it does not prevent this development from taking place,

---

[206] *Declaration of the Heads of State and Government*, Brussels, 11 January 1994, para 7.
[207] Ministerial Meeting of the North Atlantic Council/North Atlantic Cooperation Council, NATO Headquarters, Brussels, 10–11 January 1994, para 1, NATO Press Communiqué M–1 (94)–3; Berlin Final Communiqué, 3 June 1996, NATO Press Communiqué M–NAC–1(96)63.
[208] M Reichard, *The EU–NATO Relationship* (Aldershot: Ashgate, 2006), 232–5.
[209] NATO Riga Summit Declaration, 26 November 2006, para 23.
[210] S Graf von Kielmansegg, 'The Meaning of Petersberg: Some Considerations on the Legal Scope of ESDP Operations', 44 *European Foreign Affairs Review* (2007), 629; J Woodliffe, 'The Evolution of a New NATO for a New Europe', 47 ICLQ (1998), 174 at 189.

and these activities certainly respond to purposes of the Modified Brussels Treaty.[211] In practice, the WEU has carried out a number of peace operations, mainly consisting in maritime interdiction activities in support of UN sanctions against Iraq and the FRY. With the acquisition by the EU of independent crisis management and military capacities, WEU tasks and facilities have been gradually overtaken by the Community. A decision to abolish the WEU was adopted in 2010, to take effect in 2011, due to the entry into force of the Lisbon EU Treaty.[212]

(m) The European Union (EU)

The European Security and Defence Policy (ESDP) capitalizes on the European Union's long-standing aspiration to acquire an independent capability to perform collective security tasks. The origins of the ESDP can be traced back to the 1954 amendment of the Brussels Treaty establishing the WEU.[213] With the 1992 Maastricht Treaty the potential of the WEU was brought to the forefront, as a basis for developing the European Union's own defence and security arm. A Declaration on the WEU attached to the Treaty stated that the 'WEU will be developed as the defence component of the European Union'.[214] From 1999 the option of the WEU acting under the Petersberg Declaration and undertaking peace support activities under the mandate of the UN or the OSCE has been given priority over the EU developing its own conflict prevention and crisis management mechanism, which has led to the development of first the Common Foreign and Security Policy (CFSP) and then the ESDP.[215]

The current legal basis for EU crisis management operations as part of the ESDP is provided in the Consolidated TEU that incorporates the changes brought in with the Lisbon Treaty.[216] According to Article 24(1) TEU, '[t]he Union's competence in matters of common foreign and security policy shall cover all areas of foreign policy and all questions relating to the Union's security, including the progressive framing of a common defence policy that might lead to a common defence'. This policy is defined and implemented by the European Council and the Council

---

[211] L Vierucci, 'The role of the Western European Union (WEU) in the maintenance of international peace and security', 2 *International Peacekeeping* (1995), 309 at 319–20, 325.

[212] Statement of the Presidency of the Permanent Council of the WEU, Brussels, 31 March 2010. This instrument announced that State-parties had collectively decided to terminate the Modified Brussels Treaty, given that Article 42(7) of the Lisbon EU Treaty now provides a mutual defence obligation.

[213] J Wouters and T Ruys, 'EU–UN Cooperation in Crisis Management', in Wouters *et al* (eds.), *The United Nations and the European Union* (The Hague: TMC Asser, 2005), 229 at 233.

[214] *Declaration on Western European Union*, para 2.

[215] J Wouters and F Naert, 'The EU and Conflict Prevention', in V Kronenberger and J Wouters (eds.), *The European Union and Conflict Prevention—Policy and Legal Aspects* (The Hague: TMC Asser, 2004), 33 at 37–8.

[216] On the impact of the Lisbon Treaty on EU peace and security activities see, in general, R Whitman and A Juncos, 'The Lisbon Treaty and the Foreign, Security and Defence Policy: Reforms, Implementation and the Consequences of (non-)Ratification', 14 *European Foreign Affairs Review* (2009), 25; S Blockmans and RA Wessel, 'The European Union and Crisis Management: Will the Lisbon Treaty Make the EU More Effective?', 14 *Journal of Conflict and Security Law* (2009), 265.

acting unanimously, except where the Treaty provides otherwise. The adoption of legislative acts is excluded. Under Article 42 TEU,

[t]he common security and defence policy shall be an integral part of the common foreign and security policy. It shall provide the Union with an operational capacity drawing on civilian and military assets. The Union may use them on missions outside the Union for peace-keeping, conflict prevention and strengthening international security in accordance with the principles of the United Nations Charter.

These tasks, specified in Article 43, essentially replicate the Petersberg Tasks acquired by the EU from the WEU, and

in the course of which the Union may use civilian and military means, shall include joint disarmament operations, humanitarian and rescue tasks, military advice and assistance tasks, conflict prevention and peace-keeping tasks, tasks of combat forces in crisis management, including peace-making and post-conflict stabilisation. All these tasks may contribute to the fight against terrorism, including by supporting third countries in combating terrorism in their territories.

According to Article 25, the Union will conduct the common foreign and security policy by defining general guidelines, and adopting decisions defining actions and positions to be taken by the Union and arrangements for the implementation of decisions. The EU Council is tasked with framing the CFSP and implementing it in accordance with European Council decisions. The High Representative puts the CFSP into effect, using Union and national resources (Article 26(2–3)). Article 28 states that '[w]here the international situation requires operational action by the Union, the Council shall adopt the necessary decisions. They shall lay down their objectives, scope, the means to be made available to the Union, if necessary their duration, and the conditions for their implementation' (paragraph 1). These decisions 'shall commit the Member States in the positions they adopt and in the conduct of their activity' (paragraph 2).[217] Significantly, the third paragraph of Article 28 provides safeguards against unilateralism, by stipulating that

[w]henever there is any plan to adopt a national position or take national action pursuant to a decision as referred to in paragraph 1, information shall be provided by the Member State concerned in time to allow, if necessary, for prior consultations within the Council.

Furthermore, '[t]he Member States shall support the Union's external and security policy actively and unreservedly in a spirit of loyalty and mutual solidarity and shall comply with the Union's action in this area.' Article 29 provides that '[t]he Council shall adopt decisions which shall define the approach of the Union to a particular matter of a geographical or thematic nature. Member States shall ensure that their national policies conform to the Union positions.'

---

[217] This replaces the concepts of common position and joint action that guided the Union's peace and security activities before the adoption of the Lisbon Treaty. As Blockmans and Wessel, ibid, 294, clarify, the somewhat unclear and unnecessary difference between common positions and joint actions has come to an end.

Standing to bring security matters before the Council is vested in any member State, or the High Representative, possibly acting with the Commission's support. If a rapid decision is required, the High Representative is entitled to convene an extraordinary meeting of the Council within 48 hours (Article 30). The Council will take decisions unanimously. Decisions by qualified majority are possible in some cases, mostly where taken for implementing decisions defining the Union's action or position (Article 31). Article 44 validates actions undertaken by coalitions of the 'able and willing' by specifying that

the Council may entrust the implementation of a task to a group of Member States which are willing and have the necessary capability for such a task. Those Member States, in association with the High Representative of the Union for Foreign Affairs and Security Policy, shall agree among themselves on the management of the task.

The Treaty specifies decision-making powers for a Political and Security Committee (PSC) which, as allowed under Article 38, can exercise the political control and strategic direction of crisis management operations referred to in Article 43, and be authorized by the Council to take decisions accordingly. The PSC has authority over the continuing command and control of operations, but it cannot authorize the alteration or termination of an EU mission.[218] The creation of the PSC (consisting of permanent representatives based in Brussels) displaced its predecessor, the Political Committee (consisting of political directors based in national capitals), which enhances the operational effectiveness of the ESDP. As pointed out, the PSC is at the core of the process leading to the drafting of relevant decisions, Concepts of Operations, and operational plans, which together constitute the key documents guiding the implementation of an operation on the ground. The Council's role in approving PSC decisions is nominal, since it is rare that the Council will reopen issues that have been already approved by the Committee.[219]

The EU Military Committee (EUMC), established by Council Decision 2001/79/CFSP,[220] consists of the chiefs of the defence staffs of member States. It is the highest military body in the EU, makes recommendations to the PSC, and directs the activity of the European Union Military Staff (EUMS). The Decision specifies that in crisis management situations the EUMC shall draw up the response options, and once operations have commenced it monitors the proper execution of military operations conducted under the responsibility of the Operation Commander. The EUMS was established as part of the General Secretariat of the Council by Decision 2001/80/CFSP, and performs 'early warning, situation assessment and strategic planning for Petersberg tasks including identification of European national and multinational forces', as well as implementing directions from the EUMC.[221]

---

[218] A Abass, 'Extraterritorial Collective Security: The EU and Operation *Artemis*', in M Trybus and N White (eds.), *European Security Law* (Oxford: Oxford University Press, 2005), 134 at 141.
[219] AE Juncos and C Reynolds, 'The Political and Security Committee: Governing in the Shadow', 12 *European Foreign Affairs Review* (2007), 127 at 135–6, 138.
[220] OJ L 27, 4.
[221] OJ L27, 7.

Early warning in the EU operates at different levels. Some member States have more information resources than others. However, an increasing flow of information is conducted through the PSC, the EUMC, and the EUMS. The Military Staff has an intelligence division which draws on national intelligence data. Monitoring missions are able to provide information regarding the situation at state borders and ethnic conflict.[222]

The EU, like other organizations, recognizes that tasks it aims to perform are not always supported by the necessary will or resources among the membership. A flexible approach can be needed to enable the exercise of the Union's aims (for example, in relation to creating a European Army or a permanent headquarters, as well as other possible arrangements), for which purpose the Treaty enables member States who are willing and able to do so to act by way of establishing *lex specialis* on a particular matter.

Article 20(1) of the Consolidated Treaty enables member States that wish to enhance mutual cooperation within the framework of the Union's non-exclusive competences to make use of its institutions and exercise those competences. Article 20(4) provides that '[a]cts adopted in the framework of enhanced cooperation shall bind only participating Member States'. While enhanced cooperation is meant to apply across the board, permanent structured cooperation is specifically meant for enhancing the Union's capacity in the area of peace and security. According to Article 42(6),

[t]hose Member States whose military capabilities fulfil higher criteria and which have made more binding commitments to one another in this area with a view to the most demanding missions shall establish permanent structured cooperation within the Union framework.

Such cooperation is without prejudice to the Union's ability to act in pursuance of ESDP goals that replicate the former Petersberg Tasks. Member States willing to pursue permanent structured cooperation have to notify their intention to the Council and the High Representative. Decisions approving the establishment of such cooperation and enabling member States to take part in it rest with the Council. Protocol No 10 to TEU defines criteria that enable a member State's participation in permanent structured cooperation. These are contributing to defence policies and arrangements, including through the European Defence Agency and participation in EU battle groups (Article 1).

Steps have been taken towards the goal of endowing the EU with an independent military capacity.[223] The Declaration of the Franco-British Summit at St Malo on 4 December 1998 proposed the development of an autonomous capacity.[224] The Helsinki Declaration of the European Council in 1999 proclaimed the goal that 'Member States must be able, by 2003, to deploy within

---

[222] N Burgess, 'The Council's Early Warning Process', in Kronenberger and Wouters, n 215 above, 21 at 23–4.
[223] See in general M Trybus, 'With or Without the EU Constitutional Treaty: Towards a Common Security and Defence Policy?', 31 ELR (2006), 145.
[224] St Malo Declaration, 1998, para 3.

60 days and sustain for at least 1 year military forces of up to 50,000–60,000 persons capable of the full range of Petersberg tasks'.[225] The St Malo Declaration of 24 November 2003 specified that the EU

should be capable and willing to deploy in an autonomous operation within 15 days to respond to a crisis. The aim should be coherent and credible battle-group sized forces, each around 1,500 troops, offered by a single nation or through a multinational or framework nation force package, with appropriate transport and sustainability. These forces should have the capacity to operate under a Chapter VII mandate. They would be deployed in response to a UN request to stabilize a situation or otherwise meet a short-term need until peacekeepers from the United Nations, or regional organizations acting under a UN mandate, could arrive or be reinforced.

The 2004 Brussels European Council adopted the target date of 2010 for enhancing EU capacity for rapid response to military and civilian crises.[226] The 2010 Headline Goal specifies that

the ambition of the EU is to be able to take the decision to launch an operation within 5 days of the approval of the Crisis Management Concept by the Council. On the deployment of forces, the ambition is that the forces start implementing their mission on the ground, no later than 10 days after the EU decision to launch the operation.[227]

The post-Lisbon Consolidated TEU covers the pertinent requirements in Protocol No 10. So far, all EU peace operation have been conducted on an ad hoc basis, relying either on NATO assets under the Berlin Plus arrangement or on contributions by lead states, without employing resources available to or provided by the Union on a permanent basis.

(n) The Organization of Eastern Caribbean States (OECS)

The Organization of Eastern Caribbean States was established by a Treaty concluded at Basseterre, St Kitts and Nevis, on 18 June 1981.[228] The Organization appears to have a general political profile. Article 3 of the Treaty lists political, economic, security, and defence purposes and functions for it. The relevant institutions of the Organization include the supreme policy-making institution— the Authority composed of heads of government, who may be represented by designated ministers (Article 6); a Foreign Affairs Committee composed of foreign ministers—the organ responsible for the general direction and control of the executive functions of the Organization and responsible to the Authority (Article 7); and a Defence and Security Committee composed of defence

---

[225] Helsinki Declaration, 1999, para 28.

[226] EU Brussels Presidency Conclusions, 17–18 June 2004, para 62.

[227] 2010 Headline Goal, para 4. For instance, with Operation *Artemis* in the Congo, 'the European Union succeeded in overcoming a major hurdle: rapid projection of an entire force in an operational context, at a distance over 6,000 kilometres from Europe'. *The European Union and Peacekeeping in Africa*, WEU Assembly 15th Session, Doc A/1880, 1 December 2004, explanatory memorandum, para 54.

[228] 20 ILM (1981), 1166.

ministers—responsible for coordinating the efforts of member States for collective defence pursuant to Article 51 of the UN Charter, including measures to combat mercenaries (Article 8). There is no specialized security structure or procedure.

Under Article 6, the Authority can adopt decisions on the basis of unanimity, which will be binding on all member States who are obliged to give them effect; it may make such recommendations and give such directives as it deems necessary for the achievement of the purposes of the Organization. Decisions of the Foreign Affairs Committee are adopted unanimously and are binding on all subordinate institutions unless otherwise determined by the Authority; the same applies to decisions of the Defence and Security Committee (Articles 7 and 8).

(o) CIS, CSTO, and SCO

On 8 December 1991, the leaders of Russia, the Ukraine, and Belarus, then parts of the USSR, adopted the Agreement establishing the Commonwealth of Independent States (CIS), which also declared that the USSR had ceased to exist as an international legal person and a geopolitical reality. The Charter of the CIS was adopted by the CIS Summit on 22 January 1993. Articles 11 to 15 of the Charter relate to collective security arrangements. Article 12 provides for consultations if the sovereignty, security, or territorial integrity of a member State, or international peace and security, are threatened, to coordinate positions, and to adopt measures of response, including the establishment of peace-keeping forces or use of force in the exercise of the right to individual and collective self-defence under Article 51 of the UN Charter. In a somewhat ambiguous way, Article 12 also allows a decision on the use of armed force to be adopted by the Summit of Heads of State or by interested member States. There seems to be no independent competence envisaged in relation to conducting regional enforcement operations.

To enhance the security arm of the CIS, in May 1992 several state-successors to the USSR adopted a Treaty on Collective Security. Article 2 of the Treaty essentially replicates Article 12 of the CIS Charter, but without specifying the measures to be adopted in the face of a threat. Action is provided for only in Article 4, which states that

[i]f an aggression is committed against one of the States Parties by any state or a group of states, it will be considered as an aggression against all the States Parties to this Treaty. In case an act of aggression is committed against any of the States Parties, all the other States Parties will render it necessary assistance, including military [assistance], as well as provide support with the means at their disposal through an exercise of the right to collective defence in accordance with Article 51 of the UN Charter.

Article 6 specifies that decisions on the above shall be adopted by heads of state of State-parties. Most pertinently, Article 6 specifies that '[t]he Armed Forces can be used beyond the territory of the States Parties exclusively in the interests of international security in strict compliance with the Charter of the United Nations and the legislation of the States Parties to this Treaty'.

The Collective Security Treaty Organization (CSTO) was established by a Charter signed on 7 June 2002 by states party to the Collective Security Treaty. It provides an institutional framework including, above all, the Collective Security Council. It is noteworthy that an organization primarily established as a defence pact is denoted as a collective security organization; CSTO will not normally engage in internal conflicts.

The Shanghai Cooperation Organization (SCO) covers most member States of the CSTO, and China. As an organization it has a general competence but maintenance of peace and security is among its principal purposes, as specified in its Charter adopted on 7 June 2002. The Charter establishes the Council of Heads of State, a Council of Heads of Government, and a Council of Foreign Ministers (Articles 5 to 7). The SCO has not yet engaged in security-related activities, but it has expressly declared 'that stability and security in Central Asia can be provided first and foremost by the forces of the region's states on the basis of international organizations already established in the region'.[229]

---

[229] Bishkek Declaration of the Heads of State of SCO, 16 August 2007.

3
The Regime of Competence Allocation

1. General Aspects

The unity of collective security is premised on the completeness of the existing collective security framework to deal with pertinent threats, and presupposes that both the UN and regional institutions implement a single policy in relation to relevant crises. The UN Secretary-General articulated the rationale of Chapter VIII as being 'to ensure that global and regional collective security is mutually complementary and that the total effort of the international community for securing the peace is optimized through the collaboration of our various international organizations'.[1] As was pointed out in the Security Council by Mexico (who initiated the discussion), 'the multilateral system, in effect, comprises the sum of the United Nations, the regional and subregional organizations and the specialized institutions. The right cooperation and the full exploitation of their capacities and comparative advantages could create a powerful engine for finding solutions.'[2] The German representative was more specific in pointing out that 'the means to achieve, and the conceptual underpinning for, a multilateral division of labour for peace and security are already in place. What is now needed is the political will to make good use of the possibilities.'[3] The Spanish representative added that there can be no rigid model for cooperation between the UN and regional levels because every crisis is unique, thus revealing added value in the comparative advantage of each organization.[4] Still, as the Italian representative observed, while '[n]o one formula or solution is right for every crisis that might arise . . . this does not mean forgetting the importance of homogeneous standards and respect for certain basic shared principles'.[5]

Effective implementation of a single collective security policy requires the sharing of tasks between different institutions, which then bears on both the allocation of available resources and the competence of institutions to take the relevant action. As has been pertinently pointed out, it would be objectively difficult for the UN to

---

[1] *A Regional-global Security Partnership: Challenges and Opportunities*, Report by the Secretary-General, A/61/204–S/2006/590, at 16 (para 80).
[2] *Cooperation between the United Nations and regional organizations in stabilization processes*, 20 July 2004, S/PV.5007, 6 (Mexico).
[3] Ibid, 17–18 (Germany).
[4] Ibid, 32 (Spain).
[5] *Relationship between the United Nations and regional organizations, in particular the African Union, in the maintenance of international peace and security*, S/PV.5649, 28 March 2007, 20 (Italy).

develop a close working relationship with regional organizations if they are working on separate mandates and with different aims.[6] That said, different organizations having parallel functions is conducive to international security, since the inactivity of one institution—whether for lack of resources, of enforcement powers, or of political will—can be remedied by another institution; complexity of response can be ensured through a joint involvement; institutions can balance each other if their delegated authority is exceeded and thus enhance each others' accountability.

It is correctly emphasized that the more the UN involvement in crisis situations increased, the more its efforts became dependent on the contribution by regional organizations.[7] This is natural, as Chapter VIII of the UN Charter is premised on the understanding that no single organization will be able to cover all pertinent crises through its assets and resources. As has been pointed out, '[o]nly the interplay of both levels carries promise for progress towards a more effective international system for the maintenance of peace and security'.[8] For instance, NATO and the UN need each other, as 'neither can successfully ensure collective security on its own. Together, the moral force and the fighting power' complement each other.[9] Regional alliances enable states to develop specific assets of deterrence and to that effect adopt joint policies, actions, and commitments to make deterrence credible, thus complementing each other's capacity in providing security.[10] However, the capacity and resources of a particular institution do not determine the scope of that institution's competence. Lack of resources does not remove competence any more than the availability of resources establishes it.

Regionalization is defined as devolution of authority and power from the UN to regional organizations in accordance with Chapter VIII of the UN Charter.[11] This raises questions as to whether the powers of the UN can devolve, that is be alienated or abdicated. Regionalization and decentralization have been promoted in *Agenda for Peace*, where the UN Secretary-General observes that

regional arrangements or agencies in many cases possess a potential that should be utilized in serving the functions covered in this report: preventive diplomacy, peace-keeping, peace-making and post-conflict peace-building. Under the Charter, the Security Council has and will continue to have primary responsibility for maintaining international peace and security, but regional action as a matter of decentralization, delegation and cooperation with

---

[6] R Durward, 'Security Council Authorisation for Regional Peace Operations: A Critical Analysis', 13 *International Peacekeeping* (2006), 350 at 360.

[7] J Cloos, 'EU–UN Cooperation on Crisis Management—Putting Effective Multilateralism in Practice', in J Wouters *et al* (eds.), *The United Nations and the European Union* (The Hague: TMC Asser, 2006), 259 at 261.

[8] C Schreuer, 'Regionalism v Universalism', 6 *European Journal of International Law* (1995), 477 at 497.

[9] RG Mackay, 'NATO and UN', 288 *Annals of the American Academy of Political and Social Science* (1953), 119 at 125.

[10] C Wallander, 'Institutional Assets and Adaptability: NATO after the Cold War', 54 *International Organisation* (2000), 705 at 710.

[11] M Pugh, 'The World Order Politics of Regionalisation', in M Pugh and WPS Sidhu (eds.), *The United Nations and Regional Security—Europe and Beyond* (Boulder: Lynne Rienner Inc, 2003), 31.

United Nations efforts could not only lighten the burden of the Council but also contribute to a deeper sense of participation, consensus and democratization in international affairs.[12]

This approach favours the policy of decentralization. The Secretary-General pointed in another report to competing policies and aims to be balanced:

in any new division of labour, the United Nations retains its primacy in the maintenance of international peace and security, while its burden is lightened and its mission reinforced and underlined by the active involvement of appropriate regional agencies. The exact modalities of this division of labour remain to be worked out.[13]

On the other hand, as the Secretary General's report emphasizes,

[o]ften regional agencies have credibility as local actors to encourage their members to adhere to accepted international and regional norms. The international community benefits from the innovative approaches of regional organizations and from the knowledge of effective prevention strategies that are acquired in one region and that could be shared elsewhere in the world. . . . capacity exists in conflict prevention both in constitutional mandates and operational mechanisms in all such organizations.[14]

It is then cautiously observed that

[w]hile both the United Nations and regional organizations, particularly the African Union, refer to *partnership*, there remains the potential for misunderstanding and misperception concerning the meaning and scope of such a partnership. When the United Nations partners with regional organizations, the parameters of such partnerships need to be well defined and well coordinated.[15]

As for such parameters, one government pointed out before the Security Council in the wake of the adoption of Resolution 1809(2008) that 'optimally, those three levels of responsibility—global, regional and national—should, owing to their intertwining nature, act in harmony, respecting the principles of subsidiarity, division of labour and effectiveness, in order to achieve peace and security'.[16]

However, jurisdictional conflicts can arise over which institution can do what in which situation. Curiously enough, the political ethos favouring increased use of regional mechanisms in the post-Cold War period has witnessed more frequent differences between the UN and regional organizations as to the proper ways of addressing threats. Such duality of policies has illustrated that no preconceived vision of competence allocation could reasonably be adopted. Therefore, principles governing jurisdictional conflict between the UN and regional organizations acquire increasing importance. Policy principles such as autonomy, ownership,

---

[12] *An Agenda for Peace—Preventive diplomacy, peacemaking and peace-keeping*, Report of the Secretary-General pursuant to the statement adopted by the Summit Meeting of the Security Council on 31 January 1992, A/47/277–S/24111, 17 June 1992, para 64.

[13] Secretary-General's Annual Report on the Work of the Organization (New York: 1992), 44.

[14] *A Regional-global Security Partnership*, n 1 above, 6, paras 20–1.

[15] *Report of the Secretary-General on the relationship between the United Nations and regional organizations, in particular the African Union, in the maintenance of international peace and security*, S/2008/186, 7 April 2008, 6–7 (para 8, emphasis in original).

[16] S/PV.5869, 26 (Croatia).

subsidiarity, non-subordination, complementarity, or notions of partnership, division of labour, and sub-contracting, can favour the involvement of one or another organization; some of these are presumably quasi-normative principles or those derived from or recognized in provisions under constituent instruments, general practice, and policies. Others may just denote *de facto* outcomes that obtain in specific cases.

Chapter VIII serves three purposes: (1) to provide a point of departure in terms of task sharing and competence allocation between the UN and regional organizations; (2) to make organizations eligible to be employed for enforcement under Chapter VIII; and (3) to impose a prohibition on their use of coercion following from broader prescriptions under Articles 2(4), 24, and 42. For the purposes of dispute settlement, the independent competence of regional organizations is recognized under Chapter VI and Article 52. As far as enforcement is concerned, the initiation of coercive action by the UN Security Council remains the starting point.

2. The Essence of 'Regional Arrangements'

The purpose of Chapter VIII of the UN Charter is to enable threats to be effectively addressed at various levels of collective security. Hence, as the UN Secretary-General specified in *Agenda for Peace*, the Charter allows

useful flexibility for undertakings by a group of States to deal with a matter appropriate for regional action which also could contribute to the maintenance of international peace and security. Such associations or entities could include treaty-based organizations, whether created before or after the founding of the United Nations, regional organizations for mutual security and defence, organizations for general regional development or for cooperation on a particular economic topic or function, and groups created to deal with a specific political, economic or social issue of current concern.[17]

There is no generally accepted definition of a regional organization under Chapter VIII. As the Secretary-General pointed out, 'the concept of a region has never been clarified, neither during the framing of the Charter nor since. A draft definition of a regional agency proposed at the San Francisco Conference was rejected on the view that it might unduly restrict the need for flexibility.'[18] There were attempts at the San Francisco Conference to define regions. On behalf of the Arab League the Egyptian delegation put forward a definition based on a geographical area covering several countries united by proximity, community of interests, or cultural, linguistic, historical, or spiritual

---

[17] n 12 above, para 61.
[18] *A Regional-global Security Partnership*, n 1 above, 16 (para 77); the Report proceeds to state (ibid, para 81)

that [i]n addition to regional organizations, it will be of practical sense to identify also the subregional organizations within the partnership. Although the Charter is silent on this matter, it has always been clear to me and my colleagues that the provisions of Chapter VIII imply that subregional organizations are to be included. The nature of the relationship between regional and subregional organizations itself may require greater clarity in the future. This is particularly complex, given the relationship between a regional organization and its subregional partners, on one hand, and between the United Nations and both entities, on the other hand.

affinities, which makes them jointly responsible for the settlement of regional disputes and maintenance of regional peace.[19] This was meant to tie down regional action to cases involving a genuine regional unity. The relevant committee turned this proposal down as it could not provide an all-inclusive definition.

Given the Security Council's recognition of the principle of complementarity relating to the knowledge of root causes of regional problems,[20] a valid concept of a regional organization can be based primarily on a proper regional representation. Chapter VIII does not define whether a regional arrangement means an organization, the membership of which is concentrated in a particular region, or an organization, the activities of which focus on a particular region. As Kelsen explains, under Chapter VIII 'it is not required that the parties to the regional agreement be geographically neighbours. It is essential only that the actions of the organization established by the regional arrangement be restricted to a certain area, determined in the agreement.'[21]

The concept of a region under Article 52(1) should not be construed narrowly. It may comprise any limited number of like-minded states joined by a shared interest in peace and security matters. It is correctly pointed out that limited membership and the security mandate can place the arrangement concerned within the scope of Chapter VIII.[22] Thus, an organization covering more than one geographical region, such as NATO, the OSCE, the OIC, or the Arab League, could still be considered as a regional arrangement in relation to each region it covers, because its members have established it to deal with the problems arising in that region.

The reference in Chapter VIII to agencies as well as arrangements already implies broadly definable criteria. Akehurst suggests that agency is based on international superstructure while arrangement is not.[23] The Charter does not define the degree of institutionalization which an organization should possess to qualify under Chapter VIII: whether it should have separate organs or consist merely of its members' mutual cooperation. However in practice occasional groups of states have been refused Chapter VIII status.[24] As the International Court's judgment in the *Nicaragua* case indicates,

[t]he Court [did] not consider that the Contadora process, whatever its merits, can properly be regarded as a 'regional arrangement' for the purposes of Chapter VIII of the Charter of

---

[19] 12 UNCIO 850; UNCIO Doc. 533, III/4/A/9; 889, III/4/12, cited in HN Howard, 'Middle Eastern Regional Organization: Problems and Prospects', 24(4) *Proceedings of the Academy of Political Science* (1952), 101 at 104.

[20] See section 4 below.

[21] H Kelsen, 'Is the North Atlantic Treaty a Regional Arrangement?', 45 AJIL (1951), 162 at 162–3. According to Zwarenburg, the word 'regional' and reference to 'local disputes' in Article 52 imply some geographical vicinity, even though geographical contiguity is not required: M Zwarenburg, 'Regional Organisations and the Maintenance of International Peace and Security: Three Recent Regional African Peace Operations', 11 *Journal of Conflict and Security Law* (2006), 483 at 488.

[22] N Tsagourias, 'EU Peacekeeping Operations: Legal and Theoretical Issues', in M Trybus and N White, *European Security Law* (Oxford: Oxford University Press, 2005), 102 at 126.

[23] M Akehurst, 'Enforcement Action by Regional Agencies, With Special Reference to the Organization of American States', 42 *British Yearbook of International Law* (1967), 175 at 177.

[24] T Gazzini, 'NATO's Role in the Collective Security System', 8 *Journal of Conflict and Security Law* (2003), 231 at 248. This also means that occasional groups cannot count in the subsidiarity equation: see section 4 below.

the United Nations. Furthermore, it is also important always to bear in mind that all regional, bilateral, and even multilateral, arrangements that the Parties to this case may have made, touching on the issue of settlement of disputes or the jurisdiction of the International Court of Justice, must be made always subject to the provisions of Article 103 of the Charter.[25]

Akehurst develops a subjective test focusing on 'whether the parties to the arrangement have claimed that it is a regional arrangement, and whether this claim has been accepted in practice by the United Nations'.[26] Some organizations have expressly identified themselves as regional arrangements under Chapter VIII. The OAS has done so in its Charter while the CIS, the OSCE, and the League of Arab States have declared this subsequently.[27] There is some doctrinal scepticism as to whether the EU is a traditional Chapter VIII organization,[28] but it certainly gets sub-contracted by the Security Council under Chapters VII and VIII.

Article 52 of the Charter admits the existence of regional arrangements provided that their activities are consistent with the purposes and principles of the UN, such as non-use of force and non-intervention in domestic affairs. Apart from these negatively specified requirements there is no positive specification as to what purposes, tasks, or structures a regional arrangement should have to qualify under Chapter VIII. The Article 52 requirements are therefore broad and flexible, which reflects the need to preserve the freedom of groups of states to arrange themselves on regional bases in a manner suitable to their interests.

This is illustrated by the example of the Arab League. UN General Assembly Resolution 120 (1947) accepted the League as a regional arrangement. When the permanent invitation of the League to attend General Assembly meetings was discussed in 1950, Israel objected on the grounds that the League

was not accessible to all Member States in the Middle East; it was conceived on the principle of racial exclusiveness which did not accord with the basic ideas of the Charter; the Pact of the League, which had been signed prior to the Charter, did not contain any reference to acceptance by the League of obligations under the Charter; the League had failed to solve the conflicts within the area it covered; the activities of the League had been directed against the United Nations and had not been consistent with the Purposes and Principles of the Charter; and the League had not given support to the Security Council resolutions relating to the restoration of international peace and security in the Far East in connexion with the Korean question.[29]

At a later meeting Israel stated that the requirements for recognition as regional arrangements under Article 52 were as follows:

a) the existence of a clearly defined security region for which the agency assumed responsibility; b) the existence of a strong legal instrument with power to achieve its purposes; c) the

---

[25] *ICJ Reports* 1984, 440.

[26] Akehurst, n 23 above, 178.

[27] J Wouters and T Ruys, 'EU–UN Cooperation in Crisis Management', in Wouters *et al*, n 7 above, 229 at 231.

[28] Cloos, n 7 above, 265.

[29] *Repertory of Practice of United Nations Organs*, 1945–54, 446.

effectiveness of such an agency; d) the consistency of such arrangements and their activities with the Purposes and Principles of the Charter.

The League did not meet these requirements. Some other states responded that

Article 52 laid down only that regional organizations should deal with matters relating to the maintenance of international peace and security and that their activities should be consistent with the Purposes and Principles of the Charter, but did not go beyond those conditions to lay down a model to which all regional organizations should conform. Article 52 did not define the regions of the world or lay down that the organizations should be accessible to all States in the regions or exclude organizations the members of which were bound together by racial ties.... The regional arrangements to which Article 52 referred included those which had preceded the establishment of the United Nations. The holding of secret meetings was not inconsistent with the procedure of the United Nations.... Several representatives stated that the Arab League was not a racial organization, that its activities were not inconsistent with the Purposes and Principles of the Charter, that its records were published and that it had already suggested a relationship with the United Nations similar to that of the Organization of American States.[30]

The General Assembly adopted Resolution 477(V) (1950), to invite the League, by 29 votes to 1, with 5 abstentions. Israel's concerns (as set out above) are understandable, because recognizing the Arab League as a Chapter VIII organization could have risked conferring on this essentially pro-Arab institution an enhanced standing under the Charter to deal with the crisis in the Middle East.[31] But these concerns could be addressed by raising the impartiality issue in pertinent cases, as opposed to a general refusal to view the League as a Chapter VIII organization, given moreover that it could become involved in other crises without such concerns arising.

As Akehurst highlights, there have been controversies in terms of characterizing organizations such as NATO and the Warsaw Pact, because they were initially based on Article 51 of the UN Charter.[32] But collective self-defence and collective security are closely interlinked. In fact, regional arrangements can be established to pave the road for collective self-defence, and they have assumed self-defence functions. A restrictive understanding of external self-defence exceeding the regional 'internal' mandate of an organization under Chapter VIII should be rejected.[33]

NATO has not been officially established as a Chapter VIII regional arrangement. In drafting the North Atlantic Treaty the reference to Chapter VIII was deliberately avoided, to prevent NATO from being subjected to the UN veto in relation to its core tasks of collective self-defence (among other reasons).[34] At those

---

[30] Ibid, 446–7.

[31] It is pointed out that, as regional organizations, the Arab League and the OIC are not adequate to deal with protracted crises between Arab states and Israel: J Morris and H McCoubrey, 'Regional Peacekeeping in the Post-Cold War Era', 6 *International Peacekeeping* (1999), 129 at 145.

[32] Akehurst, n 23 above, 179.

[33] A Eide, 'Peace-Keeping and Enforcement by Regional Organizations: Its place in the United Nations System', 3 *Journal of Peace Research* (1966), 125 at 126, 136; Schreuer, n 8 above, 490; Y Dinstein, *War, Aggression and Self-Defence*, 4th ed. (Cambridge: Cambridge University Press, 2005), 257.

[34] D Leurdijk, 'The UN and NATO: The Logic of Primacy', in Pugh and Sidhu, n 11 above, 57. The US/UK approach prevailed over the French original inclination to qualify NATO as a regional arrangement in the preamble of the North Atlantic Treaty: Gazzini, n 24 above, 248.

early stages NATO simply did not envisage going beyond its core self-defence tasks.[35] The attitude in NATO's early years was that, as US Secretary of State Dulles had put it, 'NATO has not been organized as a regional association, nor has it any policy or jurisdiction to deal with disputes as between the members'.[36] However, such unilateral policy statements are not conclusive. According to Kelsen, NATO meets the criteria to qualify as a regional arrangement under Chapter VIII. The wording of the Charter does not exclude self-defence organizations from qualifying under Chapter VIII and NATO can certainly undertake both roles.[37] Dinstein reiterates this point, especially since NATO performed a Chapter VIII role under Security Council Resolutions 816(1993) and 836(1993). Furthermore, 'any attempt to erect a barrier between collective self-defence organizations and regional arrangements for enforcement purposes is artificial.' The only difference between the two types of activity is that collective self-defence does not require the Security Council's authorization,[38] while regional enforcement is under strict and direct control of the Security Council.[39] This is why the essence of regional arrangements should be determined by formal criteria focusing on the lowest common denominator inferable from Chapter VIII, as opposed to how these arrangements view themselves or how they are viewed in state practice at any given point in time.

Extending the constitutional mandate of a regional organization is possible through a variety of means. The consensual nature of international law can allow expanding the competence of international organizations to out-of-area activities even if such were not originally envisaged. There are reasonable grounds for considering that NATO has redefined itself in the process of UN sub-contracting, by virtue of its adoption of declarations redefining its role to assume peace and security functions.[40] To illustrate, NATO's Comprehensive Political Guidance adopted in 2006 specifies that

[t]he Alliance will remain ready, on a case-by-case basis and by consensus, to contribute to effective conflict prevention and to engage actively in crisis management, including through non-Article 5 crisis response operations, as set out in the Strategic Concept.[41]

---

[35] Against this background, the suggestion that NATO sought to characterize itself as a collective self-defence alliance in order to avoid the obligation to seek the Security Council's permission for the purposes of Article 53(1) of the Charter (D Sarooshi, *The United Nations and Development of Collective Security* (New York: Oxford University Press, 1999), 251) appears questionable. As is clear from the terms of the North Atlantic Treaty, NATO was established as a self-defence pact without any intention to prejudice the responsibility of the UN Security Council for any matter specified in the Charter. At that stage NATO did not envisage taking enforcement action.

[36] Department of State Bulletin, 34/884, 4 June 1956, 925–6.

[37] Kelsen, n 21 above, 163–4, 166; Akehurst, n 23 above, 180–3; Gazzini, n 24 above, 249; A Abass, *Regional Organisations and the Development of Collective Security: Beyond Chapter VIII of the UN Charter* (Oxford: Hart, 2004), 39.

[38] Dinstein, n 33 above, 312–13.

[39] G Bebr, 'Regional Organizations: A United Nations Problem', 49 AJIL (1955), 166 at 174.

[40] Gazzini, n 24 above, 249.

[41] NATO Comprehensive Political Guidance, 29 November 2006, para 6.

Subjectively, NATO has agreed to be a Chapter VIII organization by agreeing to undertake Chapter VIII tasks, which (having accepted this legal character) seems to amount to an estoppel. Alternatively, it is certain that NATO objectively meets the Chapter VIII requirements.

Graham suggests classifying regional organizations into two categories, depending on whether the organization in question acts exclusively within the jurisdictional zone of its own member States (regional focus) or also outside that zone (global focus). The first category can be employed by the UN under Article 53, and the second under Article 42. The first category, regional or sub-regional organizations, can become 'partners of first instance' for the UN since they are responsible for peace and security in their own regions. But if they are unable or unwilling to undertake such action, then the Security Council could call upon a 'global executive agent' such as NATO or the EU to act in 'out-of-area' zones.[42] According to Gaja, 'as the context of Chapter VIII makes it clear, Article 53 cannot be invoked when the States in which action is intended to take place [are] not a party to the regional arrangement or organization'.[43] Dinstein, on the other hand, suggests that the state that is the target of the Article 53 action does not have to be a member of that regional organization, and refers to the Security Council's request to the OAU under Resolution 217(1965) to assist in implementating the embargo against Rhodesia.[44] In fact, there is no imperative reason why regional organizations cannot get involved outside the area of their membership, if this is duly requested by the state concerned or authorized by the Security Council. However, one should warn against assigning some inherent order of preference to organizations. An arrangement of this kind might be unworkable in practice as it could be contradicted by the choice of parties and by the principle of subsidiarity.

3. Policy Arguments about Competence Allocation

Policy considerations behind the relationship between the UN and regional organizations are essentially informed by the reasons that underlie the establishment of the organization concerned, and by how its founding and driving member States see its role in relation to the UN collective security framework. This can be highlighted by a debate in the United States (soon after the adoption of the North Atlantic Treaty) over whether, in the early years of the Cold War, NATO was meant to achieve the aims of the free world through greater power than its adversaries, or whether it should serve the aims of the United Nations.[45] From the outset the UN itself was based on an uneasy compromise between universal competence to deal with all matters of peace and security, and institutions

---

[42] K Graham, 'UN–EU Cooperation on Security: In Search of "Effective Multilateralism" and a Balanced Division of Tasks', in Wouters *et al*, n 7 above, 281 at 295.

[43] G Gaja, 'Use of Force Made or Authorised by the United Nations', in C Tomuschat (ed.), *The United Nations at the Age of Fifty* (The Hague: Kluwer, 1995), 39 at 44.

[44] Dinstein, n 33 above, 311.

[45] Cf discussion in 44 *ASIL Proceedings* (1950), 22ff.

of collective self-defence and regional alliances, which express regional claims to spheres of influence which benefit regional great powers.[46]

At times, regional organizations are seen as expressing regional opposition to hegemonic policies dominating the UN agenda, while at others they are seen as instruments of regional hegemony aimed at limiting external supervision from the UN, particularly its veto-wielding members, in order to restrain a concerted regional position or a regional great power.[47] The OAS approach to hemispheric security (or security in the Americas), as witnessed by OAS decisions on the Cuban missile crisis, has been to prevent the intervention of extra-continental powers. On the other hand, a reason driving the formation of the Inter-American Security System (comprising the OAS Charter, the Rio Treaty, and the Bogota Pact) was Latin American concern and vigilance regarding US interventionism, which was expressed in the non-intervention rule enshrined in Article 18 of the Rio Treaty.[48] As witnessed in the Guatemala and Cuba situations, these policies can even be mutually incompatible.

When the League of Nations Covenant was being negotiated and discussed, President Wilson did not favour the idea of limited leagues and alliances as they could lead to counter-alliances and thus increase the causes of war. Nevertheless, he had to agree to the regional exception under Article 21 of the League Covenant, having in mind the need to preserve the Monroe Doctrine.[49] According to Article 21, the Covenant would not 'affect the validity of international engagements, such as treaties of arbitration or regional understandings like the Monroe doctrine, for securing the maintenance of peace'. This was essentially a deference clause: the League would operate subject to the role of regional arrangements whose status was at times undefined. The Monroe Doctrine and other informal arrangements could in principle be invoked to bypass Covenant arrangements for the use of force under its Articles 15 and 16. In practice such claims do not seem to have been raised.

The 1937 Chatham House Report suggested that 'if it had been possible to conclude a general treaty for automatic military support the demand for regional pacts would probably have never arisen'. Regional pacts could be useful in achieving collective security purposes only if they did not degenerate into alliances of the type seen before the First World War. For the very fact of conclusion of a regional defence pact implied the weakening of a commitment to assist, through collective security mechanisms and procedures at the universal level, the victim of aggression.[50]

In line with the universal implication of threats, during the inter-war period the universality of collective security was advocated as a guiding principle. The British

---

[46] F Kratochwil, *Rules, Norms and Decisions* (Cambridge: Cambridge University Press, 1989), 84–5.

[47] I Claude, 'The OAS, the UN and the United States', 35 *International Conciliation* (No 547, March 1964), 1 at 7–8.

[48] American Treaty on Pacific Settlement (Pact of Bogota) 1949. J Tacsan, 'Searching for OAS/UN Task-sharing Opportunities in Central America and Haiti', 18 *Third World Quarterly* (1997), 489 at 497.

[49] LM Goodrich, 'Regionalism and the United Nations', 23 *Proceedings of the Academy of Political Science* (1949), 47; Bebr, n 39 above, 168.

[50] Chatham House, *International Sanctions*, A Report by a Group of Members of the Royal Institute of International Affairs (Oxford: Oxford University Press, 1938), 132.

diplomat Noel-Baker emphasized that the obligations upon which collective security is founded must be applicable to aggression in every quarter of the world. The danger of war was not regional and aggression could not be restrained by regional limitations.[51] Likewise, Mitrany considered that reducing the possibility of wars required the commitment of the entire international community, not of selective parts of it.[52]

Lauterpacht suggested that, had the League of Nations and Article 10 of its Covenant remained effective in practice, there would have been no need for subsequent pacts of guarantee and non-aggression.[53] Noel-Baker retorted that the failure of the Covenant was due to the lack of support by states, not to any inherent systemic problem. The Covenant gaps were not addressed by states intending to provide viable rules and mechanisms to enable the League to function effectively, especially in line with the Kellogg Pact. This especially was true of the gap in Article 16 of the Covenant that allowed each state to decide for itself whether the act of aggression had been committed.[54]

The need to have regional agencies controlled through a universal framework has been asserted since then. The 1937 League of Nations Report on the application of principles of the Covenant specified that two conditions had to be fulfilled if regional agreements were not to replicate the old alliances and lead to the formation of rival groups, but serve the principles of the Covenant. The first condition was that determining the act of aggression and ensuing military and economic sanctions should rest with the League Council. After sudden armed attacks states should be given the possibility of defending themselves, as was provided, for instance, under the Locarno Pact. The League Council's rights should be reserved. The second condition was that regional pacts should allow such states to join as might wish to accede to them, which could prevent these pacts transforming into old-style alliances.[55] The first condition actually reflects the position adopted later under the UN Charter (Articles 51 and 53); the second condition is more doctrinal than juridical, as in legal terms it is left to alliance members to determine.

The geopolitical idea of organizing the world to match a pattern of regional Greater Areas was embraced in forming the United Nations. In political terms the San Francisco Conference debates were not just about doctrinal aspects of globalism and regionalism. More specific security interests were at stake and great powers were concerned that lesser powers might intrude into their security spheres of interest.[56] In addition, 'there was in fact no clear-cut distinction between regionalists and universalists. Most representatives wanted freedom for their particular

---

[51] P Noel-Baker, 'The Future of the Collective System', in Mowat *et al*, *Problems of Peace*, 10th Series (London: George Allen and Unwin Ltd, 1936), 178 at 182.
[52] Cf L Fawcett, 'The Evolving Architecture of Regionalisation', in Pugh and Sidhu, n 11 above, 11 at 13.
[53] H Lauterpacht, 'International Law after the Covenant', in Mowat *et al*, n 51 above, 37 at 52.
[54] Noel-Baker, n 51 above, 195–6.
[55] Cf Y Liang, 'Regional Arrangements and International Security', 31 *Transactions of the Grotius Society* (1945), 216 at 219–21.
[56] RL Butterworth, 'Organizing Collective Security: The UN Charter's Chapter VIII in Practice', 28 *World Politics* (1976), 197 at 199.

cause, but not for others.'[57] At that stage Winston Churchill favoured the idea of co-existence of a centralized organization and a series of regional councils, the latter allocated with the primary role of maintaining international peace and security. President Franklin Roosevelt also found this approach appealing. The opposite approach was developed by the US Secretary of State, Cordell Hull, who favoured a global organization playing the primary role in conflict management. The Dumbarton Oaks draft embodying a prohibition of regional enforcement measures without a UN mandate upheld Hull's approach.[58] There seems to be no essential difference between Section C of Chapter VIII in the Dumbarton Oaks Proposals and Chapter VIII of the UN Charter as far as the role of regional arrangements in dispute settlement and enforcement action is concerned.

It is suggested that by signing the Act of Chapultepec in the Pan-American context, the United States essentially undertook the responsibility 'for helping to secure the alternation of the Dumbarton Oaks draft in a pro-regionalist direction' to meet the desire of Latin American states to be entitled to deal with threats and aggression in that area,[59] and to eliminate the possibility of a veto by an extra-continental permanent member of the Security Council over the defensive action provided for in the Act.[60]

At the San Francisco Conference, the Latin American states had feared that extra-regional great powers would get the right to veto regional actions and affairs, and that the Security Council could override their regional peace efforts. Thus, as a compromise, the right to self-defence was singled out in what is now Article 51 of the Charter to enable groups of states to act in collective self-defence without the Security Council's authorization, in case this organ were to be paralysed by a veto.[61] The insertion of Article 51 allayed the concerns of the groups that opposed the absolute primacy of the UN over regional enforcement actions, since the Act of Chapultepec was essentially about self-defence, but the use of coercion in other circumstances had to be authorized centrally. But, given that self-defence was only part of the mandate of Inter-American institutions, the reference to self-defence resolved only part of the problem accruing to interaction between the UN and the Inter-American security framework, as developments over subsequent decades have demonstrated.[62]

---

[57] Eide, n 33 above, 133–4.

[58] AC Arend, 'The United Nations, Regional Organizations, and Military Operations: The Past and the Present', 7 *Duke Journal of Comparative and International Law* (1996–7), 3 at 6–7; the same difference in approaches characterized US political opinion, which was divided between isolationists opposing UN involvement in European or Pacific affairs, and those who envisaged a global role for America: Claude, n 47 above, 5; see also in general Eide, n 33 above, 133.

[59] Claude, n 47 above, 6–7; Arend, n 58 above, 8.

[60] Goodrich, n 49 above, 49: the Latin American position was suitable for the member States of the Arab League as well and they asked for their Pact to be referred to along with the Act of Chapultepec, though in the end the references to specific arrangements were dropped: M Khadduri, 'The Arab League as a Regional Arrangement', 40 AJIL (1946), 756 at 772–3.

[61] Akehurst, n 23 above, 175; Arend, n 58 above, 9; J Kunz, 'Individual and Collective Self-Defense in Article 51 of the Charter of the United Nations', 41 AJIL (1947), 872.

[62] See on this section 4 below.

Some delegations at San Francisco, such as Australia and France, went further than Latin American states and opposed the principle requiring the unanimity of permanent members to authorize regional enforcement. Australia especially contended that, in the case of Security Council's inaction, regional organizations should be able to take such action as they deem just and necessary to restore peace and security 'in accordance with that arrangement'.[63] The UN Charter rejects regional autonomy along those lines as it adopts the solution directly opposed to that.

The positions expressed by the Latin American states on the Dumbarton Oaks proposals evince that they did not intend to claim any form of regional autonomy from the future world organization. Statements made by 13 Latin American states on the Dumbarton Oaks proposals specified that regional organizations should comply with the UN Charter, and there was to be no regional enforcement. In disputes, the Security Council could only intervene 'if the regional agency fails or disputes in the region threaten world peace'. This viewpoint was expressly stated by Brazil, Chile, Venezuela, and Peru.[64] A clear support for subsidiarity of the UN role was thus articulated.

Post-Cold War trends towards regionalization have been caused by regional interests and assertiveness, such as the desire for a greater African autonomy in providing 'African solutions for African problems', ASEAN's closeness to the concerns of South-east Asian security, and the OAS experience with democratization and preventive diplomacy in Latin America. The empowerment of regional organizations and actors may have been influenced by the lack of or limits on UN capacity, yet it led to a degree of autonomy that discredited the UN purposes by placing peace enforcement at the hands of regional hegemons, such as the United States in NATO, Russia in the CIS, or Nigeria in ECOWAS. Regional organizations were thus understood as institutional tools for supporting and veiling the political status and agenda of regional hegemons acting in their own interest. In addition, trends to regionalization have been promoted by the fear among developing countries that the UN has been hijacked by the powerful Western states.[65] A perception has developed in a similar fashion among Western states that the use of regional arrangements is one way to evade the influence of China and Russia, who hold the veto power in the Security Council. The universality of UN collective security is reinforced, however, by the need for unanimity of permanent members before Security Council enforcement action can be launched. As Morgenthau suggests, if the UN were to undertake enforcement action without the assent of one of the permanent members, it would lose both its peace-maintenance function

---

[63] Cf Bebr, n 39 above, 171.

[64] The original Spanish version of the Mexico City conference records of the 1945 Inter-American Conference on Problems of War and Peace is referenced in J Lloyd Mecham, 'The Integration of the Inter-American Security System Into the United Nations', 9(2) *The Journal of Politics* (1947), 178 at 187–9.

[65] Fawcett, n 52 above, 14, 17–18, 19, 22; Pugh, n 11 above, 37; Nigeria was deemed to have vested interest in the mineral resources and diamonds of Sierra Leone: Durward, n 6 above, 356.

and its legal identity, and become a political and military coalition against permanent members or members.[66]

As Sir Marrack Goulding has pointed out, arguments for regionalization are specious and arguments against it are strong. It is contrary to the ethical vision of universalism that people in a particular region receive only such level of peace keeping as their regional organization can provide. Although the universal reach of the UN is questionable, decentralization is seen to be riddled with risks of fragmenting security, possibly abandoning some areas of the world to lawlessness and even fostering a peace-keeping apartheid. Peace operations deployed by most regional organizations have been ineffective.[67]

The universality of collective security is insufficient, however, as is clear from Henry Kissinger's observation that 'if everybody is allied with everybody, nobody has a special relationship with anybody. It is the ideal situation for the most ruthless seeking to isolate potential victims.'[68] Also, regional organizations offer a more feasible response to aggression where resources are more likely to be mobilized and decisions more likely to be taken than at the UN level.[69] On the other hand, it is pointed out that regional organizations

may lack the experience of UNDPKO [UN Department of Peacekeeping Operations] and may be perceived as partial or as dominated by a regional hegemon. More fundamentally, they lack the unique legitimacy of the 192-Member United Nations. For this reason, erosion of the UN's primacy role in peacekeeping and peacebuilding should be avoided; regional peacekeeping should remain the exception.[70]

The Secretary-General especially warned against viewing delegation of peace-restoration tasks to regional organizations as a panacea, since problems of resources and impartiality can arise.[71] When the majority in a regional organization is strongly biased against one of the parties to the conflict, and where such bias is shared by a great power with hegemonic influence, efforts for pacific settlement might not be quite sincere, and can end up in using a regional organization as a shield to prevent the UN from becoming involved in the context of a more or less disguised armed attack.[72] More specifically,

[w]hile regional action is preferable to coercion by individual States, there is no guarantee that it will always be benign. In fact, history tells us that control and supervision by a body not representing immediate interests in an ongoing conflict is indispensable. Therefore, regional organizations will not be able to assume a stopgap function for an ineffectual

---

[66] H Morgenthau, 'Diplomacy', 55 *Yale Law Journal* (1945–6), 1067 at 1076.

[67] Cf Pugh, n 11 above, 38; I Martin, 'Is Regionalisation of Peace Operations Desirable?', in Pugh and Sidhu, n 11 above, 47 at 53.

[68] Quoted in H McCoubrey and J Morris, *Regional Peacekeeping in the Post-Cold War Era* (The Hague: Kluwer, 2000), 10.

[69] Mackay, n 9 above, 124; Schreuer, n 8 above, 496.

[70] Wouters and Ruys, n 27 above, 254.

[71] *The causes of conflict and the promotion of durable peace and sustainable development in Africa*, Report of the Secretary-General, A/52/871–S/1998/318, 13 April 1990, 10.

[72] Eide, n 33 above, 126.

universal system. The overarching authority of a global institution is essential to check abuse and to provide the necessary coordination.

Without this, 'the Security Council could degenerate into an agency for the rubber-stamp legitimization of regional power politics by its more influential Members'.[73] The rationale for UN intervention then is to compensate for the partisan element in the regional effort through applying its universalist impartial policies.

This policy can be compromised by the problem 'that it is regional hegemonic powers that are providing the means for the operation and taking up the burden of peacekeeping'.[74] More acutely,

the concept of 'partnership' is overused, given that it is often one-sided. At times partnership is devoid of clear understanding or knowledge of the recipient's needs. The customer is not asked, primarily because the strategic interest of the bigger power decides what is needed or the limits of its assistance.[75]

Thus, there is in political terms no universal way of assuming whether the regional or universal organizations should have primacy over the matter at issue. The promotion of a power-political agenda is possible both through universal and regional mechanisms and where one such is used for a power-political purpose, the other could—and should—be used to balance it and protect the victim.

The reason why in 1954 Guatemala preferred the UN evaluation of its invasion complaint to that by the OAS was that the latter organization was dominated by the United States, which regarded the Guatemalan government as communist. Thus the OAS could offer no real response to this crisis, as it was more inclined to promote than to prevent the overthrow of the Guatemalan government, which would have been treated by the OAS as a defendant not a plaintiff. On the other hand, the United States opposed UN involvement because it accused the USSR of having 'designs on the American hemisphere', and warned against the Security Council exercising a veto over OAS activities.[76] A fairly similar contrast of positions was displayed in the crisis between the United States and Cuba in the early 1960s. As the USA claimed, in relation to enforcement measures taken by OAS against Cuba, regional organizations would be stultified if subjected to the strong control of the Security Council.[77]

Policy dilemmas arise. If regional enforcement is subjected to the requirement for UN Security Council authorization, a single hostile permanent member could block the action; conversely, a permanent member who happened to be in the regionally dominant position could get a particular regional organization to act in its interest, effectively without UN supervision.

---

[73] Schreuer, n 8 above, 497–8.
[74] Durward, n 6 above, 356.
[75] F Olonisakin and C Ero, 'Africa and the Regionalisation of Peace Operations', in Pugh and Sidhu, n 11 above, 233 at 246.
[76] I Claude, 'The OAS, the UN and the United States', 35 *International Conciliation* (No 547, March 1964), 1 at 23, 25, 27–8, 30, 52.
[77] Claude, n 47 above, 35, 56–7.

Several regional organizations—the OAS, NATO, the EU, the AU, or ECOWAS—have claimed regional autonomy to various degrees. According to Abass, the legitimacy crisis of the UN Security Council and the reluctance of the UN to carry out timely and effective interventions in Africa has caused the activation of regional organizations in the area of peace and security. The adoption in 1999 of the ECOWAS Protocol on Conflict Prevention Mechanism witnessed precisely this trend. The Protocol empowers ECOWAS to carry out enforcement measures foreseen under Article 53 of the UN Charter but arguably without UN authorization.[78] According to other commentators, 'ECOWAS members often felt reluctant to seek UN legitimacy primarily because they saw no reason to be answerable to an organisation that neither mandated nor paid for their activities'.[79]

Another side of the problem is that, despite the African autonomy and African solutions thesis, 'some African leaders have yet to define their own view of the continent's security needs, thus allowing donors to manipulate the environment and determine their needs'.[80] On the other hand, the Security Council's support for 'African solutions to African problems' is often seen in Africa as an excuse to abandon the UN's proper responsibilities in the area of peace and security in this region.[81] If there is not sufficient political will at the regional level to enable regional institutions to identify threats coherently and decide on response, this supports the enhanced rationale of the UN involvement.

The EU's involvement in the conflict prevention field is dictated by the need to ensure security within the EU itself,[82] as opposed to dealing with local threats as such. It is emphasized that 'in Brussels, the choice of means is undertaken according to Member States' interests and their ability to push through these interests at the EU level'.[83] In some circumstances, this could duplicate the collective security agenda in relation to the current crisis and undermine the unity of collective security.

The Arab League and the OAU have not been controlled by a regional *hegemon*, but both have targets that have made them appear partial in some periods. The League has its 'just cause'—liberation of Palestine—which makes it perceived as opposed to Israel. The OAU cause has been the elimination of colonialism, of remaining white minority governments in Africa, and of neo-colonial policies.[84] However, the OAU's just cause has actually been reflected in the UN policy of decolonization. African states in the UN have been among the driving forces against South Africa and Portugal.[85]

---

[78] Abass, n 37 above, 102.
[79] Olonisakin and Ero, n 75 above, 246.
[80] Ibid, 247.
[81] A Adebajo, 'Ethiopia/Eritrea', in D Malone (ed.), *The UN Security Council—From the Cold War to the 21st Century* (Boulder/London: Lynne Rienner Inc, 2004), 575 at 586.
[82] V Kronenberger and J Wouters, 'Introduction', in Kronenberger and Wouters (eds.), *The European Union and Conflict Prevention—Policy and Legal Aspects* (The Hague: TMC Asser Press, 2004), XXV; see Chapter 4 below (threats).
[83] R Rummel, 'The EU's Involvement in Conflict Prevention', in Kronenberger and Wouters, ibid, 67 at 71.
[84] Eide, n 33 above, 137–8.
[85] FO Wilcox, 'Regionalism and Collective Security', 19 *International Organisation* (1965), 789 at 802.

The relationship between universal and regional organizations can also be examined by reference to their ideological underpinnings. For instance, while the UN is based on secular universalism premised on the aim of global redemption through respect and accommodation of the other, organizations like the EU or NATO are premised on a particular ideology of democratic liberalism, acting as a vehicle for the community of democracies.[86] The preference for EU and NATO action can be motivated by their Western character. There is fear in the UN that the ESDP serves egocentric and Eurocentric purposes of the European Union.[87] The European Union expresses one cultural viewpoint on world affairs.[88] Arguably, regionalization thus contributes to a revision of the world order along the patterns of liberalism.[89]

The US administration considered it right for NATO to use force without Security Council authorization when the United States thought this a good idea. They presumably do not envisage organizations like the Arab League or the CIS to be equally free in this field. Nonetheless, distinguishing NATO from those other organizations could not be accomplished without an accepted legal principle.[90] Brunée criticizes as problematic the view of Slaughter that a permanent coalition of liberal states should be given power to authorize the use of force when the Security Council is paralysed. This idea is seen as unacceptable to developing states, contradicting the pluralist background of international law, and 'a banding together of a coalition of democratic States would only further poison international relations'.[91]

The policy aspect of the relationship between universal and regional institutions is neither one-sided nor absolutely straightforward. Inaction, power politics, and interest manipulation are possible at all levels; the constructive approach is to secure such involvement of various levels as could check abuse at other levels. There are policy reasons both for and against decentralization, none of which is inherently better or worse than others. Each policy approach is subjective and forward-looking, and does not inherently accommodate limits on its reach. As has been most pertinently emphasized,

the regional/universal debate can never be resolved. Indeed, neither side will be able to provide the necessary empirical evidence to sustain its arguments, and both sides are plagued with relativism, because none of their generalisations is free from exceptions. These exceptions are too many to sustain any important pattern.[92]

The dilemmas produced by these policy arguments are conceptually insoluble, since each policy argument is sound, and contains no indication as to how

---

[86] Graham, n 42 above, 256.

[87] Wouters and Ruys, n 27 above, 251.

[88] Graham, n 42 above, 287.

[89] Pugh, n 11 above, 33.

[90] ME O'Connell, 'The United Nations Security Council and the Authorisation of Force', in N Blokker and N Schrijver, (eds.), *The Security Council and the Use of Force* (Leiden: Martinus Nijhoff, 2005), 47 at 53.

[91] J Brunée, 'The Security Council and Self-Defence: Which Way to Global Security?', in Blokker and Schrijver, ibid, 107 at 114.

[92] Tacsan, n 48 above, 491.

conflicting—and likewise sound—policies should be accommodated. There is no international consensus on the inherent validity of such policies, nor on how conflict between these policies should be resolved. However, the principles of competence stated in or inferable from constituent instruments command more consensus and point to agreed lines for dividing tasks and labour.

4. Principles of Competence

(a) General Aspects

Addressing the problem of interaction between the UN and regional organizations, the UN High-Level Panel suggested formalizing their cooperation in an agreement.[93] The Supplement to the *Agenda for Peace* identified the parameters of the interaction between the UN and regional organizations:

(a) Agreed mechanisms for consultation should be established, but need not be formal; (b) The primacy of the United Nations, as set out in the Charter, must be respected. . . . (c) The division of labour must be clearly defined and agreed in order to avoid overlap and institutional rivalry where the United Nations and a regional organization are both working on the same conflict. In such cases it is also particularly important to avoid a multiplicity of mediators; (d) Consistency by members of regional organizations who are also Member States of the United Nations is needed in dealing with a common problem of interest to both organizations, for example, standards for peace-keeping operations.[94]

These are policy proposals. Burden sharing and labour division are rational expectations, while competence allocation needs to be examined in its normative dimension. Principles for allocating competence are necessary, to show who has the better claim to involvement under the existing legal position. A general thesis that global and regional institutions should cooperate and share the burdens of maintaining international peace and security is certainly going to be acceptable in all quarters, but can do little to indicate solutions for specific problems. Everyone is likely to agree that cooperation between institutions is a good idea. But this does not automatically translate into principles for allocating competence which are designed to apply when institutions decide to cooperate and act jointly, nor when they do not wish to cooperate with one another and get jointly involved, nor when one institution is keen on keeping another one out. Such principles are needed to resolve controversies as much as to promote cooperation, and to indicate preferences when there is a disagreement between universal and regional institutions

---

[93] High-Level Panel, 90.

[94] *Supplement to an Agenda for Peace: Position Paper of the Secretary-General on the Occasion of the Fiftieth Anniversary of the United Nations*, Report of the Secretary-General on the Work of the Organization, A/50/60–S/1995/1, 3 January 1995, para 88; on the need to ensure division of labour and prevent the UN from getting overloaded, see WA Knight, 'Towards A Subsidiarity Model for Peacemaking and Preventive Diplomacy: Making Chapter VIII of the UN Charter Operational', 17 *Third World Quarterly* (1996), 31 at 32–3.

as to what should be done in a particular case, what action, if any, is appropriate, or which institution, if any, is better placed to intervene.

The universal collective security framework is obviously important in identifying starting-point policies and presumptions on this matter. Unlike the deferential approach embodied in Article 21 of the League of Nations Covenant, the Chapter VIII framework is premised on the principle of the unity of collective security. Action can be taken at different levels, but the multilevel arrangement under Chapter VIII allowing for both interaction and reaction among parties is meant to ensure that the policy adopted in every particular case should be the only one that is genuinely needed to combat pertinent threats. To this end, the Charter enables the UN to follow regional choices, yet imposes the criterion of legality of these choices and provides for the eventuality that UN decisions will have primacy. The complexity of Chapter VIII, as opposed to the single-handedness of Article 21 of the League Covenant, is precisely what can guarantee the unity of collective security. For this unity means neither unconditional UN primacy nor unbridled regional autonomy: it means effective action through mutual control. A key description of this process is the multilevel interaction to implement any one policy. Neither UN organs nor regional agencies are ultimate judges of whether and how this policy is best served. In a world where a global government is absent and every authority could potentially exceed its competence, no organ should be able to unconditionally impose its choices and conclusively interpret its own competence.

In national legal systems the allocation of competence between various levels of government is regulated through a single legislative framework. Such arrangements are not in place internationally. As Claude suggests, the decision of the San Francisco Conference to make the UN the principal collective security agency provided no precise indication of the division of competences and responsibility between that organization and regional agencies, and there is no clear delineation of their relationships under the Charter.[95]

There is certainly no inherent division of competences to undertake particular types of action at regional rather than universal levels: for instance, by allocating robust operational tasks to one level and conciliatory tasks to another. The general pattern of competence allocation seems to require the 'the primacy of dispute settlement through regional means (Articles 33(1) and 52(2) and (3)). On the other hand, enforcement action remain[s] under the overriding jurisdiction of the Security Council (Articles 24, 25, 39–42, 53(1) and 54).'[96] However, the type of a particular jurisdiction is relevant to show how competence is allocated in a particular case. 'Exclusive jurisdiction' allows only the entity that possesses it to judge whether action is suitable or justified; 'concurrent jurisdiction' admits the exercise of judgement by different entities on the same matter concurrently; 'residual jurisdiction' is exercised by the entity unless and until another entity having the proper mandate demonstrates positively that such judgement should be replaced or overtaken.

---

[95] Claude, n 47 above, 15.
[96] Schreuer, n 8 above, 478.

Competence allocation is essentially a problem of treaty interpretation. As Goodhart explains,

> If the Constitution provides specifically that the federal power shall be exclusive then there is no problem, but what is the answer if the instrument is silent on this point? Ought there to be a presumption that when power to deal with a particular subject-matter is given to the central body this automatically excludes the constituent states, or is there a presumption in favour of concurrent exercise of power? It may be suggested on this point that powers will be construed to be exclusive only if that is expressly declared in the instrument or is a necessary implication, because it is not reasonable to hold that the constituent states have surrendered more of their power than was essential for the particular purpose. . . . All powers which have not been expressly or by necessary implication transferred to the United Nations remain in the individual States. They hold these powers not by grant but by sovereign right.[97]

Likewise, states can delegate the same rights to a regional organization on a concurrent basis. In addition, some powers expressly provided for in the constituent instrument of one organization could also constitute implied powers of another organization. The competence thus established is parallel and concurrent, but not exclusive.

From the normative perspective, outcomes depend on the interaction between constituent instruments, particularly their parallel applicability and interpretation, including the implications of silence in these instruments regarding the matter of competence in the present case. A normative conflict under Article 30 of the 1969 Vienna Convention on the Law of Treaties only arises if the operation of one treaty prevents the application of another treaty in relation to the same set of facts, more specifically if the constituent instrument of one organization were to claim competence in relation to matters over which exclusive competence is vested in another organization according to its own constituent instrument. As collective security competence is mostly concurrent and parallel, rather than exclusive, Article 30 situations should not be expected to arise frequently.

In some instances, normative outcomes are expressly prescribed, such as under Article 103 of the UN Charter or former Article 307 of the EU Treaty, as examined by the European Court of Justice in the *Kadi* case. Article 103 makes the Charter prevail over the constituent instruments of regional organizations; its real effect in particular cases must be measured by reference to what the Charter, especially Chapters VI and VIII, actually requires in terms of allocating competence. If it follows that competence is concurrent, then Article 103 does not entail the primacy of UN jurisdiction over regional arrangements. An additional agreement or understanding in state or institutional practice can be deemed to embody the attitude of the pertinent institutions' membership as to the scope of institutional competence. The process of mutual reaction by UN and regional organizations to each others' activities also has systemic value in the absence of any overarching legislative framework allocating their competences in a comprehensive way. Such reactions

---

[97] A Goodhart, 'North Atlantic Treaty Organisation', 79 *Recueil des Cours de l'Académie de Droit International de la Haye* (II–1951), 183 at 192–3.

can draw legal judgments. It will also matter whether particular views and practice relate to an area in which competence is not expressly defined, or attempt to redefine a competence that is already defined in constituent instruments. Extra-conventional factors such as consent and acquiescence to pertinent actions or positions can also explain institutional competence or give preference to one institution's involvement over that of another when otherwise both institutions are similarly entitled to get involved.

Principles of competence are residual to what is stipulated in constituent instruments; they are not meant to replace or revise consensually allocated competence, but to complement it and give such expression to it as to make it applicable to specific cases, thus enabling the entire collective security framework to respond to threats effectively. The ultimate merit of quasi-statutory and quasi-consensual principles of competence allocation is premised on their utility to implement in practice the principle that collective security is united, give effect to Chapter VIII provisions that are doctrinally deemed to be ambiguous, and consequently ensure that various levels of competence are involved with the sole aim of ensuring the proper identification of threats and adoption of the measures of response that the relevant situation requires. Such principles are needed to resolve, in a transparent and predictable manner, political disagreements over which institution should be involved first and which one should be kept out.

(b) Complementarity

Models of organizational interaction between the UN and regional organizations in giving effect to Chapter VIII are helpful in understanding how different institutional levels are mutually compatible. The *redundancy* model describes cases where the jurisdiction and operational capabilities of global and regional organizations are similar and overlapping. There would be no UN impotence *versus* regional strength and vice versa. The *complementary capabilities* model is directly opposed to the redundancy one, and describes situations where different collective security levels have different jurisdiction and capabilities. Where this model applies, no level of collective security can handle crises on its own. Under this model the relevance of politics is quite limited and the matters at hand can be disposed by objective facts— the UN cannot act if the matter does not threaten the peace beyond the particular region, and a regional action might be insufficient if the matter is too serious. A related model is that of *context specialization*, where organizations can have comparable capabilities, but one may possess the advantage of having jurisdiction more useful in a particular specialized context. This model is based on understanding UN intervention in regional conflict, not as inherent but as subsidiary to the role of regional organizations. The *comparative advantage* model refers to a 'subjective' choice by relevant actors to entrust the resolution of a crisis to an institution that will better reflect their interests, as opposed to emphasizing general goals of collective security. The issues of capability and jurisdiction will have to be adapted to fit. It is argued that Chapter VIII reflects this model, allowing that level to intervene in relation to which a better multilateral consensus can be formed. Jurisdiction of institutions arguably depends on the bargaining perception or advantage of states. As a matter of outcome, this approach reflects the connection between the geographical proximity of a crisis and the interest of states in resolving it, and thus favours most regional crises being handled through regional mechanisms.[98]

Most UN cases are indistinguishable from many regional cases in their type and character, for instance by being limited to a particular region, and in many cases neither the UN nor regional organizations have a decided advantage in handling them. This is seen as further evidence that the comparative advantage model best represents the idea behind Chapter VIII. Its operational dimension has confirmed its normative role.[99] Advantage here is defined in terms of the subjective choice of states, presumably where the actors involved wanted to keep the matter out of collective security altogether. However, Butterworth comes to recognize the objective dimension to a comparative advantage model, which he initially defines as subjective. This model is expected to lead to UN intervention where there are disagreements within the region as to the regional institutions' role and the latter do not resolve the crisis.[100] This links the comparative advantage model to subsidiarity: even if the cause behind institutional involvement is subjective, the outcome of a regional effort failing is objective.

It has to be examined how far these models are reflected in constituent instruments, and how the practice in question came to accept or reject them; and whether all four models are qualitatively different from each other, or in fact logically and structurally premised on each other. General Assembly Resolution 49/57 (1994) specifies that regional organizations, in the fields of their respective competence, can usefully complement the work of the UN in the area of peace and security. Security Council Resolution 1809(2008) specifies in paragraph 9 that

common and coordinated efforts undertaken by the United Nations and regional organizations, in particular the African Union in matters of peace and security, should be based on their complimentary capacities, making full use of their experience in accordance with the United Nations Charter and the relevant Statutes of the regional organizations.

In the Presidential Statement adopted in 2007, the Security Council 'recognize[d] that regional organizations are well positioned to understand the root causes of many conflicts closer to home and to influence the prevention or resolution, owing to their knowledge of the region'.[101] In a way similar to the Presidential Statement, General Assembly Resolution 49/57 specifies that '[c]ooperation between regional

---

[98] Butterworth, n 56 above, 199–205.
[99] Ibid, 208, 213.
[100] Ibid, 215.
[101] SC Presidential Statement S/PRST/2007/7, 28 March 2007, at 2; *In Larger Freedom*, SG Report, 52 (para 213); the same affirmed in the Secretary-General's report, S/2008/186, para 9, referring to 'compelling underlying reasons' such as 'their proximity to the crisis and their familiarity with the actors and issues involved in a particular crisis. More importantly, regional organizations have a keen interest in resolving crises that erupt in their backyard.' See also *The Security Council and regional organizations: facing the new challenges to international peace and security*, 11 April 2003, S/PV.4739, 22 (Russia); *Cooperation . . . in stabilization processes*, n 2 above, 7 (AU), 13 (China).

arrangements or agencies and the United Nations should be in accordance with their respective mandates, scope and composition and should take place in forms that are suited to each specific situation, in accordance with the Charter'. Linking the issue of complementarity with the interpretation of mandates specified under constituent instruments of organizations affirms the link between complementarity and the distribution of competence between institutions.

Some members of the Security Council have also emphasized that

regional organizations have the advantage of physical proximity to the threats, as well as a greater understanding of those threats and the political sensitivities involved. Concerted action allows them to exploit this advantage and facilitates an appropriate interpretation of the provisions of the Charter, particularly with respect to peacekeeping actions and support for the delivery of humanitarian aid. . . . The response of local actors to a regional threat can benefit from a more homogeneous socio-cultural vision. These actors have a special incentive to maintain security in the area and their proximity facilitates a timely response.[102]

It was further observed that

On the basis of the principle of complementarity, it is possible to make more rational and effective use of the comparative advantages of each organization. . . . it is necessary fully to take advantage of each regional organization's unique experience within its own sphere of action and its precise knowledge of local cultural conditions and mechanisms of under-standing for treating post-conflict situations.[103]

In another report, the Secretary-General upheld the idea of 'determining a division of labour based on their comparative advantages'.[104]

The precise parameters of complementarity have to be worked out by reference to particular areas of competence and institutional interaction in accordance with constituent instruments. More specifically, precisely what complementarity is has to be clarified: a normative or quasi-normative principle with straightforward content and requirements; a general framework of cooperation and/or resolving competence conflicts; or a principle merely to divide labour and allocate resources, but not competence?

In the pertinent Security Council discussion, the Chinese representative upheld the relevance of complementarity between UN and regional organizations. The French representative went further and made a 'general comment' suggesting that 'we need to ensure that our cooperation abides by the principle of complementarity. Each organization should intervene first and foremost in the area where it can provide real added value'.[105] Complementarity thus understood can work both ways without justifying any categorical preconception of which level ought to have initial jurisdiction. 'Real added value' presumably refers to a genuine contribution to restoring peace and security in the particular situation; no institutional involvement is justified for its own sake.

---

[102] *Cooperation . . . in stabilization processes*, ibid, 9 (Chile), 21 (Brazil).
[103] Ibid, 5 (Mexico).
[104] *A Regional-global Security Partnership*, n 1 above, 16.
[105] *Facing the new challenges*, n 101 above, 28 (China), 35 (France).

Under complementarity root causes that are region-specific lead to regional organizations being assigned the preventive function. As the Brazilian representative specified, 'regional organizations can detect potential threats faster and they can be very useful in an early-warning system'.[106] Spain identified complementarity and comparative advantage with 'faster intervention and better knowledge of the ground'. This 'can foster a heightened feeling of ownership among those populations'.[107] The representative of Benin pointed out that

a genuine complementarity [should] be developed between the actions of the Security Council and regional contributions to peace and security. Depending on the seriousness of the situation and the speed of the action required, regional organizations may offer a comparative advantage in terms of their capacity to intervene rapidly to prevent a situation from spiralling out of control.[108]

The ASEAN representative specified that the optimization of organizational potential on the basis of comparative advantage will lead to complementary efforts and the elimination of duplication.[109] Germany was more specific in treating complementarity as more a practical principle of good governance than a normative allocation of competence. Complementarity means that 'one actor—whether the United Nations or a regional organization—will offer a comparative advantage'. Division of labour will be successful if all relevant actors are involved, the most suitable one takes the lead, and funding problems are resolved.[110]

It is by now clear that comparative advantage has been viewed in state and UN practice as focusing, not on the interests of individual states, but on the need to secure the unity and consistency of collective security goals and efforts. Chapter VIII may be open to providing room to a multilateral and local choice in some respects but in other respects it is about regional subordination to the Security Council. The utility of the 'comparative advantage' and 'complementarity' approaches is to remove collective security matters from the field of purely political choices and help to use collective security institutions in genuinely multilateral interests. While complementarity does get asserted, upheld, and not contradicted, it has to be ensured that it becomes a practicable standard and not a bureaucratic cliché without identifiable content. One perspective was suggested by Belgium in the Security Council debates that led to the adoption of Resolution 1809(2008):

If a regional organization decides to establish a peacekeeping operation authorized by the Security Council under Chapter VIII of the Charter, the Council is validating the international legality of the operation. Such authorization, however, does not imply that the United Nations is substituting itself for the regional organization or that it is automatically assuming political, logistical or financial responsibility.

---

[106] Ibid, 21 (Brazil).
[107] Ibid, 31 (Spain).
[108] Ibid, 10 (Benin).
[109] Ibid, 19 (ASEAN) (the same view was expressed in UNDPKO, Lessons Learned Unit, *Cooperation between the United Nations and Regional Organisations/Arrangements*, Suggested Principles and Mechanisms, March 1999, at 14).
[110] Ibid, 17 (Germany).

The situation is somewhat different when the United Nations decides to support the operation of a regional organization. In the case of a joint operation, the United Nations and the regional organization are both responsible for the preparation and conduct of the operation. That is a particularly complex form of cooperation that can succeed only if it is based on a common political vision.

In order to avoid all misunderstandings, appropriate consultations between the organizations are vital, especially in the initial decision-making phase. Such consultations must help to prevent decisions made by one party from taking the other by surprise and to facilitate cooperation in their implementation. They should also allow us better to determine the kind of cooperation that is most appropriate, based on the nature and geographical characteristics of a given conflict.[111]

This last observation is important for the authorization of enforcement action. If there is inter-level cooperation, decisions must be taken and policy must be determined jointly, that is before the operation is deployed, as opposed to the UN approving regional operations *ex post facto*. One could not support the role of the UN by excluding it from the decision-making process.

As the UNDPKO has specified, the ways to achieve complementary action, collaboration, and division of labour can include consultation, exchange of views, diplomatic support, operational support with resources and troops, co-deployment, and joint operations. The adequacy of the mandates of UN, regional, and sub-regional organizations is also critical.[112] Allowance must still be made for cases 'when a regional or subregional body will choose to become involved not because it enjoys a comparative advantage, but for a political or other imperative'.[113] The comparative advantage model has not caused regional organizations to prevent UN interference. The division of labour has been arranged so as to let the UN intervene in a way that forestalls its more active intervention at a later point should the situation aggravate further, while regional agencies would perform a managing role.[114] Regional organizations can also undertake parts of UN-authorized missions, such as training of forces, financing, and strategic airlift, eg the EU activities in Darfur.

In Liberia, the division of responsibilities put ECOWAS in charge of the enforcement side and the UN of observation. ECOMOG forces were responsible for the military aspects of implementing the 1993 Cotonou Peace Agreement and of the arms embargo imposed by Security Council Resolution 788(1992), while the UN mission monitored ECOMOG forces for their impartiality. In paragraph 3(h) of Resolution 866(1993) the UN Observer Mission in Liberia (UNOMIL) was required '[w]ithout participation in enforcement operations, to coordinate with ECOMOG in the discharge of ECOMOG's separate responsibilities both formally, through the Violations Committee, and informally'. However, complementarity has to be assessed dynamically, considering all factors in the ongoing process. As has been emphasized,

---

[111] S/PV.5868, 21 (Belgium).
[112] UNDPKO, n 109 above, 7, 13.
[113] Ibid, 10.
[114] Butterworth, n 56 above, 213–14.

ECOMOG's activities in both Liberia and Sierra Leone included looting, widespread promiscuity and human rights abuses. It is unlikely that mandatory UN Security Council authorization on its own would improve the record of such operations unless combined with much more intrusive linkages for oversight at every level of the operation.[115]

In Sierra Leone, ECOWAS first imposed sanctions on the junta and then appealed to the UN to make these sanctions global. Security Council Resolution 1132 (1997) both adopted sanctions and entrusted ECOWAS with the task of their enforcement. This was needed because sanctions were now global and had to be observed by non-ECOWAS states.

The Security Council mission report on Sierra Leone specified that there had to be an effective consultation mechanism between the UN and ECOWAS. The Council pointed out that 'the leadership of ECOWAS is displaying energy and vision, but the organization itself—by its own admission—lacks sufficient resources and expertise to carry forward and implement its initiatives, such as the proposal to place ECOWAS military observers on the borders. As a key first step, the mission recommends an immediate package of international assistance to help the ECO-WAS secretariat to develop its capacity.'[116]

The OAU expressly applied the complementarity approach to the peace-keeping operation in Zaire. The Addis Ababa Communiqué of the Central Organ of the OAU Mechanism for Conflict Prevention, Management and Resolution at the level of ministers emphasized the humanitarian tragedy unfolding in eastern Zaire, with its far-reaching implications for peace, security, and stability in the region. The Organ specified that setting up a neutral force as recommended by the Nairobi Summit would have been the most effective manner of facilitating the creation of safe corridors and temporary sanctuaries and ensuring an effective African contribution to such a force, and regretted that the UN Security Council did not fully take into account the OAU recommendation to that effect. But the Organ added that, given the decision by the Security Council to create a multinational force, African participation in such a force would be pivotal. Most interestingly, the Organ goes on to observe that

given the resource constraints that would clearly face African contributors to the force, the Central Organ underscores the need for the Security Council and the international community at large to create a mechanism which would ensure an effective African participation. This means that financial, logistic and material resources should be provided on a very reliable, dependable and sustainable basis.[117]

The Security Council's response in Resolution 1080(1996) was to decide that

---

[115] Durward, n 6 above, 356; R May and G Cleaver, 'African Peacekeeping: Still Dependent?', 4 *International Peacekeeping* (1997), 1 at 13–14. Furthermore, it was complained that persistent bombing attacks by ECOMOG on civilian targets resulted in extensive casualties: *Report of the Secretary-general on the Question of Liberia*, S/25402, 12 March 1993, para 28.

[116] *Report of the Security Council Mission to Sierra Leone*, S/2000/992, 16 October 2000, para 55.

[117] *Communiqué issued after the fourth extraordinary session of the Central Organ of the OAU Mechanism for Conflict Prevention, Management and Resolution at the level of ministers Addis Ababa*, 11 November 1996, UN Doc S/1996/922.

the cost of implementing this temporary operation will be borne by the participating Member States and other voluntary contributions, and welcomes the establishment by the Secretary-General of a voluntary trust fund with the purpose of supporting African participation in the multinational force.[118]

The AU legal framework expressly admits the need to secure resources and capacities from outside Africa. According to Article 17(2) of the AU Peace and Security Council Protocol,

[w]here necessary, recourse will be made to the United Nations to provide the necessary financial, logistical and military support for the African Union's activities in the promotion and maintenance of peace, security and stability in Africa, in keeping with the provisions of Chapter VIII of the UN Charter on the role of Regional Organizations in the maintenance of international peace and security.

During the humanitarian catastrophe in Darfur, the AU's claims for 'ownership' of the problem were generally accepted by Western countries, because of political sensibilities involved with sending white soldiers to Africa. However, as AU members lacked military capabilities, particularly to transport troops from other parts of Africa to the region, external help was needed to fill the gap.[119] During the discussion of this topic in 2004 the AU representative put it to the Security Council that

the United Nations is not always in a position to address every crisis situation. In some situations in the past, the United Nations—and the international community as a whole, including Africa—have not been able to meet the challenge of peace in Africa. In other, more recent cases, such as in Burundi, the United Nations did not seem ready to intervene, given the lack of a peace to keep. An African peacekeeping mission had to be deployed, with great difficulty, under the aegis of the African Union until the Security Council decided to authorize the deployment of a United Nations operation, which it ultimately did. That scenario could be repeated in the future. The question therefore arises as to the extent to which the Security Council can authorize logistical and financial support for such operations as are deployed under its mandate or with its agreement, endorsement or backing.[120]

The complementarity of efforts acceptable under Chapter VIII of the UN Charter is illustrated by operations under UN mandate complemented by NATO and EU resources. In a report on the relationship between the UN and EU, the Union specified that

with the creation of a European military capacity, the question of the EU's possible contribution to UN-mandated peacekeeping and peace-making operations becomes more urgent than ever. As CFSP and ESDP are underpinned by the wish to act to uphold the principles and Charter of the UN, providing active and early support to UN-mandated or UN-led operations is a clear track for the progressive framing and deployment of the EU's security and defence policy and capabilities.[121]

---

[118] See paragraph 9. This had been the case with Chad earlier: Resolution 504(1982), trust fund.
[119] M Reichard *The EU–NATO Relationship* (Aldershot: Ashgate, 2006), 270–1.
[120] S/PV.5007, 7 (AU).
[121] *The European Union and the United Nations: The Choice of Multilateralism*, European Commission, 10 September 2003, Com (2003) 526 final, 7.

The 2004 declaration on EU–UN Cooperation in Military Crisis Management identified two options: provision of national military capabilities in the framework of a UN operation, or an EU operation in answer to a request from the UN.

Complementarity similarly operates between European and African institutions to support the leading role of African institutions in African conflicts. In March 2004 the EU member States adopted the Commission's proposal for the creation of a €250 million African Peace Facility. It aims to support African efforts to promote peace across the entire continent. It is based on the principle of African ownership and the AU will play a central role in its decision-making process. The facility will not finance European peacekeeping operations.[122] More generally, 'further enhancement and compatibility in crisis management have been discussed [between the UN and the AU] in the following areas: *(i)* planning; *(ii)* training; *(iii)* communication and *(iv)* best practices—which includes a "regularised and systematic exchange of lessons learned and best practices information, including sharing of information on mission hand-over and procurement."'[123]

Dinstein denotes the Chapter VIII involvement of regional organizations as sub-contracting,[124] which 'reflects the supremacy of a central authority while burden sharing implies a more diffuse control'.[125] Sub-contracting implies that the regional agency is involved in implementing a policy and task that is defined, or at least approved, by the UN. The EU involvement in the Congo can be denoted as complementarity through sub-contracting. The UN defined the policy basis for EU involvement and the EU moved in with its resources. Article 53 authorizations of the use of force can reflect complementarity, because the UN authority complements a regional effort that is backed by no authority comparable to that of the Security Council under Article 53 of the UN Charter.

It is suggested that the Charter originally foresaw the role of regional arrangements only within regions, which does not reflect how the EU and NATO get engaged in conflicts nowadays.[126] As Reichard explains for NATO, international peace and security is by definition a global, general interest to be pursued under the UN Charter. The security of NATO members does not necessarily extend to every case where international peace and security may be endangered.[127] Kronenberger and Wouters emphasize that the ability of the EU to manage conflicts outside its membership area forms the core of its new responsibilities.[128] Given the importance of the EU on the international scene, 'there is no doubt that the EU should

---

[122] *The European Union and Peacekeeping in Africa*, WEU Assembly 15th Session, Doc A/1880, 1 December 2004, explanatory memorandum, para 35.
[123] Ibid, para 42.
[124] Dinstein, n 33 above, 310; C Walter, 'Security Council Control over Regional Action', 1 *Max Planck Yearbook of UN Law* (1997), 129 at 192: 'in management terms', as outsourcing. 'Utilization' under Article 53 means that, while the overall responsibility for crisis management rests with the Council, the military part can be given to a regional organization; it also denotes the action of ECOWAS Liberia is sharing the burden between the UN and ECOWAS.
[125] Pugh, n 11 above, 40.
[126] Wouters and Ruys, n 27 above, 253–4.
[127] Reichard, n 119 above, 105.
[128] Kronenberger and Wouters, n 82 above, XXVII.

project stability beyond its own borders'.[129] The 1992 Lisbon European Council Conclusions clearly specified that common EU interests are determined by the proximity of the particular region to the EU, considerations of stability in that region, and the threat to the security of the EU and its members.[130] EU security is related to developments in other regions and vice versa:

An illustration of this interrelatedness is the relationship between the lack of human security in Northern or Sub-Saharan African countries, the problems of governance on a national level in several of these States, the growing strength and popularity of radical fundamentalist groups within society, the expanding recruitment basis for terrorist groups, and the growing insecurity for the West that arises from the increasingly popular fundamentalist and terrorist groups.[131]

Problems of this nature require the adoption of a structural 'root causes' approach, rather than a robust collective security action to tackle such threats. The EU intervention in the Congo was not meant to respond to those problems.

Trans-regional involvement could be required when the territorial state is reluctant to admit the UN mission on its territory. For instance, Indonesia was reluctant to accept a UN role in the Aceh situation and instead consented to the deployment of the EU Aceh Monitoring Mission.[132] Article 11(c) of the SADC Protocol provides that, in consultation with the UN Security Council and the OAU Central Organ, the SADC Organ 'may offer to mediate in a significant interior intra-state conflict that occurs outside the Region'. This is a vision of extra-regional involvement competence as limited by and contingent upon the primary responsibility of other organizations.

(c) Complementarity and the Concept of 'Primary Responsibility'

Although the 'primary responsibility' of the UN Security Council is mentioned in many instruments, it means little across the board and unless contextualized in terms of specific principles of competence and provisions of constituent instruments. The Security Council's 'primary responsibility' under Article 24 of the UN Charter reflects a structural view of 'primary responsibility'. A 'remedial' version of 'primary responsibility' focuses on the failure of the Security Council to act and the action by another organ or organization to step in. This is problematic, given that the Charter does not specify where the 'secondary' responsibility lies. Different regional organizations might then be willing to act in mutually conflicting ways. Should this be the legal position, it would support the possibility of inter-regional wars. There would be no objective measure of which organization is right.

---

[129] J Nino Perez, 'Conflict Indicators Developed by the Commission—The Check-List for Root Causes of Conflict/Early Warning Indicators', in Kronenberger and Wouters, ibid, 3 at 4.
[130] Annex I, para 3 and 12.
[131] S Keukeleire, 'EU Structural Foreign Policy', in Kronenberger and Wouters, n 82 above, 151 at 155–6.
[132] Wouters and Ruys, n 27 above, 257.

The UN–EU Joint Statement on Cooperation in Crisis Management (23 September 2004), subscribes to the primary responsibility for the maintenance of international peace and security of the Security Council.[133] Under the EU Security Strategy, the Union committed itself

> to upholding and developing International Law. The fundamental framework for international relations is the United Nations Charter. The United Nations Security Council has the primary responsibility for the maintenance of international peace and security. Strengthening the United Nations, equipping it to fulfil its responsibilities and to act effectively, is a European priority.[134]

As for the manner of EU involvement, the 2001 Göteborg Declaration specifies, in line with the complementarity approach, that 'the development of the ESDP strengthens the Union's capacity to contribute to international peace and security in accordance with the principles of the UN Charter'.[135]

The 1999 NATO Strategic Concept states that 'mutually reinforcing organizations have become a central feature of the security environment', and likewise subscribes to the Security Council's primary responsibility, also emphasizing that it 'plays a crucial role in contributing to security and stability in the Euro-Atlantic area'. The 1999 OSCE Istanbul Summit Document and the OAS Declaration on Security in the Americas affirm the same.[136]

'Primary responsibility' does not prescribe ready-made outcomes, nor define the principles of competence, nor by itself ensure the primacy of the UN across the board. This is illustrated by the African Union legal framework. Article 16 AUPSC Protocol specifies that the African Union has primary responsibility for promoting peace, security, and stability in Africa. Article 17 recognizes that the UN Security Council has primary responsibility for the maintenance of international peace and security, and commits the Union to work closely with the Council. This can be seen as mere conceptual thinking; or also as a perception of how the UN Charter allocates competence and responsibilities.[137] The AU representative explained this to the Security Council as reflecting the approach adopted by the UN Charter:

> it should be emphasized that article 16 of the Protocol of the Peace and Security Council stipulates that regional African mechanisms are an integral part of the basic security architecture of the Union, which has the primary responsibility for promoting security

---

[133] The same is reiterated in the 2007 Joint Statement on this matter, para 1; see also the EU Helsinki Presidency Conclusions 1999, Annex IV.

[134] *A Secure Europe in a Better World—A European Security Strategy*, European Council, 12 December 2003, 9.

[135] EU Presidency Conclusions, 15 and 16 June 2001, para 47.

[136] *Declaration on Security in the Americas*, 2003, para 4(z).

[137] A similar approach prevailed within the OAU. While the UN Security Council retained primary responsibility for the maintenance of international peace and security, the OAU 'remains the premier organization for promoting security, stability, development and cooperation in Africa', CCSDCA Solemn Declaration, AHG/Decl.4 (XXXVI), para 9(g), OAU, Lomé, 1999: ibid., (f): 'The responsibility for the security, stability and socio-economic development of the Continent lies primarily with African States'.

and stability in Africa. The spirit of article 16 also recalls Chapter VIII of the Charter of the United Nations.[138]

According to the preamble of the EU Council Common Position 2004/85/CFSP,

(1) The primary responsibility for prevention, management and resolution of conflicts on the African continent lies with Africans themselves. (2) The United Nations Security Council has the primary responsibility for the maintenance of international peace and security under the Charter of the United Nations.

Article 4 specifies that AU and sub-regional African organizations are central actors in prevention, management, and resolution of conflicts in Africa.[139] While the EU is not competent to pronounce on allocation of competences between two other organizations, its approach presumably restates the position specified in the AU Treaty. Another EU Common Position further spells out the relevance of complementarity:

Cooperation with the UN on crisis management shall be taken forward in line with and as a part of the implementation of the Joint Declaration on UN–EU Cooperation in Crisis Management of 24 September 2003. The EU, notwithstanding its commitment to African ownership, shall remain prepared to become involved, whenever necessary, in crisis management in Africa with its own capabilities.[140]

Thus the EU places its action within the limits of international law, and also accepts some hierarchy between African organizations and the special responsibility of the African Union:

ESDP actions should be in response to specific and well documented requests from the UN, the AU, African sub-regional organisations or African states. While fully respecting African ownership, proposals can be initiated by EU Member States. The EU shall, in response to requests from sub-regional organisations, consult with the African Union.[141]

Subsidiarity is more expressly emphasized in the WEU recommendation on the EU and peace-keeping in Africa, which

Tak[es] the view that the institutions responsible for the Union's Common Foreign and Security Policy and the European Security and Defence Policy should have a subsidiary role in coordinating bilateral and multilateral initiatives to support African military crisis-management capabilities.[142]

---

[138] *Cooperation ... in stabilization processes*, n 2 above, 7 (AU); under Article 16(1) AUPSC Protocol, the modality of partnership between AU and these organizations 'shall be determined by the comparative advantage of each and the prevailing circumstances'.

[139] Council Common Position 2004/85/CFSP of 26 January 2004 concerning conflict prevention, management and resolution in Africa and repealing Common Position 2001/374/CFSP, preambular paragraph 1; the same principle is reiterated in *Communication from the Commission to the Council*, Brussels, 23 June 2003, COM (2003) 316 final, Annex, para 2.

[140] Ibid, Article 2.

[141] *Action Plan for ESDP Support to Peace and Security in Africa*, Political and Security Committee, Brussels, 16 November 2004, Doc 10538.4/04/Rev 4, 3.

[142] Recommendation 756 on the European Union and Peacekeeping in Africa, 1 December 2004, preambular paragraph (ix).

This subscribes both to EU efforts complementing African efforts, and to subsidiary EU involvement; and illustrates the incidences of 'primary responsibility' in such contexts.

The primary responsibility of the Security Council necessarily includes its primacy over regional organizations in the area of enforcement. The German representative elaborated thus in the Security Council discussions on this point:

> the primary responsibility for the maintenance of international peace and security lies with the United Nations. The Security Council is the central forum for international conflict management. If the primacy of the Council with respect to the maintenance of international peace and security is rejected, the very foundations of international law, as represented by the Charter, will be brought into question. No other universally accepted legal basis for constraining wanton acts of violence exists.

It is imperative that regional security operations remain mandated by the Council if the legal basis of the international security system is to be maintained.[143]

This was seconded by Angola, which stated that 'regional organizations cannot substitute for the role and character of the United Nations as a universal Organization'.[144] These statements reject the 'remedial' approach mandating regional organizations to step in where the universal organization cannot act, and instead perceive 'primary responsibility' as a systemic principle of cardinal importance.

(d) The Essence and Applications of Subsidiarity

The whole rationale of dispute settlement procedures under the constituent instruments of collective security organs is to provide for institutional intervention where parties to a dispute are unwilling or unable to resolve them bilaterally. This already implies that institutional involvement is subsidiary. There are claims that subsidiarity should be considered a universal principle, accepted doctrinally from the 1931 Papal Encyclical Letter that advises against the interference of 'central' levels of authority in the operation of 'local' ones.[145] Subsidiarity as an underlying idea or a general regulatory principle is recognized in many areas. In the law of the EU, subsidiarity defines the allocation of competence between the EU and its member States. It

embraces three separate, albeit related ideas. The Community is to take action only if the objectives of that action cannot be sufficiently achieved by the member States; the Community can better achieve the action, because of the scale or effects; if the Community does take the action then this should not go beyond what is necessary to achieve the Treaty objectives. The first two parts of this formulation entail what the Commission has termed a

---

[143] *Facing the new challenges*, n 101 above, 5; a similar position was expressed by Russia, ibid, 22, and China, *Cooperation . . . in stabilization processes*, n 2 above, 13; ibid, 21 (Brazil); see also ibid, 18 (Russia): 'immutable nature of the primary responsibility of the Security Council for the maintenance of international peace and security'.

[144] S/PV.4739, 6 (Angola).

[145] Cf Knight, n 94 above, 43–4.

term of comparative efficiency: is it better for the action to be taken by the Community or the Member States? The third part of the formulation brings in a proportionality test.[146]

Subsidiarity is not a one-sided principle but allows multiple circumstances to be taken into account. Hence,

[t]here will be many areas in which the comparative efficiency calculus comes out in favour of Community action. The idea that matters should be dealt with at the level closest to those affected is fine in principle. The very *raison d'être* of the Community will, however, often demand Community action to ensure the uniformity of general approach which is of central importance to the realisation of a common market.[147]

This conveys in principle the idea that the principle of subsidiarity is not supposed to be invoked where the realization of an overarching, treaty-based mandate is at stake.

In the law following the European Convention on Human Rights, as the European Court specified in *Handyside*,

the machinery of protection established by the Convention is subsidiary to the national systems safeguarding human rights. The Convention leaves to each Contracting State, in the first place, the task of securing the rights and liberties it enshrines. The institutions created by it make their own contribution to this task but they become involved only through contentious proceedings and once all domestic remedies have been exhausted.[148]

The Court added, in *Akdivar*, that the local remedies rule

is based on the assumption, reflected in Article 13 of the Convention—with which it has close affinity—that there is an effective remedy available in respect of the alleged breach in the domestic system whether or not the provisions of the Convention are incorporated in national law. In this way, it is an important aspect of the principle that the machinery of protection established by the Convention is subsidiary to the national systems safeguarding human rights.[149]

The essence of subsidiarity is thus to check the lawfulness of national action through the involvement of the Convention machinery.

In the Statute of the International Criminal Court (ICC) the concept of complementarity is also premised on subsidiarity. As follows from Article 17 of the Statute, complementarity means that states should investigate crimes properly (and not use national proceedings to shield the accused from a genuine prosecution). If they do not investigate properly, the case would be admissible before the Court. On a general plane the ICC complements national jurisdictions competent to try the same crimes as are covered by the ICC Statute. But in individual cases the ICC jurisdiction is essentially subsidiary to national criminal jurisdictions. The ICC will not interfere in national proceedings unless the factors mentioned in Article 17 of its Statute materialize.

---

[146] P Craig, *EU Administrative Law* (Oxford: Oxford University Press, 2006), 422.
[147] Ibid, 423.
[148] *Handyside v UK*, No 5493/72, Judgment of 7 December 1976, para 50.
[149] *Akdivar*, No 21893/93, Judgment of 16 September 1996, para 65.

These frameworks are united around an underlying principle that one level of authority should not get involved in a situation that is being properly dealt with at another level, where the requirement of propriety or adequacy has to relate to factors and considerations that possess systemic legitimacy for the overarching 'upper' level and presumably also for the 'lower', and where the 'lower' level is aware that its 'first-instance' jurisdiction is not free of limits and conditions, non-compliance with which can entail supervision from the 'upper' level. Structural differences between different frameworks do not deny the principle of subsidiarity, but instead spell out the details of its operation.

Doctrinal understanding of subsidiarity in relation to collective security is essentially similar to its relevance in other areas. What matters for the purpose of collective security, however, is not just the general conceptual value of subsidiarity but also how it is specifically reflected in constituent instruments. The UN can evaluate the correctness of regional involvement against the background of the UN Charter, in terms of whether the regional effort helps to restore peace and security. To borrow the concept used in the ICC Statute, UN interference in a regional collective security effort can be justified if that effort is used to shield the problem it ought to be resolving.

First-hand knowledge by regional organizations of the background to a conflict and a greater interest in resolving it presumably require that 'the relationship between the global and regional level could be based on the principle of *subsidiarity* where the upper level takes action only if and in so far as the objectives of the proposed action cannot be sufficiently achieved at the lower level'.[150] Subsidiarity, as a principle of power allocation, favours the delegation of power to a lower tier of authority within what is understood to be 'a tiered governance system'. The whole essence of subsidiarity, thus understood, focuses on identifying an 'appropriate site of authority in a given issue area'.[151]

Subsidiarity can be relevant in the context of burden sharing and sub-contracting, but it can also apply to situations where there is no objective shared by the relevant organizations. The multiple relevance of subsidiarity has been addressed in the pertinent Security Council discussions. The representative of Chile pointed out that

> continental and regional arrangements must assume their share of responsibility within the framework of subsidiarity. The principle of subsidiarity must also be accompanied by the principles of solidarity and complementarity. Thus, when a regional organization undertakes efforts to establish or maintain peace, it must be able to benefit from the political, financial and logistical support of the continent and of the international community as a whole.[152]

According to the AU representative, 'Chapter VIII reaffirms the principle of subsidiarity and complementarity in the regulation of relations between the Security Council and regional bodies'.[153] Benin submitted that

---

[150] M Szapiro, 'International Organizations' Cooperation in the Field of Conflict Prevention', in Kronenberger and Wouters, n 82 above, 347 at 364; Abass, n 37 above, 153–4.
[151] D O'Brien, 'The Search for Subsidiarity: The UN, African Regional Organizations and Humanitarian Action', 7 *International Peacekeeping* (2000), 57 at 58–9.
[152] *Cooperation . . . in stabilization processes*, n 2 above, 7 (Chile).
[153] Ibid, 8 (AU).

from the point of view of subsidiarity . . . the member States of a given region should, through regional agreements, build up a rapid-reaction capacity in order to be in a position to deal with situations that pose serious threats or that could lead to a breach of the peace, and that the launching of United Nations peacekeeping operations would take place only in the face of an increased threat that cannot be dealt with through regional mobilization alone.[154]

A more contextual view of subsidiarity was presented by the Philippines:

The questions relating to subsidiarity and comparative advantages . . . should relate to the stages of a conflict. In conflict prevention, the regional approach should first be exhausted, because of important geopolitical considerations. However, the United Nations should monitor developments even during that stage and should ascertain if there are impediments to the regional approach, especially if a conflict is country-specific and has grave humanitarian implications.[155]

There is also evidence of the Security Council itself viewing its Chapter VII role as subsidiary. Whenever the relevant situation involves no peace agreement or cease-fire, and no regional organization deals with the issue, in principle the Council could intervene (as it did in Somalia in the 1990s), having at all pertinent stages expressed favour for the involvement of competent regional organizations.[156] But when a regional or collective effort is being undertaken, the Council will normally frame its intervention to support and complement the efforts and arrangements already in place (including under Chapter VII, where the Council's response has been based on how it perceives the parameters of that response in the agreements between the states and actors involved, especially peace agreements). This was the case with the action in Haiti (the Governor's Island Agreement), the establishment of UNTAES pursuant to the Eastern Slavonia peace agreement, the Bangui Agreement in the Central African Republic, and the Dayton Agreement in Bosnia. This can be seen, empirically at least, as the UN's perception of the subsidiarity of its role and response where the parties to the crisis have themselves designed the desired outcome. In such cases, UN involvement is meant to support the conventionally agreed effort. There is no indication in UN practice that, in a crisis, this organization would act in disregard of any consensually agreed framework applicable.

A broader recognition of the relevance of subsidiarity is witnessed by the acceptance of the thesis of African ownership of African problems. The implication is that policy has to be determined by African organizations and that the UN can step in later on the basis of complementarity. The discretion of the Security Council to choose a response based on policy is contingent, in the first place at least, on the choice of the pertinent African institution. This presumption could be reversed if the case at hand involved the unwillingness of the regional organization to act, bias, or conflict with the UN Charter.

The AU vision of complementarity through subsidiarity has been illustrated by its position in relation to the Darfur crisis. The AU Assembly addressed concerns

---

[154] Ibid, 11 (Benin).
[155] Ibid, 28 (Philippines).
[156] See, eg preamble to Resolution 733(1992).

arising out of atrocities and humanitarian crisis in Darfur, specified the need for response, and added that 'the African Union should continue to *lead* these efforts to address the crisis in Darfur and that the International Community should continue to *support* this effort'.[157] In its communiqué after the 13th meeting, the AU Peace and Security Council denoted this decision of the Assembly as the one that 'provides a framework for addressing the crisis', stressed 'the need for the AU to continue to lead the efforts to resolve the crisis in Darfur', and that the Security Council should continue supporting those efforts, through providing financial and logistical support to the AU-led Mission in Darfur, among other initiatives.[158] The fact that the AU specified these requirements imperatively effectively means its assertion of first-instance jurisdiction was reinforced by the subsidiarity approach. While in most cases the UN and the AU are agreed on important points, this process could be seen to produce a convention, to say the least, that the AU might actually have the decisive word in these matters.

Generally in dispute settlement, subsidiarity requires that 'while every opportunity is to be given to regional agencies to settle local disputes among their member-nations, the Security Council retains the right to step in at any time in order to determine whether or not the regional machinery will be efficacious in settling the disputes and to make recommendations on the appropriate procedures or methods of adjustment (Article 36)'.[159] The requirement under Article 36 of the Charter that the Security Council should take into account existing dispute-settlement procedures imposes a duty on the Council to explain why its intervention is justified even though the matter is already being dealt with under the procedures the parties chose, which might include resort to a regional organization. The burden of proving this assertion lies with the Council, and discharging it properly is required by the overriding principle of good faith. Even in relation to Article 39 situations, the role of the Council should certainly be regarded as subsidiary to the operation of those existing frameworks. If the frameworks are handling the matter properly, an Article 39 determination is simply not required and consequent measures would not be necessary, nor proportionate.[160]

As subsidiarity must be seen in the context of unity in collective security, and Chapter VIII interpreted against this background, this requires starting from the need to deal with genuinely identified dangers or threats to international peace and security. Subsidiarity thus encourages the involvement of those organizations that are impartial and do not favour one state over another for political, ideological, national, or religious reasons. If bias prevents regional agencies from performing this task properly, subsidiarity does not provide them with beneficial presumptions. In other cases, a regional agency could be otherwise unsuitable and unreliable. ASEAN's involvement in a human rights crisis might not be suitable if the EU is willing to get involved under the UN mandate.

---

[157] Decision of the AU Assembly, AU/Dec.54(III), 6–8 July 2004, para 3 (emphasis added).
[158] 13th Meeting, 27 July 2004, PSC/PR/Comm.(XIII), paras 2–3.
[159] Lloyd Mecham, n 64 above, 193.
[160] See further Chapter 4 below.

Otherwise, there is a strong systemic presumption in favour of continued regional involvement in defining and implementing collective security policies; where necessary, this involvement can be complemented by the Security Council's efforts to compensate for lack of mandate or resources at the regional level. This is where subsidiarity gives expression to complementarity. By acknowledging that regional organizations have better knowledge of the root causes of conflicts and crises in their region, the Security Council and the General Assembly effectively accept that the judgement of regional organizations on what is suitable, adequate, or necessary to maintain or restore peace and security should inform UN principal organs' judgements on the same matter. By acknowledging the principle of complementarity the UN also acknowledges the relevance of the principle of subsidiarity.

While subsidiarity in some respects is reflected in complementarity, it also has its independent regulatory relevance when complementarity does not work, that is, where the relevant regional institution is inactive and there is nothing to be complemented. Subsidiarity, depending on all relevant factors, can mean the disapproval of UN intervention where the regional organization deals with the crisis, and justification for UN intervention where the competent regional institution chooses not to act. The UN should not intervene where the regional effort is adequate in resources and mandate and where observance of the UN Charter is not at risk. Combined with complementarity, subsidiarity could result in a division of labour, under which the regional organization deploys first and the UN moves in later with a more substantial and durable arrangement.

The complementarity framework could also present some challenges. UNOMIL was deployed in Liberia to verify and ensure the impartiality of ECOMOG. The Secretary-General had specified in broader terms that this delegation of enforcement powers to regional organizations was not a panacea, because 'at times the impartiality or neutrality of their member States may be questioned, for historical reasons or for political or economic reasons'.[161] Such cases can reverse the presumption that the subsidiarity principle will otherwise prevail.

Moreover, ECOMOG withdrew from Sierra Leone abruptly, without a proper coordination with the United Nations Mission in Sierra Leone (UNAMSIL), leaving the UN force to cover the country without enough troops.[162] Similarly, the impartiality of the OAS can easily be questioned because of the enormous power asymmetry in the region. Regionalization of the security dimension in Latin America can be understood by the regional governments as a reaffirmation of US control over that part of the world.[163]

It also matters whether there is a regional appeal, eg the OAS appeal in the Haiti matter. This factor can indicate whether UN intervention is needed. General Assembly Resolution 46/7 of 11 October 1991 on Haiti specifies that the UN

---

[161] *The causes of conflict*, n 71 above, 10.
[162] J Hirsch, 'Sierra Leone', in Malone, n 81 above, 521 at 527; ECOMOG experience has been difficult, both in Liberia and Sierra Leone: Adebajo, n 81 above, 586.
[163] M Herz, 'Managing Security in the Western Hemisphere: The OAS's New Activism', in Pugh and Sidhu, n 11 above, 213 at 215, 219.

effort was based on a request from Haiti's lawful authorities and cooperation with OAS, and refers to OAS resolutions. The Assembly condemned the unlawful replacement of the Haitian government, demanded its restoration to power, and expressed support for OAS measures. OAS established its mission in Haiti in 1992; once the mission failed, OAS resolutions called upon the UN to contribute to this regional peace effort.[164] The UN was able to introduce mandatory sanctions and facilitate the conclusion of the 1993 Governor's Island Agreement, and later lift those sanctions. The Security Council authorized its mission in Haiti (UNMIH) under Resolution 862(1993), and then the situation deteriorated. The Secretary-General reported to the Security Council that the Haiti coup leaders were unwilling to comply with their obligations under the Governor's Island Agreement and thus it was necessary to restore the oil and arms embargo against Haiti originally imposed by Resolution 841(1993) and suspended by Resolution 861(1993) following the appointment of a prime minister.[165] The OAS/UN Civilian Mission in Haiti (MICIVIH) had to be evacuated and the Multinational Force under Resolution 940(1994) was deployed under Chapter VII. Only after the completion of this enforcement action could UNMIH be deployed in November 1994. Sanctions were lifted by Resolution 944(1994), after President Aristide returned to the country.

In relation to another crisis in Haiti in 2004, the Security Council got involved in the course of events leading to President Aristide again fleeing the country. Before that, regional organizations such as the OAS and the Caribbean Community (CARICOM), had proposed a solution by creating a new government. CARICOM's efforts included sending a fact-finding mission to Haiti and proposing an Action Plan, which included compliance with previous OAS resolutions, negotiation of rules for demonstrations, the release of detainees, disarmament of strong-arm groups, the strengthening of the police force, and the enjoyment of fundamental freedoms. The opposition rejected this plan. Hostilities then broke out, in which the armed opposition outnumbered the police. The Security Council initially expressed support for the CARICOM and OAS initiative to bring the crisis to an end, deplored the decision of the opposition to reject the CARICOM–OAS Action Plan, and called on both parties to accept and implement its provisions and pertinent OAS resolutions.[166] Similarly, the OAS Permanent Council in CP/RES/862 expressed concern at 'the deterioration of the situation in Haiti and its effects on the civilian population', stressed 'the important role of the initiative of the Caribbean Community (CARICOM) to help to resolve the political crisis and of the OAS Special Mission for Strengthening Democracy in Haiti', expressed 'its profound regret that the opposition has not accepted the CARICOM Plan, which offers the best prospects for a peaceful resolution to the current crisis, and expressing the hope that they will reconsider', and then called upon the UN Security Council 'to take the necessary and appropriate urgent

[164] CP/RES/594, 10 November 1994, MRE/RES, 4 December 1994.
[165] See the Secretary-General's Report S/26573 of 13 October 1993.
[166] UNYB 2004, 289.

measures, as established in the Charter of the United Nations, to address the crisis in Haiti' (paragraph 1). Paragraph 3 requested

the [OAS] Secretary General to remain in close contact with the Secretary-General of the United Nations and his representatives to ensure coordination and complementarity in the roles of the two organizations, in particular taking into account the activities of the OAS Special Mission in Haiti.[167]

This demonstrates an allegiance to the subsidiarity approach. Policy is determined within CARICOM, then the OAS gets involved, and later an appeal is made to the Security Council.

The matter was brought before the Security Council by Jamaica (the current Chair of CARICOM), suggesting that the matter had now become a threat to international peace and security and—as seems to be premised on the logic of complementarity—that while CARICOM continued to seek a political solution, its member States sought direct and immediate UN intervention, 'as the situation was one of utmost urgency and the need for decisive action was paramount. The immediate need was for the Security Council to authorize the deployment of a multinational force, in addition to addressing the growing humanitarian crisis and extending assistance to Haiti's long-term economic and social reconstruction.'[168] Thus, both the need for the Security Council's involvement through Chapter VII and the existence of a situation subsumable under Article 39 were articulated through a representative regional organization.

In its Presidential statement 2004/4, the Security Council commended OAS and CARICOM for their lead role in the crisis, and specified that the Plan of Action worked out by those two bodies 'represent[s] an important basis for a solution to the crisis'. On 29 February 2004 President Aristide resigned and left the country. On the same day the Security Council adopted Resolution 1529(2004) which established the MNF. On 3 March CARICOM made a Statement that 'expressed dismay and alarm over the events leading to the departure from office of President Aristide and the ongoing political upheaval and violence in Haiti'. They

were deeply perturbed at the contradictory reports surrounding the demission from office of the constitutionally elected President. These concerns were heightened by public assertions made by President Aristide that he had not demitted office voluntarily. Heads of Government called for an investigation under the auspices of the United Nations to clarify the circumstances leading to his relinquishing the Presidency.

CARICOM reiterated that 'no action should be taken to legitimize the rebel forces nor should they be included in any interim government', and 'that the CARICOM Prior Action Plan had been developed with the full involvement of the United States, Canada, the Organization of American States and the European Union and fully endorsed by the international community'. They 'were disappointed by the

---

[167] Resolution of 26 February 2004; for the text see S/2004/148.
[168] UNYB 2004, 290.

reluctance of the Security Council to take immediate action in response to appeals for assistance by the Government of Haiti.' Instead,

the Security Council adopted resolution 1529(2004), authorizing the deployment of a Multinational Interim Force to Haiti. This was what CARICOM had sought in the first place, but the decision was taken in circumstances quite different from those conceived in the CARICOM Plan since it followed immediately the departure from office of President Aristide.

CARICOM further 'expressed the view that the circumstances under which the President demitted office set a dangerous precedent for democratically elected Governments everywhere as it promotes the unconstitutional removal of duly elected persons from office.'[169] While the Council had adopted the regional representative's policy at the outset, its action after Aristide's resignation, which took place in uncertain circumstances, bypassed that policy.

The principle of subsidiarity was clearly adhered to within the Security Council in 2008 during discussions about imposing sanctions on Zimbabwe. Zimbabwe argued before the Security Council that pursuant to AU and SADC mandates President Mbeki was consulting the Zimbabwean leadership and 'any other separate initiatives on that matter would be counterproductive and serve to undermine the role of SADC'.[170] Zimbabwe, seconded by South Africa, argued that, while the AU had expressed concern regarding the situation in Zimbabwe, 'the African Union summit did not call for sanctions against that country', but preferred more conciliatory moves. 'Accordingly, South Africa, as a member of both SADC and the African Union, is obliged to follow the decision of those regional bodies', and vote against the draft resolution.[171] Libya also reiterated that the regional effort was under way:

SADC and the African Union are supporting the people of Zimbabwe as they strive to preserve their territorial integrity and sovereignty. However, the draft resolution before us today does not serve those objectives. It is in conflict with Article 52 of the Charter.... Imposing sanctions on Zimbabwe would hinder African efforts to resolve the crisis in the country through SADC.[172]

Burkina Faso thought that a limited intervention (such as an arms embargo) to prevent large-scale conflict would not undermine regional efforts.[173] But it had not been demonstrated that such conflict was likely. Benin's position was that the pressure that could be exerted by the Security Council would actually support regional efforts towards a conciliated solution,[174] and the United States attempted to construe the AU statement (that steps needed to be taken to prevent the situation in Zimbabwe worsening) as supporting sanctions that the Council was to adopt.

---

[169] The text is reproduced in A/58/731–S/2004/191.
[170] S/PV/5933, 3 (11 July 2008).
[171] Ibid, 4.
[172] Ibid, 5.
[173] Ibid, 6.
[174] Ibid, 13.

Four African states were among the sponsors of the draft resolution.[175] Measuring regional attitudes is a complex issue. Nevertheless, the AU representative referred to the AU position as favouring a negotiated solution rather than sanctions, and stated her expectation that the Security Council would follow the AU approach.[176] The AU Summit decision of 1 July 2008 did not impose any sanctions on Zimbabwe. The Russian view was that

[t]he sponsors of the draft resolution have not considered the opinions of the States of the region, which reject its sanctions philosophy and are calling for the search for a political solution to be continued. Indeed, the draft ignores the consensual decision of the African Union appealing to States to refrain from any act that could have a negative impact on advancing the dialogue between the Zimbabwean parties. The adoption of a resolution could lead to a realignment of the regional situation and deepen existing problems.[177]

Likewise, 'China believe[d] that the African Union resolution on the question of Zimbabwe represents an important position that reflects the consensus of African countries on the current situation. The Security Council should accord it great attention and full respect.'[178] Even if states disagreed on whether sanctions had to be imposed, there was a virtual unanimity among them that undertaking such measures has to comply with the regional attitude and be consistent with regional efforts. This is clear from statements of those states who actually sponsored and supported the vetoed resolution.

An interesting distinction in terms of subsidiarity was articulated by the Spanish representative in the relevant Security Council discussions:

We believe more in complementarity than in subsidiarity. The idea is not that the United Nations cannot or should not intervene in a given situation and that, therefore, a regional organization should step in. Rather, it may well come to pass that an analysis of the circumstances surrounding any given conflict or threat may make it desirable for a specific regional organization to intervene in place, or in support, of the United Nations.

As instances of such complementarity the UN-mandated EU Operation *Artemis* in the Congo, the similarly UN-mandated EU operation in Kosovo, and the NATO–UN collaboration in Afghanistan should be mentioned: all three examples illustrate the inter-institutional division of labour.[179] But the Spanish statement covers only part of the field within which the UN interacts with regional organizations. The same Operation *Artemis* was actually an exercise in subsidiarity. Had the African resources been adequate, the need for EU intervention under the UN mandate would never have arisen.

Complementarity is not an alternative to subsidiarity; instead it is a systemic policy making due allowance for subsidiarity. Subsidiarity, whatever shape it takes under the constituent instrument of a particular regional organization, can serve as

---

[175] Ibid, 14.
[176] Ibid, 17.
[177] Ibid, 10.
[178] Ibid, 13.
[179] *Cooperation . . . in stabilization processes*, n 2 above, 31–2 (Spain).

a standard of the propriety of external or UN involvement in regional conflicts where the views as to who should be involved differ. Complementarity, on the other hand, refers to mutually cooperative attitudes among the relevant organizations in relation to a pertinent crisis. Subsidiarity offers a straightforward equation premised on the (in)adequacy of a regional effort and consequent interference from outside, while complementarity can accommodate multiple outcomes starting from diverse initial premises varying between those that underlie the concept of subsidiarity, and those favouring sub-contracting.

Not an independent legal principle itself, subsidiarity can be relevant only to the extent that it does not require the existing legal framework that specifies the terms under which competence is allocated to be contravened. Subsidiarity does not apply where competence is exclusive under the constituent instruments, for instance under Article 53 of the UN Charter which makes the use of force part of the exclusive competence of the Security Council.

Subsidiarity normally applies only to organizations in the relevant crisis region which benefit from the knowledge of root causes of conflicts in their own region and can legitimately define a policy for regional involvement, provided that this corresponds to the purposes and principles of the UN Charter. This no longer applies to extra-regional involvement by organizations such as the EU and NATO, which do not benefit from any such primary knowledge and moreover, as is the case with the EU, profess to get involved outside their regions if their own security is affected.

(e) Subsidiarity and Jurisdictional Clauses under Constituent Instruments

(i) Under the UN Charter

The Chapter VIII framework is meant to specify, in conjunction with other pertinent Charter provisions under Chapters IV, VI, and VII, the conditions under which the UN is justified in intervening in regional efforts and what means it could lawfully use. Incidences of subsidiarity are enshrined in Article 52 of the Charter, which recognizes regional competence in relation to matters on which regional action is appropriate. Schachter states that 'the idea that disputes and threats to the peace involving States within a region should preferably be dealt with primarily by regional bodies has been [an] early and persistent influence'.[180] Apart from that, even recent Security Council debates have witnessed the submissions of some states that Chapter VIII provides for regional priority in settling regional disputes and regional organizations should be resorted to first.[181] However, Article 52 does not formulate a clear-cut division of competence between universal and regional levels; it merely suggests criteria that should help to identify principles of competence.

---

[180] O Schachter, *International Law: Theory and Practice* (Leiden: Nijhoff, 1991), 410.
[181] *The role of regional and subregional organizations in the maintenance of international peace and security*, S/PV.5776, 6 November 2007, 6 (Qatar), 18 (Panama).

The essence and limits of subsidiarity were articulated in discussions between Ethiopia and the USA regarding the Dumbarton Oaks Proposals. Ethiopia expressed its fear that the words 'first of all' would prevent the UN Security Council from interfering in a regional effort until it was too late. The US delegate opposed the dropping of these words, yet went on to explain how the competence is allocated: the parties to a dispute should endeavour to settle controversies by pacific means; 'if, however, those methods were not successful, and a threat to the peace or an act of aggression occurred, the Security Council should not delay, but should act immediately as provided by Chapter VIII, Section B', without waiting for the completion of preliminary procedures. 'The Council should and must intervene in any dispute which threatened world peace, but it should not possess such power [in] all disputes, since its competence would then be unduly and unnecessarily expanded.'[182] The US position shows that allowance was made to allot a subsidiary role to the Security Council in regional efforts: it should intervene only if statutory preconditions for such action are fulfilled; whether they are fulfilled depends on the facts of the case, in which the regional efforts also count.

It is suggested that in practice the Security Council has not declined getting involved in disputes and situations, whether or not a regional solution had first been attempted, and that it has treated the priority clause under Article 33 as a policy matter as opposed to a legal obligation.[183] However, if this were purely a policy matter, then the entire legal framework would be based on discretion as opposed to legal principles. Neither constituent instruments nor their application in practice indicate that this could be the case.

Article 33 of the UN Charter differs from the corresponding Dumbarton Oaks Proposals on dispute settlement (Chapter VIII, Sections A1–A3) in that it expressly refers to the dispute-settlement role of regional organizations. On the other hand, the role of regional organizations under Article 52 of the Charter is somewhat qualified, since this provision preserves the Council's role under Articles 34 and 35. Thus, unlike the separately defined dispute-settlement functions of the Security Council and of regional organizations under the Dumbarton Oaks Proposals, the Charter treats the roles of the UN and regional organizations as inter-linked.

In practice the Dumbarton Oaks pattern of separation would have produced controversies over how the two separately defined competences should relate to one another. The UN framework (which treats them as inter-linked) raises the complex issues of primacy, autonomy, and subsidiarity of the role of both institutional levels. Such inter-linking of responsibilities also permits diverse actors to argue in favour of the overarching primacy of Security Council jurisdiction, or for local ownership of local disputes and primacy of local institutions.

Article 52 requires the involvement of regional organizations before the pertinent dispute is referred to the Security Council, and thus envisages these organizations as

---

[182] 12 UNCIO 23, cited in D Ciobanu, *Preliminary Objections Related to the Jurisdiction of the United Nations Principal Organs* (Leiden: Nijhoff, 1975), 84 (Ethiopia was reassured by the US clarification and withdrew its proposal).
[183] Ciobanu, ibid, 83.

first-instance. The relevance of subsidiarity is affirmed by the standard-setting General Assembly declaration which specifies that 'States party to regional arrangements or members of agencies referred to in Article 52 of the Charter should make every effort to prevent or remove local disputes or situations [that can threaten international peace] through such arrangements and agencies'.[184] General Assembly Resolution 49/57 (1994) likewise considers that '[t]he Members of the United Nations entering into such arrangements or constituting such agencies shall make every effort to achieve pacific settlement of local disputes through such regional arrangements or by such regional agencies before referring them to the Security Council'. Article 52 is broad in referring not only to pacific settlement of regional disputes but in more general terms to 'such matters relating to the maintenance of international peace and security as are appropriate for regional action'. This might include not just mediation and consultation but more operational and robust action such as peace keeping. Resolution 49/57 and the declaration mentioned above also view regional organizations as first instances on such broader conditions.

General Assembly Resolution 49/57, by proscribing autonomous regional enforcement and then stating that regional arrangements or agencies can contribute to peace and security efforts including 'through the peaceful settlement of disputes, preventive diplomacy, peacemaking, peace-keeping and post-conflict peace-building', actually upholds the position that there is no UN exclusive competence in areas other than enforcement action. In fact this resolution gives expression to the competence allocation principle implied in Chapter VIII of the Charter, that outside the enforcement field essentially regional organizations, in the first place at least, may employ the range of peace-maintaining activities and operations independently of the UN. Later UN interference is justified only if the situation continues to threatening the peace *despite the regional effort*.

The 'appropriateness' criterion under Article 52 seems to be one of the keys for working out the parameters of the subsidiarity principle in this field. But who is going to decide what matters are appropriate for regional solutions under Article 52 of the Charter and what criteria should be applied in making such determinations?

In the context of his power-political approach, Morgenthau develops the view that the UN is subsidiary both to traditional methods of dispute settlement and to regional organizations. While Articles 34 and 35 establish discretionary competence for the UN, concurrent with traditional methods of dispute settlement, Article 37 reaffirms the primacy of traditional methods and the supplementary nature of UN procedures. Similarly, Morgenthau sees Articles 52 and 53 as establishing the precedence of regional dispute settlement over UN procedures and, although Article 52 refers to Articles 34 and 35, 'in point of practical application' these latter articles must be read in the light of Articles 52 and 53.[185]

---

[184] *Declaration on the Prevention and Removal of Disputes and Situations Which May Threaten International Peace and Security and on the Role of the United Nations in this Field*, A/RES/43/51, 5 December 1988, para 4.
[185] Morgenthau, n 66 above, 1073–4.

According to Eide, Articles 33 and 52(2) recognize regional organizations' priority, not exclusivity.[186] Exclusive regional competence would entail the exclusion of the UN competence, while in principle its mere priority admits recourse to the UN on the basis of subsidiarity, presupposing (of course) the existence of criteria that justify UN involvement, such as bias or insufficiency of regional effort. It is thus significant that Article 52(4) preserves the application of Articles 34 and 35, which means that, even if the relevant dispute or situation is regional in its nature, extent, and implications, the Security Council is still competent to be seised of it and investigate it anytime. Obviously the Council's power to determine the existence of a threat to peace, breach of the peace, or act of aggression under Article 39, and take appropriate measures under Articles 41 and 42, continues intact despite possible or actual action by regional organizations, even though Article 52 (4) does not specifically refer to these provisions—but then is contingent on the nature and adequacy of regional efforts.[187] Article 52(4) does not give unconditional primacy to the Council nor imply that the Council's proposed solution of the relevant situation or dispute is inherently better than one designed at the regional level. This is why Article 52 does not refer to Articles 36 to 38, which are about making recommendations and suggestions as to how a dispute or situation should be resolved.[188] The Council's role under Articles 36 to 38 is relevant only if regional efforts fail to resolve the crisis, and thus incorporates a due allowance for subsidiarity.

At the same time, Articles 34 and 35 via Article 52 deal only with referral, not with the Council's actual decision to get involved, still less impose any solution. If subsidiarity is considered, a general philosophy of Articles 34 and 35 is not to get the Council involved parallel to a regional organization's efforts and thus cause duplication, but to enable the Council to remedy a situation which a regional organization does not handle properly. In short, Articles 34 and 35 are tools which the Security Council uses to assess a regional situation along the lines of complementarity and subsidiarity. If the regional effort is adequate, the Council is supposed to leave it as it is; if it is inadequate, the Council can either complement or displace it.

It must be concluded that a matter is appropriate for regional action unless the Security Council (on the basis of criteria applicable to its decision-making under Chapters VI and VII of the Charter and of the verified factual background or of a regional appeal) positively determines that the particular situation warrants the focus of its Charter-based competence, even though the matter would otherwise be

---

[186] Eide, n 33 above, 133.

[187] As Kelsen explains, if the Council is presented with a local dispute, it will investigate it under Article 34 and then act appropriately if it identifies that a threat to international peace is likely to materialize: H Kelsen, 'The Settlement of Disputes by the Security Council', 2 *International Law Quarterly* (1948), 173 at 209. This would further raise the question of the propriety of Article 39 determinations, in the absence of which the Council could face a challenge to its excess of delegated powers. See further Chapters 4 and 8.

[188] *Per contra* Kelsen: 'the fact that only Articles 34 and 35 are mentioned in Article 52, paragraph 4, does not necessarily mean that Article 52 impairs the application of those Articles in Chapter VI which are not expressly mentioned', ibid, 207. In any case, Article 37 becomes relevant after the Chapter VIII dispute settlement effort fails.

managed within regional mechanisms. The burden rests on the Security Council to demonstrate why its interference is warranted despite a regional effort being pursued. The reasons could be that a regional organization is biased; that regional effort is backed by insufficient resources; that regional institutions cannot secure cooperation of all relevant parties; that regional efforts cannot defuse a situation involving a threat; or that regional settlement can lead or is leading to a solution that contravenes the Charter of the United Nations which, for the parties to the relevant crisis, prevails over their obligations under regional agreements. The Council is not justified in interfering just because its members do not like substantive terms of settlement adopted at the regional level.

(ii) Under Regional Instruments and Practice

Ensuring coherent interpretation of competence allocation provisions under the UN Charter and regional constituent instruments is a delicate task, guided above all by the need to avoid constructions that might place constituent instruments in conflict with one another. Any possible pattern of competence allocation—based on subsidiarity or regional autonomy, exclusive or concurrent jurisdiction—would make little sense in practical terms unless the entire normative framework of collective security competence allocation can be seen as coherent and consistent. For if conflicting outcomes are possible under different instruments, no jurisdictional principle could claim any relevance in practice. Furthermore, if regional instruments are treated as granting primacy in initial jurisdiction to regional mechanisms, this could potentially trigger a conflict with Articles 34, 35, and 52 of the UN Charter. It is also arguable that if one party to the dispute or situation chose to refer the matter to the UN, support for this party's position might by itself displace the relevance of the subsidiarity principle, since UN involvement would replace regional effort rather than complement it. The view has been expressed that, even where a regional organization seemingly possesses primary jurisdiction over a local dispute, the relevant state could resort directly to the UN if it expected a better deal from the collective organization. It would then be up to the UN to recommend resort either to regional mechanisms or to some other means of solution.[189]

The Iraqi invasion of Kuwait raised the question whether the US-led Coalition should have waited for settlement of the problem within the Arab League.[190] In the 1970s the OAU member States tended to accept the 'Try OAU First' principle,[191] which was did not succeed in developing a regional exhaustion of remedies rule, and has arguably given way to the principle of free choice.[192] But this had only a limited impact. Even though the regional leaders could not stop a determined member from airing complaints, 'in disputes between members, the African leadership neither sought nor

---

[189] Lloyd Mecham, n 64 above, 193–4.
[190] Arend, n 58 above, 19.
[191] A Henrikson, 'United Nations and Regional Organizations: "King-Links" of a "Global Chain"', 7 *Duke Journal of Comparative and International Law* (1996), 35 at 48.
[192] Schreuer, n 8 above, 491.

accepted Security Council recommendations for peaceful adjustment (Article 36), or proposals for settlement (Article 37), much less a mandate for peacekeeping'.[193]

Under Articles 34 and 35, the parties' choice does not strictly bind the Council either way and therefore it is difficult to speak of a free-standing and coherent principle of free choice that by itself displaces the initial jurisdiction of regional organizations, and the subsidiarity principle attached to it. A regional effort can be complemented or displaced, not because the parties have a free choice but only if it can be demonstrated that the regional effort is inadequate on some objective basis (bias, lack of resources, lack of competence), after taking into account those cases where the parties did claim that free choice. This corresponds to the systemic relevance of subsidiarity under Article 52.

The principle of free choice does indeed apply in international dispute settlement, but only where parties to a dispute mutually agree to a particular mode of settlement. Conversely, collective security competence deals with those situations where the choice, if any, has to be made pursuant to an overriding collective aim to deal with current threats effectively, as opposed to honouring parties' preferences as to forum. There can be no free choice where the parties failed to choose.

As was the case with the 1998 agreement between Ethiopia and Eritrea, it can happen that the parties see the problem as not just a regional concern but also a UN concern, and call for UN involvement. In that case, the agreement consistently invoked roles both for the UN and for the OAU.[194] When Ethiopia and Eritrea disagreed on the implementation of the Algiers Accords in 2000, Ethiopia insisted on an OAS role while Eritrea stated its distrust for that body, not least because of its anti-secession stand, and appealed to the UN.[195] This is similar to the OAS/UN controversies over Cuba and Guatemala.

Lebanon claimed in 1958 to have been attacked by the United Arab Republic (established through the merger between Egypt and Syria). While the Council of the Arab League claimed the exclusive control of the problem, the Lebanese Government used its right to refer the matter to the UN Security Council under Article 35 of the UN Charter.[196]

The bases for regional jurisdiction should also be examined. While the US Secretary of State John Foster Dulles considered that NATO has no jurisdiction to deal with disputes between its members,[197] NATO members subsequently agreed (following the recommendations of the Committee of Three Wise Men) to submit their disputes to procedures within NATO before resorting to any other international agency.[198] It is not immediately clear how far this can be regarded as a

---

[193] N Pelcovits, 'Peacekeeping: The African Experience', in H Wiseman (ed.), *Peacekeeping: Appraisals and Proposals* (New York: Pergamon Press, 1983), 256 at 260.

[194] Adebajo, n 81 above, 579.

[195] Ibid, 581, 583.

[196] Henrikson, n 191 above, 49; Lebanon also resorted to the Arab League but the latter made no decision: UNYB 1958, 37.

[197] Cf Henrikson, n 191 above, 50–1.

[198] *Non-Military Cooperation in NATO*, the Committee Report, at 8, quoted in Wilcox, n 85 above, 796.

binding agreement that can affect the principles and provisions underlying competence allocation, but it certainly fits within the subsidiarity-based understanding of Chapter VIII, especially Article 52.

Article 20 of the Bogota Pact prescribes that disputes should be submitted to inter-American mechanisms before being referred to the UN Security Council.[199] Article 24 OAS Charter is very similar to the arrangements under Articles 33 and 52 of the UN Charter: it also specifies that '[t]his provision shall not be interpreted as an impairment of the rights and obligations of the Member States under Articles 34 and 35 of the Charter of the United Nations'. Article 2 Rio Treaty provides in stricter terms that

the High Contracting Parties undertake to submit every controversy which may arise between them to methods of peaceful settlement and to endeavor to settle any such controversy among themselves by means of the procedures in force in the Inter-American System before referring it to the General Assembly or the Security Council of the United Nations.

The same preference for OAS procedures is expressed in Article II Bogota Pact on Dispute Settlement which states that '[t]he High Contracting Parties recognize the obligation to settle international controversies by regional procedures before referring them to the Security Council of the United Nations'. The OAS provisions thus clearly contradict the free choice principle. If free choice were to be admitted in relation to other regional organizations, then to apply Chapters VI and VIII of the UN Charter would require discrimination between regional organizations in deciding which should deal with a matter.

Is there a conflict between the Rio Treaty and the OAS Charter, which preserves the role of the Security Council, not to mention a further possible conflict between the Rio Treaty and the UN Charter itself? Is it plausible that an OAS instrument can validly exclude a dispute or situation from the Security Council's competence or curtail the right of a state to alert the Security Council? Reading Article 52 of the Charter in tandem with OAS provisions reflects the principle of subsidiarity. But then, OAS instruments should be read as being in harmony with the UN Charter in order not to prejudice the right of the Security Council to intervene if the local effort proves inadequate, and then complement or replace it. It is precisely here that the concurrent nature of jurisdiction becomes obvious.

When Guatemala became a victim of invasion from Nicaragua and Honduras in 1954, it expressly stated its preference to refer the matter to the UN Security Council and request the OAS to suspend consideration of its case. The Soviet veto prevented the Security Council from referring the case to the OAS. The Council was subsequently unable to take up the case, so long as the Inter-American Peace Committee was conducting its investigation.[200] The Security Council was unable to deal with the Guatemalan situation. The members' views of how competence

---

[199] Bogota Pact, n 48 above. For a similar approach see Article 18 of the IGAD Treaty, examined in Chapter 2 above.
[200] Claude, n 47 above, 22–3.

had been allocated between the two organizations differed. Before the Security Council Guatemala submitted that

Articles 33 and 52(2) were completely inapplicable to Guatemala's case because Guatemala had no dispute of any kind with Honduras and Nicaragua which required peaceful settlement. Guatemala was faced with 'an outright aggression'. Under the terms of Articles 34, 35 and 39, on which Guatemala had based its complaint, Guatemala had an unchallengeable right of appeal to the Council, and 'the Security Council cannot deny it its right of direct intervention by the Council, no intervention through regional organization'. Guatemala had no obligation to submit this question to the Organization of the American States.[201]

The British representative argued against abdication by the UN of its primary responsibility but perceived the role of the two organizations as mutually complementary, the UN role being subsidiary to that of the OAS:

prima facie the situation was one that could not be dismissed without investigation. For the Security Council to divest itself of its ultimate responsibility would be gravely to prejudice the moral authority of the United Nations. It was also clear that it was not at the moment open to the Security Council to take any further action in the matter without having more facts at its disposal. The question was how to establish the facts. The action of the Inter-American Peace Committee was sufficient for the moment as a means of providing the necessary information for the Council. The Committee was part of the Organization of American States, which was a regional organization within the meaning of Chapter VIII. Where such an organization took, of its own initiative, proper and constructive action, it seemed to the United Kingdom delegation entirely in accordance with the provisions of the Charter that such action should go on and that the Council should be kept informed.[202]

The New Zealand representative submitted, also in terms of subsidiarity, that

the Security Council should not, by any decision it might reach, give the appearance of abdicating the supreme responsibility and authority conferred upon it by the Charter. This was a matter of principle and cardinal importance to small nations. Any decision not to proceed with the discussion of the Guatemalan complaint at that meeting of the Council did not affect this principle and did not prejudice the Council's right to take up the question in the future if events made this necessary.[203]

There was essentially no agreement in the Guatemalan case to accept the principle that the OAS was a forum of first instance which overrode the right of an American state to appeal to the Security Council,[204] nor the exclusive jurisdiction of the OAS and the lack of its own authority to deal with the matter.[205] This is in principle a correct outcome, since its opposite would attempt to curtail the competence of the Security Council both under Chapters VI and VII. On the other hand, while the principle applied was correct, the failure of the Security

---

[201] *Repertory of Practice of the Security Council*, 1952–5, 166.
[202] Ibid, 167.
[203] Ibid.
[204] Claude, n 47 above, 33.
[205] Wilcox, n 85 above, 798.

Council to intervene in the Guatemalan situation was due to the United States being hostile to the government of Guatemala, which was actually overthrown as an outcome of this invasion by forces operating from beyond its border. The Guatemalan situation thus witnessed a correct articulation of subsidiarity but its defective application to facts.

In addition, the 'regional organizations first' principle seems to apply, by all indications, only to cases where all parties to a particular dispute are members of the same regional organization. There seems to be no similar imperative or preference if some parties to a dispute are not members. Guatemala had not finalized its adoption of the OAS Charter,[206] hence the UN presumably took priority over the OAS as Guatemala had contended.

Even though the Security Council did not engage in the Guatemalan issue, later in 1954 several Latin American states stated in the UN General Assembly that they did not agree that the OAS had exclusive jurisdiction on matters such as Guatemala's appeal. The principles of the regional system could not be invoked to deprive states of direct and immediate access to and protection under the UN system. To accept that regional organizations have exclusive jurisdiction in such cases means placing members of such organizations in a worse position than states who are not members of regional agencies, and subject their security and independence to the political characteristics peculiar to particular arrangements. A similar vision was approved in the Secretary-General's annual report.[207] These views were no doubt motivated by the dire results stemming from the Security Council's inaction.

In the Cuban missile crisis, the view expressed more often than any other was that, although the Security Council retained—had not relinquished—its competence, it should not deal with the matter until after the OAS had dealt with it. During the crisis, Cuba in its submissions to the Security Council considered it evident that any American state could choose between recourse to the Security Council and to the OAS. 'Otherwise, one would have to reach the conclusion that the American States, upon forming a regional agency, had renounced their rights under the United Nations Charter.' This would then 'place States members of a regional agency in a position of *capitis diminutio* in the United Nations, which would be legally improper.' The USA responded that 'the proper forum for the discussion of any controversies between the Government of Cuba and the Governments of other American Republics was the OAS'.[208] The US position seems to assert the subsidiarity approach in favour of the primacy of regional jurisdiction even against the choice of the affected party, treating the OAS as a forum of first instance.

Security Council Resolution 144(1960), regarding the Cuban complaint against the United States, offers some insight into how the competence provisions in the UN Charter and regional instruments (in this case those of the OAS) operate in

---

[206] CG Fenwick, 'Jurisdictional Questions Involved in the Guatemalan Revolution', 48 AJIL (1954), 597 at 598–9.

[207] For the views expressed by Ecuador, Uruguay, and Argentina, and by Secretary-General Hammarskjold, and references, see B Wood and M Morales, 'Latin America and the United Nations', 19 *International Organization* (1965), 714 at 715–19.

[208] *Repertory of Practice of United Nations Organs*, n 29 above, 277–8; UNYB 1960, 155, 157.

practice. The Council heard the Cuban statement, took 'into account the provisions of Articles 24, 33, 34, 35, 36, 52 and 103 of the Charter' and also Articles 20 and 102 of the OAS Charter, noted 'that this situation is under consideration by the Organization of American States', and '[d]ecide[d] to adjourn the consideration of this question pending the receipt of a report from the Organization of American States'. It was stressed that the Security Council could not decide on substance until the OAS conclusions were known. The adjournment had to be viewed merely as an interruption of the Council's debate rather than an attempt to deny Cuba of its right to have its case heard by the Council.[209]

The reference to Articles 33, 36, and 52 of the UN Charter, and to the OAS clauses, means that the Council construed these provisions as pointing to its own subsidiary jurisdictional role in relation to regional situations dealt with by the OAS. On this interpretation, the Council should not interfere in what belongs to a regional jurisdiction. At the same time, by referring to Article 103, the Council pointed to the UN Charter as the overarching framework for any outcome that the OAS might arrive at.

According to one assessment, the handling of the Cuban crisis at the UN represented a setback for the doctrine that the OAS had jurisdiction over local disputes, which its members had to accept and to which the UN had to defer. The Cuban case showed that the Guatemalan case had produced not a precedent but a reaction.[210]

At the initial stage of the Security Council's consideration of the complaint by Lebanon in respect of the intervention by the United Arab Republic in its internal affairs, it was pointed out that the complaint was to be discussed almost simultaneously by the League of Arab States. It was also asserted that the Security Council was duty-bound under Article 36 to take into account the peaceful means of settlement chosen by the parties when signing the Pact of the League of Arab States. The Council repeatedly postponed consideration of the complaint to permit the League of Arab States to continue its efforts.[211] While leaving the matter to the Arab League, the Council was presumably convinced of the League's comparative advantage in achieving the objectives that the UN itself would be guided by, and alluded to no reason to doubt the League's impartiality. To that extent this principle binds the Council on subsequent occasions, or at least places a burden on it to explain why in subsequent cases those circumstances are not present.

5. Subsidiarity and Regional Attitudes

Unless the Security Council is to be seen as representing the views and interests of only part of its membership, in the process of a Chapter VII action it must consider the views and reactions of all groups of states potentially affected, and know and

[209] UNYB 1960, 156.
[210] Claude, n 47 above, 43.
[211] *Repertory of Practice of United Nations Organs*, n 29 above, 475.

take into account all underlying facts, controversies, and risks on which relevant regional institutions (provided that they are impartial) might be a good source to draw from. The statement in Article 24 of the Charter that the Security Council shall act on behalf of the entire UN membership acquires a compelling importance here. If it is obvious that a Chapter VII decision of the Council does not properly represent the entire membership—for instance because it is adopted with the support of states representing some regions in the Council against those representing other regions, or because there is obvious opposition to that measure outside the Council from regional groups who consider that the decision concerned is not a matter affecting maintenance or restoration of peace and security—it could be challenged as incompatible with the requirements under Article 24. This effect of Article 24 involves regional involvement in functional duality. Regional institutions can appear as primary owners of the regional situation on the basis of subsidiarity, or as representatives of the broader membership of the UN and thus counting in the Article 24 equation.

In practice, UN and regional attitudes can differ on whether the situation at hand involves a threat; whether the measures under consideration will meet the threat; whether the impact of measures is proportionate or, on the contrary, insufficient; or whether the aim for which Chapter VII has been activated has been met and the measures should be terminated. As a working assumption, a conflict of views between the UN and regional organizations exists if there is (a) a visible and consistent opposition by one or more regional groups within the UN, and (b) an articulation of how the Council's decision falls short, for instance that a threat to the peace has not been properly determined, or that measures adopted are disproportionate, or the relevant article of the Charter has not been complied with.

The British representative has specified in Security Council discussions that 'regional and subregional organizations are key players in operationalizing the Council's work'.[212] As the Angolan representative has pointed out, 'regional consensus assists the Security Council by guiding its deliberations. When regional consensuses are taken into account, they ultimately improve compliance with, and the sustainability of, decisions that seek to prevent and resolve conflicts.'[213] The implication is that if such views are not taken into account the UN decisions may not be effective. The representative of Cameroon actually asked a more process-oriented question—'How can the Security Council take into account African Union decisions on African questions with which it is seised?'[214] This is relevant for other organizations' decisions as well. The Secretary-General of the Arab League warned against overlooking the role of particular regional organizations, specifying that 'the proper functioning of the collective international security system in the coming years will require the Council's efficient use of assistance by the regional organizations in addressing various crises'.[215] Furthermore, it is the Arab League's position that

---

[212] Ibid, 18 (UK).
[213] *Facing the new challenges*, n 101 above, 6 (Angola).
[214] Ibid, 28 (Cameroon).
[215] Ibid, 16 (LAS).

[t]he Security Council must recognize the resolutions adopted by regional organizations and promote the role of those organizations. The Security Council should turn to them and involve them in conflict resolution. The African Union and the League of Arab States can be at the forefront in playing a positive role in this respect.[216]

In a related debate before the Security Council focusing on the relationship between the UN and the AU, Benin articulated the relevance of regional attitudes in terms of a subsidiary role for the UN, by promoting the idea of synergy that 'can best be optimized only through coordination among the various elements of the decision-making hierarchy, with the Security Council taking a decision as a last resort in situations that threaten international peace and security'.[217]

In the Security Council debate on Iran's nuclear enrichment programme, Iran referred to the statements of the Non-Aligned Movement (NAM) and the Organization of the Islamic Conference. The OIC statement considered that the only way to resolve Iran's nuclear issue was to resume negotiations without preconditions. The Non-Aligned Movement had 'stressed that there should be no undue pressure or interference in the Agency's activities, especially its verification process, which would jeopardize the efficiency and credibility of the Agency', and that 'nothing should be interpreted in a way as inhibiting or restricting this right of States to develop atomic energy for peaceful purposes'. They also reaffirmed that 'States' choices and decisions in the field of peaceful uses of nuclear technology and its fuel-cycle policies must be respected'. However, the EU–3 asked Iran to 'make a binding commitment not to pursue fuel cycle activities'. Iran considered that its rejection of that illegal and unwarranted demand was the sole reason for the imposition of resolutions and statements on the IAEA Board and on the Security Council, including the adoption of Resolution 1696(2006).[218] Accordingly, Iran relied on the regional and an even broader NAM consensus to offset the claim that its refusal to suspend enrichment activities provided just cause for a Chapter VII involvement of the Security Council.[219]

6. Claims of Regional Autonomy, Primacy, and Subordination

The arguments for regional autonomy and (non-)subordination of one organization to another have been advanced at different times: the earliest case relating to Latin American concerned the relationship between the Act of Chapultepec and the Dumbarton Oaks proposals. Construing the legal notion of a regional organization having autonomy is effectively endowing the relevant power and political interest with legal primacy to act, within or outside its area of membership, without the authorization of the United Nations. Unlike the concept of subsidiarity, which applies only to areas in which the competence of different organizations is

---

[216] S/PV.5649 (Resumption 1), 20 (LAS).
[217] S/PV.5649 (Resumption 1), 16 (Benin).
[218] S/PV.5500, 9–10.
[219] For further incidences of this phenomenon see Chapters 4 and 5 below.

concurrent not exclusive, the autonomy thesis essentially aims to rearrange the allocation of competence under organizations' constituent instruments—including exclusive competence—and thus enable a regional organization to undertake an action that otherwise needs UN authorization.

Regional autonomy across the board cannot be countenanced under the UN Charter, among other documents, because when the Charter was adopted the idea of allocating regional zones of responsibility was rejected. A conceptual basis for regional organizations having autonomy from the UN Security Council could be inferred from the fact that Chapter VIII provisions and Article 103 of the UN Charter bind states, not other international organizations as such. The autonomy thesis is premised on taking institutions as starting-points, rather than their constituent instruments. What matters in reality, however, is how treaties from which institutions derive their existence interact and the ways in which they regulate the issues of primacy between institutions and their conflicting jurisdictions. The arguments on regional autonomy were rehearsed in the appeal decision of the European Court of Justice in the *Kadi* case. The Court annulled the EU regulation which had implemented Security Council Resolutions 1267(1999), 1333(2000), and 1390(2002), on the basis that the EU Treaty did not enable the implementation of UN resolutions targeting non-state entities.[220] The Court of First Instance had previously ruled that the EU was obliged to implement Security Council resolutions, because 'the Community must be considered to be bound by the obligations under the Charter of the United Nations in the same way as its Member States, by virtue of the Treaty establishing it.'[221] The reason was that, unless the relevant Security Council resolution falls outside the powers of the Security Council for its violation of the Charter or of *jus cogens*, the European institutions have to follow it, in order to avoid putting member States in breach of their higher-ranking obligations.

The ECJ, on the contrary, referred to 'the autonomy of the Community legal system, observance of which is ensured by the Court by virtue of the exclusive jurisdiction conferred on it' by the Treaty. Thus the Court had the power to review Community acts for compatibility with EU fundamental human rights principles.[222] The Court did not define its notion of autonomy, but used it to review Community acts such as implementing Security Council resolutions without pronouncing on the legality of those resolutions.[223] Thus, the ECJ considers that it has the right to review a Community act giving effect to a Security Council resolution as soon as it conflicts with higher principles of Community law, and *regardless of whether* that resolution complies with the limits on the Security Council's powers. Under this approach, even a perfectly lawful Security Council

---

[220] See Chapter 7 below.
[221] Joined Cases T-306/01 and T-315/01 *Ahmed Ali Yusuf and Al Barakaat International Foundation and Yassin Abdullah Kadi v Council of the European Union and Commission of the European Communities*, Judgments of the EC Court of the First Instance, 21 September 2005.
[222] Joined Cases C-402/05 P and C-415/05 P *Yassin Abdullah Kadi and Al Barakaat International Foundation v Council of the European Union and Commission of the European Communities*, Judgment of the European Court of Justice (Grand Chamber), 3 September 2008, paras 281–2, 286.
[223] Ibid, paras 287–8.

resolution might be unenforceable within the EU legal system on the grounds that it conflicts with the 'higher' principle of EU law.

This raises deeper questions of the relationship between the EU Treaty and the UN Charter, namely the effect on the Treaty of Article 103 of the Charter, which the ECJ did not address in its reasoning. The ECJ's assertion of the autonomy of the EU legal system disregards the fact that, this autonomy notwithstanding, member States of the EU are still obliged to give priority to the UN Charter and Security Council resolutions adopted on the basis of it. By excluding considerations of international law in reviewing European acts adopted on the basis of UN Security Council resolutions, the ECJ has mandated a systemic inconsistency by endorsing duality of the legal regime applicable to the relevant sanctions. Thus, the legal position at EU level should not affect the obligations of UN member States under the Charter and Security Council resolutions.

In relation to the OAS sanctions against Cuba, states which believed that under Article 53 of the Charter the Security Council had no competence to rule on the legality of these sanctions have voted against referring the matter to the International Court, which presumably illustrates their lack of belief that their legal position was correct. The Court was not likely to rule on the basis of 'the general political principle of regional autonomy which formed the real basis of the pro-OAS position'.[224] Policy principles were thus invoked in practice to justify reading treaty provisions out of the treaty.

As for NATO, when the North Atlantic Treaty came before the US Senate to be ratified, the Foreign Relations Committee declared that 'the treaty is expressly subordinated to the purposes, principles and provisions of the UN Charter', while Secretary of State Dulles confidently stated that the Treaty did not disturb US obligations under the Charter.[225] During the Kosovo crisis, when the new Strategic Concept was adopted in 1999, the US administration repeatedly emphasized the autonomy of NATO in its decision making and its non-subordination to any other organization, including the UN. In the wake of the NATO attack on the FRY US Under-Secretary of State Talbott warned against subordinating NATO to any other international body and favoured preserving the Alliance's freedom of action when its members so decided by consensus.[226] While NATO disregarded its real obligation to seek a UN mandate for enforcement action against the FRY, it seems likely that NATO would try to avoid narrowing its freedom of action further. Indeed, in 1998 the UK vetoed the document (NATO Doctrine for Peace Support Operations) in the North Atlantic Council (NAC) because it defined PSOs as operations authorized by the Security Council.[227] However, the failure to adopt

---

[224] Claude, n 47 above, 59; in the Dominican Republic matter, the members of the Security Council that supported the US/OAS approach had concerns as to whether Article 53 of the Charter covered their position, and thus argued that the Council should approach this issue in terms of general concept of regional autonomy, as opposed to the text of Article 53: ibid, 51.

[225] Cf Wilcox, n 85 above, 793.

[226] Cf M Zwarenburg, 'NATO, its member states and the Security Council' in Blokker and Schrijver, n 90 above, 204; Leurdijk, n 34 above, 66.

[227] Durward, n 6 above, 358.

this document was not as conclusive in confirming the NATO's position on these issues as are its repeated declarations affirming the primacy of the UN Security Council in the matters of enforcement.[228]

Nor does the Arab League legal framework subscribe to any notion of autonomy. Article 11 Arab League Joint Defence Treaty specifies that no provision of the Treaty will in any way affect the rights of League members under the UN Charter nor the responsibilities of the Security Council.

The EU autonomy discourse develops around economic sanctions and military operations. The EU Cologne Summit Document (1999) states that the EU has 'capacity for autonomous action' to undertake the full range of Petersberg Tasks in the areas of conflict prevention and crisis management, in accordance with the UN Charter.[229] This autonomous action is not the same as autonomous decision making; in this area, the EU does not claim competence to make decisions autonomously. Its relevant documents reveal no intention to that effect.

The EU Council Joint Action 2003/423/CFSP of 5 June 2003 on the European Union military operation in the Democratic Republic of Congo specifies that '[t]he Secretary-General of the United Nations has requested UN Member States to provide a temporary stabilisation force in the Ituri Region in implementation of the mandate provided in United Nations Security Council Resolution 1484(2003) of 30 May 2003', and then states that '[i]n accordance with the EU Framework Nation Concept endorsed on 24 July 2002 as a conceptual basis for the conduct of autonomous EU-led Crisis-Management Operations with recourse to a Framework Nation, a Member State should be designated as a Framework Nation'. This approach severely undermines the thesis of EU autonomy in the collective security field. If EU involvement is possible only after the UN call and authorization, and its actual action has to rely on a member State as a framework nation, this is clear evidence that EU autonomy is not manifested in any visible form.

The 2007 Joint UN–EU Statement on Cooperation in Crisis Management specifies that '[t]he EU Battlegroup Concept also provides for the possibility of EU-led Crisis Management Operations being deployed in response to requests from the UN Security Council, under a UN mandate where appropriate'. Pursuant to the European Security Strategy, the EU will seek the UN mandate for its operations, except for non-coercive operations that could be undertaken in Europe.[230]

---

[228] NATO has reaffirmed subordination of its non-Article 5 tasks to the UN by the following declarations: Final Communiqué, Brussels Ministerial Meeting, 17 December 1992, paras 4–5; Declaration of the Heads of State and Government, Ministerial Meeting of the North Atlantic Council/North Atlantic Cooperation Council, NATO Headquarters, Brussels, 10–11 January 1994, para 7; Founding Act on Mutual Relations, Cooperation and Security between NATO and the Russian Federation, Paris, 27 May 1997, Section III; NATO Strategic Concept (1999), para 31.

[229] Annex III, para 1.

[230] Wouters and Ruys, n 27 above, 252; it is however argued that the EU has not committed itself under the ESS to seek for and obtain the UN mandate in enforcement situations, because EU members are reluctant to give up their autonomy in favour of a Security Council which includes China and Russia as permanent members: S Biscop and Drieskens, 'The European Security Strategy: Confirming the Choice of Collective and Comprehensive Security', in Wouters *et al*, n 7 above, 267 at 273.

A particular process involving the arguments of autonomy and subordination has taken place in relation to the relationship between NATO and EU. Reichard speaks of NATO's treaty-based primacy over the EU, under Article 8 of the North Atlantic Treaty.[231] Article 8 specifies that '[e]ach Party declares that none of the international engagements now in force between it and any other of the Parties or any third State is in conflict with the provisions of this Treaty, and undertakes not to enter into any international engagement in conflict with this Treaty'. Still, the scope of this clause limits the original task of NATO to collective defence, and does not prevent the EU and its member States building up the military capability for collective security tasks, and getting involved in crises independently of NATO. Given that NATO's non-Article 5 tasks are not part of the North Atlantic Treaty, NATO members are not legally precluded from entering into agreements that affect NATO's ability to conduct such extra-Treaty operations.

The increase of European autonomous crisis management capabilities affects the transatlantic security framework, specifically in terms of the role of NATO and the United States in Europe. The US reaction to the 1998 St Malo Declaration aimed at forming the autonomous EU military capacity, which was later accepted as a goal by European Council 1999 summits in Cologne and Helsinki,[232] was accordingly expressed in US Secretary of State Albright's Statement in 1998. The US position has long been that the EU should avoid *d*uplicating existing NATO efforts, *d*ecoupling European defence from NATO, and *d*iscrimination against states who are members of NATO but not of the EU (known as EU 3D).[233]

Decoupling means the adoption of EU decisions independently of NATO, of which the EU already has a record, and also the assumption by the EU of tasks that are already exercisable within the NATO framework or facilities. As Reichard points out, in the years since the Albright statement, the principle of non-duplication has never been applied strictly and has given way to a more elastic notion of 'unnecessary duplication'. Since 2003, this principle has no longer covered military planning structures, even though EU planning facilities are not as great as those of NATO SHAPE.[234] EU Presidency Conclusions setting up independent ESDP structures effectively discriminate against non-EU NATO allies. The classified information available at PSC, EUMC and EUMS is not accessible to non-EU members. Similarly, decoupling has taken place through the establishment of independent ESDP institutions.[235]

Deviating from the original US position on EU 3D, the 1999 NATO Washington Summit Communiqué supports 'the European Union [having] the capacity for

---

[231] Reichard, n 119 above, 148–9.
[232] 1999 Cologne Summit Declaration, Annex 3, para 3; 1999 Helsinki Summit Declaration, paragraph 27, states the intention 'to develop an autonomous capacity to take decisions and, where NATO as a whole is not engaged, to launch and conduct EU-led military operations in response to international crises. This process will avoid unnecessary duplication and does not imply the creation of a European army.'
[233] Reichard, n 119 above, 147.
[234] Ibid, 161–2.
[235] Ibid, 156–8.

autonomous action so that it can take decisions and approve military action where the Alliance as a whole is not engaged' (para. 9(a)). This is a reference to subsidiarity, but falls short of clearly dividing competences between organizations, which could relate either to involvement in managing a particular crisis, or to means and resources needed for such involvement. It is argued that the EU can get independently involved in low-intensity operations while NATO, due to the range of its assets such as logistics, air- and sea-lifts, intelligence, and air power, should be in charge of high-intensity operations.[236] But while in abstract terms this might be a pattern for the division of labour, it is not a division of competences. There is no preconceived model of complementarity in this area and the matter rather depends on independent decisions by organizations. Moreover, EU competence under the Petersberg Tasks includes high-intensity operations involving fully-fledged combat. NATO, on the other hand, is not legally prevented from venturing into 'low-end' task action.[237]

In a partial attempt to resolve the outstanding policy controversies, the Berlin Plus agreement embodied in the NATO–EU Declaration on ESDP 16 December 2002

[w]elcome[s] the European Security and Defence Policy (ESDP), whose purpose is to add to the range of instruments already at the European Union's disposal for crisis management and conflict prevention in support of the Common Foreign and Security Policy, the capacity to conduct EU-led crisis-management operations, including military operations where NATO as a whole is not engaged.

Furthermore, 'NATO is supporting ESDP in accordance with the relevant Washington Summit decisions, and is giving the European Union, inter alia and in particular, assured access to NATO's planning capabilities'. Reichard suggests that the use of words 'inter alia and in particular' means that the EU has assured access only to planning capabilities, while it can obtain access to early-warning systems, mobile headquarters, and satellite imaging on a case-by-case basis only.[238] In principle it matters seriously whether the Berlin Plus arrangement is an international treaty: stakes for NATO relate to its legal right to claim primacy over the EU; for the EU, the assurance of access to NATO assets and facilities is at stake. However, in practice NATO cannot feasibly rely on the right of first refusal, because its members who are also EU members can prevent the Alliance from getting involved in any crisis in relation to which they prefer the EU's involvement. Moreover, if the EU conducts its operations without recourse to NATO assets, non-EU NATO allies cannot veto them. On the other hand, EU members can prevent the activation of NATO even if it never draws on EU resources and facilities.

The ECOWAS instruments do not contain an express reference to the competence of the UN in the matters of peace and security. In relation to the conflict in

---

[236] F Terpan, 'EU–NATO Relations: Interoperability as a Strategic Consideration and a Legal Requirement', in Trybus and White, n 22 above, 287; Reichard, n 119 above, 242.

[237] Reichard, ibid, 245.

[238] Ibid, 275–7.

Sierra Leone, ECOWAS expressly regarded itself as the natural organization to deal with this conflict. In the decision of the 1999 Abuja Summit of Heads of State and Government it was clearly stated that ECOMOG in Liberia was the only force in the sub-region capable of responding to requests of this kind.[239] There is a view that the ECOMOG intervention in Liberia was conducted without getting the Security Council involved because the regional governments did not trust the Security Council, considering it too removed and too slow.[240] Abass refers to the statement of its Director that the AU is not an arm of the United Nations. They accept the global authority of the UN but will not wait for the UN to authorize action the AU intends to take, especially in view of the influence of political factors in the UN Security Council. The AU Director further stressed that the AU is in tacit agreement with the UN and that there was mutual understanding to that effect.[241] Deals between officials or secretariats of international organizations cannot prejudice, still less substitute for, the strict requirements under Chapter VIII of the UN Charter.

The Rio Treaty submits to the UN Charter in its preamble, Article 1 (non-use of force contrary to the provisions of the Charter), and the reference in Article 5 to reporting under Article 54 of the Charter. It is emphasized that the United States treated the Cuban missile crisis, not as a regional crisis but as one between itself and the USSR, and seised both the Security Council and the OAS. Still, the United States considered that the OAS could introduce military sanctions without seeking UN authorization (as it did in the event). The US position resulted in asserting unlimited OAS autonomy from the UN enforcement regime, which 'argument demanded the elimination, not merely the restrictive interpretation, of Article 53' of the UN Charter, its virtual repeal.[242]

7. Conclusion

It seems on balance that, since constituent instruments do not expressly address every aspect of competence allocation, there is no substitute for recourse to such principles of competence as can be derived from the text and spirit of those instruments, the way they mutually interact, and from generally accepted practice. This chapter has demonstrated the value that principles of competence allocation possess in addition to the provisions of constituent instruments, where the validity of these principles derives from, and the limits to which they are subject.

Allocation of powers to the UN and regional organizations under Chapters VI, VII, and VIII of the UN Charter provides guidance for the operation of principles that govern collective security competences, and also substantially depends on those

---

[239] Quoted in Abass, n 37 above, 158.
[240] K Coleman, *International Organisations and Peace Enforcement* (Cambridge: Cambridge University Press, 2007), 111.
[241] Quoted in Abass, n 37 above, 166.
[242] Claude, n 47 above, 57, 60.

principles. Without this, no consistent model of collaboration between the UN and regional organizations could obtain, nor could potential conflicts between jurisdictional clauses under the UN Charter and regional instruments be resolved in areas where many organizations have concurrent competence in relation to the same matter.

4
The Identification of a Threat

1. General Aspects

Collective determination of a threat—agreement as to its existence and character-istics—is needed to trigger any collective security action. Otherwise there can be no international consensus as to whether the relevant situation warrants enforcement action. As the UN High-Level Panel Report specifies, views differ as to whether pandemic diseases constitute a security threat, whether terrorism is a threat to all states, and whether civil wars or poverty in Africa constitute a problem for interna-tional security along with having humanitarian and developmental dimensions.[1]

A policy publicly and transparently stated by a collective security institution as to the kind of threats it intends to deal with can be denoted as institutional threat perception. As there is no unified statutory regulation of how competence is allocated between collective security institutions, each institution, in the first place at least, can determine the range of threats it will deal with. This can be specified in constituent instruments, decisions, declarations, and communiqués manifesting a general agreement among the membership of a particular institution. By stating its threat perception, the relevant institution publicly conveys what it understands to be the outer limits of its competence.

2. Determination of a 'Threat to Peace' by the UN Security Council

(a) The Essence of Determination

Article 39 of the UN Charter states that

[t]he Security Council shall determine the existence of any threat to the peace, breach of the peace, or act of aggression and shall make recommendations, or decide what measures shall

---

[1] High-Level Panel Report, Synopsis, 11. The 1267 Sanctions Committee observed that states do not always have an adequate understanding of terrorist threats, and see them as remote to their own security and therefore low on their list of priorities. 'Seventeen States have said that they do not consider themselves as threat, and three believe that there is no regional threat.' Letter dated 1 December 2005 from the Chairman of the Security Council Committee established pursuant to Resolution 1267(1999) concerning Al-Qaida and the Taliban and associated individuals and entities addressed to the President of the Security Council, S/2005/761, 6 December 2005, para 54.

be taken in accordance with Articles 41 and 42, to maintain or restore international peace and security.

A determination under Article 39 is a necessary requirement for adopting enforcement measures under Chapter VII. As the nature of a threat—facts and events underlying it—is supposed to determine the type of enforcement measures, at a systemic level the Charter requires that such a determination is made explicitly.[2]

The Dumbarton Oaks Proposals provided that, should the Security Council deem that a failure to settle a dispute (in accordance with procedures or with its recommendations made under the relevant Proposal provisions) constituted a threat to the peace, it would take necessary measures in accordance with the purposes and principles of the Organization.[3] The risks of purely political determination of a threat induced small states at the Dumbarton Oaks conference to insist on mentioning in the Charter the need for the UN to comply with justice and international law, which was reflected in its Article 1(1).[4] Article 39 does not specifically require determinations to be 'in accordance with the purposes and principles of the Organization'. But this is essentially a distinction without a difference, given that in any case Articles 24 and 25 require the Council's decisions to be in accordance with the Charter. Articles 1, 2, 24, and 25, although not directly pronouncing on the content of Article 39 determinations, impose limits to their content and parameters. The Charter cannot be reasonably interpreted as requiring states, under Articles 1 and 2, to comply with international law and then admitting, under Article 39, the possibility of the Security Council's finding a threat to the peace in the conduct of a state that had complied with international law.

The Charter does not define a 'threat to the peace'. In literal terms, a threat means 'a likely cause of damage or danger' or the possibility of that; 'threaten' means to 'put at risk'.[5] To 'exist' means 'be real; be present in a place or situation'.[6] Article 39 thus requires the existence of a threat, and hence its reality. What matters here is not a subjective perception that danger and damage is likely, but the objective existence of a situation which, on its own—through its nature, scale, or gravity, and without being exacerbated by sources other than its original source—points, intelligibly to all, to the risk of danger to international peace and security.

Only the Security Council can make an Article 39 determination. The General Assembly could express a view that a particular situation involves a threat to the peace. It is contended that regional organizations can determine the existence of a

---

[2] For this reason, doctrinal views that admit the possibility of an implied determination under Article 39 appear untenable. See, for such views, H Freudenschuß, 'Article 39 of the UN Charter Revisited: Threat to Peace and the Recent Practice of the UN Security Council', 46 *Austrian Journal of Public and International Law* (1993) 31; R Lapidoth, 'Some Reflections on the Law and Practice Concerning the Imposition of Sanctions by the Security Council', 30 *Archiv des Völkerrechts* (1992) 114 at 115.

[3] Dumbarton Oaks Proposals, Chapter VIII, Section B1.

[4] R Kolb, *Ius contra bellum, Le droit international relatif au maintien de la paix* (Basle/Louvain: Helbing Lichtenhahn/Bruylant, 2003), 69–70.

[5] *Compact Oxford English Dictionary,* 3rd ed. (Oxford: Oxford University Press, 2005), 1078–9.

[6] Ibid, 347: 'existence' refers to 'the fact or state of existing'.

threat to the peace, as this is not expressly proscribed under the Charter, and then apply to the Council for authorization to take enforcement action under Article 53.[7] Thus, the determination of a threat to the peace in Rhodesia was preceded by a statement by the OAU meeting at Addis Ababa that the Rhodesian independence crisis constituted a threat to international peace and security and that sanctions should be imposed upon the illegal regime in Rhodesia.[8] But the Council could not grant that request unless it had independently arrived at the conclusion that there existed a threat of such gravity as to warrant enforcement action.

Attempts by entities other than the Security Council to determine the existence of a threat to the peace can be seen at most as the expression of a view, the statement of a policy, or an initiative directed at the UN. As such, they produce no legal consequences. However, the Security Council, which has subscribed to the thesis that regional organizations benefit from better knowledge of root causes of conflicts in their regions,[9] has to consider how these regional organizations perceive pertinent threats in their own region, or where they indicate that Chapter VII is not suitable for addressing the situation at hand.

(b) The Scope of Discretion under Article 39

Under Article 39 the Council 'shall' identify threats to the peace: in contrast, the word 'may' is used in relation to the application of enforcement measures under Articles 41 and 42. This raises the question whether determination of a threat is mandatory or discretionary.[10] The entire context of the Charter is instructive. The preamble refers to the many horrors of the Second World War and states the intention to avoid similar tragedies in the future; Articles 1 and 2 specify principles and purposes of the UN accordingly; Article 24 entrusts the Council with the task of acting promptly and effectively on behalf of the entire membership of the Organization; Article 39 then specifies the Council's competence in relation to threats to put the Charter mechanism of collective security into operation. Whatever pragmatic considerations might suggest, the structural inter-connection between the pertinent provisions of the Charter compels us to view the Article 39 determination power as part of the imperative mandate of the Council, which does not admit selectivity in confronting threats. To illustrate this position, in Resolution 294(1971), the Council was '[c]onscious of its duty to take effective collective measures for the prevention and removal of threats to international peace and

---

[7] A Abass, *Regional Organisations and the Development of Collective Security: Beyond Chapter VIII of the UN Charter* (Oxford: Hart, 2004), 53–4.

[8] Cf CG Fenwick, 'When is There a Threat to the Peace?—Rhodesia', 61 AJIL (1967), 753 at 754.

[9] See Chapter 3 above.

[10] In translation, the pertinent part of the Russian text of Article 39 reads as follows: '[t]he Security Council determines the existence of *any* threat to the peace, *any* breach of peace or act of aggression . . .'. The word 'any' is used twice which can be seen as an emphasis on the duty-oriented nature of the Council's mandate to identify threats to and breaches of peace. If coupled with 'shall' in the English text, which is stronger than the corresponding 'should' in the Dumbarton Oaks proposals (Chapter VIII, Section B2), the case for viewing this as an obligation on the Council as opposed to its mere entitlement becomes stronger.

security and for the suppression of acts of aggression'.[11] Likewise, Sir Arthur Goodhart has suggested that the Council is 'under a positive duty to reach a determination in the matter and to decide what measures should be taken. In contrast to the compulsive nature of Article 39, the choice of measures under Articles 40, 41 and 42 is permissive.'[12]

There is strong doctrinal support for viewing the permissible content of a 'threat to the peace' as completely dependent on the Security Council's discretion. A formalistic approach is often upheld, defining a threat as 'a situation which [an] organ, competent to impose sanctions, declares to be an actual threat to the peace'.[13] According to Kooijmans, the Council was designed to adopt purely political decisions when determining a 'threat to the peace'.[14] According to Reisman, the UN collective security mechanism was intended to operate at the discretion of permanent members of the Security Council.[15] Kooijmans also refers to 'the complete discretion the Security Council has with regard to the interpretation of the three concepts "threat to the peace", "breach of the peace" and "act of aggression"'.[16] Dinstein argues that 'a threat to the peace is not necessarily a state of facts: it can be merely a state of mind; and the mind that counts is that of the Security Council'.[17] It has however been emphasized that, 'when the Council fails to articulate clearly the precise basis of a threat to the peace, it risks being accused of making determinations of mere convenience'.[18]

Even if it has political and discretionary connotations, Article 39 is still a legal provision in a treaty and there have to be criteria whereby valid determinations under it can be distinguished from invalid ones. In its appeal decision on *Tadić*, the ICTY articulated limits on the Council's power to make Article 39 determinations. The Judgment specifies that

[t]he situations justifying resort to the powers provided for in Chapter VII are a 'threat to the peace', a 'breach of the peace' or an 'act of aggression'. While the 'act of aggression' is more

---

[11] The same approach was reaffirmed in Resolution 300(1971).

[12] A Goodhart, 'North Atlantic Treaty Organization', 79 *Recueil des Cours de l'Académie de Droit International de la Haye* (II–1951), 183 at 200.

[13] Definition by J Combacau, quoted in P Kooijmans, 'The Enlargement of the Concept "Threat to the Peace"', in P-M Dupuy (ed.), *The Development of the Role of the Security Council* (Leiden: Martinus Nijhoff, 1993) 111; see also A Lowenfeld, *International Economic Law* (New York: Oxford University Press, 2008), 858.

[14] P Kooijmans, 'The ICJ: Where Does It Stand'? in S Muller, D Raic, and H Thuranzsky (eds.), *The International Court of Justice. Its Future Role after Fifty Years* (Leiden: Martinus Nijhoff, 1997), 416.

[15] M Reisman, 'Peacemaking', 18 *Yale Journal of International Law* (1993), 418.

[16] Kooijmans, n 13 above, 111. But Kooijmans adds 'although the Security Council is completely free to decide whether a situation constitutes a threat to the peace, one may ask whether it is fully in conformity with the spirit of the Charter to impose sanctions if the threat is not actual and efforts to resolve the dispute have not been completely exhausted': ibid, 117.

[17] Y Dinstein, *War, Aggression and Self-Defence,* 4th ed. (Cambridge: Cambridge University Press, 2005), 284, further remarking that the ICTY Appeal Chamber's observations in *Tadić* on the limits of the Security Council Article 39 power are not particularly helpful. See also K Graham, 'UN–EU Cooperation on Security: In Search of "Effective Multilateralism" and a Balanced Division of Tasks', in J Wouters *et al, The United Nations and the European Union* (The Hague: TMC Asser Press, 2006), 281, 285, referring to Article 39 as 'a vehicle of self-empowerment through subjective judgment'.

[18] JM Farrall, *UN Sanctions and the Rule of Law* (Cambridge: Cambridge University Press, 2007), 191.

amenable to a legal determination, the 'threat to the peace' is more of a political concept. But the determination that there exists such a threat is not a totally unfettered discretion, as it has to remain, at the very least, within the limits of the Purposes and Principles of the Charter.[19]

The Appeal Chamber assigns the adjective 'political' to 'threat to the peace', but does so to denote the initial freedom of the Council to engage with threats on the basis of political consensus, and is quick to specify that this discretion is limited by the purposes and principles of the Charter, which obviously embody fundamental principles of international law.[20]

The word 'discretion' is not mentioned in Article 39 or elsewhere in the Charter. Pertinent meanings of discretion point to 'the freedom of what should be done in a particular situation', while 'discretionary' refers to whatever is 'done or used according to a person's judgement'.[21] A literal meaning of discretion can thus have multiple connotations including sheer subjective whim and desire. Exclusions from discretion should thus depend on systemic preconditions under the legal framework that confers discretion to the relevant authority.

In juridical terms discretion presupposes the incompleteness of determination by the law of the elements of applicability of the pertinent norm, and it is arguably to that extent that the organ in question is competent to make political determinations. But being based on the legal framework, this discretion is legal as much as it is political.[22] More specifically, discretion can be political in the context of the decision makers' motives, but where it derives from and how far it can reach are questions of law.

National legal systems have diverse concepts of discretion.[23] The issue arises as to how far the legislator can empower an administration to adopt discretionary decisions.[24] For the purposes of English law, discretion exists 'where there is a power to make choices between courses of action or where, even though the end is specified, a choice exists as to how that end should be reached'.[25]

Under the rule of law, an administration can enjoy neither free discretion on a whim nor discretion of opportunity, but only a dutiful discretion to effect the best possible decision under the relevant circumstances. Discretion (*Ermessen*) requires relevant factors to be weighed up, while opportunism involves an element of whim. Opportunist choices entail closing an eye to the conduct of those one views favourably, but not to others. Consequently, opportunism is antithetical to

---

[19] *Prosecutor v Tadić,* Case IT-94-1-AR72, Appeal Chamber, Decision on Jurisdiction:, 2 October 1995, para 29.

[20] See Chapter 2 above.

[21] *Compact OED*, n 5 above, 282–3; 'discretion' also refers to 'choice, option, preference, disposition, volition; pleasure, liking, wish, will, inclination, desire'. 'Discretionary' means 'optional, voluntary, at one's discretion, elective', and its opposite is 'compulsory': *Compact Oxford Thesaurus,* 3rd ed. (Oxford: Oxford University Press, 2005), 221.

[22] Kolb, n 4 above, 122.

[23] P Craig, *EU Administrative Law* (Oxford: Oxford University Press, 2006), 433.

[24] G Püttner, 'Ermessen und Ermessensausübung: Gedanken zur Weiterentwicklung der Ermessenslehre', 63 *Zeitschrift für öffentliches Recht* (2008), 345 at 348.

[25] P Craig, *Administrative Law* (London: Sweet & Maxwell, 2008), 501.

discretion and misleads in clarifying its essence.[26] The overall aim of discretionary powers is to enable the empowered authority to make the best possible decision that the legislator could not specifically provide for in advance.[27] Purpose-oriented rather than opportunist discretion thus fits better with the Security Council's mandate under the Charter.

For the purposes of EU law, discretion can derive from any Treaty provision, regulation, or directive which states that the European Commission *may* take certain action, or that it can assess economic and social conditions within the Community to attribute specific meaning to phrases in the Treaty that at first appear indeterminate, for instance to determine whether state aid should promote economic development in areas where the life of quality is 'abnormally low' or there is 'serious under-employment'—phrases used in the Treaty—so that it can then determine whether that aid is compatible with the common market. Such discretion involves the power vested in the Commission and the Council to balance objectives.[28]

The jurisprudence of international administrative tribunals pertinently explains what discretion is all about and what can and what cannot validly fall within the proper exercise of discretionary powers. The ILO Administrative Tribunal specified in the *Ballo* case that discretionary authority must not be confused with arbitrary power. Discretion must be exercised lawfully, that is in regular form and procedure, free of an error of law or fact or a misuse of authority, and by taking all essential facts into consideration.[29] The Asian Development Bank Administrative Tribunal indicated in the *Lindsey* case that, while there is 'a broad discretion to determine the policy of the Bank and its operational needs', the exercise of discretion should be based on the awareness of relevant facts, namely 'reliable first-hand evidence of any deficiencies alleged'.[30] Furthermore,

the establishment of the truth or falsehood of allegations is not itself a subject of discretion but is the consequence of an objectively verifiable and rationally explicable examination of the facts. Where the continuance or not of a staff member's livelihood is involved, it is not sufficient to rely on unexplained or unsubstantiated beliefs or vague recollections.

---

[26] Püttner, n 24 above, 347–9 ('Ermessen ausüben bedeutet "messen", abwägen, während Opportunität (verwandt mit Opportunismus) eher ein Element des Beliebens, das Entscheiden nach der Staatsraison oder auch nach Nützlichkeitskalkül zum Ausdruck bringt. Opportunität kann "Augenzudrücken" bedeuten, zB indem ein ein den ruhenden Verkehr überwachender Amtswalter nicht nur bei einem Freund, sondern auch bei einem Querulanten, der ihm schon Ärger gemacht hat, nichts unternimmt, also "die Augen zudrückt". Das kann aber im Rechtsstaat nicht richtig sein. Die Verwaltung hat im Rechtsstaat jeden ohne Ansehen der Person nach gleichem Maßstab zu behandeln, das Augen-Zudrücken ist Ermessensmissbrauch. Da aber der Begriff Opportunität nach dem allgemeinen Sprachgebrauch eher das Gegenteil zum Ausdruck bringt, sollte er nicht mit dem Begriff Ermessen gleichgesetzt, sondern im Zusammenhang mit Ermessen tunlichst nicht weiter verwendet werden, weil er irreführt.')

[27] Ibid, 349 ('Es geht nicht darum, den Beamten gleichsam eine Spielwiese zu eröffnen, sondern darum, im Einzelfall die bestmögliche Entscheidung zu ermöglichen in den Fällen, in denen der Gesetzgeber aus Sachgründen diese nicht vorweg genauer vorzeichnen kann.')

[28] Craig, n 23 above, 433–4.

[29] *Ballo v UNESCO*, (1972) ILOAT Judgment No 191, *UN Juridical Yearbook* 1972, 144.

[30] *Lindsey v ADB*, Decision No 1, 18 December 1992, paras 9, 11.

If one asserts the use of discretion, one has to prove the facts that justify a discretionary action.[31] An essential requirement for the valid exercise of discretion is that the organ in question has to specify in an open and transparent manner what specific objective its policy aims to achieve and how the conduct of the relevant legal persons adversely affects it.

Consequently, if the organ exercising discretion fails to allude to relevant facts, or relies on a combination of relevant and irrelevant facts, its approach can be judged to be an abuse of discretion which is conferred to that organ on a strict condition of acting solely pursuant to its delegated mandate), even if its action is seen as performed in good faith. In other words, discretion can be used to define a policy of institutional reaction to certain facts and situations, to identify the scope of those facts and situations, and apply that policy when those facts and situations arise; it cannot be used to make up facts and situations that fall within the stated policy, nor to draw up a policy that justifies making up facts and situations that fall within it and then designing a politically suitable response.

As can be seen, no legal framework accepting the relevance of discretion provides a public authority with power to make counter-factual determinations that fail to reflect the state of things on the ground, still less determinations that can eventually lead to violation of the law. In the case of the Security Council, systemic evidence for the relevance of the requirement for the best possible decision is provided by a joint reading of Articles 1, 2, 24, and 39 of the Charter as part of a single normative framework, leading to an outcome requiring the use of the Council's discretion to give effect to the Charter's purposes and principles in relation to the case at hand. The authors of the Charter no doubt realized that a single category covering the crises and events the Council would be dealing with was impossible to determine at once and exhaustively. Discretion under Article 39 is therefore not a purely political discretion but operational, designed to put into operation Charter provisions that have a broad scope.

A 'conventional wisdom' that Article 39 is indeterminate and thus warrants purely political determinations of a threat to the peace ignores the broader context of the Charter, which subjects the Security Council's power to legal limitations. Discretion does not imply one-sided, conclusive assertions of the existence of a threat; rather, it implies the Council's communication of its verified and transparent understanding of the situation at issue in a way that is intelligible to the rest of the UN membership.

(c) The Requirement of Genuineness for Article 39 Determinations

Even though policy reasons can attend an Article 39 determination, it has to be made in relation to such facts, events, and situations as justify adopting enforcement measures under Articles 41 and 42, so that these measures will then be both necessary and proportionate to address their object. The genuineness requirement is thus a statutory precondition on which the text and structure of Article 39, as well

---

[31] Ibid, paras 10, 36 (emphasis added); on that basis the Tribunal found that the Bank's failure to extend Lindsey's contract was contrary to due process: para 38.

as the general context of the Charter are premised. As for the text of Article 39, 'determine' as a verb means to 'establish something by research or calculation'.[32] The Council has to determine the *existence* of a threat. In relation to aggression and 'breach of the peace', 'determine' certainly means ascertaining factual existence; it cannot have a different meaning in relation to 'threats', since in a treaty provision the same word cannot be interpreted as having different meanings in the same context. An Article 39 determination is thus meant to declare what the existing situation is. In the *Namibia* case Judge Fitzmaurice emphasized that there is a broad margin for appreciation under Article 39 yet it is limited by the requirement of genuineness. Thus, the Charter 'does not limit the *occasions* on which the Security Council can act in the preservation of peace and security, provided the threat said to be involved is not a mere figment or pretext.'[33] Such limitations

are necessary because of the all too great ease with which any acutely controversial international situation can be represented as involving a latent threat to peace and security, even where it is really too remote genuinely to constitute one. Without these limitations, the functions of the Security Council could be used for purposes never originally intended.... [The Council can validly act only if there is a] threat to peace and security other than such as might be artificially created as a pretext for the realization of ulterior purposes.[34]

A UN Report further clarifies that 'the "threat" may not be determined on the basis of ulterior political motives—there must be genuine "international concern" behind the sanctions, not the foreign or domestic policy considerations of a single State or group of States'.[35] The High-Level Panel Report refers to the criterion of *seriousness of a threat* as meaning whether any 'threatened harm to State or human security [is] of a kind, and sufficiently clear and serious, to justify *prima facie* the use of military force'; whether internal threats involve genocide or other large-scale killing, ethnic cleansing, or serious violations of international humanitarian law, actual or imminent.[36]

Under the Dumbarton Oaks Proposals, the preconditions for determining a threat to the peace were the failure to settle a dispute or to carry out UN recommendations. This condition is not included in the Charter. According to Kelsen, the Council can determine that non-compliance with its recommendations under Articles 36, 37, and 38, even if not violating a state's international obligations, constitutes a threat under Article 39, and take enforcement action.[37] But whether a

---

[32] *Compact OED*, n 5 above, 270; the French text of Article 39 uses the word 'constate': *constater* means to notice as an observer, to ascertain, to establish, certify, or record: *Oxford Hachette French Dictionary* (Oxford: Oxford University Press, 1998), 129.

[33] Dissenting Opinion of Judge Fitzmaurice, *Namibia*, *ICJ Reports* 1971, 293 (para 112) (emphasis in original).

[34] Ibid, 294 (para 116).

[35] M Bossuyt, 'The adverse consequences of economic sanctions on the enjoyment of human rights', Working paper, E/CN.4/Sub.2/2000/33, 7.

[36] High-Level Panel, n 1 above, 57–78.

[37] H Kelsen, 'The Settlement of Disputes by the Security Council', 2 ILQ (1948), 173 at 213; Kelsen, 'Limitations on the Functions of the United Nations', 55 *Yale Law Journal* (1946), 997 at 1005; Kelsen, 'Sanctions under the Charter of the United Nations', 12 *Canadian Journal of Economics and Political Science* (1946), 429 at 433.

threat exists depends on its factual characteristics, gravity, and magnitude, not on whether past recommendations have been complied with. The opposite outcome would effectively end up with contending that the Charter requires states to treat UN recommendations as binding.

In 1954, the United States informed the Security Council that a US Navy aircraft, on a peaceful mission over the high seas, had been attacked without warning and destroyed by two MIG-type aircraft with Soviet markings, with ensuing casualties. The USA asserted that this matter could endanger peace and security while the USSR asserted that the conduct of the US aircraft had contravened international law, including the violation of Soviet air space. The President of the Council suggested an investigation under Article 34, which met the following reaction:

The representative of the USSR remarked that he could not see how Chapter VI of the Charter, and Article 34 in particular, could have any bearing on the incident brought to the attention of the Council. Such an incident could not be seriously considered, in his opinion, as capable of creating a threat to international peace and security. He would, therefore, reject any proposals based on the premise that the incident fell within the jurisdiction of the Security Council.[38]

For understandable reasons, the matter was not taken further; but this is an instructive case where the Council attempted to identify the minimum level of danger in a situation capable of leading to a threat to the peace. While such instances of international violence can potentially create threats to the peace, it could be asked whether incidents in which force is used, but which are not ongoing, and can be resolved within the law of state responsibility, can provide a valid cause for the Security Council's involvement. An additional question is whether, in a comparable situation, the aircraft in question had indeed violated the foreign airspace. In such a case, qualifying the relevant situation as a threat to the peace could open the door for applying Chapter VII coercion to any state which simply acts to protect its borders and thereby causes a 'threat'. Policy dilemmas emerging from this are insoluble. A structured view of international peace and security could instead indicate solutions compatible with the framework of international law, as defined in the Essential of Peace.[39]

It might be asked whether the standard for identifying possible or actual threats under Articles 37 and 39 is subjective or objective. It seems that the applicable standard is objective. If under Article 37 the Council must ascertain whether the pertinent dispute is 'in fact' likely to endanger peace and security, it is implausible to hold that it is not likewise obliged to ascertain whether an actual threat under Article 39 'in fact' exists.

Both Chapter VI and VII require that, before the Security Council proceeds with the matter in hand, it has to satisfy itself that a situation referred to in Articles 33, 34, or 39 indeed exists. In terms of proving this, no decisive allocation of the burden of proof is established under the Charter nor, as emphasized, has a

---

[38] *Repertory of the Practice of the Security Council,* 1952–5, 121.
[39] See Chapter 1 above on the General Assembly resolution on the 'Essentials of Peace'.

significant constitutional debate been conducted on this point.[40] A reference could
be made to the claim before the Council raised in 1961 by Liberia, that the
situation in Angola represented a situation under Article 34, warranting investigation, to which the UK representative replied that the burden of proving this lay
with Liberia. However Ciobanu suggests that, due to the public policy character of
the Security Council's powers, there is no need to expect any individual member to
substantiate such claims through evidence, as member States have often provided
the appropriate evidence. The Council could pronounce on such preliminary
objection *ex officio*, as the matter is not a member's exclusive concern.[41] It can be
assumed that whenever the Council proceeds with the merits of a question, by
implication it pronounces on its competence in relation to that question.[42]

The crucial point, however, is that the overall burden still lies with the Council
in the sense that in every pertinent case it has to ascertain that the situation meets
the requirements under Articles 33, 34, or 39, because its Charter mandate is linked
precisely to the existence of such situations. This burden of proof can be discharged
either by the member which raises the question or by any other member, so long as
(in the end) the Council adopts a substantiated decision; its decision would not be
substantiated, and thus consistent with the Charter, if in the process of its adoption
no one had provided proper evidence that a situation of the required nature existed,
or if assertions to the contrary made in the Council were not refuted with evidence.

Determination of an objective for the pertinent Chapter VII effort will test the
genuineness of an Article 39 determination and the necessity and proportionality of
consequent measures. Proper specification of the objective of a Chapter VII action
is a systemic requirement under the Charter. The Council has to clarify what
difference it intends to make through its Chapter VII action and how the measures
it undertakes will achieve that aim. If the Council identifies a threat, it is also
supposed to set an objective for its elimination, thereby operationalizing *in casu* its
tasks under the preamble, and Articles 1 and 24 of the Charter. This will then help
to ascertain the propriety of those measures by measuring their necessity and
proportionality. The causal connection between the objective pursued and the
measures adopted has to be demonstrated.

As has been pointed out, the objectives specified by the Council in certain
contexts involving gross and widespread human rights violations do not involve
stopping those violations, as such, but are directed at other humanitarian purposes,
such as ensuring the delivery of humanitarian assistance.[43] To illustrate, Resolutions 752(1992) and 757(1992) on Bosnia noted 'the urgent need for humanitarian assistance and the various appeals made in this connection', and that safe
conditions for this had not yet been established. Resolution 770(1992) recognized
'that the provision of humanitarian assistance in Bosnia and Herzegovina is an

---

[40] D Ciobanu, *Preliminary Objections Related to the Jurisdiction of the United Nations Principal Organs*
(Leiden: Nijhoff, 1975), 187–8.
[41] SCOR, 944th meeting, in ibid, 188–9.
[42] Ciobanu, n 40 above, 192.
[43] D Sarooshi, *The United Nations and Development of Collective Security* (New York: Oxford
University Press, 1999), 210.

important element in the Council's effort to restore international peace and security in the area'. Pursuing this goal, the Council demanded that all parties stop fighting immediately and give unimpeded access for humanitarian organizations to all camps, prisons, and detention centres (paragraphs 1 and 3).

In the matter of the Lockerbie terrorist bombing, the Security Council, initially acting under Chapter VI, adopted Resolution 731(1992) demanding that Libya extradite the bombing suspects to the UK or the USA. Libya instituted proceedings against the USA and the UK before the International Court, arguing that its decision to try suspects instead of extraditing them complied with its obligations under the 1971 Montreal Convention, and alleging that the respondents had made threats to use force against Libya. Dealing with a situation initially through a Chapter VI recommendation, as with Resolution 731,[44] demonstrates that a situation does not involve a threat to the peace, to which position the Council can *in casu* be seen as committed through estoppel. The factual circumstances leading to adoption of Resolution 748(1992), including the text of Resolution 731 (which contains no reference to threats to the peace), demonstrate that the situation addressed by that resolution had not developed in a way warranting application of coercive measures. Neither was there any peace-threatening development in Libya's conduct during the period between the adoption of Resolutions 731(1992) and 748(1992). It is thus implausible that any genuine threat to the peace existed in this situation. This raises further questions: why did the Council issue a mere recommendation in relation to something it anticipated could grow into a genuine threat to the peace? If that was not the case, then, did the Council intentionally and artificially create a 'threat to the peace' by first issuing a recommendation on a matter which, if treated through binding decisions at the outset, would have been controversial, and then use this as an excuse to resort to its enforcement powers under Chapter VII—which constitutes an abuse of powers?

Genuineness of a threat necessarily implies the requirement not to modify or expand the parameters of the originally determined threat, unless concrete facts and conduct subsequent to the original threat determination clearly justify such a decision. If a situation has initially been addressed under Chapter VI, then before that situation is engaged under Chapter VII, there has to be a genuine (even though gradual) transformation on the ground which demonstrates, for all to clearly see, that what previously had merely seemed likely to endanger peace now in fact does so.

Libya's position on this matter was to offer cooperation and alternative ways to achieve accountability for terrorists in the Lockerbie case.[45] Thus the actual difference between the Libyan view and the British/American view underlying the Council's approach was not that wide. The trigger for the Council's Chapter VII action was not the need to secure accountability for terrorist attacks, but *where* the suspects should be tried. It is thus open to doubt whether the Council's activation of

---

[44] As confirmed in the *Lockerbie* Preliminary Objections Judgment of the International Court, *ICJ Reports* 1998, 26.

[45] Letter dated 9 December 1992 from the Permanent Representative of the Libyan Arab Jamahiriya to the United Nations addressed to the Secretary-General, S/24961.

Article 39 was consistent with the Charter. The motive behind the Council's use of Chapter VII can thus be characterized as ulterior. This is even more evident from the preambular paragraph in Resolution 748, which actually makes an Article 39 determination on the basis of Libya's failure 'to demonstrate by concrete actions its renunciation of terrorism', assuming as granted that which had never been proved. Libya had already stated its readiness to undertake 'concrete actions', and to try individual suspects, or surrender them to a third country. Sanctions were thus imposed on Libya for no substantial reason. States sponsoring Resolutions 748 (1992) and 883(1993) fell short of establishing the existence of a genuine threat. In fact, Libya expressly pointed out that, not only did its proposals of cooperation meet outright refusal from the USA and the UK, but such refusal was also followed by a threat to use force that made a negotiated settlement impossible.[46] The Council dealt only with Libya's behaviour, and effectively backed up a threat to use force against Libya contrary to Article 2(4) of the UN Charter.

Another problem with the Council's involvement in the Lockerbie affair has to do with clarifying whether Libya's alleged involvement in a terrorist attack that had taken place years before could validly be considered as a threat to the peace. The Council determined that state-sponsored terrorism constitutes such a threat. The Council seems thus to have been referring to the general phenomenon of terrorism. But along with that the Council determined that Libya's non-compliance with Resolution 731, that is the failure to extradite the suspects to the USA or the UK, constituted a threat to the peace. Since the Council had determined that state-supported terrorism as such was a threat to the peace, it was supposed to adopt measures for eliminating this threat, or essentially reducing its impact on international relations. However, the Council simply linked its coercive measures to demands for the extradition of two suspects to the USA or the UK. It is thus clear that, while labelling a general phenomenon a threat to the peace, the Council directed its enforcement measures against, not that threat, but the specific fact of non-extradition, as is obvious from operative paragraphs 1, 4, 5, and 13 of Resolution 748. It is obvious that non-extradition of two suspects to a particular country cannot in itself be a threat to the peace, however wide might be the discretion of the Council in making determinations under Article 39. Thus the Council's measures were not properly directed at the elimination of a threat to the peace.

Another instance of counter-factual and opportunist determinations under Article 39 is provided by the Council's practice of requesting the International Criminal Court to defer proceedings in the interests of international peace and security pursuant to Article 16 of its Statute which, 'assuming the wisdom of staying international justice in the interests of peacemaking',[47] specifies that

---

[46] Letter dated 18 January 1992 from the Permanent Representative of the Libyan Arab Jamahiriya to the United Nations addressed to the Secretary-General, 31 ILM (1992), 728 at 729.
[47] W Schabas, *The International Criminal Court—A Commentary to the Rome Statute* (Oxford: Oxford University Press, 2010), 333.

[n]o investigation or prosecution may be commenced or proceeded with . . . for a period of 12 months after the Security Council, in a resolution adopted under Chapter VII of the Charter of the United Nations, has requested the Court to that effect.

Article 16 refers to Chapter VII and thus points to the way decisions ought to be made under this Chapter; it does not attempt to alter the required steps in Chapter VII decision making. Consequently, every single Council decision made pursuant to Article 16 of the ICC Statute is meant under Article 39 of the Charter to properly and genuinely identify the existence of a threat that can be suitably dealt with through a deferral. This condition was not observed when the Council adopted Resolutions 1422(2002) and 1487(2003), whereby, due to efforts of the United States, it exempted the personnel of UN-established or -authorized peace operations from the jurisdiction of the ICC.

The process by which these resolutions were adopted demonstrates that the Council did not discharge its duty to make a proper Article 39 determination before adopting a Chapter VII decision. The representative of Samoa observed that, in the absence of a situation threatening or breaching peace and security, the vires in the purported use of Chapter VII were questionable. It was 'very doubtful that the requisite circumstances exist in this case to bring into play Article 39 of the Charter and Chapter VII.'[48] The German representative was also of the view that Chapter VII 'requires the existence of a threat to the peace, a breach of the peace or an act of aggression—none of which, in our view, is present in this case. The Security Council would thus be running the risk of undermining its own authority and credibility.'[49] The UK shared 'the concern that actions of the Council should remain within the scope of its powers. Article 39 of the United Nations Charter is relevant in that respect.'[50] Canada was 'troubled that action would be taken in the absence of any apparent threat to international peace and security, which is the fundamental precondition for action under Chapter VII of the Charter.'[51] When, in such cases, the Council is told expressly that it cannot act without identifying preconditions required under Article 39, but it still does act without doing so, the case for the anti-statutory character of the resolution adopted becomes compelling.

The genuineness requirement also applies to remote and generic threats. As the High-Level Panel Report specifies, distant threats should not become imminent and imminent ones should not actually become destructive. This requires a framework for preventative action to address threats in line with their gravity and magnitude.[52]

A 'remote' threat is not the same as a non-existent threat. The reference to 'remote' threats enables the Security Council to address root causes of particular

---

[48] S/PV.4568, Res. 1, 7 (Samoa).
[49] Ibid, 9 (Germany).
[50] Ibid, 15 (UK).
[51] S/PV.4568, 3, S/PV.4774, 4–5 (Canada); for an identical view, S/PV.4568, 5 (New Zealand), 16 (Jordan); in relation to the adoption of Resolution 1487(2003), see S/PV.4772, 15 (Trinidad and Tobago); 20 (Netherlands).
[52] High-level Panel, n 1 above, 12.

problems and crises, and adopt a long-term prevention strategy. A generic threat can reflect a broader situation which has repeated similar manifestations on the ground, which in turn can evidence its genuine character and consequently the extent to which ensuing Chapter VII measures to combat that generic threat can then be justified. This is what justified the use of Article 39 in Resolution 1373 (2001), which required states to undertake a broad range of legislative and administrative counter-terrorist measures. Resolution 1636(2005) on the situation in Lebanon refers to Resolution 1373 and states in its preamble that the terrorist act of assassinating Prime Minister Hariri of the Lebanon 'and its implications constitute a threat to international peace and security'.

The parameters of the root causes approach (as part of the collective security process) have been identified in the Security Council discussion on climate change as an aspect of international peace and security. As Belgium pointed out,

[o]ur conventional security policies are all still often based on obsolete threat assessments and are more geared to managing crises than to preventing them. . . . To resolve the climate energy-security dilemma means that we need to rethink thoroughly the scope of our policies using a broader concept of security.[53]

Likewise, Germany observed that 'this Council usually deals with more imminent threats to international peace and security than those caused by climate change. However, less obvious and more distant drivers of conflict should not be neglected.'[54] According to Namibia, poverty and unemployment, underdevelopment and global economic imbalances 'can create tensions among nations that could threaten international peace and security'.[55] The Slovakian representative pertinently emphasized that 'the Security Council is well positioned to incorporate that new dimension of threat perception into its considerations and ad hoc discussions, while remaining within its mandate'.[56] On a somewhat different note, Venezuela observed that

[t]he Security Council should frame its actions in accordance with the spirit and letter of the Charter of the United Nations, by adopting the strictest interpretation of what really constitutes a threat to international peace and security, in accordance with Article 39 of the Charter. . . . we feel that the subject of energy is an area falling strictly under the sovereignty of States as part of their national development policies.[57]

India also considered it as obvious that 'climate change is not a threat in the context of Article 39 of the Charter; nor can we contemplate Article 41 measures'.[58] Nevertheless, it was made clear during the same discussion that global warming poses an existential threat to some states (such as small island nations), with the

---

[53] S/PV.5663, 5–6 (17 April 2007).

[54] Ibid, 19, and Switzerland, ibid, 26.

[55] Ibid, 31.

[56] Ibid, 4.

[57] S/PV.5663 (Resumption 1), 10 (17 April 2007).

[58] Ibid, 21 (according to India the main responsibility rests on developed countries, on the basis of common but differentiated responsibility).

consequent claim that this is a problem that could be encompassed by the use of Chapter VII. If the Council can adopt comprehensive resolutions on terrorism and non-proliferation, it is unclear why it cannot do so in relation to climate change.

(d) The Tools for Identifying the Genuineness of a Threat

There is no special institutionalized early warning system within the UN, but this process is inherent to the powers of UN principal organs. Fact finding is crucial to identifying threats to the peace. There is a contextual and systemic connection between Article 39 and Article 34. The investigation power under Article 34 is a general and all-encompassing one extending to both Chapter VI and Chapter VII situations. Given that the Article 34 power enables the Council to acquire information on situations that may constitute a threat to international peace, it can also be used in relation to Article 39 determinations.[59] There is an obvious similarity between Articles 34 and 39, and considerations underlying the former seem to apply equally to the latter.[60] The 1991 General Assembly Declaration on Fact-finding, which constitutes an interpretative statement of the relevant Charter rules, specifies that 'fact-finding means any activity designed to obtain detailed knowledge of the relevant facts of any dispute or situation which the competent United Nations organs need in order to exercise effectively their functions in relation to the maintenance of international peace and security'.[61] The Declaration further specifies that

[u]nless a satisfactory knowledge of all relevant facts can be obtained through the use of the information-gathering capabilities of the Secretary-General or other existing means, the competent organ of the United Nations should consider resorting to a fact-finding mission.[62]

This is further reinforced by paragraph 3 which requires that 'fact-finding should be comprehensive, objective, impartial and timely'.[63] These provisions declare the principal organs' obligation to obtain all relevant information before they proceed to determine that a threat exists or adopt relevant measures. If the Council does not conduct fact finding, this might expose motives that did not genuinely tend to the maintenance of international peace and security. This does not affect the right of the General Assembly or the Secretary-General to conduct fact finding on the same matter.

Kolb points out that fact finding is inherent to the proper exercise of the Council's Article 39 power and the credibility of its action. Still, on some occasions fact finding in the Council has been blocked, for instance by the USA after the US bombed Libya in 1986 and by France, the UK, and the USA after the US attack on

---

[59] B Conforti, *The Law and Practice of the United Nations* (The Hague: Kluwer, 2005), 155.
[60] EL Kerley, 'The Powers of Investigation of the United Nations Security Council', 55 AJIL (1961), 892 at 901.
[61] *Declaration on Fact-finding by the United Nations in the Field of the Maintenance of International Peace and Security*, UNGA Res 46/59 (1991), para 2.
[62] Ibid, para 4.
[63] Cf A Berg, 'The 1991 Declaration on Fact-Finding by the United Nations', 4 *European Journal of International Law* (1993), 107.

Iraq in 1993.[64] In the Lockerbie matter the Security Council based Resolutions 731 and 748 on the findings that resulted from inquiries conducted by the USA and the UK without involving an impartial ivestigating body. The evidence in support of the US–UK allegations was never made public.[65] An Article 39 determination was made and Chapter VII sanctions were imposed on Libya regardless. The adoption of enforcement measures by the Council without an effective investigation casts doubt on the legitimacy of that decision.

(e) Subsidiarity and the Genuineness of a Threat

In pertinent cases the Security Council should rely on regional judgement, following the principles of complementarity and subsidiarity, since regional judges are closer to and more familiar with the causes of local crises. This creates a presumption that, if a situation is being dealt with through a regular method of settlement, including a local or regional one, the existence of a threat under Article 39 is contingent on the inadequacy of those efforts, in which case there is a higher burden on the Council to demonstrate that a 'threat to the peace' exists and that Chapter VII action is required. Obviously, in most acute cases such as an ongoing aggressive war or genocide it would be implausible to insist that the regular dispute settlement procedures should be resorted to in the first place.

In particular situations, some objective characteristics possessing institutional and normative legitimacy (such as peace agreements, arrangements regarding demilitarized zones, or demarcation lines) often serve as constituents in relevant Article 39 determinations, thus reinforcing the understanding of the Council's role as subsidiary. Reference to such factors can contribute to transparency in an Article 39 determination and substantiate the genuineness of a threat. Resolution 1125 (1997) on Central African Republic takes note of the signing of the Bangui Agreements of 25 January 1997, expresses concern that nevertheless, 'in the Central African Republic, former mutineers, members of militias and other persons continue to bear arms in contravention of the Bangui Agreements', and thus '[d]etermin [es] that the situation in the Central African Republic continues to constitute a threat to international peace and security in the region'. Resolution 875(1993) contains a determination that 'the failure of the military authorities in Haiti to fulfil their obligations under the [Governor's Island] Agreement constitutes a threat to peace and security in the region'.

Another instance of the Council's subsidiary intervention through the use of Article 39 is presented by the Liberian case. In the preamble of Resolution 788

---

[64] Kolb, n 4 above, 78.

[65] H Nasu, 'Investigation *Proprio Motu* for the Maintenance of International Peace and Security', 23 *Australian Yearbook of International Law* (2004), 105 at 117–18; Quigley also suggests that the Libyan case would have been ideal for investigation, given that facts were sharply in dispute and there was no ongoing military confrontation. A conclusion about the facts by an impartial body would have carried a considerable weight: J Quigley, 'Security Council Fact-finding: A Prerequisite to Effective Prevention of War', 7 *Florida Journal of International Law* (1992), 191 at 242; see also Farrall, n 18 above, 193–4.

(1992), the Council reaffirmed 'its belief that the Yamoussoukro IV Accord of 30 October 1991 offers the best possible framework for a peaceful resolution of the Liberian conflict by creating the necessary conditions for free and fair elections in Liberia'; regretted 'that parties to the conflict in Liberia have not respected or implemented the various accords to date, especially the Yamoussoukro IV Accord'; and thus determined 'that the deterioration of the situation in Liberia constitutes a threat to international peace and security, particularly in West Africa as a whole'.

The Council then recalled the provisions of Chapter VIII of the Charter and approved sanctions proposed by ECOWAS, also emphasizing in the operative part that the role of ECOWAS was 'to assist in the peaceful implementation of this Accord'. In the preamble to Resolution 1132(1997) on Sierra Leone, the Council reaffirms its view that the Abidjan Agreement 'continues to serve as a viable framework for peace, stability and reconciliation in Sierra Leone'. The Council further

[d]eplor[es] the fact that the military junta has not taken steps to allow the restoration of the democratically-elected Government and a return to constitutional order, [is g]ravely concerned at the continued violence and loss of life in Sierra Leone following the military coup of 25 May 1997, the deteriorating humanitarian conditions in that country, and the consequences for neighbouring countries, [and d]etermin[es] that the situation in Sierra Leone constitutes a threat to international peace and security in the region.

A similar subsidiary approach was expressed in jurisprudence of the Special Court for Sierra Leone regarding the Lomé Peace Agreement:

An agreement such as the Lomé Agreement which brings to an end an internal armed conflict no doubt creates a factual situation of restoration of peace that the international community acting through the Security Council may take note of. . . . A breach of the terms of such a peace agreement resulting in resumption of internal armed conflict or creating a threat to peace in the determination of the Security Council may indicate a reversal of the factual situation of peace to be visited with possible legal consequences arising from the new situation of conflict created. Such consequences such as action by the Security Council pursuant to Chapter VII arise from this situation.[66]

A similar approach was upheld by the ICTY in its Appeal Decision in *Blaškić*, where the Tribunal held that a blatant and serious breach of the duty to cooperate with the Tribunal under Article 29 of its Statute could meet general conditions of a 'threat to the peace' if referred by the Tribunal to the Security Council.[67]

Various ways of controlling regional (in)action are open to the Council: (a) to make an Article 39 determination and thus remind regional institutions that they have to deal with the situation at hand, or entrust them with this task; or (b) make a determination premised on the insufficiency or inadequacy of the regional action and then, depending on the circumstances, either join the regional effort on the

---

[66] *Prosecutor v Morris Kallon and Brimma Bazzy Kamara*, Cases No. SCSL–2004–15–AR72(E) and SCSL–2004–16–AR72(E), Decision on Challenge to Jurisdiction: Lomé Accord Amnesty, 13 March 2004, para 43.
[67] *Prosecutor v Tihomir Blaškić*, Judgment on the Request of the Republic of Croatia for Review of the Decision of Trial Chamber II of 18 July 1997, Judgment of 29 October 1997, *sub poena* Appeal Chamber, para 36.

basis of complementarity or overtake it on the ground of its inadequacy. Both options are essentially premised on the subsidiarity of the Council's role, and neither of them justifies the Council's interfering in or overtaking a regional solution merely because the Council's membership is politically unhappy with it.

(f) The Substantive Content of Threats to Peace

Arguably 'the most typical case of a threat to the peace is that of an impending armed conflict between States, ie the imminent danger of a breach of the peace or act of aggression'.[68] If this is so, then presumably in relation to internal situations a higher threshold should be crossed before viewing them as threats to the peace. The 1992 Security Council summit statement professes that

[t]he absence of wars and military conflicts among States does not in itself ensure international peace and security. The non-military sources of instability in the economic, social, humanitarian and ecological fields have become threats to peace and security.[69]

While rarely contested in principle, this matter is not self-explanatory, however, and its historical evolution has been neither straightforward nor uncontroversial. To illustrate, Fenwick commented regarding the 1965 Security Council action imposing sanctions on Rhodesia, by asking whether, even if

admitting that some 220,000 whites are in control of some 4 million Africans, denying them what are accepted today as majority rule and other civil rights, what transformed so suddenly what was a common situation a generation ago into what is a threat to the peace today?[70]

A sound policy of dealing with internal conflicts under Article 39 has to be premised on the relevance of the purposes and principles of the Charter in the particular situation, or on the actual or possible trans-boundary implications of internal crises. Given the indeterminate and open-ended character of the notion of a 'threat to the peace', it is also necessary to demonstrate that the requisite understanding of Article 39 is defensible as a matter of treaty interpretation. Examining the Security Council's Chapter VII action in the former Yugoslavia, the ICTY in *Tadić* interpreted Article 39 in the light of subsequent practice, under Article 31(1)(b) of the Vienna Convention, which demonstrated the agreement of the UN membership:

But even if it were considered merely as an 'internal armed conflict', it would still constitute a 'threat to the peace' according to the settled practice of the Security Council and the common understanding of the United Nations membership in general. Indeed, the practice of the Security Council is rich with cases of civil war or internal strife which it classified as a 'threat to the peace' and dealt with under Chapter VII, with the encouragement or even at the behest of the General Assembly, such as the Congo crisis at the beginning of the 1960s and, more recently, Liberia and Somalia. It can thus be said that there is a common

---

[68] JA Frowein and N Krisch, 'Article 39', in B Simma (ed.), *The Charter of the United Nations—A Commentary* (New York: Oxford University Press, 2002), 722.
[69] S/PV.3046, 31 January 1992.
[70] Fenwick, n 8 above, 753.

understanding, manifested by the 'subsequent practice' of the membership of the United Nations at large, that the 'threat to the peace' of Article 39 may include, as one of its species, internal armed conflicts.[71]

This demonstrates the community consensus and sets a relatively high threshold for the relevance of subsequent practice, such as the position of the UN General Assembly. The Security Council is not entitled to lower the threshold requirement on its own to include, say, low-intensity friction. Some evidence of the international community's acceptance of the changing standard must be adduced.

There has been a general reluctance to characterize cases as threats to the peace. The case of Somalia manifests the Council's reluctance to identify, without more evidence, that an internal situation falls within Article 39. Resolution 751(1992) took note 'of the signing of letters of agreement in Mogadishu, Hargeisa and Kismayo on the mechanism for monitoring the cease-fire and arrangements for the equitable and effective distribution of humanitarian assistance in and around Mogadishu'. This gave an impetus to the Council's engagement of Article 39. Resolution 767(1992) '*[d]etermin[ed]* that the magnitude of the human tragedy caused by the conflict in Somalia, further exacerbated by the obstacles being created to the distribution of humanitarian assistance, constitutes a threat to international peace and security.' The resolution further alluded to

the continuation of conditions that impede the delivery of humanitarian supplies to destinations within Somalia, and in particular reports of looting of relief supplies destined for starving people, attacks on aircraft and ships bringing in humanitarian relief supplies, and attacks on the Pakistani UNOSOM contingent in Mogadishu.

Resolution 775(1992) further specified that provision of humanitarian assistance was an important element of the Council's efforts to maintain and restore peace and security in the area. Resolution 794(1993) authorized the deployment of international forces in Somalia while, in addition to the above,

[e]xpressing grave alarm at continuing reports of widespread violations of international humanitarian law occurring in Somalia, including reports of violence and threats of violence against personnel participating lawfully in impartial humanitarian relief activities: deliberate attacks on non-combatants, relief consignments and vehicles, and medical and relief facilities; and impeding the delivery of food and medical supplies essential for the survival of the civilian population.

Before the adoption of Resolution 794(1992), the Secretary-General clearly explained the rationale behind the Article 39 determination in this case. There were severe humanitarian problems; there was no government in Somalia that could give consent to the deployment of international forces. Thus the Council had to make an Article 39 determination given that the situation in Somalia had repercussions for the entire region.[72] At a later stage, despite improvement due to UNITAF's

---

[71]   *Tadić*, n 19 above, para 30.
[72]   Letter dated 29 November 1992 from the Secretary-General addressed to the President of the Security Council, S/24868, 30 November 1992, 3.

efforts, the situation in Somalia as a whole, according to the Secretary-General, remained insecure and improvements were not sustainable without further intervention. Therefore the threat to the peace ascertained under Resolution 794 was still present.[73]

Despite all this, in other cases the Council has not hesitated to qualify situations not crossing international borders as threats to the peace.[74] By Resolution 217 (1965), the Council imposed non-military sanctions on thegovernment of Southern Rhodesia, demanding the end of the racist regime and its replacement by a government constituted on the basis of peoples' right to self-determination in accordance with the UN General Assembly Declaration on Granting Independence to Colonial Peoples—Resolution 1514(XV) (1960).

The *coup d'état* in Haiti was also a situation taking place within the frontiers of one state. In Resolution 940(1994), the Council stated that 'the goal of the international community remain[ed] the restoration of democracy in Haiti and the prompt return of the legitimately elected President' to the country, and determined existence of a threat to international peace and security in the region. The Council was addressing in this case a purely domestic situation having no transboundary impact capable of constituting a threat to the peace in itself. In one preambular paragraph the Council referred to deterioration of the humanitarian situation and systematic violations of civil liberties causing 'the desperate plight of Haitian refugees'. This does not mean, however, that this flow of refugees by sea towards the United States as such was the decisive factor leading the Council to make a determination under Article 39. First, Resolution 940 offers no evidence that the flow of refugees was a central issue for it to address. The Council directly refers to the goal of the international community to restore democracy in Haiti. Second, the final preambular paragraph of Resolution 940 refers to 'situation in Haiti' and not their consequences as a source of a threat to the peace. These observations prompt the conclusion that, in considering Haiti, the Security Council addressed only the domestic situation under Chapter VII and applied enforcement measures to this situation alone.

The most recent practice of the Council, focusing on several internal situations as threats to the peace, includes Resolutions 864(1993) and 1173(1998), which state that the situation in Angola constitutes a threat to international peace and security. The fact that operative provisions of these resolutions prescribe certain measures only with regard to domestic actors, such as UNITA, is a further confirmation that the Council will focus on a purely internal situation as a threat. With regard to the Democratic Republic of the Congo, the Council has addressed an internal situation *prima facie*. In the preamble of Resolution 1445(2002), the Council considered that the situation in the DRC constituted a threat to the peace. On the other hand, that resolution, as well as Resolutions 1457(2003), 1468(2003)

---

[73] S/25354, para 58.

[74] One of the purposes of UN intervention in purely domestic conflicts may be, as White suggests, to prevent expansion of threats to peace beyond the frontiers of a country which is the target of intervention: N White, *Keeping the Peace* (Manchester: Manchester University Press, 1997), 34.

and 1493(2003), demonstrate that the source of a threat to the peace is not merely domestic, but also international. This holds true in terms of the plunder of the DRC's natural resources, as well as large-scale human rights violations, including through external involvement. However, in 2006, the Council addressed the purely internal situation, emphasizing, in Resolution 1671(2006), 'the importance of elections as the foundation for the longer term restoration of peace and stability, national reconciliation and establishment of the rule of law in the Democratic Republic of the Congo'. Having identified the threat to the peace in this situation, in its operative paragraphs 1 and 2 this resolution authorized deployment of a European Union force during Presidential and parliamentary elections in the Congo, determining its tasks in terms of stabilizing the internal situation.[75] The preamble of Resolution 1556(2004) on Sudan specifies that 'over one million people are in need of urgent humanitarian assistance, that with the onset of the rainy season the provision of assistance has become increasingly difficult, and that without urgent action to address the security, access, logistics, capacity and funding requirements the lives of hundreds of thousands of people will be at risk'.

Still, even later (after the *Tadic* appeal judgment), Resolution 1529(2004) on Haiti specified that 'the situation in Haiti constitutes a threat to international peace and security, and to stability in the Caribbean especially through the potential outflow of people to other States in the sub-region', still justifying the use of Article 39, partly at least, by a trans-national factor. The situation in Zimbabwe witnessed, moreover, an obstruction to activating Article 39 in relation to an internal political crisis. Zimbabwe argued, with the support of other members, that 'the situation in Zimbabwe does not warrant the adoption of a Security Council resolution under Chapter VII of the United Nations Charter. . . . the seven African leaders who attended the G8 summit stated that sanctions were not the way forward to resolve the political impasse in the country. . . . It follows therefore that the adoption of the draft resolution would be in disregard of Africa's own position.'[76] The Council adopted no resolution.

The resistance to a radical and quick expansion of UN threat perception is presumably prompted by fears of the Council's possible manipulability in one or another political interest, in which case it could attempt to act as a world government through multiple interventions, which function has never been delegated to it.

---

[75] See Chapter 7 below.

[76] S/PV/5933, 2–3 (11 July 2008); that position was seconded by Libya, suggesting that there was no threat to peace (at 5); Vietnam, suggesting that there was no threat warranting such action, and that embracing this situation within Chapter VII would create an unwelcome precedent for intervention in domestic affairs of states contrary to international law (at 7); Russia, stating that 'we are firmly convinced that the problems of Zimbabwe cannot be resolved by artificially elevating them to the level of a threat to international peace and security. The Council's application in this instance of enforcement measures under Chapter VII of the United Nations Charter is unjustified and excessive. Moreover, the draft resolution represents nothing but an attempt by the Council to interfere in the internal affairs of States, contrary to the Charter' (at 9); however, the UK and Costa Rica alluded to previous Council decisions to use Chapter VII in relation to domestic situations of humanitarian crisis and breakdown of democracy in Sierra Leone and Haiti (at 8 and 11).

(g) The Use of Article 39 and Violations of International Law

There is a widely held doctrinal assumption that the finding of a threat under Article 39 does not depend on finding a breach of international law but merely on an alteration in peaceful relations between states.[77] It is difficult to see how peaceful relations between states could be altered without force being used illegally in the first place, or at least the likelihood of this arising. Focusing on legal aspects of a particular crisis can provide an objective guide because legal principles are the only ones that bind all parties to any conflict, unlike factors related to structural causes or ideology that can be subject to a valid disagreement. To illustrate, terrorism could never be a valid cause of action under Article 39 without the predominant emphasis on its legal framework in all pertinent Security Council resolutions, because otherwise it could not be dissociated from its claimed underlying structural causes such as colonialism, invasions, interventions, or inequality. The 'Essentials of Peace' brings violation of fundamental rights of states within the range of valid causes for Article 39 determinations and even regards them as a point where the Council should begin its threat-identification exercise.

Developing this point, the UN General Assembly considers that 'States should act so as to prevent in their international relations the emergence or aggravation of disputes or situations [that can cause threat to international peace], in particular by fulfilling in good faith their obligations under international law'; the second paragraph requires that '[i]n order to prevent [such] disputes or situations, States should develop their relations on the basis of the sovereign equality of States'.[78] If compliance with international law is a precondition for avoiding threats to the peace, then it is difficult to argue that the involvement of international illegality in situations posing such threats should not be an ordinary expectation. International law contains imperatives on which states and the international community are agreed. The Security Council cannot, through the use of Article 39, design and impose policies alternative to or even conflicting with international law. Article 103 goes only so far as incidentally to enable the Council's decisions to prevail over treaties that stand in the way of enforcing a valid Chapter VII enterprise; it does not enable the Council to initiate a Chapter VII effort having a cause of action that conflicts with international law.

The view that determining a threat to the peace does not have to involve a breach of international law is arguably supported by the Council's role in contexts where the considerations of peace differ from those of justice. However, the practice of United Nations organs refutes any inherent relevance of such a dichotomy. In its Resolutions regarding the Middle East, the UN General Assembly clearly stated that the maintenance of international peace is integrally linked with the

---

[77] Kolb, n 4 above, 68, accepting, however, that the violation of peremptory norms (*jus cogens*) is adequate to subsume the pertinent situation within Article 39: ibid, 69.

[78] *Declaration on the Prevention and Removal of Disputes and Situations Which May Threaten International Peace and Security and on the Role of the United Nations in this Field*, A/RES/43/51, 5 December 1988, paras 1 and 2.

reinstatement of legal norms violated in a given situation, such as via withdrawal from occupied territories, and return of displaced persons.[79] Similarly, the Security Council stated in several resolutions that, to restore peace in the former Yugoslavia, the enforcement of the relevant legal norms, such as those on individual criminal responsibility for core international crimes, was a necessary precondition.[80] The Council thus has intertwined violations of international law and threats to the peace with each other. In Resolution 941(1994), a threat to the peace was determined on the basis of violations of international humanitarian law in Bosnia-Herzegovina. In Resolution 1638(2005), the Council emphasized that the former President of Liberia, Charles Taylor, had been indicted by the Special Court of Sierra Leone, and his return to Liberia, that is the avoidance of his trial, 'would constitute an impediment to stability and a threat to the peace of Liberia and to international peace and security in the region'. Accordingly, the Council authorized the UN peace-keeping force to arrest Taylor if he returned to Liberia and transfer him to Sierra Leone to be prosecuted before the Special Court. In Resolution 1688(2006) regarding the operation of the Special Court, the Council manifested its

determination to end impunity, establish the rule of law and promote respect for human rights and to restore and maintain international peace and security, in accordance with international law and the purposes and principles of the Charter.

The Council further pointed out that 'the proceedings in the Special Court in the case against former President Taylor will contribute to achieving truth and reconciliation in Liberia and the wider sub-region'. Consequently, the Council praised the efforts to bring Taylor before the Court and decided in paragraph 7 of the Resolution that the Special Court retained its exclusive jurisdiction over him. Clearer evidence of the Council's perception of the interdependence between peace and justice is hard to find.[81]

The argument that an Article 39 determination of a 'threat to the peace' can be made in relation to state conduct in accordance with international law projects a systemic inconsistency on the international legal system. For, if a conduct of a state is lawful yet threatens international peace, then the conclusion is that the pertinent rules of international law authorize that state to act in a way threatening international peace. Thus the operation of the 1971 Montreal Convention regime of extradition and prosecution could be viewed as potentially threatening international peace, in its turn begging the question as to why State-parties adopted it that way.

In the area of nuclear non-proliferation, it is unlikely that a valid determination under Article 39 can be made in a situation not involving a verified breach of relevant agreements, such as the 1968 Non-Proliferation Treaty. For it is this legal framework that mandates the position under which some states are entitled to have

---

[79] UNGA Res 41/162 (1986), paras 2–3; UNGA Res 39/146A (1984); UNGA Res 34/65 (1979) A, para 2.
[80] UNSC Res. 771(1992), 817(1993), 827(1993).
[81] For further examples to this effect see Chapter 1 above.

nuclear weapons and others are not. This problem arose acutely in relation to Iranian uranium enrichment, where the IAEA was unable

to conclude that there are no undeclared nuclear materials or activities in Iran. The process of drawing such a conclusion, after an Additional Protocol is in force, under normal circumstances, is a time consuming process. In view of the past undeclared nature of significant aspects of Iran's nuclear programme, and its past pattern of concealment, this conclusion can be expected to take longer than in normal circumstances.[82]

Thus the Agency treats this issue as part of its regular, core activities, without specifying any need for alarm or for urgent (let alone coercive) measures to deal with Iranian uranium enrichment.

The IAEA Board of Governors Resolution that referred the Iranian nuclear enrichment matter to the Security Council fell short of identifying any positive evidence of violation, and instead emphasized that the Agency was not yet in a position to clarify whether the Iranian nuclear programme had a military dimension. The principal problem related to the need for transparency and verification.[83] The Council adopted Resolution 1696(2006) in which it demanded that Iran cease its uranium enrichment programmes. Joyner points to the cases involving nuclear enrichment programmes in South Korea and Japan, essentially similar to that in Iran, which did not attract international condemnation. Arguably, Iran's different treatment owed, not to a breach of the NPT but rather to 'the judgment of the IAEA Board of Governors that the Iran case is somehow different'. While Iran was correct as a matter of non-proliferation law, the legal landscape changed with the adoption of Resolution 1696, especially through Article 103 of the Charter which allegedly makes Charter-based decisions prevail over Iran's rights under the NPT.[84]

Further IAEA Reports are premised on uncertainties regarding the real scope of the Iranian enrichment programme and a lack of transparency and cooperation on the Iranian side, but do not specify actual facts of Iran's violation of the NPT, nor any affirmative evidence pointing to a military dimension for Iranian nuclear enrichment. A report issued in 2006 specified that

[a]ll the nuclear material declared by Iran to the Agency is accounted for. Apart from the small quantities previously reported to the Board, the Agency has found no other undeclared nuclear material in Iran. However, gaps remain in the Agency's knowledge with respect to the scope and content of Iran's centrifuge programme. Because of this, and other gaps in the Agency's knowledge, including the role of the military in Iran's nuclear programme, the Agency is unable to make progress in its efforts to provide assurance about the absence of undeclared nuclear material and activities in Iran.[85]

---

[82] GOV/2005/67, para 51.
[83] *Implementation of the NPT Safeguards Agreement in the Islamic Republic of Iran*, Resolution adopted on 4 February 2006, GOV/2006/14, 4 February 2006, especially preamble, paras 1, 3, 7, and 8.
[84] D Joyner, *International Law and the Proliferation of Weapons of Mass Destruction* (New York: Oxford University Press, 2009), 51–4.
[85] *Implementation of the NPT Safeguards Agreement in the Islamic Republic of Iran*, Report by Director General, GOV/2006/27, 28 April 2006, para 33.

A more recent report points to 'a number of outstanding issues which give rise to concerns, and which need to be clarified to exclude the existence of possible military dimensions to Iran's nuclear programme'.[86] A subsequent report specified that, in view of lack of information requested on the matter (especially a more substantive response by Iran), 'it is critical for Iran to implement the Additional Protocol and clarify the outstanding issues in order for the Agency to be in a position to provide credible assurance about the absence of undeclared nuclear material and activities in Iran'.[87] On occasions the Agency has also proclaimed that Iran's representations were consistent with the Agency's own findings.[88]

The Security Council's treatment of the Iranian nuclear issue is marked, as a whole, by a rather nebulous treatment of the issue of whether that situation involved a threat to the peace warranting application of Chapter VII measures. Resolution 1696 speaks of proliferation risks. The Council's rhetoric goes very near to the area covered by Article 39 but does not cross its boundaries by specifying that these risks constitute a threat. The Council is thus conscious that this is not a valid case for using Article 39.

Resolution 1737(2006), imposing sanctions on Iran to address its non-compliance with the international demands to freeze its uranium enrichment programme, refers, in its preambular paragraphs, to concerns expressed by the IAEA regarding the country's nuclear programmes. The Council's entire reasoning is based, not on a concern that Iran has actually been doing something problematic, but on its failure to prove the opposite to the Council's satisfaction. The problems identified were that certain Iranian nuclear programmes '*could* have a military nuclear dimension' and that 'Iran has not established full and sustained suspension' of its presumed activities. That said, Resolution 1737 does not specify what Iranian conduct constitutes the threat to the peace: which, it may be said, is not an impeccable exercise from the viewpoint of legal certainty. Neither does the subsequent Resolution 1803(2008) identify a threat to the peace. It notes with concern that 'Iran has not established full and sustained suspension of all enrichment-related and reprocessing activities and heavy water-related projects as set out in Resolution[s] 1696(2006), 1737(2006), and 1747(2007)', is consequently concerned 'by the proliferation risks presented by the Iranian nuclear programme', and moves right to Article 41 to impose further sanctions. Unfortunately, nor has this resolution taken the matter beyond the area of speculation and allegations. Likewise, the most recent Security Council Resolution 1929(2010) reiterates presumptive statements from previous resolutions and relies on the lack of Iran's 'cooperation with the IAEA under the Additional Protocol', and

[86] *Implementation of the NPT Safeguards Agreement and relevant provisions of Security Council resolutions 1737 (2006), 1747 (2007), 1803 (2008) and 1835 (2008) in the Islamic Republic of Iran*, Report by the Director General, GOV/2009/35, 5 June 2009, para 17.

[87] *Implementation of the NPT Safeguards Agreement and relevant provisions of Security Council resolutions 1737 (2006), 1747 (2007), 1803 (2008) and 1835 (2008) in the Islamic Republic of Iran*, Report by the Director General, GOV/2009/55, 28 August 2009, paras 24 and 29.

[88] *Implementation of the NPT Safeguards Agreement and relevant provisions of Security Council resolutions 1737 (2006) and 1747 (2007) in the Islamic Republic of Iran*, Report by the Director General, GOV/2007/58, 15 November 2007, paras 11, 13, 23.

the presumptive need 'to exclude the possibility of military dimensions of Iran's nuclear programme'.

The lack of a proper cause of action in the Iranian issue was also demonstrated in discussions preceding the adoption of Resolution 1929: this resolution was rushed through, despite a joint declaration that was adopted by Brazil, Turkey, and Iran in Tehran on 17 May 2010. The Brazilian representative, while voting against Resolution 1929, quoted as one of the reasons the fact that 'the joint declaration has neither received the political recognition it deserves nor been given the time it needs to bear fruit'. The adoption of a Chapter VII resolution at that point ran counter to the successful efforts of Brazil and Turkey to engage Iran in a negotiated solution. Lack of transparency in threat identification was manifested by the fact that 'the permanent members, together with a country that is not a member of the Security Council, negotiated among themselves for months behind closed doors'.[89] The Turkish representative stated that 'the Tehran declaration has created a new reality with respect to Iran's nuclear programme' and a new opportunity for finding an agreed solution, only to be undermined by a new Chapter VII resolution.[90] The members of the Council sponsoring and voting Resolution 1929 did not properly explain why its adoption was necessary, despite the problem of nuclear enrichment proceeding to a resolution through agreed means, which reinforces the conclusion, manifested through the lack of a proper Article 39 determination in all resolutions regarding Iran, that these resolutions have been adopted as part of a parochial political agenda as opposed to being part of a proper effort under Chapter VII to confront genuinely existing threats.

The IAEA referral resolution did not refer in factual terms to a threat inherent in Iran's conduct. It was not IAEA's task to ascertain the existence of a threat to the peace and its referral of the matter to the Council cannot constitute evidence that it formed its judgement along those lines, still less absolve the Council from the duty to properly ascertain the existence of a threat before activating Chapter VII. The IAEA decision having no identified legal basis and the Security Council's decision to incorporate the IAEA decision without asking necessary questions as to that legal basis do not add up to form the legal basis required under the Charter. If a threat under Article 39 is a breach of a treaty then its existence has to be proved through specific evidence, just like that of any other internationally wrongful act.

Iran's statement on the occasion of adoption of Resolution 1737 referred to regional positions as demonstrating the unrepresentative character of this resolution under Article 24 of the Charter. Nearly two-thirds of the UN membership were also members of the NAM and the OIC 'which, at the summit level, have reaffirmed that States' choices and decisions in the field of peaceful uses of nuclear technology and its fuel cycle policies must be respected'.[91] The 2008 OIC summit statement stated a strong preference 'that Iran's nuclear issue should be settled exclusively by peaceful means and through negotiation without preconditions, within the framework of the

---

[89] S/PV.6335, 2–3 (Brazil).
[90] S/PV.6335, 3 (Turkey); Resolution 1929 acknowledges the Tehran Declaration in its preamble but falls short of according to it any importance.
[91] S/PV.5612, 12.

IAEA, and in accordance with the NPT and the Statute of the IAEA'.[92] The Havana Summit of the Non-Aligned Movement stated that

> the International Atomic Energy Agency (IAEA) [w]as the sole competent authority for verification of the respective safeguards obligations of Member States and stressed that there should be no undue pressure or interference in the Agency's activities, especially its verification process, which would jeopardize the efficiency and credibility of the Agency.[93]

The NAM Tehran Declaration is also significant in specifying that

> all safeguards and verification issues, including those of Iran, should be resolved within the IAEA framework, and be based on technical and legal grounds. They further emphasized that the Agency should continue its work to resolve the Iranian nuclear issue within its mandate under the Statute of the IAEA.[94]

By focusing on 'technical and legal' aspects, coupled with the exclusive role of IAEA in this process, the Non-Aligned Movement effectively took the position that there was no threat to peace and security involved in the Iranian nuclear enrichment controversy, and thus no valid cause of action under Article 39 of the UN Charter.

(h) Evaluation

Construing the Article 39 determination power as political and discretionary despite structural and systemic requirements under the Charter only enhances the view of it as arbitrary, and impedes the practical application of Chapter VII. The issue of whether an Article 39 determination has been made for ulterior purposes unconnected with the genuine effort to maintain peace and security should be clarified by focusing on the consistency between the situation identified as a threat, the objectives set, any demands presented, and the measures prescribed, to transparently demonstrate how it is intended to maintain or restore international peace and security in the case at issue.

3. Threat Perception by Regional Organizations

(a) The European Union

Unlike that under the UN Charter, the EU threat perception method does not look for threats to international peace and security as such, but focuses on threats to

---

[92] OIC/SUMMIT–11/2008/FC/Final, para 83; see also OIC Resolution No. 9/11–P(IS), Dakar Summit, 13–14 March 2008, paras 3–4; the identical statement can be found in the Declaration of the 33rd Islamic Conference of Foreign Ministers, Baku, 19–21 June 2006, para 12.

[93] NAM Statement on the Islamic Republic of Iran's nuclear issue, Havana, 11–16 September 2006, para 2, S/2006/1018, para 3; Ministerial Meeting of the Coordinating Bureau of the Non-Aligned Movement, Final Document, Putrajaya, Malaysia, 27–30 May 2006, para 91; reaffirmed in identical terms in the NAM Statement on the Islamic Republic of Iran's Nuclear Issue, 15th Ministerial Conference, Tehran, 27–30 July 2008, para 3.

[94] NAM Tehran Declaration, para 8.

security within the EU. In this sense, the EU's involvement outside its membership area is as an interested party. As explained in a rather Eurocentric way, promotion of the values the EU is based on, such as democracy, human rights, and economic development, is expected to reduce emerging threats and therefore act as an important conflict-preventing factor. The 2003 European Security Strategy acknowledges that there can be a need for intervention in other parts of the world where 'pre-modern' states are faced with the threat of collapse, chaos, and decomposition.[95] In a way similar to the Security Strategy, the 2003 EU Declaration on Non-Proliferation of Weapons of Mass Destruction states that such proliferation is a growing threat to international peace and security:

The risk that terrorists will acquire chemical, biological, radiological or nuclear materials adds a new dimension to this threat. . . . Meeting this challenge must be a central element in the EU external action, including the common foreign and security policy. Our objective is to deter, halt and, where possible, reverse proliferation programmes of concern worldwide.

The WEU had developed a similar external threat perception, stressing

that the current explosive situation in many African states provides a breeding ground for terrorism and extremism. Without good governance, without adequate security forces or intelligence, extremist groups and factions are free to create and expand their networks and develop into terrorist cells.[96]

The 2003 EU Security Strategy specifies the range of threats in the sense that 'nuclear activities in North Korea, nuclear risks in South Asia, and proliferation in the Middle East are all of concern to Europe', and all Europe's problems.[97] Structural causes of conflicts can be addressed through non-confrontational means, such as diplomacy, aid, and sanctions as elements of the preventive engagement approach.[98] The emphasis on the terrorist threat is made in Article 222 TEU, according to which

[t]he Union and its Member States shall act jointly in a spirit of solidarity if a Member State is the object of a terrorist attack or the victim of a natural or man-made disaster. The Union shall mobilise all the instruments at its disposal, including the military resources made available by the Member States, to:

(a) – prevent the terrorist threat in the territory of the Member States;
      – protect democratic institutions and the civilian population from any terrorist attack;
      – assist a Member State in its territory, at the request of its political authorities, in the event of a terrorist attack;

[95] J Cloos, 'EU–UN Cooperation on Crisis Management—Putting Effective Multilateralism in Practice', in J Wouters *et al* (eds.), *The United Nations and the European Union* (The Hague: TMC Asser Press, 2006), 259 at 260–61.
[96] *The European Union and Peacekeeping in Africa*, WEU Assembly 15th Session, Doc A/1880, 1 December 2004, explanatory memorandum, paras 10, 17.
[97] ESS, 6–7, 11.
[98] A Toje, 'The 2003 European Union Security Strategy: A Critical Appraisal', 10 *European Foreign Affairs Review* (2005), 117 at 127–8.

(b) assist a Member State in its territory, at the request of its political authorities, in the event of a natural or man-made disaster.

The EU Declaration on Combating Terrorism of March 2004 adds this:

The threat of terrorism affects us all. A terrorist act against one country concerns the international community as a whole.[99]

The fact that the EU has developed such a broad, indeed near-comprehensive, threat perception to address many causes of potential insecurity is balanced against the Union's policy of engaging inchoate threats by non-confrontational means, on the one hand, and of undertaking enforcement action only when authorized by the UN Security Council, on the other.

(b) ECOWAS

The ECOWAS Protocol on Mutual Assistance on Defence concluded on 29 May 1981 envisages collective action against several kinds of threat.[100] Article 16 sets out procedures of action '[w]hen an external armed threat or aggression is directed against a Member State of the Community'. Article 17 deals with the conflict between two member States. Article 18 deals with internal conflict within a member State of the Community actively maintained and sustained from outside, but specifies that Community forces will not intervene if the conflict is purely internal.

In its preamble the 1999 Protocol Relating to the Mechanism for Conflict Prevention explains the ECOWAS threat perception by providing a definition of 'member State in crisis', which refers

both to a Member State experiencing an armed conflict as well as a Member State facing serious and persisting problems or situations of extreme tension which, if left unchecked, could lead to serious humanitarian disaster or threaten peace and security in the sub-region or in any Member State affected by the overthrow or attempted overthrow of a democratically elected government.

A more detailed threat perception is specified under Article 25, which states that

[t]he Mechanism shall be applied in any of the following circumstances: In cases of aggression or conflict in any Member State or threat thereof; In case of conflict between two or several Member States; In case of internal conflict: a) that threatens to trigger a humanitarian disaster, or b) that poses a serious threat to peace and security in the sub-region; In event of serious and massive violation of human rights and the rule of law. In the event of an overthrow or attempted overthrow of a democratically elected government; [or] Any other situation as may be decided by the Mediation and Security Council.

The difference between the approaches under PMAD and the 1999 Protocol seems to reflect the gradual evolution of the notion of 'threat to the peace' under Article 39 of the UN Charter.

---

[99] EU Declaration on Combating Terrorism, March 2004.
[100] UNTS, vol. 1690, No I–29137 (1992), 52.

(c) SADC

The SADC Protocol determines the objective of its Organ on Politics, Defence and Security as being to 'protect the people and safeguard the development of the Region against instability arising from the breakdown of law and order, intra-state conflict, interstate conflict and aggression'. Article 11(2) of the Protocol specifies that

(a) The Organ may seek to resolve any significant inter-state conflict between State Parties or between a State Party and non-State Party and a 'significant inter-state conflict' shall include:
  (i) a conflict over territorial boundaries or natural resources;
  (ii) a conflict in which an act of aggression or other form of military force has occurred or been threatened; and
  (iii) a conflict which threatens peace and security in the Region or in the territory of a State Party which is not a party to the conflict.

(b) The Organ may seek to resolve any significant intra-state conflict within the territory of a State Party and a 'significant intra-state conflict' shall include:
  (i) large-scale violence between sections of the population or between the state and sections of the population, including genocide, ethnic cleansing and gross violation of human rights;
  (ii) a military coup or other threat to the legitimate authority of a State;
  (iii) a condition of civil war or insurgency; and
  (iv) a conflict which threatens peace and security in the Region or in the territory of another State Party.

(c) In consultation with the United Nations Security Council and the Central Organ of the Organisation of African Unity Mechanism for Conflict Prevention, Management and Resolution, the Organ may offer to mediate in a significant interior intra-state conflict that occurs outside the Region.

Thus there is a graduation from inter-State conflicts (at least one party to which is a SADC member), to conflicts within the member State (intra-state conflicts), and ultimately to conflicts outside the SADC membership area. Under Article 11(3)(e) a further category of crises—external military threats—is reserved to be dealt with under the SADC Mutual Defence Pact.[101]

(d) The African Union

The bottom line of the AU threat perception is enshrined in the AU Summit Declaration on Common African Defence and Security Policy, which defines African security as encompassing both 'the traditional, state-centric, notion of the survival of the state and its protection by military means from external aggression', and intra-state conflict that incorporates a dimension of human

---

[101] See Chapter 6 below.

security.[102] Common security threats pose a danger to the common defence and security interests of the continent, since they 'confront all, some, or one of the countries or regions of the continent'.[103] The Declaration then lists principal categories of threats as inter-state conflicts and tensions, intra-state conflicts and tensions, unstable post-conflict situations, other factors that engender insecurity (such as humanitarian problems, arms proliferation, and organized crime), and 'common external threats' such as aggression, mercenarism, and international terrorism.[104]

Article 1(a) of the AU Common Defence Pact defines 'Acts of Subversion' as

any act that incites, aggravates or creates dissension within or among Member States with the intention or purpose to destabilize or overthrow the existing regime or political order by, among other means, fomenting racial, religious, linguistic, ethnic and other differences, in a manner inconsistent with the Constitutive Act, the Charter of the United Nations and the Lomé Declaration.

Article 5(b) imposes obligations on states to prevent acts of subversion, but this does not get reflected in the collective threat perception under the AU PSC Protocol.

Some aspects of the AU threat perception owe their origins to threat perceptions adopted by the OAU, as embodied in the 2000 OAU Declaration on Responses to Unconstitutional Changes of Government, which expresses

grave concern about the resurgence of *coup d'état* in Africa. We recognize that these developments are a threat to peace and security of the Continent and they constitute a very disturbing trend and serious set back to the ongoing process of democratization in the Continent.[105]

The Declaration further specifies that

[i]n order to give practical effect to the principles we have enunciated, we have agreed on the following definition of situations that could be considered as situations of unconstitutional change of government:
  i) military *coup d'état* against a democratically elected Government;
  ii) intervention by mercenaries to replace a democratically elected Government;
  iii) replacement of democratically elected Governments by armed dissident groups and rebel movements;
  iv) the refusal by an incumbent government to relinquish power to the winning party after free, fair and regular elections.

The Lomé Declaration is confirmed in the preamble to the AU PSC Protocol and has thus been endowed with statutory standing. According to Article 7(1)(g) PSC Protocol, the Peace and Security Council is empowered to 'institute sanctions

---

[102] AU Summit Declaration on Common African Defence and Security Policy, Sirte (Libya), 28 February 2004, para 6.
[103] Ibid, para 7.
[104] Ibid, paras 8–9.
[105] Declaration on the Framework for and OAU Response to Unconstitutional Changes of Government, AHG/Decl.5 (XXXVI).

whenever an unconstitutional change of Government takes place in a Member State, as provided for in the Lomé Declaration'. This threat perception was put into practice when the AU responded to the unconstitutional change of government in Togo. In its Communiqué the Peace and Security Council referred to the AU Declaration of July 2000 on Unconstitutional Changes of Government, condemned the coup, and the revision of the Togolese Constitution by the *de facto* authorities, demanded the prompt restoration of lawful authorities and withdrawal of the military from interfering with the political life of the country, and stated its intention to impose sanctions if constitutional legality was not rapidly re-established.[106]

(e) The Organization of American States

In the absence of a threat, for instance under Article 6 of the Rio Treaty, the OAS has no coercive authority.[107] Within the OAS system threat perception is reflected in provisions of the OAS Treaty which prohibit intervention in domestic affairs of a state, use of coercive measures to obtain political advantage, infringement of territorial integrity, and the use of force (Articles 19–22). Under the original perception of threats, the OAS was to deal with any extra-continental attack and the Organ of Consultation was endowed with rapid reaction powers to prevent the quick victory of an aggressor. There was little anticipation of relatively minor but dangerous conflicts between OAS members themselves.[108]

Article 3 of the Rio Treaty specifies the obligations of OAS member States if aggression is offered against one of them. In broader terms, Article 6 refers to situations where

the inviolability or the integrity of the territory or the sovereignty or political independence of any American State should be affected by an aggression which is not an armed attack or by an extra-continental or intra-continental conflict, or by any other fact or situation [that] might endanger the peace of America, the Organ of Consultation shall meet immediately in order to agree on the measures which must be taken in case of aggression to assist the victim of the aggression or, in any case, the measures which should be taken for the common defense and for the maintenance of the peace and security of the Continent.

Article 6 contains to define threats broadly, but the threshold is still set so that 'in each of these three situations the inviolability or the integrity of the territory or the sovereignty or political independence of the American State must be affected',[109] The framers of the Treaty did not intend to put sanctions into effect 'unless the circumstances were of a serious and urgent character pressing, in a sense, upon the

---

[106] Declaration, ibid; PSC, 24th Meeting, Communiqué of 7 February 2005, PSC/PR/Comm. (XXIV), Section B.

[107] CG Fenwick, 'The Organization of American States: The Transition from an Unwritten to a Written Constitution', 59 AJIL (1965), 315 at 319.

[108] J Dreier, 'The Council of the OAS: Performance and Potential', 5 *Journal of Inter-American Studies* (1963), 297 at 304–5.

[109] CG Fenwick, 'Inter-American Regional Procedures for the Settlement of Disputes', 10 *International Organization* (1956), 12 at 13.

very political existence of the State'.[110] As Akehurst indicates, OAS practice confirms that Article 6 relates to subversive activities.[111] It has also been suggested that this provision covers only present threats.[112] However, it has not been clarified in practice whether the words 'fact or situation might endanger the peace of America' allow for subjective and discretionary judgement being exercised by OAS organs.

The power of investigation of facts is inherent to the convoking of a Consultation Meeting, as the Council 'must also have the necessary power to obtain the information necessary to reach a judgment on so important an issue'. The OAS Council can examine situations first, and then decide whether to apply the Rio Treaty and convoke a Meeting of Consultation 'on the basis of more solid information as to the desirability thereof',[113] which is generally similar to the relationship between Chapter VI and Chapter VII actions under the UN Charter.

Disputes that have not been found capable of bilateral handling do not, as such and because of their political element, warrant the convoking of the Organ.[114] A Meeting of the Organ of Consultation is necessary only if the cause is pressing. When the OAS Council intended to act as Organ of Consultation in relation to the controversy between Nicaragua and Costa Rica in 1948–9 on the basis of Costa Rica's complaint of being invaded by troops that had bases in Nicaragua, after investigation through the OAS committee of ambassadors the two states concluded a Pact of Amity, and so the Meeting of Consultation was called off.[115] No institutional intervention is needed when bilateral and other mechanisms can bring about the desired outcome. In the controversy between Nicaragua and Costa Rica in 1955, Nicaragua requested a Meeting of Consultation, but the Council established a Committee of Investigation, which established security zones on both sides of the border and appointed military observers to watch them. In a situation between Peru and Ecuador involving the risk of armed conflict, the Council designated Argentina, Brazil, Chile, and the USA as guarantor powers and mandated them to investigate the situation. Having heard of the measures taken by the guarantor powers, the Council held that military action by Peru had been prevented and thus there was no need to convoke the Organ of Consultation.[116] This demonstrated the OAS potential to defuse tense political situations using measures of transparency short of enforcement, similar to Chapter VI under the UN Charter, and in the spirit of subsidiarity.

In a controversy between Haiti and the Dominican Republic involving claims that a Haitian former military officer was receiving active support from within the

---

[110] CG Fenwick, 'The Issues at Punta Del Este: Non-Intervention v Collective Security', 56 AJIL (1962), 469 at 471.
[111] M Akehurst, 'Enforcement Action by Regional Agencies, With Special Reference to the Organization of American States', 42 *British Yearbook of International Law* (1967) 175 at 192.
[112] Ibid, 192–3.
[113] Dreier, n 108 above, 310–11.
[114] Fenwick, n 109 above, 18.
[115] Ibid, 14–15.
[116] Ibid, 17–18.

Dominican government, the OAS Council invoked the limits on its action imposed by the threshold under Article 6 of the Rio Treaty and persuaded the parties to resort to other procedures; it thus abstained from convoking the Organ of Consultation.[117] However, a year later the Council convoked the Organ in a controversy between the same two states but, having ascertained that the parties had agreed to remove the source of the controversy, called the meeting off.[118]

In 1950 the OAS Council declared (supplementing the threat perception pattern and structural priorities specified in OAS treaties) that, although representative democracy was important, a threat to it did not justify violating inter-American commitments embodying the principle of non-intervention.[119] An attempt to expand the conventionally stated threat perception is witnessed by the adoption, by the Tenth Inter-American Conference in 1954, of the Declaration of Caracas, which identified the spread of communism as a threat to the peace. The Declaration stated that 'the aggressive character of the international communist movement' consti-tuted 'a special and immediate threat to the national institutions and the peace and security of the American States', and to their right to develop without outside intervention in their internal or external affairs. Consequently,

the domination or control of the political institutions of any American State by the international communist movement extending to this Hemisphere the political system of an extra continental power, would constitute a threat to the sovereignty and political independence of the American States, endangering the peace of America, and would call for a meeting of consultation to consider the adoption of appropriate action in accordance with existing treaties.

This manifests the intention of the authors of the Caracas Declaration to expand the threat perception provided for under 'existing treaties'.

The Caracas Declaration was not acted upon until 1962 when Cuba was excluded from participation in the OAS;[120] it had little impact on the crisis management activities of OAS and during the missile crisis it was not formally invoked.[121] This is understandable, as the concern in that case was far more specific than a general concern at the spread of communism. But the influence of the Declaration is still visible in this case. As Fenwick observed, the focus of the Punta del Este Consultation Meeting covered a wider area than the limits prescribed under Article 6 of the Rio Treaty, as the Cuban ties to the Sino-Soviet Powers did not cross the threshold prescribed under that provision. However, the Caracas Declaration described domination of political institutions by the communist movement as a situation actionable under Article 6.[122]

---

[117] CG Fenwick, 'Application of the Treaty of Rio de Janeiro to the Controversy Between Costa Rica and Nicaragua', 43 AJIL (1949), 329 at 332.

[118] Fenwick, n 109 above, 15.

[119] Quoted in H McCoubrey and J Morris, *Regional Peacekeeping in the Post-Cold War Era* (The Hague: Kluwer, 2000), 97.

[120] Fenwick, n 107 above, 318.

[121] R Barliant, 'The OAS Peace and Security System', 21 *Stanford Law Review* (1969) 1156 at 1163.

[122] Fenwick, n 110 above, 471–2.

OAS threat perception under Article 6 has clear parameters for the political independence and territorial integrity of member States. It does not relate to internal situations within a state, even where these are seen undesirable from outside. The Caracas Declaration cannot validly be read into Article 6 because this would modify the requirements under that article. The Declaration was adopted with the aim of imposing a new OAS threat perception, even though one OAS member, Guatemala, did not agree with it (and Mexico and Argentina abstained).[123] This falls short of the requirements that a subsequent agreement must meet, as a matter of interpreting Article 6 of the Rio Treaty. The burden on any subsequent agreement is increased by structural characteristics of Article 6, which are firmly grounded on a trans-national dimension to any threats perceived. As demonstrated above, a 'threat to the peace' under Article 39 of the UN Charter is subject to no such limiting criteria and can be interpreted (through general and consistent practice of UN members and organs) to include internal armed conflicts. But the same does not apply to threats under Article 6 of the Rio Treaty. Incorporating the Caracas threat perception into this legal framework would have deep structural implications as it would require revising the entire Inter-American framework (originally based on principles of territorial supremacy, non-intervention, and non-aggression) by importing a qualitatively new perception of a threat not reaching the trans-boundary threshold laid down in Article 6, of a kind to which the Rio Treaty simply has not been designed to respond. This would require amending the treaty.

McCoubrey and Morris nevertheless attempt to assign legitimacy to the Caracas Declaration by referring to Article 23 of the OAS Charter specifying that 'measures adopted for the maintenance of peace and security in accordance with existing treaties do not constitute a violation of the principles set forth in Articles 19 and 21' and thus suggest that, while the preamble and Article 3 emphasize the importance of the representative democracy, the Caracas Declaration lawfully directs the legal position to disapply the principle of non-intervention where a non-democratic regime engages in practices threatening regional security.[124] But this misses the point that the measures that the Caracas Declaration attempted to legitimize were not those 'adopted . . . in accordance with existing treaties' as required under Article 23. The pertinent OAS treaties, such as the Rio Treaty, fall short of justifying measures against threats that do not fit within the threat perception adopted as part of those treaties. The original 1950 position of the OAS Council could only be explained by the members' understanding that the principle of non-intervention still stands in the face of claims that a particular state is not governed democratically.

OAS General Assembly Resolution 1080(1991) specifies representative democracy as another dimension of identifying threats. According to operative paragraph 1, the Assembly decides

---

[123] CG Fenwick, 'Jurisdictional Questions Involved in the Guatemalan Revolution', 48 AJIL (1954), 597.
[124] McCoubrey and Morris, n 119 above, 96–8.

[t]o instruct the Secretary-General to call for the immediate convocation of a meeting of the Permanent Council in the event of any occurrences giving rise to the sudden or irregular interruption of the democratic political institutional process or of the legitimate exercise of power by the democratically elected government in any of the Organization's member states, in order, within the framework of the Charter, to examine the situation, decide on and convene an ad hoc meeting of the Ministers of Foreign Affairs, or a special session of the General Assembly, all of which must take place within a ten-day period.[125]

It has been stated that 'the Santiago Declaration rescues an old idea from the Charter's text, that of the promotion of democracy, and upgrades it to [a] principle'.[126]

Acting, professedly, in pursuance of the threat identification criteria under the OAS constituent instruments, the Organ of Consultation has made several determinations of a threat. Resolution I of the 1962 Punta del Este meeting, paragraph I, professes to adhere to the genuineness requirement by stating that

[t]he Ministers have been able to verify that the subversive offensive of communist governments, their agents, and the organizations which they control, has increased in intensity. . . . The *outstanding facts in this intensified offensive are the declarations set forth in official documents* of the directing bodies of the international communist movement, that one of its principal objectives is the establishment of communist regimes in the underdeveloped countries and in Latin America.[127]

Resolution VIII of the Eighth Meeting, deciding to introduce an arms embargo against Cuba, is premised, in its preamble, on the genuine existence of the pertinent threat:

The Report of the Inter-American Peace Committee to the Eighth Meeting of Consultation of Ministers of Foreign Affairs states, with regard to the intense subversive activity in which the countries of the Sino-Soviet bloc and the Cuban Government are engaged in America, that such activity constitutes 'a serious violation of fundamental principles of the inter-American system'.

In another case, the Special Committee of Investigation led by the Peruvian Ambassador referred to such facts as Cuba bringing into its borders hundreds of individuals from different countries in the hemisphere (including Venezuela), to train them, and then use them in subversive activities in other states to promote the spread of its own political and economic system; to a 'well-known plan' to conduct subversion; to statements by the Cuban spokesman on the liberation of Venezuela; and to provision of arms to guerrillas in Venezuela and remittance of funds to them through travellers.[128] The Ninth Meeting of Consultation states that

[h]aving seen the report of the Investigating Committee designated on December 3, 1963 . . . the said report establishes among its conclusions that 'the Republic of Venezuela has been the target of a series of actions sponsored and directed by the Government of Cuba,

---

[125]   AG/Res 1080(XXI–O/91), 5 June 1991.
[126]   J Tacsan, 'Searching for OAS/UN Task-sharing Opportunities in Central America and Haiti', 18 *Third World Quarterly* (1997), 489 at 496.
[127]   Resolution I, Punta del Este Meeting, 1962 (emphasis added).
[128]   See details of the Report in LI *Department of State Bulletin* (1964), No 1311, 176–7.

openly intended to subvert Venezuelan institutions and to overthrow the democratic Government of Venezuela through terrorism, sabotage, assault, and guerrilla warfare,' and [t]hat the aforementioned acts, like all acts of intervention and aggression, conflict with the principles and aims of the inter-American system.

Paragraph I then declares that 'the acts verified by the Investigating Committee constitute an aggression and an intervention on the part of the Government of Cuba in the internal affairs of Venezuela'.[129] This refers to these threats as verified in terms of their existence and scale.

Resolution III of the Twelfth OAS Meeting of Consultation states that

[t]he report of Committee I of the Twelfth Meeting of Consultation of Ministers of Foreign Affairs establishes among its conclusions that 'it is clear that the present Government of Cuba continues to give moral and material support to the Venezuelan guerrilla and terrorist movement and that the recent series of aggressive acts against the Government of Venezuela is part of the Cuban Government's continuing policy of persistent intervention in the internal affairs of other American states by fostering and organizing subversive and terrorist activities in their territories'.

In addition, 'during the course of the Twelfth Meeting of Consultation the Government of Bolivia has presented proof of intervention by the Government of Cuba in the preparation, financing, and organization of guerrilla activities in its territory.'[130] On some occasions these findings of evidence were disputed as inconclusive but the practice outlined confirms the OAS organs' position that the genuine existence of a threat has to be ascertained in order to justify an enforcement action.

Guatemala, having had its motion to seize the UN Security Council defeated, appealed to the OAS, but this proved too late as the invading forces overthrew its government soon afterwards. As Fenwick interestingly queries, it can be speculated how the Organ of Consultation would have proceeded in a situation where Guatemala had made a valid claim under the Rio Treaty and earlier it had also been condemned, for example through the Caracas Declaration procedure, for permitting international communism to infiltrate the Americas.[131] The OAS has effectively been engaged in two different, mutually contradictory threat perceptions. If the OAS had approved the action by Honduras, this would contradict both the OAS Charter and the Rio Treaty; if it had disapproved it, this would render the Caracas Declaration immaterial.

(f) NATO

The key provision of NATO's original threat perception is enshrined in Article 4 of the North Atlantic Treaty which specifies that '[t]he Parties will consult together whenever, in the opinion of any of them, the territorial integrity, political independence or security of any of the Parties is threatened'. It is open to doubt whether Article 4 can justify adopting an external threat perception relating to events

---

[129] Resolution I, Ninth Meeting of the Organ of Consultation, 1964, preamble and Paragraph I.
[130] Resolution III, 24 September 1967, preamble.
[131] Fenwick, n 109 above, 16.

beyond Alliance members' territory. Scope for this can still be provided by an expansive reading of the 'security' of NATO members under Article 4, promoting the conclusion that any security threat can justify the activation of NATO under this clause. A NATO Declaration, adopted as early as 1974, specified that members' 'interests can be affected by events in other areas of the world'.[132] A countervailing consideration is, however, that both the Treaty and the 1974 Declaration have to be understood as related to NATO's original self-defence tasks.

The 1991 Strategic Concept widened the vision of threats NATO could deal with, specifying that risks to the stability of the Allies could result, not only from a calculated attack, but 'from the serious economic, social and political difficulties, including ethnic rivalries and territorial disputes, which are faced by many countries in central and Eastern Europe'. These do not directly threaten the security and territorial integrity of Alliance members, but still could 'lead to crises inimical to European stability and even to armed conflicts, which could involve outside powers or spill over into NATO countries, having a direct effect on the security of the Alliance'.[133] The 1999 Strategic Concept repeats this almost word–for–word.[134]

Another expansion of NATO's vision of threats took place after the 11 September 2001 attacks in the United States. In a 2002 Prague Summit Document the NATO announced a 'comprehensive package of measures' to meet the threat posed by terrorism and by the proliferation of weapons of mass destruction and their means of delivery. The Declaration further announced that 'we are determined to deter, disrupt, defend and protect against any attacks on us, in accordance with the Washington Treaty and the Charter of the United Nations'. For terrorism 'poses a grave and growing threat to Alliance populations, forces and territory, as well as to international security'. The Summit Document further alludes to 'the increasing missile threat to Alliance territory, forces and population centres'.[135]

The 2006 NATO Comprehensive Political Guidance document specifies that 'NATOs 1999 Strategic Concept described the evolving security environment in terms that remain valid. This environment continues to change; it is and will be complex and global, and subject to unforeseeable developments.'[136] The 2009 Declaration on Alliance Security refers to

new, increasingly global threats, such as terrorism, the proliferation of weapons of mass destruction, their means of delivery and cyber attacks. Other challenges such as energy security, climate change, as well as instability emanating from fragile and failed states, may also have a negative impact on Allied and international security. Our security is increasingly tied to that of other regions.[137]

However, the validity of NATO threat perception along the above lines depends on the organization being sub-contracted by the UN to deal with threats identified by

---

[132] Declaration on Atlantic Relations, 1974, para 11.
[133] 1991 Strategic Concept, para 9.
[134] 1999 Strategic Concept, para 20.
[135] Prague Summit Declaration 2002, paras 3–4.
[136] NATO Comprehensive Political Guidance, 29 November 2006, para 2.
[137] Declaration on Alliance Security, 4 April 2009.

the Security Council. NATO was established as a collective self-defence organization. In subsequent strategy documents, NATO has stated its readiness to undertake crisis management tasks, but always within the UN Security Council's mandate. NATO has thereby accepted that it has to follow the threat perception of the UN Security Council at least where out-of-area involvement is concerned. So far, apart from a 1999 attack on FRY that the international community largely viewed as illegal, NATO involvement in crises in the non-Article 5 sense has taken place in line with threat determinations by the UN Security Council; given that NATO does not perceive its role—in policy terms at least—as an independent enforcer of peace,[138] neither has it claimed an independent approach to threats.

---

[138] See Chapter 3 above.

5

Responses to Threats

1. The Chapter VII Competence of the Security Council

(a) The General Essence of Non-Forcible Measures under Chapter VII

Once the Security Council determines the existence of a threat to the peace, under Article 41 of the Charter it may

> decide what measures not involving the use of armed force are to be employed to give effect to its decisions, and it may call upon the Members of the United Nations to apply such measures. These may include complete or partial interruption of economic relations and of rail, sea, air, postal, telegraphic, radio, and other means of communication, and the severance of diplomatic relations.

The nature of measures under Article 41 has been explained in different ways. Kelsen suggests that Chapter VII measures are not always applied in response to a violation of the Charter, but are instead political measures used at the Council's discretion, which reflects the predominance of the political over the legal approach, with the effect that both a member which has violated its obligations under the Charter and a member which is not guilty of such violation can be subjected to enforcement actions.[1] Chapter VII sanctions could also be seen as institutional countermeasures, similar to those under the law of state responsibility.[2] But they essentially differ from both reciprocal and third-party countermeasures. Much as they are often adopted against a state that has committed an internationally wrongful act (which a 'threat to the peace' almost inevitably involves), they do not inherently involve a reciprocal violation of international obligations towards the target state. The area to which Chapter VII applies covers both inter-state relations (which derive from legal obligations of states) and those that could develop pursuant to discretionary choices of states. In the absence of an arms supply treaty between the states concerned, the imposition of an arms embargo would not involve a violation of international law affecting the target state. The same applies to economic sanctions and boycotts, since under general international law no state

---

[1] H Kelsen, 'Sanctions under the Charter of the United Nations', 12 *The Canadian Journal of Economics and Political Science* (1946), 429 at 432, 435–6.

[2] ILC's Articles 49 to 54 on State responsibility deal with 'countermeasures against a State which is responsible for an internationally wrongful act in order to induce that State to comply with its obligations': 2 *ILC Yearbook* 2001, 128ff.

is obliged to sell to or purchase from any party any sort of goods. The impact of a Security Council injunction against doing so is to transform a matter of national policy choice into one of legal prohibition under the Charter.

The relevance of Article 103 confirms precisely that. If Chapter VII sanctions had the force of countermeasures only, their legality could be sustained by the law of state responsibility alone. The difference Article 103 makes is to justify member States in implementing Chapter VII sanctions against another state even in violation of treaties in force, where the target state has not beforehand committed an act that internationally wrongs the state that implements these sanctions.

Nevertheless, when Chapter VII measures target an internationally wrongful act defined as such by an Article 39 determination, their necessity and proportionality turn on being adequate and necessary to reverse the underlying threat, just as countermeasures have to be necessary and adequate to induce the wrongdoer state to cease its wrongful act. When a wrongful act is specified in an Article 39 determination, it becomes more than a wrongful act determined to be a 'threat to the peace', but its nature and legal consequences do not alter. The Council's powers under Article 25, Chapter VII, and Article 103 of the Charter do not go as far as enabling it to modify the legal consequences of wrongful acts under general international law.[3]

In *Tadić* the ICTY adopted a textual approach to identify the scope of the sanctions competence of the Security Council under Chapter VII, pointing out that the

language of Article 39 is quite clear as to the channelling of the very broad and exceptional powers of the Security Council under Chapter VII through Articles 41 and 42. These two Articles leave to the Security Council such a wide choice as not to warrant searching, on functional or other grounds, for even wider and more general powers than those already expressly provided for in the Charter.[4]

The appellant in *Tadić* argued that Article 41 encompasses only measures generically similar to those it expressly mentions, which argument—based on restrictive interpretation—the Tribunal rejected by reference to textual interpretation. Article 41 uses the phrase 'may include', and thus 'all the Article requires is that they do not involve "the use of force"'. It 'only prescribes what these measures cannot be. Beyond that it does not say or suggest what they have to be.'[5] In general, Article 39 leaves the choice of particular means to the discretion of the Security Council; this 'choice involves political evaluation of highly complex and dynamic situations'.[6] Much as the Tribunal uses the adjective 'political', this process is fact-related and operational. The establishment of a tribunal and the specification of its judicial powers cannot be a purely political decision, given that the Council expressly sets the enforcement of the relevant international law as its objective.

---

[3] ILC's Article 59 on State responsibility preserves the relevance of the UN Charter, but the Commentary explains that the focus of Article 103 is on treaty obligations conflicting with the Charter, ibid, 143.

[4] *Prosecutor v Tadić*, Case IT-94-1-AR72, Appeal Chamber, Decision on Jurisdiction, 2 October 1995, para 31.

[5] Ibid, para 35.

[6] Ibid, para 39.

In fact, the overall structure of Chapter VII significantly emasculates the element of political discretion in the Council's decision making: under Article 39 reference has to be made to a threat that is actually present; then objective has to be stated to contain and reverse that threat; then measures from the range within Articles 41 and 42 have to be selected as necessary and adequate for achieving the stated objective. Once all that is considered, the Council's discretion is in essence a sequence of logically, causally, and structurally inter-connected steps. On balance, this reduces the room for subjective manipulation and increases the need for objective appreciation of facts. A principal implication is to proscribe Chapter VII measures based on unstated and unspoken policy objectives of Council members that might or might not coincide with the Council's stated objectives.

(b) The Requirements of Necessity and Proportionality

The requirement of necessity is inherently linked to the entire structure of Chapter VII. If Chapter VII measures are goal-related, then their legality depends on their necessity to achieve these goals. Article 39 speaks of measures that 'shall be taken' under Articles 41 and 42 to maintain or restore peace and security. Article 41 speaks of measures short of the use of armed force that 'are to be employed to give effect' to the Council's decisions. Article 42 provides for the possibility of the use of armed force when measures under Article 41 'would be inadequate or have proved to be inadequate' in relation to the objective set by the Council. General Assembly Resolution 51/242 of 26 September 1997 (Annex II) contains important statements regarding the assessment of Chapter VII measures against necessity and proportionality criteria. Sanctions should be imposed only if other peaceful options under the Charter are inadequate (paragraph 1); they should be established 'with clear objectives, provision for regular review and precise conditions for their lifting' such as steps required from the target country (paragraphs 2 and 6); their time frame should be defined with 'the objective of changing the behaviour of the target party while not causing unnecessary suffering to the civilian population' (paragraph 3); their purpose is not to punish or exact retribution; they should thus be commensurate with these objectives (paragraph 5); adverse side effects on the civilian population should be minimized by humanitarian exceptions; foodstuffs, medicines, medical supplies and equipment, agricultural equipment, and basic or standard educational items should be exempted from sanctions (paragraphs 4 and 18).[7] Early assessment is also needed to determine the humanitarian impact of sanctions.[8]

The Council's own attitude is manifested in the preamble of Resolution 1730 (2006) that sanctions are meant to serve clear objectives and 'balance effectiveness against possible adverse consequences'. According to Kolb, only such sanctions as are necessary for achieving stated goals of peace maintenance will be lawful, and

---

[7] For a similar position see *Note by the President of the Security Council: Work of the Sanctions Committees*, S/1999/92, 29 January 1999, paras 2, 11, 16.

[8] MJ Aznar-Gomez, 'A Decade of Human Rights Protection by the UN Security Council: A Sketch of Deregulation?', 13 *European Journal of International Law* (2002), 223 at 229.

among the available means the least onerous should be selected.[9] The *Supplement to an Agenda for Peace* also specifies the criteria of necessity and proportionality, by doubting whether sanctions inflicting suffering on vulnerable groups in a target country are a legitimate means of exerting pressure on political leaders whose behaviour is unlikely to be affected by the plight of their subjects. Sanctions can conflict with the development objectives of the UN by doing long-term damage to the productive capacity of the target country, and to other countries that are neighbours or major economic partners of the target country. Sanctions can also defeat their own purpose by rallying the population behind the leaders whose behaviour they are intended to modify.[10]

Proportionality is a limit on the Council's Chapter VII powers requiring that

the Council's action must be appropriate and necessary for the achievement of its stated purposes (typically, the removal of a threat to the peace), and may not affect other interests to an extent which is disproportionate to the advantage obtained or pursued.[11]

Proportionality implies a balance between the gravity of the act that generated particular Security Council measures and the gravity of those measures.[12] If the threat in question arises from an internationally wrongful act, the latter's reversal should normally translate into the objective set in the relevant resolution.

Craven develops a vision of measuring the necessity and proportionality of UN sanctions. To measure the success of sanctions, if the desired objective is to modify the conduct of a target, any claim for success is contingent upon a debatable causality between the sanctions and achievement of the objective. This is difficult to measure if sanctions are accompanied by other measures such as use of force. In cases where the objective relates to limiting the level of violence in an armed conflict, an arms embargo is a justified response. If, by contrast, the Council seeks to modify the conduct of a target regime, a limited embargo would be at best ineffective and at worst counterproductive.[13] Therefore the nature of the crisis will essentially dictate what measures are required.

Considerations underlying proportionality indicate that the response has to be directed, not against the target state as such, but at particular conduct that the Council identifies as a threat to the peace. If, for instance, Chapter VII measures are used to target the act of aggression identified as a cause of action under Article 39, it would be appropriate to impose an oil embargo on the state that had launched that aggression because the possession of this resource contributes to, indeed determines, its ability to carry on military operations. But the same oil embargo is

---

[9] R Kolb, *Ius contra bellum, Le droit international relatif au maintien de la paix* (Basle/Louvain: Helbing Lichtenhahn/Bruylant, 2003), 126.

[10] *Supplement to an Agenda for Peace: Position Paper of the Secretary-General on the Occasion of the Fiftieth Anniversary of the United Nations*, Report of the Secretary-General on the Work of the Organization, A/50/60–S/1995/1, 3 January 1995, para 70.

[11] N Angelet, 'International Law Limits to the Security Council', in V Gowlland-Debbas (ed.), *UN Sanctions and International Law* (The Hague: Kluwer 2001), 71 at 72.

[12] Kolb, n 9 above, 125.

[13] M Craven, 'Humanitarianism and the Quest for Smarter Sanctions', 13 *European Journal of International Law* (2002), 43 at 46–8.

presumably unnecessary and disproportionate in a situation where the state concerned engages in human rights violations, terrorism, or proliferation of weapons of mass destruction, because the possession of oil resources does not affect whether those activities could continue.

There is a conceptual difference between the Council's observance of the requirements of necessity and proportionality, and its compliance with international law that forms part of the limits on the Security Council's powers. Necessity and proportionality requirements are broader, since collective security decisions that do not violate specific rules of international law can still cause damage, above all economic damage, which cannot be justified by reference to the objective specified to deal with the pertinent threat. However, if Chapter VII enforcement measures violate human rights and humanitarian norms, a strong case can be made that they are disproportionate to their stated objectives.[14]

2. Chapter VII and the Security Council's Subsidiary Role

The robustness of the Council's enforcement action can go hand-in-hand with its subsidiary role in relation to crises already dealt with by regional organizations. In the crisis in Haiti, the UN showed its allegiance to the OAS position in this matter. General Assembly Resolution 47/20(1993), adopted before the Security Council's use of Chapter VII powers in this case, affirmed that the solution of the Haitian crisis should take into account the measures adopted under several OAS resolutions, including that on trade embargo against Haiti.[15] Security Council Resolution 841(1993) refers in its preamble to the same OAS resolutions, recalls the provisions of Chapter VIII, and specifies that the request of Haiti,

made within the context of the related actions previously taken by the OAS and by the General Assembly of the United Nations, defines a unique and exceptional situation warranting extraordinary measures by the Security Council in support of the efforts undertaken within the framework of the Organization of American States.

Thus the Council invoked the request from Haiti and the previous OAS action on the matter in deciding to use Chapter VII in this case,[16] and thereby intervened to complement the OAS effort through its own subsidiary role. In paragraph 3 of this

---

[14] See, for an overview of applicable standards, M Bossuyt, *The adverse consequences of economic sanctions on the enjoyment of human rights*, Working paper, E/CN.4/Sub.2/2000/33; see also A Orakhelashvili, *Peremptory Norms in International Law* (New York: Oxford University Press, 2006), Chapter 12 and references therein.

[15] For the text of the latter resolution see 86 AJIL (1992), 667; sanctions included such embargo measures as suspension of commercial flights and freezing the assets of the Haitian *de facto* regime and its supporters: *Report of the Secretary-General on the Question of Haiti*, S/1994/742, 20 June 1994, para 8. Resolution 841(1993) introduced arms and petroleum embargoes.

[16] President Aristide requested the Security Council to make the 1991 OAS sanctions universal and mandatory. However Security Council Resolution 841 only introduced weapons, oil, and petroleum sanctions. S von Einsiedel and DM Malone, 'Haiti', in D Malone (ed.), *The UN Security Council— From the Cold War to the 21st Century* (Boulder/London, 2004) 467 at 470.

resolution the Council stated that the sanctions it imposed on Haiti, 'which are consistent with the trade embargo recommended by the Organization of American States', would come into force at the specified time unless by then the Council had received a joint UN–OAS report that the imposition of sanctions would not be warranted. In Resolution 917(1994), the Council again adhered to the position of the OAS (paragraph 5), and imposed comprehensive economic sanctions on Haiti (paragraphs 6 to 9), which had a dire impact on the country's society and population. It seems that the Council used the regional position as a cover to adopt measures, the necessity and proportionality of which was not properly ascertained.

The entire story of imposing sanctions on Sudan following the attempted assassination of the President of Egypt in Addis Ababa shows the Council's adherence to the principle of subsidiarity in confronting such incidents. Security Council Resolution 1044(1996) took note of the position the OAU expressed at its session of 11 September 1995 that the attack in question was aimed both at the President of Egypt and the stability of Ethiopia. The Council's action is understood as pursuing the policy defined at the OAU level. The Council also stated its preference to have the matter resolved bilaterally, and commended the government of Ethiopia for undertaking efforts accordingly (paragraph 3). In addition, the Council called upon the government of the Sudan to comply with the requests of the OAU without further delay: to extradite to Ethiopia for prosecution the three suspects sheltering in the Sudan and wanted in connection with the assassination attempt on the basis of the 1964 Extradition Treaty between Ethiopia and the Sudan (paragraph 4). It should be noted that, unlike the Lockerbie bombing matter, the Council acted here to demand extradition in the context of the extradition treaty as part of the legal framework between the relevant states.

Resolution 1054(1996) similarly follows the OAU policies, 'taking note of the continued effort of the OAU Secretary-General to ensure Sudan's compliance with the requests of the Central Organ of the OAU'. The Council went on to determine 'that the non-compliance by the Government of Sudan with the requests set out in paragraph 4 of Resolution 1044(1996) constitutes a threat to international peace and security'. Consequently, the refusal to meet the OAU demands was seen as a threat to the peace under Article 39. Chapter VII was thus activated for the UN to complement, on the basis of subsidiarity, the OAU action (which did not itself possess the requisite enforcement potential). Diplomatic sanctions were accordingly imposed on Sudan under paragraph 3 of this resolution, to be backed up by an air embargo under Resolution 1070(1996).

The Council has also shown its willingness to be guided, to some extent, by regional organizations' views on whether it should continue or lift Chapter VII measures. The preamble of Resolution 1372(2001) lifting sanctions on Sudan specifies that the Council considered communications on behalf of the Non-Aligned Movement, the League of Arab States, and the African Group, and from the Secretary-General of the OAU. During the Council's discussion of this issue, the relevance of regional attitudes was mentioned as a factor that caused this resolution to be adopted,[17] and the Sudanese representative expressed its gratitude to the Non-aligned Movement for sponsoring this resolution.[18] The USA abstained, which demonstrates that this case has been one witnessing regional initiatives as a driving force for the Council's Chapter VII decision.

In the preamble of Resolution 1907(2009), the Security Council noted a decision of the 13th AU Assembly, 'calling on the Council to impose sanctions against foreign actors, both within and outside the region, especially Eritrea, providing support to the armed groups engaged in destabilization activities in Somalia and undermining the peace and reconciliation efforts as well as regional stability', and 'expressing its grave concern at the total absence of progress regarding the implementation by Eritrea of, inter alia, Resolution 1862(2009) regarding the border dispute between Djibouti and Eritrea.'[19] The Council consequently imposed an arms embargo on Eritrea. Its entire judgement in applying Articles 39 and 41 of the Charter, that is the nature of the threat and of the necessary measures, seems to have been pervaded by the policies proposed by the AU. The Council thus covered itself by presenting its action as following a policy determined at AU level.

3. Specific Sanctions Regimes

(a) Air Embargo against Libya

As demonstrated above,[20] Resolutions 748(1992) and 883(1993) imposing a flight embargo on Libya never properly articulated the justification for these measures, either in terms of their proportionality to the Libyan refusal to extradite the two individuals suspected of involvement in the Lockerbie terrorist attack, or their adequacy to deal with a general threat of terrorism of which Libya's position allegedly formed part.

The impact of the sanctions against Libya was to inflict serious damage on the agriculture and animal husbandry sector. Farmers and agricultural cooperatives were unable to export their surplus production, which would usually have been shipped by air. Financial losses amounted to $710,777,777. It was not possible to import fruit seedlings for planting in conditions allowing protection against plant diseases. The country's plans and programmes for developing the animal health sector through the establishment of veterinary units and clinics in various areas were also crippled, since the necessary supplies could no longer be shipped in by air freight.[21] The Libyan government explained to the Security Council that the seven-year

---

[17] S/PV.4384, 2 (Russia), referring to regional organizations' statements 'which all indicate that Sudan has fully met all of the demands that were made on it'.

[18] Ibid, 4 (Sudan).

[19] For the AU position see Thirteenth Ordinary Session, Sirte, 1–3 July 2009, Assembly/AU/Dec. 243–67 (XIII) Rev 1, paras 16–17.

[20] See Chapter 4 above.

[21] *Sixth comprehensive report on damage caused by the implementation of Security Council Resolutions 748(1992) and 883(1993) during the period from 15 April 1992 to 31 December 1995*, S/1996/717, 4 September 1996, 5, 7–8.

sanctions programme seriously disrupted operation in Libya of the global child immunization programme run by the WHO, by making it difficult to obtain vaccines; reduced the effect of vaccines due to spoilage while they were transported overland instead of by air; impeded the medical procurement programme; and prevented ambulance aircraft from being repaired and made serviceable.[22] The UN Fact-Finding Mission on sanctions against Libya further found that

although the air embargo did not apply to domestic air travel, the restrictions on the purchase of aircraft, spare parts, navigational and landing equipment and on training and certification of pilots and other crew had reduced the number of airworthy aircraft and curtailed domestic air travel. That had placed restrictions on the ability of Libyans to respond to humanitarian emergencies.... The most adverse impact of the air embargo had been on the health sector, for it had restricted emergency medical evacuation both within and outside the country.[23]

During the Security Council debate the USA argued that these sanctions

were targeted sanctions, imposed to address aspects of Libyan involvement in international terrorism, but specifically designed to prevent suffering among the Libyan people. The sanctions did not prohibit the importation of food, medicine or clothing. They did not close Libya's land or sea borders, and they did not prevent Libya from selling its oil on the open market.

In response the Arab League stated that 'the sanctions constituted a form of collective punishment of an entire people, despite the fact that there was no proof of either the guilt or the innocence of the two suspects', and called upon the Council to suspend sanctions. According to the OIC, 'the fact that the international community was mobilized behind Libya, showed that the only action worth taking was suspension of the air embargo'.[24] Russia pointed out that the four ageing Libyan planes authorized for medical evacuation purposes needed urgent replacement, as their use posed a serious threat to the safety of the flights. 'Restrictions should also be lifted on the import of spare parts for agricultural aircraft, which is necessary for supplying food to broad strata of the civilian population.'[25] The Bahraini representative observed that 'the Libyan authorities are completely unable to ensure air transport for their pilgrims or to ensure the emergency evacuation of sick people who need immediate health care abroad'.[26]

The UN sanctions against Libya were maintained in force in the face of constant and persistent opposition to them by all relevant, representative, regional organizations such as the Arab League, the OIC, and the OAU.[27] The Arab League and the OIC also called upon the Council to 'lift the ban on certain flights carried out by

---

[22] *Damage Caused by the Implementation of Security Council Resolutions 748 (1992) and 883 (1993) during the Period from 15 April 1992 to 5 April 1999*, S/2000/243.

[23] UNYB 1998, 157; see also text of the report in S/1998/201.

[24] UNYB 1998, 159; the UK position was similar to the US position: S/PV.3864, 20 March 1998, 31 (UK).

[25] S/PV.3864, 20 March 1998, 16 (Russia).

[26] Ibid, 21 (Bahrain).

[27] UNYB 1998, 156.

the Libyan authorities, such as flights of a humanitarian nature and individual flights for religious purposes',[28] before the crisis could ultimately be resolved. Likewise the OAU, on 27 February 1998, appealed to the Council to lift the sanctions imposed as a matter of urgency.[29] China also supported this 'reasonable request raised by the League of Arab States and the OAU on numerous occasions'.[30]

The Arab Summit renewed support for Libya in requesting the Security Council to 'lift the sanctions imposed on it immediately and completely, as they are no longer justified under any pretext'. The Arab states would 'consider themselves free from any commitment to these sanctions should they continue to be imposed'. They expressed support for Libya to obtain compensation for the human and material losses it sustained as a result of sanctions.[31]

In March 1998 'the Council reviewed the sanctions imposed against Libya, concluding that there was no agreement that the necessary conditions existed for modification of the measures imposed'.[32] The British position as late as 1998 was that the OAU and the Arab League objectives could only be achieved by trying the suspects 'through the Scottish courts in Scotland'.[33] The Council's presidential statement 1996/18 considered that the flight of a Libyan-registered aircraft from Tripoli to Jeddah on 16 April 1996 was a clear violation of Resolution 748(1992) and called on Libya to refrain from any further such violations. The Libya Sanctions Committee also 'decided that the flights on 22 and 23 June [1996], in disregard of Security Council Resolution 748 (1992), were serious violations of the resolution.... If a further violation occurred, it would consider recommendations to the Council on ways to increase the effectiveness of the measures contained in Resolution 748(1992).'[34]

(b) Arms Embargoes

(i) *Arms Embargo on Rwanda*

The Council has imposed comprehensive arms embargoes on Rwanda, under Resolution 918(1994) in response to a grave humanitarian crisis; on Liberia, under Resolution 788(1992) in response to a civil war; and on Sierra Leone under Resolution 1132(1997) in response to the overthrow of a democratically elected government by a military junta (in this latter case a petroleum embargo was also imposed). Resolution 1011(1995) exempted the government of Rwanda from the embargo, at that government's request, but went on to prohibit the supply of arms, or their sale to non-governmental entities in Rwanda or 'or to persons in the States

---

[28] Ibid, 158.
[29] As mentioned in S/PV.3864, 20 March 1998, 20.
[30] Ibid, 17 (China).
[31] Arab Summit Final Statement, Amman, 27–28 March 2001, para 29.
[32] Ibid, 158.
[33] S/PV.3864, 20 March 1998, 21 (UK).
[34] *Report of the Security Council Committee established pursuant to Resolution 748(1992) concerning the Libyan Arab Jamahiriya*, S/1996/1079, 31 December 1996, para 13.

neighbouring Rwanda if such sale or supply is for the purpose of the use of such arms or *matériel* within Rwanda' (paragraph 9). These embargoes were not implemented straightforwardly. The Rwanda Sanctions Committee ended its reports with a standard statement that it did not have any monitoring mechanism to ensure effective implementation of the arms embargo, but relied solely on the cooperation of states to obtain information, and during the reporting period no violations of the embargo had been brought to its attention.[35]

The Council, however, expressed in Resolution 1053(1996) 'its grave concern at allegations of the sale and supply of arms and related materiel to former Rwandese Government Forces in violation of the embargo imposed under its Resolutions 918 (1994), 997(1995) and 1011(1995)', and its determination that the arms embargo on 'nongovernmental forces for use in Rwanda should be implemented fully'. The International Inquiry Commission later concluded that 'the former Rwandan government forces, including the Interahamwe militia, are continuing to receive arms from a variety of sources in violation of the Security Council embargo'. One major source of these was Zaire. Reliable and highly reliable sources in various countries 'painted a coherent picture of huge, loose, overlapping webs of more or less illicit arms deals, arms flights and arms deliveries spanning the continent from South Africa as far as Europe, particularly Eastern Europe'.[36] The Commission recommended to the Council to enhance the effectiveness of the embargo by imposing a freeze on assets, including bank accounts, of individuals and organizations involved in raising funds to finance the insurgency.[37]

(ii) Arms Embargo in relation to Darfur

Under paragraphs 7 and 8 of Resolution 1556(2004), the Security Council imposed an arms embargo (covering weapons, vehicles, ammunition, and spare parts) against non-governmental entities and individuals, including the Janjaweed militia, operating in the states of North, South, and West Darfur, and insisted that all states prevent their nationals from providing weapons and related technical assistance, training, or manufacture to the entities and individuals covered by the embargo.

Resolution 1591(2005) reaffirmed these measures, extended them to all parties to the Ndjamena Peace Agreement of 8 April 2004,[38] and specified that they should not apply to 'supplies into the Darfur region that are approved in advance by the Committee established under paragraph 3(a) upon a request by the Government of Sudan' (paragraph 7). The Sudan Sanctions Committee, in response to a

---

[35] See, eg, *Report of the Security Council Committee established pursuant to Resolution 918(1994) concerning Rwanda*, S/1998/1219, 24 December 1998, para 5.

[36] *Third report of the International Commission of Inquiry (Rwanda)*, S/1997/1010, 24 December 1997, 9, 20 (paras 36, 90); 23–4 (paras 106ff).

[37] Ibid, 25 (para 114).

[38] Under which, along with the Abuja Protocol of 8 November 2004, the Sudanese government had undertaken to neutralize and disarm armed militias including the Janjaweed: S/2006/795, para 77.

query by the Korean government, interpreted this paragraph as allowing member States to

provide arms and military equipment to the Government of the Sudan outside the Darfur region and that the Government could move military equipment or supplies irrespective of their origin into the Darfur region on the condition that such movement was approved in advance by the Committee upon a request by the Government.[39]

This limitation was crucial for the viability of the entire arms embargo, which would have been emasculated had the Sudanese government not been subjected to it (as other states are not).

The arms embargo was violated constantly. Both the Sanctions Committee and the Panel of Experts established under Resolution 1591 reported that the Sudanese government was 'unwilling or unable' to meet its obligations under paragraph 7 of Resolution 1591, troops movements continued, and offensive helicopters were introduced into Darfur. They continued to be used to assist offensive ground operations by government forces. Neither was the embargo properly implemented in relation to supplies from neighbouring states. The Panel recommended that, in response to these flagrant violations, the arms embargo should cover the entire territory of Sudan.[40] The Sanctions Committee observed that the government of the Sudan had conducted offensive military over-flights in Darfur, including aerial bombardments.[41]

The failure to implement this arms embargo can be explained by, among other factors, the context of the Darfur conflict. Unlike other sanctions regimes against non-state entities (such as in Angola or Sierra Leone), the Sudan arms embargo targeted groups which were not inherently antagonized against the government, and therefore the latter had no interest in disarming them. The operation of the entire sanctions regime depended on the goodwill of a national government that was at liberty to deal with the movement of arms and resources within the entire Sudanese territory as it deemed fit, subject only to monitoring by international bodies. Furthermore, as the Panel of Experts stated,

---

[39] *Report of the Security Council Committee established pursuant to Resolution 1591(2005) concerning the Sudan*, S/2006/1045, 28 December 2006, para 13.

[40] *Report of the Panel of Experts established pursuant to paragraph 3 of Resolution 1591(2005) concerning the Sudan*, S/2006/65, 30 January 2006, 4–5, and paras 104–7, 110, 136 specifying, among other things, that the Sudanese government never requested the Council's authorization to move troops into Darfur. In its second report (S/2006/250) the Panel again stated that arms flow into Darfur continued unabated and Arab militia maintained their stock of weapons and ammunition. According to its report of 23 October 2006 (S/2006/795)

> the Panel has credible information that the Government of the Sudan continues to support the Janjaweed through the provision of weapons and vehicles.... Reliable sources indicate that the Janjaweed continue to be subsumed into the Popular Defence Force in greater numbers than those indicated in the previous reports of the Panel. Their continued access to ammunition and weapons is evident in their ability to coordinate with the Sudanese armed forces in perpetrating attacks on villages and to engage in armed conflict with rebel groups: para 76.

The Sanctions Committee report issued on 8 January 2010 (S/2010/16) specified that the conduct of the Sudanese government had not altered and violations persisted: para 27.

[41] *Report of the Security Council Committee established pursuant to Resolution 1591(2005) concerning the Sudan*, S/2007/779, 31 December 2007, para 25.

the Security Council's intent to deny arms to what the Council has referred to as 'Janjaweed' in its resolutions was circumvented by the fact that many of the tribal militias were already formally part of the Government security organs or were incorporated into them.[42]

The government of Sudan thus effectively claimed a liberty to determine which entities were covered by the relevant resolution and consequently to interpret it unilaterally.

Security Council Resolution 1706(2006) authorized the UN Mission in Sudan (UNMIS) to use force 'to seize or collect, as appropriate, arms or related material whose presence in Darfur is in violation of the Agreements and the measures imposed by paragraphs 7 and 8 of Resolution 1556, and to dispose of such arms and related material as appropriate'. However, UNMIS was never deployed to Darfur, and instead a hybrid UN–AU mission, UNAMID, was established.

Council Resolution 1769(2007) establishing UNAMID specified that it 'shall monitor whether any arms or related material are present in Darfur in violation of the Agreements and the measures imposed by paragraphs 7 and 8 of Resolution 1556(2004)' (paragraph 9), but then fell short of authorizing UNAMID to enforce the embargo via powers conferred on it under paragraph 15 of that resolution. Violations persisted and in further resolutions the Council has not gone beyond expressing its readiness to take action against entities impeding the exercise of UNAMID's tasks.

(iii) 'General and Complete' Embargo on Somalia

In Resolution 733(1992), the Security Council demanded 'that all States shall, for the purpose of establishing peace and stability in Somalia, immediately implement a general and complete arms embargo on all deliveries of weapons and military equipment to Somalia'. The Somalia Team of Experts' report conceded that the embargo imposed on Somalia under this resolution left 'room for national interpretation of its scope'. Paragraph 5 provided for a general and complete embargo while paragraph 6 prohibited any action that would increase tensions in the area. It was thus unclear whether 'the provision of financing to train and equip armed groupings within Somalia and the provision of services (such as training, repair and maintenance of existing equipment) are within the scope of the embargo'. Therefore, the Council 'could usefully clarify the scope of the embargo, preferably to make clear that the provision of financing and services of any kind that support military activities in Somalia is a violation of the embargo'.[43] To further enhance the embargo, 'the scope of the term "military equipment" [under paragraph 5] could usefully be clarified either through the development of a reference list or through the adoption of a military end-use principle . . . because of the widespread use of civilian vehicles in military operations'.[44]

---

[42] S/2006/65, n 40 above, para 85.
[43] *Report of the team of experts appointed pursuant to Security Council Resolution 1407(2002), paragraph 1, concerning Somalia*, S/2002/722, paras 63–7.
[44] Ibid, para 68.

In response, Resolution 1425(2002) notes 'with serious concern the continued flow of weapons and ammunition supplies to and through Somalia from sources outside the country, in contravention of the arms embargo' and, acting under Chapter VII, 'stresses that the arms embargo on Somalia prohibits financing of all acquisitions and deliveries of weapons and military equipment'; the Council furthermore 'decides that the arms embargo prohibits the direct or indirect supply to Somalia of technical advice, financial and other assistance, and training related to military activities'.

This case blurs the line between interpreting an existing embargo and amending it through an authentic—and effective—interpretation, for it is not straightfor-wardly clear whether the embargo had the scope accorded to it under Resolution 1425 because the Council so specified or the other way round. In any case, it was within the Council's gift either to effectively interpret or to consensually upgrade the existing embargo.

(iv) Arms Embargo on the Congo

In the Congo crisis the Council intervened against the background of the conclu-sion of the Global and All-Inclusive Agreement on the Transition in the Demo-cratic Republic of the Congo (signed in Pretoria on 17 December 2002), and the subsequent establishment of a Government of National Unity and Transition. By paragraph 20 of Resolution 1493(2003), the Council decided that all states, including the Congo, had to

> prevent the direct or indirect supply, sale or transfer . . . of arms and any related materiel, and the provision of any assistance, advice or training related to military activities, to all foreign and Congolese armed groups and militias operating in the territory of North and South Kivu and of Ituri, and to groups not party to the Global and All-inclusive agreement, in the Democratic Republic of the Congo.

The Group of Experts established by Resolution 1552(2004), which also extended the embargo for a further year, identified a number of problems with its operation, due mainly to problems relating to interpretation of Resolution 1493. The situa-tion on the ground witnessed several armed groups and militias exercising actual control over parts of the Congolese territory. In some cases even units of the official armed forces followed the orders of local groups and acted in accordance with their own vested loyalties and interests. The Group of Experts queried whether it would be a violation of the embargo to deliver arms to groups formally under the authority of the government in Kinshasa, or committed to the Global and All-inclusive Agreement, but in fact operating outside the command and control of the govern-ment, or building their own armed constituencies. A further question arose in relation to weapons imported into other areas of the Congo without proper notification of the unified army or Transitional Government if it was known that they might be subject to onward transfers to the embargoed region. The Group proposed monitoring options, including first delivering arms to Kinshasa and taking an inventory before they were reshipped to other locations in the Congo, and also that the embargo should apply to the entire territory of the Congo.[45] In response, the Security Council noted the Group's Report in its Resolution 1596(2005) and specified that the embargo 'shall from now on apply to any recipient in the territory of the Democratic Republic of the Congo', further reiterating that 'assistance includes financing and financial assistance related to military activities'. Later, by Resolution 1807(2008), the Congolese government was exempted from the arms embargo.

While the Council's response to the Report's findings was useful and positive, the interpretative question raised by the Group of Experts has never found conclusive clarification. By using words that the embargo 'shall from now on apply' to all recipients the Council should be seen as trying to introduce a qualitatively new embargo covering entities that had not previously been covered. The question how to interpret the embargo under Resolution 1493 relates, however, to whether the entities not as such covered by that embargo were nevertheless subjected to it if their acquisition of arms facilitated that by embargoed entities, which construction could be required by the need for effective interpretation of the resolution, so that the measures it stipulated could achieve their objectives. It seems that, under Resolution 1493, the embargo could be effectively construed as applying, not only to transfers of arms to officially embargoed entities, but also to entities having an official status not covered by the embargo, though in fact engaged in acquiring and transferring arms to serve purposes that the Council had expressly outlawed and targeted through the embargo. The same should have applied to transfers of arms to non-embargoed regions of the Congo from where they ended up in embargoed regions. This would have ensured the applicability of the embargo, not just to *de jure* embargoed entities and regions but also to those that *de facto* fell into that category. These prohibitions, deducible from the scope of the embargo under Resolution 1493, would have been strictly functional, targeting non-embargoed territories and entities only to the extent that they purported to acquire and transfer arms with a view to enabling them to reach destinations outlawed under the resolution. As we saw, the Council chose a more far-reaching response by making the arms embargo comprehensive, through its legitimate use of discretion under Article 41. But had the Council been unable to reach political agreement on this point, the only means of securing proper implementation of the arms embargo under Resolution 1493 would have been the effective interpretation of that resolution.

(c) The Use of Chapter VII in relation to the Iranian Nuclear Enrichment Issue[46]

By Resolution 1737(2006), the Council, invoking Article 41, decided that all states had to prevent the supply, sale, or transfer to Iran 'of all items, materials, equipment, goods and technology which could contribute to Iran's enrichment-related, reprocessing or heavy water-related activities, or to the development of nuclear

---

[45] *Report of the Group of Experts, in accordance with paragraph 6 of Security Council Resolution 1552 (2004) of 27 July 2004*, S/2005/30, 25 January 2005, paras 26–32.
[46] For the background see Chapters 2 and 4 above.

weapon delivery systems' (paragraph 3). Had these measures been aimed at a genuinely identified threat under Article 39, their generic nature would have created no obvious problem in terms of necessity and proportionality.

Resolution 1803(2008) imposed targeted sanctions obliging all states to prevent the entry into or transit through their territories of individuals directly associated with or providing support for Iran's sensitive nuclear activities, or for the development of nuclear-weapon delivery systems (paragraph 5). In the wake of adopting this resolution, South Africa described it as unfortunate that the Council had acted in such haste, in deciding on a series of further punitive sanctions without considering the significant progress made through the IAEA to provide factual information on the implementation of NPT safeguards in Iran.[47] Resolution 1929 (2010) requires that all states prevent the sale or transfer to Iran of 'battle tanks, armoured combat vehicles, large calibre artillery systems, combat aircraft, attack helicopters, warships, missiles or missile systems'. It seems rather odd to address the problem of proliferation of weapons of mass destruction by measures aimed at conventional arms supplies.[48] The process of adoption of Resolution 1929 indeed witnessed some doubts as to the necessity and proportionality of sanctions it contains. Brazil voted against sanctions because they did not constitute an effective instrument and only undermined prospects of resolving the nuclear enrichment problem through dialogue. It was 'unnatural to rush to sanctions before the parties concerned can sit and talk about the implementation of the declaration'. Sanctions would 'delay rather than accelerate or ensure progress in addressing the question'.[49]

(d) The Process of Consensual Upgrading of the Sanctions Regime against the FRY

In the case of the former Yugoslavia, the Council first imposed an arms embargo under Resolution 713(1991), then prohibited imports under Resolution 757 (1992), paragraph 6 of which specified that these economic sanctions would not apply 'to the trans-shipment through the FRY of commodities and products originating outside the FRY'. This exempted only commodities crossing the FRY's territory, not those bound for the FRY. The FRY Sanctions Committee permitted transhipment tolls to be paid, notably by the Greek government, since this was seen as a basic requirement for transhipment. The FRY thus obtained significant revenues in foreign currency. In addition, some goods meant for transhipment were diverted and ended up within the FRY, thus undermining the rationale of the sanctions. The Council responded by adopting Resolution 787 (1992) which narrowed the range of commodities that could be transhipped.[50] Under paragraph 9 of this resolution, the Council decided

---

[47] S/PV.5858, 7 (South Africa), 11 (Indonesia).
[48] The same problem arises with Resolution 1718(2006) regarding North Korea.
[49] S/PV.6335, 2–3 (Brazil); see, ibid, Turkey's position.
[50] Cf. M Scharf and J Dorosin, 'Interpreting UN Sanctions: The Rulings and Role of the Yugoslavia Sanctions Committee', 19 *Brooklyn Journal of International Law* (1993), 771 at 794.

in order to ensure that commodities and products transshipped through the FRY are not diverted in violation of Resolution 757(1992), to prohibit the transshipment of crude oil, petroleum products, coal, energy-related equipment, iron, steel, other metals, chemicals, rubber, tyres, vehicles, aircraft and motors of all types unless such transshipment is specifically authorised on a case-by-case basis by the Committee established by Resolution 724 (1991) under its no-objection procedure.

In addition, the Committee Guidelines required a confirmation by receiving states of the receipt of transhipped goods. But documents were frequently forged and the transhipment regime was largely unsuccessful. The Council responded by adopting Resolution 820(1993) which established a complete ban on transhipping commodities through the FRY.[51] The Council took the approach of a consensual upgrading of the sanctions regime. Even while the sanctions regime under Resolutions 757 and 787 was being violated and thus inefficient, transhipment in its various modalities was still permitted. The need for the overall effectiveness of sanctions does not justify interpreting away reserved entitlements, which could be taken away only through the Council's adoption of generically different measures, as were ultimately introduced by Resolutions 787 and 820.

(e) The Ways of Assessing the Necessity and Proportionality of Sanctions: Liberia and Afghanistan Sanctions Regimes

Security Council Resolution 1343(2001) imposed an arms embargo on Liberia since rebel movements in Sierra Leone were receiving assistance from Liberian territory. In Resolution 1478(2003) the Security Council acknowledged a finding by the Panel of Experts that the Liberian government had breached the arms embargo and carried on acquiring arms, a major source of which was Liberian timber.[52]

Consequently, paragraph 17(a) of Resolution 1478 requires that all states prevent 'the import into their territories of all round logs and timber products originating in Liberia'. This affected the industry that was responsible for more than half of Liberia's export income. In paragraph 25 the Council requested the Secretary-General to establish a Panel of Experts to assess the possible humanitarian and socio-economic impact of these measures.

The Panel reported in August 2003, stating that due to the security situation it could not establish a detailed picture of humanitarian and socio-economic conditions in Liberia. On the humanitarian implications of timber sanctions, the report is riddled with ambivalence. The Panel assessed the necessity and proportionality of sanctions as follows:

The most obvious benefit of the timber sanctions is that armed State and non-State actors are deprived of timber revenue; [v]iolations of human rights, of rural Liberians in particular,

---

[51] Cf. ibid, 795–6.
[52] *Report of the Panel of Experts pursuant to Security Council Resolution 1343(2001), paragraph 19, concerning Liberia*, S/2001/1015, 26 October 2001, paras 321ff; *Report of the Panel of Experts pursuant to Security Council Resolution 1408(2002), paragraph 16, concerning Liberia*, S/2002/1115, 25 October 2002, paras 189ff.

associated with the timber industry will decrease, as will the overharvesting of Liberian forests; [t]he negative impacts associated with the stark reduction of export income and employment may have long-term consequences for the redevelopment of Liberia; [t]hese negative impacts may currently be overshadowed by the negative effects of the civil war.[53]

This suggests that negative impact, even if admitted, could be overshadowed by alternative factors. However, what matters for necessity and proportionality of sanctions is their *current* impact. Otherwise, the whole issue could be viewed in relative terms, eroding the relevance of proportionality.

In Resolution 1521(2003) the Council reaffirmed the timber sanctions and called upon Liberia 'to take all necessary steps to ensure that government revenues from the Liberian timber industry are not used to fuel conflict or otherwise in violation of the Council's resolutions but are used for legitimate purposes for the benefit of the Liberian people, including development', and expressed its readiness to terminate timber sanctions once this had been achieved (paragraphs 10–12). Three years later, the Council noted in Resolution 1689 the progress towards compliance with Resolution 1521 and decided not to renew timber sanctions (preamble and paragraph 1).

The ways that the necessity and proportionality of sanctions against Afghanistan are assessed under Resolutions 1267(1999) and 1333(2000) are the focus of the Secretary-General's report prepared pursuant to the latter resolution. The report specifies overall vulnerability in Afghanistan as the background against which the humanitarian implications of the sanctions can be assessed. Both the economic and the humanitarian situation were dire. There was no threat of hyper-inflation, however, and the sanctions regime had not caused any inflation in the prices of basic commodities.[54] The sanctions regime had direct implications for Afghanistan's trade since it targeted international flights previously used for transporting traded goods. But this did not have a huge impact because, even before the embargo, most imports were transported into Afghanistan by land.[55] The conclusion was that the principal cause of adverse effects was not the sanctions regime but alternative factors such as drought, war, and the deprivation of human rights.[56]

(f) Comprehensive Economic Sanctions against Iraq, FRY, and Haiti

Economic sanctions were imposed on Iraq by Resolution 661(1990) to induce it to withdraw its forces from Kuwait, which it had invaded and occupied. Sanctions were maintained in force for a long period after the Iraqi withdrawal. The comprehensive nature of the sanctions, especially their inclusion of foodstuffs, medical equipment, and other civilian goods raised questions of necessity and proportionality.

---

[53] *Report of the Panel of Experts pursuant to paragraph 25 of Security Council Resolution 1478(2003) concerning Liberia*, S/2003/779, 7 August 2003, paras 4, 15.

[54] *Report of the Secretary-General on the Humanitarian Implications of the Measures Imposed by Security Council Resolutions 1267(1999) and 1333(2000) on Afghanistan*, S/2001/695, 13 July 2001, paras 3–4, 35, 51.

[55] Ibid, para 21.

[56] Ibid, para 67.

Under Article 41 the Council was supposed to adopt the measures to 'give effect to its decisions', namely to be adequate, necessary, and proportionate to achieve Iraq's withdrawal from Kuwait, which requirement economic sanctions could hardly meet. As an insider's voice confirms, these sanctions were designed as a substitute for war, defended by those keen on discouraging the US government from launching a military offensive on Baghdad.[57] It follows that the entire sanctions regime was introduced in excess of the Council's stated objective to expel Iraqi forces from Kuwait. Sanctions were adopted for an unstated—ulterior—purpose.

The preamble of Resolution 666(1990) recognized that 'circumstances may arise in which it will be necessary for foodstuffs to be supplied to the civilian population in Iraq or Kuwait in order to relieve human suffering', and emphasized that 'it is for the Security Council, alone or acting through the Committee, to determine whether humanitarian circumstances have arisen' under paragraphs 3(c) and 4 of Resolution 661. Operative paragraph 5 specifies that, if the Committee had determined that such circumstances had arisen, it should report promptly to the Council its decision as to how such need should be met. The Council thus asserted the exclusive power to make such determinations, which in essence purported to proscribe states from asserting their own judgement on this issue. But whether such a situation has actually arisen is purely a matter of fact, failing to properly ascertain which the Council would contradict its own resolution by extending sanctions further than the enabling resolution (661) actually intended, on a *de facto* basis. This attitude shows that at that point the Council did not intend to be guided by the principles of necessity and proportionality.[58]

Whatever the role of the Iraqi government, the UN has never avoided the charge that its sanctions contributed significantly to the deterioration of the humanitarian situation in Iraq. Prior to sanctions, imported food provided 70–80 per cent of Iraq's total caloric intake, and by November 1990, shortages increased food prices to about 18 times their pre-sanction level.[59] Humanitarian exceptions failed to ensure that the population had access to all required humanitarian items. Sanctions were responsible for increased infant mortality, inadequate nutritional intake, and caused a generation to grow up without the benefits of basic education. The Oil-for-Food programme was launched under Resolution 986(1995) in partial

---

[57] P van Walsum, 'The Iraq Sanctions Committee', in Malone, n 16 above, 181 at 192.

[58] A similar pattern of open-ended delegation is contained in paragraphs 3(c)–(f) of Resolution 1591(2005), which imposed targeted sanctions on individuals impeding the peace process in Darfur, and stipulated that the travel ban imposed on such individuals would not apply where the Sanctions Committee 'determines on a case by case basis that such travel is justified on the ground of humanitarian need, including religious obligation, or where the Committee concludes that an exemption would otherwise further the objectives of the Council's resolutions for the creation of peace and stability in Sudan and the region'. This pattern of delegation is problematic because it leaves the scope of Security Council sanctions to be determined by the Committee on a case-by-case basis, and also leaves the issue of observance of fundamental human rights (such as freedom of religion) to the Committee's discretion, thereby increasing the likelihood of human rights violations in this process.

[59] KE Boon, 'Coining a New Jurisdiction: The Security Council as Economic Peacekeeper', 41 *Vanderbilt Journal of Transnational Law* (2008), 991 at 1001–2.

recognition of these concerns, but the provision of basic foodstuffs remained insufficient to affect the levels of malnutrition.[60] Resolution 986, and the earlier Resolutions 706(1991), 712(1991), and 778(1992) permitted the limited sale of Iraqi oil, and made some previously frozen Iraqi assets available to fund the purchase of humanitarian items, the equitable distribution of which was to be monitored by the UN to ensure that all regions of Iraq and all sections of the Iraqi population would benefit.[61] The Report of the panel of experts established by the President of the Security Council emphasized that hospitals in Iraq had not been repaired since 1991 and that malaria and water-borne diseases (under control before the Kuwait invasion) had reappeared in epidemic form.[62]

Apart from the functional inadequacy of these sanctions to serve as necessary means of achieving Iraq's compliance with the Council's demands or constitute a proportionate response, they violated a number of rules of international law. The situation was frequently aggravated by the Council's withholding of the relevant items, which led to severe infringements on the rights of Iraqis to life, health, food, and work as provided for under the 1966 Economic and Social Rights Covenant.[63] The problem—besides attribution of responsibility for these violations—relates not only to formal arrangements as to what exceptions applied in principle, but also to the day-to-day administration of these exceptions. It is suggested that 'even if there were clear evidence that the Council's sanctions caused starvation among the Iraqi population, the specific intent on the part of the Security Council to starve the Iraqi people cannot be proven'.[64] It matters not whether the Council positively intended starvation and malnutrition effects, however, but whether it adopted measures actually causing that outcome. Moreover, the Council's actual intention can be identified from the types of information it had as to the impact of sanctions and the way it reacted to this.

The Sanctions Committee's reports list only the numbers of requests processed under humanitarian exemptions and relevant procedural issues.[65] They contain little or nothing to enable the humanitarian situation on the ground to be assessed, or the impact that the humanitarian exceptions actually had. As regards supplies to satisfy basic civilian needs (other than foodstuffs), during the one-year period from

---

[60] Craven, n 13 above, 45–6, 50; HC Graf Sponeck, 'Sanctions and Humanitarian Exemptions: A Practitioner's Commentary', 13 *European Journal of International Law* (2002), 81 at 82; DJ Halliday, 'The Impact of the UN Sanctions on the People of Iraq', 28 *Journal of Palestine Studies* (1999), 29 at 30, 32.

[61] For a description see M Matheson, *Council Unbound—The Growth of UN Decision Making in Conflict and Post-conflict Issues after the Cold War* (Washington, DC: USIP Press, 2006) 87–8; Bossuyt, n 14 above, 16. Subsequently, the UN Council's Resolution 1958(2010) decided to terminate the residual aspects of this programme.

[62] *Report of the second panel established pursuant to the note by the President of the Security Council of 30 January 1999 (S/1999/100), concerning the current humanitarian situation in Iraq*, Annex II of S/1999/356, 30 March 1999, para 21.

[63] Sponeck, n 60 above, 82–3.

[64] B Kondoch, 'The Limits of Economic Sanctions under International Law: The Case of Iraq', *International Peacekeeping—Yearbook of Peace Operations*, 267 at 290–1.

[65] *Report of the Security Council Committee Established by Resolution 661(1990) concerning the Situation between Iraq and Kuwait*, S/1996/700, 26 August 1996, 10.

1 August 1996 to 31 July 1997 the Committee considered more than a thousand applications under the no-objection procedure, and it rejected more of them than it approved.[66] The Committee rejected a request from non-aligned states to permit certain humanitarian supplies to be made to Iraq under the notification procedure rather than the no-objection procedure. It merely agreed that certain humanitarian items would receive favourable consideration.[67] Given the volume of requests the Committee had to deal with, and the humanitarian situation in Iraq, this 'concession' hardly amounted to an effective alleviation of humanitarian problems in the country. In addition, during the debate in the Sanctions Committee on humanitarian exceptions to Iraqi sanctions, Iraq, Cuba, and the Yemen suggested that access to food was a basic human right. The majority in the Committee rejected this position and settled for a criterion-based approach.[68]

Paragraph 20 of Resolution 687(1991) purports to alleviate humanitarian suffering by deciding that prohibitions on the sale or supply to Iraq of commodities or products other than medicine and health supplies, and prohibitions on financial transactions related thereto contained in Resolution 661(1990) would not apply to foodstuffs notified to the Iraq Sanctions Committee or, with the approval of that committee, under the simplified and accelerated 'no-objection' procedure, to materials and supplies for essential civilian needs. As the UN Legal Counsel confirmed, this paragraph allowed states to unfreeze Iraqi assets within their jurisdiction in order to finance the sale or supply to Iraq of foodstuffs notified to the Committee, in addition to medical supplies already allowed under Resolution 661.[69] However, the Committee's further position leaves the implications of this interpretation vague. The Committee informed several states that unfreezing Iraqi assets pursuant to paragraph 20 was 'not obligatory' and a matter of 'national policy and [a State's] particular national legislation', and would hence not constitute a violation of Resolution 687.

The Council's permission to unfreeze assets under paragraph 20 was premised on its acknowledgement of the humanitarian implications of the sanctions on Iraq, and that these were neither necessary nor proportionate for achieving the Council's objectives. This contradicts the Committee's perception that the matter was one of national discretion, resulting in an assertion that the Council allowed those humanitarian implications to continue even though it no longer considered them to be necessary and proportionate. The Committee's approach thus distorted the object and purpose of the sanctions regime by admitting a legal justification for restrictions with humanitarian implications that the Council had purely and simply abolished.

In relation to the FRY the Council admitted a humanitarian exception but not in a straightforward way; by Resolution 760(1992) it

[66] *Report of the Security Council Committee Established by Resolution 661(1990) concerning the Situation between Iraq and Kuwait*, S/1997/672, 28 August 1997, 10.

[67] S/1996/700, 11.

[68] GL Burci, 'Interpreting the Humanitarian Exceptions through the Sanctions Committees', in Gowlland-Debbas, n 11 above, 143 at 146.

[69] Reproduced in S/1996/700, 17.

[d]ecide[d] that the prohibitions in paragraph 4 (c) of Resolution 757(1992) concerning the sale or supply to the Federal Republic of Yugoslavia (Serbia and Montenegro) of commodities or products, other than medical supplies and foodstuffs, and the prohibition against financial transactions related thereto, contained in Resolution 757(1992) shall not apply, with the approval of the Committee established by Resolution 724(1991) under the simplified and accelerated 'no objection' procedure, to commodities and products for essential humanitarian need.

While this seemingly broadened the range of permitted humanitarian supplies, the operation of the humanitarian exception was again made dependent on the Committee's decision-making procedures.

In the Yugoslavian case, too, attempts to draw up a general list of exempted humanitarian items ended in failure. The FRY Sanctions Committee preferred to consider requests on a case-by-case basis. Given the Committee's no-objection procedure, any member's objection could delay the arrival of humanitarian items while discussions continued.[70] In relation to Iraq, it was only Resolution 1284 (1999) that directed the Sanctions Committee to approve lists of humanitarian items, 'including foodstuffs, pharmaceutical and medical supplies, as well as basic or standard medical and agricultural equipment and basic or standard educational items', and confirmed that, despite the requirements under Resolutions 661(1990) and 687(1991), 'supplies of these items will not be submitted for approval of that Committee'. Thanks to this resolution the restrictions on importing food and medicines into Iraq ceased, as did those on the volume of Iraqi oil to be sold for humanitarian purposes.[71] Still, the fact that the Council had bargained, exchanging this easing of sanctions for Iraq's acceptance of certain obligations in the area of disarmament, illustrates the Council's intentions *vis-à-vis* the humanitarian situation in Iraq prior to the adoption of Resolution 1284.

It is presumably right that the deterioration of conditions of life in Iraq and Haiti are testimony to the inadequate functioning of humanitarian exceptions managed by the committees.[72] Nevertheless, this outcome was not due merely to technical aspects of the operation of sanctions regimes, but also to the policy that the Council had deliberately adopted. In relation to Iraq sanctions, the Under-Secretary-General informed the Secretary-General and the Security Council in 1991 that the humanitarian situation in the country was dire. Livestock farming had been seriously affected because many feed products had previously been imported. There were problems with veterinary vaccines destroyed by bombardment, and corresponding animal disease. Iraq was heavily dependent on foreign vegetable seeds and all stocks of these were exhausted. Lack of pesticides had compromised the grain harvest. The Under-Secretary-General then recommended that 'in view of [the] bleak prognosis, sanctions in respect of food supplies should be immediately removed, as should those relating to the import of agricultural equipment and

---

[70] Aznar-Gomez, n 8 above, 232.
[71] Van Walsum, n 57 above, 181 at 187.
[72] Burci, n 68 above, 147.

supplies'.[73] In relation to the situation in Haiti after the Council imposed sanctions under Resolution 841(1993), the Secretary-General reported to the Council that

the Haitian economy is on the verge of collapse. Since last month, the national currency has lost 40 per cent of its value. There is galloping inflation, and shortages are becoming more severe. The prices of staple food products have more than doubled. According to international economists, almost four-fifths of the population are unemployed.

Humanitarian assistance continued in increasingly difficult conditions.[74] In Reisman's assessment of the impact of the sanctions imposed on Haiti, the wealthy elite and the military command heavily benefited from the black market that flourished after sanctions were imposed, while the rest of the population 'was, without exaggeration, starving to death'.[75] The naval embargo imposed on Haiti under Resolution 875(1993) did not prove effective due to Haiti's land border with the Dominican Republic. However, humanitarian and economic costs proved lastingly crippling for Haiti.[76] In general, the sanctions against the FRY, Iraq, and Haiti produced economic impact but little political compliance, and arguably caused Council members to realize that their policies made the Council's peace and security mandate clash with the prospects of human survival. The humanitarian assessment report on the implications of a possible air embargo on Sudan ultimately led to such an embargo not being imposed.[77]

The humanitarian disaster inflicted on Iraq in the 1990s has been recognized both by the UN and by the scientific community. The population was left without means of subsistence and nutrition and, just as in Haiti, a black market flourished. Sanctions were effectively a collective punishment of the Iraqi people. Despite being aimed at inducing the populations of Iraq and Yugoslavia to put pressure on their governments, sanctions profoundly failed to bring about that effect.[78]

The procedures required to authorize civilian and humanitarian supplies obviously impacted on the humanitarian situation on the ground, which may be due to the

---

[73] *Report to the Secretary-General on Humanitarian Needs in Kuwait and Iraq in the Immediate Post-Crisis Environment by a Mission to the Area Led by Mr Martti Ahtisaari, Under-Secretary-General for Administration and Management,* S/22366, 20 March 1991, 6–7, paras 13–18.

[74] *Report of the Secretary-General on the Question concerning Haiti,* S/1994/1012, 26 August 1994, paras 8 and 9.

[75] M Reisman, 'Assessing the Lawfulness of Nonmilitary Enforcement: The Case of Economic Sanctions', 89 AJIL (1996), 37.

[76] Von Einsiedel and Malone, n 16 above, 471.

[77] D Cortright and GA Lopez, 'Reforming Sanctions', in Malone, n 16 above, 167 at 167–8.

[78] M Bennouna, 'Les sanctions économiques des Nations Unies', 300 *Recueil des Cours de l'Académie de Droit International de la Haye* (2002), 40–2. It is also pointed out that 'the "theory" behind economic sanctions is that economic pressure on civilians will translate into pressure on the Government for change. This "theory" is bankrupt both legally and practically, as more and more evidence testifies to the inefficacy of comprehensive economic sanctions as a coercive tool': Bossuyt, n 14 above, 9; a House of Lords Report similarly suggests that 'when economic sanctions are relatively weak in their economic effects, they can have the overall net effect of strengthening the target regime by legitimizing it, by strengthening its control over resources, or both. Where the economic effects of sanctions are more severe, they can have the effect of weakening the target regime's overall capabilities to act, especially in foreign policy, but the regime can still turn aspects of sanctions to its advantage and increase its internal control' HL Select Committee on Economic Affairs, *The Impact of Economic Sanctions,* 2nd Report of Session 2006–7, HL Paper 96–I, para 130.

inherent nature of the relevant procedure or surrounding circumstances such as delays due to workload. With regard to the 'no-objection' procedure specifically, its description in resolutions as 'simplified and accelerated' captures only part of its essence. This procedure places emphasis, not on whether particular goods are humanitarian or civilian, but on whether the sanctions committee agrees that they should be allowed in. Given that sanctions committees work by consensus, the 'no-objection' procedure enables the relevant supply to be blocked if only one member so wishes. The 'no-objection' procedure is thus not really a step towards alleviating humanitarian implications, but essentially an excuse for the Council's failure to take account of the humanitarian dimension of sanctions on its own merit.

Another problem with the 'no-objection' procedure is that, unless the relevant humanitarian exception is substantiated through a list of goods, it allows the Council to abdicate at least part of its Chapter VII powers in favour of unilateral or group decisions within this organ. If, by a majority specified under Article 27 of the Charter, the Council allows a humanitarian exception and then leaves its meaning to be determined by committees that operate through an essentially different procedure, then it effectively gives the relevant member or group of members the power to decide what the Council's Chapter VII decisions mean and what they allow. Even more so, since liberalizing humanitarian exceptions or making them stricter essentially determines what will be the scope and impact of the sanctions to which those exceptions are admitted, and whether they will consequently achieve their objective.

(g) Problems with Necessity and Proportionality of Sanctions against the FRY and North Korea

An instance demonstrating problems with the necessity and proportionality of sanctions is provided by the Council's imposition of sporting, cultural, and scientific sanctions against the FRY under paragraphs 8(b) and 8(c) of Resolution 757 (1992), referring to persons and teams representing the FRY. These sanctions led to the exclusion of FRY teams from international sporting events such as the European football cup finals. As 1992 approached, the Olympic Committee decided to allow athletes to compete so long as they appeared in a personal capacity. While the FRY Sanctions Committee approved this decision, it allowed only athletes in individual sports to participate and exclude them from competing in group sports, contending, in a somewhat grotesque manner, that the participation of more than one athlete evoked representation of the FRY.[79] Such decisions fail necessity and proportionality tests in terms of their actual contribution to restoring peace and security in the Balkans. In terms of interpreting Resolution 757, the Committee actually expanded the scope for collective decision contained in paragraph 8(b), which refers only to athletes representing the FRY—not to those who are FRY

[79] Cf Scharf and Dorosin, 50 above, 810–11.

nationals. Even if competing in group sports under the special Olympic Committee arrangements, the relevant athletes could not be seen as representing the FRY.

The luxury goods sanctions under paragraph 8(a)(iii) of Resolution 1718(2007), whereby the Council imposed sanctions on North Korea (mainly an arms embargo), raise some problems of necessity and proportionality. The Council did not define the meaning of luxury goods and thus produced indeterminacy bordering on the arbitrary. States could allegedly interpret what luxury goods might be themselves. Had they adopted an extensive approach they might act in excess of the Security Council measures; if they adopted a narrow approach, they could let into North Korea goods and commodities that would presumably have been excluded had the Council provided a meaningful and defensible definition of luxury goods. This problematic position has been corroborated by the attitude of the Korea Sanctions Committee. As the Committee report specifies,

on 21 February 2007 the Committee addressed a letter to Member States clarifying that any definition of luxury goods as might be necessary for Member States to implement the provision would be the national responsibility of individual Member States. The Committee also reaffirmed that the measures contained in paragraph 8(a)(iii) were consistent with the objectives of the resolution and were not intended to restrict the supply of ordinary goods to the wider population of the country or to have a negative humanitarian impact on the Democratic People's Republic of Korea.[80]

There is thus no collective view of the Council's as to the meaning of paragraph 8(a)(iii). If member States can unilaterally determine what constitute luxury goods, they can also unilaterally determine what precisely has to be done to maintain international peace and security. The impact of indeterminacy is to effectively transform the imperative of dealing with 'threats to the peace' into an option, and a legal obligation to do what the Council requires for that purpose into a matter of national choice.

(h) Targeted Sanctions against Individuals and Entities Suspected of Involvement in Terrorism

Targeted sanctions are not aimed against states as such, but against individuals, whether government officials or not. Resolution 1267(1999) initiated the policy of targeting sanctions against individuals suspected of involvement in terrorist activities, such as a travel ban and freezing their funds. Resolution 1373(2001) introduced a number of general measures to deal with these problems. In the preamble to Resolution 1822(2008) the Council articulated the necessity of targeting sanctions on terrorist suspects by asserting that terrorism can only be defeated by a sustained and comprehensive approach involving the active participation and collaboration of all states 'to impede, impair, isolate, and incapacitate the terrorist threat'. By Resolution 1735(2006), adopted 'with respect to Al-Qaida, Usama bin

---

[80] *Annual report of the Security Council Committee established pursuant to Resolution 1718(2006)*, S/2007/778, 31 December 2007, para 5, at 2–3.

Laden, and the Taliban and other individuals, groups, undertakings and entities associated with them', the Council decided that, without delay, all states should freeze the funds and other financial assets or economic resources of these individuals, groups, undertakings, and entities, and ensure that such funds, financial assets, or economic resources were not made available to them (paragraph 1(a)).

While targeted sanctions differ from economic sanctions in producing little impact on populations in targeted countries, they are still governed by the principles of necessity and proportionality.[81] This has to be measured in terms of how penalizing the relevant individual promotes the attainment of the Council's stated objectives. Factors that impact on the proportionality of targeted sanctions cumulatively include their general nature, their designation and impact, the exceptions that they admit, and their impact on the legal rights of the target entities.

An inherent problem with the targeted sanctions regime is that, while the Security Council adopts these sanctions, it leaves to individual states to decide which individuals will be placed on the sanctions list, with the effect of obliging all states to apply sanctions to that individual. Thereby the Council effectively approves a unilateral determination by states of the scope of the sanctions regime. This process cannot therefore be characterized as a genuinely collective effort to maintain peace and security.

In the nature of sanctions, it is not completely obvious that 'the practice of listing really is a temporary measure'. Thus, lists can become open-ended in duration, thereby making temporary sanctions such as the freezing of funds tantamount to their permanent confiscation.[82] Targeted sanctions regimes did not originally include humanitarian exceptions. Subsequently, Resolution 1452(2002) admitted exceptions from financial measures 'necessary for basic expenses, including payments for foodstuffs, rent or mortgage, medicines and medical treatment, taxes, insurance premiums, and public utility charges', but still left these to be put into effect by decisions of member States (paragraphs 1(a)–(b)). The 1267 Sanctions Committee has repeatedly applied these exceptions. It is suggested that targeted sanctions can be considered proportionate in the sense that, because exceptions are provided for basic needs, they do not interfere inappropriately with fundamental human rights.[83] However, this humanitarian dimension is only one aspect of the problem and does not cover the issue of the proportionality of the nature and impact of sanctions as such.

Necessity and proportionality have to be measured against the stated objective of the sanctions regime, namely to prevent terrorist acts.[84] Targeted sanctions can cause economic disruption and financial hardship to targeted entities, reinforced by the stigmatizing and psychological impact of being wrongly listed. Damage to the

---

[81] *Report of the Special Rapporteur on the promotion and protection of human rights and fundamental freedoms while countering terrorism*, A/61/267, 16 August 2006, para 33.

[82] A/61/267, para 34.

[83] *Strengthening Targeted Sanctions Through Fair and Clear Procedures*, White Paper prepared by the Watson Institute Targeted Sanctions Project, Brown University, 30 March 2006, A/60/887-S/2006/331, 14 June 2006, 33.

[84] As confirmed by the Sanctions Monitoring Team, S/2005/752, para 42.

reputation of individuals adversely affects their business operations. Their families and employees suffer collateral impact. Apart from this, procedural shortcomings arise such as problems associated with prompt notification, absence of justification for listing, or information about how to appeal against designation.[85] Imposing hardship for no obviously proved reason without providing effective legal remedies is bound to be more disproportionate than just imposing hardship. On balance, any benefit to international peace and security from containing terrorism through targeted sanctions has certainly been outweighed by the hardship inflicted on targeted individuals and entities.[86]

The requirements of necessity and proportionality could be observed if the sanctions regime effectively prevented terrorist acts precisely through its adverse impact on the targeted individuals and entities. If it does not, the sanctions regime must be seen as unnecessary and disproportionate. As pointed out,

having to satisfy a proportionality test also requires posing the questions as to whether the means chosen (sanctions) are *capable* of achieving the goal (cutting off, or making more difficult terrorist financing) as well as whether these means are *proportional* to the end to be achieved.

There is a great deal of doubt whether the sanctions have *any* significant effect on terrorist financing and even the 1267 Sanctions Committee is ambiguous on the point. For 'blacklisting will not facilitate the identification of the networks financing such groups and the means by which this is done. On the contrary, blacklisting will usually make the process of *detection* much more difficult.'[87] The Sanctions Monitoring Team has admitted the difficulty in quantifying the effect of sanctions and acknowledged their symbolic importance in fighting Al-Qaida.[88] The 1267 Sanctions Committee fell short of indicating any certain effect of sanctions and articulated the outcome in terms of presumption and likelihood:

Information from States suggests that financial sanctions are having an effect. The designation of non-profit organizations that had previously provided funds to Al-Qaida, and more rigorous scrutiny of transactions in the formal banking system, *may have forced* Al-Qaida cells to rely more heavily on local criminal activity to finance their operations, rather than on

---

[85] Watson Institute Report, n 83 above, 8–9; J Almqvist, 'A Human Rights Critique of European Judicial Review: Counter-Terrorism Sanctions', 57 ICLQ (2008), 303 at 307–8. The ECJ decision in *Bosphorus* likewise observes that 'any measure imposing sanctions has, by definition, consequences which affect the right to property and the freedom to pursue a trade or business, thereby causing harm to persons who are in no way responsible for the situation which led to the adoption of the sanctions': C–84/95, 30 July 1996, para 22.

[86] A further manifestation of this is that Al-Qaida has adapted 'to the tightening of international financial structures, especially by using alternate remittance systems such as *hawala* to transfer money': *Report of the Security Council Committee established pursuant to Resolution 1267(1999) concerning Al-Qaida and the Taliban and associated individuals and entities*, S/2004/281, 8 April 2004, para 32.

[87] Council of Europe, *The European Convention on Human Rights, Due Process and United Nations Security Council Counter-Terrorism Sanctions*, Report by I Cameron, 6 February 2006, 18 (emphasis in original).

[88] *Third report of the Analytical Support and Sanctions Monitoring Team appointed pursuant to Resolution 1526(2004) concerning Al-Qaida and the Taliban and associated individuals and entities*, S/2005/572, 9 September 2005, 38.

money from elsewhere within the organisation. Large sums, while not critical to the success of an attack, are now *less likely* to be available.[89]

These discrepancies between the actual effect of sanctions and their impact on the lives of individuals has been made obvious to the Security Council over the years, but did not result in any modification of the sanctions regime resulting in a more sound balancing of the aims of sanctions against their adverse effects.

The Watson Institute Report recognizes that 'targeted sanctions may affect peoples' lives in a way comparable to penalties imposed in criminal proceedings', yet proceeds to deny that sanctions can be characterized as criminal in nature.[90] The Sanctions Monitoring Team established under Resolution 1526(2004) has likewise specified that 'the List is not a criminal list'. Rather, it contains the names of individuals 'regardless of whether any authority has formally charged them with a criminal offence'. Furthermore, 'the sanctions do not impose a criminal punishment or procedure, such as detention, arrest, or extradition, but instead apply administrative measures such as freezing assets, prohibiting international travel and precluding arms sales.'[91]

It should be pointed out at this stage that the criminal law status of the relevant sanctions measures is not crucial in assessing the proportionality of these measures. Whether criminal or administrative in nature, the relevant measure can have tangible effect on individuals and thus be disproportionate, which would be further corroborated if criminal sanctions were to be imposed without adequate procedural guarantees.[92] Still, by simultaneously admitting that 'sanctions programmes have not required their targets to have been convicted by a court of law',[93] the Sanctions Monitoring Team effectively acknowledges that the intention behind the sanctions regime has been to impact on the position and lives of these individuals without properly establishing their participation in terrorism.

A further reflection by the Analytical Team confirms the relationship between necessity and proportionality, and the relevance of legal proceedings:

States need not wait until a national administrative, civil or criminal proceeding can be brought or concluded against an individual or group before proposing a name to the List.

---

[89] Letter dated 1 December 2005 from the Chairman of the Security Council Committee established pursuant to Resolution 1267(1999) concerning Al-Qaida and the Taliban and associated individuals and entities addressed to the President of the Security Council, S/2005/761, 6 December 2005, para 18 (emphasis added).

[90] Watson Institute Report, n 83 above, 10, 16–17.

[91] S/2005/572, paras 39, 41.

[92] The Watson Institute Report, n 83 above, 17, accepts this:

If sanctions are characterized as criminal charges the required evidence for listing an individual would have to meet the standard of 'beyond reasonable doubt'. If, on the other hand, the sanctions are characterized as administrative then the evidentiary burden for listing is lower. In this case, it could still be maintained that the longer a person's name is on the list and the longer his assets are frozen, the more harmful the effect. On that basis, it might be argued that the evidentiary standard should be increased after an individual has been listed for a defined period of time, for example five years.

These observations demonstrate that the real impact of the measure may not be that different whether it is formally denoted as criminal or administrative.

[93] S/2005/752, paras 41–2.

Although occasionally a delay might be necessary for investigative or enforcement purposes, the Team believes that the preventative objectives of the sanctions regime are best served by the addition of the name as soon as a State has gathered the requisite evidence. Delays only serve to allow Al-Qaida or Taliban supporters to circumvent the sanctions by, for example, moving their assets or fleeing the jurisdiction.[94]

It is therefore admitted that the listing measures are intended to enable states to list individuals on the basis of mere allegations, that is to subject them to severe legal consequences without proper legal process. It thus becomes obscure how the preventative rationale of sanctions can be served by targeting entities whose participation in terrorist transactions is not substantiated by evidence. The Report does not define what the 'requisite evidence' means and why, if it is located, the counter-terrorist objective cannot be served better by using that evidence through proper legal procedures that can eventually lead to legal consequences including conviction in accordance with all the requirements of due process.

The same problem emerges at the international level, since the sanctions committees 'have rarely, or ever, evaluated the "evidence" that the named person is engaged in activities involving a threat to international peace and security'.[95] By asserting that targeted sanctions are not meant to be criminal proceedings the Council and the 1267 Committee have essentially obscured the real nature and impact of these sanctions.

The UN Special Rapporteur raises 'the question of whether the nature of the sanctions—civil or criminal—determine[s] the procedural safeguards, including which standards of proof, shall apply'. The confiscation of funds is 'a very serious criminal sanction which calls for proper procedural safeguards'. Having commented on the position held on this question by the Analytical Team, the Report nevertheless considers it

generally accepted that the determination of whether the charges are criminal or civil depend [s] on the seriousness of the sanction or punishment. If the sanctions linked to inclusion on the list are permanent, then no matter how they are qualified, they may fall within the scope of criminal sanctions for the purposes of international human rights law.[96]

Under international law, specifically the ECHR, 'criminal charge' is an autonomous concept and states have no discretion in determining what it is.[97] Such a discretion could not accrue to the Security Council, nor its committees. Otherwise they would end up legislating in defiance of human rights standards that bind them.

Procedures regarding listing and delisting also count in the proportionality equation. As illustrated, both listing and delisting take place on a no-objection basis, which means that any member State of the Committee can prevent a

---

[94] Ibid, para 43; see also the 1267 Committee Guidelines, n 86 above, version of 9 December 2008, para 6(c).
[95] Cameron Report, n 87 above, 5.
[96] A/61/2007, paras 34–5.
[97] *Engel and Others v the Netherlands*, No 5100/77, Judgment of 8 June 1976, paras 79–81.

particular individual from being delisted, being under no obligation to give reasons. The listing and delisting criteria are interpreted and applied by a political organ, the Sanctions Committee, and this procedure contains no legal safeguard for the individuals in question.[98]

It also matters for proportionality who can petition for delisting. For if an entity is subjected to the sanctions regime without being able to independently put its case before the relevant organ and request delisting, the burden imposed on it obviously increases. Initially, the sanctions committees received petitions of delisting only from the target's country of residence or citizenship (the 1267 Committee) or (exceptionally) would consider requests received directly from individuals (the Liberia Sanctions Committee). The parameters of 'exceptionality' in the latter case were never specified and individual requests for delisting have been unsuccessful.[99] However, later on Committee Guidelines have enabled individuals to request independent review of a case.[100] While this could matter in assessing the proportionality of sanctions, it will not go far enough to fully resolve the problem with proportionality, since the no-objection procedure still applies.

The delisting procedural guidelines attached to Resolution 1730(2006) requested the Secretary-General to establish within the Secretariat a focal point for receiving requests for delisting from petitioners, namely individuals, groups, and/or entities on the sanctions committees' lists. As the representative of France observed at the adoption of this resolution, 'there has been a widespread sense that, once a name has been added to a list, it is difficult to delist it and to plead one's case, since the procedure has been so opaque and inaccessible. That has affected the efficacy of sanctions'. The new procedure adopted under the resolution 'enables individuals and entities that have been listed to present their petitions for delisting directly to a focal point created to that end within the Secretariat'.[101]

However, the matter will not be considered by the committee if the designating government or the government of citizenship and residence opposes the request (paragraph 6). As the representative of Qatar specified, the focal point 'lacks independence, neutrality, standards or controls for delisting. Therefore, this point of contact does not at all constitute an effective means of fairness'.[102] On balance, the author of the petition has to clear two hurdles: objection by the relevant government before the matter is placed on the committee's agenda, and objection by any member of the Committee. Council Resolution 1904(2009) has obliged Committee members to provide reasons when objecting to delisting requests.

All these alterations to the targeted sanctions regime still do not go far enough to enable targeted individuals to enjoy judicial protection. Therefore, so far judicial review of relevant Security Council decisions by national, EU, or international courts remains the only way to enforce the relevant international law.

---

[98] Cameron Report, n 87 above, 6.
[99] Watson Institute Report, n 83 above, 36–8.
[100] 1267 Sanctions Committee Guidelines, n 86 above, paragraph 7(a); Liberia Sanctions Committee Guidelines, as revised and adopted by the Committee on 30 March 2010, paragraph 7(b).
[101] S/PV.5599, 2 (France).
[102] Ibid, 4 (Qatar).

While Resolutions 1730 and 1904 improved procedures in certain respects, the fact remains that the targeted sanctions system still does not include any effective judicial remedy.[103] As Lord Rodger pointed out,

[t]here is no appeal body outside the Committee to which they can complain. The individuals themselves cannot apply directly to the Committee to have their names removed from the list. Such requests now go to the Ombudsperson. And, if a State applies on their behalf, the name will still not be removed unless all members of the Committee agree. There is an obvious danger that States will use listing as a convenient means of crippling political opponents whose links with, say, Al-Qaida may be tenuous at best.[104]

In England the High Court addressed the implementation in the English legal system of paragraph 1(c) of Security Council Resolution 1373(2001), which obliges states to 'freeze without delay funds and other financial assets or economic resources of persons who commit, or attempt to commit, terrorist acts or participate in or facilitate the commission of terrorist acts'. To implement this, the Terrorism (UN Measures) Order 2006 conferred on the Treasury power to act upon the resolution requirements where they have 'reasonable grounds for suspecting that the person is or may be' committing the relevant crimes. The High Court rightly pointed out that the threshold set in the Order was very low and could not constitute a necessary means of implementing the resolution. The resolution did not extend to those who were suspected of possible involvement in terrorism, even though it was not actually limited to those who had actually been proved to be performing those acts.[105] The High Court also stated that the objective of freezing assets under Resolution 1373 was to ensure that funds were not made available for terrorist purposes: 'thus any criminal liability which could fall on those who make any assets available to a designated person should depend on whether it was or ought to have been known to the supplier that the asset in question could result in funds being available for terrorist purposes'. That at the very least was an appropriate limitation on criminal liability. The Order did not reflect the resolution's requirements and thus was not a necessary measure to implement the resolution or the obligations imposed by the Sanctions Committee.[106]

The Court of Appeal acknowledged that the reasonable suspicion standard is not warranted under the text of Resolution 1373, and insisted that the resolution is silent on the standard of proof to be met on the question whether a particular person had committed the relevant terrorist act. Thus the state could properly conclude that it was expedient to provide for the reasonable suspicion test. However, use of the words 'may be' had to be disapproved because Resolution 1373 did

---

[103] *HM Treasury* v *Mohammed Jabar Ahmed and others*, [2010] UKSC 2, 27 January 2010, para 78 (*per* Lord Hope).

[104] Ibid, para 181 (*per* Lord Rodger).

[105] *A, K, M, Q & G* v *HM Treasury*, Queen's Bench, [2008] EWCH 869 (Admin), 24 April 2008, paras 39–40. The reasonable suspicion approach is also disapproved under Resolution 1822(2008) which focuses on 'acts of activities indicating' that an individual or entity is associated with Al-Qaida, Usama bin Laden, or the Taliban (paragraph 2).

[106] Ibid, para 46.

not authorize these words to be used in implementing legislation (the 2006 Order).[107] In the appeal judgment the reasoning, as well as the evidence—or lack of it—substantiating this last point is essentially the same as that relating to the use of the reasonable suspicion standard. If use of the words 'may be' was not warranted by the resolution, nor was use of the reasonable suspicion standard.

The difference between the approaches of the two courts may not be that great if the Court of Appeal's rejection of the words 'may be' is considered. Any sensible meaning properly attaching to the reasonable suspicion approach refers, in essence, to whatever the state suspects 'may be' the case. Suspicion is a mental process focused on likelihood, potential, or possibility, and is thus definitionally different from certainty, which falls within the realm of demonstration, knowledge, and proof. One could never suspect that something *is* the case but only that something *might be* the case, and one's assertion of suspicion that something is the case in effect only means that one suspects that something may be the case. From the perspective of an external observer, expression of a suspicion not substantiated by evidence points, in any case whatsoever, to the likelihood that suspected facts could be true, whether or not the person expressing suspicion insists that it actually is the case. The use, in the 2006 Order, of the words 'suspecting that the person is' thus amounts to an oxymoron. The Court of Appeal's rejection of the words 'may be' effectively amounts to its rejection of the reasonable suspicion test as a whole, because in practice it will be very difficult to approve this test without also approving its likelihood element.[108] This judgment states that the choice of words in the 2006 Order was unfortunate.[109]

The courts' approach to interpreting Resolution 1373 is a separate issue. While the High Court rightly opposed adoption of the standard of reasonable suspicion, it also acknowledged that neither is the obvious proof standard required in Council resolutions. Thus, if the High Court's opposition to the reasonable suspicion standard is correct, it is left profoundly unambiguous what standard might actually apply to the assets-freezing requirement under paragraph 1(c) of Resolution 1373, which again, on the High Court's interpretation, supports neither of the two evidentiary standards. Therefore, under the High Court's approach, the British government effectively applied its own interpretation to paragraph 1(c) by arrogating to itself a greater power over individuals than that paragraph allocated to it.

On its face, paragraph 1(c) is sufficiently clear in referring to individuals who 'commit', 'attempt to commit', or 'facilitate the commission' of terrorist acts, as opposed to those who are suspected or presumed to be doing any of these. The text of the resolution does not mandate any presumptive approach in this regard. It is moreover doubtful whether the Council could validly subscribe to the reasonable

---

[107] *A, K, M, Q & G v HM Treasury*, [2008] EWCA Civ 1187, 30 October 2008, paras 39, 42.

[108] Unless, of course, courts were to defer to the self-judging assertion by the executive that the latter's mere belief and suspicion point to certainty rather than likelihood or possibility, without being in any position to verify this.

[109] Even more so in the Terrorism (UN Measures) Order 2006, Article 4(1) of which enables the relevant measures to be taken if the HM Treasury has 'reasonable grounds for suspecting' that a particular person 'is or may be' Usama Bin Laden or a person designated by the Sanctions Committee.

suspicion standard. Even though targeted sanctions fall within its powers under Article 41, it is still incompetent to stipulate the reasonable suspicion standard in relation to what effectively amounts to criminal liability, and consequently offend against fundamental human rights that possess peremptory status. The Court of Appeal's decision avoids construing paragraph 1(c) (via the 2006 Order) as actually entailing that result, in particular through disapproving the words 'may be' (which in practice will preclude paragraph 1(c) from being applied as if it approved the use of the reasonable suspicion standard). But, as a matter of principle, the Court of Appeal does not reject the reasonable suspicion standard as such and this approach, it can be concluded, materialized only due to the appeal judgment's avoidance of any consistent attempt to properly interpret paragraph 1(c) using the methods that govern interpretation of Security Council resolutions.

The Supreme Court judgment in this case demonstrates the ways of interpreting Security Council resolutions to prevent a unilateral modification of their meaning by states. Lord Hope held that the words of the Order must be tested against the words used in the resolution. While the Order was meant to enforce the resolution, 'it does not permit interference with the basic rights of the individual any more than is necessary and unavoidable to give effect to the SCR and is consistent with the principle of legality'. There was 'nothing to indicate that the Security Council has decided that freezing orders should be imposed on a basis of mere suspicion'. Resolution 1373 is not phrased in terms of reasonable suspicion. It instead lays down 'specific factual tests' for association with Al-Qaida and the Taliban. By introducing that test to give effect to Resolution 1373, the Treasury had acted ultra vires of that resolution as given effect in England through the UN Act 1946.[110]

This expansive interpretation also has an impact on the proportionality of actions claimed to be taken pursuant to Resolution 1373. As Lord Hope stated,

[t]he Resolution nowhere requires, expressly or by implication, the freezing of the assets of those who are merely suspected of the criminal offences in question. Such a requirement would radically change the effect of the measures. Even if the test were that of reasonable suspicion, the result would almost inevitably be that some who were subjected to freezing orders were not guilty of the offences of which they were reasonably suspected. The consequences of a freezing order, not merely on the enjoyment of property, but upon the enjoyment of private and family life are dire. If imposed on reasonable suspicion they can last indefinitely, without the question of whether or not the suspicion is well-founded ever being subject to judicial determination.[111]

Simliarly, Lord Mance observed in this context that '[a] measure [under the 2006 Order] cannot be regarded as effectively applying that core prohibition [under Resolution 1373], if it substitutes another, essentially different prohibition freezing the assets of a different and much wider group of persons on an indefinite basis'.[112]

---

[110] *Ahmed and others*, n 103 above, paras 47, 58–61, 139, 142 (*per* Lord Hope, also referring to the 1267 Committee Guidelines, n 86 above, section 6(d), which specified the type of evidence required to justify listing, which is qualitatively different from mere suspicion): ibid, para 140; ibid, paras 199–200 (*per* Lord Brown), paras 225–6 (*per* Lord Mance).

[111] Ibid, para 137.

[112] Ibid, para 230.

All this demonstrates the Supreme Court applying the accepted principles for interpretation of Security Council resolutions, above all the principle of ordinary meaning. This enabled the Court to identify the meaning and reach of measures prescribed in Resolution 1373, contrast them with a unilateral interpretation by the executive, establish that this unilateral interpretation entails consequences disproportionate in relation to the objectives set by the Security Council, and enforce the legal consequences of these findings within the English legal system.

The Canadian Federal Court's treatment of the Resolution 1267 sanctions regime is also accurate and instructive. The federal judge has added his name

to those who view the 1267 Committee regime as a denial of basic legal remedies and as untenable under the principles of international human rights. There is nothing in the listing or de-listing procedure that recognizes the principles of natural justice or that provides for basic procedural fairness. . . . the 1267 Committee listing and de-listing processes do not even include a limited right to a hearing. It can hardly be said that the 1267 Committee process meets the requirement of independence and impartiality when, as appears may be the case involving Mr Abdelrazik, the nation requesting the listing is one of the members of the body that decides whether to list or, equally as important, to de-list a person. The accuser is also the judge.

Furthermore, even though there had been an amendment to allow a listed individual to make an application personally to the 1267 Committee,

[i]t is difficult to see what information any petitioner could provide to prove a negative, ie to prove that he or she is not associated with Al-Qaida. One cannot prove that fairies and goblins do not exist any more than Mr Abdelrazik or any other person can prove that they are not an Al-Qaida associate. It is a fundamental principle of Canadian and international justice that the accused does not have the burden of proving his innocence, the accuser has the burden of proving guilt.[113]

4. The 'Legislative' Measures

Resolution 1373(2001) requires states to prevent and criminalize the financing of terrorism (paragraph 1), bring individuals involved in terrorist activities to justice (paragraph 2), and cooperate with each other to these ends (paragraph 3). The assertion of legislative character for this resolution is not supported by its characteristics: its provisions are generically similar to 'smart' targeted sanctions and only differ by their general character. Paragraph 1(c) specifies as targets those who commit, attempt to commit, or participate in terrorist attacks. Some provisions in paragraphs 2 and 3 are too general to impose specific obligations on states, stating instead general priorities within which states should adopt counterterrorist measures. The argument of 'legislation' therefore stumbles not only at the Council's lack of legislative power, but also at its lack of the actual intention to legislate. As

---

[113] *Abousfian Abdelrazik v The Minister of Foreign Affairs and the Attorney General of Canada*, Federal Court, Ottawa, 2009 FC 580, 4 June 2009, paras 51, 53.

pointed out, 'the substantive rules that the Security Council thus imposed on all states were not suddenly invented by the Council but were based, albeit somewhat loosely, on prior resolutions of the General Assembly adopted unanimously or by overwhelming majorities largely during the past decade'. Moreover, some provisions in Resolution 1373 are non-binding, such as paragraph 3.[114] Furthermore, because Resolution 1373 did not define terrorist targets against which states should apply legally binding measures, it has been exceedingly difficult for the UN Counter-Terrorism Committee to pressurize any state into implementing this resolution.[115]

The EU CFI judgment in the *Modjahedines* case likewise confirms that assuming legislative character for Resolution 1373 is unjustified. It does not specify individually the persons, groups, or entities subject to the relevant measures, nor establish specific legal rules concerning the procedure for freezing funds, nor safeguards or judicial remedies enabling the relevant persons to challenge the measures adopted by states implementing them. It was for states—and, in this case, the Community, through which states have decided to act—to identify persons, groups, and entities whose funds are to be frozen pursuant to Resolution 1373, 'in accordance with the rules in their own legal order'.[116]

Similarly, Resolution 1540(2004) on nuclear non-proliferation lacks legislative features. At the stage of adopting this resolution the Pakistani representative pointed out that Pakistan had already met the requirements specified in paragraphs 1–4 of the resolution, and then stated, in terms cautioning against implying the Council's legislative entitlement, that 'the provisions of the resolution will not serve to impose non-proliferation obligations on States or to transfer the general responsibility for global non-proliferation and disarmament to the Security Council'. In addition 'the eleventh preambular paragraph also recognizes that the binding legal obligations that are mentioned are only those arising from "treaties to which they are parties"'.[117] The Spanish representative argued that 'the resolution is not intrusive because it enables States to translate the obligations conferred by it into domestic law as they wish'.[118] Most importantly, in paragraph 5 of Resolution 1540 the Council '[d]ecides that none of the obligations set forth in this resolution shall be interpreted so as to conflict with or alter the rights and obligations of State Parties to the Nuclear Non-Proliferation Treaty, the Chemical Weapons Convention and the Biological and Toxin Weapons Convention', and effectively disclaims any intention to legislate by overriding existing international law. In any case, the propriety of a resolution depends on its 'general acceptability',[119] which militates

---

[114] P Szasz, 'The Security Council Starts Legislating', 96 AJIL (2002), 901 at 903.
[115] E Rosand, 'The UN Response to the Evolving Threat of Global Terrorism: Institutional Reform, Rivalry or Renewal?', in PG Danchin and H Fischer (eds.), *United Nations Reform and the New Collective Security* (Cambridge: Cambridge University Press, 2010), 250 at 257.
[116] *Organisation des Modjahedines du peuple d'Iran v Council of the EU*, Case T–228/02, 12 December 2006, paras 100–2.
[117] S/PV.4956, 3–4.
[118] Ibid, 8.
[119] See Chapter 2 above.

against it having legislative character. If a resolution is adopted to impose on states general obligations that they would not consensually undertake, this indicates that the resolution is not 'generally acceptable' and is thus ultra vires.

5. 'Intrusive' Measures: The Case of Territorial Administration

Over the past two decades the Security Council has adopted a number of resolutions containing measures that increasingly intrude into the domestic jurisdiction of states, namely those establishing missions with an expanded governance mandate in Bosnia, Cambodia, Kosovo, Iraq, and Afghanistan.[120] That the establishment of such ambitious missions must 'intrude' into the social and political lives of states is dictated by the seriousness of humanitarian disasters produced by internal armed conflicts.[121] At the same time, the temporary nature of such missions, and any consent by territorial states expressed in peace agreements, confirm that these 'intrusive' missions can still fit within the scope of the powers provided to the Council under the Charter and be governed by the requirements of necessity and proportionality.

The intrusive measures in some cases can actually evidence the Council's understanding of its role to complement agreed solutions. In its Article 2 the Cambodia Comprehensive Peace Agreement 1991 invited the Security Council to establish the UN Transitional Authority in Cambodia (UNTAC) and provide a mandate for it as defined in that Agreement, which the Council ultimately did under Resolution 745(1992). The UN Mission in Kosovo (UNMIK), established following Security Council Resolution 1244(1999) in the aftermath of the NATO armed attack against Yugoslavia, was endowed with far-reaching powers and extensively regulated aspects of economic life in Kosovo including taxation, currency, trade, and investment. UNMIK even repealed housing laws that had previously applied in Kosovo, because it found them being used in a discriminatory fashion.[122]

In 1999 the Secretary-General recommended in its report that the Council establish a UN Transitional Administration in East Timor (UNTAET) as an integrated, multidimensional operation to assist East Timor's transition to independence, which the Secretary-General estimated would take two to three years. Since the Indonesian government had left Timorese territory, UNTAET would have to focus on rebuilding the administration and judiciary. The Special Representative, who was to be the Transitional Administrator, was empowered to amend or repeal existing laws and introduce new ones, to ensure consistency with international

---

[120] For detail see C Stahn, *The Law and Practice of International Territorial Administration, Versailles to Iraq and Beyond* (Cambridge: Cambridge University Press, 2008); R Wilde, *International Territorial Administration: How Trusteeship and the Civilizing Mission Never Went Away* (Oxford: Oxford University Press, 2008).

[121] P Daillier, 'Les opérations multinationales consécutives à des conflits armés en vue du rétablissement de la paix', 314 *Recueil des cours* (2005), 233 at 267.

[122] M Matheson, 'The UN Governance of Post-Conflict Societies', 95 AJIL (2001), 76 at 80–81; Boon, n 59 above, 1031.

human rights.[123] Conferral of a plenary power to legislate does not appear to have been intended in Council Resolution 1272(1999) whereby UNTAET was established. The resolution defined UNTAET's mandate as providing security and maintaining law and order throughout the territory of East Timor; establishing an effective administration; assisting in the development of civil and social services; and ensuring the coordination and delivery of humanitarian assistance, rehabilitation, and development assistance. UNTAET's military component replaced the multinational force established by Resolution 1264(1999), to maintain security in East Timor (paragraphs 2 and 3).

The establishment and operation of 'intrusive' missions by the Security Council has been premised on a dynamic interpretation of the Council's Chapter VII powers, to enable this organ to cope, on a temporary basis, with major threats by taking action commensurate to these.

6. Authorization of the Use of Force under Article 42

(a) The Nature and Effect of Authorizations

Article 42 refers to operations by armed forces of member States as amounting, or constituting an alternative to, the Council's 'action by air, sea, or land forces'. There is no straightforward requirement that the use of force should be carried out by the UN and not by individual states. Doctrinal positions regarding the use of Article 42 are diverse. Dinstein takes the view that in the Security Council's practice Article 42 has never been activated, because non-mandatory authorizations do not fall within this provision.[124] It is also suggested that the authorization technique is an amendment of the Charter through practice.[125] It is also submitted that the failure to activate the Military Staff Committee and Article 43 agreements has led the Security Council to develop an alternative option of contracting individual states to provide forces under their own command once a crisis erupts.[126] As the ICTY observed in the *Tadić* appeal decision, action by member States on behalf of the UN under Article 42 is a poor substitute for operations undertaken under UN

---

[123] *Report of the Secretary-General on the Situation in East Timor*, S/1999/1024, 4 October 1999, paras 27–8, 32–3, 39; the Report also defined UNTAET's structural components including its Executive Committee, chief officials, and liaison offices: ibid, paras 40ff.

[124] Y Dinstein, *War, Aggression and Self-Defence*, 4th ed. (Cambridge: Cambridge University Press 2005), 304.

[125] J Quigley, 'The "Privatisation" of Security Council Enforcement Action: A Threat to Multilateralism', 17 *Michigan Journal of International Law* (1995–6), 249 at 277.

[126] K Kaikobad, 'Self-Defence, Enforcement Action and the Gulf Wars, 1980–88 and 1990–91', 63 *British Yearbook of International Law* (1992), 299 at 359; G Gaja, 'Use of Force Made or Authorised by the United Nations', in C Tomuschat (ed.), *The United Nations at the Age of Fifty* (The Hague: Kluwer, 1995), 38 at 41; N Blokker, 'Is the Authorisation Authorised? Powers and Practice of the UN Security Council to Authorise the Use of Force', 11 *European Journal of International Law* (2000), 541 at 549; A Pellet, 'The Road to Hell is Paved with Good Intentions. The United Nations as a Guarantor of International Peace and Security: A French Perspective', in Tomuschat, ibid, 113 at 125; C Greenwood, 'The United Nations as Guarantor of International Peace and Security: Past, Present and Future—A United Kingdom View', in Tomuschat, ibid, 58 at 70.

command proper.[127] Still, in the case of Haiti the Secretary-General regarded it as in conformance with the Charter, past practice, and established principles for the Council to adopt a Chapter VII resolution, to 'authorize a group of Member States to establish and deploy a force... to facilitate the early restoration of the legitimate authorities and the re-establishment of their structures in working order'.[128]

Sarooshi observes that if a Security Council resolution fails to refer to Article 42 this does not prevent that resolution from being constitutionally based on that provision.[129] Gaja argues in broader terms that Article 42 has to be seen as the basis of all types of military intervention, including peace keeping.[130] A further argument is developed that 'there is an implied power for the Security Council to adopt authorization resolutions',[131] and to exercise command and control of a military force made up of units voluntarily contributed by states.[132] On the other hand, as White points out, 'it is arguably legally unacceptable to imply a power which goes against the express provisions of the Charter which clearly envisage collective security in the form of the centralisation of armed force'.[133] Indeed, if a decentralized military option cannot fit within Article 42, it cannot be implied into the Charter either, for it is solely Article 42 that stipulates the option of military enforcement. In addition, while implied powers define what the Organization can do in the absence of express stipulations, the decentralized military option pursues the question of *how* the power expressly stipulated under Article 42 can be exercised: namely, whether it can be exercised in a way arguably different from that stipulated. Article 42 is broad enough to allow for enforcement action to be conducted by states. But even if this were not the case, a decentralized military option has to be viewed not as based on the Council's implied power but as an adaptation to circumstances on the ground (including the lack of Article 43 agreements) of the power expressly allocated to the Council.[134]

There is a crucial difference between the Security Council's overall control over the mandate of an operation (for instance through its right to change or terminate the operation), and its control over the actual operation (that is, military operations, command and discipline, on whether it will achieve its aims and observe legal requirements). This could justify Gaja's remark that an action under Article 42 is not taken by the UN. Control of the UN over national operations can be limited, because its resolution may state the objectives of the use of force vaguely and the

---

[127] *Tadić*, n 4 above, para 36.
[128] *Report of the Secretary-General on the United Nations Mission in Haiti*, S/1994/828, 15 July 1994, paras 9, 20, and 21.
[129] D Sarooshi, *The United Nations and Development of Collective Security* (New York: Oxford University Press, 1999), 199–200.
[130] Gaja, n 126 above, 51.
[131] Blokker, n 126 above, 554.
[132] Sarooshi, n 129 above, 78.
[133] N White, *Keeping the Peace* (Manchester: Manchester University Press, 1997), 128.
[134] For the treatment of this principle in jurisprudence see *Admissibility of Hearings of Petitioners by the Committee on South West Africa*, Advisory Opinion, 1 June 1956, *ICJ Reports*, 1956, 23 at 27–8, 30–2. The case related to the hearing of petitioners before the UN Committee for South West Africa, which had not originally been foreseen as part of the procedure, because the mandatory government (South Africa) had failed to properly cooperate with the Committee in dealing with petitions.

Rules of Engagement may afford states considerable discretion.[135] It may happen that states to which Chapter VII powers have been delegated might serve their own interest and not that of the UN. This is contrary to centring in the UN the responsibility for maintaining peace and security through collective decisions.[136]

Tools for avoiding this are control through fixing an objective in the governing Security Council resolution; control of an enforcement action in progress through fixing its time limit;[137] imposing a reporting duty;[138] and control through the Council's power to renew or terminate the operation's mandate. An authorization not containing a functional or temporal limitation will be void for its conflict with the Charter. In many cases the Security Council clearly specifies a time limit for operations authorized under Article 42. The period of authorization can vary from 11 days to a year, with the possibility of renewals.[139] In practice this is connected with the consent of the territorial state, as Resolution 1546(2004) actually specified in relation to the MNF in Iraq, confirming that the presence of that force could be terminated sooner than the stipulated time limit if the Iraqi Government so requested. There are cases where no obvious time limit is specified and thus the relevance of the collective will of the Council is diminished, as is the case with the authorization of the NATO Kosovo Force (KFOR) under Resolution 1244(1999).

It is suggested that states are not obliged to act upon the authorization of the use of force by the Council.[140] Dinstein argues that 'authorization is no less permissive than recommendation'. They both share non-mandatory status and thus neither falls within Article 42.[141] Authorization constitutes an approval of an offer by states or organizations that are able and willing to perform a task. In practice authorization is given once the relevant states make an offer to the Council to conduct an intervention or to serve as lead nation. This process manifests the Council's view that an arrangement with a lead nation serves the necessity of action to meet a stated objective of the Council, which is not characteristic of recommendations. The difference between recommendation and authorization is that the latter meets the legal conditions permitting the use of force where this otherwise would not be permitted, while the former has no such effect because it has no impact on the rights and duties of states.

---

[135] Gaja, n 126 above, 41; this has implications for command and control arrangements: see Chapter 7 below.

[136] Sarooshi, n 129 above, 153–4.

[137] Resolution 1125(1997) authorized MISAB in the Central African Republic, limited its mandate to three months, and subsequently extended it by Resolutions 1152 and 1155(both 1998).

[138] Resolution 1101(1997) on Albania required from 'the Member States participating in the multinational protection force to provide periodic reports, at least every two weeks, through the Secretary-General, to the Council'. These reports were to specify 'the parameters and modalities of the operation on the basis of consultations between those Member States and the Government of Albania' (paragraph 9).

[139] Cf Blokker, n 126 above, 562–3.

[140] Quigley, n 125 above, 262.

[141] Dinstein, n 124 above, 310; however, according to Weston, the Council 'authorized' military action under Resolution 678(1990), instead of recommending it, to reject a comparison with the Korean case: B Weston, 'Security Council Resolution 678 and Persian Gulf Decision Making: Precarious Legitimacy', 85 AJIL (1991), 516 at 521–2.

There is strong doctrinal support for the use of force acquiring legality on the basis of Security Council recommendations. As Pellet suggests, if the Council could do more, that is decide that member States must contribute troops to its operations (which Pellet suggests the Council is entitled to do), then it could do less, that is recommend an action on which it could adopt a decision.[142] This view ignores that, where the Council has determined that there is a threat under Article 39 of sufficient severity and magnitude to be best handled by the use of force, then it can only act under Article 42. The Council cannot validly take the view that there is a threat but only recommend forcible action, ie suggest that this is not necessary. Article 39 cannot include the power to recommend what can only be authorized as a matter of necessity under Articles 41 and 42. The criterion of the necessity of the force to be used under Chapter VII is the rationale for admitting, under Article 42, an exception to the otherwise comprehensive prohibition of the use of force.

Last but not least, authorization is the Council's collective decision. A unilateral interpretation of resolutions with a view to reading in authorization that is not present essentially purports to replace the Council's judgement of the propriety of a particular measure with that of individual member States or their groups. To illustrate, Resolution 688(1991) on the humanitarian situation in Iraq and its drafting process revealed no intention to authorize the use of force to protect the Kurds in Iraq. However, the US government unilaterally interpreted the resolution as permitting such a use of force.[143] The no-fly zones in Iraq were then claimed to be based on that authorization, even though none of this was mentioned in pertinent resolutions. The Secretary-General also suggested that the presence of foreign troops in Iraq required an express authorization. The Council membership was divided on the legality of this, which means that the authorization of no-fly zones would have been rejected, had it been proposed to the Council.[144]

(b) The Requirements of Necessity and Proportionality

The High-Level Panel Report formulates a number of requirements as to the necessity and proportionality of such use of force. In terms of necessity, the question relates to the proper purpose of operation: whether 'the primary purpose of the proposed military action is to halt or avert the threat in question, whatever other purposes or motives may be involved'. A related question is whether the use of force constitutes the last resort and whether every non-military option for meeting the threat in question has been explored, with reasonable grounds for believing that

---

[142] Pellet, n 126 above, 126; H Lauterpacht (ed.), *Oppenheim's International Law*, 7th ed. (London: Stevens & Sons, 1952), vol II, II, 429; Dinstein, n 124 above, 290; *per contra* H Kelsen, *The Law of the United Nations* (London: Stevens & Sons, 1950), 932.

[143] MR Hutchinson, 'Restoring Hope: UN Security Council Resolutions for Somalia and an Expanded Doctrine of Humanitarian Intervention', 34 *Harvard International Law Journal* (1994), 624 at 633–4.

[144] J Lobel and M Ratner, 'Bypassing the Security Council: Ambiguous Authorizations to Use Force, Cease-fires and the Iraqi Inspection Regime', 93 AJIL (1999) 124 at 126, 132–3; Sarooshi, n 129 above, 229, 232.

other measures would not succeed.[145] This seems to replicate the concept of necessity under *jus ad bellum*. The principle of last resort means that it is not for the decision maker to select the use of force from available alternatives, but to resort to it only if other measures hold no prospect of success, since Article 42 specifies that force can be authorized if all non-forcible measures are or would be inadequate. The burden of demonstrating that this is the case lies with the Council.

The High-Level Panel Report also addresses the issue of proportionality: whether the scale, duration, and intensity of the proposed military action are the least necessary to meet the threat in question. In balancing the consequences, it has to be ascertained whether there is 'a reasonable chance of the military action being successful in meeting the threat in question, with the consequences of action not likely to be worse than the consequences of inaction'.[146] According to Gaja, the requirement for proportionality of an Article 42 action may affect both the selection of the objectives that the use of force must achieve and the choice of means to attain these objectives.[147] Furthermore, proportionality has a humanitarian component, namely to strike a reasonable balance between achievement of the Charter objectives and preventing unnecessary loss of life and suffering, especially of civilians. If proportionality and necessity are imprecise concepts to apply, this increases the need for caution.[148]

(c) Authorization of the Use of Force to Effect Maritime Interdiction

The use of Article 42 to authorize the use of force without central UN command dates back to the Rhodesian crisis, further to the imposition of economic sanctions on Rhodesia under Article 41. Paragraphs 8 and 9 of Resolution 217(1965) called upon Britain to enforce an economic embargo against Rhodesia. But the British government regarded this resolution as an inadequate basis for detaining a ship on the high seas and Resolution 221(1966) was then adopted with that effect.[149] In Resolution 221, the Council called upon the UK 'to prevent, by the use of force if necessary, the arrival at Beira of vessels reasonably believed to be carrying oil destined for Southern Rhodesia'. Paragraph 5 of the resolution 'empowered' the UK to detain *Joanna V* 'upon her departure from Beira in the event her oil cargo is discharged there'. This word seems to be making the difference and is synonymous with 'authorizing'. This resolution is a classic instance of the Council determining that previously imposed economic sanctions under Article 41 had not been adequately implemented. The Council stated in the resolution that embargoes imposed under Resolutions 216 and 217 might not be observed because substantial shipments of oil could get through to Rhodesia, and then called upon the UK to stop the tanker by the use of force if necessary.

---

[145] High-Level Panel Report, 58.
[146] Ibid, 58.
[147] Gaja, n 126 above, 39.
[148] J Gardam, 'Legal Restraints on Security Council Military Enforcement Action', 17 *Michigan Journal of International Law* (1996), 285 at 308–12.
[149] JW Halderman, 'Some Legal Aspects of Sanctions in the Rhodesian Case', 17 ICLQ (1968), 672 at 685.

Resolution 221 cannot be seen as a general licence to stop and search vessels on the high seas. A more reasonable reading, in line with the necessity and proportionality requirements, suggests that *once* a particular ship is identified as carrying an embargoed cargo to a prohibited destination, states become entitled to prevent that ship from accomplishing this task. The ultimate objective of authorization remains that the cargo must not reach its destination port, not that the ship must be inspected, detained, or confiscated. To draw an analogy with the traditional law of blockade, the aim remains to block the ports of the target state, and unless this is effectively accomplished, detaining ships on the high seas cannot serve the purpose for which a blockade or, for that matter, an embargo was instituted.

The same issue arose in relation to Resolution 661(1990), paragraph 3 of which imposed comprehensive sanctions on Iraq, but was not being properly implemented. The USA and the UK started naval interdiction operations to intercept commodities and products moving to and from Iraq and Kuwait, and claimed this to be based on collective self-defence under Article 51, which justified the use of the 'minimum force necessary'. This has rightly been challenged by a number of states as 'there was, indeed, no indication in Resolution 661 that the Council had intended to confer upon States a power to use or threaten force against ships flying the flags of other States in order to enforce sanctions'.[150] Resolution 661 could not be interpreted to make its clauses imposing sanctions under Article 41 imply a qualitatively new measure under Article 42 on which a new Council decision would have been required. This deficiency was remedied with the adoption of Resolution 665(1990). By paragraph 1 of Resolution 665 the Council

[c]all[ed] upon those Member States co-operating with the Government of Kuwait which are deploying maritime forces to the area to use such measures commensurate to the specific circumstances as may be necessary under the authority of the Security Council to halt all inward and outward maritime shipping in order to inspect and verify their cargoes and destinations and to ensure strict implementation of the provisions related to such shipping laid down in Resolution 661(1990).

The sanctions under Resolution 665, if limited by requirements of necessity and proportionality, extended only to vessels clearly identified as heading to an Iraqi port. Along similar lines, Resolution 875(1993) on Haiti

[c]alls upon Member States . . . to use such measures commensurate with the specific circumstances as may be necessary under the authority of the Security Council to ensure strict implementation of the provisions of Resolutions 841(1993) and 873(1993) relating to the supply of petroleum or petroleum products or arms and related *matériel* of all types, and in particular to halt inward maritime shipping as necessary in order to inspect and verify their cargoes and destinations.[151]

---

[150] C Greenwood, 'New World Order or Old? The Invasion of Kuwait and the Rule of Law', 55 MLR (1992), 153 at 161.
[151] Once the Council widened sanctions against Haiti, it extended this authorization accordingly, under paragraph 10 of Resolution 917(1994).

According to Sarooshi, these requirements under Resolution 875 reflect the Council's intention to authorize the action within the limits of proportionality under *jus ad bellum* and *jus in bello*. This element of proportionality restricts both the scope of measures and the area of operation in which force may be used, the latter being limited to the region which is the subject to the Council resolution.[152]

Resolution 787(1992) prohibited the transhipment of oil and other products through the territory of the FRY and then (in paragraph 12) called upon states

to use such measures commensurate with the specific circumstances as may be necessary under the authority of the Security Council to halt all inward and outward maritime shipping in order to inspect and verify their cargoes and destinations and to ensure strict implementation of the provisions of Resolutions 713(1991) and 757(1992).

Paragraph 28 of Resolution 820(1993) 'prohibit[s] all commercial maritime traffic from entering the territorial sea of the Federal Republic of Yugoslavia'; paragraph 29

[r]eaffirms the authority of States acting under paragraph 12 of Resolution 787(1992) to use such measures commensurate with the specific circumstances as may be necessary under the authority of the Security Council to enforce the present resolution and its other relevant resolutions, including in the territorial sea of the Federal Republic of Yugoslavia (Serbia and Montenegro).

The wording 'reaffirms the authority' could raise questions whether this was already implied in previous resolutions. The 're-affirmation' under paragraph 29 cannot, however, relate to a power existing before Resolution 820 was adopted because under paragraph 28 of that resolution the Council had just approved, for the first time, the extension of the prohibition of all maritime traffic to the territorial sea of the FRY.

A 'general and complete' arms embargo on Somalia was imposed by Resolution 733(1992). Resolution 1356(2001) required states to take the necessary steps to ensure 'full implementation and enforcement' of that embargo. There is a doctrinal argument that this 'general and complete' embargo authorizes action against all potential suppliers of arms to Somalia, including through air and sea routes, and thus a maritime interdiction of arms bound to Somalia, because without this a 'general and complete' embargo could not be implemented.[153] If so, then, given that Resolution 733 is drafted in the language of obligations not rights, maritime interdiction would also become a duty, which outcome is absurd in itself.

In general, the Council's authorization to interdict vessels on the high seas would entail a radical shift in the allocation of jurisdiction under international law, which the Council should not be deemed to intend in the absence of explicit language to that effect; if it has intended this outcome, the issue of its compliance with the limits on its powers would arise, because Article 103 does not allow the Council to override customary law. Arms embargo normally means that states should

---

[152] Sarooshi, n 129 above, 205.
[153] W Heintschel von Heinegg, 'Legality of Maritime Interdiction Operations in Operation *Enduring Freedom*', in M Bothe, ME O'Connell and N Ronzitti, *Redefining Sovereignty: the Use of Force after the End of Cold War* (Leiden: Brill, 2005), 364 at 373–4.

prevent arms being exported from within their territories to the target state, not that states are entitled, still less obliged, to police the high seas to ensure that no arms are delivered to the target state. Implying the authorization of the use of force on the high seas *could* promote the overall efficiency of an arms embargo against Somalia imposed under Article 41. But such authorization is already an Article 42 matter and requires a separate decision, should the Council see this as necessary.

It is suggested that Resolutions 1373(2001) on terrorism, 1540(2004) on weapons of mass destruction, 1695(2006) and 1718(2006) on North Korea, and 1696(2006) on Iran—which require states, 'consistently with international law', to inspect cargoes containing weapons and related material, prevent these items from being exported to target states, or take measures to prevent the commission of terrorist acts—are broad enough and can be reasonably construed as granting entitlements to take action against the shipping on high seas.[154] The argument is developed that maritime interdiction on the high seas or in territorial waters, claimed to be conducted pursuant to resolutions regarding non-proliferation, would not conflict with the UN Convention on the Law of the Sea (UNCLOS) because its provisions, notably Articles 92 and 110 relating to innocent passage and high seas navigation, permit interference in navigation if that is provided for in other treaties.[155] It seems, however, that this argument puts the cart before the horse. In order to establish that the Convention validates maritime interdiction pursuant to resolutions, it has first to be established that resolutions authorize such interdiction in the first place. Even if the relevant resolution were expressly to authorize such interdiction, its legality, and consequently its impact on Convention provisions, would have to be conditional on clearing two hurdles: the insufficiency of Article 103 to override customary law reflected in most provisions of the Convention, and the requirement that interference in maritime navigation be necessary and proportionate to achieve the Council's stated objectives The Council in its practice has never considered this to be the case—otherwise it would have made the relevant authorization express. Instead, pertinent resolutions require states to act 'consistently with international law', that is, respect the freedom of the high seas. In addition, these resolutions are normally meant to oblige states to take relevant measures within their jurisdiction; the entitlement to act on the high seas, beyond the sovereignty of states, is qualitatively different and cannot be implied in a resolution.

Resolution 1929(2010) on Iran confirms this approach. Having specified in its preamble that the law of the sea, as reflected in UNCLOS, sets out the legal framework applicable to ocean activities, the Council continues in recommendatory language that states, consistent with international law, may request inspections of

---

[154] R Churchill, 'Conflicts between United Nations Security Council Resolutions and the 1982 United Nations Convention on the Law of the Sea, and Their Possible Resolution', 85 *US Naval War College International Law Studies Series* (2009), 143 at 144; see, eg paragraph 8(f) on Resolution 1718 (2006) regarding North Korea.

[155] Ibid, 146–7.

vessels on the high seas with the consent of the flag state, and calls upon all states to cooperate in such inspections if there is information that provides reasonable grounds to believe the vessel is carrying items the supply, sale, transfer, or export of which is prohibited by previous resolutions on Iranian nuclear enrichment (paragraph 15). This approach is again substantiated by the Council's treatment of the problem of piracy off the Somali coast. In paragraph 7 of Resolution 1816 (2008), the Council

[d]ecide[d] that for a period of six months from the date of this resolution, States cooperating with the TFG in the fight against piracy and armed robbery at sea off the coast of Somalia, for which advance notification has been provided by the TFG [Transitional Federal Government] to the Secretary-General, may:
  (a) Enter the territorial waters of Somalia for the purpose of repressing acts of piracy and armed robbery at sea, in a manner consistent with such action permitted on the high seas with respect to piracy under relevant international law; and
  (b) Use, within the territorial waters of Somalia, in a manner consistent with action permitted on the high seas with respect to piracy under relevant international law, all necessary means to repress acts of piracy and armed robbery.

The Council was careful to emphasize in paragraph 9 that

the authorization provided in this resolution applies only with respect to the situation in Somalia and shall not affect the rights or obligations or responsibilities of member states under international law, including any rights or obligations under the Convention, with respect to any other situation, and underscores in particular that it shall not be considered as establishing customary international law, and affirms further that this authorization has been provided only following receipt of the letter from the Permanent Representative of the Somalia Republic to the United Nations to the President of the Security Council dated 27 February 2008 conveying the consent of the TFG.

Paragraphs 10 and 11 reiterate the same approach regarding enforcement action to be conducted off the Somali coast by regional organizations such as the EU and NATO.[156]

The Council thus disclaimed any intention to affect the status quo of general international law either on a general plane or in that specific case. At the adoption of this resolution member States emphasized the need to preserve the integrity of the law of the sea. According to Indonesia, 'it is our duty to voice strong reservations if there are actions envisaged by the Council or any other forum that could lead to modifying, rewriting or redefining UNCLOS'.[157] According to Vietnam, the resolution should not be interpreted as allowing any action that is contrary to international law, including UNCLOS, to be taken within maritime areas under the jurisdiction of a coastal state.[158] In terms emphasizing the Council's subjection to international law and the interpretative relevance of this, China observed that the

---

[156] See also, to the same effect, preamble and paragraphs 3 and 10 of Resolution 1851(2008), preamble and paragraphs 6 and 8 of Resolution 1897(2009).
[157] S/PV.5902, 2 (Indonesia).
[158] Ibid, 4 (Vietnam, and ibid for the identical position of Libya).

resolution must comply with UNCLOS and should not conflict with existing international law.[159] These positions, reflecting that enshrined in the text of the resolution, have not encountered resistance from any member of the Council.

An important question of necessity and proportionality in connection with maritime interdiction operations that have been properly authorized arises in terms of the treatment of vessels found to be in violation of a sanctions regime. With regard to Iraqi vessels impounded in the Gulf, the Sanctions Committee advised the states concerned that it had no objection to their instituting legal proceedings under national law to dispose of such vessels.[160] Resolution 820 (1993) expressly specifies in paragraph 25 that

all States shall detain pending investigation all vessels, freight vehicles, rolling stock, aircraft and cargoes found in their territories and suspected of having violated or being in violation of Resolutions 713(1991), 757(1992), 787(1992) or the present resolution, and that, upon a determination that they have been in violation, such vessels, freight vehicles, rolling stock and aircraft shall be impounded and, where appropriate, they and their cargoes may be forfeit to the detaining State.

As Sarooshi observes, the Council in this case obliges states to act in the way they are already entitled to act under the 'traditional' law of maritime prize and blockade under general international law.[161] However, the Council imposes this obligation in a context different from the inter-belligerent relations to which the law of prize and blockade applies. The traditional law allows vessels to be seized when they provide services that are not neutral *vis-à-vis* the belligerent which seizes them. In the case of Resolution 820 all states were obliged to impound vessels, whether or not they had suffered anything like non-neutral service from that vessel's flag state, still less were at war with it. Giving individual states a conclusive right in relation to putative violators of sanctions inconveniently mixed a multilateral regime with unilateral enforcement.

Moreover, the objective of the Council's action under Chapter VII in this case was to ensure that the blockade against the FRY was observed. This could have been accomplished without affecting the property rights of third states over vessels. Embargo as a peace-maintenance effort requires certain goods to be prevented from reaching a designated territory (here, the FRY), which could be done without impounding, capturing, or imposing a forfeit on such vessels, any of which then amounts to a disproportionate action. The Security Council has imposed on third states an essentially new legal regulation and has done it in an obviously dispropor-tionate way.[162] However, Resolution 1851(2008), which enables states to effect

---

[159] Ibid, 5 (China).
[160] S/1996/700, 21–2.
[161] Sarooshi, n 129 above, 266.
[162] For a further example of a disproportionate decision see paragraph 16 of Resolution 1929(2010) on Iran, in which the Council obliges all states to 'seize and dispose of (such as through destruction, rendering inoperable, storage or transferring to a State other than the originating or destination States for disposal) items the supply, sale, transfer, or export of which is prohibited' by the relevant resolutions on Iranian nuclear enrichment. The rationale of the Council's non-proliferation effort is to ensure that particular items do not reach Iran. Seizure and disposal exceed this objective.

'seizure and disposition of boats, vessels, arms and other related equipment used in the commission of piracy and armed robbery at sea off the coast of Somalia' does not raise grave problems with proportionality, since pirates, being *hostis humani generis* of which international law anyway requires the elimination, cannot be equated to states.

(d) Authorization of the Use of Force to Secure the Council's Humanitarian Objectives

Security Council Resolution 781(1992) established the flight ban in the Bosnian airspace with a view to promoting the end of hostilities in Bosnia. The ban kept being violated; to enhance its effectiveness, paragraph 4 of Resolution 816(1993) authorized member States 'to take, under the authority of the Security Council and subject to close coordination with the Secretary-General and UNPROFOR, all necessary measures in the airspace of the Republic of Bosnia and Herzegovina', to ensure compliance with the ban on flights in Bosnian airspace, and 'proportionate to the specific circumstances and the nature of the flights'. The dimension of necessity and proportionality in this matter is twofold. The Council's authorization was premised on that organ's judgement that this was a necessary and proportionate response to problems created for humanitarian flights in Bosnian airspace, without which their safety could not have been guaranteed. In addition, the actual operations to secure the flight ban needed to be necessary for dealing with a challenge presented by a prohibited military flight, and be proportionate in relation to its nature and scale.

The Council also authorized enforcement action by member States to enable the protection of safe areas in Bosnia—Bihac, Gorazde, Sarajevo, Srebrenica, Tuzla, and Zepa[163]—which task primarily fell within the UNPROFOR mandate. Paragraph 10 of Resolution 836(1993) authorized member States to take,

under the authority of the Security Council and subject to close coordination with the Secretary-General and UNPROFOR, all necessary measures, through the use of air power, in and around the safe areas in the Republic of Bosnia and Herzegovina, to support UNPROFOR in the performance of its mandate.

The parameters of this authorization are specific: only measures which use air power and assist UNPROFOR when performing its mission to secure the cease-fire, protect safe areas, and ensure the withdrawal from Bosnia of all military units not under Bosnian authority.

---

[163] As determined by Resolution 824(1993), paragraph 2, specifying that these and 'their surroundings should be treated as safe areas by all the parties concerned and should be free from armed attacks and from any other hostile act'. See in general B Oswald, 'The Creation and Control of Places of Protection during United Nations Peace Operations', 83 *International Review of the Red Cross* (2001), 1013–35.

Initially, the UN Secretary-General was unable to request NATO air strikes before the NAC expressly authorized NATO forces to launch the operation.[164] While NATO confirmed its readiness to act under the authorization in Resolution 836, the Secretary-General stressed that the first decision on air strikes would be taken by himself in consultation with Security Council members.[165] Once the pertinent authorization to use force under Chapter VII is given, however, in legal terms no further conditions are required for this authorization to be discharged. For instance, Russia argued that the Secretary-General could use force only after consulting the members of the Security Council.[166] But it contradicts the rationale of the authorizing resolution to impose an additional requirement, as this could hamper the implementation of collective security decisions once they are consensually and collectively adopted.

In response to the UN request, NATO adopted its decision to support the Security Council in protecting the safe areas, specifying that

with immediate effect, if any Bosnian Serb attacks involving heavy weapons are carried out on the United Nations-designated safe areas of Gorazde, Bihac, Srebrenica, Tuzla and Zepa, these weapons and other Bosnian Serb military assets, as well as their direct and essential military support facilities, including but not limited to fuel installations and munitions sites, will be subject to NATO air strikes.[167]

NATO further reaffirmed its 'readiness to provide close air support in the event Bosnian Serb forces attack UNPROFOR or other United Nations and relief agency personnel throughout Bosnia and Herzegovina or forcibly interfere with the conduct of their mandate'. Accordingly, the NATO Southern Command was 'authorized to conduct air strikes against Bosnian Serb heavy weapons and other military targets within a 20-kilometre radius of the centre of Gorazde (but inside the territory of Bosnia and Herzegovina)'.[168]

The Secretary-General submitted to the Security Council that

the relevant Security Council resolutions call for close coordination between the United Nations and NATO on the use of NATO air power. These 'dual-key' arrangements remain in place. In order to streamline decision-making within the United Nations chain of command when air strikes are deemed to be necessary, I have decided to delegate the necessary authority in this respect to the Force Commander of the United Nations Peace Forces with immediate effect. As regards close air support to defend United Nations peace-keepers, my

---

[164] Letter dated 28 January 1994 from the Secretary-General addressed to the President of the Security Council, S/1994/94, 28 January 1994.

[165] *Report of the Secretary-General pursuant to Security Council Resolution 836(1993)*, S/25939, paras 2, 8; the NATO Council 'agrees with the position of the UN Secretary-General that the first use of air power in the theatre shall be authorized by him. With respect to NATO, the NAC shall be the political authority that will decide on the conduct of air strikes, which will be carried out in coordination with the UN.' NAC Decision of 9 August 1993, paragraph 1.

[166] S/1994/50 as quoted in Sarooshi, n 129 above, 84.

[167] *Decisions on the protection of safe areas taken at the meeting of the North Atlantic Council on 22 April 1994*, para 9, S/1994/498, 22 April 1994.

[168] *Decisions taken at the meeting of the North Atlantic Council on 22 April 1994*, para 7, S/1994/495, 22 April 1994.

Special Representative has today delegated the necessary authority to the Force Commander, who is authorized to delegate it further to the Commander of the United Nations Protection Force (UNPROFOR) when operational circumstances so require.[169]

Thus, although the Secretary-General affirmed the 'dual-key' system, he effectively 'delegated', down the chain of military command, power to authorize the use of air power in individual cases.

The dual-key arrangement means that NATO and UN shared the power to make decisions over the launching of air strikes. The actual conduct of and command and control over these air strikes rested with NATO. The UN had no involvement with the use of air power, which task was performed by NATO from its air bases and aircraft carriers outside the conflict zone. The chain of command went from the North Atlantic Council through NATO's Supreme Allied Commander Europe (SACEUR), and then Allied Forces Southern Europe (AFSOUTH) and the Commander-in-Chief South (CINCSOUTH).[170] The UN exercised influence over the command mostly through the ability of Special Representative of the Secretary-General (SRSG) Akashi to withhold UN consent under the 'dual-key' arrangement. The dual-key system meant that NATO and UNPROFOR could each propose air strikes but could veto each other's requests and proposed targets. Akashi proposed to judge the suggested air strikes using a number of criteria, some of which were purely fact- and mandate-related (whether the request was within the UNPROFOR mandate, whether the air strike would contribute to the objectives of the UN Security Council *in casu*, whether there was a clearly defined target and the proposed response was proportionate or otherwise consistent with humanitarian law), and some were purely policy-related (how the air strike would affect the overall peace-making effort and the UN reputation). At times this system led to accusations that the UN unduly rejected air strike requests.[171]

On the ground, operations to protect safe areas ended in failure and in summer 1995 NATO even considered withdrawing UNPROFOR; instead, the distinctly intensive Operation *Deliberate Force* was launched jointly by NATO and UNPROFOR against the Bosnian Serb forces. Arguably both UN and NATO

---

[169] S/1995/623, 26 July 1995. In another report, the Secretary-General observed that 'UNPRO-FOR has requested NATO to use its air power on nine occasions when my Special Representative has deemed such action necessary and appropriate. In all cases air power was used against Bosnian Serb targets or targets in Serb-controlled parts of Croatia that had been operating in support of the Bosnian Serbs': *Report of the Secretary-General pursuant to Security Council Resolutions 982(1995) and 987 (1995)*, 30 May 1995, S/1995/444, para 57. In the same report the Secretary-General raised concerns over the impact of air strikes on the dynamics of the relationship between Bosnian Serbs and UNPROFOR, especially in terms of the latter's freedom of movement and ability to conduct humanitarian operations.

[170] T Findlay, *The Use of Force in UN Peace Operations* (New York: Oxford University Press, 2002), 232, 234; JW Houck, 'The Command and Control of United Nations Forces in the Era of "Peace Enforcement"', 4 *Duke Journal of Comparative and International Law.* (1993–4), 1 at 40–1.

[171] Findlay, ibid, 234–5, 269–70; in fact on occasion Akashi rejected calls to authorize air strikes against Bosnian Serb targets even over US insistence on enforcing the pertinent resolutions, and attracted President Clinton's criticism: ibid, 243.

had to agree that their operations achieved the goals set in the Security Council resolutions and the NATO statement of 5 September 1995, before those operations could cease.[172] This does not actually appear in any related documents but might have been an informal arrangement. However, the Russian representative in the Security Council insisted that 'those arrangements gave the United Nations the right to independently put an end to the strikes'.[173] The end of air strikes came with the conclusion of the Dayton Peace Agreement in 1995.

In the aftermath of the genocide in Rwanda, the Security Council repeatedly, in Resolutions 918, 925, and 929 (all 1994), determined that the situation qualified as a threat to the peace under Article 39, and decided to reinforce the mandate of UNAMIR to enable it to meet the United Nations objectives. However, the Secretary-General's report to the Council acknowledged that

with the failure of Member States to promptly provide the resources necessary for the implementation of its expanded mandate, UNAMIR may not be in a position, for about three months, to fully undertake the tasks entrusted to it by those resolutions. Meanwhile, the situation in Rwanda has continued to deteriorate and the killing of innocent civilians has not been stopped.

The Secretary-General accordingly suggested that

the Security Council may wish to consider the offer of the Government of France to undertake, subject to Security Council authorization, a French-commanded multinational operation in conjunction with other Member States, under Chapter VII of the Charter of the United Nations, to assure the security and protection of displaced persons and civilians at risk in Rwanda.

The multinational force was to be deployed for a minimum of three months before the Chapter VI mission of UNAMIR could be brought up to the necessary strength.[174] In Resolution 929(1994), the Council welcomed the French offer

in order to achieve the objectives of the United Nations in Rwanda through the establishment of a temporary operation under national command and control aimed at contributing, in an impartial way, to the security and protection of displaced persons, refugees and civilians at risk in Rwanda[,]

and authorized the French-led force under Chapter VII to conduct the operation using all necessary means for achieving these objectives (paragraphs 2–3).

The authorization of the Multi-National Force in Haiti under Chapter VII saw the articulation in practice of criteria as to the establishment of a secure environment.[175] Paragraph 8 of Resolution 940(1994) specified that

---

[172] Sarooshi, n 129 above, 262; T Gazzini, 'NATO's Role in the Collective Security System', 8 *Journal of Conflict and Security Law* (2003), 231 at 236.

[173] S/PV.3575, 3.

[174] Letter dated 19 June 1994 from the Secretary-General addressed to the President of the Security Council, S/1994/728, 20 June 1994, paras 11–12.

[175] For the background see Chapter 3 above.

the multinational force will terminate its mission and UNMIH will assume the full range of its functions ... when a secure and stable environment has been established and UNMIH has adequate force capability and structure to assume the full range of its functions; the determination will be made by the Security Council, taking into account recommendations from the Member States of the multinational force, which are based on the assessment of the commander of the multinational force, and from the Secretary-General.

In the preamble to Resolution 944(1994), the Council reaffirmed 'the objectives of the urgent departure of the *de facto* authorities, the prompt return of the legitimately elected President Jean-Bertrand Aristide, and the restoration of the legitimate authorities of the Government of Haiti'. By Resolution 948(1994) the Council welcomed the restoration of the lawful authorities and the return of President Aristide to Haiti. On 19 January 1995, states that had contributed to the Force established under Resolution 940 wrote to the Security Council, and recommended terminating the authorization. It was pointed out that

a secure and stable environment now exists in Haiti, and the States members of the multinational force recommend that the Security Council determine that it is appropriate for the United Nations Mission in Haiti (UNMIH) to begin assuming the full range of its functions. ... Security Council Resolution 940(1994) authorized the multinational force to facilitate the departure from Haiti of the military leadership, the return of President Aristide and the restoration of the legitimate authorities of the Government of Haiti, and to establish and maintain a secure and stable environment that would permit the implementation of the Governor's Island agreement. All of these goals and more have been accomplished.[176]

In 2004, the Council once again used Article 42 in relation to Haiti. Resolution 1542 (2004) defined the principal element of the MINUSTAH mandate as follows: 'in support of the Transitional Government, to ensure a secure and stable environment within which the constitutional and political process in Haiti can take place'. MINUSTAH activity involved a combination of violations of mandate, particularly of the requirements of necessity and proportionality; and of specific breaches of international law that were not operation-related. MINUSTAH personnel committed independent breaches of international law such as murder, unlawful detention, and rape.[177]

On 6 July 2005, MINUSTAH forces led a full-fledged military attack on armed gangs in Cité Soleil, having expended a voluminous and indiscriminate 22,000 rounds of ammunition over the course of 7 hours, killed around 30 people, and caused severe damage to property. MINUSTAH has acknowledged the inevitable 'risk of civilian casualties' and 'unintended targets,' given the 'flimsy construction of homes in Cite Soleil', the 'large quantity of ammunition expended', and the 'nature of such missions in dense populated urban areas'.[178] But any regard for humanitarian law would have led MINUSTAH to consider the principles of necessity and

---

[176] *Recommendation of the States members of the multinational force in Haiti to the Security Council on the situation in Haiti*, S/1995/55, 3.

[177] For details see M Halling and B Bookey, 'Peacekeeping in Name Alone: Accountability for the United Nations in Haiti', 31 *Hastings International and Comparative Law Review* (2008), 461 at 465–7.

[178] Ibid, 464–5, 470.

proportionality, take precautions in attack, and (if excessive casualties seemed likely) then cancel it, as required by the I 1977 Additional Protocol to the 1949 Geneva Conventions. As the UN is bound by humanitarian law, the mandate conferred on forces under its Chapter VII authorization and its resolutions cannot be interpreted as contemplating or authorizing violations of this body of law.

(e) Authorizations to Use Force to Repel an Armed Attack: Korea

Under Resolution 83(1950) and while the Soviet representative was absent from the Council, the Security Council described the attack by North Korean forces against the Republic of Korea across the 38th parallel as a 'breach of the peace' under Article 39 and 'recommend[ed] that the members of the United Nations furnish such assistance to the Republic of Korea as may be necessary to repel the armed attack and to restore the international peace and security in the area'. By Resolution 84(1950), the Council authorized the deployment of a unified force under US command (the USA was also to appoint the commander), and authorized the force to use the United Nations flag (paragraphs 3–5).

The outer limit of the mandate under Resolution 83 became disputed once the operation was under way. The Secretary-General was opposed to pressing the conflict beyond the 38th parallel. However, the United States, which had 'unified command' over the forces, pressed ahead with this plan which led to Chinese intervention in the conflict, the bombing of bridges on the Yalu river, the involvement of Chinese nationalist troops, and the imposition of an economic and arms blockade on China, and culminated in a political and military stalemate.[179] This went much further than could be interpreted into the authorization under Resolution 83 or related resolutions of the Security Council.

The Korean situation also witnessed an attempt by the General Assembly to redefine the objectives set by the Council for the UN forces in Korea, lending support to the US interpretation of its UN mandate.[180] In the preamble to Resolution 376(1950), the Assembly acknowledged how the relevant Security Council resolution specified the objectives of the operation in Korea, yet proclaimed that the objective of General Assembly resolutions on the subject was the establishment of a unified, democratic, and independent Korea. Consequently, the Assembly recommended that the UN forces should stay in Korea until they accomplished these tasks (paragraph 1(a)–(c)), that is, until they could reunite Korea by force. This not only went beyond the objectives specified by the Security Council, but also contravened Article 12 of the Charter, which requires that the Assembly refrain from making recommendations in matters on which the Council has taken action.

Furthermore, the Korean case demonstrates differences in wording between objectives specified by the Assembly and those of the Council. If the Council's

---

[179] Houck, n 170 above, 14.
[180] Cf ibid.

objectives had been similar to that of the Assembly, the former would have been formulated accordingly, which would have been perfectly possible had the Council agreed to do this while the USSR was absent from its meetings. But the difference in wording demonstrates that the words 'restore international peace and security in the area' have no independent impact in determining the outer limit of the operation, let alone in providing an objective going far beyond the more specific objective to repel the North Korean armed attack.

The principal lesson of the operation in Korea—legal as well as political—is that, along with being illegal under the UN Charter, this operation was not carried out in accordance with a mandate that would have guided its legality, had its initiation been lawful in the first place. The implications of this operation went far beyond the intentions of the Security Council, and it appears unlikely that it would ever have received multilateral endorsement had those implications been foreseen in advance.

(f) The Uses and Non-Uses of Article 42 in the Case of Iraq

(i) *The Scope of the Authorization to Use Force to End the Iraqi Occupation of Kuwait under Resolution 678(1990)*

The most acute controversy over interpreting authorization clauses in resolutions arose in the context of the Iraqi invasion of Kuwait in 1990 and the US-led coalition war against Iraq in 2003. The initial cause of controversy related to interpretations of paragraph 2 in Resolution 678(1990), whereby the Council authorized member States cooperating with Kuwait 'to use all necessary means to uphold and implement Resolution 660(1990) and all subsequent relevant resolutions and to restore international peace and security in the area'. The extent of this authorization has been discussed in terms of whether the amount of force used against, and damage caused to, Iraq was proportionate to the objective of inducing Iraq to withdraw from Kuwait. A use of force not necessary within the meaning of that resolution would contravene its terms.[181] Another question is whether and to what extent coalition states were entitled to determine what the objective of the authorization was.

It is doctrinally contended that the open-ended language in Resolution 678 could, 'on its face', have been interpreted as authorizing the use of force up to the point of removing the Iraqi regime and occupying Iraq for some time, if that had been deemed necessary to restore peace in the area, just as Resolution 83 had been interpreted as permitting the crossing of the 38th parallel. It is acknowledged, however, that 'this would have been contrary to the intentions of both the Council and the coalition members at the time'.[182] Had that interpretation been correct, it would have led to coalition forces simply abandoning the tasks the Security Council had allocated to them.

---

[181] Quigley, n 125 above, 279; Kaikobad, n 126 above, 335.
[182] Matheson, n 61 above, 146–7; Houck, n 170 above, 16; Greenwood regards this as central to the justification of the use of force against Iraq in 2003: C Greenwood, 'The Legality of the Use of Force: Iraq in 2003', in Bothe, O'Connell and Ronzitti, n 153 above, 387 at 414; EV Rostow, 'Until What? Enforcement Action or Collective Self-Defence?', 85 AJIL (1991), 506 at 514, 516; Weston, n 141 above, 525–6.

According to Weston, the phrase 'to restore international peace and security in the area' left obvious room for interpretative and operational manoeuvre. This provision leaves the source of authority unstated, fails to state limitations on the means permissible to achieve the stated goal, and imposes no time limits.[183] Sarooshi considers that the allegedly open-ended and unrestricted authorization of the use of force under Resolution 678 renders unlawful that part of the resolution which authorizes an open-ended military action.[184] If Resolution 678 indeed authorized an open-ended military action, it should be treated as void on account of deliberately granting an authorization that was unnecessary and disproportionate to the objective stated in this and preceding resolutions. The use of interpretation methods, however, can clarify whether the Council intended a decision as far-reaching as that.

The argument is made that Resolution 678 has not lapsed because of the passage of time, on the ground that

there is no principle that Security Council resolutions lapse after a particular time. Unless the Council sets a time limit on the life of a resolution, it remains in force until its purpose is achieved or the Council decides to terminate it. . . . Then it necessarily follows that there remained scope for military action being taken under that resolution and thus for military action being taken without the need for an entirely fresh 'all necessary means' resolution to be adopted.[185]

However Resolution 678 should be interpreted in accordance with its object and purpose. The clear intention of the Council was to authorize the use of force to liberate Kuwait, no broader. For broader objectives a fresh authorization should have been obtained.[186] Authorization may be given either in relation to a specific time frame or in relation to specific conduct. If a conduct is authorized, authorization lapses as soon as that conduct is performed. The crucial point relates not to the resolution's duration in force, but to the performance of an act or conduct it authorizes. In the only instance where Resolution 1441(2002) substantially refers to Resolution 678, it is clear that 'Resolution 678 (1990) authorized Member States to use all necessary means to uphold and implement its Resolution 660(1990) of 2 August 1990 and all relevant resolutions subsequent to Resolution 660(1990) [and inevitably limited to those adopted before Resolution 678] and to restore international peace and security in the area'.

Greenwood contends that if the phrase 'restore peace and security in the area' refers merely to the liberation of Kuwait then it is redundant, and moreover 'the liberation of Kuwait could lawfully have been accomplished anyway by the exercise of the right of collective self-defence'.[187] Presumption against redundancy is assuredly an accepted principle of interpretation and certainly applies to Security

---

[183] Weston, ibid, 525–6.
[184] Sarooshi, n 129 above, 179–80.
[185] Greenwood, n 182 above, 406–7, 410.
[186] Lobel and Ratner, n 144 above, 124, 128, 140, 145.
[187] Greenwood, n 182 above, 405; Greenwood, n 150 above, 170; Kaikobad submits along identical lines that 'an interpretation [of Resolution 678] consistent with the fulfilment of the Council's functions is preferable to one predicated on minimizing its powers': Kaikobad, n 126 above, 355–6.

Council resolutions. However, the problem in this case can be resolved by a contextual reading of Resolution 678 which sees the 'breach of the peace' in Iraq's invasion of Kuwait—no other event—and thus authorized the Chapter VII force to deal with, and 'restore peace and security in the area' after, that 'breach of the peace'. Once this 'breach of the peace' had been reversed, peace and security in the area would be restored. No genuine problem of redundancy arises in interpreting Resolution 678, because the objective—additional to liberation of Kuwait—of 'restoring peace and security in the area' has never been detailed by the Council.

As for the self-defence argument, the only cause of action the Council identified under Article 39 was the response to an invasion. There is no obvious contradiction in an invasion of a state (which normally activates the right to self-defence) being also characterized as a 'breach of the peace' under Chapter VII. Otherwise, one must suppose that the members of the Council knew that collective self-defence was an available option and went on to authorize something else, but neither knew nor defined what it was.

If, at the time that Kuwait was occupied by Iraq, the Council had identified a threat requiring measures going beyond the liberation of Kuwait, it would have made an extended determination under Article 39 to justify such measures. Therefore the Council cannot be taken as having authorized the use of force going far beyond the need to deal with the 'breach of the peace' that was most pressing at that time. If the context of Resolution 678 is examined, it becomes clear that none of the resolutions from 660 onwards has identified any objective for Chapter VII action against Iraq other than its withdrawal from Kuwait. Resolution 678 did not justify restoring 'peace and security in the area' by pushing the offensive to Baghdad back in 1991. It is even less plausible that such an implied objective, absent in 1991, could have persisted as late as 2003.

(ii) The Claims as to the Authorization of the Use of Force to Invade Iraq in 2003

As Matheson pointed out, concerning the 2003 invasion of Iraq, the US legal justification is heavily dependent on interpretation of the relevant Security Council resolutions.[188] Normal methods of interpretation should be used. While the argument that Security Council resolutions employ intentional, or deliberate, ambiguity in justifying the use of force is popular in certain quarters, it is conceptually unsound, because it envisages that the legal position or entitlement might be pronounced through a non-decision—a decision not to decide. In realistic terms, if members of the Council decide not to decide, or agree to disagree as to, whether to authorize the use of force, then it inevitably follows that there is no collective decision that the pertinent use of force has been authorized.

The UK argument centred around the following points: Resolution 687(1991) suspended but did not terminate the authority to use force under Resolution 678; a

---

[188] Matheson, n 61 above, 150.

material breach of Resolution 687 would revive the authority under Resolution 678; Resolution 1441(2002) determined that Iraq was in material breach of Resolution 687; the authority to use force thus revived.[189] Upholding this approach, Greenwood has also argued that the restoration of peace and security under Resolution 678 required a partial disarmament of Iraq and other measures under Resolution 687.[190]

It is unclear how a breach of Resolution 687 would reactivate the authorization granted by Resolution 678, which was adopted considerably earlier and made no reference to an obligation to disarm. The revival argument is thus inevitably premised on the assumption that Resolution 687 carried forward an authorization under Resolution 678 which by then had already achieved its purpose, *and* expanded its remit to encompass the enforcement of an obligation on Iraq to disarm to which Resolution 678 had made no reference. This is too broad to be implied into Resolution 687, namely in its mere reference to cease-fire between the Coalition and Iraq. Dinstein denotes as wrong the British position that the Coalition use of force in 2003 was based on reviving the authorization to use force under Resolution 678. That resolution had nothing to do with the attacks a dozen years later.[191]

Resolution 687 was adopted *well after* Kuwait had been liberated and peace and security restored as required by Resolution 678. The preamble of Resolution 687 capitalizes on the achievement of Resolution 678's objectives. It 'welcom[es] the restoration to Kuwait of its sovereignty, independence and territorial integrity and the return of its legitimate Government' and '[r]eaffirm[s] the need to be assured of Iraq's peaceful intentions in the light of its unlawful invasion and occupation of Kuwait'. In addition, the Council identifies the essentially new objective 'of achieving balanced and comprehensive control of armaments in the region'. It was this additional objective, unrelated to the original authorization of the use of force under Resolution 678, which led the Council to impose disarmament obligations on Iraq. Resolution 687 was adopted as a forward-looking instrument designed to deal with the legacy of war in its multiple dimensions.

Resolution 1441(2002) referred in paragraph 1 to Iraq's failure to cooperate with UN inspectors and the IAEA, and to the need to complete the actions required

---

[189] *The Use of Force against Iraq*, The Attorney-General's Opinion, 52 ICLQ (2003), 811 at 811–12; see also, along the similar lines, the Memorandum on Advice to the Australian Government on the Use of Force against Iraq prepared by the Attorney-General's Department and Foreign Ministry of Australia, 4 *Melbourne Journal of International Law* (2003), paras 14–17, claiming among other things that authorization under Resolution 678 had not expired.

[190] Greenwood, n 182 above, 414.

[191] Dinstein, n 124 above, 300; further referring to Article 40 of the 1907 Hague Regulations on resuming hostilities where a cease-fire has been breached, Y Dinstein, 'Sovereignty, the Security Council and the Use of Force', in Bothe *et al.* (ed.) n 153 above, 111 at 119. But this confuses *jus in bello* with *jus ad bellum*: Article 40 refers to the belligerent action in an ongoing armed conflict while the use of force by the US-led Coalition against Iraq raised questions whether they were entitled in the first place to use force and start a new armed conflict. In addition, the cease-fire was not broken by Iraq; instead, one of the conditions on which the cease-fire was initially granted had been violated. That condition was an original condition of the cease-fire and, once a cease-fire had been agreed, it would last until breached.

under Resolution 687. Paragraph 2 afforded Iraq 'a final opportunity to comply with its disarmament obligations under relevant resolutions of the Council'. This means that the Council was to pronounce whether that final opportunity had been missed and what the implications were.

The UK Attorney-General identified 'the narrow but key question' as 'on the true interpretation of Resolution 1441, what has the Security Council decided will be the consequences of Iraq's failure to comply with the enhanced regime'?[192] The key therefore is the outcome that obtains after the meaning of Resolution 1441 has been ascertained through the proper use of interpretation methods. Given that Security Council resolutions are agreements among the Council members that express their collective will, intention, and decision, it has to be ascertained whether the text of Resolution 1441 reveals evidence that Council members agreed—that is, collectively decided—to again authorize the use of force against Iraq.

In this respect the Attorney-General referred to paragraphs 4, 11, and 12 of Resolution 1441, in which the Council determined that Iraq was in material breach of its disarmament obligations, instructed the Chairman of the United Nations Monitoring, Verification, and Inspection Commission (UNMOVIC) to report Iraq's obstruction of inspections to the Council, and stipulated that it would reconvene upon the receipt of this report. Admitting, impliedly at least, that these paragraphs did not contain anything that would resemble the authorization to use force, the Attorney-General proceeded to assert that 'the text is, however, ambiguous and unclear on what happens next'. This contrasts with a somewhat stronger position expressed earlier by the British government that paragraph 12 did not

mean that no further action can be taken without a new resolution of the Council. Had that been the intention, it would have provided that the Council would decide what is needed to be done to restore international peace and security, not that it would consider the matter. The choice of words was deliberate; a proposal that there should be a requirement for a decision by the Council, a position maintained by several Council members, was not adopted.[193]

Similarly, the Attorney-General pointed out that the French and Russian proposals to include a requirement for a second resolution were rejected.[194] But this approach hardly fits with any accepted method of interpreting Security Council resolutions. Resolutions should be interpreted in terms of what their text says *and* in a way compatible with what the Council is allowed to do under the Charter; not by reference to what they do not say. Rejection of the proposal to include the requirement for a second resolution does not amount to the Council's collective decision that a second resolution was not needed. A strong affirmation of the primacy of the ordinary meaning of the text of the resolution follows from the approach taken by the International Court in the *Namibia* case, that the failure by

---

[192] Attorney-General's Advice on the Iraq War: Resolution 1441, 54 ICLQ (2005), 767 at 770.
[193] n 189 above, 814.
[194] n 192 above, 771.

an international organ to adopt a particular proposal does not equate to its support for the opposite proposal.[195]

The issue whether a second resolution was needed to authorize the use of force is essentially the same as whether Resolution 1441 authorized it. Were a second resolution not needed, that would be the case precisely because Resolution 1441 already provided sufficient basis for the use of force, and vice versa. Against this background, the Attorney-General's Opinion locates no evidence in Resolution 1441 other than the finding of a breach of Resolution 687 and the need to discuss reports concerning it. There is simply nothing in this resolution relating to the use of force, which constitutes a separate, major, generically different issue too important to be implied into what is mentioned regarding breach, reporting, and discussion, thus requiring a separate decision in addition to that which found a 'material breach'. The very essence of operative paragraph 12 is to enable the Council to discuss the matter and design a response, as opposed to abdicating the Council's responsibility in favour of a unilateral use of force.

There was thus no collective intention expressed by the Council that this material breach revitalized any previous Article 42 authorization or granted a new one. Even if paragraph 12 is read narrowly, to require only the convening of the Council to consider the situation, that does not alter the position, because authorization of the use of force under the Charter remains the decision of the Council only and Resolution 1441 contains no trace of such authorization having been given. It is the Council that had threatened Iraq with 'serious consequences' and only the Council could authorize action in consequence.[196] It cannot be sensibly assumed that the Council collectively identified material breach of the cease-fire under Resolution 687 and then abdicated the right to decide on response to individual states. On the whole, the text of Resolution 1441 contains no indication that the use of force was thereby authorized, which conclusion is reinforced by the heavy difference of views within the Council, both at the time when this resolution was adopted and in March 2003.

Since the Council made cease-fire with Iraq, only the Council could determine the existence of a material breach and resume hostilities.[197] The Attorney-General's Opinion actually confirms this point by referring to the difference between the US and British views, the former asserting that the Council's inaction coupled with the determination of a 'material breach' under Resolution 1441 already constituted authorization, and the latter holding that it is actually the discussion within the Council under operative paragraph 12 that will clarify 'that military action is appropriate', but 'no further decision is required because of the terms of Resolution 1441'.[198] The US position is premised on some general right to unilaterally enforce Security Council resolutions, at times put forward together with the self-defence

---

[195] *Namibia, ICJ Reports*, 1971, 36, para 69.
[196] In fact, Resolution 1154(1998) likewise threatened Iraq with 'severest consequences' but this has not been regarded as justifying unilateral uses of force.
[197] Lobel and Ratner, n 144 above, 150; *per contra* Dinstein, n 124 above, 299–300.
[198] n 192 above, 773.

argument (as per the US statement in the Council). As for the British position, the only way the Council could clarify that anything was appropriate is to adopt a collective decision or statement manifesting its collective position. If such a decision is not adopted, it cannot be sensibly contended that the Council has thought that any action is 'appropriate'. If, on the other hand, the terms of Resolution 1441 actually amount to an authorization, it becomes unclear why the Council's additional discussion of the appropriateness of what had already been authorized would be needed. The matter then reverts to analysis of the terms of Resolution 1441 to clarify whether they authorize the use of force and, as becomes clear, they do not.

The statement of explanation of vote for Resolution 1441 by US Ambassador Negroponte specifies that the resolution contained no 'hidden triggers' and no 'automaticity' of the use of force. The procedure to be followed was laid out in the resolution. If the Council failed to act decisively in the event of further Iraqi violations, the resolution did not constrain any member State from acting to defend itself against the threat posed by that country, or to enforce relevant resolutions and protect world peace and security.[199]

Thus, the United States conceded that the resolution contained neither direct nor suspended authorization of the use of force against Iraq. No recourse thus had been made to Article 42. Nonetheless, the statement claimed the right to 'act' against a 'threat' posed by Iraq in a sense broader than the use of force in self-defence in response to an armed attack, and also claimed the right to unilaterally enforce Security Council resolutions even though those resolutions, on their faces and according to the US view in the Security Council, did not contain any authorization of the use of force against Iraq. Thus the US representative did not claim Resolution 1441—nor any other justification available under the Charter— as the basis for attacking Iraq; it was merely claimed that this resolution did not proscribe the attack, which was allegedly lawful on other grounds; if afterwards the Council did not grant authorization, the USA and its allies would act in self-defence against the threat, in other words pre-emptively. It seems that reliance has been placed on pre-emptive self-defence without any armed attack having been demonstrated,[200] for it is difficult to see what other meaning the words 'defend the United States' could possess in the context of international law. By claiming this extra-Charter justification for the use of force, the US position amounts to an invalid claim. This is further confirmed by the British position that, much as the USA had been arguing for pre-emptive self-defence, beyond imminence this doctrine is not part of international law.[201] There is also a doctrinal opinion that the pre-emptive nature of the US and coalition action does not render an otherwise lawful action unlawful.[202]

---

[199] Security Council 4644th Meeting, SC Press Release SC/7564; S/2003/351.
[200] Greenwood, n 182 above, 401–2, disputes the point that the US government used the self-defence argument.
[201] n 192 above, 768.
[202] Greenwood, n 182 above, 402; W Taft and T Buchwald, 'Preemption, Iraq and International Law', 97 AJIL (2007), 557.

This compellingly evidences that the basis for the Iraq war claimed by the US Government was both pre-emptive self-defence and the unilateral enforcement of a Security Council resolution which does not itself authorize the use of force. The British argument on the other hand relied on revival of the authorization of the use of force under Resolution 678 and consequently on the automaticity of the use of force under Resolution 1441, but did not rely on self-defence. Thus, states who went to war against Iraq in 2003 advanced diverse and to some extent mutually exclusive justifications for that war. This precludes even the remote possibility of identifying any general practice or legal judgment as the basis on which the war against Iraq could be considered as lawful.

According to the statement jointly issued on the same occasion by Russia, China, and France,

Resolution 1441(2002) adopted today by the Security Council excludes any automaticity in the use of force. In this regard, we register with satisfaction the declarations of the representatives of the United States and the United Kingdom confirming this understanding in their explanations of vote.... In case of failure by Iraq to comply with its obligations, the provisions of paragraphs 4, 11 and 12 will apply. Such failure will be reported to the Security Council by the Executive Chairman of UNMOVIC or the Director General of the IAEA. It will be then for the Council to take position on the basis of that report.[203]

This statement was not contradicted by anyone during the process of adopting Resolution 1441.

The Attorney-General's Opinion suggests that Iraq's acceptance of disarmament obligations under Resolution 687 was a condition for the declaration of formal cease-fire.[204] Resolution 687 stated in paragraph 33 that, upon official notification by Iraq to the Secretary-General and to the Security Council of its acceptance of the disarmament and other obligations under that resolution, 'a formal cease-fire is effective between Iraq and Kuwait and the Member States cooperating with Kuwait in accordance with Resolution 678(1990)'.[205] Dinstein argues that the cease-fire under Resolution 687 had been contingent on observance by Iraq of these disarmament conditions. Under this view, 'sundry air strikes' against Iraq in the 1990s should be seen as a resumption of the use of force in response to Iraqi violations of the cease-fire. Dinstein is disinclined to view the use of force against Iraq in 2003 as pre-emptive because there is nothing pre-emptive in reacting to a breach of cease-fire. Therefore, Dinstein maintains, the violation of a cease-fire by Iraq, the adoption by the Council of Resolution 1441 in which it threatened Iraq with serious consequences, and the Iraqi refusal to cooperate justified the US-led use of force against Iraq in 2003, even though that was not specifically authorized in any

---

[203] The Arab League subsequently expressed the identical position: that Resolution 1441 did not trigger war 'either implicitly or explicitly': *The Security Council and regional organizations: facing the new challenges to international peace and security*, 11 April 2003, S/PV.4739, 15 (LAS).

[204] n 189 above, 812.

[205] Accordingly, care should be taken since, if the 'post-cease-fire revival' logic is pursued, under Resolution 687(1991) authorization of the use of force could also be revived if other arrangements were breached, such as compensation of war victims or boundary demarcation.

resolution.[206] Sarooshi, on the other hand, considers that, even though the Council's authorization under Resolution 678 was in wider terms than self-defence, it terminated with the conclusion of the cease-fire under Resolution 687 and the acceptance of its terms by Iraq.[207]

A preliminary but necessary question to ask is whether, in 1991, the Coalition would have been entitled to continue combat operations up to the point of overthrowing the Iraqi government had the latter not accepted those disarmament obligations under Resolution 687. An affirmative answer to this question cannot sensibly be given in the absence of a Council decision on this point. If one is inclined to view the effect of paragraph 33 merely as a suspension of the use of force, it would follow that a collectively authorized use of force was 'suspended' by a collective decision and its resumption (if possible at all) would likewise have needed a collective decision. This is one reason why, in the absence of any such collective decision at the time Resolution 1441 was adopted, the US representative spoke of self-defence and unilateral enforcement of Security Council resolutions. This is just a matter of speculation, however, because it was precisely Resolution 687 that welcomed the achievement of the objectives of Resolution 678 and impliedly—but inevitably—acknowledged that this authorization of the use of force had terminated.

In addition, a cease-fire was adopted under Resolution 687, but a breach of its conditions could not revive the authorization under Resolution 678, because (a) Resolution 678 was about the use of force in self-defence and the claimed use of force in 2003 was qualitatively different, having nothing to do with self-defence; (b) the standard meaning of cease-fire in international law is that it is broken and hostilities can resume when one of the belligerents acts in a way that violates the cease-fire itself. For instance, if two belligerent parties agree a cease-fire for a specified period on the condition that one belligerent frees 50 prisoners captured from another belligerent, and later frees only 25 prisoners, that would certainly be a proper reason not to take that belligerent's promises at face value on subsequent occasions, but not for the actual resumption of hostilities before the specified period expires, because the cease-fire has not actually been violated.

The 1907 Regulations respecting the Laws and Customs of War on Land (Hague Regulations) confirm this approach, as they treat cease-fire as violated only once a belligerent actually resumes hostilities and say nothing about the right of an adversary to resume hostilities merely in response to the breach of conditions on which the cease-fire was agreed. According to Article 40, the threshold for resuming hostilities is high, because only a 'serious violation of the armistice by one of the parties gives the other party the right of denouncing it, and even, in cases of urgency, of recommencing hostilities immediately'.[208] If so, it is plainly obvious that the mere violation of an antecedent condition upon which the

---

[206] Dinstein, n 124 above, 296–300.
[207] Sarooshi, n 129 above, 181–2.
[208] The distinction between a cease-fire and an armistice is blurred in practice. The regulations governing armistice are applied analogously to cease-fires. The right to resume hostilities in response to a breach of armistice or cease-fire operates as an aspect of self-defence, not a punitive right. Hostilities may be resumed only if necessary and proportionate as a matter of self-defence: C Greenwood, 'Scope

cease-fire was agreed—still less a presumed and unproved violation as was the case with Iraq in 2003—can have no such effect.

Consequently, even if, in 2002–3, Iraq had been in material breach of Resolution 687, this material breach could only relate to its substantive obligations under that resolution, not to the cease-fire in a war between itself and Kuwait that had long been over by then. The remedy for such cases is given in paragraph 34 of the resolution (the Council to take further steps), as opposed to reading in a non-existent authorization of the use of force.

In addition, and despite the semantics, what happened in 1991 between the Coalition States and Iraq was not really a cease-fire but a termination of hostilities, an end to a war. Resolution 686(1991) specified in its preamble and paragraph 8 'the rapid establishment of a definitive end to the hostilities' as an aim. Even if Resolution 687 had spoken of a cease-fire, this has to be seen as a stage towards 'a definitive end to the hostilities' as envisaged earlier, not as a temporary break in hostilities, if the Council's entire position is to be construed consistently. Both the preamble and paragraph 6 of Resolution 687 manifest the Council's intention to bring the 'military presence in Iraq to an end as soon as possible consistent with paragraph 8 of Resolution 686'. In line with this, Coalition troops soon left the war zone, which ended the cease-fire and resulted in the definitive end to hostilities. The 'revival' argument advanced in 2003 is essentially not about resumption of hostilities after cease-fire as a matter of *jus in bello*, but the start of a new armed conflict as a matter of *jus ad bellum*.

(iii) The Scope of the Article 42 Authorization after the Invasion: Resolutions 1483(2003) and 1546(2004)

After the US-led invasion of Iraq and the overthrow of the Hussein regime, the Security Council engaged with this situation to meet realities that again required its Chapter VII action. Resolution 1483(2003) does not validate the presence of US-led coalition troops in Iraq after they invaded that country in March 2003. By a letter of 8 May 2003, the US and UK governments informed the Council that a provisional coalition authority had been established in Iraq to enable the performance of disarmament and humanitarian tasks. They defined the tasks of the authority as deterring hostilities, maintaining the territorial integrity of Iraq and securing Iraq's borders, disabling and rendering harmless the Iraqi weapons of mass destruction, combating terrorism, and improving the humanitarian situation.[209] Whether or not this was actually intended by the leaders of the coalition, the Security Council approved a somewhat different vision of the coalition presence. The Council fell short of granting a Chapter VII mandate to the coalition states, and instead recognized in the preamble of Resolution 1483 'the specific authorities,

---

of Application of Humanitarian Law', in D Fleck (ed.), *The Handbook of International Humanitarian Law* (New York: Oxford University Press, 2008), 67–9.

[209] Letter from the Permanent Representatives of the UK and the US, 8 May 2003, S/2003/538.

responsibilities, and obligations under applicable international law of these States as occupying powers under unified command', even though the coalition letter had not referred to the law of occupation. The Council's attitude is thus premised on a simple distinction between approval of the coalition presence as part of a UN exercise of the relevant powers, and recognition of the mere fact that coalition troops were already in Iraq, their presence being governed—independently of the Council's intervention—by the law of occupation. This body of law can obviously justify the coalition's powers over the security of the population, but only to the extent that this follows from the Fourth Geneva Convention and correlates with other responsibilities of the occupying power. It is thus important to see that the Council did not give the coalition any new Chapter VII powers, nor in any way approve their invasion of or presence in Iraq in legal terms.

The British government's position has been that Resolution 1483 did not give the Coalition 'full legislative and executive authority in Iraq', nor any authority to control the political process in Iraq, nor engineer any outcome. The call in paragraph 4 to establish an 'effective administration' in Iraq did not substantially add to the powers that the coalition possessed as an occupying power. The resolution allocated an advisory role to the Iraqi Interim Administration in relation to the disbursement of monies from the Development Fund established under paragraphs 13 and 14 of this resolution.[210] This went hand-in-hand with a requirement under paragraph 9 that the progressive transfer of power had to be effected from the Coalition to IIA. Still, the Coalition possessed some discretion in disbursing the funds, owing to the residual category 'other purposes' to which paragraph 14 referred. It was therefore important to ensure that the US government took no action in relation to the Fund that was incompatible with the resolution.[211] Even though these arrangements could at times look ambiguous, the resolution has clearly set a limit on what the occupying powers are allowed to do. This is because Resolution 1483 does not authorize any deal regarding natural resources to be made without the consent of the Iraqi people, and requires respect for their right to self-determination and permanent sovereignty over their natural resources.[212]

---

[210] According to paragraph 14, the 'Development Fund for Iraq shall be used in a transparent manner to meet the humanitarian needs of the Iraqi people, for the economic reconstruction and repair of Iraq's infrastructure, for the continued disarmament of Iraq, and for the costs of Iraqi civilian administration, and for other purposes benefiting the people of Iraq'. Paragraphs 17 and 20 specify that Iraq's petroleum revenues would be transferred to the Fund. A total of $9 billion was eventually transferred: Matheson n 61 above, 89. The arrangements regarding the Development Fund were terminated by the Council by its resolution 1956(2010), with effect from 30 June 2011.

[211] This position was articulated in a letter from Catherine Adams of the Legal Secretariat to the Law Officers, Attorney-General's Chambers, to the Foreign Office, *Iraq: Effect of Security Council Resolution 1483 on the Authority of the Occupying Powers*, 9 June 2003, paras 6, 8, 11–16.

[212] This point was the most acutely raised in deliberations, and the need to safeguard the permanent sovereignty of Iraq over its natural resources was explicitly emphasized by representatives of the United Kingdom, Spain, Mexico, the Russian Federation, Guinea, Chile, Angola, and Pakistan: S/PV.4761, at 5–15. The representatives emphasized that the Iraqi people are the owners of their oil resources, and some even linked this issue with the right of peoples to self-determination (Guinea, Russian Federation, Spain: S/PV.4761, at 6–9). The representative of Mexico was more specific in saying that Resolution 1483 'does not authorize the establishment of long-term commitments that would alienate the sovereignty of the Iraqi people over its petroleum resources': S/PV.4761, 7.

This conclusion is reinforced by the fact that under Resolution 1483 the powers of the authority are regarded as conditional on the formation of an Iraqi government to take over administration of the country, and the supervision of the coalition authority by the UN Mission in Iraq. Likewise, paragraph 1 of Resolution 1511 (2003) states that the presence of the coalition in Iraq is temporary. Corresponding limits on the Council's powers were articulated by the French representative in the Council when Resolution 1546(2004) was adopted, specifying that 'the sovereign Government may at any time ask that the mandate of the multinational force be revised or that it end, and such a request will be binding on the Security Council'.[213]

Resolution 1546 proclaimed the end of the occupation of Iraq, granted Chapter VII status to the presence of the US-led Multinational Force, since that had been agreed to by the new Iraqi government, and subjected that Force to the law of occupation under the Fourth Geneva Convention, even though the state of occupation had formally come to an end. The Council's emphasis on the Iraqi government's consent confirms that it has viewed that consent as a condition of the legality of the Force's presence in Iraq and consequently of its own competence in terms of approving that presence. The Council's overall approach thus seems to be premised on the need to act within the limits of applicable international law— including the principle of territorial supremacy of states and humanitarian law— which also factors in the proportionality equation.

Paragraphs 10 and 11 regarding the entitlements of coalition forces may be far-reaching but they fall short of authorizing the coalition to undertake military operations without the consent of the Iraqi government and must hence be construed as requiring that consent for coalition operations either as the government's policy decision or in individual cases.[214] As France pointed out when Resolution 1546 was adopted,

the resolution indicates that the interim Government and the multinational force will have to reach an agreement, but it does not specify what would happen in the event of disagreement. That is why France would have preferred that the text state that the Iraqi interim Government, sovereign in the territory of Iraq, would have the final say in such a case. As that provision was not explicitly requested by the Iraqi leaders, France was satisfied at the final adjustment made to paragraph 11 of the provision. Moreover, France cannot imagine that the multinational force would go against the opinion of Iraq's sovereign Government.[215]

As the *Namibia* approach also confirms, not including a 'final say' clause does not represent denial of the Iraqi government's right to have a final say on operations.

In general a strict construction of the authorizing clauses under Resolution 1546 is most appropriate. In the *Al-Jedda* case before the UK House of Lords,[216] the

---

[213] S/PV.4987, 7.

[214] Indeed, as the British representative pointed out in the Council, 'the aim will be agreement on the full range of fundamental security and policy issues, including policy on sensitive operations': ibid, 3.

[215] Ibid, 8.

[216] *R (on the application of Al-Jedda) (FC) (Appellant)* v *Secretary of State for Defence (Respondent)*, Appellate Committee, [2007] UKHL 58, Judgment of 12 December 2007; see further A Orakhelashvili, case review on *Al-Jedda*, 103 AJIL (2008).

issue arose as to whether the detention of Mr Al-Jedda by British troops in Iraq had been consistent with the authorization under paragraph 10 of Resolution 1546 that

the multinational force shall have the authority to take all necessary measures to contribute to the maintenance of security and stability in Iraq in accordance with the letters annexed to this resolution expressing, inter alia, the Iraqi request for the continued presence of the multinational force and setting out its tasks, including by preventing and deterring terrorism.

But it is not clear at all that the pertinent Security Council resolutions have actually authorized and justified detentions like the one involved in *Al-Jedda*. Security Council resolutions must be interpreted in accordance with the plain and ordinary meaning of their text.[217] To apply this approach to the House of Lords' analysis, and broad as the authorization of the MNF under paragraph 10 of Resolution 1546 may be, it does not specifically refer to, nor inherently imply, the power of the MNF to intern or detain individuals in violation of the applicable human rights and humanitarian law. The letter of the US Secretary of State, by reference to which Resolution 1546 was adopted and of which it forms part, emphasizes that the MNF needs to be able to intern individuals 'where this is necessary for imperative reasons of security, and the continued search for and securing of weapons that threaten Iraq's security'. However, the letter of the Secretary of State proceeds to state that 'the forces that make up the MNF are and will remain committed at all times to act consistently with their obligations under the law of armed conflict, including the Geneva Conventions'. Thus, the Security Council itself subjected the enforcement activities of the MNF to the requirements of the Geneva Conventions. The detention in question was approved by the House of Lords even though it offended against human rights and humanitarian law, since the House of Lords deemed the authorization to detain notwithstanding these bodies of law—not granted in reality—prevailed over Mr Al-Jedda's right. In this respect the *Al-Jedda* case results in a unilateral interpretation of a Security Council resolution by a state, to the detriment of the collective decision on which that resolution is based.

(g) The Use of Force under Chapter VII and the Humanitarian Crisis in Somalia

Resolution 794(1992) was adopted after the Secretary-General reported to the Council that the UN, through UNOSOM I, established in April 1992 under Resolution 751(1992), had been unable to perform its humanitarian mission in Somalia, due to the aggressive position of the faction led by General Aidid, especially its attacks on UN troops and humanitarian missions.[218] The Secretary-General's reports suggest parameters of necessity and proportionality for the UN-authorized operation, observing that the principal task was to ensure the

---

[217] See Chapter 2 above.
[218] Hutchinson, n 143 above, 628–9; for a useful analysis see C Philipp, 'Somalia—A Very Special Case', 9 *Max-Planck Yearbook of UN Law* (2005), 517.

uninterrupted delivery of humanitarian assistance.[219] One option was to continue the deployment of UNOSOM as a consensual peace-keeping mission requiring the consent of the factions; but the situation had deteriorated beyond the point at which consensual peace keeping remained suitable; there was hardly anyone firmly in control with whom the UN could negotiate. The second option was to abandon the international military presence and let humanitarian missions negotiate with warring factions as best they could. But the Secretary-General stressed that, even though expectations for UNOSOM had not been met, an international military presence remained necessary. The Council had no alternative but to adopt more forceful measures. One possibility was to perform a show of force in Mogadishu; however, the factions operated throughout the country with substantial force and the achievement of UN objectives likewise required a country-wide operation. This brought up a fourth option—an authorized operation conducted by member States, which the United States government was ready to carry out. The Secretary-General specified that authorization for such an operation can only be granted for the purpose of securing humanitarian supplies. As soon as this security issue had been resolved, weapons brought under control, and irregulars disarmed, the US-led force would be replaced by a proper UN-led peace keeping mission. The fifth option was to authorize a UN operation under UN command and control. But under any of these options, troop deployments under Chapter VII had to be functionally and temporarily limited.[220]

Given such an identification of objectives for UN involvement, these suggestions are guided by what is necessary and proportionate for achieving these objectives. The objectives of UN involvement have been interpreted as allowing far-reaching measures such as disarmament, weapons control, and de-mining. Resolution 794 shares

the Secretary-General's assessment that the situation in Somalia is intolerable . . . , and that UNOSOM's existing course would not in present circumstances be an adequate response to the tragedy in Somalia.

The Council, acting under Chapter VII, authorized the Secretary-General and member States to take up the US offer, suggesting they 'use all necessary means to establish as soon as possible a secure environment for humanitarian relief

---

[219] Letter dated 29 November 1992 from the Secretary-General addressed to the President of the Security Council, S/24868, 30 November 1992, 1.

[220] Ibid, 2–6; it is noteworthy that, in relation the coup in Haiti and the junta's compliance with the Governor's Island Agreement (ultimately addressed through a Chapter VII operation under Resolution 940(1994)), the Secretary-General proposed two options. The first was to expand the mandate of the existing UN mission in Haiti and give it additional tasks. While this would require a Chapter VII decision, UNMIH would remain under UN command vested in the Secretary-General. This option would raise organizational and financial difficulties and thus was not recommended. The second option was a multinational force composed of troops from states which were able and willing to provide them, possibly within the OAS framework as an inter-American force. The third option was a combination of the first two options: first an action by a multinational force and then the deployment of UNMIH as a consensual peace-keeping body: *Report of the Secretary-General on the Situation in Haiti*, S/1994/828, 15 July 1994, paras 18–23.

operations in Somalia' (paragraphs 8 and 10). A Unified Task Force (UNITAF), consisting of 37,000 troops, was deployed in southern and central Somalia but not in the northern part of the country and its border areas. By January 1993, the UNITAF Commander had declared that 'all areas are stable or relatively stable'. Some disarmament operations had been carried out, but the Secretary-General emphasized that UNITAF controlled only 40 per cent of the country's territory. While UNITAF had made a positive impact on the security situation, that impact was not irreversible and conditions were still volatile.[221]

After the deployment of UNITAF the Secretary-General articulated the necessity of UNOSOM enlargement, considering that without improved security humanitarian operations would remain vulnerable to disruption. Therefore the Council had to redefine the UNOSOM mandate and authorize its enlargement. The proportionality aspect of the problem is visible from the observation that the mandate of UNOSOM II should cover the whole territory of Somalia and include disarmament.[222]

Disagreements arose over the scope of the mandate given the forces deployed to establish a 'secure environment' in Somalia under Resolution 794. The US position focused merely on humanitarian supplies. This was seen as an ambiguity, and the Secretary-General regarded the mandate as covering disarmament and de-mining tasks.[223] This posed the question whether, if the warring factions had effectively disrupted the only route through which aid can be distributed in Somalia, UN-authorized forces could move beyond their expressly designated task and break the power of the factions themselves.[224] The answer should be affirmative, because that would be encompassed by 'all necessary means' under Resolution 794, and these actions would be necessary to achieve the stated objectives. As the Secretary-General's report specified,

the objectives of the Unified Task Force would not have been achieved, nor the conditions created for the transition to peace-keeping operations, if heavy weapons and lawless gangs simply withdrew from parts of Somalia controlled by the Unified Task Force to continue their action in other parts while waiting to return and resume their harassment and exploitation of the international relief effort after the Unified Task Force had handed over control to a less numerous and powerful United Nations force.[225]

---

[221] *Further Report of the Secretary-General submitted in pursuance of paragraphs 18 and 91 of Resolution 794(1992)*, S/25354, 3 March 1993, paras 6, 55, 58.

[222] Ibid, paras 56–7.

[223] Hutchinson, n 143 above, 632, further referring to the US–UN disagreement at the stage of negotiating and adopting Resolution 794: the UN insisted on disarmament and de-mining, while the USA emphasized the priority of humanitarian supplies; Sarooshi, n 129 above, 214–15.

[224] Hutchinson, ibid, 634.

[225] *Report of the Secretary-General submitted pursuant to Paragraphs 18 and 19 of Security Council Resolution 794 (1992)*, S/24992, 19 December 1992, 9; consequently, the Secretary-General suggested that when UNOSOM took over from UNITAF, its mandate would have to be enlarged to include preventing resumption of hostilities, protecting humanitarian supply centres, de-mining, control of weapons, and protection of ports and airports: ibid, paras 31–2. The preamble to Resolution 837 (1993) also acknowledged 'the fundamental importance of completing the comprehensive and effective programme for disarming all Somali parties, including movements and factions'.

It has been suggested that the Secretary-General acted in this case as an agent of the Security Council and effectively could adopt his own interpretation of the mandate the Council had enacted, the meaning of 'secure environment' under Resolutions 794 and 837(1993) being subjected to his discretion.[226] However, apart from flying in the face of the regime for interpreting Security Council resolutions, this approach leaves open the question what the legal outcome would have been had the Secretary-General preferred a narrower interpretation of the objective stated and mandate approved by the Council? It also permits, on the face of matters and in principle at least, the possibility that two mutually conflicting interpretations as to the meaning of 'secure environment' could exist.

This controversy cannot be resolved by focusing on the role of interpretative agencies alone, because this question is only about who interprets, not which interpretation is correct. The latter question can only be clarified by reference to general principles of interpretation, among which the effectiveness principle is most prominent. It is the effective construction of 'secure environment', taking into account the factor of proportionality, which ultimately indicates the correctness of the Secretary-General's interpretation. The possibility that the Secretary-General could misconstrue the meaning of a resolution and thus be validly contradicted by an interpretation advanced by states cannot be discarded altogether—to do so is only possible by viewing the Secretary-General, or the UN as a whole, as *legibus solutus*. It is instead the effective construction of the Council's objective of ensuring the safety of humanitarian supplies—as applied to outstanding threats and disruptions by armed factions on the ground—that makes the Secretary-General's interpretation correct.

Unilateral interpretations of the mandate have occurred during the US-led operation. The US aim was to defeat Aidid's forces. Italy criticized the US for its helicopter assault on the Aidid command headquarters in Mogadishu, which resulted in 50 civilian deaths, and called upon the UN to suspend combat operations in the city.[227] The mandate and activities of UNOSOM II—the expanded UNOSOM under Resolution 814(1993)—offer an instructive view of how necessity and proportionality requirements are relevant on the ground. Under Chapter VII the enforcement power (part of the mandate of UNOSOM II) applied specifically to military matters such as disarmament and securing humanitarian supply routes. These powers did not extend to Somalia's political process.[228] UNOSOM II interpreted its mandate, not merely as authorizing but also requiring militias to be disarmed, which was directly opposite to the way UNITAF had interpreted its mandate.[229]

While General Aidid's faction (known as the Somali National Alliance) was under an obligation to disarm, UNOSOM II did not exhaust peaceful remedies

---

[226] Sarooshi, n 129 above, 215–17.
[227] Quigley, n 125 above, 281.
[228] *Report of the Commission of Inquiry Established pursuant to Security Council Resolution 855(1993) to Investigate Armed Attacks on UNOSOM II Personnel Which Led to Casualties Among Them*, S/1995/653, 1 June 1994, 15.
[229] Ibid, 37.

such as reminding the SNA that they had to disarm, and imposed forcible disarmament without warning, since they felt that they had the power to do so anyway and there was no need to negotiate with the SNA. As for building Somalia's future, UNOSOM's role was to assist rather than impose solutions. The problem was further exacerbated by UNOSOM's decision to declare the 1962 Criminal Code to be applicable law in Somalia. In all these cases it went beyond assisting and imposed its measures. The Report of the Commission of Inquiry concludes that it mattered 'not whether the substance of UNOSOM II's actions were for the benefit of the Somali people, but whether they were accepted by all Somali parties or within UNOSOM II's mandate'.[230]

On this issue, UNOSOM II maintained that the 1993 Addis Ababa Agreements entitled it to enforce upon Somali political groups the various legal commitments they had assumed. The conclusion however was that

the invoking by UNOSOM II of these Agreements of the factions as a basis of its powers might lead to some confusion if viewed independently of the Security Council Resolution 814(1993) which established UNOSOM II. Resolution 814(1993) spells out UNOSOM II's mandate which only the Security Council can alter or expand. Since the resolution did not grant UNOSOM II powers to impose political solutions on the Somali people, none of the Somali factions could empower UNOSOM II to do so. UNOSOM II's mandate in the political area was to assist the Somalis achieve political reconciliation and rebuild political structures. For UNOSOM II to effectively carry out its mandate of assisting the Somalis, there had to be the agreement or at the very least the acquiescence of all Somali parties. If the Addis Ababa Agreements were adhered to by all political movements UNOSOM II could assist them implement it; once they disagreed as to its implementation UNOSOM II could not force them.

That would have been inconsistent with the mandate granted under Resolution 814.[231] This approach raises an important question of relationship between the Council's powers and consent, and projects limits on the Council's powers in the face of disagreement over its enforcement action either by states or by non-state entities.

Ultimately UNOSOM II was unable to prevail over the opposition of the Aidid faction and, after a number of US and Pakistani casualties, the Council adopted Resolution 954(1994), whereby it stated that the lack of cooperation by Somali factions no longer justified the presence of UNOSOM II in Somalia, and it was withdrawn after its final period of deployment expired on 31 March 1995.[232]

(h) The Use of Article 42 in relation to Afghanistan

The signatories to the 2001 Bonn Agreement, concluded after the fall of the Taliban regime, agreed that responsibility for providing security in Afghanistan rested with the Afghans themselves, but also acknowledged that as

---

[230] Ibid, 37–9.
[231] Ibid, 39–40.
[232] Matheson, n 61 above, 153–4.

some time may be required for the new Afghan security and armed forces to be fully constituted and functioning, the participants in the UN Talks on Afghanistan request the United Nations Security Council to consider authorizing the early deployment to Afghanistan of a United Nations mandated force. This force will assist in the maintenance of security for Kabul and its surrounding areas. Such a force could, as appropriate, be progressively expanded to other urban centres and other areas.

Consequently, in a more far-reaching way of expressing consent, 'the participants in the UN Talks on Afghanistan pledge to withdraw all military units from Kabul and other urban centers or other areas in which the UN mandated force is deployed. It would also be desirable if such a force were to assist in the rehabilitation of Afghanistan's infrastructure.'[233] Even though the Council has subsequently acted under Chapter VII, as is clear from the wording of the Bonn Agreement as acknowledged in Resolution 1386(2001) its action—as well as the necessity and proportionality thereof—was premised on agreement with the Afghan government and factions, not on exercising Chapter VII powers whether or not such agreement were given. It is unlikely that a Chapter VII deployment like the International Security Assistance Force (ISAF) would have been conducive to peace and security in Afghanistan had it been undertaken by overriding local actors' will. For Chapter VII is not a rough tool enabling the Security Council to take a wide range of non-consensual, coercive actions across the board, but instead provides for a more nuanced process of response to threats, where the necessity and proportionality of a particular action has to be weighed in every single instance. The factor of consent by actors on the ground, governments above all, indeed influences the calculation of what kind of response is necessary or proportionate. By comparison, in the Somalian situation, the Security Council (based on the Secretary-General's report) authorized military intervention because there was no government to give consent. Had there been one, the Council's judgment would presumably have been different.[234]

The first Security Council authorization of the use of force in Afghanistan was based on Resolution 1386. The British Foreign Secretary declared that the UK was prepared to serve as the initial lead nation for three months, to exercise command of the ISAF, yet the US Central Command would have authority over the ISAF to 'ensure that ISAF activities do not interfere with the successful completion of Operation *Enduring Freedom*'. The ISAF was to have a mission 'distinct from Operation *Enduring Freedom*',[235] which had not been authorized by the Council.

The mission of ISAF was determined in paragraph 1 of Resolution 1386 as being 'to assist the Afghan Interim Authority in the maintenance of security in Kabul and its surrounding areas, so that the Afghan Interim Authority as well as the personnel of the United Nations can operate in a secure environment'. Throughout the ISAF

---

[233] *Agreement on Provisional Arrangements in Afghanistan Pending the Re-establishment of Permanent Government Institutions*, Annex I, paras 3–4, S/2001/1154, 5 December 2001.
[234] See on this point in general Chapter 2 above.
[235] Letter dated 19 December 2001 from the Secretary of State for Foreign and Commonwealth Affairs of the United Kingdom of Great Britain and Northern Ireland addressed to the President of the Security Council, S/2001/1217, 19 December 2001, 2–3.

deployment, the security situation has remained tense and unstable. Part of the job in this respect was being performed by Operation *Enduring Freedom*, which focused on the Taliban; improvement of the overall security situation in the country was not its principal task. Accordingly, the North Atlantic Council agreed that expansion of the ISAF beyond Kabul would help the Afghan government to improve the degree of security in the country.[236] In line with this, Resolution 1510(2003) recalled that the Bonn Agreement 'provides for the progressive expansion of ISAF to other urban centres and other areas beyond Kabul', and 'the importance of extending central government authority to all parts of Afghanistan, of comprehensive disarmament, demobilization and reintegration of all armed factions'. The government also requested ISAF's deployment to be extended outside Kabul. In operative paragraph 1, the Council authorized expansion of the ISAF mandate to allow it to support the Afghan Transitional Authority and its successors in the maintenance of security in areas of Afghanistan outside Kabul and its environs, so that both the Afghan authorities and international personnel could operate in a secure environment. Up to the point that Resolution 1746(2007) was adopted (which declared this expansion completed), the ISAF expansion to cover essentially all of Afghanistan was carried out with the consent of the Afghan government. Still, complex issues remained as to the Chapter VII mandate and the need for a uniform collective security policy in the Afghan conflict. The Secretary-General pointed out that, while US command of ISAF improved coordination between Operation *Enduring Freedom* and ISAF, 'the inherent dangers of two forces operating in the same battle space with different mandates requires more proactive coordination to ensure success of the ISAF mission'.[237]

(i) External Limits of Article 42 Authorizations Tested: the Case of Côte d'Ivoire

Resolution 1528(2004) contains two separate though interrelated authorizations to use force in Côte d'Ivoire, one peace-keeping and the other under Article 42. UNOCI—a UN peace-keeping force—is authorized 'to use all necessary means to carry out its mandate, within its capabilities and its areas of deployment' (paragraph 8). The French forces present in the country are also authorized, under paragraph 16,

to use all necessary means in order to support UNOCI in accordance with the agreement to be reached between UNOCI and the French authorities, and in particular to: [c]ontribute to the general security of the area of activity of the international Forces; [i]ntervene at the request of UNOCI in support of its elements whose security may be threatened; [i]ntervene against belligerent actions, if the security conditions so require, outside the areas directly controlled by UNOCI; [h]elp to protect civilians, in the deployment areas of their units.

---

[236] UNYB 2003, 309–10.
[237] *The situation in Afghanistan and its implications for international peace and security*, Report of the Secretary-General, A/62/345–S/2007/555, 21 September 2007, para 34. A similar factor was present in Somalia where, in the Secretary-General's words, the UNOSOM and UNITAF commanders were working closely to ensure coordination between the two forces: S/25354, 3.

As the Secretary-General's report specified, while the French forces contributed to maintaining cease-fire and providing security for members of the government, they were not willing to perform the tasks involved in disarmament, policing, and election security.[238] The clause in paragraph 16 regarding 'the agreement to be reached between UNOCI and the French authorities' could be interpreted as making the mandate dependent on an additional agreement.

The protracted lack of progress in the peace process affected the military and security situation. France was seen as behind this and there were attacks on French troops. On 7 and 11 October 2004, demonstrations targeted both UNOCI and French *Licorne* troops, who were forced to intervene to disperse the protestors. In Abidjan, groups of 'young patriots' protested the delayed commencement of the disarmament process, but were contained by the Ivorian security forces.[239] On 4 and 5 November there was intense fighting between UNOCI and the Coalition *Forces nouvelles*, which was partly contained by UNOCI.[240] On 6 November, government armed forces continued air operations against *Forces nouvelles* positions in the north of the country, professedly aimed 'at the recapture of specific towns', following which the Ivorian government requested the UN to ensure the security of those towns. During a raid by government fighter aircraft on the town of Bouaké, a base of the French *Licorne* force was bombed, resulting in the deaths of 9 French soldiers and an American citizen, while 38 French soldiers were wounded. French forces responded by destroying the planes used by FANCI (the Ivorian national army) during the air raids, as well as military helicopters on the ground in Yamoussoukro. On 9 November a confrontation took place between *Licorne* troops and 'young patriots', which resulted in numerous deaths and injuries among the demonstrators. The Ivorian authorities accused the *Licorne* soldiers of a disproportionate use of force in response to a 'mistake' caused by the Ivorian security and defence forces, and asked for an international inquiry into 'violations of the sovereignty and territorial integrity' of the country by the French military in Côte d'Ivoire. The French Minister of Defence explained the actions of the French forces as legitimate self-defence, and indicated that France had no alternative but to respond to the attack.[241]

Resolution 1528 could potentially be seen as covering the action by French troops. As a matter of the law of self-defence, an armed attack certainly occurred. It has to be noted that, despite the intensity of hostilities, French forces did not intervene before they were attacked. The Security Council Presidential statement 2004/42 condemned the attack on the French forces, expressed 'full support for the action undertaken by French forces and the United Nations Operation in Côte d'Ivoire', and confirmed that the French and UN forces were authorized to use all necessary means to carry out their mandate in accordance with Resolution 1528.

---

[238] S/2004/3, 6 January 2004, paras 52–3.
[239] *Second report of the Secretary-General on the United Nations Operation in Côte d'Ivoire*, S/2004/697, 27 August 2004, para 3; *Third progress report of the Secretary-General on the United Nations operation in Côte d'Ivoire*, S/2004/962, 9 December 2004, para 7.
[240] UNYB 2004, 185–6.
[241] S/2004/962, paras 17–18.

Furthermore, Resolution 1572(2004), adopted unanimously, '*[c]ondemns* the air strikes committed by the national armed forces of Côte d'Ivoire (FANCI) which constitute flagrant violations of the ceasefire agreement of 3 May 2003...; *[r]eiterates* its full support for the action undertaken by UNOCI and French forces in accordance with their mandate under Resolution 1528(2004)' (paragraphs 1 and 2). In addition, paragraph 7 imposed an arms embargo on Côte d'Ivoire, applying to arms or any related *matériel*, in particular military aircraft and equipment, as well as the provision of any assistance, advice, or training related to military activities.

During the debates on this resolution, China condemned 'the air raid conducted against the French peacekeepers'.[242] The African Union did not expressly criticize the attack on the French, yet its statement '*[u]rges* the Government of Côte d'Ivoire and all the parties involved in the crisis to exercise maximum restraint' and '*[c]alls upon* all the parties to fully cooperate with UNOCI and the *Licorne* forces in maintaining peace and security in the country'.[243]

7. Enforcement Action by Regional Organizations

(a) The Essence of Authorization under Article 53 of the UN Charter

Article 53 of the UN Charter provides that the Security Council can utilize 'regional arrangements or agencies for enforcement action under its authority. But no enforcement action shall be taken under regional arrangements or by regional agencies without the authorization of the Security Council.' The phrase 'under its authority' underlines the primacy of the Council's role in designing the policy behind an authorized enforcement operation, its mandate, and powers. As Halderman observed, the 'authorization' clause under Article 53 reflects 'the principle of universality which is indispensable to the United Nations if it is ever to fulfil its major purposes'.[244]

Under paragraph 8 of Resolution 1132(1997), having targeted the military junta in Sierra Leone with sanctions, the Council, acting under Chapter VIII,

authorize[d] ECOWAS, cooperating with the democratically-elected Government of Sierra Leone, to ensure strict implementation of the provisions of this resolution relating to the supply of petroleum and petroleum products, and arms and related *matériel* of all types, including, where necessary and in conformity with applicable international standards, by halting inward maritime shipping in order to inspect and verify their cargoes and destinations, and calls upon all States to cooperate with ECOWAS in this regard.

---

[242] S/PV.5078, 15 November 2004, 2 (China).
[243] *Communiqué of the nineteenth session of the Peace and Security Council*, S/2004/896, 11 November 2004, 2, paras 3 and 6.
[244] JW Halderman, 'Regional Enforcement Measures and the United Nations', 52 *Georgetown Law Journal* (1963), 89 at 91–2; see also C Schreuer, 'Regionalism v Universalism', 6 *European Journal of International Law* (1995), 477 at 490; U Villani, 'The Security Council's Authorisation of Enforcement Action by Regional Organisations', 6 *Max-Planck Yearbook of UN Law* (2002), 535 at 537.

Under paragraph 9 ECOWAS was to report to the Council every 30 days. The Council Resolution was premised on the ECOWAS action being in support of the legitimate government of Sierra Leone. In the matter of piracy off the Somali coast, paragraph 9 of Security Council Resolution 1846(2008) authorized regional organizations to conduct enforcement action on an 'able and willing' basis,

by deploying naval vessels and military aircraft, and through seizure and disposition of boats, vessels, arms and other related equipment used in the commission of piracy and armed robbery off the coast of Somalia, or for which there is reasonable ground for suspecting such use.[245]

Resolution 1846 provided the legal basis for Operation *Atalanta*, led by the EU to combat piracy off the Somali coast.[246]

Article 53's restriction of regional enforcement manifests 'the unlimited subordination' of regional arrangements to the UN.[247] Villani argues that Article 53 foresees an autonomous role for regional organizations, but acknowledges that within the scope of Article 53 regional organizations are in a complementary and subordinate position in relation to the Security Council,[248] which contradicts the autonomy thesis by definition. The whole point of Article 53 is to ensure that enforcement measures are not *taken* without the Security Council authorization, which must be obtained before the enforcement begins. Otherwise, by circumventing the Article 53 requirement, regional organizations could arrogate to themselves the power to make decisions under Articles 39, 41, and 42, and even to determine the necessity and proportionality of the relevant action. The Security Council can no longer perform any of these evaluations if the action that has already commenced.

It has been contended that Security Council authorization of a regional action does not need to be in advance because this would compromise the essence of regional arrangements under Chapter VIII and run counter to the flexibility of the authorization requirement under Article 53(1) of the Charter.[249] But the authorization requirement under the Charter shows no trace of flexibility: it simply states, in the plainest possible terms, that no regional enforcement action can be taken until and unless it has the approval of the Security Council. As Dinstein confirms,

---

[245] See EU Joint Action 2008/851/CFSP of 10 November 2008 on a European Union military operation to contribute to the deterrence, prevention, and repression of acts of piracy and armed robbery off the Somali coast; and the Council Decision 2008/918/CFSP of 8 December 2008 on the launch of a European Union military operation to contribute to the deterrence, prevention, and repression of acts of piracy and armed robbery off the Somali coast (Operation *Atalanta*).

[246] S/PV.6026, 4 (Italy); the EU Joint Action defined the operation's mandate as including the power to 'take the necessary measures, including the use of force, to deter, prevent and intervene in order to bring to an end acts of piracy and armed robbery which may be committed in the areas where it is present': Joint Action 2008/851/CFSP, 10 November 2008, Article 2.

[247] G Bebr, 'Regional Organizations: A United Nations Problem', 49 AJIL (1955), 166 at 169; see also J Kunz, 'The Inter-American System and the United Nations Organization', 39 AJIL (1945), 758 at 763.

[248] Villani, n 244 above, 536–7.

[249] A Abass, *Regional Organisations and the Development of Collective Security: Beyond Chapter VIII of the UN Charter* (Oxford: Hart, 2004), 54–5.

Chapter VIII interlocks with Chapter VII to preserve the monopoly of the Security Council over the use of force. Like any single state, regional organizations are allowed to engage in enforcement actions only if they get 'a clear-cut go-ahead signal from the Council'.[250]

The impermissibility of enforcement operations not authorized in advance by the UN was confirmed after the Cold War, as the General Assembly specifically pointed out in paragraph 1(d) of its Resolution 49/57(1994). The Secretary-General's Report specified that 'the obligation to obtain Security Council authorization prior to the use of force is clear'.[251] Akehurst considers that subsequent authorization is not permitted:

> To hold otherwise would be to encourage illegal acts, because regional agencies would be tempted to initiate enforcement action in the hope that the Security Council would give its authorisation afterwards, but this hope might not always be fulfilled. In other cases the Security Council might feel that it would be politically awkward to withhold authorisation for what has already been done; confronting the Security Council with *faits accomplis* would therefore fetter the discretion which Article 53 intended it to enjoy.[252]

There are various ways in which regional frameworks state their subjection to the requirements of Article 53. The SADC approach is expressed in Article 11(3) of its Politics, Defence and Security Cooperation Protocol (adopted 14 August 2001), specifying that

> [t]he [SADC] Summit shall resort to enforcement action only as a matter of last resort and, in accordance with Article 53 of the United Nations Charter, only with the authorization of the United Nations Security Council.

Such a clause is not an inevitable consequence of the need to obtain the Security Council authorization, for it simply reflects what the legal position under Article 53 is. According to Article 10 of the Rio Treaty, '[n]one of the provisions of this Treaty shall be construed as impairing the rights and obligations of the High Contracting Parties under the Charter of the United Nations'. This creates a presumption that the Rio Treaty defers to the arrangements regarding the use of force under the Charter.

The argument supporting the legality of regional enforcement inevitably by-passes the evidence of the views of most states that rejected the legality of NATO's attack against the FRY. The NATO attack against the FRY in 1999, without authorization by the Security Council, was a test case to confirm that the community of states does not view regional enforcement as lawful unless it is based on previously obtained authorization under Article 53. In relation to this attack, the

---

[250] Dinstein, n 124 above, 311; in matters of self-defence, regional organizations can act only once an armed attack is launched: ibid, 312; see also Villani, n 244 above, 536; S Deen-Racsmany, 'A Redistribution of Authority between the UN and Regional Organisations in the Field of the Maintenance of Peace and Security?', 13 *Leiden Journal of International Law* (2000), 297 at 309; Sarooshi, n 129 above, 148.

[251] *The causes of conflict and the promotion of durable peace and sustainable development in Africa: Report of the Secretary-General*, A/52/871–S/1998/318, 13 April 1990, 10.

[252] M Akehurst, 'Enforcement Action by Regional Agencies, With Special Reference to the Organization of American States', 42 *British Yearbook of International Law* (1967) 175 at 214.

Brazilian representative in the Security Council explained that regional organizations are subject to 'Article 53, which imposes on them the obligation of seeking Security Council authorization beforehand'.[253] After the Kosovo bombing campaign had started, the Chinese representative observed in the Council that 'is only the Security Council that can determine whether a given situation threatens international peace and security and can take appropriate action. We are firmly opposed to any act that violates this principle and that challenges the authority of the Security Council.'[254] The Indian representative observed that the NATO attacks against the FRY

are in clear violation of Article 53 of the Charter. . . . Among the barrage of justifications that we have heard, we have been told that the attacks are meant to prevent violations of human rights. Even if that were to be so, it does not justify unprovoked military aggression. Two wrongs do not make a right.[255]

The Communiqué issued by the Rio Group on 25 March 1999 expressed regret that the use of force in the Balkans was conducted in contravention of Articles 53 and 54 of the UN Charter.[256]

The US interpretation of paragraphs 31 and 32 of the 1999 NATO Strategic Concept, shared at the time by the UK, is that these provisions do not 'suggest that NATO must have permission from the United Nations or any other outside body before it can act', while France insisted that UN assent is necessary before enforcement operations may be conducted.[257] It would be misleading, tempting though it might be, to take these mutually exclusive statements in isolation, point to the lack of agreed position, and then propose that the legal position is ambiguous, that it prevented a clear legal judgment being drawn on whether NATO should have carried on using force without a UN mandate. These statements have to be read in relation to the Strategic Concept, which does not claim autonomy from Chapter VII, and against the background of the UN Charter to which all NATO states are party and which is clear in its Article 53 that advance authorization is necessary.

Some authors take it as a starting point that the Security Council can authorize a use of force before the event, which logically entails that it could do the same after the event (*ex post facto*), and that therefore the temporal element is not decisive.[258] There is, however, an important difference: an initial authorization under Article 53 does not involve any illegality because force has been authorized before it is used. A subsequent authorization is inevitably premised on validating a violation of Article 2(4) of the Charter and could be a possible option—conceptually and

---

[253] S/PV.3937, 24 October 1998, 10–11.
[254] S/PV.3988, 23 March 1999, 12.
[255] Ibid, 15.
[256] Letter dated 26 March 1999 from the Permanent Representative of Mexico to the United Nations addressed to the Secretary-General, A/53/884, S/1999/347, 2.
[257] Gazzini, n 172 above, 257; see further Chapter 3 above.
[258] N Ronzitti, 'The Current Legal Status of Legal Principles Prohibiting the Use of Force and Legal Justifications of the Use of Force', in Bothe *et al*, n 153 above, 91 at 107; I Osterdahl, 'Preach What You Practice: The Security Council and the Legalisation *ex post facto* of the Unilateral Use of Force', 74 *Nordic Journal of International Law* (2005), 231 at 233, 237.

normatively—only if the Council stood above the Charter. In addition, the issue of subsequent or implicit validation of an initially illegal use of force involves a more principled question as to precisely what the Council should say, fail to say, or do for its action or inaction to be considered a subsequent or implied authorization of the use of force. Should it express approval, approve any subsequent involvement in the situation in question, or merely remain silent?

Resolution 156(1960) takes note of the Final Act of the OAS Sixth Meeting of Consultations of Ministers of Foreign Affairs, 'of resolution I approved at the aforesaid Meeting, whereby agreement was reached on the application of measures regarding the Dominican Republic'. The USSR argued that, by 'taking note' of the OAS sanctions against the Dominican Republic (severance of diplomatic relations and a partial embargo), the Security Council implicitly approved these sanctions.[259]

Osterdahl seems to contend that in every single case where the Security Council engaged with a situation that had previously involved an illegal unilateral use of force it has to be seen as approving this use of force. This is clear from the observation that 'the only possibility [for the Security Council] of not risking to legalize the previous unlawful action would be to abstain from taking measures *ex post facto*'.[260] There is another suggestion that 'implied authorization can only flow from a resolution passed on the matter that also contains language pointing towards an implied authorization',[261] which amounts to an oxymoron, because a decision to authorize such an enterprise is a separate decision that requires a transparent and intelligible expression of the Council's intention and judgement pursuant to Articles 39, 42, and 53 of the Charter, which can only be done overtly. It is too separate and important to be inferred from mere involvement by the Council after a conflict.

Meeker claims, citing the example of the UN Security Council 'endorsement' of the OAS-authorized quarantine against Cuba, that advance Security Council authorization is not a necessary requirement. Nor have authorizations to be express. The Security Council let the quarantine continue and did not suppress it, and thus granted authorization by the course it adopted.[262] However, the Council did not collectively express the view that the quarantine was lawful. It would certainly not have adopted that decision had it been asked to do so. The same applies to the Russian position on Resolution 156; and also to the Security Council's failure to adopt a resolution condemning the NATO attack against the FRY in 1999. This approach is supported in jurisprudence. In *Namibia*, the International Court clearly emphasized that 'the fact that a particular proposal is not adopted by an international organ does not necessarily carry with it the inference that a collective pronouncement is made in a sense opposite to that proposed'.[263]

---

[259] Akehurst, n 252 above, 190; I Claude, 'The OAS, the UN and the United States', 35 *International Conciliation* (No 547, March 1964), 1 at 52.

[260] Osterdahl, n 258 above, 237, 255.

[261] G Ress and U Bröhmer, 'Article 53', in Simma, B (ed.), *The Charter of the United Nations—A Commentary* (New York: Oxford University Press, 2002), 866.

[262] L Meeker, 'Defensive Quarantine and the Law', 57 AJIL (1963), 515 at 520, 522.

[263] *Namibia*, *ICJ Reports*, 1971, 36, para 69; see for further detail and analysis, A Orakhelashvili, n 14 above, Chapter 13.

Resolution 1244(1999) cannot be interpreted as having retrospectively approved the NATO attack on the FRY, because this resolution focuses on a prospective political solution. Mere silence of the Council on the matter of the use of force cannot be seen as validation, because this falls short of the requirement that the Council's position should be collectively expressed, satisfying the requirements of Article 27 of the Charter; besides, the failure to state a condemnation does not amount to a statement of justification. According to Dinstein, the inaction of the Council in the face of NATO action against the FRY does not amount to authorization of those measures. If the term 'authorization' under Article 53 is to be seen as including tacit acquiescence, the supremacy of the Security Council in the province of international peace and security could be utterly eroded. In general, the NATO action in Kosovo is a source of considerable disquiet.[264]

The principal problem that the thesis of subsequent authorization of the use of force fails to confront relates to the will of the Security Council as a collective institutional body, and the requirement to identify whether and how that will has been expressed. Acquiescence is not a political tool with which to construct, on the basis of political or ideological suitability, a deemed approval where none has actually been given. Instead, acquiescence is a legal device referring to the separate identity of the entity claimed to have acquiesced and the need to evidence that it has done so.[265]

(b) The EU Sanctions Regimes

Sanctions adopted by the European Union are premised on complementarity pursuant to the primacy of the UN in the area of enforcement. As an EU policy document specifies, in order to implement UN sanctions action has to be taken at EU level and a higher level of EU coordination is required.[266] The complementarity pattern in relation to UN and EU sanctions is demonstrated by the way the EU implements UN Security Council decisions.

An early discussion of this issue in relation to Rhodesia started from the EC's role complementing the UN sanctions. Pursuant to the EC Treaty, the Council would adopt a common position or joint action specifying the objective of any measures to be undertaken.[267] In debating sanctions against Rhodesia 'the Community considered that it had neither the competence nor indeed any responsibility for implementing Security Council decisions'. The EC could not act on the basis of what was then Article 113 of its Treaty because, although the UN had imposed sanctions against commercial activities, the Security Council's measures were taken

---

[264] Dinstein, n 124 above, 314–15.

[265] On the concept, requirements, and implications of acquiescence in international law see A Orakhelashvili, n 14 above, Chapter 11.

[266] *The European Union and the United Nations: The Choice of Multilateralism*, Communication from the Commission to the Council and the European Parliament, Brussels, 10 September 2003, COM(2003) 526 final, 7.

[267] I Anthony, 'Sanctions Applied by the European Union and the United Nations', *Stockholm International Peace Research Institute Yearbook* 2002, 203 at 210.

for the purpose of maintaining peace and security and therefore did not fall within the scope of that article. However, in response to the Falkland crisis an EEC Council regulation introduced economic measures without the UN Security Council's authorization and cited Article 113 as its legal basis. The same has been the case in relation to sanctions imposed against Iraq, Libya, the FRY, and Haiti, now pursuant to UN resolutions.[268]

During the 1990s, the EC contribution to enforcing Security Council sanctions was limited owing to limits on EC competence in the field of capital movement and cooperation in areas such as science, technology, culture, and sport, as well as diplomatic relations. To illustrate, EC measures relating to the sanctions on Haiti reflected the oil embargo under Resolution 841(1993), but not the financial sanctions.[269] An EC regulation on sanctions against the FRY specifies in its preamble that, while the Security Council was imposing mandatory sanctions on the FRY, 'the Community's economic relations with the Republics of Serbia and Montenegro must be halted'.[270] This manifests not only the complementarity approach but also the EC's acceptance of its activities being undertaken as part of the UN framework and subordinate to it. No inclination for independent EC action is manifested.

The preamble to a subsequent Council regulation explains the legal basis for the EC action, which is the adoption of further Security Council resolutions and a request from the President of Bosnia. The Community had to strengthen the embargo against the FRY 'to ensure a uniform implementation throughout the Community of certain of these measures'. The regulation bans imports and exports, commercial traffic, and non-financial services (paragraph 1).[271] Paragraphs 8 and 9 of this regulation relate to impounding vessels. Article 113 is named as the regulation's legal basis. It becomes arguable that the Community might have derived its implied power to act in order to respond to the need to participate effectively in UN sanctions under Chapter VII on the basis of complementarity.

The EU acted independently in imposing sanctions against the FRY in relation to the Kosovo crisis. The Council considered that 'the use of force against the Kosovar Albanian Community in Kosovo represent[ed] an unacceptable violation of human rights and put the security of the region at risk'. The Council specified in Articles 1 to 4 that '[n]o equipment which might be used for internal repression or for terrorism will be supplied to the Federal Republic of Yugoslavia', and that '[n]o visas shall be issued for senior FRY and Serbian representatives responsible for repressive action by FRY security forces in Kosovo', as determined in the Annex.[272]

---

[268] H Fox and C Wickremasinghe, 'UN Implementation of UN Economic Sanctions', 42 ICLQ (1993), 945 at 952.

[269] Ibid, 953.

[270] Council Regulation (EEC) No 1432/92 of 1 June 1992 prohibiting trade between the European Economic Community and the Republics of Serbia and Montenegro, OJ L 151, 3 June 1992, 4–6.

[271] Council Regulation (EEC) No 990/93 of 26 April 1993 concerning trade between the European Economic Community and the Federal Republic of Yugoslavia (Serbia and Montenegro), OJ L 102, 28 April 1993, 14–16.

[272] Common Position of 19 March 1998, 98/240/CFSP.

This was expanded in the Common Position of 7 May 1998, which determined that '[f]unds held abroad by the Federal Republic of Yugoslavia and Serbian Governments will be frozen' with immediate effect (Article 1).

Regulation 1081/2000 prescribes, owing to serious violations of civil and political rights in Burma,

freezing of the funds of senior members of the State Peace and Development Council, Burmese authorities in the tourism sector, senior members of the military, the Government or the security forces who formulate, implement or benefit from policies that impede Burma/Myanmar's transition to democracy, and their families, and by a prohibition of sales, supplies and exports of equipment which might be used for internal repression or terrorism.[273]

Consequently, Article 1 of the regulation prohibits selling or otherwise providing to any Burmese person equipment such as body armour, anti-riot helmets, grenades, and many other items that can be used for political repression. Articles 2 and 3 provide for the freezing of the assets of the same circle of people.

Another instance of independent EU action is provided by the sanctions against Zimbabwe under Common Position 2002/145/CFSP. Preambular paragraphs 1 and 2 register a 'serious concern about the situation in Zimbabwe, in particular the recent escalation of violence and intimidation of political opponents and the harassment of the independent press'. Article 1 imposes an arms embargo on Zimbabwe, which covers '[t]he supply or sale of arms and related material of all types including weapons and ammunition, military vehicles and equipment, para-military equipment, and spare parts for the aforementioned'. Article 2 stipulates that '[n]o equipment which might be used for internal repression will be supplied to Zimbabwe'. Article 4 provides for freezing the funds and assets of persons engaged in activities that seriously undermine democracy, respect for human rights, or the rule of law in Zimbabwe.

EU complementary action in respect to lifting sanctions is expressed in Common Position 2004/698/2004 in which the Union is guided by the fact that Security Council Resolution 1506(2003) lifted sanctions on Libya, 'while leaving in place the measures set forth in [its] paragraph 8'. The EU Council consequently decided that all EU sanctions should be lifted apart from those implementing the UN sanctions that the Security Council had decided to leave in place.

In the aftermath of the adoption of Security Council Resolution 1267(1999), the EU adopted Common Position 1999/727/CFSP pursuant to the provisions on the Common Foreign and Security Policy (CFSP) which prescribed the freezing of funds under Resolution 1267. The common position was swiftly followed in February 2000 by Council Regulation 337/2000 concerning a flight ban and the necessary freezing of funds.[274] As for the EU competence to adopt these measures, the Regulation relied both on the Treaty and on the need to implement UN Security Council resolutions:

---

[273] OJ L 95, 27 March 1998, 1.
[274] PJ Cardwell, D French, and N White, 'Case-note on *Kadi* (ECJ)', 58 ICLQ (2009), 229.

The measures set out in paragraph 4 of Resolution 1267(1999) fall under the scope of the Treaty and, therefore, notably with a view to avoiding distortion of competition, Community legislation is necessary to implement the relevant decisions of the Security Council as far as the territory of the Community is concerned.[275]

As a further illustration of the complementarity approach, Article 2 of the Regulation specifies that '[t]his Regulation shall apply to any funds, other financial resources, and aircraft designated by the Taliban Sanctions Committee'. Article 6 provides that the freezing of funds 'shall not apply to funds and other financial resources for which the Taliban Sanctions Committee has granted an exemption'.

This 'unconditional' complementarity pattern is broken with *Kadi*. The action related to Security Council Resolutions 1267, 1333(2000), and 1390(2002), which the EU had implemented in its own legal order by Regulations 467/2001, 2062/2001, and 2199/2002, which the applicants sought to have annulled.[276] The legality under EU law of the measures at stake depended on whether, having been adopted pursuant to Security Council resolutions, they could be subsumed within the terms of Article 301 of the EC Treaty, which entitles the Council to adopt an action by the Community to interrupt or to reduce, in part or completely, economic relations with one or more third countries. The Court held, pursuant to the appellant's submissions, that

the restrictive measures provided for by Resolution 1390(2002), which the contested regulation was intended to put into effect, are measures notable for the absence of any link to the governing regime of a third country. Following the collapse of the Taliban regime, those measures were aimed directly at Usama bin Laden, the Al-Qaeda network and the persons and entities associated with them, as they appear in the summary list. They do not, therefore, as such, fall within the ambit of Articles 60 EC and 301 EC.[277]

The regulations in question were annulled. The position at the time the ECJ adjudicated on this case was that under Article 301 the EU possessed no competence to take sanctions against non-state actors. To remedy this position, the Lisbon Treaty provides for the smart sanctions regime in Article 215(2) (previously Article 301) of Title IV on restrictive measures, which specifies that the Council may adopt restrictive measures against natural or legal persons and groups or non-state entities.

Additionally, in response to Resolution 1373(2001), the Council of the European Union created its own list of persons believed to be involved in terrorist activities, whose assets should be targeted even though it was under no international obligation to do so. The difference between UN and EU procedures in their original versions was that from the outset the EU procedure provided an extensive

---

[275] Council Regulation No 337/2000 of 14 February 2000 concerning a flight ban and a freeze of funds and other financial resources in respect of the Taliban of Afghanistan, OJ L 43, 16 February 2000, 1, preambular paragraph 3.

[276] Joined Cases C-402/05 P and C-415/05 P *Yassin Abdulah Kadi and Al Barakaat International Foundation v Council of the European Union and Commission of the European Communities*, Judgment of 3 September 2008, para 46.

[277] Ibid, para 167; see further Chapter 3 above and Chapter 8 below.

definition of individuals and entities to be targeted, including a specification of which kinds of 'terrorist act' they must be believed to be involved in. It specified as acceptable bases for listing decisions: (1) the instigation of investigations or prosecution for a terrorist act; (2) an attempt to perpetrate, participate in, or facilitate such an act 'based on serious and credible evidence or clues'; and (3) condemnation of such deeds.[278] These criteria are somewhat more specific than those applied in the UN targeted sanctions regime.

In the *Modjahedines* decision the CFI examined the necessity and proportionality of these measures. The Court accepted that the

notification of the evidence adduced and a hearing of the parties concerned, before the adoption of the initial decision to freeze funds, would be liable to jeopardise the effectiveness of the sanctions and would thus be incompatible with the public interest objective pursued by the Community pursuant to Security Council Resolution 1373(2001). An initial measure freezing funds must, by its very nature, be able to benefit from a surprise effect and to be applied with immediate effect.

It was still the case that 'in order for the parties concerned to be able to defend their rights effectively . . . it is also necessary that the evidence adduced against them be notified to them, in so far as reasonably possible, either concomitantly with or as soon as possible after the adoption of the initial decision to freeze funds'. The *Modjahedines* decision concluded that the procedure violated fundamental human rights requirements, such as the right to a fair hearing.[279] In reaction to this, the EU announced that it would now provide the affected individuals with reasons for listing and enable them to apply for de-listing.[280]

(c) Sanctions Adopted by ECOWAS and AU

By Decision A/DEC.1/10/92 of the ECOWAS Standing Committee of Mediation, the Committee of Five imposed economic sanctions against Liberian factions that did not comply with the Yamoussoukro IV Accord. Member States agreed to impose sanctions against any Liberian party which failed to comply with the Accord. Sanctions included preventing exports from the territories of member States 'to the territory of Liberia under NPFL [National Patriotic Front of Liberia] control of weapons or any other military equipment', and the importing into the territories of member States 'of all commodities and products originating from the territory of Liberia under NPFL control'. Member States would not make available to Taylor's authorities, nor 'to any commercial, industrial or public utility undertaking in areas under NPFL control any funds or any other financial or economic resources'. Further, they would refrain from any action or dealing that might be construed as recognition of the authority and control of Taylor's authorities 'over

---

[278] Almqvist, n 85 above, 310–11.
[279] *Organisation des Modjahedines*, n 116 above, paras 126–7, 137.
[280] Council Notice 2007/C144/01 of 29 June 2007, OJ C144, 29 June 2007, 1; Almqvist, n 85 above, 311.

any part of the territory of Liberia'.[281] As the UN Secretary-General pointed out, the Security Council supplemented ECOWAS action by imposing an arms embargo under Resolution 788(1992).[282] The embargo was lifted from Liberia under Resolution 1343(2001), after the Security Council has noted that 'the conflict in Liberia has been resolved, that national elections have taken place within the framework of the Yamoussoukro IV Agreement of 30 October 1991'.

Concerned with the breakdown of negotiations with the illegal regime in Sierra Leone after the coup in that country, the ECOWAS Authority adopted a package of sanctions and blockade to ensure the return of the legitimately elected President of Sierra Leone. State and government heads specifically mandated ECOMOG to monitor the cease-fire, sanctions, and embargo with a view to securing peace in Sierra Leone, taking all necessary means.[283]

Policy-wise, the AU PSC '[a]ffirm[ed] its determination, in conformity with Article 7(g) of the Protocol relating to the establishment of the PSC and the July 2000 Declaration, to impose the sanctions envisaged in case of unconstitutional changes, should the *de facto* authorities fail to ensure the rapid restoration of constitutional legality'.[284] In a related problem, the PSC regretted the rejection by the authorities of Anjouan (which had attempted unilaterally to secede from the Comoros) of proposals that would have led to reconciliation in the Comoros, and imposed targeted sanctions against Anjouan's leaders, including a travel ban and a freeze on assets. The government of the Comoros was to draw up a list of people to be subjected to sanctions. Furthermore, 'all air and sea transport to or from Anjouan shall be monitored to ensure that they do not, in any way, benefit . . . the illegal authorities of Anjouan and to their supporters, bearing in mind the need to limit, as much as possible, the impact of these measures on the civilian population'.[285] The matter was ultimately resolved through an AU-supported use of force by the Comoros authorities in 2008 to reintegrate the island into the country.

(d) The AU and ECOWAS Legal Frameworks Relating to the Use of Force

The AU Constitutive Act of 2000 provides '[t]he right of the Union to intervene in a Member State pursuant to a decision of the Assembly in respect of grave circumstances, namely war crimes, genocide and crimes against humanity', and '[t]he right of Member States to request intervention from the Union in order to

---

[281] *Decision A/DEC.1/10/92 relating to the implementation of decision A/DEC.8/7/92 on sanctions against parties to the Liberian conflict which fail to comply with the implementation of the Yamoussoukro Accord of 30 October 1991*, adopted by the First Joint Summit Meeting of the ECOWAS Standing Mediation Committee and the Committee of Five, 20 October 1992, preamble and Articles 1 to 4, reproduced in S/24811, 16 November 1992.

[282] *Report of the Secretary-General on the Question of Liberia*, S/25402, 12 March 1993, para 41.

[283] Final Communiqué of the ECOWAS Summit held at Abuja on 28 and 29 August 1997, S/1997/695, 8 September 1997, 12–13.

[284] 24th Meeting, 7 February 2005, PSC/PR/Comm.(XXIV), Section B5.

[285] PSC/PR/Comm(XCV) of 10 October 2007, paragraphs 2 and 5.

restore peace and security' (Articles 4(h) and 4(j)). Under Article 7 of the PSC Protocol, the Council can

recommend to the Assembly, pursuant to Article 4(h) of the Constitutive Act, intervention, on behalf of the Union, in a Member State in respect of grave circumstances, namely war crimes, genocide and crimes against humanity, as defined in relevant international conventions and instruments,

[and] approve the modalities for intervention by the Union in a Member State, following a decision by the Assembly, pursuant to article 4(j) of the Constitutive Act.

Under Article 13(3)(c) the mandate of AU stand-by forces includes 'intervention in a Member State in respect of grave circumstances or at the request of a Member State in order to restore peace and security, in accordance with Article 4(h) and (j) of the Constitutive Act'.

According to Abass, it is up to the member State to request intervention under Article 4(j). But the absence of such requests will not prevent the African Union from acting under Article 4(h).[286] It is argued that nothing in the PSC Protocol explicitly requires the African Union to seek advance authorization from the UN Security Council before launching its own interventions, and the decision not to include such a requirement was a conscious decision by AU leaders, following debacles faced by the UN in Somalia and Rwanda in the first half of the 1990s, not to bind themselves by rules and systems that had failed Africa.[287] Levitt also argues that the competence of the African Union to use force under Articles 4(h) and 4(j) is not inconsistent with Article 103 of the UN Charter, because 'both instruments recognise the primacy of the UN in maintaining international peace and security, and both reinforce its core mission: keeping international peace through regional action in accordance with Article 52 of the Charter'.[288] However, what matters is the outcome of normative conflict between the two treaties. If one provision prohibits regional organizations from acting as enforcers without Security Council authorization, and the other claims that a regional organization can act this way regardless, a normative conflict obviously exists, to be resolved in the way Article 103 of the Charter requires.

However, it seems that the above clauses do not necessarily have to be seen as the African Union's assertion of a right to use of force against states without the Security Council's authorization; instead, they contemplate action with the government's consent, which position is further reinforced by statements made on behalf of the AU that the AU legal framework does not affect the rights and obligations under the UN Charter.[289]

---

[286] Abass, n 249 above, 165.

[287] J Levitt, 'The Peace and Security Council of the African Union and the UNSC', in N Blokker and N Schrijver (eds.), *The Security Council and the Use of Force* (Leiden: Martinus Nijhoff, 2005), 229; J Levitt, 'The Peace and Security Council of the African Union: The Known Unknowns', 13 *Transnational Law and Contemporary Problems* (2003), 109 at 125–6.

[288] Levitt in Blokker and Schrijver, ibid, 213 at 231; Levitt, *TLCP*, 127.

[289] See Chapter 3 above.

The power of AU organs to authorize intervention, even if dependent on state consent, faces yet another hurdle. In order to act under Article 4(h), the PSC and the Assembly need to act in a quasi-judicial manner to determine that crimes against humanity, war crimes, and genocide have been committed in the pertinent situation. The manner in which the AU can determine that Article 4(h) crimes have occurred is not obvious.[290] But this remains a statutory condition, and not one that can be easily met unless a competent subsidiary organ is established to that end.

It has been argued that ECOWAS (like other regional organizations) can conduct enforcement action (including military intervention) without the authorization of the UN Security Council. A reason invoked is that the Security Council's primary responsibility ceases when it fails to act in the face of a crisis, and states can resort to force as a matter of their right residual to the Charter.[291] The preamble to the ECOWAS Protocol was adopted with 'the United Nations Charter, with particular reference to its Chapters VI, VII and VIII' in mind. Under Article 2, 'Member States reaffirm their commitment to the principles contained' in the UN Charter. Their allegiance to Article 53 is thus statutorily confirmed and ECOWAS members are no doubt aware of the effect of Article 103 should their regional treaties contradict the Charter. To view the Protocol consistently, it has to be accepted that the instances of intervention provided for in the Protocol refer only to action that either does not result in enforcement against a state or, if it does, is premised on the necessity of obtaining Security Council authorization. The actual provisions listing the ways intervention can be undertaken should be understood accordingly. While both the ECOWAS and the AU instruments contain intervention clauses that have been interpreted (doctrinally) as allowing the institutions in question to intervene forcibly even against the will of a target state, these provisions have not been used to this end in practice.[292]

(e) Enforcement Action by the WEU in Support of the UN Security Council's Chapter VII Measures

Article VIII(3) of the WEU Modified Brussels Treaty 1954 has normally been considered as the basis for WEU actions in support of Chapter VII sanctions regimes of the UN Security Council. During the 1990–91 Gulf War, the WEU took part in naval operations in the Gulf under UN Security Council resolutions, and later in the 1990s it took part in Operations *Sharp Vigilance* and *Sharp Guard* to monitor the enforcement of the embargo against Serbia and Montenegro.

The WEU coordinated the implementation of naval operations pursuant to paragraph 1 of Resolution 665(1990). WEU ministers had expressed the intention to act in support of that resolution. Likewise, the WEU's role in implementing

---

[290] A Abass, 'The United Nations, the African Union and the Darfur Crisis: Of Apology and Utopia', 54 *Netherlands International Law Review* (2007), 415 at 426.
[291] A Abass, 'The New Collective Security Mechanism of ECOWAS: Innovations and Problems', 5 *Journal of Conflict and Security Law* (2000), 211 at 223ff.
[292] On ECOMOG practice as peace-keepers see Chapter 7 below.

Resolution 678(1990) was undertaken to implement the requirements of its paragraph 2. More specifically, WEU countries supplied munitions, spare parts, and equipment to British and French forces in Saudi Arabia and appointed a permanent WEU coordination authority.[293]

The decision to assist the implementation of sanctions under Resolutions 713 (1991) and 757(1992) was adopted by the WEU Extraordinary Council of Ministers session at Helsinki on 10 July 1992. Paragraph 1 of the Decision specifies that

surveillance of the embargo set by UNSC Resolutions 713 and 757 will involve the participation of at least 5–6 ships, 4 MPA, one support ship, ground base helicopters. Such surveillance will be carried out in international waters, in the Otranto Channel and on other points off the Yugoslav coast, including off the Montenegro coast, following consultation with UNPROFOR.

Operation *Sharp Vigilance* was launched on 16 July 1992 with a twofold purpose: to ensure implementation of the embargo on deliveries of weapons and military equipment to Yugoslavia under Resolution 713 and to monitor execution of the economic sanctions on Yugoslavia in compliance with Resolution 757. The WEU's activity in support of these two resolutions consisted in the identification via radio of the nationality of ships in the areas listed above, their port of departure, destination, and cargo. The WEU was not mandated to intervene if violations of the embargo were suspected: these were reported to the Sanctions Committee established by Resolution 724(1991) to monitor the measures undertaken in application of the embargo.[294]

The WEU Council of Ministers Declaration on Former Yugoslavia adopted in Rome on 20 November 1992 stated that

since 16 July 1992, warships and aircraft of WEU member states, under Italian operational control, have been carrying out operations to monitor at sea compliance with the embargo established by UN Security Council Resolutions 713 and 757. So far 3,649 ships have been monitored by WEU operations and 71 suspected violations have been reported.

Ministers therefore welcomed the adoption of UNSC Resolution 787[1992]. They decided that WEU will contribute to its implementation and that, to this end, warships and aircraft of WEU member States, on the basis of approved joint planning, will start operations aimed at ensuring the strict implementation of the embargo at sea. These will include stop and search actions and other measures as necessary.

Operation *Sharp Guard* was launched by WEU jointly with NATO, to support the implementation of the sanctions regime under Resolution 820(1993).[295] The WEU saw its role as complementing the UN sanctions regime. Following the initialling of the Dayton Accord on 21 November 1995, Operation *Sharp Guard*

---

[293] L Vierucci, 'The role of the Western European Union (WEU) in the maintenance of international peace and security', 2 *International Peacekeeping* (1995), 309 at 311–12.
[294] Ibid, 313.
[295] J Woodliffe, 'The Evolution of a New NATO for a New Europe', 47 ICLQ (1998), 174 at 189; see also the WEU Council of Ministers Communiqué, Rome, 19 May 1993, para 6.

was adapted in accordance with suspending economic sanctions and phasing out the arms embargo, which led to this operation's termination.[296]

(f) Enforcement Action by OAS

Article 6 of the Inter-American Treaty of Reciprocal Assistance provides that, having identified the existence of the relevant threat, the 'Organ of Consultation shall meet immediately in order to agree on the measures which must be taken in case of aggression to assist the victim of the aggression or, in any case, the measures which should be taken for the common defense and for the maintenance of the peace and security of the Continent'. Article 8 states that

[f]or the purposes of this Treaty, the measures on which the Organ of Consultation may agree will comprise one or more of the following: recall of chiefs of diplomatic missions; breaking of diplomatic relations; breaking of consular relations; partial or complete interruption of economic relations or of rail, sea, air, postal, telegraphic, telephonic, and radiotelephonic or radiotelegraphic communications; and use of armed force.

A contextual reading could indicate that Article 6 relates to threats not necessarily limited to an armed attack and Article 8 permits the use of force as an enforcement measure, without these two Articles specifying which particular measures are mandated in response to a threat of a particular kind. It is thus possible to interpret the Rio Treaty as authorizing the OAS organs to approve the use of force even if this is not mandated as self-defence under Article 51 of the UN Charter. Under this reading, the Rio Treaty would be seen as expressly mandating a use of force that is neither allowed under general international law nor authorized by the UN Security Council. This would put the Rio Treaty in conflict with, and therefore over-ruled by, the UN Charter by virtue of the latter's Article 103.

A 1960 OAS Resolution, reacting to acts of the Dominican Republic against Venezuela, decided that all member States should break diplomatic relations with the Dominican Republic, and partially interrupt economic relations with it, including an immediate suspension of the trade in arms.[297] The 1962 Punta del Este Resolution decided '[t]o suspend immediately trade with Cuba in arms and implements of war of every kind'.[298] As Halderman observed, the Punta del Este decision imposed an arms embargo on Cuba by essentially circumventing Article 53 of the Charter.[299]

The OAS Council Resolution of 23 October 1962 recommended that

the member States, in accordance with Articles 6 and 8 of the Inter-American Treaty of Reciprocal Assistance, take all measures, individually and collectively, which they may

---

[296] D Leurdijk, 'Before and after Dayton: The UN and NATO in the Former Yugoslavia', 18 *Third World Quarterly* (1997), 457 at 460.
[297] Resolution I, Sixth Meeting of Consultation of Ministers of Foreign Affairs, Final Act, San Jose, 16–21 August 1960, operative paragraph 1.
[298] Resolution VIII, Eighth Meeting of Consultation of Ministers of Foreign Affairs, Final Act, Punta del Este, 22 to 31 January 1962, operative paragraph 1.
[299] Halderman, n 244 above, 117.

deem necessary to ensure that the Government of Cuba cannot continue to receive from the Sino-Soviet powers military material and related supplies which may threaten the peace and security of the Continent and to prevent the missiles in Cuba with offensive capacity from ever becoming an active threat to the peace and security of the Continent.[300]

The US proclamation of a 'defensive quarantine' against Cuba was based on the US belief that it was authorized by this OAS resolution.[301] The words 'they may deem necessary' presumably leave individual members some discretion as to what particular measures they should apply, and thus contemplate an open-ended though unspecified licence to use force.

The 1964 Ninth Meeting of Consultation of Ministers of Foreign Affairs in Washington (serving as Organ of Consultation) decided, in response to Cuban actions against Venezuela,

to apply, in accordance with the provisions of Articles 6 and 8 of the Inter-American Treaty of Reciprocal Assistance, the following measures:
  a. That the governments of the American States not maintain diplomatic or consular relations with the Government of Cuba;
  b. That the governments of the American states suspend all their trade, whether direct or indirect, with Cuba, except in foodstuffs, medicines, and medical equipment that may be sent to Cuba for humanitarian reasons; and
  c. That the governments of the American states suspend all sea transportation between their countries and Cuba except for such transportation as may be necessary for reasons of a humanitarian nature.[302]

The resolution instructed the OAS Secretary-General to notify the Security Council in accordance with Article 54 of the UN Charter.

As for the termination of these measures, paragraph 3 of the 1962 Punta del Este Resolution authorizes the OAS Council to discontinue, after an affirmative vote of two-thirds of its members, the measures stipulated in that resolution, 'at such time as the Government of Cuba demonstrates its compatibility with the purposes and principles of the Charter'. This is a somewhat broad and more open-ended requirement than simply that a specific threat should have disappeared. The 1964 Washington decision stipulates a similarly open-ended condition: the OAS Council is authorized, after an affirmative vote of two-thirds of its members, 'to discontinue the measures adopted in the present resolution at such time as the Government of Cuba shall have ceased to constitute a danger to the peace and security of the hemisphere'.

As Claude has illustrated, the OAS was keen on increasing regional autonomy through attempting to liberalize the requirement for Security Council approval of regional enforcement measures that was eventually embodied in Article 53.[303]

---

[300] Resolution of 23 October 1962, 47 *Department of State Bulletin* (1962), 722–3.
[301] Meeker, n 262 above, 517.
[302] Resolution I, Ninth Meeting of Consultation of Ministers of Foreign Affairs, Final Act, Washington DC, 22–6 July 1966, operative paragraph 3.
[303] Claude, n 259 above, 8.

Various strategies may be employed to this end. For instance, if a regional organization is keen on taking action it would contend that this action does not constitute enforcement, as was the case with the OAS action against the Dominican Republic and Cuba.[304]

It was argued by states supporting the legality of OAS Punta del Este measures that they did not constitute enforcement measures under Article 53, because they were steps any state could legally take, individually or collectively, without authorization from anyone.[305] Argentina submitted that giving regional agencies an efficient role would require them to be prohibited only from undertaking forcible measures (without an Article 53 authorization), but not those 'like the breaking of diplomatic relations, which was within the exclusive right of a sovereign State'.[306] The UK representative pointed out that the OAS acts against the Dominican Republic were 'acts of policy perfectly within the competence of any sovereign State and, therefore, were within the competence of the OAS members acting collectively', and that Article 53 outlawed forcible action only.[307] These statements relate only to a relatively minor part of the OAS sanctions, and thus effectively disclaim an entitlement to undertake regional enforcement beyond the limits they specify.

In terms of another, related, strategy, invoking the *Certain Expenses* Opinion,[308] US government lawyers maintained that, just like peace-keeping missions established by the UN with the consent of the host state, the OAS measures against Cuba (such as quarantine) did not constitute enforcement action, since the OAS had only recommended that states take these measures, instead of obliging them to do so. Hence it did not need advance authorization from the UN Security Council.[309] But this argument flies in the face of UN peace-keeping being consensual, since the OAS measures in question were not. They were directed against Cuba as a state and potentially against other states that might have tried to bypass the quarantine.

The quarantine constituted a threat or use of force within the meaning of Article 2(4) of the Charter. In institutional terms, as an OAS action the quarantine constituted an enforcement action in terms of the International Court's specification in the *Certain Expenses* case—it was undertaken without Cuba's consent.[310] It is suggested that the OAS Council actually authorized armed intervention on Cuban soil, by using the words 'to prevent the missiles in Cuba with offensive capability from ever becoming an active threat to the peace and security of the Continent'. For this reason, Mexico, Bolivia, and Brazil abstained on this part of the resolution.[311] Overall, in relation to Cuba, eight members of the Council

---

[304] A Eide, 'Peace-Keeping and Enforcement by Regional Organizations: Its place in the United Nations System', 3 *Journal of Peace Research* (1966), 125 at 127–8.
[305] *Repertory of Practice of United Nations Organs*, 1955–66, 295.
[306] Ibid, 291.
[307] *Repertory of Practice of the UN Security Council*, 1959–63, 318.
[308] *ICJ Reports* 1962.
[309] Meeker, n 262 above, 121; Deen-Racsmany, n 250 above, 301.
[310] Akehurst, n 252 above, 198–9, 202; Villani, n 244 above, 541.
[311] P Pirrone, 'The Use of Force in the Framework of the Organization of American States', in A Cassese (ed.), *The Current Legal Regulation of the Use of Force* (Leiden: Nijhof, 1986), 223 at 227.

expressed scepticism at the view that OAS sanctions short of armed force required no authorization from the Council.[312]

Schreuer is certainly right in suggesting that 'the coercive element is relevant primarily in relation to the State which is the object of the sanctions and not in relation to States participating in them'.[313] Enforcement involves a particular type of measure, not simply the legal force of a decision on which it is based; even when recommending particular measures, the OAS effectively approved the resort by its members to measures coercing a state.

(g) The OECS-authorized Intervention in Grenada

There has been a doctrinal attempt to qualify the US-led intervention in Grenada in 1983 as, not enforcement action but regional peace keeping under Article 52 of the UN Charter. One reason invoked was the invitation to OECS forces by the Governor-General of Grenada, which has not been quite substantiated. Moore refers to states viewing the 1965 US action in the Dominican Republic as not being an enforcement action and applies that projected position to Grenada.[314] The Governor-General's request was received two days after the OECS decided to 'authorize' intervention. It thus had no impact on the decision to use force in Grenada. On 21 October the OECS member States made a decision to invade Grenada; President Reagan's provisional decision on intervention was made on 23 October; while the Governor-General's request was made on 24 October, and the actual intervention began on 25 October.[315] Presumably, the US government thought that a regional authorization alone was insufficient and 'waited' for the request. International reaction to this intervention has been overwhelmingly negative.

The OECS Statement justified the intervention in Grenada on the basis of Article 8 of the Treaty founding the OECS. The statement emphasized the spread of armaments in Grenada which was deemed to pose a threat to the security of the members of OECS, justifying urgent steps to remove this threat. A 'multinational pre-emptive defensive strike' was thus undertaken under Article 8 of the OECS Treaty, which deals with defence and security in the region. Once the threat had been removed the OECS states would invite the Governor-General to assume the executive powers in Grenada.[316] By determining, in the OECS statement, the existence of a 'dangerous threat to peace and security' as the basis for intervention, the OECS effectively attempted to arrogate the UN Security Council's power to determine threats under Article 39 of the UN Charter, with a view to undertaking enforcement action, and thus encroached upon the exclusive competence of the Security Council under that article.

---

[312] Claude, n 259 above, 53; Halderman, n 244 above, 104, also states that the quarantine was essentially an enforcement measure.

[313] Schreuer, n 244 above, 492.

[314] JN Moore, 'Grenada and the International Double Standard', 78 AJIL (1984), 145 at 153–6.

[315] M Hakimi, 'To Condone or Condemn? Regional Enforcement Actions in the Absence of Security Council Authorization', *Vanderbilt Journal of Transnational Law*, 40 (2007), 643 at 664–5.

[316] OECS Statement of 25 October 1983, 83 *Department of State Bulletin* (December 1983), 67–8.

6
Self-Defence and Collective Security

1. General Aspects

Self-defence concentrates on actual armed attacks that have already occurred, while collective security 'proper' deals with threats in a broader sense.[1] This difference does not manifest a dichotomy. Self-defence is at the heart of the collective security process, since nearly all security institutions either originated as defensive alliances or have, simultaneously or subsequently, acquired a defence element. It is only natural that by creating a collective security institution states focus on their security from armed attacks. It is appropriate to conduct a collective security action in situations that warrant the exercise of the right to self-defence under Article 51 of the UN Charter. Collective security action can also usefully complement an action in self-defence and facilitate its success, as was the case with the Iraqi invasion of Kuwait.

2. Individual Self-Defence under Article 51

The starting point is provided by Article 51 of the Charter which specifies that '[n]othing in the present Charter shall impair the inherent right of individual or collective self-defence if an armed attack occurs against a Member of the United Nations'. Both Kelsen and Kunz consider that Article 51 prohibits preventive war and that even imminent attacks are excluded from the scope of this provision,[2] while a Secretary-General's report specified that Article 51 applies to imminent attacks but does not justify anticipatory, preventative, or pre-emptive action.[3]

Article 51 mandates the use of force in self-defence only in response to an armed attack that has been launched by one state on another. This principle came under increasing challenge after the terrorist attacks against the United States on 11 September 2001, especially after the adoption of Security Council Resolutions 1368(2001) and 1373(2001) which prescribe counter-terrorist measures and

---

[1] C Stahn, 'Collective Security and Self-Defence after the September 11 Attacks', 10 *Tilburg Foreign Law Review* (2002–3), 10 at 11, 34.

[2] J Kunz, 'Individual and Collective Self-Defense in Article 51 of the Charter of the United Nations', 41 AJIL (1947), 872 at 878; H Kelsen, 'Limitations on the Functions of the United Nations', 55 *Yale Law Journal* (1945–6), 997 at 1010.

[3] *A More Secure World: Our Shared Responsibility,* Report of the Secretary-General's High-level Panel on Threats, Challenges, and Change, A/59/565, December 2004.

recognize that states enjoy their right to self-defence.[4] However, nothing in these resolutions states that non-state actors on their own can be the source of an 'armed attack'. On closer look, Resolutions 1368 and 1373 recognize the inherent right to self-defence in the context of anti-terrorist measures and also reaffirm the responsibility of states and non-state actors for terrorist acts. This has been emphasized, however, by two separate principles, and the fact that they were mentioned together does not establish a conceptual or normative link between them.

The International Court has repeatedly affirmed in its jurisprudence that self-defence can be exercised only against an armed attack launched by a state.[5] The doctrinal reaction to the Court's clear and consistent position has been either to overlook the content of the Court's pronouncements and suggest that it has not expressly pronounced on the issue, or to describe the Court's findings as inadequate by not justifying action that states might take against terrorist networks around the globe.[6] But both categories of criticism fail, because the Court was straightforwardly and consistently clear on the principles it upheld, and there is no international authority that postulates the law of self-defence any differently from the way it is presented in the Court's jurisprudence.

3. The Security Council's Interference with the Exercise of Self-Defence

Article 51 also provides that an action in self-defence can validly last 'until the Security Council has taken measures necessary to maintain international peace and security'. The meaning of this clause has been widely debated. Kelsen claims that, because Article 51 is part of Chapter VII, self-defence is thus subordinated to the Council's collective security measures.[7] Dinstein suggests that Article 51 enables the Security Council to review self-defence claims made by states. Such a review offers the following options: retrospective approval of self-defence; to impose a

---

[4] Eg W Heintschel von Heinegg, 'Legality of Maritime Interdiction Operations in Operation *Enduring Freedom*', in M Bothe, ME O'Connell, and N Ronzitti, *Redefining Sovereignty: the Use of Force after the End of Cold War* (Leiden: Brill, 2005), 364 at 385, suggesting that Resolution 1373 'has made sufficiently clear . . . that self-defence is not restricted to armed attacks attributable to given State'.

[5] *Legal Consequences of the Construction of the Wall in the Occupied Palestinian Territory*, 9 July 2004, Advisory Opinion, General List No 131, para 138; *Case Concerning the Armed Activities on the Territory of the Congo (Democratic Republic of the Congo v Uganda)*, 19 December 2005, General List No 116, para 146. For an analysis of these decisions see A Orakhelashvili, 'Legal Stability and Claims of Change: The International Court's Treatment of *Jus ad Bellum* and *Jus in Bello*', 75 *Nordic Journal of International Law* (2006), 371.

[6] E Wilmshurst *et al*, 'The Chatham House Principles of International Law on the Use of Force in Self-Defence', 55 ICLQ (2006), 963; M Wood, 'Towards New Circumstances in Which the Use of Force May be Authorised? The Cases of Humanitarian Intervention, Counter-Terrorism and Weapons of Mass Destruction', in N Blokker and N Schrijver (eds.), *The Security Council and the Use of Force* (Leiden: Martinus Nijhoff, 2005), 75; M Wood, 'The Law on the Use of Force: Current Challenges', 11 *Singapore Year Book of International Law* (2007), 1.

[7] H Kelsen, 'Collective Security and Collective Self-Defence under the Charter of the United Nations', 41 AJIL (1948), 783 at 793.

cease-fire; to demand the withdrawal of forces to original positions; to insist on the defending state ceasing any measures it has taken, supplanting these with collective security measures; or to decide that the state claiming self-defence is in reality the aggressor.[8]

One group of writers claims that belligerent parties have no choice but to comply with Council calls for cease-fire, there being no further room for invoking self-defence.[9] According to Rostow, under the Charter the Security Council has the last word and can stop a war in self-defence if it decides that the war has become a breach of the peace.[10]

For instance, Kaikobad suggests that Iran was bound to accept Security Council Resolution 598(1986) ordering a cease-fire in the Iran–Iraq war, even though Iraq was the aggressor and Iran could otherwise have claimed its inherent right to self-defence under Article 51. If the resolution seemed capable of producing successful practical consequences in stopping the aggression, Iran was bound to comply even though otherwise it was acting under Article 51.[11] The resolution demanded, in its Articles 39 and 40, that 'as a first step towards a negotiated settlement, Iran and Iraq observe an immediate cease-fire, discontinue all military actions on land, at sea and in the air, and withdraw all forces to the internationally recognized boundaries without delay'. However, by itself a binding statement of the Council will not suffice to take away the right to self-defence, without providing the victim state with a viable alternative.

Halberstam notes that in American legal literature overwhelming support is lent to the view that the Council can bar a state from using force against an aggressor, but concludes that this is a far-reaching interpretation not reflecting the design and intention behind the Charter.[12] The state acting in self-defence is not obliged to desist until the Security Council's 'necessary' measures prove effective.[13] According to White, a realistic interpretation of Article 51 is that only measures that do not leave the victim state defenceless will suspend the right to self-defence. The right must revive if the measures prove ineffective.[14] Matheson argues along similar lines that

the more reasonable interpretation of Article 51 is that self-defence is suspended only when the Council has taken actions that effectively restore and maintain international peace and security, or that are inconsistent with separate national military action. For example, where the Council authorises major military operations under unified command, it would be

---

[8] Y Dinstein, *War, Aggression and Self-Defence*, 4th ed. (Cambridge: Cambridge University Press, 2005), 212, 214.

[9] Ibid, 215–16.

[10] EV Rostow, 'Until What? Enforcement Action or Collective Self-Defence?', 85 AJIL (1991), 506 at 513.

[11] K Kaikobad, 'Self-Defence, Enforcement Action and the Gulf Wars, 1980–88 and 1990–91', 63 *British Yearbook of International Law* (1992), 299 at 343.

[12] M Halberstam, 'The Right to Self-defence Once the Security Council Takes Action', 17 *Michigan Journal of International Law* (1995–6), 229 at 236–7.

[13] D Greig, 'Self-Defence and the Security Council: What Does Article 51 Require?', 40 ICLQ (1991), 366 at 389.

[14] N White, *Keeping the Peace* (Manchester: Manchester University Press, 1997), 56.

reasonable to conclude that States may not conduct separate military operations that would interfere with or compromise those directed by the Council.

However, lesser measures (such as the imposition and enforcement of sanctions not intended to supersede the exercise of self-defence) do not, as such, constrain or terminate aggression and thus preclude national military actions in pursuit of the same objective.[15]

If the Council censures an exercise of self-defence without effectively countering the aggressor's action, it effectively puts the aggressor and the victim on the same footing. In the context of an international armed conflict, a Chapter VII situation will inevitably be produced by armed aggression. Restoration of peace will then necessarily presuppose taking action, or at least taking sides, against the aggressor.

In order to interfere with the exercise of self-defence under Article 51, the Council has to engage the relevant situation by making an Article 39 determination. The 'measures necessary' to restore peace and security under Article 51—which, by definition, are about the context where the act of aggression has been committed (and where the Security Council has addressed that situation as a threat to or breach of the peace under Article 39)—necessarily amount to measures required to eliminate the implications of the act of aggression, measures adequate for that purpose. Only in such a case could the state acting in self-defence be lawfully expected to suspend or terminate its defensive military action.

Article 51 also requires that a state acting in self-defence report to the Security Council accordingly. In practice reporting is infrequent.[16] In *Nicaragua* the International Court treated the reporting duty as a substantive condition of the right to self-defence by stating that, if a state fails to report to the Council its exercise of the right to self-defence, it is precluded from invoking that right.[17] Judge Schwebel claimed that self-defence measures may be covert and impossible to report; the reporting duty is thus procedural and cannot upset the substantive right to self-defence.[18] Whichever option is correct, failure by a state to report to the Council can possess important evidentiary value because it can evidence whether the state concerned was confident of its legal position and of having its claims internationally assessed as a necessary and proportional response to armed attack.

4. Collective Self-Defence

As the International Court specified in the *Nicaragua* case, collective self-defence can be activated if the state that has been attacked declares this, and requests assistance from other states.[19] The legality of collective self-defence depends on

---

[15] M Matheson, *Council Unbound—The Growth of UN Decision Making in Conflict and Post-conflict Issues after the Cold War* (Washington, DC: USIP Press, 2006), 133.
[16] Dinstein, n 8 above, 216.
[17] *ICJ Reports*, 1986, 121–2.
[18] Ibid, 377–8; see also Greig, n 13 above, 381, 384, 387.
[19] *ICJ Reports*, 1986, 103–4.

whether the state in whose favour it is exercised has the right to individual self-defence in the first place.[20] A careful assessment of state claims is required, against the standards of *jus ad bellum*. For otherwise, as Kelsen points out, there might be conflict between two Chapter VIII organizations, each of them claiming to be acting pursuant to Article 51.[21]

There is a considerable doctrinal debate over whether the armed action to expel Iraq from Kuwait (based on Security Council Resolution 678(1990)) was authorized as collective self-defence, or as a use of force as a matter of collective security under Article 42. One group of writers regards this as an action in collective self-defence.[22] Dinstein remarks, regarding Resolution 678, that 'an interpretation of a Council's resolution and collective self-defence, far from being mutually exclusive, are interlinked in this instance'. Article 51 rights were exercised in the context of the Council's collective security action.[23] White instructively indicates that the position of the United States and other coalition members during the Iraq–Kuwait war in 1990–91 was that they were entitled to resort to collective self-defence to protect Kuwait, even though the Security Council had already engaged with the situation and imposed sanctions, and that authorization was sought under what subsequently became Resolution 678 owing to a desire to make the forcible action, as opposed to a legal obligation to wait until the Council had authorized a self-defence action, politically acceptable to the world.[24]

Another group of writers regards the action pursuant to Resolution 678 as a collective security action, given that the Security Council did not specify limits on the authorized action as is required under the law of self-defence.[25] It is certainly correct that, when the Security Council grants authorization of the use of force under Article 42, it should not be seen as authorizing the action in self-defence per se (since this needs no authorization, being an inherent right of states). But what matters is that, as has already been clarified,[26] the Coalition action against Iraq had the sole purpose of reversing the consequences of Iraqi aggression against Kuwait, and was thus a self-defence action. Thus it was bound, both as such and through the parameters of Article 42 authorization as stated in Resolution 678, to observe the limits of necessity and proportionality that apply to any exercise of the right to self-defence against an armed attack.

---

[20] Kunz, n 2 above, 875.

[21] Kelsen, n 7 above, 795.

[22] O Schachter, *International Law: Theory and Practice* (Leiden: Nijhoff, 1991), 402; G Gaja, 'Use of Force Made or Authorized by the United Nations', in C Tomuschat (ed.), *The United Nations at the Age of Fifty* (The Hague: Kluwer, 1995), 39 at 44; Dinstein, n 8 above, 294–5.

[23] Dinstein, ibid, 274–5.

[24] White, n 14 above, 57.

[25] C Greenwood, 'New World Order or Old? The Invasion of Kuwait and the Rule of Law', 55 MLR (1990), 153 at 169; D Sarooshi, *The United Nations and Development of Collective Security* (New York: Oxford University Press, 1999), 176.

[26] See Chapter 5 above.

5. Self-Defence and Regional Organizations

Providing collective defence for its members has been one of the principal purposes for which the Arab League was established. According to Article 6 of the League Pact,

[i]n case of aggression or threat of aggression by a State against a member State, the State attacked or threatened with attack may request an immediate meeting of the [League] Council. The Council shall determine the necessary measures to repel this aggression. Its decision shall be taken unanimously. If the aggression is committed by a member State the vote of that State will not be counted in determining unanimity. If the aggression is committed in such a way as to render the Government of the State attacked unable to communicate with the Council, the representative of that State in the Council may request the Council to convene for the purpose set forth in the preceding paragraph. If the representative is unable to communicate with the Council, it shall be the right of any member State to request a meeting of the Council.

As we see, Article 6 provides for action against both outside aggression and disturbances of peace within the Arab region.[27]

According to the Joint Defence and Economic Cooperation Treaty (1950) between the states of the Arab League, tasks of the League encompass collective defence. Article 2 stipulates that

[t]he Contracting States consider any (act of) armed aggression made against any one or more of them or their armed forces, to be directed against them all. Therefore, in accordance with the right of self-defense, individually and collectively, they undertake to go without delay to the aid of the State or States against which such an act of aggression is made, and immediately to take, individually and collectively, all steps available, including the use of armed force, to repel the aggression and restore security and peace. In conformity with Article 6 of the Arab League Pact and Article 51 of the United Nations Charter, the Arab League Council and UN Security Council shall be notified of such act of aggression and the means and procedure taken to check it.

According to Article 3 of the Treaty,

At the invitation of any one of the signatories of this Treaty the Contracting States shall hold consultations whenever there are reasonable grounds for the belief that the territorial integrity, independence, or security of any one of the parties is threatened. In the event of the threat of war or the existence of an international emergency, the Contracting States shall immediately proceed to unify their plans and defensive measures, as the situation may demand.

Collective defence arrangements are included in the African Union legal framework, such as the 2005 AU Non-aggression and Common Defence Pact. The preamble to the Pact includes a comprehensive definition of aggression. Under

---

[27] A Eide, 'Peace-Keeping and Enforcement by Regional Organizations: Its Place in the United Nations System', 3 *Journal of Peace Research* (1966), 125 at 137.

Article 4, states party to the Pact undertake to 'individually and collectively, to respond by all available means to aggression or threats of aggression against any Member State'. Articles 10 and 11 task the Peace and Security Council with implementation of the Pact, by the use (inter alia) of the African Standby Force, pursuant to the PSC Protocol. These provisions emphasize the strong link between collective defence and collective security arrangements within the AU.

The ECOWAS arrangements contain elements both of collective self-defence and of collective security. The Protocol on Mutual Assistance on Defence concluded on 29 May 1981 states that 'any armed threat or aggression directed against any Member State shall constitute a threat or aggression against the entire Community' (Article 2) and undertakes to provide mutual aid in such circumstances (Article 3).[28] Article 16 requires that the head of a state that is a victim of aggression shall direct a written request to the current chairman of the ECOWAS authority, which means that the authority has duly been notified. Article 6 allows the Authority to discuss the issue at an extraordinary meeting and provides that its decisions will be binding on members, and under Article 6(3), it 'shall decide on the expediency of the military action and entrust its execution to the Force Commander of the Allied Forces of the Community (AAFC)'.

According to Article 6 of the SADC Mutual Defence Pact,
1. An armed attack against a State Party shall be considered a threat to regional peace and security and such an attack shall be met with immediate collective action.
2. Collective action shall be mandated by Summit on the recommendation of the Organ.
3. Each State Party shall participate in such collective action in any manner it deems appropriate.
4. Any such armed attack, and measures taken in response thereto, shall immediately be reported to the Peace and Security Council of the African Union and the Security Council of the United Nations.

According to Article 17 '[n]o action shall be taken to assist any State Party in terms of this Pact, save at the State Party's own request or with its consent, except where the Summit decides that action needs to be taken in accordance with the Protocol'. Thus, like the ECOWAS framework, this provision mandates a collective self-defence action only if expressly requested by the victim state.

The OAS security mechanism under the Inter-American Treaty on Reciprocal Assistance 1947 (Rio Treaty) combines collective security and collective defence features. One of its purposes is 'to provide for effective reciprocal assistance to meet armed attacks against any American State, and in order to deal with threats of aggression against any of them'. Article 3 of the Treaty provides that

1. The High Contracting Parties agree that an armed attack by any State against an American State shall be considered as an attack against all the American States and, consequently, each one of the said Contracting Parties undertakes to assist in meeting the attack in the exercise of the inherent right of individual or collective self-defense recognized by Article 51 of the Charter of the United Nations.

---

[28] UNTS, vol 1690, No I–29137 (1992), 52.

2. On the request of the State or States directly attacked and until the decision of the Organ of Consultation of the Inter-American System, each one of the Contracting Parties may determine the immediate measures which it may individually take in fulfilment of the obligation contained in the preceding paragraph and in accordance with the principle of continental solidarity. The Organ of Consultation shall meet without delay for the purpose of examining those measures and agreeing upon the measures of a collective character that should be taken.
3. The provisions of this Article shall be applied in case of any armed attack which takes place within the region described in Article 4 or within the territory of an American State. When the attack takes place outside of the said areas, the provisions of Article 6 shall be applied.
4. Measures of self-defense provided for under this Article may be taken until the Security Council of the United Nations has taken the measures necessary to maintain international peace and security.

Article 6 states that if any American state should be the subject of an aggression which is not an armed attack, or an extra-continental or intra-continental conflict, the Organ of Consultation shall meet to consider the measures to assist the victim of the aggression. This provision has been more importantly applied—or misapplied—in practice.[29] However, neither Article 6 nor Article 3 has ever been invoked for the purposes of self-defence proper.

According to Article 5 of the North Atlantic Treaty,

The Parties agree that an armed attack against one or more of them in Europe or North America shall be considered an attack against them all and consequently they agree that, if such an armed attack occurs, each of them, in exercise of the right of individual or collective self-defence recognised by Article 51 of the Charter of the United Nations, will assist the Party or Parties so attacked by taking forthwith, individually and in concert with the other Parties, such action as it deems necessary, including the use of armed force, to restore and maintain the security of the North Atlantic area.

Thus, the occurrence of an armed attack is required to activate the collective defence clause. As pointed out, it is up to individual members to decide whether they will turn their national contingents over to NATO command should an Article 5 action be necessary.[30] Article 5 does not include a straightforward duty of member States to assist each other if attacked by a third state, but only refers to 'such action as it deems necessary, including the use of armed force'. Furthermore, under Article 5 decision making is premised on a consensus within the North Atlantic Council. Given this, a victim state has no legal guarantee that it will receive the desired assistance from its NATO allies. The absence of a strict commitment to assist the victim of an armed attack is explained by the unwillingness of the USA to commit itself to a more specific obligation to engage in armed action should the conditions foreseen under Article 5 materialize.[31]

---

[29] See Chapters 4 and 5 above.
[30] E Stein and D Carreau, 'Law and Peaceful Change in a Subsystem: "Withdrawal" of France from the North Atlantic Treaty Organization', 62 AJIL (1968), 577 at 607.
[31] M Reichard, *The EU–NATO Relationship* (Aldershot: Ashgate, 2006), 182–3.

The North Atlantic Council invoked Article 5 of the 1949 Treaty after the terrorist attack against the United States on 11 September 2001,[32] but the precise implications of that invocation remain unclear. NATO was not part of Operation *Enduring Freedom*, which the USA unilaterally launched that year against Afghanistan, and got involved only at a later stage when peace operations (ISAF) were established under the Security Council's mandate, under Resolution 1386(2001). Neither did NATO specify the precise context in relation to which it invoked Article 5, such as the fact of an armed attack; so therefore this invocation is largely symbolic.

On occasions NATO has stated its vision on pertinent aspects of the law of self-defence. The NATO Strategic Concept seems to disclaim an entitlement to resort to self-defence against non-state actors suspected of involvement in terrorism, stating that '[a]ny armed attack on the territory of the Allies, from whatever direction, would be covered by Articles 5 and 6 of the Washington Treaty'. However, 'Alliance security interests can be affected by other risks of a wider nature, including acts of terrorism, sabotage and organized crime'.[33] Therefore terrorism is not an armed attack prompting self-defence but one of the 'other risks'.

The 2004 Declaration on Terrorism explains the rationale of NATO collective defence framework thus:

Defence against terrorism may include activities by NATO's military forces, based on decisions by the North Atlantic Council, to help deter, defend, disrupt and protect against terrorist attacks, or threat of attacks, directed from abroad, against populations, territory, infrastructure and forces of any member state, including by acting against these terrorists and those who harbour them. Any operations undertaken in the defence against terrorism will have a sound legal basis and fully conform with the relevant provisions of the United Nations Charter and all relevant international norms and standards.[34]

The NATO Comprehensive Policy Guideline adopted in 2006 elaborates upon this problem the following way:

Collective defence will remain the core purpose of the Alliance. The character of potential Article 5 challenges is continuing to evolve. Large scale conventional aggression against the Alliance will continue to be highly unlikely; however, as shown by the terrorist attacks on the United States in 2001 following which NATO invoked Article 5 for the first time, future attacks may originate from outside the Euro-Atlantic area and involve unconventional forms of armed assault. Future attacks could also entail an increased risk of the use of asymmetric means, and could involve the use of weapons of mass destruction. Defence against terrorism and the ability to respond to challenges from wherever they may come have assumed and will retain an increased importance.[35]

---

[32] As reaffirmed in the 2002 NATO Prague Summit Declaration, 21 November 2002, para 3.
[33] 1999 NATO Strategic Concept, para 24.
[34] Declaration on Terrorism issued at the Meeting of the North Atlantic Council in Foreign Ministers Session held in Brussels on 2 April 2004.
[35] NATO Comprehensive Political Guidance, 29 November 2006, para 5.

These declarations manifest the collective position of the Alliance and its members. The requirement of a 'sound legal basis' for defensive action against terrorism and the statement of intention to comply with the UN Charter and international law obviously imply that NATO is not contemplating a genuine Article 5 action in situations that are not covered by Article 51 of the Charter, as interpreted by the International Court. The 2006 declaration refers to unconventional forms of attack. That said, none of these documents contain an express statement that NATO collectively approves the use of fully-fledged armed force against an attack not launched by a state.

Following the invocation of Article 5 after September 11, NATO took specific measures at the request of the United States (such as intelligence sharing, granting US aircraft rights to fly over Allied territories, and the deployment of AWACS aircraft).[36] It is difficult to see these as actions genuinely covered by Article 51 of the UN Charter. Operation *Active Endeavour* in the Eastern Mediterranean is the only NATO action ever conducted under Article 5 of the North Atlantic Treaty after the attacks of 11 September: it was launched pursuant to the invocation of, and in order to implement, Article 5. Since this was a collective action to put Article 5 into operation, the NATO Secretary-General specified in his statement on 4 October 2001 that 'the Alliance is ready to deploy elements of its Standing Naval Forces to the Eastern Mediterranean in order to provide a NATO presence and demonstrate resolve'.[37] The naval force deployed in the Eastern Mediterranean was charged, not just with surveillance and monitoring tasks, but also with enforcing responsibilities on vessels suspected of being engaged in international terrorism, no matter what flag they were flying.[38]

It is difficult to match these measures with the concept of self-defence to which Article 5 gives expression, or to NATO policy statements that its defensive action should have a 'sound legal basis'. These naval operations did not respond to an obvious armed attack, being instead premised on a suspicion of involvement in terrorism, which makes it difficult to judge their necessity or proportionality. There has been no definitive assessment of this operation through state practice, partly due to its limited geographical ambit and impact, and it is premature to regard it as a valid precedent expanding the meaning of self-defence.

The 1954 WEU Modified Brussels Treaty provided in Article V that

[i]f any of the High Contracting Parties should be the object of an armed attack in Europe, the other High Contracting Parties will, in accordance with the provisions of Article 51 of the Charter of the United Nations, afford the Party so attacked all the military and other aid and assistance in their power.

This clause, unlike Article 5 of the North Atlantic Treaty, provides a straightforward obligation on WEU members to provide military aid in the case of aggression. A view has been expressed 'that Article V imposes a stronger obligation to provide mutual

---

[36] M Zwarenburg, 'NATO, its member states and the Security Council', in Blokker and Schrijver, n 6 above, 189 at 207; Reichard, n 31 above, 187–8.
[37] *Statement to the Press by NATO Secretary General*, 4 October 2001.
[38] T Gazzini, 'NATO's Role in the Collective Security System', 8 *Journal of Conflict and Security Law* (2003), 231 at 240.

assistance than Article 5 of the Washington Treaty'.[39] Despite an aspiration to that effect, before the EU's Lisbon Treaty (Treaty on the Functioning of the European Union, 13 December 2007) the EU treaty framework never included a proper collective defence provision.[40] The Lisbon Treaty contains a clause stating that the development of the European Security and Defence Policy might lead to common defence and acknowledges in Article 42 that some members of the Union see their common defence realized within NATO. Article 42(7), however, states that

[i]f a Member State is the victim of armed aggression on its territory, the other Member States shall have towards it an obligation of aid and assistance by all the means in their power, in accordance with Article 51 of the United Nations Charter.

The reference to 'armed aggression' confirms that this arrangement is meant only to counter attacks launched by states.

The EU rarely manages to formulate a uniform stance on the law of self-defence. In somewhat broad terms, the 2003 European Security Strategy provides that:

our traditional concept of self-defence—up to and including the Cold War—was based on the threat of invasion. With the new threats, the first line of defence will often be abroad. The new threats are dynamic. The risks of proliferation grow over time; left alone, terrorist networks will become ever more dangerous. State failure and organised crime spread if they are neglected—as we have seen in West Africa. This implies that we should be ready to act before a crisis occurs. Conflict prevention and threat prevention cannot start too early.[41]

The Strategy does not specify implications for the law of self-defence as part of general international law. It is unclear whether by this document the EU claims that it is entitled to deviate from the general law of self-defence. Instead, it appears that the purpose of this statement is to underline the importance of EU taking a crisis-management role as opposed to launching an action in response to an attack against a member State. Similarly, the EU Counter-Terrorism Strategy does not include any reference to military action in general, or self-defence in particular.[42] The terrorism-related Solidarity Clause under Article 222 Lisbon Treaty mentions the possibility of providing assistance to a state affected by a terrorist threat, 'including the military resources made available by the Member States'. However, this clause is not part of the self-defence commitment under the EU Treaty (which relates to an 'armed aggression') and is formulated separately from it. The Solidarity Clause thus can encompass multiple types of inter-state collaboration, including by military means, but falling short of the use of force against third states. Given that the EU Treaty does not admit such, it would be fruitless to try and infer the existence of any collective self-defence requirement in the face of terrorist attacks not attributable to a state.

---

[39] Cf J Woodliffe, 'The Evolution of a New NATO for a New Europe', 47 ICLQ (1998), 174 at 188.

[40] 'The European Council acknowledges that the Treaty on European Union does not impose any binding mutual defence commitments', Seville European Council, Brussels, 21–2 June 2002, Annex IV, para 4; nor did the Petersberg Tasks include action in self-defence: S Graf von Kielmansegg, 'The Meaning of Petersberg: Some Considerations on the Legal Scope of ESDP Operations', 44 *European Foreign Affairs Review* (2007), 629 at 642.

[41] *European Security Strategy*, 2003, p 7.

[42] EU Counter-Terrorism Strategy, Brussels, 20 November 2005.

7

Peace Operations

1. Nature and Definitions

The two types of UN-mandated force operating in practice—peace-keeping forces and coalitions of the able and willing—are not mentioned in the Charter. In the *Agenda for Peace*, peace keeping is defined as a UN presence in the field, with the consent of all parties concerned, involving UN military and/or police personnel.[1] The UK Peace Support Manual defines peace keeping as operations 'established in a permissive environment where the level of consent and compliance is high, and the threat of disruption is low'.[2] There is also a strong doctrinal trend to sharply distinguish peace keeping from peace enforcement. It is argued that peace enforcement is another name for fighting a war and thus the engagement of peace-keeping forces in enforcement activities can be risky;[3] and that peace keeping depends on cooperation, not enforcement.[4] Generally subscribing to this view, Dinstein still acknowledges that, the original restrictive design notwithstanding, the concept of peace keeping is now multidimensional.[5] As Matheson explains, not even in the Cold War period were the 'essential characteristics' of peace keeping under Chapter VI—consent, impartiality and non-interference with internal affairs—clear and immutable. It has always been open to the UN to resort to a more aggressive style of peace keeping and deploy forces in situations where there was no peace to keep.[6]

---

[1] *An Agenda for Peace—Preventive diplomacy, peacemaking and peace-keeping*, Report of the Secretary-General pursuant to the statement adopted by the Summit Meeting of the Security Council on 31 January 1992, A/47/277–S/24111, 17 June 1992, para 20.

[2] *The Military Contribution to Peace Support Operations*, Joint Warfare Publication 3–50 (2nd ed., 1994), para 103(f).

[3] Cf T Findlay, *The Use of Force in UN Peace Operations* (New York: Oxford University Press, 2002), 155.

[4] A James, 'Painful Peacekeeping: The United Nations in Lebanon 1978–1982', 38 *International Journal* (1982–3), 613 at 629.

[5] Y Dinstein, *War, Aggression and Self-Defence*, 4th ed. (Cambridge: Cambridge University Press, 2005), 307, referring to the UNAMSIL mandate, which included safeguarding the free movement of people and goods as well as protection of civilians.

[6] M Matheson, *Council Unbound—The Growth of UN Decision Making in Conflict and Post-conflict Issues after the Cold War* (Washington, DC: USIP Press, 2006), 119, 127–8; S Graf von Kielmansegg, 'The Meaning of Petersberg: Some Considerations on the Legal Scope of ESDP Operations', 44 *European Foreign Affairs Review* (2007), 629 at 638, speaks of IFOR and SFOR as peace-keeping operations with a mandate for potential peace enforcement.

The Secretary-General's 1958 report suggested that a peace-keeping force, unless established under Chapter VII, 'must constitutionally be a non-fighting force', operating on the basis of consent.[7] A residual and more accurate definition, which encompasses a variety of missions, would refer to a broader category of forces including all kinds of UN military operation, 'provided that they do not fall within the restricted definition of enforcement actions' under Chapter VII.[8] Elements of this definition of peace keeping can be inferred from the 1994 UN Convention on the Safety of the United Nations and Associated Personnel, whose Article 1(c)(i) defines, in its pertinent part, a 'United Nations Operation' as 'an operation established by the competent organ of the United Nations in accordance with the Charter of the United Nations and conducted under United Nations authority and control'. The Convention

shall not apply to a United Nations operation authorized by the Security Council as an enforcement action under Chapter VII of the Charter of the United Nations in which any of the personnel are engaged as combatants against organized armed forces and to which the law of international armed conflict applies.

This is does not prejudice the position of peace-keeping units not initially designed to confront organized armed forces, especially those deployed in internal armed conflicts, which are later led by circumstances to exercise their right to self-defence in its various manifestations. In other words, a peace force, even if robust, conducted within a state, and using force with the consent of the government (even though not of all parties to the conflict), can still be a peace-keeping force. In addition, peace-keeping operations can be established by organs other than the Security Council, while only the Council can conduct an enforcement action designed to engage the organized armed forces of a state. The Convention's approach broadly responds to that developed by the International Court in *Certain Expenses*. Thus, whatever the semantics, international law draws a line separating forces that are used against a government from those that are not. The former are enforcing peace and the latter are keeping it.

2. Legal Basis for Peace Operations

The Charter is silent as to the legal basis of peace keeping but this is more an absence of pertinent Charter provisions than a feature of the Charter as a whole and its purposes. Instead, the silence in the Charter as to which principal organ is competent to establish peace-keeping forces means that it does not restrict to one principal organ the power to establish peace forces, nor exclude that the potential competence of other principal organs.

---

[7] Cited in JW Halderman, 'Some Legal Aspects of Sanctions in the Rhodesian Case', 17 ICLQ (1968), 672 at 677; see also R Zacklin, 'The Use of Force in Peace-keeping Operations', in N Blokker and N Schrijver (eds.), *The Security Council and the Use of Force* (2005), 91–2.
[8] Halderman, ibid, 680.

In state practice, the reference to Chapter VI as the basis for peace keeping has become traditional.[9] The UN Operation in the Congo (ONUC), not being a Chapter VII enforcement measure directed against a state as clarified by the International Court in *Certain Expenses*, was thus established under Article 36(1) of the Charter as a *method to adjust* the situation in the Congo, which endangered the international peace and security.[10] Security Council Resolutions 143(1960) and 161(1961) manifested the intention of the Council to assist the government of the Congo in fighting the groups and entities opposing it. By Resolution 169 (1961), the Council further authorized the Secretary-General 'to take vigorous action, including the use of the requisite measure of force, if necessary, for the immediate apprehension, detention pending legal action and/or deportation of all foreign military and paramilitary personnel and political advisers not under the United Nations command'. Thus ONUC was not a provisional measure under Article 40, because these 'shall be without prejudice to the rights, claims, or position of the parties concerned', and ONUC was not.

The UN Protection Force in Yugoslavia (UNPROFOR) was established under Resolution 743(1992). The preamble to Resolution 743 invoked Article 25 and Chapter VIII. UNPROFOR was UN-directed, at least originally. Resolution 836 (1993) further authorized it, under Chapter VII,

in order to enable it, in the safe areas referred to in Resolution 824(1993), to deter attacks against the safe areas, to monitor the cease-fire, to promote the withdrawal of military or paramilitary units other than those of the Government of the Republic of Bosnia and Herzegovina and to occupy some key points on the ground, in addition to participating in the delivery of humanitarian relief to the population.

This can be seen as an instance of transforming a peace-keeping force into a Chapter VII enforcement force, given that the entitlement to use force under paragraph 9 of Resolution 836 to protect safe areas could possibly be seen as entitling UNPROFOR to use force against a state.[11] However, the parameters of an authorization under paragraph 9 are limited, applying only to action 'in reply to bombardments against the safe areas by any of the parties or to armed incursion into them or in the event of any deliberate obstruction in or around those areas to the freedom of movement of UNPROFOR or of protected humanitarian convoys'. Whether this entitlement can then be interpreted as encompassing the use of force to disarm a particular faction or compel them to withdraw, should they persist in actions specified in paragraph 9—echoing the controversy that arose between the UN and the USA regarding the interpretation of the term 'secure environment' in

---

[9] G Gaja, 'Use of Force Made or Authorised by the United Nations', in C Tomuschat (ed.), *The United Nations at the Age of Fifty* (The Hague: Kluwer, 1995), 39 at 50.

[10] For further analysis see A Orakhelashvili, 'The Legal Basis of the United Nations Peace-Keeping Operations', 43 *Virginia Journal of International Law* (2003), 484 at 498–501.

[11] As the Secretary-General pointed out, 'UNPROFOR is not obliged to seek the consent of the parties for operations which fall within the mandate conferred upon it under Security Council Resolutions 836(1993) and 844(1993)': Letter dated 28 January 1994 from the Secretary-General addressed to the President of the Security Council, S/1994/94, 28 January 1994.

Somalia as part of the mandate of UNITAF under Resolution 794(1993)[12]—has never conclusively been clarified. It is also relevant that, for the purposes of further enforcement, under paragraph 10 of Resolution 836 the Council authorized member states to use force to support UNPROFOR in the exercise of its mandate.

It has been suggested that mixing the uses of Chapters VI and VII in the same context is fraught with dangers.[13] Arguably the adoption of a 'wider peace keeping' vision based on mixing Chapter VI and Chapter VII authorizations, as was done with UNPROFOR, produces a confusing operational environment for peace keepers on the ground, where they act on the basis of the consent of the territorial state in some cases and without such consent in other cases.[14] In his report the Secretary-General emphasized that the mixed environment in Bosnia (combining UNPROFOR as a peace-keeping force and NATO's enforcement air strikes) created problems for UNPROFOR performance of mainline tasks, given especially the need for pre-emptive action against Bosnian Serb air defences to ensure the safety of NATO aircraft.[15] While in principle legitimate, these concerns relate more to overall policy decisions on the crisis, to be taken by the Security Council in considering the mandate of relevant operations, than to the inherent nature of those operations. Moreover, by now mixing the use of Chapters VI and VII has become normal, as manifested by operations in Albania, Sudan, Rwanda, or Croatia.

Pellet argues that 'the safer legal ground' for all peace-keeping operations is Chapter VII.[16] It is indeed possible that a fully-fledged threat to the peace determined under Chapter VII can be addressed through the deployment of peace-keeping forces endowed with such 'classic' functions as observation and separation of warring factions. The wording of Article 42 excludes no peace-keeping operations, even in their most traditional sense.

Chapter VI situations can likewise be addressed through robust peace-keeping operations that, on their face, can be seen as enforcement actions. However, in practice, peace-keeping forces have been established as Chapter VI measures—in situations where Chapter VII is also invoked via Article 39—which proves that Article 42 is not the only approach for the Security Council might take after it has engaged Chapter VII. This approach enables the full use of jurisdictional potential available to principal organs of the UN under various headings provided for in the Charter. Peace operations conducted within this legal framework should be conceptualized and analysed without employing preconceived abstract categories, through interpretation of constituent instruments and decisions of collective security organs which establish peace operations, to ascertain systemic requirements and point to the normative possibilities of establishing new operations. Projecting

---

[12] See Chapter 5 above.

[13] C Greenwood, 'The United Nations as Guarantor of International Peace and Security: Past, Present and Future—A United Kingdom View', in Tomuschat, n 9 above, 58 at 75.

[14] Findlay, n 3 above, 263.

[15] *Report of the Secretary-General pursuant to Security Council Resolutions 982(1995) and 987(1995)*, 30 May 1995, S/1995/444, paras 40, 62ff.

[16] A Pellet, 'The Road to Hell is Paved with Good Intentions. The United Nations as a Guarantor of International Peace and Security: A French Perspective', in Tomuschat, n 9 above, 130.

conceptual clichés unnecessarily curtails the ability and mandate of the UN principal organs to deal with actual or potential threats to the peace.

A strict adherence to a black-and-white difference between peace keeping and peace enforcement, between Chapter VI and Chapter VII authorizations, between absolute impartiality and robust action, can in practice produce dire results. As is known, the UN Assistance Mission for Rwanda (UNAMIR) was established as a Chapter VI peace-keeping force under Resolution 872(1993), with a mandate to monitor peace accords and the security situation, establish a weapons-secure zone in the Rwandan capital, and (most importantly) to 'investigate at the request of the parties or on its own initiative instances of alleged non-compliance with the provisions of the Arusha Peace Agreement relating to the integration of the armed forces, and pursue any such instances with the parties responsible and report thereon as appropriate to the Secretary-General' (operative paragraph 3(e)). On 11 January 1994, the DPKO received 'unequivocal warnings' from informants in Rwanda that weapons were being stockpiled for the mass killings of Tutsi, that lists of those to be eliminated were being compiled, and that assaults on Belgian troops were also envisaged. The UN Secretariat questioned the credibility of the information and showed no enthusiasm in investigating it. When UNAMIR requested authorization to seize weapons with overwhelming force, this was refused on the grounds that the UN mandate did not permit it; UNAMIR had to avoid any forcible action.[17] Large-scale massacres followed, purely because the UN Secretariat had been so closely attached to the strict distinction between Chapter VI and Chapter VII operations.

It is arguably right that 'the consensual nature of UN peacekeeping operations means that without an express change in its mandate a peacekeeping force cannot be used to carry out [a] military enforcement mission'.[18] While this can be true of empowering a peace force to carry out a qualitatively new enforcement operation, this does not prejudice the right of that force to carry out a robust armed action to safeguard its existing mandate, which understanding is dictated by the need to interpret the UN resolution establishing that force in line with the principle of effectiveness to construe the pertinent principal organ's decision as intending to enable the force in question to exercise its mandate effectively. As the Secretary-General pointed out in relation to UNAMSIL in Sierra Leone, the presence of a robust and determined peace-keeping force in the country should be part of a strategy to induce armed groups to disarm.[19]

Resolution 745(1992) established UNTAC in Cambodia under the Security Council's authority but without specifying its Charter basis (paragraph 2). Resolution 1545(2004) established ONUB—a peace-keeping force to act in cooperation with the Burundian government—on the basis of Chapter VII and authorized it to use all necessary means to carry out its mandate (paragraph 5). UNMISET in East Timor, comprising civilian, police, and military elements, was established by Security

---

[17] Findlay, n 3 above, 279.
[18] D Sarooshi, *The United Nations and Development of Collective Security* (New York: Oxford University Press, 1999), 77.
[19] *Sixth Report of the Secretary-General on the United Nations Mission in Sierra Leone*, S/2000/832, 24 August 2000, para 52.

Council Resolution 1410(2002) without recourse to Chapter VII and given comprehensive powers to assist the exercise of internal and external functions of the newly independent East Timorese state. Paragraph 6 of the resolution authorizes UNMISET, under Chapter VII, 'to take the necessary actions, for the duration of its mandate, to fulfil its mandate'. UNMISET was established with the consent of the East Timorese government. The intention to endow UNMISET with enforcement powers against the host state government does not follow from the terms of the UNMISET mandate, as specified in paragraph 2 of the resolution. As another example, Resolution 1037(1995) describes UNTAES as a Chapter VII peace-keeping operation.

In *Certain Expenses* the International Court effectively justified the UfP resolution pattern of establishing peace-keeping forces, albeit only in relation to the role of the General Assembly in non-coercive operations.[20] The key to the Court's outcome was that peace-keeping operations do not constitute 'action' under Article 11(2) of the Charter—that is, enforcement action undertaken against a state—which falls within the exclusive competence of the Security Council.[21] Thus, the Assembly is not legally precluded from establishing peace-keeping forces so long as they are not directed against a state. As for particular bases in the Charter, *Certain Expenses* points to the relevance for the establishment of UNEF of Articles 11 and 14, which refer to the Assembly's adoption of measures to adjust situations peacefully.

There is also a strong doctrinal support for implied powers as a basis for establishing peace-keeping operations.[22] The relevance of the implied powers doctrine is to reinforce the effective interpretation of specific Charter provisions, pursuant to the object and purpose of the Charter, as was clarified in *Certain Expenses*. According to Akehurst, there is no reason why regional agencies should not possess the same implied powers as the UN to take peace-keeping action with the consent of the states concerned.[23] The frameworks of the EU, the AU, and ECOWAS include detailed provisions on institutional competence to establish peace-keeping forces. However, the OAU peace-keeping force in Chad was set up despite the lack of reference to peace keeping in the OAU Charter.[24] As Arechaga observes,

it is permissible for a regional organization to carry out a peacekeeping operation at the regional level, provided such an operation does not amount to an enforcement action, which would require the authorization of the Security Council pursuant to Article 53 of the Charter. Consequently, a regional peace-keeping operation would only be lawful if the forces are sent and stationed with the consent or at the request of the territorial State and assigned a strictly non-fighting function.[25]

---

[20] Gaja, n 9 above 48.

[21] *ICJ Reports* 1962, 171–2.

[22] M Zwarenburg, 'Regional Organisations and the Maintenance of International Peace and Security: Three Recent Regional African Peace Operations', 11 *Journal of Conflict and Security Law* (2006), 483 at 487; R Kolb, *Droit humanitaire et opérations de paix internationales* (Louvain: Bruylant 2006), 27.

[23] M Akehurst, 'Enforcement Action by Regional Agencies, With Special Reference to the Organization of American States', 42 *British Yearbook of International Law* (1967), 175 at 208, 213.

[24] R Wolfrum, 'Der Beitrag regionaler Abmachungen zur Friedenssicherung: Möglichkeiten und Grenzen', 53(3) *Zeitschrift für ausländisches öffentliches Recht und Völkerrecht* (1990), 576 at 586.

[25] E Jimenez de Arechaga, 'International Law in the Past Third of a Century', 159 *Recueil des Cours de l'Académie de Droit International de la Haye* (1978), 13 at 138.

The dynamics of regional peace keeping have however required broader peace-keeping operations that can use force as soon as they are deployed and operate with the consent of the territorial government.

3. Peace Keeping and the Subsidiary Role of the UN Security Council

(a) MISAB in the Central African Republic

Operating the principles of subsidiarity and complementarity, the Security Council can adopt as its own a peace operation established by states, if it considers that this is in the interest of maintaining and restoring peace and security, and that the regional or inter-state effort alone cannot deal with the relevant threat effectively. The Inter-African Mission to Monitor the Implementation of the Bangui Agreements (MISAB) was established by few African states. In Resolution 1125(1997) the Council considered UN intervention necessary due to the fact that, in the Central African Republic, various persons continued to bear arms in contravention of the Bangui Agreements, and that the President of the Republic had written to the UN Secretary-General requesting assistance. On that basis, the Council

approve[d] the continued conduct by Member States participating in MISAB of the operation in a neutral and impartial way to achieve its objective to facilitate the return to peace and security by monitoring the implementation of the Bangui Agreements in the Central African Republic as stipulated in the mandate of MISAB (S/1997/561, Appendix I), including through the supervision of the surrendering of arms of former mutineers, militias and all other persons unlawfully bearing arms.

Therefore, acting under Chapter VII, the Council authorize[d] 'the Member States participating in MISAB and those States providing logistical support to ensure the security and freedom of movement of their personnel' (paragraphs 2 and 3).

(b) ECOMOG in Liberia

The Security Council can also complement an existing regional peace-keeping operation by adding its own peace-keeping component, as occurred with the ECOWAS operation in Liberia from 1990 onwards. All relevant actors in the Liberia conflict took the view that the ECOWAS force in Liberia was a peace-keeping force. The ECOWAS decision A/DEC.1/10/92 adopted in 1991 reaffirmed 'the right of ECOMOG, as a peace-keeping force, to defend itself against armed attacks from any quarter'.[26] Security Council Resolution 788(1992) condemned the continuing attacks on 'the peace-keeping forces of ECOWAS in Liberia by one of the parties to the conflict' (paragraph 4). In paragraph 9, 'the peace-keeping forces of ECOWAS' were exempted from the arms embargo

---

[26] S/24811, 8 (Annex II, para 10).

imposed on Liberia. In Resolution 866(1993), the Security Council restated that the ECOWAS force was the first peace-keeping force of another organization with which the UN mission (UNOMIL) got involved in the same situation.

The ECOMOG intervention in Liberia originated with an appeal, on 14 July 1990, by President Doe to ECOWAS to deploy a peace-keeping force in Liberia to deal with the civil war in the country.[27] At that point the governmental forces supportive of Doe were practically overwhelmed by the forces of the National Patriotic Front of Liberia (NPFL), which controlled almost the entire country apart from its capital Monrovia, and objected to the deployment of ECOWAS forces.[28] The ECOWAS decision of 7 August 1990 on the Cease-fire and Establishment of ECOMOG gave that body the task of 'assisting the ECOWAS Standing Mediation Committee in supervising the implementation and in ensuring the strict compliance by the parties with the provisions of the cease-fire throughout the territory of Liberia'. The troop commander was given the power 'to conduct military operations for the purpose of monitoring the cease-fire, restoring the law and order to create the necessary condition for free and fair elections to be held in Liberia'.[29] On 10 August 1990 the Chairman of ECOWAS informed the UN Secretary-General that the Banjul summit had decided to establish ECOMOG. The Secretary-General notified the Security Council on 13 August that, according to ECOWAS, the ECOMOG functions did not conflict with the UN Charter.[30] ECOMOG included troops from 11 ECOWAS and 2 non-ECOWAS states, although weapons and troops were largely provided by Nigeria. Having faced the reality of the Liberian conflict culminating in fully-fledged civil war, and the capture and killing of President Doe, ECOMOG gradually became drawn into the conflict and its initial complement of 3,500 soldiers rose to a total of 12,000 by 1993.[31]

ECOMOG troops landed on 27 August 1990, and undertook full-fledged combat in self-defence and against Taylor's attempt to capture Monrovia. On 29 August, the National Conference of All Liberian Political Parties declared Amos Sawyer interim president, basing this decision on the collapse of Doe's government.[32] As is further noted, ECOWAS had intervened in Liberia to secure a

---

[27] For the history of the conflict see *Report of the Secretary-General on the Question of Liberia*, S/25402, 12 March 1993, paras 4ff.

[28] J Levitt, 'Humanitarian Intervention by Regional Actors in Internal Conflicts: the Cases of ECOWAS in Liberia and Sierra Leone', 12 *Temple International and Comparative Law Journal* (1998), 333 at 343.

[29] Decision A/Dec.1/8/90 quoted in S Deen-Racsmany, 'A Redistribution of Authority between the UN and Regional Organisations in the Field of the Maintenance of Peace and Security?', 13 *Leiden Journal of International Law* (2000), 297 at 313–14; see also the ECOWAS statement dated 9 August 1990, on the conclusion of the first session of the ECOWAS Standing Committee on the conflict in Liberia, S/21485, 10 August 1990, 2.

[30] Deen-Racsmany, ibid, 315.

[31] B Nivet, *Security by Proxy? The EU and (sub-)regional organisations: the case of ECOWAS*, ISS Occasional Paper No 63, March 2006, 14–15.

[32] Levitt, n 28 above, 343–4; as the ECOWAS summit stated, ECOMOG succeeded in re-establishing calm in Monrovia and its environs: *First Extraordinary Session of the Authority of Heads of State and Government*, Bamako, 27 and 28 November 1990, Final Communiqué, para 5, reproduced in A/45/894–S/22025, 20 December 1990.

compromise between political factions. ECOMOG fell short of overrunning Taylor's NPFL forces after their failed attempt to capture Monrovia, even though this was well within ECOMOG's capabilities.[33] The ECOWAS Treaty, the Non-Aggression Protocol, and the Defence Protocol do not expressly entitle ECOWAS to intervene in internal conflicts not involving external interference.[34] However, ECOWAS could presumably act in such cases if the operation in question were supported by the consent of the territorial state. It is argued that Doe lacked legal authority to invite the intervention of ECOWAS, as he was no longer an effective head of state at the date he requested this, controlling only the capital of the country. ECOMOG could only have been invited by Taylor, who controlled the most of the country.[35] This view is exclusively fact-related and overtly Hobbesian, since any coup could then have deprived the regular government of its capacity to represent the state in its external relations.

It is also contended that, as Council Resolution 788 refers to Chapter VIII of the Charter, it clearly approved the ECOMOG action as enforcement under Article 53.[36] But this instrument divulges no such intention. While ECOWAS was commended, its action was approved as regional peace keeping under Article 52 of the Charter, part of Chapter VIII, given that (its forcible nature notwithstanding), this action was not directed against a state.

In its Enclosure the Yamoussoukro IV Accord, adopted on 30 October 1991, defined the mission of ECOMOG as being to cover Liberia as a whole and supervise the 'encampment' and disarmament of all warring factions. The Enclosure also specified that

ECOMOG shall enjoy freedom of movement throughout the territory of Liberia; [a]ll warring factions will willingly abandon their fighting positions and move into designated camps; . . . [and a]ll parties concerned will recognize the absolute neutrality of ECOMOG and demonstrate their trust and confidence in it.[37]

---

[33] Levitt, ibid, 345 (by reference to D Wippman).

[34] Ibid, 346–7. ECOWAS Revised Treaty 1993; ECOWAS Protocol on Non-Aggression, Lagos, 22 April 1978; ECOWAS Protocol on Mutual Assistance on Defence, 29 May 1981, UNTS, vol 1690, No I–29137 (1992).

[35] Ibid, 348–9 (also denying, in more awkward terms, that Sawyer could authorize ECOMOG intervention because 'Doe was still considered the *de jure* Head of State"). How so, one wonders, if the only authority entitled to invite intervention was Taylor? Even more awkwardly, Levitt considers that ECOMOG intervention in Sierra Leone in 1997 was lawful as it had been invited by President Kabbah (ibid, 367), who at that time was in exile, while Taylor was at least in the country albeit embattled.

[36] Ibid, 347; U Villani, 'The Security Council's Authorisation of Enforcement Action by Regional Organisations', 6 *Max-Planck Yearbook of UN Law* (2002), 535 at 543; T Franck, *Recourse to Force* (Cambridge: Cambridge University Press, 2002), 156, 159; see also D Wippman, 'Military Intervention, Regional Organisations and Host-State Consent', 7 *Duke Journal of Comparative and International Law* (1996–7), 209 at 228; C Walter, 'Security Council Control over Regional Action', 1 *Max-Planck Yearbook of UN Law* (1997), 129 at 180–1; for a more balanced view see AC Arend, 'The United Nations, Regional Organizations, and Military Operations: The Past and the Present', 7 *Duke Journal of Comparative and International Law* (1996–7), 3 at 25–6.

[37] See, for the same position, the ECOWAS statement, adopted by the Committee of Five on 20 October 1992 at Cotonou, reproduced in S/24735, 29 October 1992; and the *Final Communiqué of ECOWAS at the informal consultative group meeting in Geneva, 6–7 April 1992*, paragraph 4(c), reproduced in S/23863, 30 April 1992.

This further confirms the consensual basis for ECOMOG operations as opposed to their enforcement nature. After the ECOWAS Authority of Heads of State and Government exerted pressure on Taylor to honour the agreement, Taylor's faction mounted a full-scale attack on Monrovia in October 1993, which was again repelled by ECOMOG. At the same time, ECOWAS states imposed an arms embargo and economic sanctions against the part of the Liberian territory controlled by NPFL and persuaded the Security Council to do the same, which culminated in the adoption of Resolution 788.[38] The preamble to Resolution 788 actually relies on requests from ECOWAS member States to make ECOWAS sanctions mandatory on a universal basis, to which the Council responded favourably.[39]

The Security Council confirmed in Resolution 866(1993) that the roles of ECOWAS and the UN in Liberia were based on complementarity and the division of roles within the framework of the Peace Agreement signed by three Liberian parties in Cotonou on 25 July 1993. The preamble to this resolution stated that

the Peace Agreement assigns ECOMOG the primary responsibility of supervising the implementation of the military provisions of the Agreement and envisages that the United Nations role shall be to monitor and verify this process.[40]

The Peace Agreement was seen as the framework for peace and security in the Liberian situation.

The ECOMOG operation in Liberia was not directed against the Liberian state, nor undertaken without its consent, and did not qualify as an enforcement action under Article 53 of the UN Charter. Hence no authorization from the Council was required, none was requested from ECOWAS, and in Resolution 788 the Security Council merely commended the outcome of ECOMOG operations, as ones that ECOMOG could in principle undertake under the mandate of ECOWAS. The facts of the Liberian case were complex, but its surrounding legal framework was straightforward. The government invited a regional organization to help to maintain order in the country, and the Security Council took note of the consensual operation conducted by ECOMOG.

Even the gradual evolution of ECOMOG's activities is compatible with its nature as a peace-keeping operation. Having initially been based on the consent of the Liberian government, ECOMOG faced attacks on the ground, responding to which (including by fully-fledged combat operations) reflected an effective interpretation of the original decision to establish ECOMOG. That decision carried with it the implied requirement—further reaffirmed in the peace agreement—that all parties to the conflict should refrain from impeding the operation of ECOMOG, and the right of the latter to self-defence (in the way this right normally applies to peace-keeping operations).

---

[38] G Nolte, 'Restoring Peace by Regional Action: International Legal Aspects of the Liberian Conflict', 53(3) *Zeitschrift für ausländisches öffentliches Recht und Völkerrecht* (1993), 603 at 611; Walter, n 36 above, 143.
[39] See preamble to Resolution 788 and Nolte, ibid, 634.
[40] For further instances of complementarity see paragraphs 3(g–h), 4, and 12 of the resolution.

The expansion of ECOMOG tasks took place gradually. The Lomé Cease-Fire Agreement of 13 February 1991 (signed by all faction leaders) recognized the monitoring role of ECOMOG and contained clear obligations on parties to not oppose the exercise of ECOMOG's mandate.[41] It would be unsound not to view ECOMOG as a peace-keeping operation merely because, having encountered resistance from Taylor's forces, it did not elect to leave Liberia under the pretext that there was 'no peace to keep', but instead proceeded to implement its mandate in the face of that resistance.

The UN was involved in Liberia alongside ECOWAS through its own peace-keeping mission in Liberia (UNOMIL). One of the functions of UNOMIL was to keep an eye on ECOMOG forces, which were accused of looting and human rights violations.[42] In Resolution 866 the Security Council listed control over the application of the Cotonou Agreement and thus over ECOMOG conduct as one of the UNOMIL's functions.[43] This resolution also welcomed 'ECOMOG's stated commitment to ensure the safety of UNOMIL observers and civilian staff and urges the Liberian parties to take all necessary measures to ensure the security and safety of UNOMIL personnel' (paragraph 8). The UN Secretary-General still insisted on the lead role of ECOWAS, since (in accordance with the Peace Agreement) ECOMOG had primary responsibility for ensuring implementation. The deployment of its troops was crucial for that purpose, while the UNOMIL role was to monitor the implementation procedures in order to verify their impartial application.[44]

(c) ECOMOG in Sierra Leone

After elections in 1996 in Sierra Leone that brought President Kabbah to power, fighting continued between the government and the Revolutionary United Front (RUF). On 30 November 1996, the Abidjan Peace Agreement was concluded after mediation by ECOWAS, the OAU, and the UN. On 25 May 1997, a coup led by Major Koromah deposed Kabbah, who had to flee to Guinea. Before fleeing, Kabbah officially requested Nigeria and ECOWAS to intervene and restore him to power.[45]

ECOWAS troops under Nigerian command were deployed in Sierra Leone and their tasks included defending Freetown against attacks.[46] The coup was condemned by the 66th Ordinary Session of the OAU Council of Ministers, who also appealed to ECOWAS to assist the people of Sierra Leone in restoring constitutional order.[47] As for the ECOWAS position,

---

[41] *Agreement on Cessation of Hostilities and Peaceful Settlement of Conflict*, 13 February 1991, Articles 1, 2, and the Annex.
[42] J Hirsch, 'Sierra Leone', in D Malone (ed.), *The UN Security Council—From the Cold War to the 21st Century* (Boulder/London: Lynne Rienner Inc, 2004), 521 at 523.
[43] Walter, n 36 above, 189.
[44] Report of the Secretary-General on Liberia, S/26422, 9 September 1993, para 39, at 10; *The causes of conflict and the promotion of durable peace and sustainable development in Africa: Report of the Secretary-General*, A/52/871–S/1998/318, 13 April 1990, 10.
[45] Levitt, n 28 above, 364–5.
[46] Deen-Racsmany, n 29 above, 316.
[47] 28–30 May, Harare, CM/Draft/Dec.(LXVI) Rev 1, 18.

the Ministers for Foreign Affairs agreed that as far as Sierra Leone is concerned, the following objectives should be pursued by ECOWAS: early reinstatement of the legitimate government of President Ahmed Tejan Kabbah, the return of peace and security and the resolution of the issues of refugees and displaced persons.[48]

The same position was reaffirmed in the final Communiqué of the ECOWAS summit held at Abuja on 28 and 29 August 1997 and the Decision on sanctions against the military junta in Sierra Leone issued at the summit.[49] In its Presidential Statement of 11 July 1997 the UN Security Council reiterated that the overthrow of an elected president was unacceptable and, in line with the subsidiarity principle,

strongly support[ed] the decision of the Thirty-third Summit of the Organization of African Unity (OAU) held in Harare, Zimbabwe, from 2 to 4 June 1997 which appealed to the ECOWAS leaders and the international community to help the people of Sierra Leone to restore the constitutional order in that country and which underlined the imperative need to implement the Abidjan Agreement which continues to serve as a viable framework for peace, stability and reconciliation in Sierra Leone.[50]

The Council's reaction to the ECOMOG actions in Sierra Leone was expressed in the Presidential Statement of 26 February 1998:

The Security Council commends the important role that the Economic Community of West African States (ECOWAS) has continued to play towards the peaceful resolution of this crisis. The Security Council encourages the Military Observer Group of ECOWAS (ECOMOG) to proceed in its efforts to foster peace and stability in Sierra Leone, in accordance with relevant provisions of the Charter of the United Nations.[51]

Thus the UN endorsed regionally determined policy, and the same line was later reiterated in Resolution 1132(1997).

After the failure of all peaceful attempts to solve the situation stemming from the coup, on 30 August 1997 at its summit held at Abuja in Nigeria ECOWAS decided to establish an ECOMOG for Sierra Leone. The force's mandate was defined as enforcement of economic sanctions against Koromah and his government, with the aim of ensuring the return of the legitimate government. Accordingly ECOMOG resorted to the use of force. After the junta attacked in February 1998, ECOMOG engaged it, expelled it from Freetown, and in the following month successfully established itself across most of the country, which was followed by the return of President Kabbah.[52] The Security Council had authorized ECOWAS under Chapter VIII to intervene before ECOMOG forces engaged in a fight, and they so engaged only after attacked by the junta. The issue of retrospective or implied

---

[48] Final communiqué, Meeting of the Foreign Ministers of ECOWAS on the situation in Sierra Leone, Conakry, 26 June 1997, para 8 (S/1997/499, 27 June 1997). The same objective is reaffirmed in Declaration of the ECOWAS Committee of Four Foreign Ministers on Sierra Leone of 30 July 1997, para 2 (S/1997/646, 15 August 1997).

[49] S/1997/695, Annexes I and II.

[50] S/PRST/36 (1997); the same position was reiterated in S/PRST/42 of 6 August 1997.

[51] S/PRST/5 (1998).

[52] *Fourth Report of the Secretary-General on the Situation in Sierra Leone*, S/1998/249, 18 March 1998, para 6; Levitt, n 28 above, 343, 346; Deen-Racsmany, n 29 above, 317.

authorization does not arise. There is no trace of the ECOMOG action having constituted, or been regarded as, an enforcement action authorized subsequently. ECOMOG's peace-keeping role was expressly referred to in paragraph 16 of Resolution 1181(1998).

Under Resolution 1270(1999), which established the UN peace-keeping mission in Sierra Leone (UNAMSIL), the Security Council adopted an approach based on mutual complementarity between the UN and ECOWAS. Paragraph 11 commends

the readiness of ECOMOG to continue to provide security for the areas where it is currently located, in particular around Freetown and Lungi, to provide protection for the Government of Sierra Leone, to conduct other operations in accordance with their mandate to ensure the implementation of the Peace Agreement, and to initiate and proceed with disarmament and demobilization in conjunction and full coordination with UNAMSIL.

In operative terms, the UN had to live with a more influential ECOMOG in charge for security in various parts of the country and on whom the UN had to rely for its own security. After ECOMOG departed its forces were absorbed into UNAMSIL.[53] A joint ECOMOG/UNAMSIL command was not established, there was insufficient cooperation and communication, and no clear division of competences. Nigeria was unwilling to tolerate two peace-keeping forces in the country and ultimately withdrew in 2000,[54] after which the remaining parts of ECOMOG were integrated into UNAMSIL through Security Council Resolution 1289(2000).

(d) ECOMOG in Côte d'Ivoire

As the conflict in Côte d'Ivoire progressed and a number of international actors sought its resolution, the parties agreed to cease hostilities so that a comprehensive peace agreement could be negotiated, and to accept the deployment of ECOWAS troops and other personnel in a buffer zone during the ceasefire. On 23 January 2003 a round table of Ivorian politicians adopted the Linas–Marcoussis Agreement aimed at resolving the ongoing crisis and root issues stemming from the political system that had given rise to domestic instability; the round table also agreed the deployment of ECOWAS forces, supported by French troops, and demanded strict compliance with it. In their communiqué, the ECOWAS heads of state expressed the wish that the Security Council endorse the joint peace-keeping operation, and authorize that operation to ensure the freedom of movement and security of its personnel and to guarantee the protection of civilians facing the imminent threat of violence.[55] This was a regional view of complementarity—the UN mandate was

---

[53] F Olonisakin and C Ero, 'Africa and the Regionalisation of Peace Operations', in M Pugh and WPS Sidhu (ed.), *The United Nations and Regional Security—Europe and Beyond* (Boulder: Lynne Rienner Inc, 2003), 233 at 243–4.

[54] M Goldmann, 'Sierra Leone: African Solutions to African Problems?', 9 *Max Planck Yearbook of UN Law* (2005), 457 at 481.

[55] UNYB 2003, 166–7.

needed to provide all necessary powers to enable the ECOWAS force to properly exercise its functions.

In its statement of 31 January 2003, ECOWAS agreed to play the role assigned to it by the Linas–Marcoussis Agreement. The AU Central Organ of the Mechanism for Conflict Prevention, Management and Resolution welcomed the signing of the Linas–Marcoussis Agreement and mandated ECOWAS to continue the initiatives taken by leaders of the region to bring peace to Côte d'Ivoire.[56]

Security Council Resolution 1464(2003) refers to 'the decision taken by the Economic Community of West African States (ECOWAS) Summit held in Accra on 29 September 2002 to deploy a peacekeeping force in Côte d'Ivoire'. The Council also welcomed the above decision of ECOWAS. Under paragraph 9,

[a]cting under Chapter VII of the Charter of the United Nations, and in accordance with the proposal contained in paragraph 14 of the conclusions of the conference of Heads of State on Côte d'Ivoire, authorizes Member States participating in the ECOWAS forces in accordance with Chapter VIII together with the French forces supporting them to take the necessary steps to guarantee the security and freedom of movement of their personnel and to ensure, without prejudice to the responsibilities of the Government of National Reconciliation, the protection of civilians immediately threatened with physical violence within their zones of operation.

This peace-keeping force was deployed under Chapters VII and VIII simultaneously, affirming the link between the two Chapters, and contained a robust mandate to use force within the operation which was expressly denoted by the Council as peace keeping. By Resolution 1528(2004) and on the basis of the ECOWAS request, the Security Council '*[d]ecide[d]* to establish the United Nations Operation in Côte d'Ivoire (UNOCI) for an initial period of 12 months as from 4 April 2004, and requested the Secretary-General to transfer authority from the ECOWAS forces to UNOCI on that date' (paragraph 1).

(e) AU and UN Peace Keeping in Sudan

African Union peace-keeping practice has manifested a vision of subsidiarity and complementarity in relation to peace operations. The AU PSC stressed, in relation to the crisis in Darfur,

the need for the AU to continue to lead the efforts to resolve the crisis in Darfur and, in this respect, welcomes the support extended by the international community, including the UN Security Council. The Council calls on the latter and all the AU partners to continue to support these efforts, including financial and logistical assistance to sustain the AU-led mission deployed in Darfur and to enhance its effectiveness.[57]

The PSC consequently defined the mandate of its mission in Sudan (AMIS) as improving the general security situation in Darfur including the protection of

---

[56] Ibid, 167–8.
[57] 13th Meeting, 27 July 2004, PSC/PR/Comm.(XIII), para 3.

civilians, monitoring compliance with peace agreements, and assisting the process of confidence building. The Council then requested the AU Commission 'to immediately take all necessary steps for the consistent, flexible, broad and robust interpretation of [this] mandate' and 'the tasks deriving thereof...in order to ensure a more forceful protection of the civilian population'.[58] Calling for a purposive interpretation of this kind is meant to preclude any possible excuses based on lack of mandate from justifying any failure to protect civilians in the conflict zone. The basis on which AMIS was established could be Article 7(c) of the PSC Protocol, which empowers this organ to authorize the deployment of peace support missions. As the government of Sudan expressly invited the AU intervention, there was no need for the Union to resort to enforcement action.[59]

The PSC stated that 'the African character of the mission, including through its composition and leadership', as well as 'the lead role of the African Union in the overall peace process' should be 'maintained in order, as much as possible, to secure the cooperation of all the parties, which is necessary to achieve a lasting solution to the conflict in Darfur'.[60] This seems to reflect the approach that regional organizations have a better sense of root causes and local realities. The 46th Meeting of the PSC also decided 'to support in principle the transition from AMIS to a UN Operation, within the framework of the partnership between AU and the United Nations in the promotion of peace, security and stability in Africa'.[61] In this respect, the PSC seems essentially to lay down guidance for Security Council decision making in the sense

that the decision on the mandate and size of any future UN peacekeeping operation in Darfur is informed by the evolving situation on the ground. In this respect, a successful outcome of the Abuja Peace Talks and a significant improvement in the security and humanitarian situation on the ground *will be key factors in any decision* by the UN Security Council on the nature of the peacekeeping operation in Darfur.[62]

An earlier UN peace-keeping presence in Sudan included UNMIS, established under Resolution 1590(2005) with the task of supporting implementation of the peace agreement, the return of displaced persons to their homes, and the delivery of humanitarian assistance. Resolution 1706(2006) expanded the mandate of UNMIS to cover Darfur, including monitoring the movement and trans-border activities of armed groups (paragraph 8). Owing to the opposition of the Sudanese government, UNMIS was unable to deploy to Darfur because it was a purely UN mission. Therefore, the deployment of a joint UN–AU mission became part of the agenda.

In a subsequent decision, the AU requested the Security Council 'to urgently authorize the deployment of the African Union–United Nations hybrid operation, to be funded through United Nations assessed contributions and managed

---

[58] PSC 46th Meeting, Communiqué, 10 March 2006, PSC/MIN.Comm.(XLV), paras 3 and 4(b)(i).
[59] A Abass, 'The United Nations, the African Union and the Darfur Crisis: Of Apology and Utopia', 54 *Netherlands International Law Review* (2007), 415 at 422.
[60] PSC, n 58 above, PSC/MIN/Comm.(XLVI), para 6.
[61] Ibid, PSC/MIN/Comm.(XLVI), para 2.
[62] Ibid, para 6 (emphasis added).

according to the United Nations procedures, rules and regulations'. At the same time, 'the operation has a predominantly African character, in keeping with the relevant decisions of the Peace and Security Council'.[63] In line with this approach, Security Council Resolution 1769(2007) endorses AU decisions including that adopted at the 79th meeting; the Council specified in the preamble that 'the Hybrid operation should have a predominantly African character and the troops should, as far as possible, be sourced from African countries'.

The case of the UN–AU Mission in Darfur (UNAMID) thus involves a complex complementarity approach. The UNAMID mandate was agreed between the UN and the AU and specified in their joint report before the Security Council approved it. Truly complementary competences were emphasized by specifying that the hybrid operation required the approval of its mandate by the AU Peace and Security Council and the UN Security Council. The hybrid operation had to 'focus on the protection of civilians, the facilitation of full humanitarian access and the return of refugees and internally displaced persons to their homes. It should also contribute to the restoration of security in Darfur, inter alia, through the implementation of the Darfur Peace Agreement.' The mandate was informed by policies stated both in UN and AU documents, and its tasks included

[t]o promote the re-establishment of confidence, deter violence and assist in monitoring and verifying the implementation of the redeployment and disengagement provisions of the Darfur Peace Agreement, including by actively providing security and robust patrolling of redeployment and buffer zones, by monitoring the withdrawal of long-range weapons, and by deploying hybrid police, including formed police units, in areas where internally displaced persons are concentrated, in the demilitarized and buffer zones, along key routes of migration and in other vital areas, including as provided for in the Darfur Peace Agreement; [t]o monitor, investigate, report and assist the parties in resolving violations of the Darfur Peace Agreement and subsequent complementary agreements through the Ceasefire Commission and the Joint Commission.[64]

The report also specified that the force commander would be African, and defines command and control arrangements.[65]

The rather broad security mandate of UNAMID was reinforced by its entitlement to use force. Resolution 1769, which authorized the deployment of UNAMID, added to that the task of monitoring the implementation of an arms embargo imposed under Resolution 1556(2004) (paragraph 9). Paragraph 5 specified the process by which AMIS would hand over to UNAMID in three stages: initial deployment of UNAMID, preparation for assuming operational capability, and finally the achievement of full operational capacity culminating with the transfer of authority from AMIS to UNAMID.

Paragraph 15 provided a broad Chapter VII authorization to use force and conveys the impression that UNAMID constituted a Chapter VII enforcement

---

[63] AU PSC 79th Meeting, 22 June 2007, PSC/PR/Comm(LXXIX), paras 8, 11.
[64] *Report of the Secretary-General and the Chairperson of the African Union Commission on the hybrid operation in Darfur*, S/2007/307.Rev 1, 5 June 2007, paras 53–5.
[65] Ibid, paras 57–9.

action. However this was referred to as peace keeping when Resolution 1769 was adopted,[66] and can more plausibly be described as a robust peace-keeping force with coercive powers. Arguably, if UNAMID were to have used these powers against the government, it would have engaged in an enforcement action. But this would not really be the position because UNAMID was not *initially* meant to act against the government but was deployed with government consent. If, then, the government had interfered adversely in its activities, UNAMID should have been able to enforce its mandate, even against the government. This fits with the authorization to use force as agreed with the Sudanese government that consented to UNAMID's deployment. The robustness of the mandate does not contradict the consensual nature of UNAMID but instead follows from it. This approach is based on the effective interpretation of UNAMID's mandate under Resolution 1769—an interpretation which would require UNAMID to withdraw if there were 'no peace to be kept' would have frustrated the design of its deployment and of the entire Resolution 1769. The underlying principle seems to be the same as that relating to the activities of ECOMOG in Liberia. Abass argues that the exercise of robust action could have been hampered by China's position (when Resolution 1769 was adopted) that this operation was not meant to exert pressure or impose sanctions.[67] But this does not alter the position that was actually adopted as part of Resolution 1769. One member's view pointing to an abstract qualification of this force cannot affect what was agreed in the resolution.

(f) AU and UN Peace Keeping in Burundi

When establishing the African Union Mission in Burundi (AMIB), the African Union was likewise guided by the principles of subsidiarity and complementarity in relation to UN involvement. It mandated the deployment of AMIB 'pending the deployment of the UN Peacekeeping Force to be mandated by the UN Security Council as envisaged in the Agreements'.[68] The AU also specified that 'the African Mission would have fulfilled its mandate after it has facilitated the implementation of the Ceasefire Agreements and the defence and security situation in Burundi is stable and well-managed by newly created national defence and security structures', and that then its presence in Burundi would no longer be required.[69] AMIB was eventually replaced by ONUB. Paragraph 3 of Resolution 1545(2004) ordered under Chapter VII that AMIB forces be incorporated into the UN command and instructed the Secretary-General to ensure that authority over this operation was transferred to the UN Special Representative.

---

[66] S/PV.5727, 2(SG), 6 (Belgium), 7 (USA), 8 (Italy), 9 (South Africa).
[67] Ibid, 10 (China); Abass, n 59 above, 434.
[68] AU Central Organ, 91st Ordinary Session, 2 April 2003, Central Organ/MEC/AMB/Comm. (XCI), para 5.
[69] Ibid, section 5(i).

(g) AU and UN Peace Keeping in Somalia

The AU Peace and Security Council authorized 'IGAD to deploy a Peace Support Mission in Somalia to provide security support to the TFG, in order to ensure its relocation to Somalia, guarantee the sustenance of the outcome of the IGAD peace process, and assist with the reestablishment of peace and security, including the training of the police and the army'.[70] The IGAD Mission was meant to operate pending the deployment of an AU Peace Support Mission.

Complementarity subsequently worked out in peculiar ways as indicated by the example of the deployment of AMISOM in Somalia. The Communiqué of the 69th meeting of the AU Peace and Security Council saw the deployment of AMISOM as necessary to enable the Transitional Federal Government (TFG), which had just secured control over Mogadishu, to extend its control over the entire country. The Council authorized the deployment of AMISOM to enable stabilization and distribution of humanitarian assistance. The PSC specified AMISOM's composition and that AMISOM was to be deployed for six months (contributing to initial stabilization in Somalia), and then evolve into a UN operation with a mandate to support long-term stabilization and post-conflict reconstruction. The PSC requested the Security Council to provide all the support necessary for the speedy deployment of AMISOM and the effective accomplishment of its mandate, including financial support, 'bearing in mind that in deploying a mission in Somalia the African Union is acting on behalf of the entire international community'.[71]

Initially the Security Council, by Resolution 1725(2006), authorized the deployment in Somalia of the IGAD Peace Support Mission in Somalia (IGASOM). Security Council Resolution 1744(2007) noted the AU PSC Communiqué and accordingly '[d]ecide[d] to authorize member States of the African Union to establish for a period of six months a mission in Somalia' (paragraph 4). The Security Council's unique role is also manifested by its decision to exempt AMISOM supplies from the arms embargo imposed on Somalia under Resolution 733 (1992). Both organs stated that they 'authorize' the deployment of AMISOM. The legal basis of AMISOM thus consisted of elements mutually entangling decisions of the AU and the UN. The initiative came from the AU, while the UN created the legal environment in which AMISOM could properly operate. The AU document did not mention the role of Ethiopia at all, while the Security Council resolution specified that the deployment of AMISOM is aimed (among other things) at replacing the withdrawing Ethiopian troops. Resolution 1744 viewed AMISOM as replacing the IGAD training mission, and cancelled this (paragraph 12).

AMISOM could not operate effectively, given that it never received the number of troops that had been authorized by the AU. The Secretary-General's initial reaction demonstrated the UN's understanding of these problems. His Report stated that the AU was

---

[70] 24th Meeting, 7 February 2005, PSC/PR/Comm.(XXIV), Section A4.
[71] Communiqué of 19 January 2007 is reproduced in UN Document S/2007/34.

facing a considerable challenge in raising the forces required, with the necessary equipment and logistical support provided by designated partners, and the necessary resources to finance the operation. The African Union urgently needs to reinforce the Ugandan contingent in order to facilitate the withdrawal of the remaining Ethiopian forces and to expand its area of operations both within Mogadishu and beyond to complete the first of the operation's anticipated four phases.[72]

The AU Commission President addressed the UN in terms consistent with the principle of complementarity, specifying the need for 'a financial, logistical and technical support package for AMISOM, within the context of the provisions of Chapter VIII of the Charter of the United Nations'.[73] However, the Secretary-General's response was that

under the prevailing political and security situation, I believe that the deployment of a United Nations peacekeeping operation cannot be considered a realistic and viable option. . . . Given the complex security situation in Somalia, it may be advisable to look at additional security options, including the deployment of a robust multinational force or coalition of the willing. . . . In due time, such a force could be built to a level that would enable Ethiopian forces to commence a partial, then complete withdrawal from the country.[74]

In other words, the UN was not willing to properly complement the regional effort that was under way. Its view was that this could be complemented, but by someone else.

4. Peace-Keeping Operations by NATO

In 1995 the Dayton Peace Treaty envisaged Nato's role as being the guarantor of its implementation. The actors involved in this process viewed NATO as the only possible guarantor of a settlement based on the Dayton Peace Treaty and its involvement has made the enforcement of these arrangements more credible.[75] At the same time, the documents adopted in this process, along with the attitudes of NATO stated on a more general plane, evidence that all relevant actors viewed the role of NATO within the overarching framework of the UN collective security framework under Chapters VII and VIII of the UN Charter.

Annex 1A of the Dayton Peace Treaty ('Military Aspects of the Peace Settlement') specified that

[t]he United Nations Security Council is invited to adopt a resolution by which it will authorize Member States or regional organizations and arrangements to establish a multinational military Implementation Force (hereinafter 'IFOR'). The Parties understand and

---

[72] *Report of the Secretary-General on the situation in Somalia pursuant to paragraphs 3 and 9 of Security Council Resolution 1744(2007)*, S/2007/204, 20 April 2004, para 33.

[73] Letter dated 4 August 2007 from the President of the African Union Commission addressed to the Secretary-General, S/2007/499.

[74] *Report of the Secretary-General on the situation in Somalia*, S/2007/658, 7 November 2007, paras 33–4.

[75] N Figa-Talamanca, 'The Role of NATO in the Peace Agreement for Bosnia and Herzegovina', 7 *European Journal of International Law* (1996), 164 at 170.

agree that this Implementation Force may be composed of ground, air and maritime units from NATO and non-NATO nations, deployed to Bosnia and Herzegovina to help ensure compliance with the provisions of this Agreement (hereinafter 'Annex'). The Parties understand and agree that the IFOR will begin the implementation of the military aspects of this Annex upon the transfer of authority from the UNPROFOR Commander to the IFOR Commander (hereinafter 'Transfer of Authority'), and that until the Transfer of Authority, UNPROFOR will continue to exercise its mandate.

In addition, Annex 1A specified that 'NATO may establish such a force, which will operate under the authority and subject to the direction and political control of the North Atlantic Council (NAC) through the NATO chain of command', and that 'other States may assist in implementing the military aspects of this Annex. The Parties understand and agree that the modalities of those States' participation will be the subject of agreement between such participating States and NATO.'[76]

The Implementation Force was established in the context of the withdrawal of foreign armed forces from Bosnia, redeployment of the forces of the conflicting factions, and demilitarization of a number of areas within Bosnia.[77] The Dayton Agreement authorized IFOR 'to take such actions as required, including the use of necessary force, to ensure compliance with this Annex, and to ensure its own protection'. The agreement further specified that both parties 'shall be equally subject to such enforcement action by the IFOR as may be necessary to ensure implementation of this Annex and the protection of the IFOR'.[78]

The Security Council noted in its Resolution 1031(1995) the invitation to deploy the Implementation Force for Bosnia and authorized 'the Member States acting through or in cooperation with the organization referred to in Annex 1–A of the Peace Agreement to establish a multinational implementation force (IFOR) under unified command and control in order to fulfil the role specified in Annex 1–A and Annex 2 of the Peace Agreement'.[79] Thus, the Council effectively gave its authorization to the NATO forces under Article 53 of the UN Charter. Furthermore, the Council reaffirmed the enforcement powers of IFOR enumerated in the Dayton Agreement and especially 'note[d] that the parties have consented to IFOR's taking such measures'.[80]

It is noteworthy that, while the parties to the Dayton Agreement deemed it necessary to have UN Security Council authorization to deploy the troops of a regional organization such as NATO, the Security Council itself felt it necessary to emphasize that the deployment of NATO forces took place on the basis of the consent of the parties. Such deployment could arguably be effected by means of the Council's enforcement powers under Chapters VII and VIII, but even so the Council felt it necessary to stress the relevance of consent. It thus appears exaggerated to suggest that this deployment is 'wholly independent' of the General

---

[76] Annex 1A, Article I, paras 1(a)–(c).
[77] Ibid, Articles II–IV.
[78] Ibid, Article I, paras 2b and 3.
[79] SC Resolution 1031 (1995), paras 13–14.
[80] Ibid, para 15.

Framework Agreement and was solely based on Security Council resolutions.[81] For the Council confirmed that the legal basis of IFOR crucially included consent to it under the Agreement. This made it necessary to measure the necessity and proportionality of its decisions to approve the IFOR's deployment.

The need for UN Security Council involvement to assure legitimacy for a mandated presence of NATO forces in Kosovo was recognized at all relevant stages of the conflict. The Military Technical Agreement between the NATO Kosovo Force (KFOR) and the government of Yugoslavia referred to the prospective adoption of a Security Council resolution on the basis of which the KFOR would be deployed in the province of Kosovo.[82]

Under the Military Technical Agreement, the KFOR had the right 'to monitor and ensure compliance with this Agreement and to respond promptly to any violations and restore compliance, using military force if required', and to this end to

1. Enforce withdrawal of FRY forces;
2. Enforce compliance following the return of selected FRY personnel to Kosovo;
3. Provide assistance to other international entities involved in the implementation or otherwise authorised by the UN Security Council.

The consent of Yugoslavia to NATO operations in Kosovo was given subject to the prospective authorization of the KFOR mandate by the UN Security Council. By Resolution 1244(1999) the Council, welcoming the acceptance by Yugoslavia of the international security presence in Kosovo, 'authorize[d] Member States and relevant international organizations to establish the international security presence in Kosovo'.[83] As for the composition of the Force, paragraph 4 of Annex II to the Resolution specified that '[t]he international security presence with substantial North Atlantic Treaty Organization participation must be deployed under unified command and control and authorized to establish a safe environment for all people in Kosovo and to facilitate the safe return to their homes of all displaced persons and refugees'.[84]

5. Peace-Keeping Operations by the EU

(a) Operation *Concordia* in Macedonia

The first EU peace-keeping mission was launched after NATO's mission *Allied Harmony* to uphold the 2001 Ohrid Agreements between Slav and Albanian sides to the Macedonian crisis, and was based on the consent of the Macedonian

---

[81] As argued by J Woodliffe, 'The Evolution of a New NATO for a New Europe', 47 ICLQ (1998), 174 at 185.
[82] Military Technical Agreement between the International Security Force (KFOR) and the Governments of the Federal Republic of Yugoslavia and the Republic of Serbia, 9 June 1999.
[83] SC Resolution 1244(1999), paras 2, 4, and Annex II.
[84] In addition, NATO conducted two more peace-keeping operations: in Albania in 1999 to defuse a humanitarian crisis and in Macedonia in 2001–3 to assist the government to control the security situation in the country. In both cases, NATO acted on the request of the relevant governments. See T Gazzini, 'NATO's Role in the Collective Security System', 8 *Journal of Conflict and Security Law* (2003), 233.

government. *Concordia* was also the first instance of EU–NATO cooperation under the Berlin Plus arrangements. The EU relied on the planning capabilities and operative command structures of NATO,[85] and a small number of NATO troops stayed in Macedonia. Doubts were raised as to whether the EU Command element in AFSOUTH was genuinely under EU control.[86]

Joint Action 2003/92/CFSP specified that 'the Political and Security Committee should exercise political control of and provide strategic direction to the EU-led operation and take the relevant decisions in accordance with Article 25, third paragraph of the Treaty on European Union'. Article 4 further specified that '[t]his authorization shall include the powers to amend the operation plan, the chain of command and the rules of engagement. The powers of decision with respect to the objectives and termination of the operation shall remain vested in the Council, assisted by the Secretary General/High Representative.' Under Article 10 (2), '[t]he entire chain of command will remain under the political control and strategic direction of the EU throughout the operation'.

The 2003 EU Presidency Report ranked this operation as a success, given that the EU had achieved all its objectives; the EU and NATO had cooperated successfully in implementing EU–NATO permanent arrangements, including Berlin Plus, enabling the EU to launch an operation with recourse to NATO assets and capabilities.[87]

(b) Operation *Artemis* in the Congo

The EU Operation *Artemis* in Bunia, the Congo, was authorized by UN Security Council Resolution 1484(2003) as an enforcement action. The mandate is defined in paragraph 1 of Resolution 1484:

to contribute to the stabilization of the security conditions and the improvement of the humanitarian situation in Bunia, to ensure the protection of the airport, the internally displaced persons in the camps in Bunia and, if the situation requires it, to contribute to the safety of the civilian population, United Nations personnel and the humanitarian presence in the town.

Paragraph 4 accordingly '*[a]uthorizes* the Member States participating in the Interim Emergency Multinational Force in Bunia to take all necessary measures to fulfil its mandate'.

The question has been raised whether it was within the competence of the EU to act outside its area of membership, and accordingly whether it was within the competence of the Security Council to authorize Operation *Artemis*.[88] There seems to be no limit

---

[85] Article 2(3) of the Joint Action 2003/92/CFSP states that 'NATO will be invited to agree that the EU Operational Headquarters be at the Supreme Headquarters of Allied Powers in Europe (SHAPE)'.

[86] M Reichard, *The EU–NATO Relationship* (Aldershot: Ashgate, 2006), 248–50.

[87] ESDP Presidency Report, Brussels, 9 December 2003, para 4.

[88] For discussion see A Abass, 'Extraterritorial Collective Security: The EU and Operation *Artemis*', in M Trybus and N White (eds.), *European Security Law* (Oxford: Oxford University Press, 2005), 134 at 143ff.

envisaged in Chapters VII and VIII (in terms of the area where the crisis takes place) on the types of organization the Security Council can authorize to get involved in any particular crisis. On the contrary, the need to get regional organizations involved extra-territorially, and authority to do so, follow from the need for the Security Council to exercise its Chapter VII mandate effectively. If an organization from the region where the crisis is taking place lacks capability or will, it would be justified to authorize extra-regional involvement to cover the security gap.

Operation *Artemis* was authorized under Chapter VII (presumably Article 42) and not Chapter VIII, presumably because both members and non-members of the EU were involved. In terms of command and control, the EU did not subordinate its PSC to the UN Security Council. France was the 'Framework Nation' and consequently provided the headquarters and operational command. Reichard illustrates how Berlin Plus arrangements were tested, using the example of the EU operation in the Congo. Under those arrangements, the EU was to be engaged only if NATO was unwilling to be. In the Congo case the EU was acting with its own facilities and assets, and it adopted decision to get involved without officially enabling NATO to exercise its right to first refusal. NATO Secretary-General Robertson considered this a circumvention of the permanent arrangements between NATO and the EU. But in the end NATO did not protest and acknowledged support for the EU by wishing its operation success.[89]

The 2003 ESDP Presidency Report assesses Operation *Artemis* as having improved security conditions to allow for the timely deployment of a reinforced UN presence, and the setting-up of the transitional institution in Kinshasa. The EU had demonstrated that it could intervene in a timely manner in support of the UN.[90] The EU has regarded this operation as a measure and evidence of its independent crisis management capability.

(c) EU Peace Keeping in Bosnia

In 1995, when an international military presence was established in Bosnia, NATO was the only organization that could reasonably be expected to perform this task. The ESDP was not fully functional and any international military presence had to be conducted as a (NATO) Combined Joint Task Force (CJTF). Since the early 2000s, calls for the EU to take over have been intensified but did not initially meet enthusiasm from NATO. In 2004, at the Istanbul Summit, NATO decided to terminate SFOR and hand over the mission to the EU under the Berlin Plus agreement, which envisages the operation being carried out with recourse to NATO assets. The operation was essentially a continuation of the SFOR operation (since 80 per cent of troops on the ground remained the same).[91] By its Resolution 1551(2004), the UN Security Council referred to NATO and EU positions coming together over the replacement of a NATO mission with an EU one, and

---

[89] Reichard, n 86 above, 267.
[90] ESDP Presidency Report, Brussels, 9 December 2003, para 3.
[91] Reichard, n 86 above, 256–8.

renewed the mandate for the international presence in Bosnia. The EU Joint Action on EUFOR is premised on the agreement of both NATO and the UN Security Council to the EU deployment in Bosnia, and treats it as crucial that Resolution 1551 confirmed the applicability to EU forces of the SFOR Status of Forces Agreement contained in the Dayton Agreement.[92] The Joint Action also specifies command and control arrangements.

By Resolution 1575(2004), the Security Council acknowledged the consent of the authorities of Bosnia that both the EU force and the remaining NATO troops in Bosnia 'can take such actions as are required, including the use of force, to ensure compliance with Annexes 1–A and 2 of the Peace Agreement and relevant United Nations Security Council resolutions' (preamble and paragraph 7). In paragraph 3 the Council further stresses the consensual dimension of the whole international presence in Bosnia by reminding the parties

that, in accordance with the Peace Agreement, they have committed themselves to cooperate fully with all entities involved in the implementation of this peace settlement, as described in the Peace Agreement, or which are otherwise authorized by the Security Council.

Thus even though particular missions are authorized by the Security Council, its authority over the parties stems mainly from the peace agreement. Paragraph 10

[a]uthorizes the Member States acting through or in cooperation with the EU to establish for an initial planned period of 12 months a multinational stabilization force (EUFOR) as a legal successor to SFOR under unified command and control, which will fulfil its missions in relation to the implementation of Annex 1–A and Annex 2 of the Peace Agreement in cooperation with the NATO HQ presence in accordance with the arrangements agreed between NATO and the EU as communicated to the Security Council in their letters of 19 November 2004, which recognize that the EUFOR will have the main peace stabilization role under the military aspects of the Peace Agreement.

Paragraph 11 states that 'the EUFOR will have the main peace stabilization role under the military aspects of the Peace Agreement'.[93] Pursuant to Berlin Plus

---

[92] Joint Action 2004/570/CFSP of 12 July 2004 on the European Union military operation in Bosnia and Herzegovina, preambular paragraph 8.

[93] See also Resolution 1639(2005); Letter dated 17 November 2004 from the Secretary-General of NATO to the High Representative of the European Union (S/2004/915) specifies that 'NATO and EU will both have access to the full authorities under Annexes 1–A and 2 of the General Framework Agreement for Peace in Bosnia and Herzegovina'. NATO welcomes the fact that EUFOR will thus have the main peace stabilization role under Dayton with NATO staying in the background. 'NATO headquarters Sarajevo will also undertake certain operational supporting tasks: counter-terrorism while ensuring force protection; support to the International Criminal Tribunal for the Former Yugoslavia with regard to the detention of persons indicted for war crimes; and intelligence-sharing with EU, NATO, acting through its Senior Military Representative will exercise its authorities only when necessary to fulfil its tasks, including for force protection', and 'NATO headquarters Sarajevo will also assess progress towards the fulfilment of the objectives mentioned in Annexes 1–A and 2 of the General Framework Agreement'. The Deputy SACEUR is designated as the EUFOR Operation Commander. 'NATO should continue to be held responsible for any liabilities incurred by SFOR, and NATO should not be held responsible for liabilities incurred by EUFOR.' The EU High Representative accepted these conditions in its letter of 18 November 2004 to the NATO Secretary-General, S/2004/916.

arrangements, NATO Deputy SACEUR is the EU Operational Commander and headquarters are located at SHAPE.[94]

Paragraph 14 authorizes the mission to use all necessary means to enforce the peace agreement on parties, while the right of the mission, and of the NATO presence, to use force in self-defence is provided on separate grounds under paragraph 15. The dividing line between the two kinds of use of force seems to be blurring, given that the vision of peace forces' self-defence has expanded from the Waldheim memorandum onwards.[95] While the two entitlements may overlap, there still is a conceptual difference between the two kinds of use of force in peace operations. Action in self-defence is inherent to the very deployment of a peace force while action to implement peace agreements has to be provided for by an agreement, including the consent by the host state.

(d) EUFOR RD Congo

The Security Council authorized EUFOR RD Congo under Chapter VII to support the UN Operation *MONUC* during the initial period of its activity covering the elections in the Congo. EUFOR was authorized to take all necessary steps to support MONUC in stabilizing the situation, for instance by helping individuals in danger. The Joint Action of the EU refers expressly to UN Security Council Resolution 1671(2006), which authorized the EU to deploy forces in the DRC in support of MONUC during the election process, and stated that '[t]he DRC authorities have welcomed a possible EU military support to MONUC during the electoral process'.[96]

Viewing the EU deployment in the context of the broader UN mandate is demonstrated by the provisions in the Joint Action requiring the EUFOR commander to liaise in the course of EUFOR activities with the MONUC command and the DPKO, but more importantly by the articles according to which '[t]he status of the EU-led forces and their personnel, including the privileges, immunities and further guarantees necessary for the fulfilment of their mission, will be determined in accordance with the relevant provisions of United Nations Security Council Resolution 1671(2006)' (Articles 9 and 12). Moreover, the Joint Action states that '[t]he SG/HR is hereby authorized to release to the United Nations, MONUC and to other third parties, associated with this Joint Action, EU classified information and documents' (Article 14).

6. The Inter-American Peace Force

The United States unilaterally intervened in the Dominican Republic on 28 April 1965, initially with 405 marines, but within a week there were over 30,000 US

---

[94] Reichard, n 86 above, 259.
[95] S/11502/Rev/1, 27 October 1973.
[96] Joint Action 2006/319/CFSP, 27 April 2006, preambular paras 7–8, and Article 1.

troops in the Republic.[97] Initially the USA claimed to be protecting US nationals, and later claimed its intervention had been motivated by the need to avert the threat of communism. After the intervention, the OAS established the Inter-American Peace Force. The resolution establishing it did not officially approve the US use of force and the Force was established for reasons different from those claimed by the USA in support of its intervention, even though the international neutral refugee zone in which the Force operated was initially established through the US forcible action.[98]

Resolution III of the Tenth Meeting of Consultation states the OAS aim as re-establishment of peace and normal conditions in the territory of the Dominican Republic, and states that 'the formation of an inter-American force will signify *ipso facto* the transformation of the forces presently in Dominican territory into another force that would not be that of one State or of a group of States but that of the Organization of American States'. Accordingly, the Meeting requested member States

that are willing and capable of doing so to make contingents of their land, naval, air or police forces available to the OAS, within their capabilities and to the extent they can do so, to form an inter-American force that will operate under the authority of this Tenth Meeting of Consultation.

The 'sole purpose' of this force was defined as 'cooperating in the restoration of normal conditions in the Dominican Republic' and restoring security and an atmosphere of peace. The intention was to establish a unified command for the Force to ensure coordinated and effective action. As for the Force's composition, a progressive equalization of national contingents was required.[99]

The Inter-American Force was not formed pursuant to the Rio Treaty and for this reason certain Latin American states argued that its formation was ultra vires, being contrary to the principle of non-intervention under that Treaty.[100] However, the principal problem with the legal basis of this Force was that it was difficult to dissociate it from the original unilateral—and unauthorized—intervention by the United States. As Arechaga has most pertinently stated,

the 'Inter-American Peace Force' in the Dominican Republic in 1965 cannot be considered as a lawful peace-keeping operation. The forces entered the territory of the Dominican Republic without the consent of its Government; the bulk of the forces had been sent unilaterally by the United States without the consent of or a request from the affected Government and were sent before any decision had been taken by the regional organization. Furthermore, the mission performed by these forces went beyond a mere interposition

[97] P Pirrone, 'The Use of Force in the Framework of the Organization of American States', in A Cassese (ed.), *The Current Legal Regulation of the Use of Force* (Leiden: Nijhoff, 1986), 223 at 229.
[98] Akehurst, n 23 above, 208, 210–11.
[99] Resolution on Inter-American Force, adopted on 6 May 1965, third plenary session of the Tenth OAS Consultation Meeting, 1 May 1965–6 March 1970, Final Act, OAS Official Records, OEA/Ser C/II.10 (English), preamble and paragraphs 1 to 3, 338–9.
[100] Pirrone, n 97 above, 229 (and fn. 3).

between fighting adversaries: it carried out fighting activities to the detriment of one of the factions in the conflict.[101]

These factors also point to important differences between the Inter-American Force and the NATO-led KFOR in Kosovo. The latter was qualitatively different—in its mandate and composition—from the 1999 NATO attack against the FRY, and was established with the consent of FRY.

7. The Arab Deterrent Force

The Riyadh Summit of 17–18 October 1976, attended by heads of state from Egypt, Kuwait, Lebanon, Saudi Arabia, and Syria, was not held within the formal framework of the Arab League. It decided to transform the 'token' Arab Security Force into the Arab Deterrent Force. The resolution to this effect required that 'the present Arab security force be strengthened to become a deterrent force', to be 30,000 strong. These summit conclusions were then endorsed at the Arab League summit held in Cairo on 25–26 October 1976. The ADF mandate was to deter the parties to conflict in Lebanon from resorting to conflict again, and included the tasks of maintaining cease-fire, collecting heavy weapons, and supporting the Lebanese government in maintaining its authority.[102]

8. The Issue of Consent

The intersection of peace keeping with state sovereignty naturally raises the requirement for the host state's consent to any deployment. Despite protecting the domestic jurisdiction of states under Article 2(7), the UN Charter does not specify which UN operations require the consent of a territorial state and which do not.

When the UN initiated its peace-keeping practices, it was taken for granted that consent of the host state was required. UNEF was established under the UfP resolution and consent was required before the Assembly could request for it to be stationed.[103] It has been contended, in the post-Cold War context, that there is 'a real tendency on the part of the Security Council to weaken the requirement of consent as a basis for UN involvement' in peace operations including those under Chapter VII.[104] But this has not really been the case, since both peace-keeping and peace-enforcement forces authorized by the UN under Chapter VII (such as IFOR (Resolution 1031(1995)), KFOR (Resolution 1244(1999)), UNTAET (Resolution 1264(1999)), or UNAMID

---

[101] Arechaga, n 25 above, 138.
[102] J-P Issele, 'The Arab Deterrent Force in Lebanon, 1976–1983', in Cassese, n 97 above, 179 at 186–7.
[103] *Summary Study of the Experience Derived from the Establishment and Operation of the Force: Report of the Secretary-General*, A/3963, 9 October 1958, 10–11, para 15.
[104] M Berdal, 'The Security Council, Peacekeeping and Internal Conflict after the Cold War', 7 *Duke Journal of Comparative and International Law* (1996–7), 71 at 76.

in Sudan (Resolution 1769(2007)) have been premised on the consent of territorial states. The consent of the host state to the deployment of IFOR on the territory of Bosnia is acknowledged in Resolution 1031. By emphasizing in the Dayton Peace Agreement that the UN Security Council had to authorize this peace operation, states party to the agreement acknowledged that the UN Security Council possesses exclusive competence in terms of approving deployments of forces under Chapter VII. On its part the Security Council based the deployment of IFOR on the consent of states party to the Dayton Agreement.

Some Chapter VI peace-keeping forces (such as UNOSOM I and UNOSOM II) were not established by consent, as Somalia had no government. Resolution 918 (1994) expanded the mandate of UNAMIR, under Chapter VI, without requiring additional state consent to that effect. There seems to be nothing inherent in particular types of operation being or not being subject to the requirement for consent; what matters is how a particular operation is located in the overall context of the exercise by the Security Council of its peace and security mandate, including the necessity and proportionality of underlying decisions.

Akehurst considers that consent given to the deployment of a peace-keeping force by both sides in a civil war is as good as consent from the established territorial government.[105] Consent by conflicting sides other than the host government is not a requirement, however. As Matheson specifies, had the ONUC depended on the consent of the Belgian government, secessionist entities, and foreign mercenaries, it would never have become a feasible operation.[106]

The host state is free to withhold consent from a peace-keeping force. But the initial withholding of consent cannot be placed on the same footing as its withdrawal once deployment has been agreed. The initial grant of consent is a matter of grace, after which the matter moves into the dimension of legal rights and obligations. In relation to UNEF, the Egyptian government's position at the stage of deployment was that UNEF would have to withdraw if the government so decided at a later stage. Secretary-General Hammarskjold's view was that the consent of Egypt was given to UNEF as a mission approved by the General Assembly to perform certain tasks and thus it could not be withdrawn until those tasks were discharged. Secretary-General U Thant took a different view at the time that UNEF was actually withdrawn.

Hammarskjold's *aide mémoire* specified that, as Egypt endorsed the General Assembly resolution establishing UNEF and thereby consented to UNEF's exercise of its tasks, they could not ask for UNEF's withdrawal before the completion of these tasks. Withdrawal of Egypt's consent before that would run counter to its acceptance of the initial resolution. This was further reinforced by the UN commitment to Egypt to maintain the Force until it could achieve its tasks, which brought about Egypt's reciprocal obligation to respect the presence of the Force.[107] As further emphasized in Hammaskjold's Summary Study on UNEF, Egypt's acceptance of the Assembly resolution meant its acceptance of an

---

[105] Akehurst, n 23 above, 212.
[106] Matheson, n 6 above, 122.
[107] *Aide mémoire* of 5 August 1957, 6 ILM (1967), 595 at 595–7, 599–600.

international force under terms fixed by the United Nations. The correspondence between Egypt and the UN in 1956 confirmed that there was a mutual understanding between both parties regarding that point,[108] which was not denied until 1967.

The termination of UNEF's presence in Egypt and the Gaza Strip was initiated in 1967 by the Egyptian Foreign Minister notifying the UN Secretary-General U Thant, who in his turn attached conclusive importance to Egypt's position and held that UNEF had to withdraw, because it was a peace-keeping operation dependent on the basic principle of the consent of territorial states, not a peace-enforcement operation. It could not function without the continued consent and cooperation of the host country. UNEF was based

entirely on its acceptance by the governing authority of the territory on which it operates and that is not in any sense related to Chapter VII of the Charter. It is a fact beyond dispute that neither UNEF nor any other United Nations peace-keeping operation thus far undertaken would have been permitted to enter the territory involved if there had been any suspicion that it had the right to remain there against the will of the governing authority.[109]

This position does not accord with U Thant's earlier position; he took issue with the Egyptian government over its actions to impede the effective operation of UNEF.[110] The divergence between the Hammarskjold and U Thant positions is about whether sovereignty of the territorial state should be allowed to undermine an effective interpretation of the peace-keeping mandate agreed as between that state and the UN, by causing its restrictive interpretation—essentially a treaty interpretation point dealt with, and rejected, in international jurisprudence from the *Wimbledon* case onwards.[111]

Consent given to a peace-keeping operation is not just agreement that a pertinent force should be deployed, but a broader consent that certain objectives should be achieved through the deployment of that force. Holding that the territorial state has an unlimited power to request withdrawal of a peace-keeping force essentially approves the host state's right to interpret its rights and obligations in relation to that force unilaterally. If the host state has an unrestricted right to withdraw consent, it can effectively use this as a bargaining tool to influence how the mandate of a peace-keeping force operates as part of the collective security effort and thus

---

[108] *Summary Study*, n 103 above, 12, 25 paras 23, 133.

[109] *Special Report of the Secretary-General on UNEF*, A/6669, 18 May 1967, 9; *Report of the Secretary-General*, S/7896, 19 May 1967, 3–4, para 12; U Thant also referred to Egypt's understanding that without its consent UNEF would no longer be entitled to stay deployed: *Report of the Secretary-General on the Withdrawal of the United Nations Emergency Force*, A/6730/Add.3, 26 June 1967, 12, 22, paras 34, 72; and another *Report by the Secretary-General*, S/7906, 26 May 1967, 3, para 7, although it is doubtful whether this unilateral position could overrule Egypt's agreement with the UN on UNEF's tasks, as referred to by Hammarskjold, and thus whether U Thant was justified in according such significance to Egypt's unilateral position. See also *Statement of Secretary-General U Thant on Hammarskjold Aide Mémoire*, published in *NY Times*, 20 June 1967, at 19 and reproduced in 6 ILM (1967), 603.

[110] See section 10 below.

[111] *SS Wimbledon*, Judgment of 17 August 1923, *PCIJ Series A*, No. 1, 15. See for detail A Orakhelashvili, *Interpretation of Acts and Rules in Public International Law* (New York: Oxford University Press, 2008), Chapter 11.

unilaterally affect the underlying collective security policy determined by the relevant organ of the UN.

The Secretary-General has no power to terminate a peace-keeping operation established by a UN resolution, because such a decision can only be made by the Security Council or on the basis of its delegation of powers. Termination is required once the pertinent force has fulfilled its mandate. Accordingly, the Secretary-General's unilateral decision to order the withdrawal of UNEF from the Egyptian territory was ultra vires.[112] Along similar lines, even before the powers of UNPROFOR's were upgraded to enforcement level, the Secretary-General specified that UNPROFOR's early withdrawal was possible only on the basis of a Security Council decision.[113] This recommendation was then implemented in paragraphs 3 and 4 of Resolution 743(1992) establishing UNPROFOR.

9. The Mandate of Peace Operations

Instruments establishing peace operations also approve their mandate, including referring to the mandate as specified in the agreement concluded in relation to the relevant crisis. There are instances of progressive consensual expansion of a mandate, while in other cases its effective interpretation can be needed to enable the force established under it to exercise its tasks properly. The nature of the situation on the ground can be important for indicating whether and how the mandate of a peace force can be interpreted effectively or, in the alternative, that the scope agreement behind the mandate is not commensurate to the nature of the threat on the ground and thus needs to be upgraded, progressively and consensually.

Under Resolution 186(1964), the mandate of UNFICYP was 'to prevent a recurrence of fighting and, as necessary, to contribute to the maintenance and restoration of law and order and a return to normal conditions'. In addition to its original mandate under Resolution 743(1992), Resolution 776(1992) authorized enlargements of UNPROFOR's mandate and strength in Bosnia to perform the functions outlined in the Security Council's report, including the protection of convoys of released detainees if requested by the Red Cross (paragraph 2). In relation to the UNPROFOR mandate to protect safe areas, the Secretary-General pointed out that

when a safe area has strategic importance in ongoing military operations launched or provoked by the forces defending the area, it would be unrealistic to expect the other party to avoid attacking that area, even with full knowledge of the likely consequences of violating the relevant Security Council resolutions. In these circumstances, the efforts of UNPROFOR to defend the safe area make it necessary to obstruct only one of the hostile forces, which considers itself to be merely reacting to offensives launched by the other. In

---

[112] Sarooshi, n 18 above, 125.

[113] *Further Report of the Secretary-General pursuant to Security Council Resolution 721(1991)*, S/23592, 15 February 1992, para 30.

such circumstances, the impartiality of UNPROFOR becomes difficult to maintain and there is a risk of the Force being seen as a party to the conflict.[114]

The tasks of the Rapid Reaction Force, placed at the disposal of UNPROFOR as an integral part of it, included emergency action to assist isolated or threatened United Nations units, helping redeployment of UNPROFOR elements; and facilitating their freedom of movement where necessary. On a note different from the previous report, the Secretary-General specified that

the purposes of the RRF would be to give the commander a capacity between 'strong protest and air strikes'; it would increase tactical operational flexibility and would be intended to have a deterrent effect but it would not change the United Nations role to peace-enforcement; the status of UNPROFOR and its impartiality would be unaffected.[115]

The merit of making these fine distinctions in this case is unclear. Security Council Resolution 998(1995), which authorized the Secretary-General to incorporate the RRF into UNPROFOR, was adopted in the context of the existing authorization of UNPROFOR under Resolution 836(1993) to use force in self-defence as broadly understood, including the protection of safe areas.

UNOSOM I was established under Resolution 751(1992) to monitor the ceasefire in Mogadishu and escort deliveries of humanitarian assistance. Resolution 775(1992) entitled UNOSOM I to protect humanitarian convoys and distribution centres. As the situation in Somalia deteriorated further, and the existing efforts were no longer adequate, the Security Council decided to complement the activities of UNOSOM I by authorizing the US-led UNITAF to establish safe conditions for humanitarian assistance. The mandate of UNOSOM II was defined in operative paragraph 4 of Resolution 814(1993) in a broad manner, and included diverse tasks from monitoring hostile factions to controlling heavy weapons, from seizing small arms to maintaining the security of ports, from clearing mines to assisting the repatriation of refugees. Paragraph 14 of the same resolution requested the Secretary-General

to direct the Force Commander of UNOSOM II to assume responsibility for the consolidation, expansion and maintenance of a secure environment throughout Somalia, taking account of the particular circumstances in each locality, on an expedited basis . . . in this regard to organize a prompt, smooth and phased transition from UNITAF to UNOSOM II.

UNTAC's Rules of Engagement for the first time identified the prevention of crimes against humanity as a task for a UN force, warranting the use of 'all necessary means'.[116] After the genocidal massacre in Rwanda, in Resolution 912 (1994) the Security Council decided

in the light of the current situation in Rwanda, to adjust the mandate of UNAMIR as follows: (a) To act as an intermediary between the parties in an attempt to secure their

---

[114] *Report of the Secretary-General pursuant to Security Council Resolution 959(1994)*, S/1994/1389, para 37.
[115] Letter Dated 9 June 1995 from the Secretary-General addressed to the Security Council, 9 June 1995, S/1995/470, at 4.
[116] Findlay, n 3 above, 125.

agreement to a cease-fire; (b) To assist in the resumption of humanitarian relief operations to the extent feasible; and (c) To monitor and report on developments in Rwanda, including the safety and security of the civilians who sought refuge with UNAMIR.

A further expansion of the UNAMIR mandate took place under Resolution 918 (1994)

to include the following additional responsibilities within the limits of the resources available to it: (a) To contribute to the security and protection of displaced persons, refugees and civilians at risk in Rwanda, including through the establishment and maintenance, where feasible, of secure humanitarian areas; (b) To provide security and support for the distribution of relief supplies and humanitarian relief operations.

The Council '[r]ecognize[d] that UNAMIR may be required to take action in self-defence against persons or groups who threaten protected sites and populations, United Nations and other humanitarian personnel or the means of delivery and distribution of humanitarian relief' (paragraphs 3–4).[117] The preamble to Resolution 925(1994) defined the parameters of the mandate of UNAMIR by pointing out that UNAMIR was not to have the role of a buffer force between the two parties and that its expanded military component would continue only as long as and to the extent that it was needed to carry out the tasks defined in Resolution 918.

The United Nations Mission in Sierra Leone (UNAMSIL) was established under Security Council Resolution 1270(1999) to monitor the implementation of the Lomé Peace Agreement; to assist the government of Sierra Leone in the implementation of the disarmament, demobilization, and reintegration plan; to establish a presence at key locations throughout Sierra Leone, including at disarmament/reception centres and demobilization centres; to ensure the security and freedom of movement of United Nations personnel; to monitor adherence to the cease-fire and to facilitate the delivery of humanitarian assistance (paragraph 8). In paragraph 14, the Council,

acting under Chapter VII of the Charter of the United Nations, decide[d] that in the discharge of its mandate UNAMSIL may take the necessary action to ensure the security and freedom of movement of its personnel and, within its capabilities and areas of deployment, to afford protection to civilians under imminent threat of physical violence, taking into account the responsibilities of the Government of Sierra Leone and ECOMOG.

UNAMSIL was a peace-keeping mission with a robust mandate.[118] Resolution 1313(2000) specified its mandate further, its main objectives being to maintain the security of the Lungi and Freetown peninsulas, and their major approach routes; to deter and, where necessary, decisively counter the threat of RUF attack by responding robustly to any hostile actions or threat of imminent and direct use of force to assist the efforts of the government of Sierra Leone to extend state authority; to restore law and order and stabilize the situation progressively throughout the entire

---

[117] The same is reiterated in paragraphs 3–4 of Resolution 925(1994).
[118] Findlay, n 3 above, 298.

country; and to assist in the promotion of the political process, including a disarmament, demobilization, and reintegration programme (paragraph 3).

The Mandate of UNMISET under paragraph 2 of Resolution 1410(2002) was broad and

shall consist of the following elements: (a) To provide assistance to core administrative structures critical to the viability and political stability of East Timor; (b) To provide interim law enforcement and public security and to assist in the development of a new law enforcement agency in East Timor, the East Timor Police Service (ETPS); (c) To contribute to the maintenance of the external and internal security of East Timor.

The task of UNMISET was effectively to assist the East Timorese state to keep functioning. However, the resolution does not specify how the competences of UNMISET would interact with those of the East Timorese government, which entailed a presumption that UNMISET's tasks were circumscribed by cooperation with and the consent of the host state.

The robustness of the mandate given to some peace-keeping operations, from ONUC onwards, raises the question of the relevance of their impartiality in performing their tasks. It has to be borne in mind that the impartiality of peace-keeping forces is not a preconceived principle applicable across the board, but instead means impartial implementation of the mandate of the relevant force. For instance, if one particular force is mandated to disarm both sides to a conflict, disarming one side only would be a breach of impartiality; but if it is mandated to disarm only one side, doing just that would not offend the impartiality requirement.

Operational problems can still arise where the relevant operation is initially established with limited impartial tasks and is later on endowed with more robust tasks. As the Secretary-General observed in relation to UNPROFOR,

the decisions of Member States to provide troops to UNPROFOR were based on the existing Security Council resolutions and on the assumption that the mandate of the Force would be implemented as a peace-keeping operation. Any attempt to redefine radically the conditions in which UNPROFOR's mandate is implemented and which could have implications for the security of its personnel may, therefore, lead the contributing States to exercise their sovereign right to terminate their contribution to the Force. Although some troop-contributing nations have expressed their willingness to continue their participation even in changed circumstances, I do not believe it to be in the interests of the United Nations for a peace-keeping force to be converted into one which, by mandate and composition, becomes a party to the conflict it was originally deployed to help the parties to bring to an end.[119]

The Secretary-General's position raises the old dilemma between observing impartiality by compromising the efficiency of the mission in question, and endangering the operation as such. This is a complex problem which in practice is most often resolved by consensually upgrading the mandate of the relevant operation to enable

---

[119] *Report of the Secretary-General Pursuant to Resolution 908(1994)*, S/1994/1067, 13.

it to face challenges on the ground that might not have been present when the mission was originally established. In this sense, the abstract concept of impartiality does not affect the dynamic evolution of peace-keeping mandates and their inclusion of a robust element in support of one of the sides in the conflict in question. As the Brahimi Report specified, for UN operations impartiality is not the same as neutrality or equal treatment of all parties in all cases for all time, which could amount to a policy of appeasement, but adherence to the principles of the Charter. Where one party to a peace agreement clearly and incontrovertibly violates its terms, the continued equal treatment of all parties by the UN 'can in the best case result in ineffectiveness and in the worst may amount to complicity with evil'.[120] Furthermore,

in some cases, local parties consist not of moral equals but of obvious aggressors and victims, and peacekeepers may not only be operationally justified in using force but morally compelled to do so. Genocide in Rwanda went as far as it did in part because the international community failed to use or to reinforce the operation then on the ground in that country to oppose obvious evil. . . . If a United Nations peace operation is already on the ground, carrying out those actions may become its responsibility, and it should be prepared.[121]

This approach is reflected in the practice of framing peace-keeping mandates the way to enable them using all necessary means to implement it.

10. Command and Control

Command and control over military operations led or authorized by collective security institutions matters in two respects: it determines who actually is in charge of the relevant operation; and which entity—a state or an international organization—is responsible for its acts. As for the UN system, the Charter does not specify command and control arrangements relating to peace-keeping forces established, or multinational forces authorized, by the UN. It is suggested that 'the authority for the command and control of UN peacekeeping forces established by the Security Council rests solely with the Security Council', as they are the Council's subsidiary organs.[122] In relation to enforcement action, the Secretary-General stated in the *Supplement to the Agenda for Peace* that neither the Security Council nor the Secretary-General at present has the capacity to deploy, direct, command, or control peace operations, except perhaps on a very limited scale.[123] When the Security Council refers to 'unified command' in the case of peace-enforcement

---

[120] *Report of the Panel on United Nations Peace Operations* (Brahimi Report), A/55/305–S/2000/809, 21 August 2000, page IX.
[121] Ibid, para 50.
[122] Sarooshi, n 18 above, 67.
[123] *Supplement to an Agenda for Peace: Position Paper of the Secretary-General on the Occasion of the Fiftieth Anniversary of the United Nations*, Report of the Secretary-General on the Work of the Organization, A/50/60–S/1995/1, 3 January 1995, para 77.

troops composed of coalitions of the able and willing, it means authorizing an operation under national command of a lead state.

Although the unified command of the United States over troops in Korea was in practice referred to as the UN command,[124] in essence no UN command has ever been established. As commander of the US Forces in Korea General McArthur specified, the US Government was acting in Korea as an agent of the UN, but orders came from the US Joint Chiefs of Staff.[125] Security Council Resolutions 83 and 84(both 1950) recommended that the military units to be deployed in the Korean War should be made available under the unified command of the United States, and requested the United States to designate a commander of the UN-authorized force.[126] If, as suggested, the force in Korea was under the overall authority and control of the UN,[127] it was so in terms of its overall mandate, not its operations.

In the Iraq–Kuwait war the command pattern established under Resolution 678 (1990) was arguably complex. Apart from the dual US-Saudi command structure, the Coalition was 'managed' rather than single-state, the principal evidence of which pattern is said to be the fact that the American commander collaborated to a greater extent with coalition partners regarding the conduct of operations and consulted them.[128] Whether this 'managed coalition' pattern constitutes a separate kind of command and control is questionable. At most this can evidence that decisions were made after consultation. What matters, however, is who actually took decisions and if it was, again, the American commander who did so (even after consulting other coalition partners), it still would be the case that the coalition against Iraq was under a US 'unified command'. The 'managed' nature of decision making in the conduct of operations also leaves unaffected the issue of control of operations on the ground, and thus of responsibility for acts committed during these operations. The state providing the 'unified command' would then be responsible for the acts of its own troops and also—as a matter of joint responsibility shared with other coalition partners—for any unlawful act that was caused, as such, by decisions taken through that 'unified command'.[129]

Resolution 794(1992) on Somalia reveals no intention of the Council to establish a UN command. UNITAF was meant to be under unified command and control, and subject to the US military command line. Of course, the Security

---

[124] Cf R Higgins, *United Nations Peacekeeping*, vol. 2 (Oxford: Oxford University Press, 1970), 197, specifying that the UN resolutions, the correspondence, and the agreements of contributing states with the United States referred to UN force and UN command.

[125] Referred to in Sarooshi, n 18 above, 110; see ibid, 114 for the extract from the Dutch-US agreement regarding the participation of Dutch troops in the Korean war under US command, stating clearly that Dutch troops would be receiving orders from the US commander.

[126] Resolution 84(1950) was adopted by the Council after the USA rejected the idea of having the operation directed by the Committee of Coordination of Assistance to Korea whose establishment the Secretary-General had suggested; ibid, 173; the USA had both political control (*de jure* and *de facto*) and strategic direction over the operation in Korea: JW Houck, 'The Command and Control of United Nations Forces in the Era of "Peace Enforcement"', 4 *Duke Journal of Comparative and International Law* (1993–4), 1 at 13.

[127] Sarooshi, n 18 above, 111.

[128] Houck, n 126 above, 17–19.

[129] On responsibility see further Chapter 8 below.

Council could change the mandate of UNITAF, or even terminate the operation, but the actual acts done during that operation would not be attributable to the UN. This view is reinforced by paragraph 10, in which the Council authorizes the pertinent states under chapter VII to undertake all necessary means to achieve the stated aims. On the basis of the US leading the operation, paragraph 12 of the resolution instructs the Secretary-General to 'make the necessary arrangements for the unified command and control of the forces involved'. There was to be appropriate coordination between UNITAF and the UN and the latter's liaison group should be present at the headquarters of the unified command (paragraphs 13 and 15). The Secretary-General did not exercise any effective control and command powers over UNITAF.[130] In fact, the Secretary-General's proposal to have UN command and control was rejected, because states were reluctant to place their soldiers and equipment under UN control.[131]

As for peace-keeping operations, there is no indication in the Charter of any presumption in favour of, let alone requirement for, UN command and control over these forces. For a long time the prevailing pattern has been based on the model proposed by Secretary-General Waldheim when the Security Council established UNEF II in 1973. The Council has ultimate control over peace-keeping forces, including the establishment and specification of mandate, while the Secretary-General exercises day-to-day supervision of operations. Command in the field is exercised by a force commander appointed by the Secretary-General with the consent of the Security Council.[132] In relation to UNOSOM II, the Secretary-General specified that brigade commanders should report to the Force commander and the latter to SRSG,[133] who would exercise political control over UN troops in the field, while the Force Commander translated these political directives into military commands addressed to national contingents.[134]

One cardinal principle is that UN personnel are not supposed to receive instructions from national authorities. As emphasized in Secretary-General Hammarskjold's Summary Study on UNEF, the commander has direct command authority over the relevant force and its operations. During the period of their assignment to a UN force, members of that Force (although remaining in their national service) are international personnel subject to the instructions only of the commander and his chain of command.[135] A member State cannot instruct its national commander to disobey the force commander's instructions.[136] In more

---

[130] Sarooshi, n 18 above, 213.

[131] S/24868, 5–6.

[132] *Report of the Secretary-General on the Implementation of Security Council Resolution 340 (1973)*, S/11052/Rev 1, 27 October 1973, 2, para 4(a); *Report of the Secretary-General on the Implementation of Security Council Resolution 425(1978)*, S/12611, 19 March 1978, para 4(a); the same approach is reiterated in *Supplement to the Agenda for Peace*, n 123 above, para 38; Houck, n 126 above, 22–3.

[133] S/25354, para 78.

[134] D Sarooshi, 'The Role of the United Nations Secretary-General in United Nations Peace-Keeping Operations', 20 *Australian Yearbook of International Law* (1999), 279 at 291.

[135] *Summary Study*, n 103 above, 24, para 128.

[136] Sarooshi, n 134 above, 290.

specific terms, Secretary-General U Thant observed in relation to UNEF that the commander could not comply with any requests affecting the disposition of UNEF forces emanating from any source other than UN headquarters. The host state had no right to give such instructions and the Secretary-General took issue with the Egyptian government for attempting to do so.[137]

This approach was confirmed in the Secretary-General's report on the Model Agreement between the UN and Member States Contributing Personnel and Equipment to UN Peacekeeping Operations, specifying that, during the period of assignment to the UN, the personnel remain in the national service but fall under UN command, ultimately responsible to the Secretary-General who shall have 'full authority over the deployment, organization, conduct and direction' of the operation. The forces shall not seek, nor accept instructions in respect of the performance of their duties from an authority external to the UN, nor shall governments give them such instructions.[138]

For all the effort to ensure a viable division of roles, these arrangements still leave the notion of 'ultimate control' and 'full control' profoundly unclear; neither do they specify which entity should be deemed to exercise actual control over operations and forces.

The command pattern within the EU depends on whether an EU operation draws on NATO resources or is led by a framework nation. Where the EU acts using NATO assets, the Deputy SACEUR acts as EU Operation Commander from NATO SHAPE and reports to the EUMC. The Nice European Council specified that for autonomous operations operational planning 'will be carried out within one of the European strategic level headquarters'. This means national headquarters, which can also operate as multinational operational headquarters.[139]

The EU Joint Action on the deployment of EUFOR RD Congo expressly stated that 'the Political and Security Committee (PSC) should exercise political control of the EU military operation in the DRC in support of MONUC, provide it with strategic direction and take the relevant decisions in accordance with third sub-paragraph of Article 25 of the EU Treaty'.[140] Article 6(1) of this Joint Action specified how the powers would be shared between different levels of the EU hierarchy. The authorization of the PSC under Article 25 EU Treaty

shall include the powers to amend the planning documents, including the Operation Plan, the Chain of Command and the Rules of Engagement. It shall also include the powers to take further decisions on the appointment of the EU Operation Commander and/or EU Force Commander.

Powers of decision over the objectives and termination of the EU military operation remain vested in the Council. According to Article 7(1), '[t]he EU Military

---

[137] S/6669, 3–4, para 6.
[138] A/46/185, paras 7 and 9 (23 May 1991).
[139] C Gourlay, 'European Union Procedures and Resources for Crisis Management', 11 *International Peacekeeping* (2004), 404 at 409.
[140] Joint Action 2006/319/CFSP, 27 April 2006, preambular para 9.

Committee (EUMC) shall monitor the proper execution of the EU military operation conducted under the responsibility of the EU Operation Commander'.

ECOMOG in Liberia proved to have no established and ready-made command structures.[141] The 1999 Protocol specified the ECOWAS model of command and control. As applied to peace keeping, under this model the Defence and Security Commission (which consists of representatives of the defence staffs of member States) appoints a force commander and determines the composition of the force (Articles 18–19). For ECOMOG, '[o]n the recommendation of the Executive Secretary an ECOMOG Force Commander shall be appointed by the Mediation and Security Council and in consultation with the Defence and Security Commission for each operation'. The ECOMOG Commander is responsible for the efficiency of operational, administrative, and logistical plans of the mission, issues instructions to contingent commanders for all operational activities and receives reports from them, and is accountable to the Executive Secretary, through the Special Representative (Articles 33 and 34).

The AU legal framework is also somewhat open-ended. In relation to African Standby Forces, the AU PSC Protocol states that '[f]or each operation undertaken by the African Standby Force, the Chairperson of the Commission shall appoint a Special Representative and a Force Commander, whose detailed roles and functions shall be spelt out in appropriate directives, in accordance with the Peace Support Standing Operating Procedures'. The Force Commander reports to the Special Representative who reports to the Chairperson of the Commission. Contingent Commanders report to the Force Commander, while the civilian components report to the Special Representative (Article 13, paragraphs 6 and 7).

As can be seen, none of the underlying legal frameworks prescribe criteria regarding the actual control of troops and their conduct. What is required in the first place is to identify the meaning of terms such as 'command', 'control', and 'authority'. To illustrate, a peace force is protected by the 1994 UN Convention on the Safety of the United Nations and Associated Personnel if it is under the 'authority *and* control' of the UN. This is a comprehensive requirement that, depending on the factual context in which they operate, would leave many peace operations outside the scope of the Convention.

Both authority and control could relate to mandate or to actual conduct of operations. Command is defined as the legal authority to issue orders and to compel obedience, and thus entails the power and responsibility for accomplishing the planned mission. Control, on the other hand, is the process through which a commander, assisted by staff, organizes and directs the activities of the forces.[142] According to another view, 'command' refers to operational or tactical control of

---

[141] Olonisakin and Ero, n 53 above, 237.

[142] R Murphy, *UN Peacekeeping in Lebanon, Somalia and Kosovo: Operational and Legal Issues in Practice* (Cambridge: Cambridge University Press, 2007), 115–16; the pertinent Force regulations are usually supposed to clarify these issues *in casu*, but they are not always issued, as (until 1995) was often the case with UNIFIL: ibid, 143. It is also argued that 'command' in the peace-keeping context has 'a somewhat different meaning' from what it means in a conventional military operation: Houck, n 125 above, 25. But the precise difference is not explained.

forces in the field.[143] Control can be exercised through the appointment and dismissal of commanders, circumscribing their powers through regulations, determining the size and composition of the force, imposing restrictions on movement, or imposing a reporting duty.[144] This presumably refers to the manner in which the mandating institution can control the peace operation at issue. Overall, both command and control remain concepts that have no clear-cut, authoritative meaning, and could refer either to legal authority or to factual control over directing the conduct of a force.

The right to command and control troops comprises political, strategic, and operational control over them, which definition is central to determining who is responsible for the actions of those personnel, whether on peace-keeping or peace-enforcement missions. It is important to see who controls the forces. The UN command and control model is premised on a network of national contingents under UN political and strategic control.[145] But there seems to be no obvious guidance for taking matters any further. What if the UN Regulations leave the enforcement of discipline to the discretion of contributing states?[146] How does this impact on who actually is in effective command and control of troops? Similar considerations apply to phrases frequently used in Security Council resolutions, such as 'Security Council's (overall) authority and control'; although frequently used in practice, they are coined unfortunately and could never be adequate to clarify the actual position.

The term 'strategic direction' in relation to forces placed at the Security Council's disposal is used in Article 47 of the Charter in relation to the role of the abortive Military Staff Committee under the Security Council. This is presumably due to the civilian nature of the Council, which led the drafters of the Charter to foresee a need for professional military assistance. The Charter does not define 'strategic direction', but a plausible meaning for it seems to be serving as a vital link in the chain of command between the Council and an operational commander, by advising the former on the basis of views of the latter.[147] As Bowett specified, strategic direction is the translation of political directives into military terms.[148] That 'strategic direction' is different from 'command' follows from Article 47(3), which defers the determination of the latter to subsequent decisions.

It is observed that when national forces are placed under the mandate of international organizations, national governments normally maintain full command, which is more comprehensive, and grant the international organization

---

[143] Houck, n 126 above, 10 (referring to Seyersted).

[144] D Bowett, *United Nations Forces* (London: Stevens & Sons, 1964), 354–5.

[145] J Peck, 'The UN and the Laws of War: How Can the World's Peacekeepers be Held Accountable?', 21 *Syracuse Journal of International Law and Commerce* (1995), 283 at 293–4. There was a dual command structure in the Gulf War in 1991: US forces were under American command, Islamic forces under Saudi operational command; British and French forces were under political control of their national command authorities, but their troops operated under the tactical command of Americans and Saudis: ibid, 292–3.

[146] Cf ibid, 309.

[147] Houck, n 126 above, 8–10.

[148] Bowett, n 144 above, 359.

only operational command and control.[149] In Presidential Statement 1994/22 the Security Council considers it a 'leading principle' that UN peace-keeping forces should be under the operational command of the UN. In Resolution 1313(2000) on UNAMSIL, the Council stated that successful achievement of the UN objectives in that conflict depended on the provision of 'fully equipped, complete units, with the required capabilities, effective command and control structure and capacity, a single chain of command, adequate resources and the commitment to implement the mandate of the mission in full as authorized by the Security Council' (paragraph 6). Resolution 1769(2007) specifies, in relation to UNAMID, that 'unity of control and command' means, in accordance with basic principles of peace keeping, 'a single chain of command'. The Council further decides that 'command and control structures and backstopping will be provided by the UN' (paragraph 7).

Operational control of troops by a mandating organization through a 'single chain' of command has to be distinguished from effective control over the conduct of troops. In order for particular conduct to be attributed to a state or an international organization, that conduct must be performed under its effective control. Given that international forces are composed of national contingents, there must be a presumption that the mandating organization does not have effective control over them. This presumption is not irrefutable, however. It is perfectly possible that in the final analysis the arrangements made in a particular case will enable it to be concluded that an organization effectively controls the pertinent force and its actions. But this requires it to be demonstrated that there is an effective connection between the institutional (eg UN) command of the force and what those forces do on the ground.[150]

As Kolb states, UN forces have never been subjected to exclusive UN command and control. Peace-keeping units are under double command and control. Officially, they are deemed to be subsidiary organs of the UN; in factual terms, however, they are organs of their states. Supreme command, which includes strategic and operational aspects, rests with the UN. But then command devolves to national commanders in charge of transmitting orders, preparing contingents for duty, discipline, administration, and law enforcement. In order for a peace force to be considered a UN force, it should be under the principal, not the exclusive control of the UN, as was the case with UNOSOM in Somalia.[151] Under this pattern, the UN does not have effective control and command over its peace-keeping operations. Even where strategic command is performed by the UN, all pertinent activities on the ground relating to the conduct of operations were effectively performed by national authorities.

In *Attorney-General v Nissan* Lord Pearce specified that UN peace-keeping forces are in the UN chain of command and the force is always international; yet individual components remain under national discipline regulations and in national

---

[149] Murphy, n 142 above, 116, 120.
[150] See further Chapter 8 below.
[151] Kolb, n 22 above, 23.

service.[152] The House of Lords did not draw a precise line nor specify implications for how the allocation of command and control affects responsibility. This approach keeps all questions on command and control and ensuing responsibilities open.

The presumption thus goes against the UN being in control and command of peace operations. If the Security Council intends to assume its own control and command over an operation, with the effect that it becomes responsible for whatever is done during that operation, it will have to indicate in its resolution, expressly and straightforwardly, that it assumes such command and control, and to specify through what kind of arrangements this will be implemented.

A further problem is that Rules of Engagement do not always reflect the tasks and obligations specified in the mandate, and in some cases the pertinent force is not even covered by a single set of Rules of Engagement. For instance, each contingent of KFOR has its own ROE based on the KFOR ROE, which allow for KFOR activities and commitments to be distinguished, depending on national policies and priorities. As pointed out,

the separate KFOR brigades are controlled like independent fiefdoms, with little or no central command, and significant variations in policy and procedures. There is no real effort to subordinate the military operation to NATO procedures or command. Even within brigade areas here are no common standing operations procedures, and national policies take precedence.

KFOR is not a unified peace force, because each of its multi-national brigades has broad discretion over operational policies and procedures in its area. The same applied to UNOSOM II.[153] In Kosovo, national contingents of KFOR interpreted their mandate individually, which prevented KFOR from performing its mandate task to provide a secure environment. Likewise, some UNOSOM II troop contingents appeased the warlord General Aideed, while others bombed his headquarters.[154] As pertinently pointed out, the 'UN needs to avoid micromanagement of its missions by troop contributors, lest its operations become even more unwieldy'.[155]

UNOSOM was under the command of the SRSG, and so was UNOSOM II meant to be, pursuant to Resolution 814(1993). Nevertheless, the SRSG post (and the UNOSOM II deputy commander post) were occupied by a retired US admiral, which reinforced the leading role of the United States in this operation. UN orders to US troops in UNOSOM II were transferred through that deputy commander, who also served as the Commander of US Forces in Somalia, reporting directly to Commander in Chief at US Central Command. While Secretary-General Boutros-Ghali was keen to retain close control, US forces under UN command were the only logistics forces unlikely to encounter direct combat. The US rangers deployed in October 1993 came with their own commanding US general. All this was meant

---

[152] *Attorney-General v Nissan*, AC (1970), 179 at 223.
[153] Murphy, n 142 above, 113, 170–1, 212.
[154] Gaja, n 9 above, 56.
[155] Findlay, n 3 above, 367.

to keep US forces firmly under US operational control, and to eliminate any misperception that those forces were under UN command.[156] Furthermore, as Findlay states, 'the interpretation of the UNOSOM II mandate was apparently never formally discussed between the political and military wings of the mission. Policy guidelines and interpretation of the mandate fell to the respective contingents, who operated according to their own perspectives and understanding.'[157]

Furthermore, German forces in Somalia remained under the full command authority of the German Defence Ministry, and also came under its 'operational control', while Canadian forces came under Canadian operational command and control. The US forces in UNOSOM remained under the full command of the USA, including operational control. Different UNOSOM contingents continued to receive instructions from their national governments. Therefore the UN had no effective command and control of UNOSOM or operations in Somalia in general. Some national contingents maintained back-channel communications links with their home governments, and on occasions the UN acquiesced in such practices. The Spanish battalion in Bosnia was known to refer all operational issues arising on the ground to the Spanish government; Indonesian forces in Cambodia took their directions from the Indonesian ambassador in Phnom Penh; and the Italian UNOSOM commander in Somalia referred to the Italian government before carrying out UN orders on aspects of military action.[158]

The acuteness of the problem is vividly illustrated by the observations in the Brahimi Report on command and control problems in Sierra Leone:

> The problems of command and control that recently arose in Sierra Leone are the most recent illustration of what cannot be tolerated any longer. Troop contributors must ensure that the troops they provide fully understand the importance of an integrated chain of command, the operational control of the Secretary-General and the standard operating procedures and rules of engagement of the mission. It is essential that the chain of command in an operation be understood and respected, and the onus is on national capitals to refrain from instructing their contingent commanders on operational matters.[159]

The Security Council's control over the mandate of an operation conducted, on the basis of authorization, by individual states or regional organizations (also doctrinally referred as 'overall authority and control') essentially differs from the command and control of that operation itself. If the Council authorizes another entity to conduct the operation, the control and command of that operation will rest with that entity. The role of the Security Council is only to decide on the duration of the mandate.

To illustrate, under Resolution 1244(1999) there is no provision for UN control over the NATO forces in Kosovo that form the core of KFOR. According to Annex II of this resolution, the international security presence with substantial NATO

---

[156] Ibid, 189; Houck, n 126 above, 36–7.
[157] Findlay, ibid, 212.
[158] Murphy, n 142 above, 107, 124–5, 129; R Kolb, *Ius contra bellum, Le droit international relatif au maintien de la paix* (Basle/Louvain: Helbing Lichtenhahn/Bruylant, 2003), 100, adding that 'on imagine aisément les cacophonies qui résultent de la multiplicité de telles chaînes de commandement'.
[159] Brahimi Report, n 120 above, para 267.

participation is deployed 'under unified command and control'. According to Article 1(b) to Annex I of the Dayton Peace Agreement, IFOR 'will operate under the authority and subject to the direction and political control of the North Atlantic Council ("NAC") through the NATO chain of command'. Thus, although IFOR is deemed to be under the overall authority and control of the Security Council, the essence of that overall authority and control is rather narrow and limited to decisions on the duration of the IFOR mandate or possibly pronouncement on its compliance with that mandate. The Security Council had no effective say in the overall direction of the policies and conduct of IFOR operations, this role having been assumed (with the Security Council's assent) by the North Atlantic Council. As pointed out, NATO forces in Yugoslavia 'were fully integrated in the Alliance military structure, and operated under NATO rules of engagement and NATO chain of command. The NAC exercised political control and strategic direction over the operations, while the troops were under exclusive NATO command and control.'[160]

According to one view, even if IFOR had been under NATO command and control, contributing states were still directly accountable to the Security Council. Resolution 1031(1995) authorized individual states, not NATO, to take military action on Bosnian territory.[161] This case thus provides a basis for distinguishing between the exercise of control over the direction of an operation through mandate and command arrangements (which was allocated to NATO), and actual and effective control over the conduct of troops (which remained with participating states).

Similarly, there has been no prospect of the USA accepting a UN command in ISAF under Resolution 1386(2001), even though ISAF is a UN-authorized operation. ISAF command and control involved a complex network of powers and responsibilities allocated between various actors. As of 2003, NATO nations contributed approximately 95 per cent of ISAF's troops. NATO, on the basis of the NAC decision, provided

an in-theatre deployed composite headquarters, including the required communications and logistics support; a force commander from a troop-contributing allied nation; and strategic coordination, command and control exercised by the supreme headquarters of the allied Powers in Europe, with an ISAF operations coordination cell to involve participating nations. The political direction and coordination responsibilities would be undertaken by the North Atlantic Council in close consultation with non-NATO contributors to ISAF. Increased involvement by NATO would be within the context of ISAF's UN mandate and NATO would operate according to Security Council resolutions. ISAF would therefore continue to operate distinct from Operation *Enduring Freedom*.[162]

As is clear, the mandate of ISAF is constrained by Security Council resolutions, but control over operations is shared between NATO and its member States.

---

[160] Gazzini, n 84 above, 249.
[161] Figa-Talamanca, n 75 above, 168–70.
[162] UNYB 2003, 309.

11. Use of Force by Peace-Keeping Forces

The nature of the right of peace-keeping forces to defend themselves has long been a contested question. The Secretary-General's reports defined the parameters of this right to self-defence without alluding to any authority and effectively took its existence as granted. Other powers such as the freedom of movement may be incidental to the principal mandate; hence, the effective interpretation of pertinent Security Council resolutions can justify implying certain such powers even though they are not expressly stated.

As Dinstein explains, peace-keeping forces' right to self-defence is more specific than, and essentially different from, the right of states to self-defence under Article 51 of the UN Charter.[163] The extent to which force may be used by peace-keeping forces in self-defence depends on their mandate. The parameters of self-defence depend, not necessarily on that force being directly attacked, but on its tasks being substantially hampered.

Peace-keeping forces can defend themselves against actual or imminent attacks. It is readily admitted by military experts that effective defensive action may have to be anticipatory and is frequently resorted to in combatant activities.[164] The mandate of some troop contingents in UNEF (eg the Swedish contingent) contained standing orders permitting them to open fire, not just when fired upon but also when armed personnel approached them 'with the obvious intention of attacking them'.[165] In 1962, UNEF Commander Gyani set out the principles of the use of force requiring the existence of justification for every forcible act and insisted on any coercion having a preventative as opposed to punitive nature.[166]

Secretary-General Hammarskjold specified that the broad interpretation of the right to self-defence might blur the distinction between peace-keeping and peace-enforcement operations, and insisted that the matter was governed by the injunction against any initiative by peace keepers in using force. They could instead respond to attacks or to attempts to make them withdraw from the positions they occupied under their commanders' orders.[167] Secretary-General U Thant authorized UNFICYP to use force if there were an attempt to disarm them by force or prevent them from carrying out their responsibilities as ordered by their commanders, but also to maintain the freedom of movement necessary for the unimpeded implementation of their mandate, and to remove fortified positions and installations that would endanger the peace. At a later stage Secretary-General Waldheim authorized UNFICYP, allegedly without having first consulted the

---

[163] Dinstein, n 5 above, 308.
[164] GIAD Draper, 'The Legal Limitations upon the Employment of Weapons by the United Nations in the Congo', 12 ICLQ (1963), 401.
[165] Findlay, n 3 above, 27.
[166] Cf ibid, 32.
[167] *Summary Study of the Experience Derived from the Establishment and Operation of the Force*, Report of the Secretary-General, A/3962, 9 October 1958, para 179. The ONUC directive prohibited the initiative in using force: Findlay, n 3 above, 60.

Security Council, to use force against either side in the conflict if any of them attempted to seize Nicosia airport.[168]

Where the UN has been given the task of overseeing the departure of foreign armies, the normal procedure is for the Organization to discuss with the state concerned the arrangements and timetable for withdrawal, and to oversee it.[169] If the withdrawal does not then materialize, that state's conduct breaches the peace-keeping force's mandate and entitles the latter to resort to self-defence. For example, since (under Resolutions 425 and 426(both 1978)) UNIFIL's task was to help the Lebanese government to re-establish its control over the Lebanon, and UNIFIL had the right of self-defence against any activity that would have hampered the performance of its tasks, it follows that UNIFIL could lawfully have countered by force attempts against the re-establishment of Lebanese control over the Lebanon. Practice, however, hampered the effective interpretation of the authority to act in self-defence under Resolutions 425 and 426. On the ground the resolutions and the Secretary-General's guidelines were restrictively interpreted, since UNIFIL was unwilling to confront the PLO in the Tyre area.[170]

Resolution 467(1980) is an instance of retrospectively acknowledging the need to empower UNIFIL to act in a way necessary to carry out its mandate. The preamble to the resolution refers to the pertinent provisions in the Secretary-General's 1978 report that 'the Force must be able to function as an integrated and efficient military unit . . . must enjoy the freedom of movement and communication and other facilities that are necessary for the performance of its tasks . . . shall not use force except in self-defence', and that 'self-defence would include resistance to attempts by forceful means to prevent it from discharging its duties under the mandate of the Security Council'. The premise underlying this approach is that 'the force will proceed on the assumption that the parties to the conflict will take all the necessary steps for compliance with the decisions of the Security Council'.[171] These parameters of self-defence thus imply the binding force of Security Council decisions. Similar factors matter in relation to ECOMOG in Liberia, which was a peace-keeping force with a robust mandate, not an enforcement operation of the kind that falls within Chapter VII. When attacked by the RUF in Sierra Leone, ECOMOG invoked self-defence and in February 1998 used massive force against this faction to drive it out of Freetown, which example demonstrates that, if attacked, peace-keeping forces can lawfully adopt a full-scale military response that can go beyond protecting the peace-keeping force itself. Thus, the importance of UNIFIL's entitlement to use force for meeting its ends was emphasized at

---

[168] Cf Findlay, ibid, 92, 98.

[169] James, n 4 above, 629.

[170] Murphy, n 142 above, 174–7; however, Murphy's suggestion (ibid) that the text of Resolution 425 allowed for this restrictive interpretation and doing otherwise would offend the principle of impartiality cannot stand the test, because the tasks were clearly defined in the resolution and self-defence applied to those tasks. This is further confirmed by Resolution 426(1978), which specified that UNIFIL was to be established along the lines of the Secretary-General's report, which defined the parameters of self-defence.

[171] S/12611, 2, para 4(d); regarding UNEF II, see the same approach in S/11052/Rev 1, para 4(d).

the initial stage but the Council only articulated this expressly two years later, and after several incidents UNIFIL had not been able to make as much difference on the ground as it was required to under the its mandate.

Resolution 467 expressly reflected in its preamble the parameters for self-defence of UNIFIL specified in the Secretary-General's report. In paragraph 1, the Council adopted a stance conducive to effective interpretation of its previous resolutions and '[r]eaffirm[ed] its determination to implement the above-mentioned resolutions, particularly Resolutions 425(1978), 426(1978) and 459(1979), in the totality of the area of operations assigned to UNIFIL, up to the internationally recognized boundaries'. This approach prevents viewing the tasks of UNIFIL as limited to any particular area of the conflict zone and thus excluding it from zones where it might face military confrontation. Such a view would effectively divide the deployment zone into the area where UNIFIL could be peacefully deployed and that in which *de facto* armed units could be active without UNIFIL confronting them. This interpretation would have destroyed the design and intention of the Council resolutions which established UNIFIL: these aimed precisely for the force to be active over the entire zone in question, and to confront *de facto* forces wherever they might interfere with enforcement of its mandate.

In paragraph 2 the Council condemned '[a]ll obstructions of UNIFIL's ability to confirm the complete withdrawal of Israeli forces from Lebanon, to supervise the cessation of hostilities, to ensure the peaceful character of the area of operation, to control movement and to take measures deemed necessary to ensure the effective restoration of Lebanon's sovereignty'. Paragraphs 6 and 7 point 'to the provisions in the mandate that would allow the force to use its right to self-defence; [and] to the terms of reference of UNIFIL which provide that the Force will use its best efforts to prevent the recurrence of fighting and to ensure that its area of operation is not utilized for hostile activities of any kind'.

In 1973, in relation to the UNEF II mandate, Secretary-General Waldheim proposed expanding the entitlement of the peace-keeping mission to use force beyond narrow self-defence situations to cover attempts to prevent it from discharging its duties under the mandate of the Security Council.[172] As the UN General Guidelines for Peace-Keeping Operations specify,

Since 1973, the guidelines approved by the Security Council for each peace-keeping force have stipulated that self-defence is deemed to include resistance to attempts by forceful means to prevent the peacekeeping force from discharging its duties under the mandate of the Security Council. This is a broad conception of self-defence which might be interpreted as entitling United Nations personnel to open fire in a wide variety of situations.[173]

Along similar lines, the Brahimi Report confirms that, in defining the parameters of self-defence to be exercised by peace-keeping forces,

---

[172] See n 95 above.
[173] *General Guidelines for Peace-keeping Operations*, UN Doc 95–38147, October 1995, 20–1.

rules of engagement should not limit contingents to stroke-for-stroke responses but should allow ripostes sufficient to silence a source of deadly fire that is directed at United Nations troops or at the people they are charged to protect and, in particularly dangerous situations, should not force United Nations contingents to cede the initiative to their attackers.[174]

In practice, the broad concept of self-defence has been accepted. As Zacklin explains, because of the experiences of the UN in Bosnia, Rwanda, and Somalia, the Security Council felt subsequently that the mandates of peace forces should now include the right to use force (beyond self-defence) to protect civilians.[175] Paragraph 9 of Security Council Resolution 836(1993) authorized UNPROFOR

acting in self-defence, to take the necessary measures, including the use of force, in reply to bombardments against the safe areas by any of the parties or to armed incursion into them or in the event of any deliberate obstruction in or around those areas to the freedom of movement of UNPROFOR or of protected humanitarian convoys.

The UNPROFOR Rules of Engagement authorized the use of necessary and proportionate force, not just to disarm an armed group where necessary to prevent an attack on UNPROFOR, but also if hostile intent (that is, action that appeared preparatory to an aggressive action) so warranted.[176] Paragraph 9 of Resolution 871 (1993) similarly

[a]uthorize[d] UNPROFOR, in carrying out its mandate in the Republic of Croatia, acting in self-defence, to take the necessary measures, including the use of force, to ensure its security and its freedom of movement.

As for KFOR, Resolution 1244(1999) is silent on the right to use force. However, Annex II of the 1999 Military Technical Agreement between NATO and the FRY specifies that

the international security force ('KFOR') commander shall have the authority, without interference or permission, to do all that he judges necessary and proper, including the use of military force, to protect the international security force ('KFOR'), the international civil implementation presence, and to carry out the responsibilities inherent in this Military Technical Agreement and the Peace Settlement which it supports.

After the excessive use of force by UNOSOM II in Somalia, the Secretary-General's report suggested that the Security Council re-design the UNOSOM II mandate by excluding the entitlement to use force and limiting its military activity to protecting ports and personnel. The Secretary-General specified that he favoured continuing the UNOSOM II original mandate to use force, but that this option should be excluded because neither available resources nor local attitudes supported it.[177] Security Council Resolution 897(1994) redefined the UNOSOM II mandate

---

[174] Brahimi Report, n 120 above, para 49.
[175] Zacklin, n 7 above, 96.
[176] Findlay, n 3 above, 133.
[177] *Further Report of the Secretary-General submitted in pursuance of paragraph 4 of Resolution 886 (1993)*, S/1994/12, 6 January 1994, paras 56–7.

accordingly, mainly limiting it to protecting ports and airports, humanitarian relief, and protection of UN personnel (paragraph 2).

Paragraph 4 of Resolution 918(1994) on Rwanda specified that

UNAMIR may be required to take action in self-defence against persons or groups who threaten protected sites and populations, United Nations and other humanitarian personnel or the means of delivery and distribution of humanitarian relief.

Thus the Security Council confirmed UNAMIR's power to use force to protect humanitarian supplies, but still denoted this as self-defence. The resolution does not contain a broader authorization to use force against interferences with the mandate and duties of UNAMIR. In any case, UNAMIR possessed the 'expanded' right to self-defence even though it was not a Chapter VII mission. Similarly, the Security Council decided that, under Chapter VII and paragraph 16 of Resolution 1590(2005)

UNMIS is authorized to take the necessary action, in the areas of deployment of its forces and as it deems within its capabilities, to protect United Nations personnel, facilities, installations, and equipment, ensure the security and freedom of movement of United Nations personnel, humanitarian workers, joint assessment mechanism and assessment and evaluation commission personnel, and, without prejudice to the responsibility of the Government of Sudan, to protect civilians under imminent threat of physical violence.

Paragraph 12 of Resolution 1706(2006) intended to endow UNMIS with the right to use all necessary means to protect UN facilities, and prevent disruption of the peace process and attacks against civilians (paragraph 8). In Resolution 1769 (2007), the Security Council, acting under Chapter VII,

(a) *decides* that UNAMID is authorised to take the necessary action, in the areas of deployment of its forces and as it deems within its capabilities in order to: (i) protect its personnel, facilities, installations and equipment, and to ensure the security and freedom of movement of its own personnel and humanitarian workers; (ii) support early and effective implementation of the Darfur Peace Agreement, prevent the disruption of its implementation and armed attacks, and protect civilians, without prejudice to the responsibility of the Government of Sudan.

What this practice most significantly indicates is that the difference between the concept of self-defence (at times narrowly understood but expanded in practice to enable troops to protect the exercise of their mandate) and the authorization in Council resolutions to use 'all necessary means' or take 'the necessary action' to enforce the relevant mandate, gets increasingly and inevitably blurred. It can be concluded that the practice of peace keeping has gradually overcome the precon-ception of viewing the use of force as inimical to its nature.

8

Legal Consequences of Illegal Collective Security Acts and Decisions

1. Excess of Competence

Given that the powers of collective security organs are conferred by delegation from states, any excessive limits imposed on these powers will result in an excess of competence (ultra vires).[1] No other preliminary objection to the jurisdiction of UN organs has been raised as frequently as the objection ultra vires, which is inherent in the Charter's definition of the powers of political organs.[2] Difficulties in raising the objection ultra vires are arguably twofold. UN organs frequently fall short of citing the source of their authority. It is suggested that a decision's 'general reference to goals, functions and powers provides the objector with less support than particular texts indicating specific powers',[3] but if anything this factor has a directly opposite legal relevance. The underlying, or projected, uncertainty does nothing to limit or curtail the relevance of an objection of ultra vires, but instead enhances its relevance by requiring greater caution and increasing the burden of proving that the decision at issue has indeed been adopted pursuant to delegated powers.

The issue of abuse of the Council's competence (or action ultra vires) can be raised when the Council adopts a decision inimical to the aims stated in the Charter or bypassing the 'due process' requirements, especially through any bargain behind the decision making which is alien to the Charter purposes.[4] As the ICTY Trial Chamber specified in *Tadić*, 'if the Security Council acted arbitrarily or for an ulterior purpose it would be acting outside the purview of the powers delegated to it in the Charter'.[5]

The broad character of the UN's purposes substantially reduces the risk of one of its acts being considered ultra vires, but the *Certain Expenses* Opinion still emphasizes the limited and delegated nature of UN powers by postulating the presumption of

---

[1] See Chapter 2 above.
[2] *Report of the Special Committee on Reference to the International Court of Justice of Questions of United Nations Competence*, 44 *ASIL Proceedings* (1950), 256 at 257; D Ciobanu, *Preliminary Objections Related to the Jurisdiction of the United Nations Political Organs* (Leiden: Nijhof, 1975), 72.
[3] Ciobanu, ibid, 73–5.
[4] B Weston, 'Security Council Resolution 678 and Persian Gulf Decision Making: Precarious Legitimacy', 85 AJIL (1991), 516 at 524.
[5] *Prosecutor v Tadić*, Trial Chamber, 10 August 1995, para 15.

an act performed pursuant to those purposes not being ultra vires, as opposed to being unconditionally valid.[6] Compliance with the purposes of the UN is relevant for judging the legality of decisions that do not breach express requirements of the Charter. As Judge Winiarski pointed out, this means interpreting the Charter in terms of its text and purposes, which deprives of validity any approach that plays purpose against text. It had been asserted that 'the maintenance of international peace and security may provide a legal justification for certain decisions, even if these are not in conformity with the Charter'. Compliance with the UN's purposes, however, does not suffice to render a UN action lawful. The Charter is a carefully negotiated treaty specifying limited competences.[7]

Judge Spender's Opinion in *Certain Expenses* contains a clear-cut articulation of what renders an action by a principal organ ultra vires:

the General Assembly may in practice construe its authority beyond that conferred upon it, either expressly or impliedly, by the Charter. It may, for example, interpret its powers to permit it to enter a field prohibited to it under the Charter or in disregard of the procedure prescribed in the Charter. Action taken by the General Assembly (or other organs) may accordingly on occasions be beyond power.... In practice, if the General Assembly (or any organ) exceeds its authority there is little that the protesting minority may do except to protest and reserve its rights whatever they may be. If, however, the authority purported to be exercised against the objection of any Member State is beyond power it remains so.[8]

As Rama-Montaldo further observes, the test establishing that a decision is not ultra vires is that 'it must be demonstrably adopted to carry out one of the purposes of the Organisation'.[9] Presumably following this approach, the International Court specified in *Certain Expenses* that the establishment of peace-keeping forces by principal organs served the purposes of the UN and hence was not ultra vires. The ICTY Appeal Chamber ruled that the Tribunal's establishment did not exceed the Security Council's Chapter VII powers. The High Court in England has ruled that targeted sanctions against non-state actors are not (as such) ultra vires Article 41.[10]

Judge Spender also clarified that, when the International Court

is called upon to pronounce upon a question whether certain authority exercised by an organ of the Organization is within the power of that organ, only legal considerations may be invoked and *de facto* extension of the Charter must be disregarded.[11]

The practice of the Council is thus treated as a factual matter, the legality of which has to be examined against the term of the Charter which determines the scope of

---

[6] *Certain Expenses*, ICJ Reports 1962, 167–8.
[7] Ibid, 230.
[8] Ibid, Separate Opinion of Judge Spender, 196.
[9] Ibid, 168; M Rama-Montaldo, 'Contribution of the General Assembly to the Constitutional Development and Interpretation of the United Nations Charter', in R St J Macdonald, *Towards World Constitutionalism: Issues in the Legal Ordering of the World Community* (Leiden: Nijhof, 2005), 491 at 511–12.
[10] *A, K, M, Q & G v HM Treasury*, Queen's Bench, [2008] EWCH 869 (Admin), 24 April 2008, para 15.
[11] Judge Spender, n 8 above, 197.

competences. Thus an illegal Security Council resolution would not protect acts performed by states or organs of organizations in defiance of the legal limitations that UN organs are bound to observe. Responsibility for such acts must be properly attributed to each entity concerned.

Decisions based on an improper purpose constitute one of the categories of acts exceeding delegated powers. Assessing the propriety of an act's purpose requires the interpretation and application of all provisions in constituent treaties that enable decision making (expressly or by implication) by determining the purpose of a relevant decision through a use of discretion and the assessment of factual situations. This involves assessing whether the relevant decision is based on a proper use of discretion, for instance when identifying a threat or designing measures of response that are necessary and proportionate to a clearly identified objective.

A complex case of adopting decisions ultra vires reinforced by ulterior motives is offered by Security Council Resolutions 731(1992) and 748(1992) on Libya. As the above analysis has demonstrated, these resolutions:

(a) were adopted with the intention of circumventing regular dispute-settlement procedures under Articles 33 and 36 of the Charter, and the adoption of the resolutions was rushed, so proceedings before the International Court could be influenced;

(b) did not properly identify a threat to the peace under Article 39 to justify the consequent activation of Chapter VII;

(c) did not set a clear objective for this Chapter VII effort, nor present Libya with a demand that could be straightforwardly complied with; and

(d) caused disproportionate economic and humanitarian damage.[12]

In addition, as Judge Ajibola illustrated, Security Council resolutions on the Lockerbie matter included UK/US demands that Libya 'surrender for trial all those charged with the crime; accept complete responsibility for the actions of Libyan officials', and also 'pay appropriate compensation'. It was unclear

how the State of Libya could be urged to pay compensation when the 'suspects' or even to put it higher than that the 'accused persons' have not been found guilty by any competent court or tribunal and have not been proved to have acted in complicity with Libya. The presumption of innocence until guilt is established is still an integral part of the due administration of criminal justice the world over.[13]

No straightforward compliance could be expected with demands framed like this. Therefore, Resolutions 731 and 748 constitute a clear-cut case of ultra vires actions that do not command the binding force that accrues to resolutions under Article 25 of the Charter.

---

[12] See for detail Chapters 2, 4, and 5 above.
[13] *Lockerbie (Libya v UK)*, Provisional Measures, Dissenting Opinion of Judge Ajibola, *ICJ Reports* 1992, 86–7.

Another case of a decision taken for an ulterior motive is provided by Resolution 1422(2002) which exempted US personnel from the jurisdiction of the International Criminal Court pursuant to a power granted to the Security Council under Article 16 of the Rome Statute of the International Criminal Court, 17 July 1988. The legality of Resolution 1422 depends on the parameters within which this power was conferred. This provision was meant to enable the Council to decide whether to defer proceedings, but it does not displace the criteria by which the Council has to be guided when it adopts a Chapter VII decision. Therefore, a lawful Chapter VII decision under Article 16 has to properly identify a genuinely existing threat, clearly specify the objective to be met, and then decide on deferral as a necessary and proportionate measure.

Resolution 1422 was in fact adopted because (up to that point) the US position had been to block the renewal of peace-keeping mandates unless its concerns about ICC jurisdiction over US personnel serving with various peace missions were addressed. In particular, the USA vetoed extension of the UNMIBH mandate.[14] In its preamble Resolution 1422 specifies that 'it is in the interests of international peace and security to facilitate Member States' ability to contribute to operations established or authorized by the United Nations Security Council'. That said, the withdrawal of one nation from peace operations may be regrettable but not so critical as to justify their deferral under Article 16. This is not a genuine reason for adopting a Chapter VII resolution with far-reaching effects. As the representative of Jordan submitted to the Council,

should the Council consider again the adoption of a draft resolution on the ICC falling under Chapter VII, it will edge itself toward acting ultra vires—that is, beyond its authority under the Charter. After all, how could it adopt a Chapter VII resolution on the Court when the latter cannot by any stretch of the imagination be considered a threat to international peace and security?[15]

This demonstrates that Resolution 1422 was adopted for an ulterior motive, which cannot be without consequences for its legal effect.

Given that Resolution 1422 refers, not to existing situations but to future operations, and that a case-by-case analysis was not entered into as to whether the particular situation warranted deferral, the resolution is contrary to the ICC Statute.[16] As the Colombian representative elaborated (on the relationship between extension of the UNMIBH mandate and the ICC jurisdiction), 'a Security Council resolution issued under Chapter VII cannot ignore the content of the provisions of the Rome Statute'.[17]

---

[14] N White and R Cryer, 'The Security Council and the International Criminal Court: An Uneasy Relationship?' in MC Bassiouni, J Doria, H-P Gasser, and N Jdanov (eds.), *The Legal Regime of the International Criminal Court: Essays in Memory of Igor Blishchenko* (The Hague: Brill, 2008), 457 at 467.

[15] S/PV.4568, 16; for an identical view ibid, 3 (Canada).

[16] White and Cryer, n 14 above, 468–9; see also R Cryer, 'Sudan, Resolution 1593, and International Criminal Justice', 19 *Leiden Journal of International Law* (2006), 195.

[17] S/PV.4568, Res. 1, 6 (Colombia).

Resolution 1422 fails to articulate the basis required under Article 39. Discussions in the Security Council demonstrated a lack of the preconditions required under Article 39 for the Council to adopt a decision under Article 16 of the ICC Statute, even in the face of countervailing concerns related to the sustainability of peace operations. Taking into account also the circumstances of its adoption, Resolution 1422 does not identify the existence of statutory preconditions for the Council's action. It is precisely the political nature of Resolution 1422 that evidences its anti-statutory character. According to Conforti, in approving impunity for crimes that fall within the jurisdiction of the ICC, Resolution 1422 has to be evaluated by reference to *jus cogens,* which binds the Security Council.[18]

Resolutions 1422(2002) and 1487(2003) do not go as far, in some important respects, as Resolutions 1497(2003) and 1593(2005), adopted in relation to conflicts in Liberia and Sudan. In paragraph 7 of Resolution 1497, which deployed a Multi-National Force to deal with the situation in Liberia, the Council

[d]ecides that current or former officials or personnel from a contributing State [to the Multinational Force in Liberia], which is not a party to the Rome Statute of the International Criminal Court, shall be subject to the exclusive jurisdiction of that contributing State for all alleged acts or omissions arising out of or related to the Multinational Force or United Nations stabilization force in Liberia, unless such exclusive jurisdiction has been expressly waived by that contributing State.

In paragraph 6 of Resolution 1593, which referred the situation in Sudan to the ICC, the Council

[d]ecides that nationals, current or former officials or personnel from a contributing State outside Sudan which is not a party to the Rome Statute of the International Criminal Court shall be subject to the exclusive jurisdiction of that contributing State for all alleged acts or omissions arising out of or related to operations in Sudan established or authorized by the Council or the African Union, unless such exclusive jurisdiction has been expressly waived by that contributing State.

Several problems arise with the legality of these provisions. They neither refer to, nor are subsumable within, Article 16 ICC Statute, given that they are not time-limited. They leave open the impunity option, as prosecution by the state of nationality is not guaranteed. Furthermore, by upholding the exclusive jurisdiction of the contributing state, they purport to displace ordinary jurisdictional arrangements under general international law, over and above simply preventing the ICC from trying crimes normally falling within its jurisdiction. It is doubtful that the Council is authorized to adopt such decisions, since this goes well beyond the scope of Article 103. As these two resolutions do not provide for proper deferrals (as the ICC Statute does), that Court does not have to act upon them. Therefore, these resolutions are defensible neither under regular Chapter VII powers of the Council, nor under an ad hoc conferral of powers under Article 16.

In the process of adopting Resolution 1497, the Council expressly heard from the German representative that paragraph 7 of the resolution violated not only the

---

[18] B Conforti, *The Law and Practice of the United Nations* (The Hague: Kluwer, 2005), 201.

ICC Statute but also jurisdictional arrangements under general international law.[19] The Mexican government expressly stated that

paragraph 7 fails to provide guarantees for the attainment of one of the international community's most dearly held objectives—the elimination of impunity—since it does not establish an obligation for troop contributing countries to try officials or personnel who have committed crimes or other offences.[20]

This points to a blanket impunity and evidences the ultra vires nature of the Council's decision, with the consequence that the clause exclusively reserving the right to exercise jurisdiction over deployed personnel to their national state is opposable neither to other states nor to the ICC. States' opposition to any arrangement envisaging impunity and excessive impact on national criminal jurisdictions has been rigorously expressed. Germany stated its preference, in relation to paragraph 7 of Resolution 1497, for the Council 'to have voted on the draft resolution paragraph by paragraph to make clear that the Security Council has consensus on all parts of the draft resolution except paragraph 7'.[21] In relation to Resolution 1593, Brazil considered that preserving exclusive jurisdiction for states of nationality was contrary to international law.[22] Denmark proposed an interpretation of paragraph 7 of Resolution 1593 consistent with international law,[23] specifying that 'with regard to the language on exclusive jurisdiction, it is our interpretation that it does not affect the universal jurisdiction of Member States in areas such as war crimes, torture and terrorism'.[24]

These statements envisage the possibility of separating the impugned clauses from the parent resolutions; the underlying debates in the Security Council did not point to these clauses being, structurally or systemically, inherent parts of the respective Chapter VII efforts, much as it could be arguable that without these provisions the two resolutions would not have commanded the required majority under Article 27 of the Charter. Under the law of treaties, Article 44 of the 1969 Vienna Convention specifies that a void clause can be separated from the rest of the treaty unless that clause has been an essential condition for the acceptance of the treaty by the relevant party. While separability is presumably admissible under general international law outside the Vienna Convention, and moreover is not undesirable in the case of resolutions,[25] it is not obvious at all whether the position under the law of treaties could be applied by analogy to Security Council resolutions, by contending that a void clause in the relevant resolution was an essential

---

[19] S/PV.4803, 4 (Germany).
[20] Ibid, 2 (Mexico).
[21] Ibid, 4 (Germany).
[22] S/PV.5158, 11.
[23] See Chapter 2 above.
[24] S/PV.5158, 6 (Denmark); France emphasized, along similar lines, 'that the jurisdictional immunity provided for in the text we have just adopted obviously cannot run counter to other international obligations of States and will be subject, where appropriate, to the interpretation of the courts of my country': ibid, 8.
[25] See A Orakhelashvili, *Peremptory Norms in International Law* (New York: Oxford University Press, 2006), Chapters 6 and 14, on the issues of invalidity.

requirement for a permanent member to vote for that resolution as a whole. A more plausible test for establishing whether the impugned clause is separable from the rest of a resolution thus relates, not so much to the voting intentions of Council members, but to the structure of the resolution at issue, as it embodies a collective security effort. Under this view, the exclusive jurisdiction clauses under Resolutions 1497 and 1953 are void and separable from the rest of these resolutions, leaving those remaining parts intact.

In the process of adopting Resolution 1559(2004) concerning withdrawal of foreign forces from Lebanon, and prescribing a number of requirements regarding political and constitutional requirements in that country, Lebanon considered that the concerns expressed in the resolution were outside the Council's mandate and called for its withdrawal.[26] Brazil abstained on account of this resolution being ultra vires, pleading that

Resolution 1559(2004) deals with matters that are essentially within the domestic jurisdiction of Lebanon. The existence of a dispute likely to endanger international peace and security has not been properly characterized in the text. If it had been, the Security Council would have had to take into consideration the procedures for settlement of the dispute already adopted by the parties.[27]

Even if the Council had found a threat to the peace to exist, it would still have been bound (by the principle of subsidiarity) to identify that threat. If the Council interferes in the internal affairs of a state without intelligibly demonstrating how that internal situation constitutes a threat to the peace, its decision will be open to refusal on the basis of excess of power. Lebanon's own submissions confirm just that:

The legitimacy of the United Nations, the Charter and the Council's rules of procedure provide no justification for this draft resolution, which constitutes interference in the internal affairs of a State Member of the Organization. The draft resolution also discusses bilateral relations between two friendly countries, neither of which has filed any complaint with regard to those relations, which are guided by the agreement on coordination and cooperation they have signed. We therefore call for the withdrawal of the draft resolution.[28]

Once it is established that a collective security decision is either ultra vires or constitutes an abuse of discretion and cannot consequently be based on the affected organ's delegated powers, that decision no longer has a legal basis. As pointed out, a resolution vitiated by a manifest excess of powers is invalid and no longer binding.[29] As the ASIL Special Committee Report specified, there is no unique method for resolving doubts about the constitutionality of UN resolutions.[30] There is no regular judicial jurisdiction over any principal organ. What remain are options generally available under international law for resolving disputes regarding treaty

---

[26] S/PV.5028, 3.
[27] Ibid, 6–7 (Brazil); see also a similar submission by Philippines, ibid, 7.
[28] Ibid, 3 (Lebanon).
[29] *Certain Expenses,* Separate Opinion of Judge Morelli, *ICJ Reports* 1962, 223; Ciobanu, n 2 above, 80.
[30] *Report: Questions of UN Competence,* n 2 above, 257.

interpretation, which refer to the relevance of the views both of member States and of principal organs, and the right of principal organs such as the Security Council, the General Assembly, or the International Court to deal with these issues when they are raised in the course of their exercise of their regular jurisdiction.

2. Refusal by States to Implement Ultra Vires Decisions

It can be taken as a starting position that, while the Charter is silent on termination and modification of Security Council resolutions, power to decide to do this rests with the Council.[31] An early position to this effect was expressed by US Ambassador Goldberg in relation to the Rhodesian case: the Security Council's decision under Article 39 'is conclusive and not to be contested by any member'.[32]

However, this starting position goes hand-in-hand with the Council's duty to act in accordance with the Charter and relevant international law, failing which unilateral non-compliance can no longer be ruled out. As Judge Bustamante observed in *Certain Expenses*, the real reason for obedience by states to UN decisions is the conformity of the latter with the text of the Charter. Under Article 25, the duty to accept institutional decisions is conditional upon the conformity of those decisions with the Charter. There is therefore a legal presumption that each organ complies with the prescriptions of the Charter; 'but when, in the opinion of one of the Member States, a mistake of interpretation has been made or there has even been an infringement of the Charter, there is a right to challenge the resolution in which the error has been noted for the purpose of determining whether or not it departed from the Charter'.[33] Following the same approach, the ASIL Special Committee Report specified that a UN member may refuse to execute a UN decision 'if he feels strongly that the decision is unconstitutional'.[34] Conforti suggests that 'each member State may question an interpretation of the Charter made by one of the organs in taking a specific measure'.[35] If so, then states can actually challenge the Council's resolutions, because every such resolution is inevitably premised on the interpretation of the Charter by the Council.

The grounds for disregarding economic sanctions under Chapter VII would be the resolution's ultra vires character, owing to either its disproportionate impact or its violation of human rights. If humanitarian exceptions do not work properly, a valid ground for disregarding a resolution that had introduced sanctions could arise. According to one view, at least as of 2000 states were entitled to reject the binding character of sanctions imposed on Iraq, given the Security Council's unwillingness for more than a decade to amend them to remedy its violation of the right to life

---

[31] D Caron, 'The Legitimacy of the Collective Authority of the Security Council', 87 AJIL (1993), 552 at 578.

[32] Cf CG Fenwick, 'When is There a Threat to the Peace?—Rhodesia', 61 AJIL (1967), 753 at 755.

[33] *Certain Expenses*, Dissenting Opinion of Judge Bustamante, *ICJ Reports* 1962, 304.

[34] *Report: Questions of UN Competence*, n 2 above, 267.

[35] Conforti, n 18 above, 16; see further Chapter 2 above.

and right to health in Iraq. This entitlement arises because on the basis of Article 25 of the Charter states must comply with Security Council resolutions when these resolutions accord with the Charter, and the violations of human rights in Iraq violated the Charter.[36]

In the Lockerbie matter, Libya initially argued that the bombing had to be resolved as a legal dispute through the means available under Article 33 of the Charter.[37] After repeated attempts by the USA and the UK to requalify this legal dispute as a political one (through the adoption of Security Council Resolutions 731 and 748(both 1992)), Libya resorted to the remaining options under Article 33 and brought the matter before regional organizations: the OAU, the LAS, the NAM, and the OIC. Mediation efforts undertaken by and within these organizations were rejected or disregarded by the USA and the UK, which continued to rely on their position as permanent members of the Security Council. Libya then persuaded the OAU, the Arab League, and others that the Libyan suspects would never receive a fair trial in the UK or the USA.[38] Libya's proposal was to try the two terrorist suspects in The Hague before Scottish judges and in accordance with Scottish law. This position was supported by the OAU and the Arab League. These organizations also took the position that sanctions imposed on Libya should be lifted.[39] The resolution adopted at the 1996 Addis Ababa meeting of the OAU stated its solidarity with Libya and deplored 'the maintenance of sanctions against Libya despite that country's flexibility and efforts in meeting the conditions set by the United Nations Security Council for lifting the sanctions',[40] whereby it registered its direct opposition to the Security Council's judgement on this issue. An resolution that the OAU adopted at its Yaoundé session in 1996 called upon 'the Security Council to lift the sanctions imposed on the Libyan Arab Jamahiriya since the continued implementation of such sanctions may compel African States to look into possible means of sparing the Libyan Arab people further suffering'.[41]

A similar position was expressed at the 1997 OIC Tehran Summit, which appealed to the Security Council to lift the embargo imposed on Libya.[42] The OIC Seventh Casablanca Summit Declaration called 'for the holding of just trial of the two suspects by Scottish Judges in accordance with Scottish law at the seat of the International Court of Justice in The Hague'.[43] The Non-Aligned Movement Cartagena Declaration also

---

[36] De Wet, *Chapter VII Powers of the UN Security Council* (Oxford: Hart, 2004), 385; see further Chapter 5 above.

[37] See Chapter 2 above.

[38] S/PV.3864, 20 March 1998, 6 (Libya); M Plachta, 'The *Lockerbie* Case: The Role of the Security Council in Enforcing the Principle *Aut Dedere Aut Judicare*', 12 *European Journal of International Law* (2001), 125 at 135.

[39] UNYB 1996, 143–4.

[40] CM/Res 1623(LXIII), paras 1–2, 26–8 February 1996.

[41] CM/Res 1652(LXIV), preamble, paras 1 and 3, 1–5 July 1996.

[42] 1997 OIC Tehran Summit Declaration, para 61.

[43] Declaration of 13–15 December 1994, para 77.

urged the Security Council to lift the air embargo and the other measures imposed on Libya, in response to the decisions and resolutions adopted by regional organizations on the dispute of Libya with France, the United Kingdom and the United States. . . . They called upon the three concerned Western countries to respond to the positive initiative calling for dialogue and negotiations and for a just and fair trial of the two suspects in a neutral country to be agreed upon by all parties. Unless the Western countries concerned respond to the request of regional organizations, the proposals for the peaceful settlement of the crisis, and the flexibility shown by the Libyan Arab Jamahiriya, the States Members of the Non-Aligned Movement will not be able to continue to abide by the sanctions resolutions, especially that these resolutions have caused not only the Libyan people, but also several peoples of States Members of the Non-Aligned Movement great human and economic loss.[44]

The Ouagadougou Decision of the Assembly of Heads of State and Government of the OAU expressed regret 'for lack of positive response by the United States of America and the United Kingdom to the International and Regional initiatives and efforts aimed at finding a solution to the dispute based on the principles of international law', and decided

not to comply any longer with Security Council Resolutions 748(1992) and 883(1993) on sanctions, with effect from September 1998, if the United States of America and the United Kingdom refuse that the two suspects be tried in a third neutral country pursuant to the verdict of the International Court of Justice by July 1998, date on which sanctions will be due for review, owing to the fact that the said resolutions violate Article 27 paragraph 3, Article 33 and Article 36 paragraph 3 of the United Nations Charter, and the considerable human and economic losses suffered by Libya and a number of other African peoples as a result of the sanctions.[45]

Sanctions on Libya did not work and, as time passed, the prospects of a successful criminal prosecution of the alleged perpetrators also faded.[46] Chad, Niger, and Gambia flouted the US air embargo when their leaders flew to Tripoli; and in the summer of 1998, 53 members of OAU voted to release themselves from the observance of Security Council sanctions against Libya. At the same time, the rejection of the Libyan proposal to try suspects on neutral territory put the USA and the UK in an inconvenient position, seen as obstructing the settlement of this problem.[47] Non-compliance with sanctions increased and the air embargo was disregarded. In this respect, the Sanctions Committee

---

[44] Non-Aligned Movement, Cartagena Declaration, NAC 11/Doc.1/Rev.3, 18–20 October 1995, para 163; see ibid, for reservations to that position expressed by Colombia, Panama, Peru, Thailand, Malaysia, and Chile. See also Cartagena Ministerial Summit Document, 8–9 April 2000, para 127, supporting 'the right of Libya for compensation of the damages it suffered as a result of the sanctions'. This was adopted after a compromise was agreed (to try the suspects in the Netherlands) and sanctions on Libya had been suspended.

[45] *The Crisis between the Great Socialist People's Libyan Arab Jamahiriya and the United States of America and the United Kingdom*, AHG/DEC 127 (XXXIV), 8–10 June 1998, 6 *African Yearbook of International Law* (1998), 390–1.

[46] JB Schwartz, 'Dealing With a "Rogue State": the Libya Precedent', 101 AJIL (2007), 553 at 565–6.

[47] Plachta, n 38 above, 135.

took note of the fact that some States had invoked the decision of a regional organization as overriding Security Council resolutions. The Committee sent letters to the Member States concerned (Burkina Faso, Chad, Eritrea, Mali, Niger, Sudan), reminding them of their obligations under the Charter and under Resolution 748(1992), and noting that the flights in question were unacceptable breaches of the sanctions regime.[48]

There is no immediate indication that these states complied with the demands of the Sanctions Committee. On the contrary, the OAU decision to cease to comply with sanctions was adopted after the committee expressed its position. In the same year, the UK and the USA agreed, 'in the interest of resolving this situation in a way which will allow justice to be done', and 'as an exceptional measure, to arrange for the two accused to be tried in the Netherlands'.[49] This was the position that they had consistently opposed during the previous years.[50] The United Kingdom enacted the necessary statutory instruments and concluded an agreement with the Netherlands with a view to arranging the trial in that country.[51] On 27 August 1998, the Security Council adopted Resolution 1192. Paragraph 1 of this resolution demanded 'once again' that Libya comply with Resolutions 731(1992), 748 (1992), and 883(1993). Paragraph 4, however, demanded Libya 'ensure the appearance in the Netherlands of the two accused'. These two paragraphs required Libya to do different things. It was clear, however, that extradition of the suspects to the United States or the United Kingdom was not really the goal which the Council or the sponsoring states were trying to achieve. That had proved to be unrealistic. Therefore, upon arrival of the suspects in the Netherlands on 5 May 1999, the sanctions imposed on Libya by Resolutions 748 and 883 were suspended in accordance with paragraph 8 of Resolution 1192, which meant in practical terms that they were lifted because to reimpose them would have required a further decision by the Security Council.[52] It was, in the end, the regional attitudes that determined how the Security Council concluded its Chapter VII enterprise in the Lockerbie matter.

It has been submitted that, doctrinally, challenging the action of the Security Council through national courts is almost impossible.[53] However, the UK Supreme Court held in the *Targeted Sanctions* case that a Chapter VII resolution that is ultra vires because of its conflict with *jus cogens* does not command the effect that accrues to Security Council decisions in the English legal system on the basis of the 1946 UN Act. It is thus open to domestic courts in the UK to review the vires of Security Council resolutions.[54]

---

[48] UNYB 1998, 97.
[49] Letter dated 24 August 1998 from the Acting Permanent Representative of the UK and the USA to the UN addressed to the Secretary-General, S/1998/795, para 3.
[50] A Aust, '*Lockerbie*: The Other Case', 49 ICLQ (2000), 283; for the text of the UK/US Letter to the UN Secretary-General embodying these proposals, see 117 *ILR* 687–9.
[51] For the texts of these documents see 117 *ILR* 666ff.
[52] Aust, n 50 above, 295–6.
[53] A Reinisch, 'Developing Human Rights and Humanitarian Law Accountability of the Security Council for the Imposition of Economic Sanctions', 95 AJIL (2001), 866.
[54] *HM Treasury v Mohammed Jabar Ahmed and others*, [2010] UKSC 2, 27 January 2010, para 151.

3. Judicial Review

(a) Arrangements and Options within the UN System and Beyond

Statutory prerequisites for judicial review within the UN system are premised on the Security Council's subjection to international law under Articles 24 and 25 of the Charter, and the International Court's general competence to administer law under Articles 36 and 38 of its Statute. There are no statutory provisions excluding judicial review. As there is no subordination of the Council to the Court or vice versa, each organ can exercise its function independently of the other. Matters of legal interpretation of the Charter, including the scope of discretion of the Security Council under Chapter VII, would ultimately rest with the Court. The absence of a regular procedure to review Security Council acts does not prejudice the Court's existing—contentious, advisory, or incidental—jurisdiction to state the law in relation to underlying facts, actions, and positions, which includes the Council's decisions.

The *Certain Expenses* case acknowledged that the amendment favouring the ultimate interpretation of the competence of UN organs by the International Court had been rejected at the San Francisco conference. Still, the Court went on to specify the criterion for undertaking judicial review: compliance of the relevant decision with the purposes of the Charter, in which case it can be seen as covered by the relevant organ's delegated mandate.[55] The contention that the International Court cannot review Security Council resolutions necessarily equates to viewing the Court's powers as subordinated to the Council, and bringing in the *litis pendens* doctrine through the back door. To illustrate this perception, Judge Bedjaoui specified that Resolution 748(1992) has negated the effects of the potential list of provisional measures that the Court might have ordered in the *Lockerbie* case.[56]

Dugard proceeds from the silence of the UN Charter on the International Court's power to review Security Council decisions. In the way it regulates the relationship between the Security Council and the General Assembly in Article 12, the Charter does not exclude judicial review of the Security Council's acts by the Court. In addition, the Charter-based powers of the Council are not unlimited, and are further subject to *jus cogens*. From here there is a short step to the conclusion that the Court is the appropriate body to review the Council's resolutions.[57] Dugard's approach seems to rightly link the issue of principle—the Council being subjected to the Charter and *jus cogens*—to the institutional outcome of the Court being competent to review its resolutions. Dinstein likewise suggests that the International Court is entitled to review the vires of Security Council resolutions, or for conflicting with a superior rule of *jus cogens*.[58]

---

[55] *ICJ Reports* 1962, 167–8.
[56] Dissenting Opinion of Judge Bedjaoui, *ICJ Reports* 1992, 47–8; see also Dissenting Opinion of Judge Ranjeva, ibid, 73–4 (para 8).
[57] J Dugard, 'Judicial Review of Sanctions', in V Gowlland-Debbas (ed.), *UN Sanctions and Internationa Law* (The Hague: Kluwer, 2001) 83 at 85–6.
[58] Y Dinstein, *War, Aggression and Self-Defence*, 4th ed. (Cambridge: Cambridge University Press, 2005), 325.

As for the pattern of review, Dugard observes that in principle the Court could interfere where the Council makes an Article 39 determination in bad faith, that is commits an abuse of rights, but that this is unlikely to happen. In reviewing actual sanctions, the Court would have to address the issue of proportionality.[59] According to Franck, 'judicial review for "gross abuse of discretion" would enhance significantly the authority of the Council by assuring the members of the UN— especially those not on the Council—that its actions remain accountable to the Charter and the membership'.[60]

On a different note, Matheson argues that, since the Council's decisions are informed by political judgement, they are not readily subject to judicial review.[61] Likewise, Judge Schwebel in *Lockerbie* contended that judicial review can upset the operation of the collective security mechanism, suggesting that 'the conclusions to which the *travaux préparatoires* and text of the Charter lead are that the Court was not meant to be invested with a power of judicial review of the legality or effects of decisions of the Security Council'. Only the Council can determine what constitutes a threat to the peace under Article 39, and adopt consequent measures. Contentious cases may come before the Court that call for its passing judgment upon questions of law raised by Council decisions, or interpreting pertinent resolutions. But that power cannot be equated with an authority to review the decisions of the Security Council.[62]

It is right that, as a matter of constitutional allocation of powers under the Charter, only the Council can make an Article 39 determination, and that no other principal organ can set Chapter VII in motion. But this does not translate into the position that, in performing its Chapter VII role, the Council has unlimited discretion to denote anything it likes a threat to the peace. The repeated affirmation in jurisprudence that the Council is not *legibus solutus* applies to all areas of its activities including Chapter VII.[63] The Council's exercise of Chapter VII powers does not determine whether the Court should act; instead, it is for the Court to ascertain the limits of the Council's binding powers.

In the same *Lockerbie* case, Judge ad hoc Jennings expressed similar scepticism at the reviewability of Chapter VII decisions, arguing that if

the Security Council, exercising the discretionary competence given to it by Article 39 of the Charter, has decided that there exists a 'threat to the peace', it is not for the principal judicial organ of the United Nations to question that decision, much less to substitute a decision of its own, but to state the plain meaning and intention of Article 39, and to

---

[59] Dugard, n 57 above, 88.

[60] T Franck in C Tomuschat (ed.), *The United Nations at the Age of Fifty* (The Hague: Kluwer, 1995), 25 at 37.

[61] M Matheson, *Council Unbound—The Growth of UN Decision Making in Conflict and Post-conflict Issues after the Cold War* (Washington, DC: USIP Press, 2006), 38.

[62] *Lockerbie (Libya v UK)*, Preliminary Objections Judgment, Dissenting Opinion of Judge Schwebel, *ICJ Reports* 1998, 80.

[63] This point is even more noteworthy, since Judge Schwebel's opposition to judicial review in this context is accompanied by a statement that in the Chapter VII context the Security Council is unbound by law.

protect the Security Council's exercise of that body's power and duty conferred upon it by the law; and to protect the exercise of the discretion of the Security Council to 'decide what measures not involving the use of armed force are to be employed to give effect to its decisions'.[64]

If, however, the Court can go so far as 'to state the plain meaning and intention of Article 39', then it certainly can apply that plain meaning and intention to underlying facts and see whether the Council has made the proper use of this provision. If the Court lets stand a determination made for ulterior purposes or on a counter-factual basis, essentially it upholds an decision made by the Council outside its powers, which is not justified under the mandate delegated to it by the Charter. After all, Article 39 is a treaty provision fully within the Court's jurisdiction.

This approach to the reviewability of Chapter VII decisions, including Article 39 determinations, has prevailed in practice. The Trial Chamber of the ICTY some-what deferentially observed in *Tadić* that

the validity of the decision of the Security Council to establish the International Tribunal rests on its finding that the events in the former Yugoslavia constituted a threat to the peace. This finding is necessarily fact-based and raises political, non-justiciable issues.[65]

It has not been explained, however, why a factual matter should be exempted from judicial review. The Appeal Chamber, on the other hand, proceeded to state that

the wider the discretion of the Security Council under the Charter of the United Nations, the narrower the scope for the International Tribunal to review its actions, even as a matter of incidental jurisdiction. Nevertheless, this does not mean that the power disappears altogether, particularly in cases where there might be a manifest contradiction with the Principles and Purposes of the Charter.[66]

Therefore, the Security Council's discretionary decisions are reviewable when they offend the principles and purposes of the Charter, and *a fortiori* fundamental principles of international law that these principles and purposes incorporate.

Decisions of the UN Administrative Tribunal specify the parameters set for judicial review of discretionary decisions. The Tribunal claimed the competence to review the Secretary-General's broad discretion in personnel matters, if this is exercised in a discriminatory, arbitrary manner or for improper purposes.[67] In another Judgment, the Tribunal specified the principle of proportionality, proce-dural irregularity, and a significant mistake of fact as grounds for judicial review.[68] More specifically, the reasons given for the exercise of discretion can be examined 'for their truthfulness'. Relying upon 'an unsupported reason' means that the entity

---

[64] Dissenting Opinion of Judge ad hoc Sir Robert Jennings, *ICJ Reports* 1998, 110 (emphasis in original).

[65] *Prosecutor v Tadić*, Case IT-94-1-AR72, Appeal Chamber, Interlocutory Decision on Appeal, 2 October 1995, para 24.

[66] *Prosecutor v Tadić*, Case IT-94-1-AR72, Appeal Chamber, Judgment, 15 July 1999, para 31.

[67] Judgment No 1425, 30 January 2009, 6.

[68] Judgment No 1428, 30 January 2009, 8; *Lindsey v ADB*, Asian Development Bank Administra-tive Tribunal, Decision No 1, 18 December 1992, para 12.

in question 'improperly exercised [its] discretion', and then the Tribunal may vitiate the impugned decision and invalidate it.[69] The exercise of discretion 'in the interest of the Agency' finding serious misconduct which had been neither alleged nor proved can constitute an abuse of powers, leading to a decision being nullified or quashed.[70] The Asian Development Bank Tribunal stated in *Lindsey* that its right to review institutional discretion was based on its competence to determine its own competence.[71] This can explain the power of international tribunals to review counter-factual determinations by the Security Council or unsubstantiated assertions by it that a threat to the peace exists in a particular situation.

The issue of review of Security Council decisions arose acutely in the *Kadi* case before the EU courts.[72] The Court of First Instance refused to admit, in the first place, that the Security Council's decisions can be reviewed by the EU judiciary, because the UN Charter, due to its Article 103, prevails over EU treaty instruments. Therefore, EU courts could review Security Council resolutions only if these acts offend a higher rule of *jus cogens*.[73] The ECJ, on the other hand, annulled the contested regulation due to its conflict with fundamental human rights as part of EU law. The Court overruled the objections of France, the Netherlands, and Britain that, insofar as Community measures implement UN Chapter VII measures (which enjoy primacy both for member States and the Community), they escape all review by the Community judicature, even review of the observance of fundamental rights, and enjoy immunity from jurisdiction; no review of Security Council resolutions could be carried out by the Community judicature even if resolutions offend against *jus cogens*.[74] The Court's dismissal of this deference argument was based on its perception of the autonomy of the EU legal order, in the sense that the legality of EU instruments implementing Security Council resolutions must be judged solely by reference to the compliance of these instruments with EU fundamental rights, whatever the position under the UN Charter. The ECJ thus avoided directly confronting those aspects of United Nations law regarding the review of Security Council resolutions.

(b) Judicial Review and the International Court's Provisional Measures Proceedings

The 1992 Order in *Lockerbie* conveys the impression that a distinction is drawn between the various types of proceedings. The Court seemed to mix and match to

---

[69] Judgment No 1429, 30 January 2009, 7–8.
[70] Judgment No 1238, 30 September 2005, 8.
[71] *Lindsey*, n 68 above, para 11.
[72] For further detail see Chapters 3 and 5 above.
[73] *Ahmed*, n 54 above, paras 276–7, 281–2, 337; Joined Cases T-306/01 and T-315/01 *Ahmed Ali Yusuf and Al Barakaat International Foundation and Yassin Abdullah Kadi v Council of the European Union and Commission of the European Communities,* Judgment of 21 September 2005, paras 225–6, 230–1, 282.
[74] *Kadi*, ibid, paras 262–9, 276.

create what it presumably intended as a compromise solution—to avoid interference with Security Council decisions under Resolutions 731 and 748(both 1992) by declaring them valid *prima facie* and at the same time to preserve its judicial function by emphasizing the purely interim character of both its proceedings and the validity of the resolutions at hand. The compromise nature of this approach does not, however, dispense with the need to examine its internal consistency as well as its compatibility with the imperatives of the Court's judicial function under its Statute.

In its Order the Court specified that

both Libya and the United Kingdom, as Members of the United Nations, are obliged to accept and carry out the decisions of the Security Council in accordance with Article 25 of the Charter;...[therefore] the Court, which is at the stage of proceedings on provisional measures, considers that *prima facie* this obligation extends to the decision contained in Resolution 748(1992);...[and] in accordance with Article 103 of the Charter, the obligations of the Parties in that respect prevail over their obligations under any other international agreement, including the Montreal Convention;...consequently the Court, while thus not at this stage called upon to determine definitively the legal effect of Security Council Resolution 748(1992), considers that, whatever the situation previous to the adoption of that resolution, the rights claimed by Libya under the Montreal Convention cannot now be regarded as appropriate for protection by the indication of provisional measures.

This led to the conclusion that 'an indication of the measures requested by Libya would be likely to impair the rights which appear *prima facie* to be enjoyed by the United Kingdom by virtue of Security Council Resolution 748(1992)'.[75] The Court's Order is clear that Articles 25 and 103 of the Charter operate in a *prima facie* manner, not in a conclusive and definitive manner. Libya's rights were neither appropriate for protection through the grant of provisional measures, nor inappropriate for judicial protection as such. The same approach is further corroborated by the Court's express statement that at the provisional measures stage the Court could not 'make definitive findings either of fact or of law on the issues relating to the merits, and the right of the Parties to contest such issues at the stage of the merits must remain unaffected by the Court's decision'.[76]

Another plain inconsistency in the Court's Order is that, while the Court invokes Article 103 to affirm that 'the obligations of the Parties in that respect prevail over their obligations under any other international agreement, including the Montreal Convention', it then turns the matter on its head, declaring that 'the rights claimed by Libya under the Montreal Convention cannot now be regarded as appropriate for protection by the indication of provisional measures'. What were initially obligations covered by Article 103 have suddenly become rights. Apart from that, the view upheld in the Court's Order of Articles 25 and 103 precluding the Court's indication of provisional measures is a simple, straightforward, and

---

[75] *Lockerbie, ICJ Reports* 1992, 15 (paras 39–41).
[76] Ibid, 14 (para 38).

intelligible argument that carries with it the inference of correctness and persuasion. On closer inspection, however, this inference proves misguided.

The Court's approach that its Order had an interim and *prima facie*, not a definitive, effect was shared by individual judges. According to Judge Shahabudd-een, 'the validity of the resolution, though contested by Libya, *has, at this stage, to be presumed*'.[77] Judge Ajibola was also clear that the issue of validity of the relevant resolutions 'will be resolved one way or the other when the matter comes up for argument on its merits'.[78] However, Judge Bedjaoui explained the opposite implication of Resolution 748 for Libya's rights under the Montreal Convention:

if this right is not protected by provisional measures, the possibility that it may disappear purely and simply cannot be rejected, so that, from this viewpoint, the prejudice would be irreparable in that the right that has been lost could not thereafter be restored. The threat of disappearance of this right was so real that it subsequently became a reality with the adoption of Resolution 748(1992), which in effect put an end to it![79]

Judge Ranjeva likewise stated that the Court had to indicate provisional measures to protect rights that were under threat of disappearance.[80] If, as was the case, a party's rights are threatened with elimination, the *prima facie* analysis and interim decision allegedly performed in the Court's order would no longer be a *prima facie* and interim decision, once implemented. If, in the meantime, Libya were to comply with Resolutions 731 and 748, its rights would be irreversibly destroyed, which would then produce a result inimical to what Article 41 of the Statute requires, namely preserving rights while the case is pending.

If the Court's task under Article 41 is to preserve the rights of parties, its inherent and principal task is also to look at the ways in which those rights are endangered in particular situations. What Article 41 requires from the Court is to protect rights, not in the abstract, but in a practical way wherever they are threatened. Thus the problem is not really whether Resolution 748 is binding on Libya *prima facie*. A closer inspection of the text and effects of this resolution can indeed reveal that the Council's intention was no less than to override Libya's Convention rights in the Lockerbie case with a conclusive and irreversible effect. Upholding these effects in an interim way can entail their permanent consolidation. The annihilation of rights that can be protected under Article 41 of the Statute is not justified under the Charter; the effect of Article 103 covers obligations rather than rights, let alone those expressly protected under a Statute which forms the part of the Charter. It is questionable whether, in the absence of hierarchy between the two organs, Article 103 could override the Court's powers under Article 41 of the Statute. By portraying its approach as limited to the interim aspect of the case, the Court effectively lost sight of the interim nature of its proceedings. On this account the 1992 Order is faulty under both the Charter and the Statute.

---

[77] Separate Opinion of Judge Shahabuddeen, ibid, 28 (emphasis added).
[78] Dissenting Opinion of Judge Ajibola, ibid, 91–2.
[79] Dissenting Opinion of Judge Bedjaoui, ibid, 39; see also ibid, 44 (para 23).
[80] Dissenting Opinion of Judge Ranjeva, ibid, 73 (para 7).

(c) Judicial Review and the International Court's Jurisdictional Proceedings

The 1998 preliminary objections judgment dismissed objections advanced by the USA and the UK that Libya's submissions based on the Montreal Convention were beyond the Court's jurisdiction, inadmissible, or moot. The Court ruled that the dispute under Article 14 of the Montreal Convention had survived the adoption of Resolution 748. Judge Schwebel claimed that

> the Court should have held Libya's claims to be inadmissible, or at any rate moot, on the ground that the issues between it and the Respondent have been determined by decisions of the Security Council which bind the Parties and which, pursuant to Article 103 of the Charter, prevail over any rights and obligations that Libya and the Respondent have under the Montreal Convention.[81]

Being inadmissible means, however, that a claim exists which can affect the substance of a dispute, indeed constitute a dispute, but that the way it is brought before the Court (for instance in an untimely manner, without exhausting local remedies, or without demonstrating a legal interest) prevents its adjudication. What renders the claim inadmissible are grounds that make the case structurally unfit for international adjudication. While the International Court's Statute specifies no conditions for admissibility of claims, the Court can validly declare a case inadmissible only on conditions generally accepted in international law, whether in the context of an adjudication or outside it, as recognized in judicial practice as well as in the law of state responsibility.[82] It is not for the Court to invent new grounds for admissibility; criteria for admissibility can be only those upholding which does not require the Court to pronounce on the merit of the dispute.

For a claim to be moot, on the other hand, means that the real dispute between the parties (in terms of a disagreement on a point of fact or law, and mutual opposition of claims) has disappeared, so there is nothing to adjudicate upon. The implication is that if a claim is inadmissible, it cannot be moot, and vice versa. It is possible that a claim is neither inadmissible nor moot; but it is impossible for it to be both.

The effect of Security Council resolutions is a question of merits, specifically of validity and interpretation, which has to be gone through properly before the issue is decided. It is not a preliminary issue of admissibility. Indeed, the Court has specified that

> [b]y maintaining that Security Council Resolutions 748(1992) and 883(1993) have rendered the Libyan claims without object, the United Kingdom ... is requesting, in reality ... on the one hand a decision establishing that the rights claimed by Libya under the Montreal Convention are incompatible with its obligations under the Security Council

[81] *Lockerbie (Libya v UK)*, Preliminary Objections Judgment, *ICJ Reports* 1998, 71.
[82] Cf ILC's Article 44 on State responsibility (Admissibility of Claims), and commentary thereto, *Yearbook of the ILC* 2001, volume 2, 120ff.

resolutions; and, on the other hand, a decision that those obligations prevail over those rights by virtue of Articles 25 and 103 of the Charter.[83]

This would involve resolving the merits at the preliminary objections stage. This is further underscored by the UK submission that 'Resolutions 748 and 883 are legally binding and they create legal obligations for Libya and the United Kingdom which are determinative of any dispute over which the Court might have jurisdiction', and 'the relief which Libya seeks from the Court under the Montreal Convention is not open to it'.[84] This is essentially a merits language framed in terms of a conflict between the two treaties.

The impact of Article 103 on conflicting treaties is a matter of substantive law and, if it indeed had primacy over Libya's rights in the case at hand, at the merits stage the Court would have had to pronounce accordingly. Proceeding with the merits of this case would not have prejudiced the effect of Article 103, but precisely enabled its proper effect to be displayed and enforced. Requiring the Court to declare the case inadmissible or moot due to the effect of Article 103 is to put the cart before the horse.

The Preliminary Objections Judgment in *Lockerbie* holds that the date on which the application was filed determines the admissibility of the application. The Judgment thus might be seen as indicating that the case would have been inadmissible, had it been instituted after the adoption of Resolution 748, due to the impact of Articles 25 and 103 of the Charter. The Court's approach necessarily means that while, had Libya submitted its application at a later date, that Security Council resolution would have made its claims inadmissible, in the actual case the same resolutions could be dealt with at the merits stage with the possibility of being struck down. Under this approach, the Council's resolutions, and broader considerations of maintaining peace and security under Chapter VII, have no inherent impact on proceedings; all that matters is the timing of their adoption. It is unclear why the timing of the application should be crucial if a resolution could in principle displace treaty rights and make a claim based on those rights inadmissible. Even if the case were admissible initially, a post-seisin resolution produces a normative conflict and purports to displace treaty rights: if the Court ruled the case admissible it would risk adopting a decision that contradicted a resolution binding under the Charter.

The Court could be seen as offering a deal to the Council: the Court will not adjudicate on Chapter VII resolutions adopted before the case was brought before it, and thus will refrain from interfering in the Council's work; conversely, since the Council is not supposed to use Chapter VII to frustrate proceedings that had already started before the Court, if it does this the Court will adjudicate. The Court can thus be seen as asserting its constitutional significance, and an institutional role that is independent of the Council. But, in doing so, it seems to compromise its own judicial duty to apply law to facts. In other words, the Court here asserts that it is important but in some cases can be impotent. The policy behind this approach is

---

[83] *Lockerbie, ICJ Reports* 1998, 29.
[84] Ibid, 24.

to ensure, not the Council's compliance with the overarching legal framework, but that it does not encroach upon the Court's *institutional role*.

This approach could be seeing as admitting, in relation to cases brought after a Chapter VII resolution had been adopted, a broader criterion of admissibility (or of mootness) which could exempt from the Court's adjudication all Security Council decisions, whether or not they are in accordance with the Charter, and covered by Article 103. The impact of this would be, not to affirm the legal effects of a contested resolution, but merely to prevent adjudication on that resolution. Unless the Court were to decide merits at the jurisdiction stage, it would not result in establishing that the state in question should abide by a resolution, and thus legally protect the Council's Chapter VII action; it would only preclude judicial consideration of the issue whether it should be so protected.

This conclusion seems inferable from the Court's approach, but for the fact that the respondents did not argue the case that way, instead choosing a substantive 'mini-merit' approach: the Court cannot be deemed to have adopted a defence which the respondent did not propose.

The broader context also illustrates that the Court did not reject Libya's first two submissions (which were framed in constitutional terms) but rather acceded to its third submission as to the timing of the application;[85] it simply did not address them, not least because none of those submissions were preliminary in character, instead relating to merits (just like the UK/US admissibility submissions did). The timing argument was the only admissibility submission framed in terms suitable for preliminary proceedings. Thus, disposal of the case was possible only by answering the third submission, which was the only admissibility criterion proper raised by Libya, and because the time factor was the only point by reference to which the Court could avoid deciding, at the preliminary objections phase, the merits point of normative conflict between the Montreal Convention and Security Council resolutions. This is further reinforced by the Court's reference to Resolution 731(1992) having recommendatory, as opposed to binding, force, on which both parties actually agreed during the proceedings. There simply was no correlation between the Court's rejection of the UK/US submissions (which did not argue the timing point) and its acceptance of Libya's third submission (which did). Therefore in this particular respect the Court's approach has to be seen as closely tied to the context of the case and the peculiarity of the parties' submissions, which constrained the Court in developing options for its reasoning. Its conclusion on the timing point, therefore, does not lend itself to generalization.

(d) The Actual Implications of the Court's 1998 Judgment on Preliminary Objections

It is a separate question whether the 1998 Judgments on Preliminary Objections in *Lockerbie*, in that they did not pronounce on merits, constituted a judicial review, which

---

[85] Libya presented its argument regarding constitutionality and interpretation of the relevant resolutions as its principal argument: ibid, 130.

was thought to be the case, for instance, by Judge Schwebel. After the Judgment was handed down, Libya relied on it in the Security Council as evidence that the legal dispute between itself and states that had sponsored Resolutions 731 and 748—regarding the interpretation of the 1971 Montreal Convention—survived the adoption of those resolutions. The USA and the UK were thus bound by this position: the implication of the Judgment was that sanctions under Resolutions 748(1992) and 883(1993) became irrelevant, had to be rescinded, and the dispute had to be settled as a legal dispute which would allow for substantiation of all pertinent allegations should they be true.[86] The Arab League representative observed, in addition, that 'the Libyan Arab Jamahiriya has, from the very start, followed the correct path as it resorted to the International Court of Justice, in accordance with Articles 33 and 36 of the Charter of the United Nations'. Sanctions were no longer acceptable, and Resolutions 748 and 883 had to be suspended.[87] The OAU and the OIC representatives reiterated this view at some length.[88] On behalf of the African Group, Mali submitted that the Court's judgment rejected the claims that the Security Council action made the Montreal Convention inapplicable to the dispute; the dispute subsisted and 'the sanctions provided for in Resolutions 748 (1992) and 883(1993) no longer have any *raison d'être*'.[89]

The US position was that 'the rulings of the Court involved technical, procedural issues. Contrary to the assertions of the Libyan Government, the Court is not calling for the review or suspension of Security Council resolutions. The Court has made clear that it was not dealing with the substance or the merits of the case.'[90] Japan argued that the rulings 'cannot prejudice the power of the Security Council on an issue of which the Council has been legitimately seised'.[91]

The judgment certainly does not pronounce on substantive legal questions, and thus does not perform a substantive legal review of resolutions, which question could only be dealt with at the merits stage. But its implication is to confirm that the course of action chosen by the Security Council does not correspond to the constitutional allocation of competence under the Charter. The division of competence between the Council and the Court is governed by Articles 33 and 36 which recognize that legal disputes should be submitted to the Court. The Court's recognition that the legal dispute subsisted despite having been rebranded through Chapter VII Resolutions 731 and 748 constitutes a recognition that those resolutions were adopted in breach of structural limitations enshrined in Articles 33 and 36. The Court effectively reviewed the Council's handling of the issue (as opposed to the content of the resolutions at issue), namely its circumvention of Articles 33

---

[86] S/PV.3864, 20 March 1998, 9–11 (Libya); see also ibid, 21–2 (Bahrain).

[87] Ibid, 35 (LAS).

[88] Ibid, 36–9 (OAU and OIC).

[89] Ibid, 41 (Mali on behalf of the African Group).

[90] Ibid, 12 (US); 29 (France); 31 (UK); 40 (EU).

[91] Ibid, 23 (Japan); the UK also submitted that 'Libya's claims that the ruling relieves Libya of its obligations to hand over the two accused for trial in Scotland or the United States are simply false. Indeed, an application by Libya that it should no longer be called upon to surrender the two accused because of these proceedings has already been rejected by the International Court, in a previous decision of 1992': ibid, 32 (UK). However, the 1992 Order spoke only of a *prima facie* allocation of obligations and said nothing of a substantive decision as to a venue for the trial.

and 36, which was not in accordance with the Charter and hence not opposable to the Court. The dispositive effect of the Court's judgment is broader than a potential review of the substantive content and effect of resolutions, namely that Resolutions 731 and 748 should not have been adopted in the first place, and even after they were adopted, they lacked the intended effect. The affirmation that a dispute is suitable to be dealt with under Chapter VI provisions of dispute settlement such as Articles 33 and 36, more specifically under the Montreal Convention, inherently presupposes that circumstances justifying the use of Chapter VII (such as under Article 39) are also lacking.

This is confirmed by Ghana's submissions before the Security Council, that the Court's decision

appears to us to weaken the foundations of the Council's Resolutions 748(1992) and 883 (1993)....For if, as is evident from the decision of the Court, there is a dispute as to judicial competence to establish responsibility for the tragic incidents, then it was premature for this Council to impose sanctions on one of the parties to the dispute in support of the rival claims advanced by the other parties.

We therefore disagree with those who hold the view that the preliminary, or procedural, judgment of the ICJ does not affect the Security Council resolutions imposing sanctions on one of the parties. In the light of the foregoing, we propose that the Council should, as a matter of urgency, revisit Resolutions 731(1992), 748(1992) and 883(1993) with a view to suspending or lifting the sanctions imposed on one of the parties pending the determination of the substantive issues involved in the dispute between the parties, or pending the establishment of responsibility in accordance with the fair and just compromise proposal advanced by the Organization of African Unity, the League of Arab States, the Organization of the Islamic Conference and the Non-Aligned Movement.[92]

The majority of interventions during the debate, which also covered the greater part of the world, affirmed that the Security Council had bypassed the constitutional allocation of power between itself and the Court by rebranding the dispute, that the Court validly maintained both the proper characterization of the dispute and its own constitutional position, and that the implication of the judgment was that sanctions now had to be rescinded. The judgment effectively determined that the dispute under the Montreal Convention (as to where suspects should be tried) had subsisted and hence contradicted the US/UK position backed up by Chapter VII resolutions that purported to conclusively establish that the trials necessarily had to be in Scotland; instead, the suspects could be tried anywhere permitted by the Montreal Convention.

4. Collective Security Decisions and Responsibility of the Entities Involved

There is no principle in international law that a wrongful act committed by a state ceases to be its internationally wrongful act because it is committed in the context of

---

[92] Ibid, 56 (Ghana).

implementing a decision of an international organization. To allocate responsibility in the context of peace operations, it is necessary to identify where the effective command of troops and control of activities lies. There is an argument that the performance of particular conduct under an authorization by an international organization should play a role in determining responsibility. Sarooshi argues that

the question of who exercises *operational* command and control over the force is immaterial to the question of responsibility. The more important enquiry is who exercises *overall* authority and control over the forces. In the case of forces from Member States exercising delegated Chapter VII powers, it is the Security Council that exercises overall authority and control over the forces. Accordingly, it is the Council which must accept the primary responsibility for the acts of the force.

There is then secondary responsibility of states which have actually carried out the authorized tasks. The Council is placed at the centre of the operations and is obliged to ensure that delegated powers are exercised in a way that will achieve their objective.[93] But this position does not accord with the law of international responsibility, under which attribution requires demonstrating a causal connection between the conduct and a violation.

In a way that reflects these considerations, Zacklin suggests that when an operation is under UN command and has the status of a subsidiary organ of the Security Council, violations of humanitarian law are the responsibility of the UN. Where there is national command and control, responsibility lies with the states that have direct command and control. The UN, having authorized the operation, retains a residual responsibility for the conduct of an operation.[94] But still, being a subsidiary organ of the UN means only that this organ performs a mandate defined by the UN, not that its actual actions while performing that mandate are under UN control. Whether the action outside the scope of the Council's authorization has taken place is essentially a matter of substantive law. Responsibility is not affected by whether action in question properly falls within the scope of a Council-authorized mandate, but whether it is actually performed by the designated entity.

General Comment No 31 of the UN Human Rights Committee, which confirms that states party to the International Covenant on Civil and Political Rights (ICCPR) are obliged to ensure the rights laid down in the Covenant to anyone within their power or effective control, affirms that

---

[93] D Sarooshi, *The United Nations and Development of Collective Security* (New York: Oxford University Press, 1999), 163–5 (emphasis in original), 186; it should be noted that Sarooshi mentions overall control first and effective control later (at 164): these are essentially different. For the sake of clarity and accuracy it will further be assumed that the Council's control and command over authorized Chapter VII and VIII operations is 'overall' (possessing competence to change and terminate the mandate) and not 'effective' (having the ability to influence what is being done and how).

[94] R Zacklin, 'The Use of Force in Peace-keeping Operations', in N Blokker and N Schrijver (eds.), *The Security Council and the Use of Force* (Leiden: Martinus Nijhoff, 2005), 105–6; see also *Bici v MOD*, [2004] EWCH 786, 7 April 2004, para 2, noting that 'the defendant has conceded that it is vicariously liable for any wrongs committed by any of the soldiers. The Crown retained command of the British forces notwithstanding that they were acting under the auspices of the UN.'

[t]his principle also applies to those within the power or effective control of the forces of a State Party acting outside its territory, regardless of the circumstances in which such power or effective control was obtained, such as forces constituting a national contingent of a State Party assigned to an international peace-keeping or peace-enforcement operation.[95]

This supports the principle that the liability of member States participating in UN operations is primary. This also reinforces the idea of effective control in the sense that being a contingent of national forces inherently implies being under the effective control of the relevant state.

These considerations were not properly taken into account in the European Court's decision in *Behrami*, before which there had existed a relatively consolidated position that the acts of IFOR, SFOR, and KFOR outside their official duties were attributable to member States as opposed to the Alliance. This case related both to the US decision to make an *ex gratia* payment to China for the bombing of the Chinese embassy in Belgrade as part of the NATO operation, and to unlawful acts committed by IFOR and KFOR outside their duties.[96]

In the *Behrami* case, the European Court of Human Rights held that the acts committed by KFOR national contigents in Kosovo (FRY) were not attributable to the relevant State-parties to which the contingents belonged. This was explained by the fact that KFOR operated under the UN Security Council mandate.[97] The European Court asserted that 'that the key question is whether the UNSC retained ultimate authority and control so that operational command only was delegated'.[98] The Court further specified that

the UNSC was to retain ultimate authority and control over the security mission and it delegated to NATO (in consultation with non-NATO member states) the power to establish, as well as the operational command of, the international presence, KFOR. NATO fulfilled its command mission via a chain of command (from the NAC, to SHAPE, to SACEUR, to CIC South) to COMKFOR, the commander of KFOR. While the MNBs were commanded by an officer from a lead TCN, the latter was under the direct command of COMKFOR. MNB action was to be taken according to an operational plan devised by NATO and operated by COMKFOR in the name of KFOR.[99]

But this refers to mandate, delegation, and formal authority, not to the actual commission of the wrongful act and the actual effective control over it. In order to find that the UN and not individual states had been responsible for the relevant wrongful act, it had to be established that the UN had actually committed it. Otherwise, the responsibility would have rested with the individual states whose troops actually committed that act. No UN resolution authorized KFOR to

---

[95] General Comment No. 31, Nature of the General Legal Obligation on States Parties to the Covenant, UN Doc CCPR/C/21/Rev 1/Add.13 (2004), para 10.

[96] For an overview see T Gazzini, 'NATO's Role in the Collective Security System', 8 *Journal of Conflict and Security Law* (2003), 231 at 242.

[97] *Behrami & Saramati v France*, Nos 71412/01 and 78166/01, Admissibility Decision of 2 May 2007.

[98] Ibid, para 133.

[99] Ibid, paras 134–6.

perform conduct that violates the European Convention on Human Rights. The outcome of *Behrami* is that the states that actually violated the European Convention were effectively excused, with the possibility of speculation on whether the UN has to be held responsible even though it neither performed nor authorized the offending acts.

It seems plainly obvious that once the UN Security Council has delegated to someone else effective command over a peace operation, the United Nations can no longer be seen as performing any of the actions that are undertaken during that peace operation. The authorization and mandate by the United Nations means only that the UN has approved the existence and general powers of the relevant organs, not that the UN is itself responsible for whatever is done during the authorized peace operation. The delegation of powers to another organization or subsidiary organ over which Security Council maintains some authority in terms of accountability, reporting, or termination of mandate, is never tantamount to the assuming of actual and effective control over the activities of that organ or military contingent. The whole question of delegation is thus beside the point in determining who is responsible for any particular activity.

This explains why, in the commentary to its Articles on the Responsibility of International Organizations, the UN International Law Commission disapproved *Behrami* because the judgment did not focus on effective, that is operational, control over particular conduct.[100] The ILC's Articles 3 and 5 and commentary to these articles specify the basis by which wrongful acts should be attributed to international organizations based on the organization's effective control of the conduct in question. Most pertinently, Article 6 then provides that

[t]he conduct of an organ of a State or an organ or agent of an international organization that is placed at the disposal of another international organization shall be considered under international law an act of the latter organization if the organization exercises effective control over that conduct.

The Commission specifies in the commentary that in principle the UN has 'exclusive control of the *deployment* of national contingents in a peacekeeping force'. However, '[a]ttribution of conduct to the contributing State is clearly linked with the retention of some powers by that State over its national contingent and thus on the control that the State possesses in the relevant respect.' Thus, 'when an organ or agent is placed at the disposal of an international organization, the decisive question in relation to attribution of a given conduct appears to be who has effective control over the conduct in question.'[101] Such effective control over the conduct of troops is not the same as control over their deployment. In clarifying the parameters of that effective control *in casu*, the extent to which the contributing state 'ret[ains] some powers' can also matter.

---

[100] For a similar line of reasoning see A Orakhelashvili, review of the UK House of Lords judgment in *Al-Jedda*, 103 AJIL (2008).
[101] Commentary to Article 6, paras 5 to 7, *ILC Report* 2009, 63–4 (emphasis added).

The Commission went on to specify that the UN cannot be held responsible for any conduct of some of its authorized operations, such as UNOSOM II, because the commander was not in effective control of some of its contingents, and observes, most importantly, that

[w]hat has been held with regard to joint operations, such as those involving UNOSOM II and the Quick Reaction Force in Somalia, should also apply to peacekeeping operations, insofar as it is possible to distinguish in their regard areas of effective control respectively pertaining to the United Nations and the contributing State. While it is understandable that, for the sake of efficiency of military operations, the United Nations insists on claiming exclusive command and control over peacekeeping forces, attribution of conduct should also in this regard be based on a factual criterion.[102]

This factual matter can be evidenced by reference to factors such as jurisdiction, actual control, disciplinary, and other control. Most importantly, 'when applying the criterion of effective control, "operational" control would seem more significant than "ultimate" control, since the latter hardly implies a role in the act in question.'[103] The ILC Commentary treats this as a question of fact and evidence, not of status and formal affiliation.

ILC Article 7 specifies that an international organization is responsible for its acts even if these exceed its competence. As the commentary specifies, '[e]ven if the act was considered to be invalid, it may entail the responsibility of the organization', so third parties are duly protected.[104] Article 16 is about responsibility for decisions and thus proposes certain rules that supplement, but in no way replace, the ordinary rules of attribution. Article 16 specifies that an international organization incurs international responsibility if it adopts a decision binding a member State to commit an act that would be internationally wrongful if committed by the organization and would circumvent its international obligations (paragraph 1). The same applies if an organization authorizes, or recommends, a member State to commit a wrongful act and that state commits that act because of that authorization or recommendation (paragraph 2).[105] Thus, an organization incurs responsibility for any decision that authorizes, obliges, or recommends conduct that is contrary to that organization's constituent instrument. This essentially includes all ultra vires decisions and recommendations (which decisions covered by Article 16 would necessarily be), which leads to the conclusion that states remain responsible for their nationals' conduct carried out pursuant to such acts. Responsibility of an organization under paragraph 1 is straightforward, while under paragraph 2 it is conditional on the requisite conduct of states. Still, in both cases the states performing the conduct at issue remain responsible.

---

[102] Ibid, para 8.
[103] Ibid, para 9.
[104] Commentary to Article 7, para 5, *ILC Report* 2009, 71.
[105] As paragraph 10 of the Commentary to Article 16 specifies in relation to the rule under paragraph 2, 'this condition requires a contextual analysis of the role that the authorization or recommendation actually plays in determining the conduct of the member State or international organization': ibid, 91.

In general, acts unlawful for an organization can include any that go beyond their delegated powers (acts ultra vires) and any that are lawful as such but involve, as a matter of fact, violations of international law in the course of their performance. Acts under Article 16 that would be unlawful if committed by an organization are acts exceeding substantive legal limits on the delegated powers of organizations, such as provisions in constituent instruments, functional limitations, or *jus cogens*. This would be the position, for instance, if the UN Security Council were to decide to impose sanctions or authorize a use of force under Chapter VII that would go beyond what was necessary and proportionate to deal with a validly identified threat under Article 39; or if a regional organization were to authorize a military enforcement operation against a state which would be clearly beyond the competence of such organization due to the restriction contained in Article 53 of the UN Charter.

Not all decisions are structurally identical, however. For instance, disproportionate civilian damage caused by a national contingent in a Chapter VII armed operation is essentially an action that can be committed by contingents controlled by states as well as those controlled by mandating organization. In order to attribute such conduct to the UN, it would need to be demonstrated that the UN decision as such had mandated the disproportionate action, which is hardly possible given that pertinent Chapter VII resolutions normally incorporate references to proportionality by requiring the action to be commensurate to a threat; even if they were not to incorporate such a limit, the latter would still apply given that it constitutes a structural and systemic requirement under the Charter for any Chapter VII operation.[106]

By contrast, human rights violations in Iraq caused by the UN sanctions regime were not acts that can be committed by a single state. Child mortality in Iraq might not rise if, for instance, Denmark or Portugal decided, on its own, not to deliver any medical equipment to Iraq. Child mortality has risen, however, because the arrangement of the sanctions regime by the Security Council (including the operation of humanitarian exceptions) effectively prevented *all states* from supplying Iraq with the necessary material. These were thus truly collective violations of international law covered, in their essence, by the Security Council's decisions, repeatedly confirmed and ratified by this organ through its refusal, directly or via the sanctions committee, to ease the delivery of humanitarian and related supplies. Collective sanctions bring about such an outcome because they are coordinated through a binding decision of the Security Council, and thus the breach can be attributed to the UN.

Along similar lines, if (for instance) Serbia were to claim reparations from NATO and its member States for the 1999 bombing campaign, then under Article 16(2) NATO would be responsible for the decision authorizing the attack as a breach of *jus ad bellum*, since member States would not have performed it without that decision. Its member States who participated in the campaign would then be responsible both for the breach of *jus ad bellum* (given that states have autonomous capacity to judge whether Article 53 of the UN Charter had proscribed NATO

---

[106] See Chapter 5 above.

from launching this war),[107] and for the actual bombing campaign and disproportionate civilian damage it caused (in accordance with the rules on state responsibility, now as a matter of *jus in bello*). This would then raise a question of division of
reparations between the responsible entities.[108]

Article 16 is thus concerned only with the acts that directly follow from an
authorization or mandate granted by an organization to a state. It is not concerned
with acts committed while that authorization or mandate is being discharged.
Article 16 is not a clause immunizing states for their conduct if it takes place in
the context of operations authorized by the UN. If a peace-keeping unit (controlled
by an organization) commits a violation of international law going beyond what has
been authorized, for instance exceeding the necessity and proportionality prescribed under its mandate or in terms of its right to self-defence (or by specifically
violating human rights such as the right to life), such violation would not fall within
any principle enunciated under Article 16(2), because it would simply not be an act
authorized by an organization nor, consequently, would have been committed
because authorized or recommended by an organization. To illustrate, MINUS-
TAH in Haiti had a mandate under Security Council Resolutions 1529(2004) and
1542(2004) to ensure a secure and stable environment in the country. The two
resolutions provide no obvious basis for MINUSTAH to use force to such ends. In
practice, as illustrated above,[109] MINUSTAH engaged in large-scale combat
operations which caused heavy and disproportionate damage including the loss of
lives. It cannot be plausibly argued that the ILC's Article 16 means that the Security
Council's decision to authorize the deployment of MINUSTAH engaged its
responsibility for the acts of this force, for there is nothing in the Council's decision
to authorize the disproportionate use of force; had it been otherwise, the Council's
decision would in that respect have been ultra vires and thus failed anyway to
provide a legal basis for those actions. In any case, the attribution of, and responsibility for, such disproportionate acts should be conducted on the basis of the ILC's
Articles 3 and 5 and their effective control test; if these provisions do not cover the
act in question, this should be attributed to the relevant state(s).

As pointed out, the various options for assigning responsibility in this case are
not mutually exclusive. One option is to sue Brazil as the largest troop-contributing
nation and the top operation commanders. Alternatively, the responsibility of
Brazil with the UN can be concurrent. MINUSTAH is 'a military contingent of

---

[107] See further Gazzini, n 96 above, 244, 246, stating that 'following the NAC decision, member
states remain free to participate in and eventually to withdraw at any time from these operations. In
order to have the decision implemented, therefore, a further expression of will must be manifested at
least by some of the member states. The forces voluntarily provided for by member states are put under
the command of the civilian and military authorities of the Alliance, acting as common organs of these
states.'

[108] On which see A Orakhelashvili, 'Division of Reparation between Responsible Entities', in
J Crawford, A Pellet, and S Olleson (eds.), *The Law of International Responsibility* (Oxford: Oxford
University Press, 2010), 647, also dealing with questions of primary and secondary responsibility of the
relevant entity.

[109] See Chapter 5 above.

member states acting within an international organization where each member state is mandated to be individually responsible for the actions of its troops.'[110]

The International Law Commission specified in its Articles 40 and 41 that a 'serious breach by an international organization of an obligation arising under a peremptory norm of general international law' can produce no valid consequences. States and other organizations shall not recognize as lawful a situation created by such a serious breach, nor render aid or assistance in maintaining that situation.[111] The rationale of Articles 40 and 41 is to prevent decisions from producing a legal effect and consolidating a legal position that attempts to derogate from *jus cogens*; they actually affirm that *jus cogens* produces absolute invalidity of acts by international organizations that offend against *jus cogens*; this is implied in the duty not to recognize such acts. Articles 40 and 41 perfectly suit the allocation of responsibility to international organizations for their decisions, as opposed to a specific action, as provided for in Article 16. If an Article 16 decision meets the requirements under Article 40 defining violations of *jus cogens*, the consequences under Article 41 apply, with the effect that the impugned decision does not serve as a valid authorization of a conduct that violates *jus cogens*, and makes no difference, so does not shift the responsibility from states performing that conduct to organizations that authorize it. The organization, however, would remain responsible for the decision as such, as part of Article 16. This entire regime is little more than a reaffirmation of generally accepted principles that international organizations are bound by *jus cogens* and their acts conflicting with *jus cogens* are void.

---

[110] M Halling and B Bookey, 'Peacekeeping in Name Alone: Accountability for the United Nations in Haiti', 31 *Hastings International and Comparative Law Review* (2008), 461 at 472–3, 475–6.
[111] *ILC Report* 2009, 125–8 (text and commentary).

Conclusion

This study has demonstrated that the multilevel and multidimensional process of collective security is as much about conflict and competition between institutions as it is about the sustainable division of labour. Given that the mandate of all collective security institutions is subject to contractually specified limits, the possibility of their action exceeding that mandate, and encroaching on that of another institution, is inherent.

The experience of past decades has shown that collective security institutions can either be established as such, or evolve into such having originated as self-defence pacts or economic unions. The constituent instruments of some organizations expressly confer on them powers which are exercised by other institutions on the basis of the implied powers doctrine. The mandate and efforts of institutions can be complemented by the efforts of states acting on an 'able and willing' basis. All these developments fall within the parameters dictated by the consensual imperative underlying the international legal system. Constituent instruments have to be interpreted in accordance with the principle of effectiveness to allow certain types of action when the possibility of other types of action is stalled; or action by one organ when another organ is paralysed. Contempt for this approach, especially in the area of peace-keeping operations, has led to grave humanitarian consequences.

But the same consensual imperative produces an insurmountable limit on this process expressed, above all, by the duty of collective security organs to abide by the letter and spirit of their constituent instruments; they have to observe specific restrictions stated in the text, as well as act in good faith when they use their discretion. To illustrate this problem, the UN Secretary-General's High-level Panel has emphasized that 'the [Security] Council's decisions have often been less than consistent, less than persuasive and less than fully responsive to very real State and human security needs'.[1] A related problem arises with sanctions programmes that at times inflict greater harm than the benefit they produce in achieving their objectives. This process has prompted increased acceptance of the principle that decisions taken by principal organs of the UN, if they involve an exceeding of delegated powers, can be disregarded by states and regional organizations, and reviewed by national and international courts with a view to establishing their lawfulness and effects.

---

[1] Report of the Secretary-General's High-level Panel on Threats, Challenges and Change, 2 December 2004, A/59/565, 56.

The process by which collective security institutions multiply has indicated several ways of arranging the allocation of labour and consequences between them. Regional security institutions and capabilities have developed in response to problems specific to a particular region or, as is the case with the European Union, to contribute to peace and security out-of-area. The conclusion that follows from the analysis in this study is that, subject to the exclusive competence of the UN Security Council over enforcement actions against a state, the relationship between the UN and regional organizations (both under the UN Charter and general international law) permits every kind of collective security decision to be taken at every pertinent level, whether universal or regional. The implication is that, if one level fails to take an action needed in the interest of peace and security, other levels may step in. At the same time, regional organizations increasingly emphasize limits on the powers of the United Nations, especially of the Security Council, with implications for the general acceptability of UN decisions and their impact on the ground.

Bibliography

Abass, A, 'The New Collective Security Mechanism of ECOWAS: Innovations and Problems', 5 *Journal of Conflict and Security Law* (2000), 211.

——*Regional Organisations and the Development of Collective Security: Beyond Chapter VIII of the UN Charter* (Oxford: Hart, 2004).

——'The United Nations, the African Union and the Darfur Crisis: Of Apology and Utopia', 54 *Netherlands International Law Review* (2007), 415.

Adler, E and Barnett, M (eds.), *Security Communities* (Cambridge: Cambridge University Press, 1998).

Akehurst, M, 'Enforcement Action by Regional Agencies, With Special Reference to the Organization of American States', 42 *British Yearbook of International Law* (1967) 175.

Almqvist, J, 'A Human Rights Critique of European Judicial Review: Counter-Terrorism Sanctions', 57 ICLQ (2008), 303.

Anthony, I, 'Sanctions Applied by the European Union and the United Nations', *Stockholm International Peace Research Institute Yearbook* (2002), 203.

Arend, AC, 'The United Nations, Regional Organizations, and Military Operations: The Past and the Present', 7 *Duke Journal of Comparative and International Law* (1996–7), 3.

Aust, A, '*Lockerbie*: The Other Case', 49 ICLQ (2000), 283.

Aznar-Gomez, MJ, 'A Decade of Human Rights Protection by the UN Security Council: A Sketch of Deregulation?', 13 *European Journal of International Law* (2002), 223.

Bailey, SD and Daws, S, *The Procedure of the UN Security Council* (New York: Oxford University Press, 1998).

Barliant, R, 'The OAS Peace and Security System', 21 *Stanford Law Review* (1969), 1156.

Bebr, G, 'Regional Organizations: A United Nations Problem', 49 AJIL (1955), 166.

Bennouna, M, 'Les sanctions économiques des Nations Unies', 300 *Recueil des Cours de l'Académie de Droit International de la Haye* (2002).

Berdal, M, 'The Security Council, Peacekeeping and Internal Conflict after the Cold War', 7 *Duke Journal of Comparative and International Law* (1996–7), 71.

Berg, A, 'The 1991 Declaration on Fact-Finding by the United Nations', 4 *European Journal of International Law* (1993), 107.

Beveridge, F, 'The Lockerbie Affair', 41 ICLQ (1992), 907.

Blockmans, S and Wessel, R, 'The European Union and Crisis Management: Will the Lisbon Treaty Make the EU More Effective?', 14 *Journal of Conflict and Security Law* (2009), 265.

Blokker, N, 'Is the Authorisation Authorised? Powers and Practice of the UN Security Council to Authorise the Use of Force', 11 *European Journal of International Law* (2000), 541.

——and Schrijver, N, (eds.), *The Security Council and the Use of Force* (Leiden: Martinus Nijhoff, 2005).

Boon, KE, 'Coining a New Jurisdiction: The Security Council as Economic Peacekeeper', 41 *Vanderbilt Journal of Transnational Law* (2008), 991.

Borchard, E, 'The Impracticability of "Enforcing" Peace', 55 *Yale Law Journal* (1945–6), 966.

Borquin, M (ed.), *Collective Security, A Record of the Seventh and Eighth International Studies Conferences*, Paris 1934–London 1935 (Paris: International Institute of Intellectual Cooperation, 1936), 3.

Bothe, M, O'Connell, ME, and Ronzitti, N (eds.), *Redefining Sovereignty: the Use of Force after the End of Cold War* (Leiden: Brill, 2005).

Bowett, D, *United Nations Forces* (London: Stevens & Sons, 1964).

Brierly, JL, 'The Covenant and The Charter', 23 *British Yearbook of International Law* (1946), 83.

Butterworth, RL, 'Organizing Collective Security: The UN Charter's Chapter VIII in Practice', 28 *World Politics* (1976), 197.

Campbell, AIL, 'The Limits on the Powers of International Organisations', 32 ICLQ (1983), 523.

Cardwell, PJ, French, D, and White, N, 'Case-note on *Kadi* (ECJ)', 58 ICLQ (2009), 229.

Caron, D, 'The Legitimacy of the Collective Authority of the Security Council', 87 AJIL (1993), 552.

Carr, EH, 'The League of Peace and Freedom—An Episode in the Quest for Collective Security', *International Affairs* (1935), 836.

Cassese, A (ed.), *The Current Legal Regulation of the Use of Force* (Leiden: Nijhoff, 1986).

Chatham House, *International Sanctions*, A Report by a Group of Members of the Royal Institute of International Affairs (Oxford: Oxford University Press, 1938).

Churchill, R, 'Conflicts between United Nations Security Council Resolutions and the 1982 United Nations Convention on the Law of the Sea, and Their Possible Resolution', 85 *US Naval War College International Law Studies Series* (2009), 143.

Cilliers, J, 'Towards a Continental Early Warning System for Africa', ISS Paper 102 (Pretoria: Institute for Security Studies, April 2005).

Ciobanu, D, *Preliminary Objections Related to the Jurisdiction of the United Nations Principal Organs* (Leiden: Nijhoff, 1975).

Claude, I, *Swords Into Plowshares*, 3rd edn. (New York: Random House, 1964).

——'The OAS, the UN and the United States', 35 *International Conciliation* (No 547, March 1964), 1.

Coleman, K, *International Organisations and Peace Enforcement* (Cambridge: Cambridge University Press, 2007).

Collins, A (ed.), *Contemporary Security Studies* (New York: Oxford University Press, 2007).

Conforti, B, *The Law and Practice of the United Nations* (The Hague: Kluwer, 2005).

Craig, P, *EU Administrative Law* (Oxford: Oxford University Press, 2006).

——*Administrative Law* (London: Sweet & Maxwell, 2008).

Craven, M, 'Humanitarianism and the Quest for Smarter Sanctions', 13 *European Journal of International Law* (2002), 43.

Cryer, R, 'Sudan, Resolution 1593, and International Criminal Justice', 19 *Leiden Journal of International Law* (2006), 195.

Daillier, P, 'Les opérations multinationales consécutives à des conflits armés en vue du rétablissement de la paix', 314 *Recueil des cours* (2005), 233.

Deen-Racsmany, S, 'A Redistribution of Authority between the UN and Regional Organisations in the Field of the Maintenance of Peace and Security?', 13 *Leiden Journal of International Law* (2000), 297.

van Dijk (ed.), *Supervisory Mechanisms in International Economic Organisations* (The Hague: TMC Asser Press, 1984).

Dinstein, Y, *War, Aggression and Self-Defence*, 4th ed. (Cambridge: Cambridge University Press, 2005).

Draper, GIAD, 'The Legal Limitations upon the Employment of Weapons by the United Nations in the Congo', 12 ICLQ (1963), 401.

Dreier, J, 'The Council of the OAS: Performance and Potential', 5 *Journal of Inter-American Studies* (1963), 297.

Durward, R, 'Security Council Authorisation for Regional Peace Operations: A Critical Analysis', 13 *International Peacekeeping* (2006), 350.

Eagleton, C, 'The Jurisdiction of the Security Council over Disputes', 40 AJIL (1946), 513.

——'The Pacific Settlement of Disputes under the Charter', 246 *Annals of the American Academy of Political and Social Science* (1946), 24.

Eide, A, 'Peace-Keeping and Enforcement by Regional Organizations: Its place in the United Nations System', 3 *Journal of Peace Research* (1966), 125.

Farrall, JM, *UN Sanctions and the Rule of Law* (Cambridge: Cambridge University Press, 2007).

Fenwick, CG, 'Application of the Treaty of Rio de Janeiro to the Controversy between Costa Rica and Nicaragua', 43 AJIL (1949), 329.

——'The Competence of the Council of the Organization of American States', 43 AJIL (1949), 772.

——'Jurisdictional Questions Involved in the Guatemalan Revolution', 48 AJIL (1954), 597.

——'Inter-American Regional Procedures for the Settlement of Disputes', 10 *International Organization* (1956), 12.

——'The Issues at Punta Del Este: Non-Intervention v Collective Security', 56 AJIL (1962), 469.

——'The Organization of American States: The Transition from an Unwritten to a Written Constitution', 59 AJIL (1965), 315.

——'When is There a Threat to the Peace?—Rhodesia', 61 AJIL (1967), 753.

Figa-Talamanca, N, 'The Role of NATO in the Peace Agreement for Bosnia and Herzegovina', 7 *European Journal of International Law* (1996), 164.

Findlay, T, *The Use of Force in UN Peace Operations* (New York: Oxford University Press, 2002).

Fox, H and Wickremasinghe, C, 'UN Implementation of UN Economic Sanctions', 42 ICLQ (1993), 945.

Franck, T, *Recourse to Force* (Cambridge: Cambridge University Press, 2002).

Freudenschuß, H, 'Article 39 of the UN Charter Revisited: Threat to Peace and the Recent Practice of the UN Security Council', 46 *Austrian Journal of Public and International Law* (1993), 492.

Gardam, J, 'Legal Restraints on Security Council Military Enforcement Action', 17 *Michigan Journal of International Law* (1996), 285.

Gazzini, T, 'NATO's Role in the Collective Security System', 8 *Journal of Conflict and Security Law* (2003), 231.

Goldmann, M, 'Sierra Leone: African Solutions to African Problems?', 9 *Max-Planck Yearbook of UN Law* (2005), 457.

Goodhart, A, 'North Atlantic Treaty Organisation', 79 *Recueil des Cours de l'Académie de Droit International de la Haye* (II–1951), 183.

Goodrich, LM, 'From League of Nations to United Nations', 1 *International Organization* (1947), 3.

—— 'Regionalism and the United Nations', 23 *Proceedings of the Academy of Political Science* (1949), 47.

—— 'The UN Security Council', 12 *International Organization* (1958), 273.

Gourlay, C, 'European Union Procedures and Resources for Crisis Management', 11 *International Peacekeeping* (2004), 404.

Gowlland-Debbas, V (ed.), *UN Sanctions and International Law* (The Hague: Kluwer, 2001).

Greenwood, C, 'New World Order or Old? The Invasion of Kuwait and the Rule of Law', 55 MLR (1990), 153.

—— 'Scope of Application of Humanitarian Law', in Fleck, D (ed.), *The Handbook of International Humanitarian Law* (New York: Oxford University Press, 2008).

Greig, D, 'Self-Defence and the Security Council: What Does Article 51 Require?', 40 ICLQ (1991), 366.

Haas, EB, 'Types of Collective Security: An Examination of Operational Concepts', 49 *American Political Science Review* (1955), 40.

Hakimi, M, 'To Condone or Condemn? Regional Enforcement Actions in the Absence of Security Council Authorization', 40 *Vanderbilt Journal of Transnational Law* (2007), 643.

Halberstam, M, 'The Right to Self-defence Once the Security Council Takes Action', 17 *Michigan Journal of International Law* (1995–6), 229.

Halderman, JW, 'Regional Enforcement Measures and the United Nations', 52 *Georgetown Law Journal* (1963), 89.

—— 'Some Legal Aspects of Sanctions in the Rhodesian Case', 17 ICLQ (1968), 672.

Halliday, DJ, 'The Impact of the UN Sanctions on the People of Iraq', 28 *Journal of Palestine Studies* (1999), 29.

Halling, M and Bookey, B, 'Peacekeeping in Name Alone: Accountability for the United Nations in Haiti', 31 *Hastings International and Comparative Law Review* (2008), 461.

Henrikson, A, 'United Nations and Regional Organizations: "King-Links" of a "Global Chain"', 7 *Duke Journal of Comparative and International Law* (1996), 35.

Higgins, R, *United Nations Peacekeeping*, vol. 2 (Oxford: Oxford University Press, 1970).

—— 'The Place of International Law in the Settlement of Disputes by the Security Council', 64 AJIL (1970), 1.

—— 'The Advisory Opinion on Namibia: Which UN Resolutions Are Binding under Article 25 of the Charter?', 21 ICLQ (1972), 270.

van Hoof, GJH and de Vey Metsdagh, K, 'Mechanisms of International Supervision', in P van Dijk (ed.), *Supervisory Mechanisms in International Economic Organisations* (The Hague: TMC Asser Press, 1984).

Houck, JW, 'The Command and Control of United Nations Forces in the Era of "Peace Enforcement"', 4 *Duke Journal of Comparative and International Law* (1993–4), 1.

Howard, HN, 'Middle Eastern Regional Organization: Problems and Prospects', 24(4) *Proceedings of the Academy of Political Science* (1952), 101.

Hutchinson, MR, 'Restoring Hope: UN Security Council Resolutions for Somalia and an Expanded Doctrine of Humanitarian Intervention', 34 *Harvard International Law Journal* (1994), 624.

James, A, 'Painful Peacekeeping: The United Nations in Lebanon 1978–1982', 38 *International Journal* (1982–3), 613.

Jenks, W, 'The Conflict of Law-Making Treaties', 30 *British Yearbook of International Law* (1951), 401.

Jimenez de Arechaga, E, 'International Law in the Past Third of a Century', 159 *Recueil des Cours de l'Académie de Droit International de la Haye* (1978), 13.

Johnson, HC and Niemeyer, G, 'Collective Security: The Validity of an Ideal', 8 *International Organization* (1954), 19.

Joyner, D, *International Law and the Proliferation of Weapons of Mass Destruction* (New York: Oxford University Press, 2009).

Juncos, AE and Reynolds, C, 'The Political and Security Committee: Governing in the Shadow', 12 *European Foreign Affairs Review* (2007), 127.

Kaikobad, K, 'Self-Defence, Enforcement Action and the Gulf Wars, 1980–88 and 1990–91', 63 *British Yearbook of International Law* (1992), 299.

Kelsen, H, 'Limitations on the Functions of the United Nations', 55 *Yale Law Journal* (1946), 997.

—— 'The Preamble of the Charter—A Critical Analysis', 2 *Journal of Politics* (1946) 134.

—— 'Sanctions under the Charter of the United Nations', 12 *Canadian Journal of Economics and Political Science* (1946), 429.

—— 'Collective Security and Collective Self-Defence under the Charter of the United Nations', 41 AJIL (1948), 783.

—— 'The Settlement of Disputes by the Security Council', 2 *International Law Quarterly* (1948), 173.

—— *The Law of the United Nations* (London: Stevens & Sons, 1950).

—— 'Is the North Atlantic Treaty a Regional Arrangement?', 45 AJIL (1951), 162.

Kerley, EL, 'The Powers of Investigation of the United Nations Security Council', 55 AJIL (1961), 892.

Khadduri, M, 'The Arab League as a Regional Arrangement', 40 AJIL (1946), 756.

Kielmansegg, S Graf von, 'The Meaning of Petersberg: Some Considerations on the Legal Scope of ESDP Operations', 44 *European Foreign Affairs Review* (2007), 629.

Kirgis, F, 'NATO Consultations as a Component of National Decision-making', 73 AJIL (1979), 372.

Knight, WA, 'Towards A Subsidiarity Model for Peacemaking and Preventive Diplomacy: Making Chapter VIII of the UN Charter Operational', 17 *Third World Quarterly* (1996), 31.

Kolb, R, *Ius contra bellum, Le droit international relatif au maintien de la paix* (Basle/Louvain: Helbing Lichtenhahn/Bruylant, 2003).

—— *Droit humanitaire et operations de paix internationales* (Louvain: Bruylant 2006).

—— 'The Eternal Problem of Collective Security: From the League of Nations to the United Nations', 26 *Refugee Studies Quarterly* (2007), 221.

Kondoch, B, 'The Limits of Economic Sanctions under International Law: The Case of Iraq', 6 *International Peacekeeping—Yearbook of Peace Operations* (2001), 267.

Kooijmans, P, 'The Enlargement of the Concept "Threat to the Peace"', in Dupuy, P-M (ed.), *The Development of the Role of the Security Council* (Leiden: Martinus Nijhoff, 1993), 111.

—— 'The ICJ: Where Does It Stand'? in Muller, S, Raic, D, and Thuranzsky, H (eds.), *The International Court of Justice. Its Future Role after Fifty Years* (Leiden: Martinus Nijhoff, 1997), 407.

Koskenniemi, M, 'The Place of Law in Collective Security', 17 *Michigan Journal of International Law* (1995–6), 455.

Kratochwil, F, *Rules, Norms and Decisions* (Cambridge: Cambridge University Press, 1989).

Kronenberger, V and Wouters, J (eds.), *The European Union and Conflict Prevention Policy and Legal Aspects* (The Hague: TMC Asser Press, 2004).

Kunz, J, 'The Inter-American System and the United Nations Organization', 39 AJIL (1945), 758.

——'Individual and Collective Self-Defense in Article 51 of the Charter of the United Nations', 41 AJIL (1947), 872.

——'The Bogota Charter of the OAS', 42 AJIL (1948), 568.

——'The Idea of "Collective Security" in Pan-American Developments', 6 *Western Political Quarterly* (1953), 658.

LTG, 'A Microcosmic View of the OAS: The Honduras–El Salvador Conflict', 57 *Virginia Law Review* (1971), 291.

Lapidoth, R, 'Some Reflections on the Law and Practice Concerning the Imposition of Sanctions by the Security Council', 30 *Archiv des Völkerrechts* (1992), 114.

Lauterpacht, H (ed.), *Oppenheim's International Law*, 7th ed. (London: Stevens & Sons, 1952), vol II.

Leurdijk, D, 'Before and after Dayton: The UN and NATO in the Former Yugoslavia', 18 *Third World Quarterly* (1997), 457.

Levitt, J, 'Humanitarian Intervention by Regional Actors in Internal Conflicts: the Cases of ECOWAS in Liberia and Sierra Leone', 12 *Temple International and Comparative Law Journal* (1998), 333.

——'The Peace and Security Council of the African Union: The Known Unknowns', 13 *Transnational Law and Contemporary Problems* (2003), 109.

Liang, Y, 'Regional Arrangements and International Security', 31 *Transactions of the Grotius Society* (1945), 216.

Lloyd Mecham, J, 'The Integration of the Inter-American Security System Into the United Nations', 9(2) *The Journal of Politics* (1947), 178.

Lobel, J and Ratner, M, 'Bypassing the Security Council: Ambiguous Authorizations to Use Force, Cease-fires and the Iraqi Inspection Regime', 93 AJIL (1999) 124.

Lowenfeld, A, *International Economic Law* (New York: Oxford University Press, 2008).

Mackay, RG, 'NATO and UN', 288 *Annals of the American Academy of Political and Social Science* (1953), 119.

Malone, D (ed.), *The UN Security Council—From the Cold War to the 21st Century* (Boulder/London: Lynne Rienner Inc, 2004).

Matheson, M, 'United Nations Governance of Postconflict Societies', 95 AJIL (2001), 76.

——*Council Unbound—The Growth of UN Decision Making in Conflict and Post-conflict Issues after the Cold War* (Washington, DC: USIP Press, 2006).

May, R and Cleaver, G, 'African Peacekeeping: Still Dependent?', 4 *International Peacekeeping* (1997), 1.

McCoubrey, H and Morris, J, *Regional Peacekeeping in the Post-Cold War Era* (The Hague: Kluwer, 2000).

McDougal, M and Gardner, R, 'The Veto and the Charter: An Interpretation for Survival', 60 *Yale Law Journal* (1951), 258.

Meeker, L, 'Defensive Quarantine and the Law', 57 AJIL (1963), 515.

Morgenstern, F, 'Legality in International Organisations', 48 *British Yearbook of International Law* (1975–6), 241.

Morgenthau, H, 'Diplomacy', 55 *Yale Law Journal* (1945–6), 1067.

Moore, JN, 'Grenada and the International Double Standard', 78 AJIL (1984), 145.

Morris, J and McCoubrey, H, 'Regional Peacekeeping in the Post-Cold War Era', 6 *International Peacekeeping* (1999), 129.

Mowat *et al*, *Problems of Peace*, 10th Series (London: George Allen & Unwin Ltd, 1936), 178.

Murphy, R, *UN Peacekeeping in Lebanon, Somalia and Kosovo: Operational and Legal Issues in Practice* (Cambridge: Cambridge University Press, 2007).

Nasu, H, 'Investigation *Proprio Motu* for the Maintenance of International Peace and Security', 23 *Australian Yearbook of International Law* (2004), 105.

Nincic, D, *The Problem of Sovereignty in the Charter and in the Practice of the United Nations* (Leiden: Nijhoff, 1970).

Nivet, B, *Security by Proxy? The EU and (sub-)regional organisations: the case of ECOWAS*, ISS Occasional Paper No 63, March 2006.

Nolte, G, 'Restoring Peace by Regional Action: International Legal Aspects of the Liberian Conflict', 53(3) *Zeitschrift für Ausländisches öffentliches Recht und Völkerrecht* (1993), 603.

O'Brien, D, 'The Search for Subsidiarity: The UN, African Regional Organizations and Humanitarian Action', 7 *International Peacekeeping* (2000), 57.

Orakhelashvili, A, 'The Legal Basis of the United Nations Peace-Keeping Operations', 43 *Virginia Journal of International Law* (2003), 484.

——'Legal Stability and Claims of Change: The International Court's Treatment of *Jus ad Bellum* and *Jus in Bello*', 75 *Nordic Journal of International Law* (2006), 371.

——'The Legal Framework of Peace Operations by Regional Organisations', 11 *International Peacekeeping: Yearbook of International Peace Operations* (2006), 111.

——*Peremptory Norms in International Law* (New York: Oxford University Press, 2006, paperback 2008).

——'The Power of the UN Security Council to Determine the Existence of a "Threat to the Peace"', 1 *Irish Yearbook of International Law* (2006), 61.

——'The Acts of the Security Council: Meaning and Standards of Review', 11 *Max-Planck Yearbook of United Nations Law* (2007), 143.

——'The *Al-Jedda* case (House of Lords, UK)', 103 AJIL (2008).

——*Interpretation of Acts and Rules in Public International Law* (New York: Oxford University Press, 2008).

——'Statehood, Recognition and the United Nations System: A Unilateral Declaration of Independence in Kosovo', 12 *Max-Planck Yearbook of United Nations Law* (2008), 1.

——'Threat, Emergency, and Survival: The Legality of Emergency Action in International Law', 9 *Chinese Journal of International Law* (2010), 345.

——'Division of Reparation between Responsible Entities', in J Crawford, A Pellet, and S Olleson (eds.), *The Law of International Responsibility* (Oxford: Oxford University Press, 2010), 647.

Osterdahl, I, 'Preach What You Practice: The Security Council and the Legalisation *ex post facto* of the Unilateral Use of Force', 74 *Nordic Journal of International Law* (2005), 231.

Oswald, B, 'The Creation and Control of Places of Protection during United Nations Peace Operations', 83 *International Review of the Red Cross* (2001), 1013.

Packer, CAA and Rukare, D, 'The New African Union and Its Constitutive Act', 96 AJIL (2002), 365.

Peck, J, 'The UN and the Laws of War: How Can the World's Peacekeepers be Held Accountable?', 21 *Syracuse Journal of International Law and Commerce* (1995), 283.

Pelcovits, N, 'Peacekeeping: The African Experience', in Wiseman, H (ed.), *Peacekeeping: Appraisals and Proposals* (New York: Pergamon Press 1983), 256.

Philipp, C, 'Somalia—A Very Special Case', 9 *Max-Planck Yearbook of UN Law* (2005), 517.

Plachta, M, 'The *Lockerbie* Case: The Role of the Security Council in Enforcing the Principle *Aut Dedere Aut Judicare*', 12 *European Journal of International Law* (2001), 125.

Pogany, I, 'The League of Arab States: An Overview', 21 *Bihar Law Journal* (1989), 41.

Pugh, M and Sidhu, WPS (eds.), *The United Nations and Regional Security—Europe and Beyond* (Boulder: Lynne Rienner Inc, 2003), 31.

Püttner, G, 'Ermessen und Ermessensausübung: Gedanken zur Weiterentwicklung der Ermessenslehre', 63 *Zeitschrift für öffentliches Recht* (2008), 345.

Quigley, J, 'Security Council Fact-finding: A Prerequisite to Effective Prevention of War', 7 *Florida Journal of International Law* (1992), 191.

——'The "Privatisation" of Security Council Enforcement Action: A Threat to Multilateralism', 17 *Michigan Journal of International Law* (1995–6), 249.

Rama-Montaldo, M, 'Contribution of the General Assembly to the Constitutional Development and Interpretation of the United Nations Charter', in R St J Macdonald, *Towards World Constitutionalism: Issues in the Legal Ordering of the World Community* (Leiden: Nijhof, 2005), 491.

Ratner, S, 'The Cambodia Settlement Agreements', 87 AJIL (1993), 9.

Reichard, M, *The EU–NATO Relationship* (Aldershot: Ashgate, 2006).

Reinisch, A, 'Developing Human Rights and Humanitarian Law Accountability of the Security Council for the Imposition of Economic Sanctions', 95 AJIL (2001), 866.

Reisman, M, 'Peacemaking', 18 *Yale Journal of International Law* (1993), 415.

——'Assessing the Lawfulness of Nonmilitary Enforcement: The Case of Economic Sanctions', 89 AJIL (1996), 37.

Rosand, E, 'The Security Council as "Global Legislator": Ultra Vires or Ultra Innovative?', 28 *Fordham International Law Journal* (2004–5), 542.

——'The UN Response to the Evolving Threat of Global Terrorism: Institutional Reform, Rivalry or Renewal?' in PG Danchin and H Fischer (eds.), *United Nations Reform and the New Collective Security* (Cambridge: Cambridge University Press, 2010), 250.

Rostow, EV, 'Until What? Enforcement Action or Collective Self-Defence?', 85 AJIL (1991), 506.

Sarooshi, D, *The United Nations and Development of Collective Security* (New York: Oxford University Press, 1999).

——'The Role of the United Nations Secretary-General in United Nations Peace-Keeping Operations', 20 *Australian Yearbook of International Law* (1999), 279.

——'Conferrals by States of Powers on International Organisations: The Case of Agency', 74 *British Yearbook of International Law* (2003), 291.

Schabas, W, *The International Criminal Court—A Commentary to the Rome Statute* (Oxford: Oxford University Press, 2010).

Schachter, O, 'The Relation between Law, Politics and Action in the United Nations', 109 *Recueil des Cours de l'Academie de Droit International de la Haye* (1963), 169.

——'The Quasi-Judicial Role of the Security Council and the General Assembly', 58 AJIL (1964), 960.

——*International Law: Theory and Practice* (Leiden: Nijhoff, 1991).

Scharf, M and Dorosin, J, 'Interpreting UN Sanctions: The Rulings and Role of the Yugoslavia Sanctions Committee', 19 *Brooklyn Journal of International Law* (1993), 771.

Schraga, D, 'UN Peacekeeping Operations: Applicability of International Humanitarian Law and Responsibility for Operations-Related Damage', 94 AJIL (2000), 406.

Schreuer, C, 'Regionalism v Universalism', 6 *European Journal of International Law* (1995), 477.

Schrijver, N, 'The Future of the Charter of the United Nations', 10 *Max-Planck Yearbook of UN Law* (2006), 1.

Schwartz, JB, 'Dealing With a "Rogue State": the Libya Precedent', 101 AJIL (2007), 553.

Schwarzenberger, G, 'The North Atlantic Pact', 2 *Western Political Quarterly* (1949), 309.

Seyersted, F, *Common Law of International Organisations* (Leiden: Brill, 2008).

Simma, B (ed.), *The Charter of the United Nations—A Commentary* (New York: Oxford University Press, 2002).

Sponeck, HC Graf, 'Sanctions and Humanitarian Exemptions: A Practitioner's Commentary', 13 *European Journal of International Law* (2002), 81.

Stahn, C, 'Collective Security and Self-Defence after the September 11 Attacks', 10 *Tilburg Foreign Law Review* (2002–3), 10.

——*The Law and Practice of International Territorial Administration, Versailles to Iraq and Beyond* (Cambridge: Cambridge University Press, 2008).

Stein, E and Carreau, D, 'Law and Peaceful Change in a Subsystem: "Withdrawal" of France from the North Atlantic Treaty Organization', 62 AJIL (1968), 577.

Stromberg, R, 'The Idea of Collective Security', 17 *Journal of the History of Ideas* (1956), 250.

Szasz, P, 'The Security Council Starts Legislating', 96 AJIL (2002), 901.

Tacsan, J, 'Searching for OAS/UN Task-sharing Opportunities in Central America and Haiti', 18 *Third World Quarterly* (1997), 489.

Taft, W and Buchwald, T, 'Preemption, Iraq and International Law', 97 AJIL (2007), 557.

Thompson, KW, 'Collective Security Re-examined', 47 *American Political Science Review* (1953), 753.

Tierney, MJ, 'Delegation Success and Policy Failure: Collective Delegation and the Search for Iraqi Weapons of Mass Destruction', 71 *Law and Contemporary Problems* (2008), 283.

Toje, A, 'The 2003 European Union Security Strategy: A Critical Appraisal', 10 *European Foreign Affairs Review* (2005), 117.

Tomuschat, C (ed.), *The United Nations at the Age of Fifty* (The Hague: Kluwer, 1995).

Trybus, M, 'With or Without the EU Constitutional Treaty: Towards a Common Security and Defence Policy?', 31 ELR (2006), 145.

—— and White, N, *European Security Law* (Oxford: Oxford University Press, 2005).

Vallat, F , 'The General Assembly and the Security Council of the United Nations', 29 *British Yearbook of International Law* (1952), 63.

Vierucci, L, 'The role of the Western European Union (WEU) in the maintenance of international peace and security', 2 *International Peacekeeping* (1995), 309.

Villani, U, 'The Security Council's Authorisation of Enforcement Action by Regional Organisations', 6 *Max-Planck Yearbook of UN Law* (2002), 535.

Wallander, C, 'Institutional Assets and Adaptability: NATO after the Cold War', 54 *International Organisation* (2000), 705.

Walter, C, 'Security Council Control over Regional Action', 1 *Max-Planck Yearbook of UN Law* (1997), 129.

Weston, B, 'Security Council Resolution 678 and Persian Gulf Decision Making: Precarious Legitimacy', 85 AJIL (1991), 516.

de Wet, E, *Chapter VII Powers of the UN Security Council* (Oxford: Hart, 2004).

White, N, *Keeping the Peace* (Manchester: Manchester University Press, 1997).

—— and Cryer, R, 'The Security Council and the International Criminal Court: An Uneasy Relationship?' in Bassiouni, MC, Doria, J, Gasser, H-P, and Jdanov, N (eds.), *The Legal Regime of the International Criminal Court: Essays in Memory of Igor Blishchenko* (The Hague: Brill, 2008) 457.

Whitman, R and Juncos, A, 'The Lisbon Treaty and the Foreign, Security and Defence Policy: Reforms, Implementation and the Consequences of (non-)Ratification', 14 *European Foreign Affairs Review* (2009), 25.

Wilcox, FO, 'Regionalism and Collective Security', 19 *International Organisation* (1965), 789.

Wilde, R, *International Territorial Administration: How Trusteeship and the Civilizing Mission Never Went Away* (Oxford: Oxford University Press, 2008).

Wilmshurst, E *et al*, 'The Chatham House Principles of International Law on the Use of Force in Self-Defence', 55 ICLQ (2006), 963.

Wippman, D, 'Military Intervention, Regional Organisations and Host-State Consent', 7 *Duke Journal of Comparative and International Law* (1996–7), 209.

Wolfrum, R, 'Der Beitrag regionaler Abmachungen zur Friedenssicherung: Möglichkeiten und Grenzen', 53(3) *Zeitschrift für ausländisches öffentliches Recht und Völkerrecht* (1990), 576.

Wood, B and Morales, M, 'Latin America and the United Nations', 19 *International Organization* (1965), 714.

Wood, M, 'The Interpretation of Security Council Resolutions', 2 *Max-Planck Yearbook of UN Law* (1998), 74.

——'The Law on the Use of Force: Current Challenges', 11 *Singapore Year Book of International Law* (2007), 1.

Woodliffe, J, 'The Evolution of a New NATO for a New Europe', 47 ICLQ (1998), 174.

Wouters, J *et al* (eds.), *The United Nations and the European Union* (The Hague: TMC Asser, 2005), 229.

Wulf, H and Debiel, T, 'Conflict Early Warning and Response Mechanisms: Tools for Enhancing the Effectiveness of Regional Organisations? A Comparative Study of the AU, ECOWAS, IGAD, ASEAN/ARF and PIF', Crisis States Research Centre Working Paper Series No, 2, Working Paper No. 49, May 2009.

Zimmern, A, *The League of Nations and the Rule of Law* (London: Macmillan, 1936).

Zwarenburg, M, 'Regional Organisations and the Maintenance of International Peace and Security: Three Recent Regional African Peace Operations', 11 *Journal of Conflict and Security Law* (2006), 483.

Index